JOSEPH II

Frontispiece Joseph, 1762. J. E. Liotard, pastel, collection of prince Schwarzenberg. The archduke is shown wearing a rich civilian *habit habillé* such as he seldom wore in later life.

JOSEPH II

I

In the Shadow of Maria Theresa
1741–1780

DEREK BEALES

Professor of Modern History, University of Cambridge,
and Fellow of Sidney Sussex College

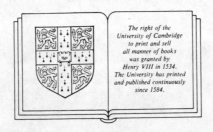

The right of the
University of Cambridge
to print and sell
all manner of books
was granted by
Henry VIII in 1534.
The University has printed
and published continuously
since 1584.

CAMBRIDGE UNIVERSITY PRESS

Cambridge
London   New York   New Rochelle
Melbourne   Sydney

Published by the Press Syndicate of the University of Cambridge
The Pitt Building, Trumpington Street, Cambridge CB2 IRP
32 East 57th Street, New York, NY 10022, USA
10 Stamford Road, Oakleigh, Melbourne 3166, Australia

First published 1987

Printed in Great Britain at the University Press, Cambridge

British Library cataloguing in publication data

Beales, Derek
Joseph II.
1: In the shadow of Maria Theresa, 1741–1780
1. Joseph, II, Holy Roman Emperor
2. Holy Roman Empire – Kings and rulers
– Bibliography
I. Title
943'.057'0924   DB74

Library of Congress cataloguing in publication data

Beales, Derek Edward Dawson
Joseph II
Bibliography: v. 1
Includes index
Contents: 1. In the shadow of Maria Theresa, 1741–1780
1. Joseph II, Holy Roman Emperor, 1741–1790
2. Austria – Kings and rulers – Bibliography. 3. Austria –
History – 1740–1789. I. Title. II. Title: Joseph the Second
DB74.5.B42 1986   943'.057'0924 [B]   86-17103

ISBN 0 521 24240 1

*To Kitty and Richard
who advised, encouraged
and warned*

Contents

Plates

Maps and figures

Preface

When I started working on Joseph II, I had no idea of producing a general study of his life and work. But I came to think, for reasons explained in the Introduction, that it was just such a book that was most needed, as it was certainly what I most wanted to write. When I began writing, I did not dream that the project would run to two volumes. But I found that, under examination, the received account of almost every aspect of his multifarious activity proved to be misleading, and that I could not demonstrate the fact and put forward a new interpretation without discussing each topic at some length. Even on this scale, I know very well that I have left much undone and unsaid, perhaps especially on the army, the partition of Poland, the problems of Bohemia and the affairs of the Holy Roman Empire; but each of these issues deserves a monograph to itself. I am thankful that Dr Peter Dickson's *Finance and Government under Maria Theresa, 1740–1780* will appear at roughly the same time as this book. He very generously gave me a copy of his typescript, which has not only taught me much, but has made me feel justified in passing lightly over the subjects he has covered so magisterially. However, my aim has been to deal both with Joseph as ruler and with Joseph the man, and I believe I have shown that the biographical and the historical approaches illuminate each other. I hope that this book is sufficiently full and reliable to provide a new foundation on which other students of the period can build. At worst, I take comfort from a remark of archbishop Laud's: 'Fifteen years' study cannot but beat out something.'

I owe thanks to a very large number of both institutions and individuals. I have received generous financial assistance for travel and research expenses from the British Academy, the Leverhulme Trust, the British Council, my College, Faculty and University. Unhappily, whenever I go abroad, sterling takes a dive; and more and more archives and libraries hamper research by ridiculously restricting the number of files and books that may be consulted on any one day. But I have been given help beyond the call of duty by archivists and librarians wherever I have worked: at the Haus-, Hof- und Staatsarchiv and the Österreichische Nationalbibliothek in Vienna, the Hungarian

National Archives and the National Museum in Budapest, the Archivio di
Stato and the Biblioteca Marciana in Venice, the Biblioteca nazionale at
Florence, the Žitenice division of the Litoměřice provincial state archive in
Czechoslovakia, the Bibiliothèque royale in Brussels, the Austrian Studies
Institutes at Stanford University and the University of Minnesota, the
Brotherton Library of the University of Leeds, and the British Library and
the Public Record Office in London. I should like to record that I have learned
much in bookshops and from their catalogues. Two debts to institutions stand
out: the first to Cambridge University Library, its invariably helpful staff, its
unique borrowing facilities and its incomparable Acton collection; the second
to my College for the friendship and assistance of its Masters, Fellows and
students, and for the grant of rooms in which books can be accumulated and
writing done. I doubt whether this volume could have been written at all
without these special local advantages.

Abroad, I have received most generous help, kindness and hospitality, in
particular from Count Arese, Professor Éva Balázs, Professor Vieri Becagli,
Professor Giacomo Becattini, Professor Kálmán Benda, Dr Peter Frank, Dr
Eva Irblich, Dr György Kelényi, Professor Grete Klingenstein, Professor Béla
Köpeczi, Professor Domokos Kosáry, Dr Elisabeth Kovács, Professor Stan-
ford Lehmberg, Dr Jaroslav Macek, Dr Klaus Peters, Dr Hedwig Szabolsci,
Dr Christiane Thomas, the Marquis de Trazegnies, Professor Adam Wan-
druszka and Dr Anna Zádor. In Britain, I owe much to the guidance,
encouragement and support of Miss Betty Behrens, the late Sir Herbert
Butterfield, the Reverend Professor Owen Chadwick, OM, Dr Nicholas Cox,
Professor William Doyle, Dr Robert Evans, Mr George Gömöri, Professor
Ragnhild Hatton, Professor Sir Harry Hinsley, Professor Ralph Leigh, Dr
John Leslie, Mr Robert Oresko, Professor Quentin Skinner, the late Dr R. C.
Smail, Dr Bernhard Stillfried, the late Professor Walter Ullmann, Professor
Ernst Wangermann and Dr Robert Wokler. Dr John Barber, Professor Linda
Colley and Dr Nicholas Davidson procured microfilms for me from foreign
archives. Dr Boyd Hilton took on my teaching for a term while I went on
sabbatical leave. Dr John Hatcher and the Reverend Dr Edward Norman
spared me some examining and so enabled me to finish the book. I have often
trespassed on the tolerance of the modern linguists of my College: Professor
Jostein Børtnes, Dr Peter Collier, Frau Ingrid Hassler, Dr Vivien Law,
Professor Barry Nisbet, Dr Sean O'Cáthasaigh and Mr Tom Wyatt.

Three individual debts must be singled out. Dr Hamish Scott not only lent
me his notes on French diplomatic documents but also commented on drafts
of chapters 9 and 13. Dr Dickson has read my whole typescript, some of it
more than once, saving me from error while supplying both information and
inspiration. The same is true of Dr Tim Blanning, who has also placed at my
disposal with complete unselfishness his time, his library and his unrivalled

knowledge of the period. His presence at Sidney has constituted my greatest single local advantage. But of course neither he, nor any of the scholars mentioned, should be held responsible for anything in my final text.

I apologise to those who as undergraduates took my Special Subject on 'Joseph II, Enlightenment and Revolution' in the years 1970–6 for the fact that most of the specific contributions they made will not be visible until volume II appears.

Mrs Ann Robson typed and re-typed my scruffy typescripts with great patience and skill.

I am grateful to Mrs Patricia Williams, then of the Cambridge University Press, for her warm initial encouragement. Mrs Elizabeth O'Beirne-Ranelagh as subeditor has corrected countless mistakes, inconsistencies and infelicities. Mrs Jane Williams and Mr Reginald Piggott have taken immense trouble over the illustrations and the admirable maps. Mr William Davies has displayed all the qualities an author seeks in a publisher: patience until the typescript arrives; enthusiasm, liberality and efficiency thereafter.

My wife has read and criticised several drafts of the book, usually at the moment of their completion, and has much improved their clarity and style. But this is only a small part of what she has done to make the whole enterprise possible. My greatest debt is to her.

Acknowledgements

The author and publisher would like to acknowledge the following for their permission to use the plates.

Kunsthistorisches Museum, Vienna, for Plates 1, 2, 5a, 7, 8a, 10, 11, 13, 16a; Schönbrunn for 3a, 3b, 6 and 8b; Bildarchiv of the Nationalbibliothek, Vienna, for 4a, 18b, and 21a; the British Museum for 4b, 14a, 16b, 21b and 23; the marquis de Trazegnies, Château de Corroy, Belgium, for 5b; Österreichisches Bundesdenkmalamt, Vienna, for 9a and 15b; Historisches Museum der Stadt Wien for 9b, 15a and 17b; Graphische Sammlung Albertina, Vienna, for 12, 14b and 18a; Sammlungen des regierenden Fürsten von Liechtenstein, Vaduz, for 17a; Generallandesarchiv, Karlsruhe, for 19b; the Syndics of the Cambridge University Library, for 20a; Château de Beloeil, Belgium, for 20b; Haus-, Hof- und Staatsarchiv, Vienna, for 22a and 22b; and the Benedictine abbey at Michaelbeuren for 24. In addition, Lichtbildwerkstätte 'Alpenland' photographed Plates 4a, 18b and 21a, and Alfred Jenderka of the Nationalbibliothek, Vienna, photographed 22a and 22b. Plate 19a is the author's own.

Abbreviations

AAE, CP	Archives des Affaires Etrangères [Paris], Correspondance Politique
AMMP	*Atti e memorie delle RR. deputazioni di storia patria per le provincie modenesi e parmensi*
AÖG	*Archiv für österreichische Geschichte*
Arneth	Alfred Ritter von Arneth
GMT	*Geschichte Maria Theresias* (10 vols., Vienna, 1863–79)
JuK	*Joseph II. und Katharina von Russland: Ihr Briefwechsel* (Vienna, 1869)
JuL	*Joseph II. und Leopold von Toscana: Ihr Briefwechsel von 1781 bis 1790* (2 vols., Vienna, 1872)
MAJL	*Marie Antoinette, Joseph II. und Leopold II.: Ihr Briefwechsel* (Vienna, 1866)
MTKuF	*Briefe der Kaiserin Maria Theresia an Ihre Kinder und Freunde* (4 vols., Vienna, 1881)
MTuJ	*Maria Theresia und Joseph II.: Ihre Correspondenz sammt Briefen Joseph's an seinen Bruder Leopold* (3 vols., Vienna, 1867–8)
Arneth & Flammermont	Arneth & J. Flammermont (eds.), *Correspondance secrète du Comte de Mercy-Argenteau avec l'Empereur Joseph II et le Prince de Kaunitz* (2 vols., Paris, 1889, 1891)
Arneth & Geffroy	Arneth & M. A. Geffroy (eds.), *Marie-Antoinette. Correspondance secrète entre Marie-Thérèse et le Cte de Mercy-Argenteau, avec les lettres de Marie-Thérèse et de Marie-Antoinette* (3 vols., 2nd edn, Paris, 1874–5)
ASI	*Archivio storico italiano*
ASPP	*Archivio storico per le province parmensi*
ASV	Archivio di Stato, Venice

Beer, *JLuK*   A. Beer (ed.), *Joseph II., Leopold II. und Kaunitz: Ihr*
                      Briefwechsel (Vienna, 1873)

Beer & Fiedler,   A. Beer & J. von Fiedler (eds.), *Joseph II. und Graf*
    JuLC   *Ludwig Cobenzl: Ihr Briefwechsel* (2 vols., Vienna,
                      1901)

BSSHNC   *Bulletin de la Société des Sciences Historiques et*
                      Naturelles de la Corse

Christoph,   P. Christoph [D. Pollack], *Maria Theresia und*
    MTuMA   *Marie Antoinette: Ihr geheimer Briefwechsel* (Vienna,
                      1952)

Conrad, *RuV*   H. Conrad, *Recht und Verfassung des Reiches in der Zeit*
                      Maria Theresias. Die Vorträge zum Unterricht des Erz-
                      herzogs Joseph im Natur- und Völkerrecht sowie im
                      Deutschen Staats- und Lehnsrecht (Cologne, 1964)

CSS   *Canadian Slavic Studies*

EEQ   *East European Quarterly*

E.L.   Eleonore Liechtenstein

FBPG   *Forschungen zur brandenburgischen und preussischen*
                      Geschichte

Ferd.   Ferdinand, son of Maria Theresa

FRA   Fontes rerum austriacarum

GV   *Gesamtdeutsche Vergangenheit, Festgabe für H. Ritter*
                      von Srbik zum 60. Geburtstag (Munich, 1938)

HHSA   Haus-, Hof- und Staatsarchiv, Vienna
  FA   Familien-Archiv
  HBP   Handbilletenprotokolle
  NL   Nachlass Lacy
  Sbde   Sammelbände
  SKV   Staatskanzlei Vorträge
  TG   Tableau général
  TZ   Tagebuch Zinzendorf

HJ   *Historical Journal*

HZ   *Historische Zeitschrift*

J.   Joseph II

JMH   *Journal of Modern History*

K.   Kaunitz

KAW   Kaiserliche Akademie der Wissenschaften

KHM   Kunsthistorisches Museum, Vienna

K-M   Graf R. Khevenhüller-Metsch and H. Schlitter (eds.),
                      Aus der Zeit Maria Theresias. Tagebuch des Fürsten
                      Johann Josef Khevenhüller-Metsch, kaiserlichen Oberst-
                      hofmeisters, 1742–1776 (8 vols., Vienna, 1907–72)

L.	Leopold, son of Maria Theresa and grand duke of Tuscany
L.K.	Leopoldine Kaunitz
M.A.	Marie Antoinette, daughter of Maria Theresa and queen of France
MARB in-8o	*Mémoires couronnés et autres mémoires, publiés par l'Académie Royale des sciences et des lettres et des beaux-arts de Belgique, collection in-8o*
M.C.	Marie Christine, daughter of Maria Theresa
MIÖG/MÖIG	*Mitteilungen des Instituts für österreichische Geschichtsforschung/Mitteilungen des österreichischen Instituts für Geschichtsforschung*
Mitrofanov	P. von Mitrofanov, *Josef II. Seine politische und kulturelle Tätigkeit*, trans. from the Russian 1907 edn by V. von Demelic (2 vols., Vienna, 1910)
MOL	Magyar Országos Levéltár (Hungarian National Archives, Budapest)
AG	Acta Generalia
MÖSA	*Mitteilungen des österreichischen Staatsarchivs*
M.T.	Maria Theresa
MTIZ	W. Koschatzky (ed.), *Maria Theresia und ihre Zeit* (2nd edn, Vienna, 1980)
MVGSW	*Mitteilungen des Vereins für Geschichte der Stadt Wien*
NCMH	*The New Cambridge Modern History* (14 vols., Cambridge, 1957–70)
ÖAW	Österreichische Akademie der Wissenschaften
ÖGL	*Österreich in Geschichte und Literatur*
ÖNB	Österreichische Nationalbibliothek, Vienna
OPBA	*Ordonnances des Pays-Bas autrichiens*
ÖZKJ	*Österreich zur Zeit Kaiser Josephs II.* (catalogue of the exhibition held at Melk, 1980)
PC	G. B. Volz and others (ed.), *Politische Correspondenz Friedrichs des Grossen* (46 vols., Berlin, 1879–1939)
PJ	*Preussische Jahrbücher*
PRO	Public Record Office, London
FO	Foreign Office
SP	State Papers
RH	*Revue historique*
RHD	*Revue d'histoire diplomatique*
RSI	*Rivista storica italiana*
SIRIO	*Sbornik imperatorskogo russkogo istoricheskogo obshchestva* (St Petersburg, 1867–1916)

SOALpZ, LRRA	Státní oblastní archiv v Litoměřicích, pobočka Žitenice (Czech state archives at Litoměřice, Žitenice branch), Lobkowitz family archive
SR	*Slavonic and East European Review*
SVEC	*Studies in Voltaire and the Eighteenth Century*
TAPS	*Transactions of the American Philosophical Society*
TRHS	*Transactions of the Royal Historical Society*
VC	T. Besterman (ed.), *Voltaire's Correspondence* (107 vols., Geneva, 1953–65)
VKNGÖ	*Veröffentlichungen der Kommission für neuere Geschichte Österreichs*
VSWG	*Vierteljahrschrift für Sozial- und Wirtschaftsgeschichte*
WBGN	*Wiener Beiträge zur Geschichte der Neuzeit*
Wurzbach	C. von Wurzbach, *Biographisches Lexikon des Kaiserthums Österreich 1750–1850* (60 vols., Vienna, 1856–91)
WZ	*Wiener Zeitung* (until 1780 *Wienerisches Diarium*)
ZBL	*Zeitschrift für bayerische Landesgeschichte*
ZKG	*Zeitschrift für Kirchengeschichte*

Notes on names of persons and places

Where an English form exists, I have used it. Otherwise, following my sources, I have generally used German versions, where such exist, of East European place names. My main aim has been internal consistency.

Introduction

Joseph II is the classic example of a radical monarch who tried to transform society from above. For one authority he ranks as 'perhaps the completest enlightened despot in European history', for another as 'the revolutionary emperor' who on the eve of the French Revolution anticipated much of its programme.[1] This book tells the story of his life, and investigates his policies, their origins and their fate.

He became emperor at the age of twenty-four when his father, Francis I, died in 1765. For the next twenty-five years until his death in 1790, Joseph presided over the vast and ancient 'Holy Roman Empire of the German Nation' and claimed precedence as the first of Europe's lay sovereigns. But in fact he possessed little power, and played no great role, in that capacity.

He set his mark on history not as emperor, but as ruler under numerous other titles of the immense agglomeration of lands in Central and Eastern Europe, Italy and the Netherlands accumulated by the Austrian branch of the Habsburg dynasty, a complex which he and his contemporaries generally called either 'the Austrian Monarchy' or simply 'the Monarchy'.[2] In 1765 he

---

[1] See p. 6 and n. 13 below.

[2] I believe it to be true that J. and M.T. never used the word 'Empire' of the lands inherited under the Pragmatic Sanction. It was normal to speak of the Russian and Ottoman empires, but in relation to central Europe the term 'Empire' was reserved for the *Reich*.

My first two quotations from J. show that he talked sometimes of his *patrie* and of *l'état*, but by far the commonest term for the whole complex of Habsburg (or Habsburg-Lorraine) territories was 'the Monarchy' or 'the Austrian Monarchy', though 'the lands of the House of Austria' and 'the Austrian states' were also employed.

I do not know of a detailed discussion of this terminology for the eighteenth century, but there are interesting points in O. Stolz, 'Wesen und Zweck des Staates in der Geschichte Österreichs', in *Festschrift zur Feier des zweihundertjährigen Bestandes des Haus-, Hof- und Staatsarchivs*, ed. L. Santifaller, vol II (Vienna, 1951), pp. 94–110. He finds a first use of 'Empire' to refer to the Monarchy in 1786. Certainly the author of the 'Constantinople letters' (see below, p. 9) so uses it.

I know that there is some question whether it is right to speak of the 'Holy Roman Empire of the German Nation', but the phrase was used at the time. See J. F. Noël, 'Traditions universalistes et aspects nationaux dans la notion de Saint-Empire Romain Germanique au XVIIIe siècle', *RHD*, LXXXII (1968), 193–212.

When people talked of leaving Vienna to go *en empire*, they obviously meant in fact southern Germany (cf. H. Raab, *Clemens Wenzeslaus von Sachsen und seine Zeit 1739–1812* (Freiburg, 1962), p. 1).

Map 1. The Austrian Monarchy and the Holy Roman Empire from the 1740s to 1780.
The political boundaries, especially within the Empire, have had to be simplified for
the sake of clarity.

Sea

Danzig

EAST PRUSSIA

Generally accepted boundary of the Empire (Reich)
Principal ecclesiastical states
Prussian gains by partition of Poland in 1772
Prussia from the 1740s
The Monarchy from the 1740s
The Monarchy's gains in the 1770s
Military frontier regions

0   100   200 miles
0   100   200   300 km

Vistula

Warsaw

P   O   L   A   N   D

SILESIA

Breslau

Neisse

SILESIA

Teschen

Wieliczka

GALICIA
(1772)

Lemberg

Sereth

Dniester

Olmütz

MORAVIA

Brünn

ZIPS
(1770)

Pruth

MOLDAVIA

VER

Pressburg

Danube

Vác

BUKOVINA
(1775)

k

ienna

TRIA

Buda · Pest

H   U   N   G   A   R   Y

TRANSYLVANIA

Hermannstadt

rlstadt

Temesvár

BANAT

SLAVONIA

WALLACHIA

Belgrade

Old Orsova

LITTLE

Save

Passarowitz

WALLACHIA

B   O   S   N   I   A

O   T   T   O   M   A   N

Danube

LMATIA
to Venice

SERBIA

EMPIRE

MONTENEGRO

became 'co-regent' of these territories with his mother, Maria Theresa. When she died in 1780 he succeeded her as their absolute sovereign for the last decade of his life.

His double role creates difficulties both of understanding and of terminology. Map 1 will clarify the geographical position: the Empire included virtually the whole of modern Germany and much else besides; but only about half of the Monarchy lay within it. As for terminology, I shall follow the practice, universal in the eighteenth century and thereafter, of using 'the emperor' as a straightforward synonym for Joseph II in all his capacities after 1765. I shall also call Maria Theresa 'the empress', as her contemporaries did, although her sole right to the title was as wife and widow of Francis I. But when I write of 'the Empire' or 'the *Reich*', I shall invariably be referring to the Holy Roman Empire. What is often nowadays known as 'the Austrian Empire' or 'the Habsburg Empire' I shall always call 'the Monarchy' or, where no confusion can arise with the region or republic of the same name, 'Austria'.

From the moment when Joseph became involved in affairs of state, he maintained that the Monarchy needed drastic reform, and worked to achieve it. In 1768 he wrote to his brother Leopold, grand duke of Tuscany,

Love of country, the welfare of the Monarchy, that is genuinely ... the only passion I feel, and I would undertake anything for its sake. I am so committed to it that, if I cannot satisfy myself that its condition is good and that the arrangements we are making are beneficial, my mind cannot be at peace nor my body in good health.[3]

He set about trying to expand and improve the army, to reform and control the Roman Catholic Church within the Monarchy, to extend religious toleration and relax censorship, to improve the position of the serfs, to introduce a tax system that took no account of social privilege, and to impose on the variegated provinces of his dominions homogeneous laws and a unified, centralised administration. He asserted that, as the sovereign, he knew better than anyone else what was for the good of his people. In 1783 he published a manifesto or 'pastoral letter' addressed to his officials:

I have sought to implant in all servants of the state the love that I have for the general good and the zeal that inspires me to promote it; from which it necessarily follows that, in accordance with my example, each man should have no other aim in all his actions but utility and the welfare of the greatest number.[4]

[3] Arneth, *MTuJ* I, p. 225 (25 July 1768).
[4] This document was published at the time in at least French, German, Italian and Hungarian, e.g. *Joseph des Zweyten Erinnerung an seinen Staatsbeamten am Schluss des 1783ten Jahres* (Vienna, [1784]). The original (French) text in J.'s hand is in HHSA SKV 138 (1783). It is published in *OPBA*, 3rd series, XII (1910), 333–8 (as a footnote). German text in J. Wendrinsky, *Kaiser Joseph II.* (Vienna, 1880), pp. 330–6.

As late as June 1789 he told his recalcitrant subjects in the southern Nether-lands: 'I do not need your consent for doing good.'[5]

Yet in January 1790, with Belgium lost and Hungary in ferment, he had to admit disillusionment and acknowledge defeat:

I confess to you [he told Leopold] that, humiliated by what has happened to me, seeing that I am unfortunate in everything I undertake, the appalling ingratitude with which my good arrangements are received and I am treated – for there is now no conceivable insolence or curse that people do not allow themselves to utter about me publicly – all this makes me doubt myself, I no longer dare to have an opinion and put it into effect, I allow myself to be ruled by the advice of the ministers even when I don't think it is the best, since I dare not hold out for my own view and indeed I haven't the strength to impose it and argue for it.[6]

A few days later he rescinded most of his reforms. Within a month he was dead, aged only forty-eight. His failure seemed abject.

Few rulers have evoked stronger and more diverse reactions. In Hungary his entire reign was written off as a usurpation.[7] In rebellious Belgium he was likened to every notorious villain of history: Tiberius, Caligula, Nero, Cara-calla, Alaric, Attila, Mahomet, Amurath, Machiavelli, Alva and Oliver Crom-well.[8] But he was also extravagantly admired – and not only in the early days of his rule. Foreign writers as well as his chief minister, prince Kaunitz, flattered him as another Trajan, Marcus Aurelius or Henri Quatre. To Da Ponte, Mozart's librettist, Joseph was a man of discerning taste, approach-able, affable, 'this adorable prince'.[9] Although his death came as a relief to most government officials, Roman Catholic clergy, nobles, Belgians and Hungarians, he was regretted by many, especially among groups like Prot-estants, Jews, Romanians and former serfs whose status he had tried to improve.[10] His contemporaries did not all accept that he had failed. Beet-

---

5 J. to the Estates of Brabant, 7 June 1789: P. A. F. Gérard, *Ferdinand Rapedius de Berg ... Mémoires et documents pour servir à l'histoire de la révolution brabançonne* (2 vols., Brussels, 1842–3), vol. II, p. 210. I shall use 'Belgium' as shorthand for 'the Austrian possessions in the southern Netherlands', except where confusion might result. See *MTIZ*, p. 21, for a reference to 'Belgium Austriacum' in 1770.
   I am using 'province' very loosely, to mean 'region in some way constitutionally distinct'.
6 Arneth, *JuL* II, p. 312 (21 Jan. 1790).
7 His laws are simply omitted from some Hungarian constitutional compilations, on the ground that he was never crowned king and never took an oath to maintain the constitution.
8 Some of these comparisons, such as those with Tiberius and Nero, appear very frequently in the pamphlet literature of the revolution in Belgium. One of the richest sources is [S. N. H. Linguet], *Choix des lettres paternelles de Joseph Néron, second du nom, Empereur des Romains, à Richard D'Alton, son Assassin en Chef, aux Pays-Bas, en 1788, & 1789* [Brussels, 1790]. Cromwell is cited in *Joseph II aux enfers, et son entrevue avec Richard D'Alton* ([Brussels], 1790).
9 Beer, *JLuK*, p. 48 (K. to J., 24 Mar. 1781). Cf. J. Lanjuinais, *Le Monarque accompli, ou prodiges de bonté, de savoir, et de sagesse qui font l'éloge de ... Joseph II* (3 vols., Lausanne, 1774), vol. I, pp. 6, 14 etc. A. Livingston (ed.), *Memoirs of Lorenzo da Ponte* (New York, 1967), esp. pp. 151–3.
10 These groups were not of course unanimous or without reservations. See for those favourable to J., e.g. Mitrofanov II, pp. 647–59, 771–5; C. H. O'Brien, 'Ideas of religious toleration at the

hoven set to music an ode on the emperor's death which contained this passage:

A monster, whose name was Fanaticism, rose from the caverns of Hell, got between the earth and the sun, and it was night. Then came Joseph ... dragged the frenzied monster down ... and crushed it. Then mankind rose up into light.[11]

The Viennese writer Caroline Pichler remembered his reign, in a classic mixed metaphor, as 'that period of burgeoning intellectual life in Austria, quickened by the sparks that fell on it from Joseph's genius'.[12]

Not only his contemporaries but also historians have vied with one another in minting colourful phrases to characterise the man and his work. Three of his twentieth-century biographers, Fejtö, Magenschab and Padover, label him 'revolutionary'. The author of the best book about his rule, the Russian Mitrofanov, called him 'a democrat from head to toe'. For Taylor he is 'the [French Revolutionary] Convention in a single man'. It was Macartney, who wrote the best account of the modern development of the Monarchy, who described him as 'perhaps the completest enlightened despot in European history'. 'Sovereignty bound up with the idea of renovation', wrote the great Ranke, 'has never had a more decided proponent than this monarch. He certainly became a martyr for it.'[13]

All these historians' judgements reflect a measure of admiration for Joseph. But the same writers also find in him thoroughly unattractive traits. Macartney, for example, remarks on his meanness and rudeness, and detects in him a

time of Joseph II', *TAPS*, new series, LIX (1969), part 7; *Politisch-kirchliches Manch Hermaeon von den Reformen Kayser Josephs überhaupt vorzüglich in Ungarn* ... [n.p., 1790]; R. Mahler, *A History of Modern Jewry, 1780–1815* (London, 1971), esp. pp. 229–333; D. Prodan, *Supplex Libellus Valachorum* (Budapest, 1971).

11 The text from *Ludwig van Beethoven's Werke. Serie 25: Supplement* (Leipzig, 1887), pp. 1–54. The author was apparently S. A. Averdonk. The Bonn *Lesegesellschaft* commissioned it, but it was not in fact performed, as had been intended, at the Society's commemoration of the emperor in 1790, or indeed until 1884. See E. Forbes (ed.), *Thayer's Life of Beethoven* (Princeton, 1967), pp. 119–20. The sentiments it embodied, however, resembled those in elegies given before the Society and elsewhere by its most active member, Eulogius Schneider. Bonn was of course the capital of Max Franz, J.'s brother, as elector of Cologne, and the Society was under his patronage. On the other hand, Schneider was soon afterwards in trouble, partly because of the radical opinions he had expressed in the course of these tributes. See J. Hansen, *Quellen zur Geschichte des Rheinlandes im Zeitalter der französischen Revolution*, vol. I (Bonn, 1931), esp. pp. 563–5, 575–6, 615–19. Strangely, the Ode is mentioned neither by Hansen nor in F. Engel-Jánosi, 'Josephs II. Tod im Urteil der Zeitgenossen', *MÖIG*, XLIV (1930), 324–46.

12 C. Pichler, *Denkwürdigkeiten aus meinem Leben*, ed. E. K. Blümml (2 vols., Munich, 1914), vol. II, p. 398; originally published in 4 vols., Vienna, 1844.

13 F. Fejtö, *Un Habsbourg révolutionnaire, Joseph II. Portrait d'un despote éclairé* (Paris, 1953); H. Magenschab, *Josef II. Revolutionär von Gottes Gnaden* (Graz, 1979); S. K. Padover, *The Revolutionary Emperor: Joseph II of Austria* (2nd edn, London, 1967). Mitrofanov II, p. 582. A. J. P. Taylor, *The Habsburg Monarchy, 1809–1918* (Harmondsworth, 1964), p. 22. C. A. Macartney, *The Habsburg Empire, 1790–1918* (London, 1968), p. 119. L. von Ranke, *Die deutschen Mächte und der Fürstenbund: Deutsche Geschichte von 1780 bis 1790* (2 vols., Leipzig, 1871–2), vol. II, p. 161.

streak of sadism; moreover, he says, 'the noun in the phrase [enlightened despot] is quite as fully operative as the adjective'. It is often claimed, too, that there were irreconcilable contradictions in Joseph's character and plans. 'Of all the eighteenth-century rulers', declared Ogg, 'he was the most complicated, because he was at once militarist, absolutist, liberal and humanitarian.' 'The humane egalitarian', writes Blanning, 'is countered by the brutal martinet, the disciple of the Enlightenment by the crude aggressor.' Some historians condemn him out of hand, most crushingly Crankshaw in his *Maria Theresa*: 'his reforms . . . sprang from self-love tempered by abstract ideals of justice and from disdain of all who differed from him . . . As a human being he seems hardly to have existed.'[14]

The stridency of these judgements is a natural response to the challenging tone and actions of the emperor himself. The wide variation of opinion largely reflects inevitable differences of approach among historians arising from their emotional, national, political and religious attitudes. But it stems in part from the wayward development of historiography, and to some degree from sheer ignorance and error.

There exists, first, a broad distinction between historians who have written in English or French and those who have written in Central and East European languages. For most of the former, the context within which Joseph II is to be considered is that of 'enlightened despotism', together with his great contemporaries, Catherine II of Russia and Frederick II of Prussia, and many lesser rulers and ministers of the second half of the eighteenth century; and the Enlightenment in question is primarily the movement in France and Britain, which owed little to the governments of those countries, often assailed them, was generally constitutionalist, commonly libertarian and sometimes free-thinking. Many of the historians concerned, most particularly Padover, author of the best-known biography of the emperor in English, have sought to identify Joseph with this movement.[15]

For most historians writing in German, Italian, Hungarian and so on, the frame of reference is quite different. They commonly insist on the usage 'enlightened *absolutism*' as opposed to 'enlightened despotism'; and it is an important truth that Joseph, like most of his fellow rulers, condemned 'despotism' and regarded himself as bound in general to observe his own and his territories' laws. However, to the confusion of scholars and their terminology, he himself describes the regime he favours as '*despotisme lié*', 'tied

---

[14] Macartney, *Habsburg Empire*, pp. 119–20. D. Ogg, *Europe of The Ancien Régime 1715–1783* (London, 1965), p. 211. T. C. W. Blanning, *Joseph II and Enlightened Despotism* (London, 1970), p. 116. E. Crankshaw, *Maria Theresa* (London, 1971), pp. 275–292.

[15] Padover, *Revolutionary Emperor*, pp. 17–18 is a blatant example, but the whole book, as we shall see, is tainted. Those other English and French historians who have notably exaggerated J.'s enthusiasm for the *philosophes* mostly depend on Padover. Some of the principal cases are mentioned in D. Beales, 'The false Joseph II', *HJ*, XVIII (1975), 467–95. See also n. 19 below.

despotism'.[16] Further, these historians think of the Enlightenment in its
Central European, and especially its German and Italian manifestations: a
movement among employees of governments, such as bureaucrats, priests and
professors, often anti-clerical but rarely freethinking, who expected reform to
come from above and not from below. In the Monarchy the Enlightenment is
associated with a movement for change named after Joseph, 'Joseph(in)ism',
affecting many aspects of life, but especially associated with claims made and
measures taken by the state to control and reform the Roman Catholic Church
within its borders, involving not only obviously ecclesiastical matters like the
exclusion of papal bulls, the dissolution of monasteries and the introduction of
religious toleration but also wider issues such as the reform of education in all
its aspects, the liberalisation of censorship and the reorganisation of poor
relief.[17]

I must make it clear that I have drawn the distinction between these two
groups of historians too crudely. There are of course writers in English and
French who themselves belong to the Central and East European tradition,
like Wangermann[18] and Fejtö; and others who, like Macartney and Blanning,
have steeped themselves in it. Contrariwise, there are writers in German who
have been influenced by the English and French tradition. But there is a very
marked difference of approach between some well-known books in English
and French, and most of those in other languages. In so far as the former are

---

[16] In the document called 'Rêveries', dating (I think) from 1763. See D. Beales, 'Joseph II's
"Rêveries"', *MÖSA*, XXXIII (1980), 142–60. The phrase quoted is on p. 156.
  For 'enlightened absolutism' see K. O. Freiherr von Aretin (ed.), *Der aufgeklärte Absolutismus* (Cologne, 1974), esp. the editor's introduction. There is a difficult recent discussion in
English by L. Krieger, *An Essay on the Theory of Enlightened Despotism* (Chicago, 1975). For
the contrast between German and French Enlightenment see the excellent *exposé* in T. C. W.
Blanning, *Reform and Revolution in Mainz, 1743–1803* (Cambridge, 1974), pp. 1–38.

[17] For Josephism the best treatments in English are in Blanning, *J. II and Enlightened Despotism*,
esp. ch. 2, and E. Wangermann, *The Austrian Achievement, 1700–1800* (London, 1973). The
three classics are E. Winter, *Der Josefinismus und seine Geschichte* (Brünn, 1943), revised as *Der
Josefinismus. Die Geschichte des österreichischen Reformkatholizismus, 1740–1848* (Berlin, 1962);
F. Valjavec, *Der Josephinismus. Zur geistigen Entwicklung Österreichs im achtzehnten und
neunzehnten Jahrhundert* (2nd edn, Munich, 1945); and F. Maass (ed.), *Der Josephinismus.
Quellen zu seiner Geschichte in Österreich, 1760–1850*, FRA (5 vols., Vienna, 1951–61). See the
valuable surveys of R. Bauer, 'Le Joséphisme', *Critique*, XIV (1958), 622–39; K. Benda,
'Probleme des Josephinismus und des Jakobinertums in der Habsburgischen Monarchie',
Südost-Forschungen, XXV (1966), 38–71; E. Kovács, 'Giuseppinismo', in *Dizionario degli Istituti
di Perfezione*, ed. G. Pelliccia and G. Rocca (Rome, 1974–), vol. IV, cols. 1357–67; S. F.
Romano, 'Studi su Giuseppe II e il "Giuseppinismo"', *RSI*, LXIX, 110–27. See further for a
subtle discussion in relation to censorship, G. Klingenstein, *Staatsverwaltung und kirchliche
Autorität im 18. Jahrhundert* (Vienna, 1970).
  I am sorry to learn from K. Vocelka in *Austrian History Yearbook*, XIV (1978), 328, that
'Josephism' seems an unacceptable term to Austrian scholars. I cannot prefer the German-
derived form 'Josephinism'. I note that the French generally use 'Joséphisme' and that
'Josephism' is well established in English-language writing. In J. Pezzl's *Faustin* (3rd edn,
n.p., 1785), p. 344, occurs the phrase 'die Josephische Aere'.

[18] His main contributions are: *From Joseph II to the Jacobin Trials* (2nd edn, Oxford 1969) and
Austrian Achievement.

preoccupied with placing Joseph against a background of British and French Enlightenment and with assessing his work by the criteria usually applied to British, French and even American history of the same period, it is evident that they are adopting inappropriate standards.

Further, many historians have failed to appreciate that the remarks most frequently ascribed to the emperor are spurious. He did not proclaim 'I have made philosophy the legislator of my empire', a statement which, ever since it was fathered on him, has naturally been accorded pride of place in many accounts of his reign. He did not say 'prejudice, fanaticism, partiality, and slavery of the mind must cease, and each of my subjects be re-instated in the enjoyment of his native liberties'; or 'I have to reduce the host of monks, I have to transform Fakirs into men.' Nor did he make the famous pronouncement which ends:

Tolerance is an effect of that beneficent increase of knowledge which now enlightens Europe, and which is owing to philosophy and the efforts of great men; it is a convincing proof of the improvement of the human mind, which has boldly reopened a road through the dominions of superstition, which was trodden centuries ago by Zoroaster and Confucius, and which, fortunately for mankind, has now become the highway of monarchs.

All these resounding utterances, which appear to stamp him as a devotee of the French Enlightenment in its more radical phase, derive, together with much else in the same vein, from a collection called *Newly Assembled Letters of Joseph II, Emperor of the Germans*, published in the year of his death, with the manifestly false imprint 'Constantinople, printed in the private Court press'. Of the forty-nine letters it contains, probably only seven derive from genuine originals. Almost all of the remainder are demonstrably pure invention, the work of a clever and mischievous author who has yet to be identified with certainty. But they are so lively and trenchant, and have tallied so well with what many people believed or hoped about the emperor's views, that they have become the prize exhibits of biographers and historians. Although they were declared suspect over a century ago, they continue to make a good showing in history books, especially in English.[19] Even Taylor, on one of the

[19] I have discussed the spuriousness of the Constantinople collection, its authorship, the use made of it by historians (esp. Padover) and its impact on their views of J. in *HJ* (1975), 467–95. I should like to add three points here. First, I have now seen the original of the letter to the magistrates of Ofen, discussed on pp. 482–3 of my article. It is a furious scribble on MOL AG 1784/7049 (26 June 1784). I think *Circulation* is the correct reading, but it is one of the most difficult of J.'s annotations to decipher.

I should, secondly, like to acknowledge that I was unfair to Bibl on p. 467: he knew that the letter to Herzan was spurious (V. Bibl, *Kaiser Josef II. Ein Vorkämpfer der grossdeutschen Idee* (Vienna, 1943), p. 141).

Thirdly, when I wrote the article, I had not seen F. Engel-Jánosi, 'Kaiser Josef II. in der Wiener Bewegung des Jahres 1848', *MVGSW*, XI (1931), 65–6 and 65n, where both the spuriousness and the influence of the collection are stressed, though not with reference to the

two occasions when he claims to quote directly from Joseph in *The Habsburg Monarchy*, picks a 'Constantinople letter'. Crankshaw relies on others to show how insufferable the emperor could be. Magenschab, author of the latest Austrian biography, trundles out all the well-known faked passages.[20] But the worst offender was Padover. About a quarter of all his numerous quotations come from this collection, and he gives extracts from twenty-six out of its forty-nine letters. His biography has been widely treated as a standard work, and so the lengthy portions he reproduced have been much copied. There is other spurious material in the field, including several volumes of letters from Marie Antoinette, Joseph's sister and queen of France, which were forged in the middle nineteenth century, and two bogus *Political Testaments* ascribed to the emperor.[21] Many of the anecdotes told about him must also be regarded as dubious.[22] Historians' judgements of Joseph have in many cases been vitiated by reliance on these discredited sources.

Because of these problems of evidence, it is peculiarly unfortunate that the emperor's biographers have been so sparing with note references. Padover provides just two, to sources located in the United States. Otherwise, apart from Mitrofanov, only Bernard conforms to scholarly practice in this respect.[23] Here is a clear instance where the effort to avoid pedantry has allowed errors to flourish and made them unusually hard to detect and eradicate. Partly for this reason, I have been careful to supply very full references.

Of course, much of high quality has been written on related topics, especially in German. From the 1860s the bulk of the Austrian archives became available to historians. Many substantial portions were published,

---

other writings about J. published immediately after his death, nor to the authorship of the *Briefe*, nor entirely accurately.

20 Taylor, *Habsburg Monarchy*, p. 20; Crankshaw, *Maria Theresa*, pp. 293, 314; Magenschab, *J. II.*, the lengthy quotations on pp. 150–2, 162, 181, 187, 250–1, 253–4, 291.

21 See Christoph, *MTuMA*, pp. 9–13; H. von Sybel, 'Briefwechsel der Königin Maria Antoinette', *HZ*, XIII (1865), 164–78, and 'Die Briefe der Königin Marie Antoinette', *HZ*, XIV (1865), 319–50; A. Geffroy (ed.), *Gustave III et la cour de France* (2 vols., Paris, 1867), vol. II pp. 303–48. The forgery was disseminated in P. V. d'Hunolstein, *Correspondance inédite de Marie Antoinette* (Paris, 1864) and F. S. Feuillet de Conches, *Louis XVI, Marie Antoinette, et Madame Élisabeth* (5 vols., Paris, 1864–9). Padover, in *The Life and Death of Louis XVI* (London, 1963), pp. 354, 356–7, showed himself aware of these and other spurious collections relating to Louis and his queen.

The *Testament de Joseph II ... Traduit par M. Linguet* (Brussels, 1790) could deceive no one; but *Testament politique de l'Empereur Joseph II, Roi des Romains* (2 vols., Vienna, 1791) was accepted as authentic by at least one participant in the Joseph II bicentenary conference in Vienna, October 1980, though the Jacobin Martinovics claimed its authorship (Wangermann, *From J. II. to the Jacobin Trials*, p. 23n).

22 Cf. R. Pick, *Empress Maria Theresa: The Earlier Years, 1717–1757* (London, 1966), p. 14, warning against anecdotes about M. T. that 'bear the stamp of the bourgeois sentimentality of a much later period'. See pp. 87n, 263, 335, 377n below.

23 P. P. Bernard, *Joseph II* (New York, 1968). Fejtö, *J. II*, however, uses some unpublished sources.

notably by the director of the Haus-, Hof- und Staatsarchiv in Vienna, Alfred Ritter von Arneth, who edited, among other collections, Joseph's letters to Maria Theresa, Leopold, Marie Antoinette and Catherine II. He also wrote a life of Maria Theresa in ten volumes, which is unlikely ever to be superseded. The reader of this vast work, though he will notice that the author can scarcely contain his admiration for his subject and that he treats the whole imperial family with nineteenth-century decorum, must be impressed by the breadth of documentation, the clarity of organisation and the generally balanced judgement which a busy archivist deployed in this pioneering enterprise. It has served as a quarry to many later historians, and has been indispensable to me.[24] Down to the fall of the Monarchy in 1918, publication of the documents of this period continued on an extensive scale, many of them edited by Hanns Schlitter.[25] After 1918 the flow diminished, but important collections have appeared on the central administration and on Josephism.[26] So far as monographs are concerned, many date from the heroic age of the 1870s. Mitrofanov's book came out in 1907. The most striking productions since the Second World War have been a clutch of works on Josephism, Adam Wandruszka's *Leopold II.* and Leslie Bodi's book on Viennese literature during the years of relaxed censorship (1781–95).[27] The impressive contribution of scholars writing in other languages, particularly Hungarian, ought to be stressed.[28] But all this activity has had little influence on recent biographies of Joseph, or on English and French historians – with significant exceptions, among whom Macartney is pre-eminent.

Joseph, then, has been exceptionally ill served by his biographers. Historians have been lamenting for at least a century that no satisfactory life exists.[29] This book is an attempt – to adapt a phrase of Macartney's – not so much to fill the gap as to put something into it.[30]

---

[24] For full references to Arneth's various editions and writings see the list of abbreviations and the bibliography. He wrote an autobiography, *Aus meinem Leben* (2 vols., Vienna, 1891–2). E. Reimann, *Neuere Geschichte des preussischen Staates*, vol. II (Gotha, 1888), pp. 681–700, criticises and corrects Arneth (and also Beer) in detail and in general. S. Schüller's extremely interesting PhD dissertation, 'Kaiser Joseph II. Beiträge zur Charakteristik seiner politischen Ideen', University of Vienna, 1931, based almost entirely on J.'s authentic writings, some of them now apparently lost, attributes some of Arneth's omissions to censorship (p. 3).

[25] See bibliography for details. Schlitter's editions are rendered both more valuable and more difficult to use by his practice of printing many interesting but barely relevant documents in extensive end-notes.

[26] For the administrative studies, published mainly by the Kommission für neuere Geschichte Österreichs (in *VKNGÖ*), see under Kallbrunner and under Walter in the bibliography. Maass in *Josephinismus* prints five volumes of documents.

[27] See n. 17 above for works on Josephism. A. Wandruszka, *Leopold II.* (2 vols., Vienna, 1963, 1965). L. Bodi, *Tauwetter in Wien: Zur Prosa der österreichischen Aufklärung 1781–1795* (Frankfurt, 1977), p. 163.

[28] A brief introduction to the Hungarian literature can be found in the bibliography to the short study of J. by J. Barta, *A nevezetes tollvonás* (Budapest, 1978).

[29] Recently, Bodi, *Tauwetter in Wien*, p. 29.

[30] Macartney, *Habsburg Empire*, p. xiii.

I know that this is a foolhardy undertaking on many counts. First, Mitrofanov's book, though nearly eighty years old, is by no means easy to rival. He says that it took him eight years to write,[31] and it is remarkable that he accomplished the task so quickly. He was not one of Chekhov's feckless, unproductive Russian professors. The two volumes are vigorous, intelligent, wide-ranging, and based for the most part on unimpeachable sources. But no book dating from so long ago could escape having been superseded in some respects. Moreover, it 'is a detailed study of [Joseph's] reforms, not a biography';[32] and it does not deal with the period of the co-regency. In any case, Mitrofanov had not used the full range of Joseph's published, let alone unpublished, correspondence. He cited neither the emperor's letters to his ambassador in Russia, count Ludwig Cobenzl, nor those to the minister plenipotentiary in the Netherlands at the end of the reign, count Trauttmans-dorff, although both collections are large and had appeared in print several years before his own work.[33] He seems not to have known of the manuscript letter-books which contain copies of most of the emperor's official correspon-dence for the period of his sole reign.[34] He relied heavily on the comments of French and German diplomats, but did not make use of English or Italian reports. He was well versed in the troubles of Belgium, but not in Hungarian affairs. Further, his approach betrayed the 'limitless Muscovite fanaticism' that led him to denounce in 1914 the Austro-German plan to encircle Russia.[35]

Secondly, the surviving material for the study of Joseph and his reign is vast. I doubt whether a historian who devoted a lifetime to it would be able to claim at the end that he had mastered it. Although fires and wars have destroyed important records, and peace treaties have required the dispersal of documents once preserved in Vienna to the farthest corners of the old Monarchy,[36] what remains in the Haus-, Hof- und Staatsarchiv is sufficiently

---

31 Mitrofanov I, p. xiii.
32 G. P. Gooch, *Maria Theresa and Other Studies* (London, 1951), p. 118.
33 Beer & Fiedler, *JuLC*; H. Schlitter (ed.), *Geheime Correspondenz Josefs II. mit . . . Trauttmans-dorff. 1787–1789* (Vienna, 1902).
34 For each year of the sole reign there is a thick volume in HHSA entitled (with minor variations) 'Protocollum separatum aller Handbillets'. For the earlier years of the sole reign there are additional volumes, each covering two years, of which the first is called 'Protocoll separ. aller Staatsräthl. Handbillets pro Annis 1781 & 1782'.
35 The quotation is from Delbrück's republication of Mitrofanov's pre-war article: H. Delbrück (ed.), *Die Motive und Ziele der russischen Politik nach zwei Russen* (2nd edn, Berlin, 1915), p. 17. The article had originally appeared in *PJ*, CLVI (1914), 388–96.
   There are good reviews of Mitrofanov's book in *PJ*, CXLIV (1911), 515–20 and in *Századok*, XLVI (1912), 298–307. See also K. Schünemann, 'Die Wirtschaftspolitik Josephs II. in der Zeit seiner Mitregentschaft', *MÖIG*, XLVII (1933), 17.
36 There is a huge and unwieldy *Gesamtinventar des Wiener Haus-, Hof- und Staatsarchivs*, ed. L. Bittner (5 vols, Vienna, 1936–40), but much of its classification is now out-of-date. On war losses in one important section of the *Archiv* see A. Coreth, 'Das Schicksal des k.k. Kabinettsarchivs seit 1945', *MÖSA*, XI (1958), 514–25. A little is said about dispersion after Versailles in *The New Guide to the Diplomatic Archives of Western Europe*, ed. D. H. Thomas and L. M. Case ([Philadelphia], 1975), pp. 5–6.

daunting. There are other repositories in Vienna that I have not been able to visit; I have used a mere handful of Belgian, Czech and Hungarian collections; and outside the lands of the Monarchy I have worked only in Britain, the United States and Venice. Although the English sources that I have studied are of considerable interest, I know those of France and Germany, which must be more significant, only at second hand. However, I believe that I have seen virtually all of Joseph's extant and accessible private letters and a good proportion of his official correspondence. This book is essentially based on identified original material, with much assistance from the very large amount of published secondary work. Since spurious documents figure so prominently in the literature, I have deliberately made full quotations from Joseph's genuine writings.

Thirdly, it is notorious that the study of the Monarchy poses acute linguistic problems. Macartney tells us that he was at first put off writing his general history because he did not know fourteen languages.[37] But there are mitigating circumstances. For Joseph's reign, nearly all original sources are in one of four languages: French for his private and family correspondence, for most documents relating to foreign policy, and for the affairs of Belgium; German for the administration of the central core of lands, and after 1784 for Hungary and the eastern provinces; Latin for Hungary and the eastern provinces before 1784, and for some church questions; and Italian for the affairs of Lombardy and for some dealings with the papacy. As for secondary writing, knowledge of these four languages together with English, Flemish and Hungarian makes it possible to read the great bulk of it.[38]

Fourthly, there is a special risk for an Englishman in taking up this subject. The dangers are underlined in the criticism made by a Hungarian reviewer of Padover's *Revolutionary Emperor*:

He confronts the economic, social, intellectual and political life of eighteenth-century Europe like an East European writing the history of the United States who has never been to America, knows no English and relies entirely on works published in his own country. Just as the latter is hardly in a position to compose a successful biography of Jefferson, so Padover should not have allowed himself to stand forward as an interpreter of Joseph II ... Not only has the European atmosphere naturally remained completely unfamiliar to him, but so have the emperor's immediate surroundings, the Court of Vienna, and also his sphere of operation, the Habsburg Monarchy, with its many nations, customs, laws and patterns of life.[39]

Historians based within the lands of the Monarchy can spend much longer in their archives than foreign students dependent on travel grants and sabbatical leave. I must have missed many points that are obvious to those who

[37] Macartney, *Habsburg Empire*, p. xi.
[38] I have read only what seemed absolutely necessary in Flemish and Hungarian, the latter with the generous aid of Dr G. Gömöri.
[39] J. Berlász in *Századok*, LXXVIII (1944), 517.

live on the spot and speak some of the languages fluently. But I would claim in compensation certain advantages. Especially since 1918, much of the writing on the history of the Monarchy has deserved Macartney's adjective 'tribal'.[40] Historians from the Austrian Republic have annexed the whole story to the small territory now ruled from Vienna. Historians from other parts of the Monarchy have often seemed interested only in their own nationality's experience within it. A complete outsider can perhaps more easily consider the whole state as it was in the eighteenth century. He may also be able to look more dispassionately than most Austrians at Joseph's church policies, which remain closely bound up with contemporary controversies. Bodi is not alone in suggesting that 'the Austrian academic Establishment still today reacts somewhat touchily to the political and social radicalism and anti-clericalism of Joseph's period'.[41]

Certain other issues deserve mention at this point. Distaste for Joseph tends to go with veneration of Maria Theresa. Moreover, the figure of his mother is so dominating that it often occludes him, and their personalities clashed so violently that it is hard to be just to both. Arneth omitted from his editions some of the passages in which Joseph put his side of the case.[42] If I single out for refutation some remarks of Crankshaw's, it is because he is the most accessible representative for the English reader of the school that admires the mother to the point of refusing a hearing to the son. More generally, I believe that the spell Maria Theresa exercises across the centuries has seduced historians into making unbalanced assessments of the co-regency.

Frederick the Great, too, often puts Joseph in the shade, partly because the Prussian has received a better press than the Austrian. The Protestants were on Frederick's side against the emperor, and they were more articulate than the Roman Catholics. Further, just when historians were beginning to plunder the Viennese archives, Prussia defeated Austria in the struggle for control of Germany, and Catholic historical scholarship was blighted by schism over the Vatican decrees and by the *Kulturkampf*.[43] Ranke was uniquely objective among Protestant scholars. Modern accounts of 'enlightened despotism' are commonly based on Prussia under Frederick and pay little heed to the Monarchy under Joseph.

A more fundamental problem is posed by two fine historians, who have cast doubt on the value of writing about Joseph at all. For the late Professor Soboul 'enlightened absolutism' was a social movement, worth serious study only from below.[44] For Miss Behrens 'enlightened despotism' no longer merits

[40] Macartney, *Habsburg Empire*, p. xii.
[41] Bodi, *Tauwetter in Wien*, p. 22.
[42] See Beales, *MÖSA* (1980), 146–7, and below pp. 207–9, 214–16, 269, 341–2, 354–6.
[43] W. O. Chadwick, *Catholicism and History* (Cambridge, 1972), p. 92.
[44] A. Soboul, 'Sur le système du despotisme éclairé', in *Les Lumières en Hongrie, en Europe centrale et en Europe orientale* (Budapest, 1977), pp. 19–29.

scholarly consideration: it is the economic and social histories of the lands concerned that should be examined instead.[45]

These views rest first on the assumption that the attention devoted to the monarchs of the late eighteenth century has ensured that we know all that matters about them – an assumption manifestly false in the case of Joseph II. Many of his letters and memoranda remain not only unpublished but unstudied. On the one hand, his biographers have troubled themselves little about questions of authenticity. On the other, the historians of administration, society and the economy have concentrated on bureaucratic documents and often ignored even those of the emperor's personal or semi-official writings that have been published. Yet this was an absolute monarch surrounded and influenced by cronies, courtiers and relations as well as by officials.[46]

Soboul and Behrens of course are raising a still bigger issue, suggesting that what went on at the top in the Monarchy and in the other supposedly enlightened states of the period was mostly or entirely a reflection of social and economic trends. This view is axiomatic among the massed cohorts of Marxist historians, and has led to the publication of much useful work on such topics as peasant agriculture. But the Monarchy, perhaps more than any other state, was a standing defiance of its peoples' predilection or tendency to distinct development. It cut across every sort of boundary, legal, customary, religious, national, linguistic, geographical and economic. Joseph was pre-eminent in challenging them all, and class boundaries too. Since he was an absolute ruler his commands could not be ignored. Hence it is impossible to write even the social and economic history of the Monarchy's provinces during his reign without giving an important place to his attitudes and actions.

Finally, it is only by studying the emperor himself, his mother and a few officials working directly under them, most prominently Kaunitz, that it is possible to discover how foreign policy was made and how it was related to domestic affairs. Diplomatic history of this period has been neglected for some time, and it has become fashionable to write it off, rather like the study of monarchs, as either unimportant or sufficiently known, or both.[47] I believe on the contrary that it is in need of drastic revision, and that no aspect of the Monarchy's history is more significant. 'If the Austrian Empire had not existed it would have been necessary to invent it.'[48] To put the point the other way round, the Monarchy was a state which owed not only its greatness but its very survival to the conflicting interests of other states, all of which had a sounder domestic base than the Habsburgs'. Further, the facts of geography and the provisions of treaties gave other Powers exceptional opportunities to

[45] B. Behrens, 'Enlightened despotism', *HJ*, XVIII (1975), 401–8.
[46] This criticism applies sometimes to Maass, *Josephinismus*, and often to the *VKNGÖ* volumes.
[47] Macartney, *Habsburg Empire*, p. xiii.
[48] Quoted in E. Crankshaw, *The Fall of the House of Habsburg* (London, 1963), p. 4.

interfere in its internal affairs. So neither the ruler of the Monarchy nor his peoples had the freedom of manoeuvre in domestic matters enjoyed by some other governments and nations. If the role of the Monarchy's sovereigns is ignored, an essential key to the understanding of its history is lost. The ruler was the state – not in the sense that he could always get his way, but in the sense that no one else had concerns coterminous with the state. He was the only person involved in every aspect of its activity as it affected every province, as well as in relations with other Powers.[49]

In this first volume I shall deal with the period down to Maria Theresa's death in 1780. When I began work on this book, I had no idea that there would prove to be so much to say about these early years. But in the first place, the story of a man's upbringing, education, loves and friendships alone gives him reality as a person. Secondly, Mitrofanov was right when he wrote that the co-regency was Joseph's apprenticeship in government.[50] It certainly should not be treated as a period when he was in control – as was sometimes suggested in older writings.[51] But nor, as has been claimed since, was it a period when he had little or no influence.[52] Thirdly, I have found many gaps, and much that is misleading, in the historiography of Maria Theresa's later years. Joseph's role as co-regent has never been adequately appraised; and partly for this reason, the conventional picture of this period needs to be redrawn.

[49] It is interesting to compare the argument of A. Sked, 'Historians, the nationality question, and the downfall of the Habsburg Empire', *TRHS*, 5th series, XXXI (1981), 175–93.
[50] Mitrofanov I, pp. 94–7.
[51] J. F. Bright, *Joseph II* (London, 1897), covers 1765 to 1790.
[52] For example, L. von Pastor, *History of the Popes* (Eng. trans., 40 vols., London, 1938–53), vol. XXXIX, p. 430, says M. T. excluded J. from 'educational and ecclesiastico-political affairs'.

CHAPTER 1

The Austrian succession

Maria Theresa wrote on Joseph's birthday in 1777:

Great day for me, which thirty-six years ago reinforced all my actions and reinvigorated me, since [it proved that] the good God, this divine Providence, still desired to maintain the sceptre in our House, granting me at the most critical juncture a son, when I no longer possessed any undisputed lands, so that in the following year I didn't know where to go for the birth of my next child, as I couldn't stay in Vienna, with Bohemia and Upper Austria lost, Lower Austria threatened by the Bavarians, Italy and the Netherlands invaded, and Hungary so plague-ridden that, when my baggage arrived at Pest, the gates were shut because of the contagion and it had to be sent back.[1]

The birth of a male heir to a throne always evokes special rejoicing. But Joseph's arrival on 13 March 1741 had been awaited with unparalleled anxiety, was welcomed with quite exceptional joy and relief, and had an unusually immediate influence on the course of politics. It is important to understand why the event mattered so much, both because his character was affected by the devotion he in consequence commanded, and because the desperate situation of the dynasty and the Monarchy at the time of his birth – which partly explains the enthusiasm – survived as a nightmare recollection in the minds of his parents and older advisers and always affected his own thinking.[2]

The great Habsburg dynasty had produced male heirs for at least twenty-three consecutive generations since the early Middle Ages. But the run came to an end in the eighteenth century. Figure 1 will help to explain the position. The Spanish Habsburg line died out in 1700 with king Charles II, 'the Bewitched', a pathetic, handicapped invalid who, though twice married, had fathered no children. As for the Austrian branch, when Charles VI succeeded his brother, Joseph I, as ruler of the Monarchy in 1711, he was the only surviving male Habsburg – or, as he himself put it in his diary, 'Of our House I

---

[1] Arneth, *MTKuF* II, p. 73 (to Ferdinand). This chapter has particularly benefited from the criticism of Dr P. G. M. Dickson.
[2] See pp. 24, 95, 293–4 and 294n below; A. Beer (ed.), 'Denkschriften des Fürsten Wenzel Kaunitz-Rittberg', *AÖG*, XLVIII (1872), 115–19.

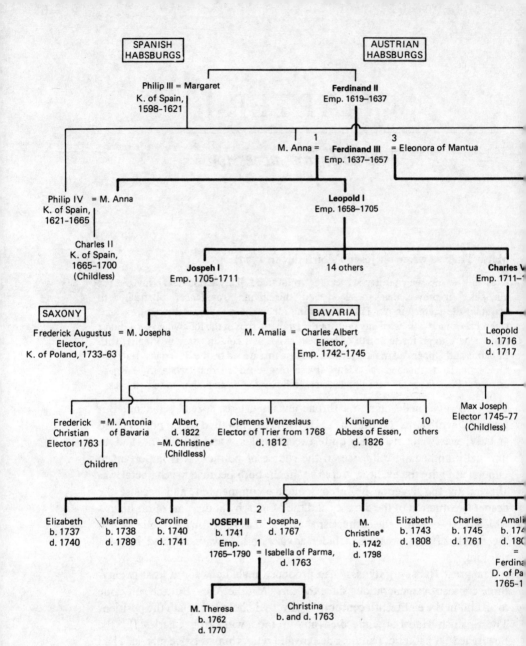

Figure 1. Genealogical table of the Austrian succession.

Heavy lines indicate rulers of the Monarchy (in bold) and their children.

* indicates the appearance of the same person twice.

K. = king, G.D. = grand duke, D. = duke, M. = Maria/Marie.

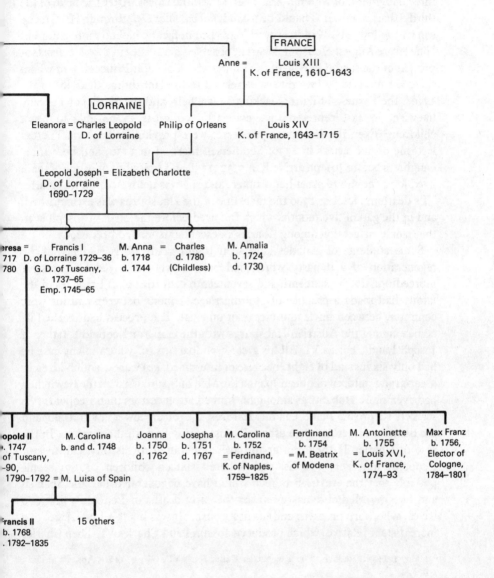

FRANCE

Anne = Louis XIII
K. of France, 1610–1643

LORRAINE

Eleanora = Charles Leopold
D. of Lorraine

Philip of Orleans

Louis XIV
K. of France, 1643–1715

Leopold Joseph = Elizabeth Charlotte
D. of Lorraine
1690–1729

...eresa =   Francis I   M. Anna =   Charles   M. Amalia
...717   D. of Lorraine 1729–36   b. 1718   d. 1780   b. 1724
...780   G. D. of Tuscany,   d. 1744   (Childless) d. 1730
         1737–65
         Emp. 1745–65

...opold II   M. Carolina   Joanna   Josepha   M. Carolina   Ferdinand   M. Antoinette   Max Franz
... 1747   b. and d. 1748 b. 1750   b. 1751   b. 1752   b. 1754   b. 1755   b. 1756,
of Tuscany,   d. 1762   d. 1767   = Ferdinand,   = M. Beatrix   = Louis XVI,   Elector of
...-90,   K. of Naples,   of Modena   K. of France,   Cologne,
1790–1792 = M. Luisa of Spain   1759–1825   1774–93   1784–1801

...rancis II   15 others
b. 1768
. 1792–1835

alone am left.' A son born to him in 1716 was dead within the year. Then came
three daughters, of whom Maria Theresa was the eldest. After the birth of the
third, Charles wrote: 'Thanks be to God, *fiat voluntas Dei*, through His Grace a
son will follow, His Will in everything.'[3] But in fact he had no more children.
'The entire August House of Austria', observed a traveller in 1729, 'consists at
present of the sacred Person of the Emperor and of eight Princesses, of whom
three are married.'[4] Two dynasties related to the Habsburgs died out in the
1730s: the Farnese of Parma, lacking a male heir, and the Medici of Tuscany
likewise, its last representative evidently too gross to be able to beget
children.[5] Even the Habsburg princesses were proving frail. Maria Theresa
lost one of her sisters in 1730. She herself married in 1736, and bore three
daughters before Joseph arrived, in 1737, 1738 and 1740; but only one of them
lived long enough to greet her brother, and she was deformed.[6] With Charles
VI's death in October 1740 the male line of the Habsburgs was extinguished,
and in the gap of five months which followed before the birth of Joseph even
the female succession among Charles's descendants looked precarious.

   Some students of genetics have seen Joseph's advent as evidence of the
regeneration of a dynasty which had been nearly destroyed by excessive
inbreeding.[7] In the sixteenth and seventeenth centuries both branches of the
family had made a practice of intermarriage. Unions between cousins were
common, between uncle and niece not unusual. The process had reached its
climax among the Austrian Habsburgs with the emperor Leopold I, father of
Joseph I and Charles VI. All his great-grandparents (of whom in any case he
had only six instead of eight, because of intermarriage) were grandchildren or
great-grandchildren of queen Joanna the Mad of Spain. Charles the Bewitched
had even more Habsburgs among his immediate ancestors then Leopold. It is
scarcely surprising that the family features, the jutting lower jaw and chin and
the hanging underlip, were especially disfiguring in both these rulers. In the
case of Charles II they appear to have contributed to his physical misery.
Leopold, however, was fit, and fathered sixteen children. But it seems
possible that the Austrian branch would have degenerated like the Spanish
and like the Medici dynasty but for the early deaths of Leopold's first two
wives, who were his niece and his first cousin. It was his third marriage, to a
more distant relative, which produced Joseph I and Charles VI. Then Charles

---

[3] 1 May 1711: O. Redlich, 'Die Tagebücher Kaiser Karls VI', *GV*, p. 146. 5 Apr. 1724: *ibid.*,
p. 144.
[4] *The Memoirs of Charles-Lewis, Baron de Pollnitz* (2 vols., London, 1737), vol. I, p. 233.
[5] W. Strohmayer, 'Die Vererbung des Habsburger Familientypus', *Nova Acta Leopoldina*, neue
Folge, v (1937), 266–78, 293–4.
[6] Arneth, *GMT* I, pp. 23, 254; Pick, *Maria Theresa*, p. 221; J. Hrazky, 'Die Persönlichkeit der
Infantin Isabella von Parma', *MÖSA*, XII (1959), 187–8. See Figure I.
[7] See literature cited in Strohmayer, *Nova Acta Leopoldina* (1937); Julius Wolf, *Blut und Rasse des
hauses Habsburg-Lothringen* (Zurich, 1940); A. Wandruszka, *The House of Habsburg* (London,
1964), pp. 137, 139–40.

VI married a princess quite unconnected with his own family. Hence Maria Theresa was the least inbred Habsburg ruler for centuries.

On the other hand, her husband, Francis Stephen of Lorraine, the future Francis I, brought a new infusion of Habsburg blood, both as a grandson through his father of Leopold I's half-sister, and less directly through his mother. This did not prevent Maria Theresa bearing him sixteen children, including five sons, nor her son Leopold II fathering legitimately another sixteen offspring, of whom twelve were sons, and yet more illegitimately. But it no doubt helped to impart to some of her own children and, through a renewal of intermarriage in that and later generations, to more of her descendants the family lip, and in a few cases the jaw as well. So Joseph was rather fortunate to display no trace of either, except possibly in early childhood.[8]

However, the perils of excessive inbreeding, and the remarkable evidence for them available in the history and portraiture of the Habsburg dynasty, appear to have been totally unsuspected by contemporaries. Charles VI and Maria Theresa attributed their failures and successes in producing children simply to the will of God, which they sought to influence by pilgrimages, votive offerings and prayers to saints. Joseph owed his name to his mother's gratitude to St Joseph, to whom she had repeatedly prayed for a son during her pregnancy.[9] She positively favoured inbreeding.[10] It is presumably coincidental that Joseph showed a special aversion for three of his relatives who were distinctively Habsburg in features: his first cousins Josepha (who became his second wife) and Clemens Wenzeslaus (elector of Trier); and his nephew the archduke Charles.[11]

What obsessed contemporaries were the risks to a dynasty and to the state it ruled when the male line failed. Female successions were virtually certain to be disputable and disputed, to lead to war, and to result in territorial losses for the state concerned. It is possible to see in retrospect that two main principles had to be reconciled in the numerous succession questions of the early eighteenth century. No one could envisage a large state being satisfactorily governed except by a hereditary monarchy, and the principle of male primogeniture was generally accepted. On the other hand, the vagaries of inheritance could not be allowed to destroy the rough balance of power that existed between the main states of Europe. When the Spanish line died out, the majority of the Powers were determined to prevent the union of its lands

[8] For this whole section, see Strohmayer's impressive article, *Nova Acta Leopoldina* (1937), 219–96.

[9] Pick, *Maria Theresa*, pp. 23, 41. Arneth, *GMT* I, pp. 255, 400.

[10] See p. 86 below.

[11] See his letters to the elector of Trier, published as a pamphlet in 1782 and by D. G. Mohnike in *Zeitschrift für die Historische Theologie*, IV (1834), 241–90; the discussion of his second marriage on pp. 85–8; L. to J., 5 June 1786 (Arneth, *JuL* II, p. 26) and 4 Oct. 1787 (HHSA FA Sbde 7, unpublished by Arneth).

either with France, as might have happened under Charles II's will, or with the Monarchy, as the rule of male primogeniture would have required. After a decade of war a separate dynasty was established in Spain, but Charles VI was compensated for the denial of his hereditary claims to the whole Spanish empire with its Italian portion and with Belgium. Similar considerations were to apply to the Austrian succession.

When Charles VI became ruler of the Monarchy in 1711, he had no children of either sex. A son would have succeeded him without question, but in default of a male heir Joseph I's two daughters had a claim arguably better than that of any daughters Charles might father. So did Leopold I's surviving daughters. However, in 1713, when still childless, Charles declared in a document known as the Pragmatic Sanction that Joseph's daughters should take precedence over Leopold's, and further that if he (Charles) had no son to succeed him but had daughters, they would take precedence over Joseph's. By the time Joseph's elder daughter, Maria Josepha, was married to the future elector of Saxony and king of Poland in 1719, and was made to renounce any prior claims to the Monarchy, Charles had two baby daughters living. Joseph's younger daughter, Maria Amalia, was also compelled to declare her acceptance of the Pragmatic Sanction when she married the future elector of Bavaria in 1722. Between 1720 and 1725 Charles obtained the consent of all the constituted representative assemblies of his provinces to the new order of succession. He meanwhile set about trying to procure its ratification by all significant European states.

Internally, he got his way at little if any cost. The Hungarian diet insisted on special terms, including a promise that the ruler would deploy all his or her strength in defence of Hungary if the country were attacked. But otherwise the net domestic effect of the Pragmatic Sanction was to strengthen the position of the sovereign and the central government, since the document asserted, for the first time, the indivisibility of the lands of the Monarchy. In other words, it was now being treated, at least for this purpose, as one state, rather than just as a collection of territories which happened all to have the same ruler.[12]

Externally, however, the Pragmatic Sanction had damaging effects on the Monarchy. Charles had succeeded to the throne at a most favourable moment. A major rebellion in Hungary had just been put down. The Monarchy and its allies were at the peak of their victories in the war of the Spanish succession. In addition to the formerly Spanish lands in Italy and Belgium which Charles added to the Monarchy, his armies under prince Eugene extended his eastern frontiers far into modern Romania and Yugoslavia, forcing the Turks to acknowledge these conquests by the peace of Passarowitz in 1718. The

---

[12] For the Pragmatic Sanction, its origins and ratification, see O. Redlich, *Das Werden einer Grossmacht: Österreich, 1700–1740* (4th edn, Vienna, 1962), ch. 8 and the literature there cited.

Habsburgs of the Austrian branch had never seemed so powerful. Charles's dominions are still full of churches and other public buildings celebrating with extravagant inscriptions and grandiose baroque frescoes his triumphs, even his apotheosis. The two in which he took the greatest interest early in his reign were the superb royal library and the Karlskirche in Vienna, both of them studied glorifications of himself (the 'Spanish Hercules'), his dynasty and the church with which he was identified. Later on, he transferred his attention to converting the old monastery at Klosterneuburg, founded by his ancestor duke Leopold, the patron saint of Austria, into a vast imperial residence, half palace, half religious community, 'a gigantic project with four great court-yards overlooked by nine cupolas, each topped by a Habsburg Crown'.[13]

Barely a quarter of this last scheme had been finished when Charles died, conscious of his failures. Even as the frescoes of the library and the Karlskirche were being completed in the late 1720s, events had begun to mock at them. The price of England's guarantee of the Pragmatic Sanction in 1731 was the dissolution of his Ostend trading company, which was to have revived the economy of Belgium and given the Monarchy a share of colonial trade. Spain succeeded in recovering most of her old Italian lands, though on behalf of princes other than the heir to the Spanish throne. In order to buy off France, Charles had to compel his future son-in-law to surrender his sovereignty over Lorraine in return for the promise of succession to Tuscany. 'No renunciation', he was told, 'no archduchess.'[14] Admittedly, the extinction of the Medici line came quickly, in 1737, leaving Francis Stephen grand duke of Tuscany. But in the same year the Monarchy went to war against the Turks, who won massive victories culminating in the capture of Belgrade in 1739. Late in that year the governor of the southern Netherlands wrote: 'We are without allies and without advisers, after having lost part of the state of Milan, the kingdom of Naples, and Sicily, Lorraine, Bar, Serbia, Wallachia, a part of Banat and terrain two leagues in width extending all along the Save.'[15]

This catalogue of disaster was not purely the result of Charles's attempts to obtain from other Powers guarantees of the Pragmatic Sanction. The Italian territories, especially Naples and Sicily, were bound to be difficult for a Court based at Vienna to defend. Prince Eugene's death in 1736 deprived the

---

13 For the background to this period of triumph, R. J. W. Evans, *The Making of the Habsburg Monarchy, 1550–1700* (Oxford, 1979). See also H. Sedlmayr, 'Die politische Bedeutung des deutschen Barocks', *GV*,esp. pp. 135–40; and, more grandiosely, F. Matsche, *Die Kunst im Dienst der Staatsidee Kaiser Karls VI.* (2 vols., Berlin, 1981). Quotation from the guidebook *Stift Klosterneuburg* by F. Röhrig (3rd edn, Munich, 1967).

14 Arneth, *GMT* I, p. 23.

15 Quoted in V. L. Tapié, *The Rise and Fall of the Habsburg Monarchy* (London, 1971), p. 164 (F. Harrach to Liechtenstein, 6 Oct. 1739). For the Turkish recovery, L. Cassels, *The Struggle for the Ottoman Empire, 1717–1740* (London, [1966]) and K. A. Roider's two books, *The Reluctant Ally* (Baton Rouge, 1972) and *Austria's Eastern Question, 1700–1790* (Princeton, 1982), ch. 5.

Monarchy of by far its greatest general. It is clear that the state's resources had been overstretched. Moreover, the other Powers were unlikely to tolerate for long such a large extension of Austrian rule as they had permitted in the 1710s. To go to war with Turkey at all was evidently a bad mistake. But Charles's obsession with the Pragmatic Sanction distorted all aspects of his policy, contributing to his diplomatic and military defeats and taking precedence over domestic reforms which might have prepared the Monarchy more effectively for the dangers of a disputed succession.[16] From Vienna the English ambassador reported in August 1739:

Every thing in this court is running into the last confusion and ruin; where there are as visible signs of folly and madness as ever were inflicted upon a people whom heaven is determined to destroy, no less by domestic divisions, than by the more public calamities of repeated defeats, defencelessness, poverty, and plague.[17]

Early in 1740 one of Francis's gentlemen remarked: 'The only event we can pin our hope on is the birth of a prince. The situation might change once people have such an object to fasten their loyalty on.'[18] But Maria Theresa's current pregnancy produced only another princess. By contrast, Joseph I's daughters now possessed between them six sons.[19]

Charles's death, which was quite unexpected, occurred at the worst possible moment for the Monarchy. The succession after Maria Theresa seemed in doubt, and the run of military defeats and territorial losses had terribly damaged the strength, morale and prestige of the state. More threatening still, Frederick II had just succeeded as king of Prussia. No ruler in history has displayed greater genius or more ruthless ambition. They were soon to be turned against the Monarchy.

Nearly all the Powers had in the end guaranteed the Pragmatic Sanction. But the failure of Charles's policy was demonstrated almost as soon as Maria Theresa succeeded him. She found herself, in her own high-flown words, 'without money, without credit, without army, without experience and knowledge of my own and finally, also without any counsel, because each one of them at first wanted to wait and see how things would develop'.[20] In the five

---

[16] Redlich, *Werden einer Grossmacht*, p. 236. It is clear that Charles VI is a ripe subject for revaluation. The process has begun in relation to the origins of Josephism. See Klingenstein, *Staatsverwaltung und kirchliche Autorität*, pp. 57–9.

[17] W. Coxe, *History of the House of Austria* (2 vols., London, 1807), vol. II, p. 201 (Robinson to Walpole, 19 Aug. 1739). This ancient work, in many respects quite outdated, remains of special value for its quotations from unpublished English archives, and its treatment of the Monarchy as a whole, particularly its foreign policy.

[18] Quoted in Pick, *Maria Theresa*, p. 51.

[19] The elector of Bavaria had one son, the king of Poland no fewer than five. See Strohmayer, *Nova Acta Leopoldina* (1937), 259–60, 263–4.

[20] Quoted from one version of her political testament in C. A. Macartney (ed.), *The Habsburg and Hohenzollern Dynasties in the Seventeenth and Eighteenth Centuries* (London, 1970), p. 100. See p. 52 and n below.

months between Charles VI's death and his grandson's birth, the situation of the Monarchy deteriorated still further. Not only the husbands of Joseph I's daughters, the king of Poland and the elector of Bavaria, but also the king of Spain laid claim to Maria Theresa's entire inheritance, and the king of Sardinia to part of it; France and some other Powers made difficulties about acknowledging her accession; and Frederick II, professing friendship, seized the greater part of Silesia, one of the wealthiest and strategically most vital provinces of the Monarchy. As well as many foreign statesmen, some of Maria Theresa's own ministers clearly anticipated that her heritage would be dismembered.[21]

Charles had illustrated what was evidently a general prejudice when he made no attempt to acquaint his daughter with affairs of state. Francis, on the other hand, was appointed viceroy of Hungary in 1732, and then a member of the chief policy-making body, the Conference.[22] Women rulers were virtually unknown in the history of Central Europe. It was supposed that any such would be weak, and in practice under the control of their husbands. Maria Theresa at once showed her ministers that she intended to be the effective ruler. But she blurred the issue by long retreats during her almost annual pregnancies, by relying on Francis in certain fields and by insisting that he be given the title of *Mitregent*, co-regent, so that in theory he shared all her responsibilities. To win acceptance for this scheme created additional difficulties for her, as it was hard to reconcile with the terms of the Pragmatic Sanction.[23] Clearly, the sole rule of a woman was thought unnatural, and a second female succession inconceivable.

One inescapable drawback to a female succession in the Monarchy was the incapacity of a woman to become Holy Roman Emperor. For 302 years and for the last thirteen tenures, the electors had always chosen as emperor the head of the Austrian branch of the house of Habsburg. It was believed in Vienna that the shadowy power and influence of the emperor brought real advantages to the dynasty and the state.[24] Francis was a possible candidate, but as yet an unlikely one, since he was resented in Germany as a man of French

---

[21] The Venetian ambassador's expectations of 'la separazione di si vasta Monarchia, che da se medesima, mancata il capo, non potrà reggersi' in Arneth, *GMT* I, p. 369 (18 Oct. 1740); the papacy's in Pastor, *History of the Popes*, vol. xxxv, p. 83; and the British ambassador's account in Coxe, *House of Austria*, vol. II, p. 266 (Robinson to Harrington, 22 Oct. 1740); 'The Turks seemed to [her ministers] already in Hungary; the Hungarians themselves in arms; the Saxons in Bohemia; the Bavarians at the gates of Vienna.' Cf. Macartney, *Habsburg and Hohenzollern Dynasties*, p. 100.

[22] Macartney, *Habsburg and Hohenzollern Dynasties*, p. 97; Macartney, *Maria Theresa and the House of Austria* (London, 1969), p. 30.

[23] Arneth, *GMT* I, pp. 92, 171–3, 287–8, 303–6.

[24] E.g. Redlich, *Werden einer Grossmacht*, pp. 207–8; Arneth, *GMT* I, pp. 175–6; Arneth, *GMT* III, p. 432. Cf. pp. 119–23 below.

background and education, and lacked a sizeable principality of his own within the generally accepted confines of the Empire.[25]

Amid all these difficulties the long-awaited prince, the future Joseph II, was born at two o'clock in the morning of Monday, 13 March 1741, in the Hofburg in Vienna, the main residence and administrative headquarters of the Habsburg dynasty. On the next day the papal nuncio, assisted by no fewer than sixteen other prelates, baptised him Joseph Benedict Augustus Johann Anton Michael Adam. Proxies acted for the godfathers, pope Benedict XIV and king Augustus III of Poland. Special emissaries were dispatched to carry the good news to all tolerably friendly rulers.[26]

It was almost the only piece of pure good fortune that the dynasty experienced between 1730 and 1745.

As soon as the news spread [reported the Venetian ambassador], the people crowded to the royal palace with shouts of joy, and ran through the streets almost madly, celebrating their exultation. The hopes of the whole nation had been directed to this moment, and with the fatal loss of the Emperor it was regarded as the only reparation. The House of Austria appears confirmed, as does the elevation of the grand duke, the father.[27]

The official *Wienerisches Diarium* at once published a supplement describing the ceremonies and festivities associated with the birth. At the baptism, it recorded, there was water from the river Jordan, and relics of the Holy Blood, the nail, the thorn and the milk. The baby was at once created a Knight of the Golden Fleece. They heard the news in Pressburg, the Hungarian capital, later on the Monday. In Prague they had to wait until the Thursday, when the archbishop celebrated the event by scattering several hundred gulden out of the window of his palace to the happy crowd.[28] A volume of over 300 pages records the illuminations and decorations with which Vienna saluted Maria Theresa when she reappeared in public at the end of April.[29]

Nevertheless, despite the boost she received from Joseph's birth, Maria Theresa had to endure terrible moments before her position was secured. At

---

[25] Arneth, *GMT* I, pp. 175–6; *GMT* III, pp. 38–9. He possessed nothing grander than the principality of Teschen, since he had renounced Lorraine and since Tuscany did not count within the Empire. When he was eventually made emperor, he rode to the cathedral as king of Jerusalem, a still less meaningful dignity claimed by the house of Lorraine (Arneth, *GMT* III, p. 108).

[26] Arneth, *GMT* I, pp. 254–6, 400. Wurzbach VI, p. 296. *WZ*, 25 Mar. 1741 (*Beschreibung deren ... Tauf-Ceremonien des neu-geborenen ... Printzen ... Josephi ...*).

[27] Arneth, *GMT* I, p. 400 (Capallo's report 13 Mar. 1741).

[28] *WZ*, 25 Mar. 1741 (special *Beschreibung* as n. 26).

[29] *Wiennerische Beleuchtungen oder Beschreibung Aller deren Triumph- und Ehren-Gerüsten, Sinn-Bildern und anderen sowohl herzlich- als kostbar und annoch nie so prächtig geschenen Auszierungen welche bey denen zu Ihren der Höchst-gewünschten Geburt Des Durchleutigsten Ertz-Hertzogs zu Oesterreich ec. JOSEPHI Den 13 Martii das erstemal und sodann Bey Allerhöchst Ihro Majestät der Königin von Hungarn ... MARIAE THERESIAE ... Beseegneten Hervorgang ...*, ed. Ghelen (Vienna, 1741). This work has recently been republished in facsimile.

the end of 1741 the elector of Bavaria held both Linz and Prague, was acknowledged as archduke of upper Austria and was crowned king of Bohemia. Next year he became the emperor Charles VII. The Prussian army repeatedly defeated the Austrian. The southern Netherlands were soon overrun by France, and territory was lost in Italy.

In these years of crisis Joseph was a useful pawn in Maria Theresa's often desperate manoeuvres. She knew very well that his mere existence greatly strengthened her chances of holding on to her inheritance. She showed herself very ready to exploit the fact. She tried to impress old cardinal Fleury of France with it.[30] At a critical point she displayed the baby to the Hungarian diet. They dutifully applauded the tender, squirrel-like archduke.[31] She sent his picture and the following appeal to field-marshal Khevenhüller as he advanced against the Bavarians: 'Here you have before your eyes a queen abandoned by the whole world, with her male heir; what do you suppose will become of him?'[32] She had him dressed up in Hungarian clothes.[33]

From 1743 onwards, proposals were made that he might be elected king of the Romans, a title which automatically ensured the holder's succession as emperor. When Charles VII died in 1745, some wanted to see Joseph elected emperor. The aim in both cases was to keep out his father. But Maria Theresa was determined to procure the imperial title for her husband. He was duly crowned as Francis I in October 1745.[34]

Joseph's survival – which, given the level of infant mortality in this period, was very fortunate – remained of priceless advantage to the dynasty at least until Maria Theresa bore a second son, Charles, early in 1745. Two more daughters had intervened between the two sons, and the succession had become yet more precarious when Maria Theresa's only surviving sister died in 1744 after giving birth to her first child, stillborn.[35] Charles was followed by yet another daughter, but in May 1747 a third son, Leopold, was born.[36]

Maria Theresa's international standing was now much improved. In 1745 peace had been made between Prussia and the Monarchy. In 1746 the papal nuncio was able to present, five-and-a-half years late, the consecrated swaddling-clothes accompanying his master's formal congratulations on the birth of his godson! For the whole of the intervening period, the pope and Vienna had been at loggerheads about various claims of Maria Theresa's to

[30] Pick, *Maria Theresa*, p. 78.
[31] Arneth, *GMT* I, pp. 305, 406 (21 Sep. 1741 – not, as has been asserted, earlier). See H. Marczali, 'Vitam et sanguinem!', *HZ*, CXVII (1917), 413–31 and A. Weber, 'Maria Theresia auf dem Pressburger Reichstag', *Ungarische Jahrbücher*, III (1923), 354–82.
[32] Arneth, *GMT* II, p. 9.
[33] K–M I, p. 194 (12 Dec. 1743) mentions the first occasion he wore it. One of the costumes is in the Hungarian National Museum in Budapest. See Plate 1.
[34] Arneth, *GMT* II, pp. 288–9; *GMT* III, chs. 1–4.
[35] Arneth, *GMT* III, p. 10; *GMT* II, pp. 452–6.
[36] Wandruszka, *L. II.*, vol. I, p. 15.

territory and other rights, some purely secular, others arguably ecclesi-astical.[37] In 1748 she acquiesced in the peace of Aachen or Aix-la-Chapelle, under which the Powers recognised her succession to the lands of the Monarchy as Charles VI had left them, with the exceptions of most of Silesia and some small areas in Italy. No doubt it was the rivalries of the Powers which had most to do with this comparatively satisfactory outcome for the empress. But there had been moments when only her own extraordinary spirit and flair had preserved the Monarchy from disintegration. And all her actions had been reinforced by the birth and survival of Joseph.

[37] K–M II, pp. 132, 419; Pastor, *History of the Popes*, vol. xxxv.

CHAPTER 2

Upbringing and education

THE LIFE OF THE COURT

Under Charles VI, according to the traveller already quoted, Vienna possessed 'the greatest and most magnificent Court in Europe. Nevertheless Ceremonies, and the Etiquette, a Name by which they call ancient Usages, give it an Air of Constraint that is to be seen no where else.'[1] The etiquette derived, through the dynastic connexion, from Spain. Its most conspicuous feature was the wearing of black 'Spanish mantles' on state occasions. On the frequent 'gala' days the emperor dined in public, wearing his hat. The empress ate at a separate table. They alone were seated. Everyone else stood, hatless of course, while forty-eight dishes were served. At imperial audiences the visitor had to make three genuflections as he approached, was offered the emperor's hand to kiss, and was then required, after perhaps a few distant if dignified words from the monarch, to make three further genuflections while withdrawing from the presence backwards. Charles VI took a personal interest in maintaining this exceptional degree of stiffness.[2]

Pride, however, appeared to go with poverty. The main imperial palace, the Hofburg, seemed 'so wretched a Mansion that few Monarchs are lodged worse than the Emperor'. The best pictures, tapestries and furniture were stored away in cupboards, presumably in deference to 'the Etiquette'. The Favorita, Charles VI's preferred residence in what was then a suburb of Vienna, resembled nothing so much as a vast Capuchin monastery. Schönbrunn, further out, designed in the 1690s to be a palace worthy of emperors, rivalling Versailles, remained unfinished and neglected.[3] Charles spent a good deal of

[1] *Memoirs of Pollnitz*, vol. I, p. 224.
[2] *Memoirs of Pollnitz*, vol. I, pp. 225–7; J. G. Keysler, *Travels through Germany, Bohemia, Hungary, Switzerland, Italy and Lorrain* (4 vols., 2nd edn, London, 1756–7), vol. IV, pp. 28, 30; J. W. Stoye, 'Emperor Charles VI: the early years of the reign', *TRHS*, 5th series XII (1962), 84; Redlich, *GV*, p. 144. See Plate 20a.
[3] *Memoirs of Pollnitz*, vol. I, pp. 234–5; Sedlmayr, *GV*, pp.130–5; O. Raschauer, *Schönbrunn, eine denkmalkundliche Darstellung seiner Baugeschichte: Der Scholossbau Kaiser Josephs I* (Vienna, 1960), pp. 104–12; J. Glaser, *Schönbrunner Chronik* (Vienna, 1969), pp. 27–34; E. Schlöss, *Das Theresianum* (Vienna, 1979).

time at Laxenburg, a hunting lodge ten miles from Vienna popular with many
generations of his family, where he could indulge both his notorious passion
for sport, particularly 'baiting the heron', and his better-concealed penchant
for the simple life. But this house was 'not worth seeing either for its
architecture or furniture'.[4] The imperial horses appeared to be more grandly
housed than their master, who had commissioned the two Fischers von Erlach
to build for them both vast new stables and what is now regarded as an
exquisite winter riding school.[5] But even this went unappreciated: the
baroque architecture of the place and period, with its bold assimilation of
classical, Italian, French and even oriental elements, was condemned by most
foreign contemporaries as appropriate rather to 'the days of the Goths'.[6]

Vienna had become the permanent capital of the Monarchy only in the late
seventeenth century. What turned out to be the last siege of the city by the
Turks had been raised in 1683,[7] but the need to protect it against attack from
several quarters constrained its development long after that. It was to reach a
population of over 200,000 in the late eighteenth century, but the increase was
accommodated in distinct suburbs. The centre was still confined within
massive walls and bastions, surrounded by a wide esplanade, and many of the
streets remained narrow and winding.[8] However, as the great noble families
had established themselves in the city in the last years of the seventeenth and
the early decades of the eighteenth centuries, its appearance had been
transformed by their splendid new palaces, the finest of them conceived by
two great architects, Johann Bernhard (the elder) Fischer von Erlach and
Johann Lukas von Hildebrandt.[9] Fischer's new building for the Bohemian

4 Keysler, *Travels*, vol. IV, pp. 10, 29; Redlich, *GV*, pp. 141, 143; J. Zykan, *Laxenburg* (Vienna, 1969), esp. pp. 18–25.
5 *Memoirs of Pollnitz*, vol. I, p. 235; K. Oettinger (ed.), *Reclams Kunstführer Österreich*, vol. I pp. 556–7, 574; E. Hempel, *Baroque Art and Architecture in Central Europe* (Harmondsworth, 1965), p. 95.
6 *Memoirs of Pollnitz*, vol. I, p. 235; Hempel, *Baroque Art and Architecture*, esp. pp. 88–95. The elder Fischer's *Entwurff einer historischen Architektur* (Vienna, 1721) displays his eclecticism. It is remarkable that it should have been published in an English edition in 1730 (*A Plan of Civil and Historical Architecture*, now available in facsimile (Ridgewood, NJ, 1964)).
7 The obvious and admirable account for the English reader is J. W. Stoye, *The Siege of Vienna* (London, 1964).
8 An interesting discussion, with useful references, is G. Klingenstein, 'Vienna nel Settecento. Alcuni aspetti', *Quaderni storici*, XXVII (1974), 803–15. The volumes of the *Geschichte der Stadt Wien*, esp. H. Srbik and R. Lorenz, *Die geschichtliche Stellung Wiens, 1740–1918* (Vienna, 1962) (vol. I of the Neue Reihe), are obvious sources. Wangermann, *Austrian Achievement* contains some material on Vienna, as does R. E. Dickinson, *The West European City* (London, 1951), esp. pp. 184–7. There are contemporary accounts in *Memoirs of Pollnitz*, vol. I, pp. 224–57; Keysler, *Travels*, vol. IV, pp. 10–39; later, N. W. Wraxall, *Memoirs of the Courts of Berlin, Dresden, Warsaw, and Vienna, in the Years 1777, 1778, and 1779* (2 vols., 3rd edn, London, 1806), vol. I, pp. 357–61. Professor Linda Colley very kindly obtained for me from Yale the MSS of Wraxall's *Memoirs* on microfilm. It has helped to persuade me of the reliability of his information, and I have used him heavily.
9 Hempel, *Baroque Art and Architecture*, esp. pp. 88–98; H. Sedlmayr, *Johann Bernhard Fischer von Erlach* (Vienna, 1956); B. Grimschitz, *Johann Lucas von Hildebrandt* (Vienna, 1932).

Court Chancery presented visual evidence of another trend, the growing centralisation of the Monarchy's administration.[10]

Beside these secular works, visitors also noticed a strikingly large number of highly ornate churches and substantial monasteries, many of them new or recently rebuilt or enlarged. Charles VI's reign roughly coincided with the last phase of the late flowering of the Counter-Reformation in the central lands of the Monarchy, especially those included in modern Austria. The most conspicuous monuments of this age are the great abbeys of the old monastic orders, which, after a period of decay, were rebuilt on a colossal scale between about 1680 and about 1740. Perhaps the grandest are the Augustinian abbey at St Florian near Linz and the Benedictine abbey of Melk. The latter still astounds the tourist by its size and its fantastic position on a rock dominating the Danube valley between Linz and Vienna. Not only the churches but also the libraries and living quarters of these magnificent institutions outshone in their day even the greatest colleges of Oxford and Cambridge, reflecting growing wealth, security and confidence, as well as an increase in monastic professions and a genuine religious revival. They illustrated too the closeness of church–state relations by incorporating sumptuous suites for the reception of the emperor. In his plans to create for himself a palace-monastery at Klosterneuburg Charles VI was only carrying to a logical conclusion one of the main tendencies of his time.[11]

Newer religious orders flourished too. The Jesuits dominated education, especially at university level. Militant Roman Catholicism followed the imperial flag into the eastern provinces of Hungary to do battle not only against Islam but also against Protestantism and Greek Orthodoxy, which had benefited from the toleration accorded to them under Turkish rule.[12] Although Charles VI himself was not a complete bigot, and prince Eugene actually took an interest in English deists,[13] the Monarchy, and even Vienna,

[10] Klingenstein, *Quaderni storici*, XXVII (1974), 811; Oettinger, *Reclams Kunstführer Österreich*, vol. I, p. 566.

[11] On these monasteries Hempel, *Baroque Art and Architecture*, pp. 88, 98–100; Sedlmayr, *GV*, p. 135; H. Hantsch, *J. Prandtauer* (Vienna, 1926). See, in general, H. Sedlmayr, *Österreichische Barockarchitektur* (Vienna, 1930), and the sources listed in n. 14. Cf. Matsche, *Die Kunst im Dienst der Staatsidee Kaiser Karls VI*. For the comparison with Oxford and Cambridge, E. Gibbon, *Memoirs of my Life*, ed. G. A. Bonnard (London, 1966), pp. 51–2. Melk was the venue of a royal meeting in 1739, and was suggested by M.T. to Maria Antonia of Saxony for a projected meeting in 1760 (W. Lippert, *Kaiserin Maria Theresia und Kurfürstin Maria Antonia von Sachsen: Ihr Briefwechsel* (Leipzig, 1908), p. 81 and n.). Joseph and his father stayed there on the way to and from Frankfurt in 1764 (Arneth, *MTuJ* I, pp. 19–20, 121–2; K-M VI pp. 6, 28) and heard an opera or Latin serenade, a musical drama and 'a Musica bernesca, to make the emperor laugh'.

[12] H. Marczali, *Hungary in the Eighteenth Century* (Cambridge, 1910), ch. 4. For this point and the previous paragraph Evans, *Making of the Habsburg Monarchy*, esp. chs. 4, 7 and 12.

[13] On Charles VI, for example, H. Benedikt, *F.A. Graf von Sporck* (Vienna, 1923), esp. pp. 190–216. On prince Eugene and Toland, F. Venturi, *Utopia and Reform in the Enlightenment* (Cambridge, 1971), p. 60. See also E. Winter, *Frühaufklärung* (Berlin, 1966), esp. pp. 124–36.

seemed to foreign visitors to be intellectually backward, stifled by Jesuit censorship and surfeited with religious observance. Witch-hunting was still rife, especially in Hungary, and many even of the Austrian and Bohemian nobility displayed a 'strange credulity'.[14]

All the same, Vienna offered the visitor some cultural compensations. The Court was multilingual. The stranger could manage perfectly well with any one of German, French, Italian or Spanish.[15] The theatre was notable, the music and opera outstanding – often Italian in language, almost always in style.[16] And the blood sports were on a stupendous scale.[17]

We know an immense amount about the ways of Maria Theresa's Court, mainly because many volumes survive of a diary kept almost throughout her reign by one of the chief officers of the imperial household, count Khevenhüller (later prince Khevenhüller-Metsch), full of detail especially on matters of form and ceremony.[18] During over thirty years in office, he fought to preserve and even to reinstate all the old usages: the wearing of the Spanish mantle, the kissing of royal hands, the eating of formal meals by the ruler and his family in public, the regular ceremonial attendances at appropriate churches on numerous great festivals. But events conspired against him. There were no precedents available to meet the case of a female ruler, a prince consort or a co-regent. It was a grave embarrassment that for the first five years of Maria Theresa's reign there was no emperor at Court, and unsatisfactory in other ways when first her husband and then her son held the superior title but had to be treated as subordinate to her in the affairs of the Monarchy. In any case, Maria Theresa was decidedly less attached to the old etiquette than her father had been. She mitigated it, and was often glad to take advantage of her pregnancies, and later of her widowhood, to modify or escape it. Already in 1745 Khevenhüller was writing, in the variegated German characteristic of the time and place, of the 'so sehr ruinirte Etiquette'.[19]

---

[14] The quotation from Keysler, *Travels*, vol. IV, p. 98. On witch-burning, *ibid.*, p. 80. Other passages on religion, *ibid.*, pp. 12–16, 83, 85; *Memoirs of Pollnitz*, vol. I, pp. 216, 228, 249–53. For a modern account of the religious history of the reign see J. Wodka, *Kirche in Österreich* (Vienna, 1959), pp. 244–5, 265, 268–74, 276–80, 288–90; Winter, *Frühaufklärung*; on witch-hunting Evans, *Making of the Habsburg Monarchy*, esp. pp. 400–17.

[15] *Memoirs of Pollnitz*, vol. I, p. 224.

[16] *Memoirs of Pollnitz*, vol. I, p. 234; Keysler, *Travels*, vol. IV, p. 31; C. Burney, *A General History of Music*, ed. F. Mercer (2 vols., New York, 1957), vol. II, pp. 941–2. Cf. Macartney, 'The Habsburg dominions', *NCMH*, VII, p. 399. For Italian influence in general, see A. Wandruszka, *Österreich und Italien im 18. Jahrhundert* (Vienna, 1963) and E. Garms-Cornides, 'Zwischen Giannone, Muratori und Metastasio', *WBGN*, III (1976), 224–50.

[17] Keysler, *Travels*, vol. IV, p. 29; Redlich, *GV*, p. 141. Charles's *Jagdtagebuch* survives.

[18] For bibliographic details, see list of abbreviations. The diary forms the basis of A. Wolf, *Aus dem Hofleben Maria Theresia's* (2nd edn, Vienna, 1859). Khevenhüller finally became *Obersthofmeister* in 1770 after many years as *Obersthofmarshall* and *Oberstkämmerer*. He had become prince in 1764. See Plate 20a.

[19] The references for this paragraph in K-M are numerous and scattered. Perhaps it is sufficient to cite the introduction (I, pp. 93–4), where the last phrase is quoted. See A. H. Benna, 'Von der erzherzoglichen Durchlaucht zur kaiserlichen Hoheit', *MÖSA*, XXIII (1970), esp. 11, and

She defied convention in a number of other ways. She froze her courtiers with the draught from the windows she insisted on keeping open; she loved to walk and talk in the gardens of her palaces; early in her reign, she danced, rode and sledged with abandon.[20] She was relatively accessible, and won the devotion of many by her spontaneity and generosity.[21] She liked to exempt friends and favoured visitors from rules of etiquette.[22] She had her old governess, a mere countess Fuchs, buried in the family vault of the Habsburgs.[23] She exploited what seem to have been elaborate conventions enabling the ruler and her family to appear incognito more or less when they pleased.[24] She loved referring to herself as the mother of her subjects rather than their ruler.[25] She showed at times a passionate devotion to her children, especially in nursing them during attacks of illness, even including smallpox, which Joseph had in 1757 and Charles two years later.[26] She and her husband cultivated simplicity in the family circle, in the style captured by her daughter Marie Christine in her painting of their exchange of Christmas presents.[27] She was described as wanting to run *un ménage bourgeois*, that is, she was unfashionably jealous of Francis's female acquaintances.[28]

Francis positively hated Court formality, and he somewhat simplified imperial etiquette.[29] In some tracts which he left among his papers he described the discomforts of a monarch's situation, and his own attempts to remain serene and devout amid flattery, pomp and crowds – to be true to himself, 'a hermit in the world'.[30] Khevenhüller records that on receiving days he generally went off to hunt in summer and play billiards in winter. He was very often at the theatre, and 'has the patience to stay from the beginning to

E. Kovács, 'Kirchliches Zeremoniell am Wiener Hof des 18. Jahrhunderts im Wandel von Mentalität und Gesellschaft', *MÖSA*, XXXII (1979), esp. 125–9.

[20] Adam Wolf, 'Relationen des Grafen von Podewils, Gesandten K. Friedrich's II. von Preussen, über den Wiener Hof in den Jahren 1746, 1747, 1748', *Sitzungsberichte KAW*, V (1850), 493, 489, 491; T. G. von Karajan, 'Maria Theresia und Graf Sylva-Tarouca', *Feierliche Sitzungsberichte KAW* (1859), 10.

[21] Wolf, *Sitzungsberichte KAW* (1850), 184, 489; L. von Ranke, 'Maria Theresia, ihr Staat und ihr Hof im Jahre 1755. Aus den Papieren des Grosskanzlers Fürst' (originally published in *Historisch-politische Zeitschrift*, II, 4 (1836)), *Sämmtliche Werke*, vol. XXX (Leipzig, 1875), pp. 7–8.

[22] E.g. Arneth, *GMT* IV, p. 143.   [23] Macartney, *M.T. and the House of Austria*, p. 5.

[24] K-M, *passim*. Incognito seems to be worthy of study, as an aspect of the history of monarchy and also of privacy.

[25] E.g. Arneth, *GMT* IV, p. 104; Macartney, *Habsburg and Hohenzollern Dynasties*, pp. 100, 131. Dr P. G. M. Dickson has pointed out to me, however, that male Habsburgs often called themselves *Landesvater*.

[26] E.g. K-M IV, pp. 63–5 (Jan.–Feb. 1757) and V, p. 136 (9 Nov. 1759). Cf. Lippert, *M.T. und Maria Antonia von Sachsen*, pp. 482–3 (Albert to Maria Antonia, 27 May 1767).

[27] See Plate 3b.

[28] Wolf, *Sitzungsberichte KAW* (1850), 493. See K-M V, p. 74 (19 Nov. 1758) for M.T.'s later efforts to obstruct the emperor's *parties fines*.

[29] Ranke, *Sämmtliche Werke*, vol. XXX, p. 10 (report by Fürst).

[30] A. Wandruszka, 'Die Religiosität Franz Stephans von Lothringen', *MÖSA*, XII (1959), esp. 165. See Plate 4a.

the end of a German comedy, which pains the least delicate spirits'.[31] He bought himself not only some more hunting lodges – while his wife gave him a rather grand one at Schlosshof – but also a private house in Vienna, which enjoyed diplomatic immunity as belonging to the grand duchy of Tuscany. There he ran his highly successful financial operations, dabbled in science and alchemy, gambled and perhaps womanised.[32] He had been initiated as a freemason on a visit to England and Holland, and is presumed to have practised the craft in Vienna, though it was outlawed there.[33]

Yet in their own fashion the imperial couple were ostentatious enough. Maria Theresa, it is true, went to Laxenburg at least once a year for perhaps a month, partly because her husband loved the sport there, but also partly because she liked the place as being too small and remote to stage the full panoply of the Court. But its simplicity faded as she adorned the house and park with new structures, including a theatre.[34] She also refurbished the royal apartments in the Hofburg, which she used as her winter palace, and made plans for massive rebuilding there.[35] On the other hand, she never resided in the Favorita after her accession; and, although she paid an annual visit to Klosterneuburg in honour of Austria's patron saint, she showed not the slightest desire to live there.[36] But in the summer palace that she came to love, Schönbrunn, she spent lavishly on repairs, extensions, decoration and furnishing. In 1745 the remodelled chapel was consecrated. In the following year major Court ceremonies were first held there. In 1747 the theatre was opened. Another wing was soon occupied, and then a new floor inserted to accommodate her growing family. Bellotto's painting of 1759 shows the exterior complete, with the royal party standing on the balcony, waiting to receive the despatch announcing the victory over Prussia at Kunersdorf, the high point of her reign. The garden was redesigned more than once. The zoo was restored by Francis, with a central pavilion in which the emperor and empress used to eat their breakfast while observing the animals. In the sixties a most extravagant scheme of internal decoration was carried out, involving the use of countless mirrors, woods specially imported from the West Indies, and lacquer panels and vellum miniatures from the East, to create one of the most spectacular displays of chinoiserie in Europe. 'All the diamonds in the world are nothing to me', she wrote. 'It is only what comes from the Indies, especially lacquer but also tapestries, that gives me pleasure.' It is no wonder

[31] K-M II, p. 156 (13 Dec. 1746); Wolf, *Sitzungsberichte KAW* (1850), 499.
[32] F. Hennings, *Und sitzet zur linken Hand* (Vienna, 1961), esp..pp. 331–3, 337–9; Arneth, *GMT* IV, p. 147.
[33] M. C. Jacob, *The Radical Enlightenment* (London, 1981), p 111.
[34] Zykan, *Laxenburg*, pp. 26–34.
[35] For the plans see R. Wagner-Rieger, 'Gedanken zum fürstlichen Schlossbau des Absolutismus', *WBGN*, II (1975), esp. 66–8.
[36] Arneth, *GMT* IV, p. 141.

that the most exotic room is known as the *Millionenzimmer*[37]. Extensions or improvements were also put in hand before Francis's death at other royal houses more distant from Vienna: at Hetzendorf, used first by her mother and then by the surplus of her own children when there was not enough room for them all at Schönbrunn;[38] at Schlosshof, her gift to her husband; and at various castles and palaces in the provinces, such as at Buda, Prague and Brussels.[39] If she and her husband somewhat reduced the religiosity, formality and ceremony of the Court, they greatly increased its comfort and opulence. The age of monastic and church building was nearly over. Many nobles were content with the palaces inherited from previous generations. This was most conspicuously a period of royal building.

Long before her widowhood provided her with a special justification for seclusion, Maria Theresa was accused of avoiding contact with the world at large, as by her confidant, count Silva-Tarouca, in 1754:

'What can I do?' Your Majesty would forcefully say to me. 'What others everywhere (I can reply in advance) sensibly do, who are not shutting themselves up out of disgust and unnecessarily; what Maria Theresa herself, here at Schönbrunn and Vienna, found it possible to do ten or eleven years ago, at the age of 24 or 25, having many enemies, very little money and assistance, and also little experience. I said then that, so to speak, abandoned to yourself, and in process of learning the ABC of sovereignty, working as hard as four people, Your Majesty found the time to relax and to cheer us all by her presence. She rode almost too much, danced, played cards, talked, ate in company in the evening as well as at midday, made several short journeys, in addition had a child every year.'[40]

Maria Theresa never lost the common sense which kept her in touch with her subjects' opinions. She always spent some of the year in Vienna itself. But her addiction to living at Schönbrunn exposed the dynasty to some of the risks of alienation which Versailles involved for the Bourbons. More and more as her reign proceeded, she cocooned herself in grandeur.[41]

Francis, for all his dislike of ceremony, took part in it often enough – more often than his wife, in fact. He frequently did duty for her on state occasions,

---

[37] Glaser, *Schönbrunner Chronik*, esp. pp. 35–44. There are many references to developments at Schönbrunn in K-M. The quotation is from Arneth, *MTKuF* IV, pp. 304–5 (9 Feb. 1753, to prince J. W. Liechtenstein). The Bellotto is in the Kunsthistorisches Museum, Vienna. (Cf. Lippert, *M.T. und Maria Antonia von Sachsen*, p. 98n. The date was 16 Aug. 1759.) See Plates 2, 8a, 8b.

[38] J. Brunner, *Hetzendorf und sein Schloss* (Vienna, 1972); K-M III, p. 233 (4 Apr. 1755).

[39] M.T.'s building has not, so far as I know, been studied as a whole. I rely chiefly on guidebooks, but see R. Wagner-Rieger, 'Architektur im theresianischen Zeitalter' in *MTIZ*, pp. 259–67. See p. 196 below for her later building. I do not know what Macartney means (*NCMH* VII, p. 412) in talking of a palace she built at Pest.

[40] Karajan, *Feierliche Sitzungsberichte KAW* (1859), 27–8. Cf. report by Fürst in Ranke, *Sämmtliche Werke*, vol. XXX, p. 7.

[41] This seems to me a more just appreciation than the picture given by E. Wangermann in A. G. Dickens, *The Courts of Europe* (London, 1977), where greater emphasis is placed on the simplification and *embourgeoisement* of Court life, even before 1765.

especially those involving religious observances in the churches of Vienna. He regularly attended the Vespers and other services of the Order of the Golden Fleece, of which she had made him the sovereign.[42] His role as emperor was necessarily ceremonious. She thought his imperial coronation 'a comedy', and it looked to spectators as though he himself held up the regalia to her as a joke during the subsequent procession, which she watched from a balcony.[43] But he continued to play his assigned part; and when in 1764 he attended Joseph's coronation as king of the Romans in a magnificent and costly set of new vestments, he outshone his son and won Khevenhüller's admiration.[44] No doubt this punctiliousness was felt to be important in view of the weakness of his hereditary claims to the offices concerned. But it is in any case wrong to place too much emphasis on the decay of formality. Under Charles VI, the Court ceremonially attended church services on eighty-six occasions a year; under Francis Stephen the number had been reduced only to seventy-eight.[45] When prince Albert of Saxony first saw the Court of Vienna in 1760, what struck him most was the continuing practice of wearing 'Spanish mantles'.[46]

These matters of form and ceremony and of outward show may seem trivial. In fact they were of enormous significance, both in themselves and because they symbolised and reflected political attitudes and relationships. Monarchy was personal. Ritual was an integral part of secular as well as religious acts. Disputes about etiquette invariably raised more fundamental issues. It was not a quaint survival, but a natural and practical arrangement,

[42] Again, the references to the Golden Fleece functions in K-M are numerous and scattered. On Maria Theresa's reluctance to take part in state ceremonial, see esp. K-M II, p. 280 (15 Oct. 1748) and III, p. 88 (28 Jan. 1753). Cf. Arneth, *GMT* II, p. 106. K-M remarks on 13 Apr. 1756 that Maria Theresa that day attended the Holy Tuesday services for the first time in her reign, having always previously missed them on account of pregnancy or other good cause (K-M IV, pp. 13–14).

[43] Ulfeld to Francis Stephen, 22 Aug. 1745 (Arneth, *GMT* III, p. 431); *Goethes Werke*, vol. IX (Hamburg, 1961), p. 201.

[44] See p. 113 below. K-M VI, p. 18 (3 Apr. 1764).

[45] The emphasis is usually placed, and was generally placed by Khevenhüller, on the emperor's dereliction of ceremonial duties and the criticism this provoked (see Hennings, *Und sitzet zur linken Hand*, esp. p. 296, relying heavily on Khevenhüller). But it is clear from Francis Stephen's writings (Wandruszka, *MÖSA* (1959), 162–73) that he did a great deal more than ideally he would have liked to do. It cannot be too much emphasised how weak his personal standing was, as titular king of Jerusalem, dispossessed duke of Lorraine, grand duke of Tuscany by way of consolation prize, co-regent and emperor only through his wife's efforts. It may be significant too that there was a rival Order of the Golden Fleece in Spain. See H. O. Kleinmann, 'Titelführung und Rechtsanspruch: Bemerkungen zum österreichischen Titel des Katholischen Königs im 18. Jahrhundert', in *Beiträge zur neueren Geschichte Österreichs*, ed. H. Fichtenau and E. Zöllner (Vienna, 1974), esp. pp. 141–2. Cf. Kovács, *MÖSA* (1979), 125, 128 and nn. Hennings's ch. 11 brings together many of K-M's best remarks. Though he usefully emphasises the separation of the two Courts of the emperor and of the ruler of the Monarchy, he does not seem to allow enough for the co-regency.

[46] Albert's unpublished memoirs (MDL). I am very grateful to Dr O. Sashegyi for his help in procuring me a microfilm of the surviving portions of this work.

that Khevenhüller, the expert on ceremony, ranked as one of Maria Theresa's chief advisers.[47]

THE BOY JOSEPH AT HIS PARENTS' COURT

No monarch has ever felt more strongly about such matters than Joseph II. His hatred of formality and ceremony was integral to his whole approach to ruling – and contributed to the ultimate defeat of his plans. Khevenhüller's diary enables us to see him as a boy at Court, a victim of its traditions and habits, of the tensions between the old and the new etiquette, and of the strains between his mother and father which they helped to create. To depict this comedy is not merely to describe the circumstances of his childhood but also to trace the origins of some of his most significant attitudes.

Khevenhüller, of course, sought to prescribe how the child heir apparent should be treated on the basis of records from the last period when such a person had existed – namely the end of the previous century.[48] He tried to maintain the precedence of the title 'archduke' and the form 'Archducal Highness', distinctive of the House of Habsburg, as against the common or garden usage 'Royal Highness'.[49] He disliked the practice of putting princes in uniform and giving them regiments. Like most of the innovations introduced into Court behaviour at this time, he saw it as a French mode, reaching Vienna by way of Lorraine.[50]

Joseph duly took part in a public meal *nach der alten Etiquette* in honour of the emperor's sister's birthday on 17 December 1747.[51] But at the end of the same month he first put on the uniform of the Althannische Regiment and received the compliments of the Court for it.[52] A year later he appeared on horseback at the head of his regiment in the presence of his parents.[53] A separate household was created for him, roughly in accordance with old tradition.[54] On 19 March 1749, his name-day, he 'for the first time *in publico* and wearing a mantle went to the *Hofkapelle* immediately preceding the emperor'.[55] In 1753 he was confirmed in public.[56] In the following year he went with his father for the first time both to visit eighteen cribs on Easter Eve

---

[47] This discussion raises very broad issues. Other work in which they are discussed includes: J. M. Beattie, *The English Court in the Reign of George I* (Cambridge, 1967); G. R. Elton, 'Tudor government: the points of contact. III. The court', *TRHS*, 5th series, XXVI (1976); H. D. Molesworth, *The Princes* (London, 1974); Kovács, *MÖSA* (1979).

[48] K-M II, p. 312 (30 Mar. 1749). Benna, *MÖSA* (1971), 16–18.

[49] K-M III, esp. pp. 203 (12 Oct. 1754), 467–70; 232–3 (30 Mar. 1755). Benna, *MÖSA* (1970), 19–26.

[50] K-M II, p. 291 (10 Dec. 1748).   [51] K-M II, pp. 156–7.

[52] K-M II, p. 198 (31 Dec. 1747).

[53] K-M II, p. 290 (10 Dec. 1748).

[54] There is much discussion of this matter in K-M II, esp. pp. 182–3, 288, 312, 448–50.

[55] K-M II, p. 309.   [56] K-M III, p. 128 (25 July 1753).

and to attend, in knight's habit, the great Vespers of the Order of the Golden Fleece.[57] After years of debate, the title 'Royal Highness' won the day.[58]

Somewhat less formally, Joseph had by now taken part in numerous plays, masked balls and other entertainments, including one in which he was a chess-piece.[59] He had replied formally to the official compliments of ambassadors and others.[60] In 1754 he first went on military manoeuvres, in Bohemia.[61] He was initiated into some forms of hunting.[62]

Court life not only had touches of *Alice*; it was strongly reminiscent of *The Marriage of Figaro*. The emperor had to call the guard through the window of the *Spiegelzimmer* at Schönbrunn to expel an intruder.[63] The prince de Ligne, as a young Court chamberlain, was dressed up by emperor and empress as the prospective bride of an unfortunate groom.[64] More or less confidential notelets passed from one part of the huge palace to another, often with instructions to the recipient to burn them.[65] When the Court paid what many thought a tiresome visit to Kaunitz's country seat near Austerlitz in 1755, the buildings were found to be unfinished and the service inadequate; and the boredom was only intensified by a specially produced peasant festival featuring a local dance and lasting all of half-an-hour.[66]

Joseph's lifelong aversion to Court ceremonial was first noticed when he was only five.[67] But, despite the weight of etiquette, religious observance and artificiality, his upbringing was exceptionally fortunate and happy by the general standards of the period, and especially by that of princes who were his approximate contemporaries. Both Louis XVI's parents died before he was thirteen; they had not valued him highly, and had made their attitude plain; and they had been at loggerheads with the king, his grandfather, partly because they disapproved of the royal mistresses.[68] George III's father died when the boy was twelve; he was thereafter kept in close seclusion by his mother, and brought up to believe that George II, his grandfather, was an ogre.[69] Christian VII of Denmark lost his mother when he was three, had an

57 K-M III, p. 169 (13 Apr. 1754); p. 213 (29 Nov. 1754). On the significance of cribs see O. Chadwick, *The Popes and European Revolution* (Oxford, 1981), pp. 59–64.
58 K-M III, p. 232 (30 Mar. 1755). See Benna, *MÖSA* (1970), pp. 24–7.
59 E.g. K-M II, p. 194 (7 Dec. 1747); III, p. 4 (20 Jan. 1752).
60 E.g. K-M II, pp. 308, 316 (13 Mar. and 19 Apr. 1749).
61 K-M III, p. 188 (17 Aug. 1754).
62 K-M IV, pp. 1 ('Früh-Baitz'), 41 ('Creisjagd') (18 May and 30 Aug. 1756).
63 K-M III, pp. 131–3 (6 Aug. 1753).
64 Prince de Ligne, *Fragments de l'histoire de ma vie*, ed. F. Leuridant (2 vols., Paris, 1927–8), pp. 72–3.
65 Hrazky, *MÖSA* (1959) gives examples of letters of this type from Joseph's first wife to Marie Christine (e.g. p. 230). Some of Maria Theresa's letters to Kaunitz in HHSA FA Sbde 70 qualify.
66 K-M III, pp. 252–5 (28 July–1 Aug. 1755).   67 K-M II, p. 156 (13 Dec. 1746).
68 P. Girault de Coursac, *L'Education d'un roi: Louis XVI* (Paris, 1972) has described his upbringing.
69 See J. Brooke, *King George III* (London, 1972), esp. pp. 15, 34, 41–2.

alcoholic father and a sadistic tutor.[70] Paul of Russia may have been illegit-
imate, but it was his legal father, the drunken Peter III, whom his mother,
Catherine II, deposed and allowed to be murdered; she showed her contempt
for her son, and he his dislike of his mother.[71] Frederick the Great was beaten,
reviled, imprisoned and threatened with death by his coarse and puritanical
father.[72] Joseph, on the other hand, was adored by both his parents, who were
still living when he came of age; and only death broke the solidarity of their
gifted family.

'Poor boy', exclaimed a hard-bitten Cambridge tutor about one of his
pupils, 'he has both a mother and a father.'[73] United families generate their
own tensions. It is easy to see that there was a special problem in Joseph's
upbringing. Everyone around him was conscious of the peculiarity of the
situation in which his mother, rather than his father, was the ruler. Many
people, like Charles VI himself, had assumed that after her accession Francis
would take control. After her husband's death, it was expected by some that
she would abdicate in favour of her son.[74] She certainly felt it necessary to
make first Francis and then Joseph co-regent.[75] She showed resentment at
being a woman, asserted that she would have gone into battle herself if she had
not been nearly always pregnant, and offered as a reason for not letting herself
be crowned empress with Francis that, having been declared king of Hungary
and Bohemia already, she did not choose to change sex in her coronations.[76]
But it was she who transacted most of the business, devoting most of every day
to it while her husband was unoccupied to the point of boredom.[77] His
spelling, even in French, and even by Maria Theresa's standards, was
grotesque, and she was ashamed of it.[78] His advice was rejected on important
occasions. He was sometimes allowed to take the field as a general, but what

---

[70] H. W. Chapman, *Caroline Matilda, Queen of Denmark* (London, 1971), pp. 45–7.
[71] See e.g. E. M. Almedingen, *So Dark a Stream* (London, 1959). J. himself actually told his
mother how lucky he was not to have the sort of relationship with her that Paul had with
Catherine II (Arneth, *MTuJ* III, p. 271: 4 July 1780).
[72] E.g. W. F. Reddaway, *Frederick the Great and the Rise of Prussia* (London, 1954), ch. 2.
[73] The remark is attributed to Dr B. T. D. Smith, tutor of Sidney Sussex College, Cambridge,
from 1929 to 1945. I owe it to Dr R. C. Smail.
[74] E.L. to L.K., 28 Aug. 1765 (SOALpZ, LRRA P. 16/19).
[75] But see F. Reinöhl, 'Die Übertragung der Mitregentschaft durch Maria Theresia an
Grossherzog Franz Stephan und Kaiser Joseph II.', *MÖIG Ergänzungsband* XI (1929), 650–1,
and pp. 135–7 below.
[76] Ulfeld to Francis Stephen, 22 Aug. 1745 (Arneth, *GMT* III, p. 431). Cf. Benna, *MÖSA*
(1970), 15, and E. Holzmair, 'Maria Theresia als Trägerin "männlicher" Titel. Eine
numismatische Studie', *MÖIG* LXXII (1964), 122–34. It perhaps has significance that the first
medal on which her masculine royal titles are flaunted was issued in honour of her husband's
imperial coronation (*ibid.*, p. 126). Macartney, *Habsburg and Hohenzollern Dynasties*, p. 115.
[77] This impression (e.g. in Hennings, *Und sitzet zur linken Hand*, and Crankshaw, *Maria Theresa*)
seems well justified by K-M.
[78] On rejection of his advice, Macartney, *M.T. and the House of Austria*, pp. 81–2. On his spelling
see H. L. Mikoletzky, 'Kaiser Franz I. Stephan in Briefen (an seine Mitarbeiter)' in *Etudes
européennes: Mélanges offerts à Victor Tapié* (Paris, 1973), pp. 270–1, and n. 84 below.

little prospect there was of his distinguishing himself in that capacity was reduced by her practice of beseeching him to return from the front at the earliest opportunity.[79]

Even so, there was more substance to the co-regency than is often allowed. Francis was the architect of her private fortune and had much to do with the comparative success of her public financial arrangements.[80] He introduced many of her most notable servants to her, including Haugwitz and Kaunitz.[81] She credited him with the extremely important contribution of having opened her eyes to the true attitude of the Hungarians at the beginning of her reign.[82] Although he was never given ultimate responsibility, it is clear from the following passage in Khevenhüller's diary, written in explanation of the military disasters of December 1757, that he was far from being a nullity:

We have two masters, the emperor and the empress. Both want to rule. But, although the former directs the military, and also *d'une certaine façon* financial affairs – or at least in both these branches of government nothing significant is lightly undertaken without his knowledge and agreement – he is too easy-going to be able to support so great a burden. The empress for her part is by contrast much too fiery, cannot be patient about anything, and hence does not stick to any plan.[83]

He was given more to do in the 1760s, as a member of the *Staatsrat*, where he spent painfully long hours, and as a sort of financial overlord.[84] But he remained manifestly subordinate to his wife.

As a father, Francis was affectionate and concerned – too indulgent, according to the empress[85] – but he was not allowed much influence. He and Joseph went out hunting and attended church together, but the idle emperor was less often on hand than the busy empress when the heir was examined formally by his tutors.[86] Maria Theresa cared about her children to an extent scarcely to be paralleled among eighteenth-century queens, but she cannot possibly have devoted to them even as much as the two hours a day recommended by her confidant.[87] Moreover, she blew hot and cold. Having had Joseph dressed up in his regiment's uniform for the admiration of the Court, she decided that he was being paid too many compliments for his own

[79] Hennings, *Und sitzet zur linken Hand*, pp. 239–40.

[80] H. L. Mikoletzky, *Kaiser Franz I. Stephan und der Ursprung des habsburgisch-lothringischen Familienvermögens* (Vienna, 1961). Dr P. G. M. Dickson has considerably modified Mikoletzky's picture in his forthcoming book.

[81] Macartney, *Habsburg and Hohenzollern Dynasties*, p. 118; G. Klingenstein, *Der Aufstieg des Hauses Kaunitz* (Göttingen, 1975), p. 273.

[82] Arneth, *GMT* VII, p. 574.   [83] K-M IV, p. 141.

[84] Arneth, *GMT* VII, pp. 156–7. On 10 Nov. 1762 he wrote to his brother Charles: 'Je vous écris hore du conseil d'eta lequel man fourni le tan, care ordinereman ille dur 5 ou 6 heure . . . come celuy d'ou je vous écri cour asteur la 6hiem heur' (*ibid.*, VII, p. 518).

[85] Beer, *JLuK*, p. 432.

[86] This emerges from the numerous references in K-M to Joseph's examinations, esp. vol. IV, p. 242 (28 May 1755).

[87] Karajan, *Feierliche Sitzungsberichte KAW* (1859), 5.

good and sent him off to eat in his own room.[88] She had him beaten at least once. When told that it was contrary to all precedent to chastise archdukes, she said it was high time the experiment was made.[89] She loved to hear him praised, but often felt it necessary to be hypercritical of him herself.[90] In the circumstances, the mother–son relationship was bound to be exceptionally intense and complex.

The Prussian ambassador, Podewils, wrote for Frederick the Great a description of Joseph at the age of six, on which historians have naturally fastened. He reported that the heir to the throne was haughty with everyone, invariably addressing people with the condescending *Du*; and that 'in a room adorned with portraits of his ancestors he said to someone: "That is the emperor my grandfather, that is empress such and such," and, turning to the other side, with an air of disdain, "That is only a duke and duchess of Lorraine".' The ambassador continued that Joseph was stubborn and hated admitting error; that he showed little sign of liveliness of mind, disliked studying, and positively refused to learn French; that he cared only for military matters and soldiers; but that at least he was generous with his mother's money.[91]

It is impossible to credit all of this condemnation. The Prussian envoy admitted that it had not been easy for him to gather his information,[92] and the prince must have been well shielded from prying enquirers, especially if they were connected with the arch-enemy of the Habsburg dynasty. If some of what Podewils learned has the ring of truth, such as the report that Joseph liked military matters, there is a degree of absurdity in attaching significance to the tastes and opinions of a boy of six. Joseph's situation was almost certain to make him, in Khevenhüller's words, 'shy of people and embarrassed', as was the case with other young princes of that and all periods;[93] and it seems reasonable to interpret the remark in which he appeared to show contempt for his father's origins as a child's inopportune repetition of a lesson well learned. While Maria Theresa herself was soon to remark on the obstinacy, self-righteousness and censoriousness which remained characteristic of Joseph throughout his life, the statement that he was recalcitrant about studying French seems to be simply false,[94] and this is almost the only occasion on which he was ever accused of prodigality with anyone's money. If he appeared

[88] K-M II, p. 199 (31 Dec. 1747).   [89] Wolf, *Sitzungsberichte KAW* (1850), 493 (Podewils).
[90] Albert's memoirs (MOL); Arneth, *GMT* VII, p. 56.
[91] Wolf, *Sitzungsberichte KAW* (1850), 503–5.
[92] Wolf, *Sitzungsberichte KAW* (1850), 484.   [93] K-M II, p. 301 (9 Feb. 1749).
[94] Two months earlier than this report, K-M reports J. taking part in a French play, admittedly not very well; and later in the year he records J. reciting a French verse compliment and performing 'markedly better than last time' in another French play (K-M II, pp. 142 (26 Jan. 1747), 170 (4 Oct.) and 197 (7 Dec.)). In his *relazione* of 1746 the Venetian ambassador, Contarini, particularly mentioned J.'s skill at languages (Arneth (ed.), *Die Relationen der Botschafter Venedigs über Österreich im achtzehnten Jahrhundert* (Vienna, 1863), p. 306).

to lack liveliness of mind at this age, he certainly showed it very soon afterwards.[95] As for the use of *Du*, he was to become notable among monarchs for the politeness he displayed towards visitors and correspondents.[96]

Presumably in 1748, when Joseph's household was set up, Maria Theresa gave to his *Ajo* or guardian, field-marshal count Batthyány, lengthy instructions in which she spoke of the prince's faults:

Because my son, a pledge so dear and important to us all, has been brought up from the cradle with the greatest tenderness and love, it must be admitted that his desires and requests have been deferred to too easily in many ways, particularly by those who serve him, who have flattered him too much and allowed him to develop a premature conception of his exalted station. He expects to be obeyed and honoured, finds criticism unpleasant, indeed almost intolerable, gives way to all his own whims, but behaves discourteously, even rudely, to others.

Although these tendencies have now been somewhat corrected, partly through the care and teaching of his diligent Abbé [Weger], and my son also displays many signs of a good heart, it is certain that his great vivacity, which had not previously been suspected, and which can be exploited in many ways to his benefit, is growing markedly. From this stems in the first place the passionate longing to get his own way in all his petty desires, with which he is so occupied that he scarcely hears reprimands, forgets them and especially his youth a thousand times, and also is often hard to bring to the necessary diligence, at any rate by means of what might be called the dry harshness and manner which most teachers use in the schools. By that method he would only lapse into a state of passivity in which he would doubtless obey but would never flourish – as has time and again been proved. But with periodic recreation and appeal to his ambition he has already often performed better than was expected of him . . .

The empress particularly stressed the perniciousness of his habit of observing and mocking everyone's physical weaknesses or faults of personality: not only was it unfair to the persons concerned, who could not repay him in the same coin, but it would prevent him from forming a true appreciation of their essential merits.[97]

These criticisms are worth quoting at length because of their source, and because they have been used, especially by Edward Crankshaw, to justify savage denunciations of the boy Joseph, 'the horrid youth'.[98] They ought to be seen in perspective. The faults mentioned are common enough even in children who are spared the special stresses of a royal upbringing. Some parents feel bound to exaggerate the weaknesses of their children, and Maria

[95] M.T. admitted (see below) that J.'s liveliness by 1748 had not been suspected earlier. But K-M called him *sehr lebhafft und distract* on 4 Oct. 1747 (II, p. 170), and Contarini had called him very able in the previous year (Arneth, *Relationen*, p. 306).

[96] See below, pp. 258, 308–9.

[97] Arneth, *GMT* IV, pp. 159–62. For the first paragraph I have used Crankshaw's translation (*Maria Theresa*, p. 176). The original is in Arneth, *MTKuF* IV, pp. 5–13, where it is dated 1751, surely wrongly.

[98] Crankshaw, *Maria Theresa*, p. 277.

Theresa was later criticised by her daughter-in-law on just this ground.[99] The instructions to Batthyány about Joseph are mild in comparison with remarks made about his brothers. Charles, wrote Batthyány himself to the empress, was most inattentive, and subject to violent tempers.[100] Leopold was said by his mother to be 'lazy and corrupt', to have too high an opinion of himself, and to try to get his way by devious means.[101] These comments in their turn pale into insignificance beside what Frederick William I, George II and Catherine the Great thought of their sons. Louis XVI obtained little recognition from his father, and the level of his intelligence and the quality of his education were until very recently obscured by historical writers' too ready reliance on the more jaundiced remarks of contemporaries.[102] To some degree Joseph is in the same case. He had faults, of course, the most disagreeable of which was his readiness to criticise and mock at others. But they did not vitiate his whole character.

JOSEPH'S EDUCATION

His education is embarrassingly well documented. Numerous discussions about it between his parents, ministers and tutors are recorded. Copious memoranda on the subject survive from various stages in the process. A charming illustrated alphabet-book, from which he learned to read and write in German, has recently been reprinted. Several weighty scholarly works specially written for use by Joseph's teachers, some of which were later published, are extant. A substantial report of 1759 exists which surveyed the 'method followed in the education of His Royal Highness' as it neared its end.[103]

[99] Arneth, *GMT* VII, p. 56.
[100] Arneth, *GMT* IV, pp. 178–9. Khevenhüller complained of the monstrous things he said to the servants (K-M V, p. 87 (1 Feb. 1759)). Albert in his memoirs spoke of his *causticité*.
[101] Wandruszka, *L. II.*, vol. 1, pp. 47–8.
[102] On Louis XVI Girault de Coursac, *Éducation d'un roi*.
[103] Conrad, *RuV* prints many of the documents associated with J.'s education, especially so far as his study of law of all kinds is concerned. The report of 1759 is on pp. 85–107. Conrad here and in other work (see bibliography) has put the subject on an entirely new footing.
    Cf. A. H. Benna, 'Der Kronprinzenunterricht Josefs II. in der inneren Verfassung der Erbländer und die Wiener Zentralstellen', *MÖSA*, XX (1967), 115–79, where the whole process is summarised and many useful points about it are brought out, but the emphasis is on the last stages. J.'s instruction in religious and ecclesiastical matters is discussed in Benna, 'Zur Situation von Religion und Kirche in Österreich in den Fünfzigerjahren des 18. Jahrhunderts – eine Denkschrift Bartensteins zum Kronprinzunterricht Josefs II.' in *Sacerdos et pastor semper ubique. Festschrift Franz Loidl* (Vienna, 1972), pp. 193–224.
    The alphabet-book is J. B. von Antesperg, *Das Josephinische Erzherzogliche A.B.C. oder Namenbüchlein* (1741), ed. G. Mraz (Dortmund, 1980).
    I am grateful to the editors of the *Wiener Beiträge zur Geschichte der Neuzeit* for allowing me to re-use material I published in that journal in 1979. My account of his education here is rather fuller and more broadly based.
    Unfortunately, it is not possible to take seriously prince Chula of Thailand, *The Education of the Enlightened Despots* (London, 1948).

As early as 1750 a medal was struck to celebrate the progress so far made by Joseph in his studies.[104] The report of 1759 pictures the rapid and orderly development of an outstanding pupil pursuing an enlightened course under the instruction of excellent teachers. It is convenient first to follow broadly this retrospective account, even though its blandness arouses the well-justified suspicion that it is sometimes describing not what had actually occurred but what the authorities wished to pretend had occurred.

Until Batthyány was brought in, the prince had been entrusted to the care of two successive countesses, who were said to combine with all other appropriate good qualities 'much religion'. Formal religious instruction, however, was in the hands of a Jesuit, Father Höller, who stayed on in later phases both in that capacity and as Joseph's confessor. The boy had the same doctor as his parents, and so from 1745 he was treated by the great reformer, Gerard van Swieten, whom Maria Theresa had charmed into coming from the Netherlands to look after her family in Vienna.[105]

In 1748 the regime was altered. Under the general direction of Batthyány, assisted by the numerous conferences already mentioned, the Augustinian Canon Weger was put in charge of education. A second Jesuit, Father Weickhard, joined Father Höller to teach Joseph Latin and literature. An engineer colonel, Bréquin, taught him mathematics. There was also musical and physical training.[106] 'His Royal Highness did not as yet make a particular study of the French language; the majority of those around him spoke it in society ... He soon learned it with almost the same facility as his mother tongue.'[107]

His teachers spared him detail which was considered unnecessary, such as 'all the subtleties of grammar and syntax' in Latin, and in history 'thorny and superfluous questions of chronology' and 'all little facts'. In mathematics, which he specially enjoyed, he was assisted by the provision of three-dimensional geometrical figures made of wood and card.[108]

This was the pattern of his day:

---

[104] [Erzherzogin Maria Anna von Österreich], *Schau- und Denkmünzen Maria Theresias* (Vienna, 1782) (reprinted with an introduction by G. Probszt-Ohstorff (Graz, 1970)), p. 127. The archduchess is very loyal about it all, speaking of the efforts of her parents to give their illustrious children 'la plus parfaite éducation', and of J.'s having given in his public examination of 1750 'des preuves non équivoques des progrès qu'il avoit déjà faits dans diverses sciences'. On the medal, J. is 'habillé à l'hongroise'. He is represented as declaring that he will follow his mother in the spheres both of Pallas and Bellona. The archduchess modestly remarks: 'ces mêmes Princes & Princesses sont aujourd'hui le bonheur non seulement des pays héréditaires, mais encore de plusieurs autres royaumes et états de l'Europe'.

[105] Conrad, *RuV*, pp. 86–7; Arneth, *GMT* II, pp. 565–6.

[106] Conrad, *RuV*, p. 88. It appears that the Court tried to get the services as J.'s tutor of J. D. Schöpflin: see J. Voss, *Universität, Geschichtswissenschaft und Diplomatie im Zeitalter der Aufklärung* (Munich, 1979), p. 87.

[107] Conrad, *RuV*, p. 91.   [108] Conrad, *RuV*, pp. 90–2.

I

HRH rises at 6.45 and immediately says his prayers.
He dresses until nearly 7.30.
He has breakfast at 7.45.
He returns at 8.0.

II

He learns Latin until 9.30.
He has a quarter of an hour's break.
He does history until 10.30 with Father Weickhard, including a quarter-of-an-hour of German reading.
He has a short break.
He practises writing with his teacher Steiner until 11.30
He has a break until noon.
He dines and remains in conversation until 2.0.

III

He has a geography lesson until 3.0.
On Mondays and Wednesdays he will be with Father Höller until 4.0, on Tuesdays, Thursdays and Saturdays with Bréquin.
He learns Latin and history from 4.0 until 5.0, or, if he has had a break before this lesson, until 5.30.

IV

Rosary at 6.0.
At 6.30 Reutter will give him his music lesson on Mondays and Wednesdays; on Tuesdays, Thursdays and Saturdays this time is devoted to dance.
He concludes with some amusements until 8.0.
He has supper until 8.30.
He plays billiards until 9.15.
He retires for evening prayers.
He undresses and goes to bed at 9.45

The riding school will be attended on Mondays, Wednesdays and Saturdays at the writing-master's time, since HRH can practise that lesson during an odd quarter-of-an-hour.
On Sundays and Feast-Days Father Höller takes the period before noon, and M. Bréquin will come from 2.0 to 3.30.
As for the reading necessary to assist study, acquire useful knowledge and amuse the mind, that can be done during the unoccupied parts of the day, especially on Feast-Days and Sundays.[109]

A set of instructions to the domestic servants insists that he be made to wash his face and hands night and morning, and his feet once a week. The dentist will come to clean his teeth on Tuesdays and Fridays after breakfast.[110]

The retrospective account asserts that until Joseph's tenth or eleventh year he was educated on the principle that all his studies, as is appropriate for children, must take the form of games or amusements. However implausible

[109] Arneth, *GMT* IV, pp. 522–3.   [110] K-M II, p. 450.

that claim must seem in the light of what the prince had already experienced, it is clear that the next phase of his education was still more demanding. In order to ensure agreement among the tutors and the best possible supervision of the prince's studies, weekly meetings were henceforth held between Maria Theresa, Francis Stephen, the guardian and the teachers. Every day, it is claimed, reports were made to Their Majesties about his progress.[111]

Christian instruction was now given in Latin instead of German. Daily reading of extracts from the best Latin authors resulted in Joseph's having studied large portions of the following writers by the age of fourteen or fifteen: Sulpicius Severus, Justinus, Cornelius Nepos, Eutropius, Velleius Paterculus, Florus, Aulus Gellius, Valerius Maximus, Vegetius, Frontinus, Vitruvius, the two Plinys, Curtius Rufus, Caesar, Sallust, Suetonius, Livy, Tacitus, Cicero – 'and some others'! The works read in their entirety included Curtius Rufus's *History of Alexander*; the *Panegyric of Trajan*, 'masterpiece of Pliny the Younger'; Tacitus's *Annals* and *Germany*; the finest speeches of Cicero and so on. Prose composition was also studied. 'The time available for the education of sovereigns being too precious to be spent in acquiring sterile knowledge, from which they and their peoples can derive no advantage, it was thought proper to pass lightly over poetry.' Joseph was not expected to write Latin verse, and was encouraged to read only portions of Ovid, Virgil, Horace, Plautus and Terence. However, he showed a particular liking for the *Aeneid*, which he is supposed to have read more than once for his own pleasure.[112]

In contrast to poetry, it was believed that rhetoric and philosophy deserved solid study, as contributing to elevation of mind, judgement, reasoning capacity, ability to express oneself, and appreciation of the true and the beautiful. To the twentieth-century student it is of special interest to know what was meant by 'philosophy'. Its teaching was entrusted to another Jesuit, Father Frantz.

The little treatise on philosophy expressly written for the use of HRH included only the necessary minimum. Care was taken to avoid all the subtleties that are more ingenious than useful, like categories, universals . . . and a hundred others of this sort, which only lead to knowledge of how to quibble over questions of words which are as ridiculous as they are frivolous . . . Barbaric jargon and the disputations of the schools were also banished . . . As much as possible, terms common in the fashionable world and the clearest and most natural expressions were used, and the attempt was made to convert the dry disputations of pedants into polite but nonetheless instructive conversations. The *Abrégé* of philosophy . . . included two principal parts, that is, logic or the art of discovering and proving the truth by a process of reasoning, and metaphysics, both established on simple but solid principles and explained in a very intelligible manner

---

[111] Conrad, *RuV*, pp. 94–5. Cf. K-M III, pp. 121 (20 June 1753) and 166–7 (12 Mar. 1754), and the earlier documents in Conrad, *RuV*, pp. 25–76.
[112] Conrad, *RuV*, pp. 95–6.

... In the second part were treated among other things basic truths about knowledge of God and of Man, which led HRH ... towards the study of natural law, which immediately succeeded that of philosophy.

It is obvious from this statement, and still more so from his 'little treatise', that Father Frantz did not dream in his philosophy of anything resembling the thought of the French *philosophes* or their English mentors. For them, metaphysics – and every all-embracing philosophical system derived from first principles – were obstructions in the way of attaining, by observation and experience, to knowledge and understanding of the world as it is. Frantz is very severe on scepticism, but he associates it not with recent Enlightened writing but with the attitudes of Spinoza, who died in 1677. On the other hand, Frantz distanced himself from the pure scholastic tradition associated with the Jesuits. His philosophy resembles what was now widely taught in French universities, a Christianised form of Cartesianism. In 1735 the Vienna government had ordered the Jesuits to teach Cartesian metaphysics, and Frantz's compendium proves that the directive was duly carried out. It is striking that the passage about avoiding subtleties quoted above from the official account of Joseph's education is taken almost verbatim from the French Jansenist handbook of philosophy, *L'Art de penser*. Naturally, Frantz wrote about recent German thinkers, especially Leibniz, rather than about Descartes's French successors. But he made only passing reference to Christian Wolff, whose philosophical writings now dominated study of the subject in Protestant north German universities. By Viennese criteria, Frantz was an able and enlightened Jesuit, and his compendium was progressive. By the standards of contemporary Protestant Europe they were completely outdated. Even by comparison with Catholic France and Italy, they were rather behind the times. It is symbolic that the treatise was written in Latin.[113]

A good deal of time in this phase was spent on Italian language and literature, including 'a part of the works of the learned Muratori' and the plays of Metastasio, who resided at the Court of Maria Theresa. French was now seriously studied, and Joseph read widely – astonishingly widely, the account says – in its literature. In this context it is poems and plays that are mentioned, not prose works, even in the case of Voltaire. Mathematics, civil and military

---

113 Conrad, *RuV*, pp. 97–8. Frantz's treatise was edited and published by T. M. Wehofer as 'Das Lehrbuch der Metaphysik für Kaiser Josef II., verfasst von P. Josef Frantz' in *Jahrbuch für Philosophie und spekulative Theologie*, Ergänzungsheft II (Paderborn, 1895).

On the Jesuits and scholasticism, see for example Winter's *Frühaufklärung* and *Josefinismus*; H. Sturmberger, 'Studien zur Geschichte der Aufklärung des 18. Jahrhunderts in Kremsmünster', *MÖIG*, LIII (1939), 423–80; Klingenstein, *Staatsverwaltung und kirchliche Autorität*, esp. pp. 165, 180, 185, 188, 190–1.

On French university education in philosophy, L. W. B. Brockliss, 'Philosophy teaching in France, 1600–1740', *History of Universities*, I (1981), 131–68.

See my essay 'Christians and "philosophes": the case of the Austrian Enlightenment' in D. Beales and G. Best, *History, Society and the Churches* (Cambridge, 1985), pp. 161–94.

architecture, geography and physical exercise formed part of the timetable. Physical sciences and natural history were counted as amusements.[114]

History had a special role. Since there was plenty of time, the account tells us, progress through the centuries was leisurely. By the time Joseph was fourteen, he had reached the end of the Roman Empire in the west. 'Elevating his mind to contemplate the designs of Providence, in the manner of the incomparable Bossuet, the principal object was to show him the true causes of the rise and fall of empires.'[115]

After renewed discussions, a last phase of academic education began in 1754, and continued until after his eighteenth birthday in 1759. The main subjects now were law, the teaching of which was entrusted to one Beck, and history, under Leporini. But both these men had to work under the direction of Bartenstein, the chief minister of Charles VI and until recently of Maria Theresa.[116]

First came the law of nature and of nations. The works of Puffendorff [sic], Heineccius, Burlamaqui and Holberg on this part of law served as models for the compilation expressly made for the Most Serene Prince. However, neither the order nor the particular sentiments of these different authors were rigidly adhered to; and all captious and frivolous questions, which have no real utility in human life, were totally omitted ... Exact and detailed study was made of the duties of a prince towards his people, as well as of his virtues and personal qualities. In treating the various forms of government, their strengths and weaknesses were displayed, and the different ways in which the rights of sovereignty can be exercised ...

The precepts of the law of nations were shown to be always compatible with sound policy.[117]

Civil, canon and feudal law were also treated, chiefly in the context of Germany and the Empire. It was said that they were dealt with 'summarily', which meant that they were covered in about a thousand pages all told. Special reference was made to the rights of the sovereign and particularly of the emperor in these fields, to the privileges and prerogatives of the House of Austria, and to the need for legal reform within the Empire.

These studies merged into his historical lessons, which now concentrated on developments in Germany but supplied also such information as was deemed necessary and useful to him about the other states of Europe. It was claimed that the errors and weaknesses of the Habsburgs were emphasised no less than those of other rulers.[118]

---

[114] Conrad, *RuV*, pp. 98–100.   [115] Conrad, *RuV*, pp. 100–1.

[116] Conrad, *RuV*, *passim*; Arneth, 'Johann Christof Bartenstein und seine Zeit', *AÖG* XLVI (1871), pp. 55–214; Arneth, *GMT* IV, pp. 169–75; J. Hrazky, 'Johann Christoph Bartenstein, der Staatsmann und Erzieher', *MÖSA*, XI (1958), 242–51; W. Högl, 'Bartenstein als Erzieher Joseph II', University of Vienna PhD dissertation, 1959 (disappointing); Benna's article in *Festschrift F. Loidl*.

[117] Conrad, *RuV*, p. 104.   [118] Conrad, *RuV*, pp. 104–6.

In this stage of his education, Joseph had to learn 'the Sclavonian language', or Czech, both because many of his future subjects spoke it, and to please the empress of Russia, the Monarchy's ally. It may be significant that no mention was made of the requirement in the Golden Bull of 1356 that a prince destined to rule Bohemia and the Empire must be taught this language.[119] He devoted the time previously spent on mathematics to the study of the best authors on the art of war, Caesar, Vegetius, Vauban, Quinci, Puységur and marshal de Saxe; and he read the lives of such great warriors as Peter the Great, Turenne and prince Eugene.[120]

It is now proposed [concludes the retrospective account of 1759] to give him also an exact knowledge of the internal constitution of each province of the Monarchy; after which it is believed that he will be ready to receive much more important lessons still, on the art of ruling, from the very mouths of His August Parents, to whom it belongs to put the finishing touches to his education and to carry so great a work to perfection.[121]

If this formidable programme of education is examined as it actually developed, certain blemishes are seen to have been concealed in the official account. Joseph's performance in his examinations was variable, and sometimes a boy who shared his lessons did better than the prince.[122] There were many 'rows and disagreements' among his mentors along the road.[123] At each new stage, those principally concerned found it extremely difficult to obtain decisions from the emperor and empress.[124] Moreover, the compilation of the special manuals which were deemed essential always took longer than had at first been hoped. In the case of the historical works for which Bartenstein was directly responsible, this will cause no surprise, particularly when it is realised that he took twelve volumes containing six thousand sides of manuscript, not counting six volumes of supporting documentation from the archives of the Monarchy, to reach the reign of Frederick III (1452–93). For the sixteenth century, although in principle Bartenstein thought the most recent periods the most worthy of study, pressure of time forced him to lower his sights and confine himself to producing a mere eight hundred sides of questions and answers. He never got beyond Ferdinand III (1637–57) in this format.[125] A still more damaging hiatus arose from his advice that Joseph should be spared

---

[119] E. F. Henderson (ed.), *Select Historical Documents of the Middle Ages* (London, 1910), p. 261. Italian was similarly prescribed.

On the position of the languages in Bohemia, F. M. Pelzel, *Kurzgefasste Geschichte der Böhmen* (Prague, 1771), pp. 618–20. I am grateful to Professor L. R. Lewitter for his help here.

[120] Conrad, *RuV*, pp. 103–4.   [121] Conrad, *RuV*, p. 107.

[122] K-M III, p. 53 (31 July 1752).

[123] E.g. K-M III, p. 167 (12 Mar. 1754): 'Disturbi und Uneinigkeiten'.

[124] Conrad, *RuV*, pp. 37–76, prints documents ranging from June 1753 to May 1754, in which it seems to me that the urgency of the tone of Bartenstein, Batthyány and the whole Conference mounts steadily. The entries in K-M give me the same impression. Cf. Arneth, *GMT* IV, p. 170.

[125] Arneth, *GMT* IV, pp. 171–5; Benna, *MÖSA* (1967), 123–8.

much study of civil and canon law, on the ground that Maria Theresa was on the point of replacing the existing arrangements in her German states by a Codex Theresianus. Unhappily, this work was still incomplete when Joseph died.[126]

In certain other respects the grand scheme of his education was in practice marred. The selection of his mentors seems perverse. One of the two highly religious countesses proved to be incompetent in dealing with children.[127] It seems at first sight curious that Maria Theresa should have chosen such an old man as Batthyány for her son's *Ajo*. He was fifty when appointed, and over sixty when Joseph came of age. Bartenstein was older still. It was also a strange arrangement to entrust the writing of manuals to him, for others to teach from. The tutors themselves, while acknowledging Bartenstein's transcendent abilities and his unique competence in the relevant fields, declared that it was only those familiar with Joseph's ways who could possibly decide how he should be taught.[128]

Still, it was an impressive, thorough and in certain respects advanced education which he had received by the time when at the age of nineteen, in 1760, he entered upon a further stage of his training for the throne. It was then that he began to learn about the working of the Monarchy's government in practice, both from his parents and from the officials of the various departments.[129]

THE EDUCATION OF AN ENLIGHTENED DESPOT?

There are many points of view from which it would be profitable for scholars of various disciplines to consider this elaborate and well-recorded scheme of tuition. It deserves, for example, a place in general educational history for its attempt to treat the child's early studies as games, for its avoidance of rote learning and encumbering detail, for its overriding emphasis on the criterion of utility, and in particular for its stress on the usefulness of historical study. It is significant also in European cultural history for its approach to the languages and literatures of the principal nations. The fact that Joseph received no systematic instruction in German literature, and little in German language, is symptomatic of the contempt in which they were held at this period by the upper classes. French, on the other hand, was now pre-eminent as a polite language at the Court, though perhaps less so than at Berlin. No doubt the influence of the emperor and the making of the French alliance in 1756

[126] Conrad, *RuV*, p. 51. Cf. H. E. Strakosch, *State Absolutism and the Rule of Law* (Sydney, 1967), p. 51.

[127] K-M III, p. 58 (6 Sept. 1752).

[128] Batthyány was born in 1697, Bartenstein in 1690. Wurzbach I, p. 178. Conrad, *RuV*, pp. 64–5. M. Braubach, 'Bartensteins Herkunft und Anfängen', *MÖIG*, LXI (1953), 99–149.

[129] Conrad, *RuV*, pp. 107, 111–21; Benna, *MÖSA* (1967),117–18. See below pp. 90–1.

assisted its rise in Vienna. But the phenomenon was observable all over the European continent.[130] In the case of the Monarchy, it involved the supersession not of just one but of many languages previously more or less of equal standing. In the southern Netherlands Flemish was at such a low ebb that some expected it to die out altogether.[131] In Hungary Magyar became even less respectable than before, as the competition of French was added to that of Latin and German.[132] At the Court the influence of Spain and its language had steadily declined after its exaltation in the early years of Charles VI, and even Italian inevitably became less important after the loss of Naples and Sicily.[133] It is striking how many of the texts used by Joseph were French or, like most of the English books known to him, in French translation.[134] So far as the classical languages were concerned, there was no question of his learning any Greek or of his discovering much about the ancient Greeks other than Alexander.[135] This is doubtless unsurprising, since Winckelmann's first work in praise of their achievements did not appear until 1755. But it would have been inconceivable at earlier periods for so little to have been taught of Aristotle.[136]

For the purposes of this book, however, the most relevant questions to ask about Joseph's education, and more generally about his upbringing, are: what sort of an attitude to governing was inculcated in him? In what sense, if any, was he groomed for the role of an 'enlightened despot'? And how much impact did the whole process actually make on his outlook and behaviour? An attempt will be made to answer these questions here, though a full discussion of some points will have to be deferred.

Maria Theresa claimed to have devoted herself, once the desperate problems of the early 1740s had been overcome, to two causes, the reform of the

---

[130] Information on this question is collected in L. Réau, *L'Europe française au siècle des lumières* (Paris, 1938) book I. Cf. W. H. Bruford, *Germany in the Eighteenth Century* (Cambridge, 1965), esp. pp. 291–327. For a contemporary comment see Ligne, *Fragments*, vol. I, pp. 245–6.
   A 'précis du plan' of J.'s education, of 1753, does envisage instruction in German rhetoric (K-M III, p. 403).
   Some discussion of the oddities of German princes' and princesses' French in this period, especially their spelling, is to be found in Lippert, *M.T. und Maria Antonia von Sachsen*, pp. xliii–xlvii. Cf. Mikoletzky in *Études européennes*.
[131] J. Shaw, *Sketches of the History of the Austrian Netherlands* (London, 1786), pp. 224–5.
[132] Cf. Marczali, *Hungary in the Eighteenth Century*, ch. 3; G. F. Cushing, 'Books and readers in eighteenth-century Hungary', *SR*, XLVII (1969), esp. 58–60.
[133] Cf. Redlich, *Werden einer Grossmacht*, p. 244; F. Venturi, *Settecento riformatore*, (5 vols., Turin, 1969) vol. I, p. 24.
[134] Locke, Pope, Shaftesbury, Temple are all cited in French, Bacon and Hobbes in French and Latin, Wollaston in Latin. Most of the Germans' works are cited in Latin, though Frederick the Great's of course in French.
[135] There is a very small number of references to translated works of Aristotle and Plato.
[136] D. Irwin (ed.), *Winckelmann: Writings on Art* (London, 1972), p. 4. I am grateful to Professor Q. R. D. Skinner for many illuminating comments on an earlier version of this section.

government of her central provinces, and the education of her children.[137] It is instructive first to consider the relationship between these two processes.

She described her reforms frankly and idiosyncratically in two versions of a political testament, the first written in about 1750 and the second in about 1756.[138] Her programme was grounded on the advice of count Haugwitz, who dominated internal policy-making in the late forties and fifties.[139] She imposed a reorganisation of the financial administration of her central provinces, so that their various representative assemblies, or 'Estates', could no longer prevent her levying and collecting taxes adequate to maintain an army deemed big enough to defend her territories. Clergy and nobles were now required to pay something more like a fair share of the principal tax, the *contributio*, in peacetime. She hoped also to eliminate the continual disputes between the provinces and between the separate ministries that ran their affairs in Vienna. As she said, 'I determined to alter the whole rotten Constitution, central and provincial, completely and to set up new institutions designed to put the system on a firm footing.'[140] The changes involved the establishment of a single *Directorium* which fused the Chancelleries of Austria and Bohemia, and dealt with both finance and general administration for these provinces. On the other hand, judicial business was now made separate from executive activity. The chief local officials became subordinate to the government in Vienna rather than servants of the provincial Estates. All these measures struck at provincial autonomy and variety, at the Estates and at the nobles who dominated them. This programme of change had many limitations. Most important, it applied to only half the Monarchy: Belgium, the Italian lands and the vast kingdom of Hungary were excluded from it. But

---

[137] She was capable of claiming that 'L'éducation de mes enfants a été toujours mon grand et le plus cher objet' (to archduke Maximilian, [?] April 1774; Arneth, *MTKuF* II, p. 317).
Cf. Macartney, *Habsburg and Hohenzollern Dynasties*, pp. 99–100, 115.
I use the formula 'central provinces' to refer to Austria and Bohemia as opposed to Belgium, Italy, Hungary etc. It is a deliberately vague formula, which I employ even when, say, one of the Austrian duchies ought to be excepted but it seems to complicate matters unnecessarily to make the point. I have avoided using the term *Erbländer* because in my period it was sometimes used to include Hungary and sometimes to exclude it.

[138] The text is to be found in Arneth, 'Zwei Denkschriften der Kaiserin Maria Theresias', *AÖG*, XLVII (1871), 267–354, and in a more careful edition by J. Kallbrunner, *Kaiserin Maria Theresias politisches Testament* (Vienna, 1952). The latter contains some useful commentary on the curious German forms to be found in the *Testament* and in other contemporary writing.
Macartney has published an English translation of the first version of the Testament in *Habsburg and Hohenzollern Dynasties*, pp. 96–132, which on the whole I have followed.

[139] A convenient short account is F. Walter, *Die theresianische Staatsreform von 1749* (Vienna, 1958). Longer and fuller treatment is to be found in F. Walter, *VKNGÖ*, vol. XXXII (Vienna, 1938), with supporting documents in J. Kallbrunner and M. Winkler, *VKNGÖ*, vol. XVIII (Vienna, 1925). But see H. Haussherr, *Verwaltungseinheit und Ressorttrennung vom Ende des 17. bis zum Beginn des 19. Jahrhunderts* (Berlin, 1953), ch. 3, and P. G. M. Dickson, *Finance and Government under M.T.*, *1740–1780* (Oxford, forthcoming).
On Haugwitz himself, Ranke, *Sämmtliche Werke*, vol. XXX, pp. 21–3 (report by Fürst).

[140] Macartney, *Habsburg and Hohenzollern Dynasties*, p. 128.

even so it greatly strengthened the power of the ruler, notably increased the centralisation of the administration, and substantially raised the state's income and thus the size of its army.[141]

Maria Theresa was also displaying radicalism in other directions. It has been claimed that a section of her first testament – especially its unwieldy last sentence – foreshadows all her later ecclesiastical reforms, if not Joseph's as well. Her predecessors, she says, in their great piety donated vast lands to the church,

which at that time served a good purpose ... Since, however, God has now so blessed us in the German Hereditary Lands that both the Catholic religion is most flourishing and the condition of the clergy is good and assured, this principle no longer holds good. And I should therefore consider it ... culpable to give or transfer more property to the clergy. For first they do not need it, and secondly, they do not – alas! – use what they have as they should, and so they constitute a heavy burden upon the public. For no monastic house observes the limitations of its statutes, and many idlers are allowed in. All of this will require a great reform, which I intend to carry out in time and after due consideration. I except, however, from such measures the Kingdom of Hungary, where much still remains to be done for religion, in which task I shall require the clergy there to cooperate, but not work with them alone, but concert chiefly with·laymen on the principles to be followed, the chief aim of which must be to introduce seminaries, colleges, academies, hospitals for the sick and injured, establishments, like those in Italy for unmarried women, for the better instruction of the young, etc., taking careful pains to support and develop what is useful to the public, and not what profits the private advantage of the clergy, monks and nuns in any province, it being well understood that even this salutary intention cannot be realised until the military has been put completely on the footing necessary to secure the preservation of the Monarchy and the welfare of its Provinces and subjects.

Alarmed by an apparent resurgence of Protestantism in the Austrian duchies, she made approaches on church reform to the pope in the middle fifties.[142] But these proved abortive, and while Joseph's education was in progress, very little ecclesiastical reform was actually accomplished, in Hungary or anywhere else in the Monarchy. The most notable measures of these early years in this field were a reduction in the number of feast-days, ratified by papal bull, which Maria Theresa exploited (so far as popular opposition permitted) to

[141] On the significance of the reforms, in English: Strakosch, *State Absolutism and the Rule of Law*; Blanning, *J. II and Enlightened Despotism*, pp. 24–5.
[142] Macartney, *Habsburg and Hohenzollern Dynasties*, p. 106. See Maass, *Josephinismus*, vol. I, pp. 5–9 and *Der Frühjosephinismus* (Vienna, 1969). Cf. Wangermann, *Austrian Achievement*, pp. 74–9; R. Reinhardt, 'Zur Kirchenreform in Österreich unter Maria Theresia', *ZKG* LXXVII (1966), 105–19; Benna in *Festschrift F. Loidl*; A. Wandruszka, 'Geheimprotestantismus, Josephinismus und Volksliturgie in Österreich', *ZKG*, LXXVIII (1967), 94–101; E. Wangermann, 'Josephinismus und katholischer Glaube', in *Katholische Aufklärung und Josephinismus*, ed. E. Kovács (Vienna, 1979), esp. pp. 333–5, and 'Reform Catholicism and political radicalism in the Austrian Enlightenment' in *The Enlightenment in National Context*, ed. R. Porter and M. Teich (Cambridge, 1981), esp. pp. 128–9.

increase the number of days worked;[143] and the beginnings, under the aegis of Van Swieten, of reform of the censorship system and of the University of Vienna, directed against the virtual monopoly held by the Jesuits in both spheres.[144]

In foreign affairs, she obtained in 1749 agreement from the Conference for her new policy of working to reverse the traditional foreign alliances of the Monarchy by cultivating the friendship of France. This change had the approval of Bartenstein but was most effectively advocated by the young Kaunitz. He spent the next four years in Paris, trying with no obvious success to win French support. Then in 1753 he was recalled to Vienna to become foreign minister (*Staatskanzler*, state chancellor).[145] This appointment involved a major reshuffle of the higher officials, the raising of salaries for the new men and the payment of massive golden handshakes to those who were relegated.[146] The 'Diplomatic Revolution' duly occurred in 1756, provoking the Seven Years War.[147]

Maria Theresa's activity between 1748 and 1756 was a remarkable example of the imposition from above of a radical programme of change. She was proud of the ruthlessness of her internal measures, despite the unpopularity they brought her.[148] But they were only part of the wider plan of creating a large army and engineering an international situation in which it could be used to recover Silesia and humble Prussia. The policy could be regarded as defensive in two senses: first, that Frederick the Great had been the aggressor in 1740, and Maria Theresa was now only trying to get her own back; and secondly, that a larger army was needed merely to protect her territories adequately. But it was aggressive in that she countenanced schemes for deliberately provoking

[143] Wangermann, *Austrian Achievement*, p. 74.
[144] See esp. Winter, *Josefinismus*, Klingenstein, *Staatsverwaltung und kirchliche Autorität* and P. Hersche, *Der Spätjansenismus in Österreich* (Vienna, 1977). See below, pp. 441–2.
[145] Arneth, *GMT* IV, ch. 10 esp. pp. 272–80, and n. 329 on pp. 535–6; G. Klingenstein, 'Kaunitz kontra Bartenstein: Zur Geschichte der Staatskanzlei, 1749–1753', in *Beiträge zur neueren Geschichte Österreichs*, ed. Fichtenau & Zöllner.

    The principal source is H. Schlitter (ed.), *Correspondance secrète entre le Comte W. A. Kaunitz-Rietberg et le Baron Ignaz de Koch, 1750–1752* (Vienna, 1899). In English W. J. McGill, 'The roots of policy: Kaunitz in Vienna and Versailles, 1749–1753', *JHM*, XLIII (1971), 228–44.

    J. Strieder in *Kritische Forschungen zur österreichischen Politik vom Aachener Frieden bis zum Beginn des siebenjährigen Krieges* (Leipzig, 1906) and 'Maria Theresia, Kaunitz und die österreichische Politik von 1748–1755', *Historische Vierteljahrschrift*, XIII (1910), 494–509, makes *inter alia* a telling case that it was M.T. who was consistent in pursuit of the French alliance and that K. often despaired of achieving it.
[146] K-M III, pp. 69–71 (31 Oct. 1752), 108–11 (13 May 1753). Klingenstein's article cited in the previous note.
[147] In English, D. B. Horn, 'The diplomatic revolution' in *NCMH*, vol. VII, and H. Butterfield, 'The reconstruction of an historical episode: the history of the enquiry into the origins of the Seven Years War' in *Man on his Past* (Cambridge, 1955).
[148] For the pride, the political testaments (see n. 138). For the unpopularity, Karajan, *Feierliche Sitzungsberichte KAW* (1859), 21; Ranke, *Sämmtliche Werke*, vol. XXX, p. 10 (report by Fürst).

Frederick into war and for dismembering and partitioning Prussia.[149] Her absorption in these far-reaching projects was associated with her growing seclusion at Schönbrunn in the fifties.

An important aspect of her policies was the employment of servants from unorthodox backgrounds. Silva-Tarouca was a Portuguese. Van Swieten was a Roman Catholic Dutchman by birth, and therefore excluded by religion from opportunities in his own country. Haugwitz was a Protestant German by origin, from a part of Silesia conquered by Frederick the Great, who converted to Roman Catholicism to become an official under Maria Theresa. The two Zinzendorfs, financial administrators under her and (in the case of the younger) her three successors, had much the same background. Bartenstein had travelled a similar road in an earlier generation, having graduated from the University of Strasburg, the town of his birth, and converted to Roman Catholicism only after seeing how necessary the change was to his prospects of advancement in Vienna. Kaunitz was at least a member of the Moravian aristocracy but, like Haugwitz and the Zinzendorfs, had been educated at German Protestant universities. Maria Theresa's reforms were not merely imposed from above; many of them were imported from abroad. The example was often Prussia;[150] the reformers were more varied in origin. Samuel von Brukenthal, the empress's most trusted official in Transylvania, actually remained a Protestant.[151]

Historians have not grasped how little of the radicalism that Maria Theresa was displaying during the late forties and fifties in her policies and in the choice of her servants rubbed off on to her arrangements for Joseph's education. The avowed object of her political testaments is to inform her successor and to urge him to maintain her system. Yet one of them includes a specific injunction that it should not be opened until after her death,[152] and it seems clear that she did not pass on the contents of either to her son during the fifties. He was kept at his books until he was nineteen, and seems to have known nothing of her deeper plans and to have taken no part in policy-making at this stage. He was able to assert in his first extant political memorandum in 1761 that he totally lacked knowledge of both the old and the new systems of administration.[153] The schemes of reform and education were distinct, often complementing each other but in some respects mutually contradictory. This conclusion puts in doubt the account usually given of a

---

[149] Butterfield, *Man on his Past*, ch. 5.
[150] See F. Walter, 'Preussen und die österreichische Erneuerung von 1749', *MÖIG*, LI (1937), 415–29.
[151] Crankshaw, *Maria Theresa*, pp. 183–4, has made this point in a slightly different way. On the individuals, F. Walter, *Männer um M.T.* (Vienna, 1951); G. A. Schuller, *Samuel von Brukenthal* (2 vols., Munich, 1967).
[152] Kallbrunner, *M.T.'s politisches Testament*, p. 5.
[153] Arneth, *MTuJ* I, p. 1 (J. to M.T., 3 Apr. 1761).

close relationship between mother and son, in which the reticence was all on Joseph's side.[154]

That modernity was no particular object in the plans for Joseph's instruction is easily proved by the attention paid to the precedents, first, of Joseph I's education and, secondly, of the descriptions of France prepared for Louis XIV's heir, both dating from the 1690s.[155] Maria Theresa's choice of mentors for her son tells the same story. It was for a long time believed that Martini, the theorist of natural law, was his tutor, but this is now known to be untrue.[156] There is no sign that Van Swieten, who was being allowed to reform public education, was consulted about her son's. Despite her apparently advanced intentions in ecclesiastical matters, she cheerfully employed three Jesuits among Joseph's tutors. The *Ajo*, Batthyány, from a great Hungarian noble family, had made his name as a general under Charles VI. Khevenhüller had been sent to various courts by that monarch to press the Pragmatic Sanction.[157] Perhaps most surprising of all is the position accorded to Bartenstein, who was clearly the prime mover in all the plans made for the heir's education after 1751. Maria Theresa and Francis Stephen simply rubber-stamped Bartenstein's numerous and wordy memoranda, and turned them into directives.[158] Yet he had been Charles VI's favoured minister, was generally disliked as a gauche upstart, 'loved all that was Benedictine', and had been only a lukewarm supporter of Haugwitz's reforms.[159] When Kaunitz replaced him as the effective foreign minister in 1753, Bartenstein became more fully involved with Joseph's education. He was still writing memoirs for the prince about the events of the last forty years as late as 1762.[160] It illuminates Maria Theresa's priorities that she should have used responsibility for her son's education as a means of providing prestigious occupation for a superseded minister.[161]

It is true that in 1753 the new man, Kaunitz, became one of the three ministers who deliberated together regularly about the heir's studies. He also attended some of the boy's examinations. It was believed that Kaunitz made an impression on Joseph from the start by his supposed scepticism, his French manners, his disregard of etiquette in his dress and his unpunctuality.[162] But since in 1763 the crown prince wanted his influence curbed, and Maria

---

[154] E.g. in Bernard, *Joseph II* and Crankshaw, *Maria Theresa.*

[155] Benna, *MÖSA* (1967), 128, 133–6.

[156] Conrad, *RuV*, p. 6 and the references in nn. 12–14. Winter's account of J.'s views in his *Josefinismus* very largely depends on the assumption that Martini was J.'s tutor.

[157] K-M I, pp. 76–9.   [158] Conrad, *RuV*, pp. 25–74 etc.; Benna, *MÖSA* (1967).

[159] Klingenstein in Fichtenau and Zöllner, *Beiträge zur neueren Geschichte Österreichs*, pp. 147–8; Arneth, *AÖG* (1871), 9; Hrazky, *MÖSA* (1958), 239; Benna, *MÖSA* (1967), 154, 162.

[160] Arneth, *AÖG* (1871), 65–7, 72–214.

[161] Thus did Lord Butler become Master of Trinity College, Cambridge, in time for the admission of prince Charles.

[162] K-M III, pp. 114 (23 May 1753), 119 (9 June 1753) and Ranke, *Sämmtliche Werke*, vol. XXX, pp. 17–18 (report by Fürst) describe these traits, but not their effect on J.

Theresa thought her son still hostile to him in 1765, the opposite must be the case.[163] The other two ministers concerned were Bartenstein and Khevenhüller. Admittedly, Joseph's legal tutor, Beck, was a convert from Protestantism. But his appointment was the result of a recommendation from Khevenhüller to Bartenstein.[164]

Maria Theresa and Francis Stephen were preoccupied with other matters than the education of their eldest son. Neither of them had much experience of formal education.[165] That Maria Theresa had become in some respects politically radical was the result of her practical experiences, not of theoretical study. They were concerned that Joseph should be a devoted Roman Catholic of a particular tinge. They wanted him to see to the defence of the Monarchy, and to be himself militarily active. They wished him to be taught to look after the wellbeing of all the provinces, and of all classes within them. He should make himself personally agreeable to his subjects, choose his servants with great care and treat them generously.[166] But, even in so far as these precepts concerned his formal education as opposed to his upbringing, his parents were content to leave all the details to Bartenstein and the tutors working under him.

It was Bartenstein, then, who was chiefly responsible for the scheme of Joseph's education during his adolescence. He exerted his influence to have the philosophical element reduced, in particular the metaphysics, 'the most useless to a sovereign and the most disagreeable of all those [subjects] which are usually taught in the schools'. He said it had in any case declined 'since literature gained pre-eminence', and had recently been restricted by the empress in Austrian universities.[167] He ensured instead that history should dominate Joseph's studies – the most useful of all subjects because it would supply him with information of which he would be in constant need, about Germany, the House of Austria and international relations. It would also furnish him with a sufficiency of moral and political reflections. Bartenstein took pride that, in place of the teaching which Fénelon's *Télémaque* sought to pass on by way of fable, Joseph had received more appropriate lessons from the study of history itself. However, the sort of historical writing put before the prince by Bartenstein owed little to the new approaches of Enlightened authors.[168]

---

163 J. in his *Rêveries* (see ch. 4 below); M.T. to K., 5 or 6 June 1766 (Beer, *JLuK*, p. 502).
164 Benna, *Festschrift F. Loidl*, p. 196. Conrad, *RuV*, pp. 7, 55–6.
165 Pick, *Maria Theresa*, pp. 17–19; Hennings, *Und sitzet zur linken Hand*, ch. 8.
166 These aims emerge from the political testaments (see n. 138), from Wandruszka's accounts of Francis's views and instructions (*MÖSA* (1959) and *L. II.*, vol. I, pp. 81–8) and from Arneth, *MTKuF*.
167 Conrad, *RuV*, pp. 50–1.
168 Conrad, *RuV*, pp. 48–55. It was not Khevenhüller but Bartenstein who made the remark about *Télémaque* (cf. Bernard, *Joseph II*, p. 18). See E. Cassirer, *The Philosophy of the Enlightenment* (Boston, 1955), ch. 5.

Bartenstein was old-fashioned, pedantic and prolix, but he was a good scholar and a broad-minded man. Beck, who was less long-winded[169] and more up-to-date, was allowed some independence. It is possible to form a very good idea from the latter's compilation on natural, international and imperial law of what Joseph was taught about political theory and the rights and duties of sovereigns.[170]

Beck's work was heavily based on Pufendorf's *De jure naturae et gentium* of 1672. Joseph was taught that it was primarily the individual's need for security and his fear of exploitation which had led to the formation of states.[171] Hobbes is cited with approval for maintaining this view, and for his general assertion that the position and powers of the sovereign derive from natural law, though it is pointed out that he was a dangerous rationalist and heretic.[172] Locke's apparent belief that there existed contracts between rulers and ruled is gently disposed of as unhistorical.[173] The various forms of government are described. It is concluded that in general, though not everywhere and at all times, monarchy has been found the most serviceable. The monarch may be, and is best left, uncontrolled. He ought himself to rule. But his rule is not properly described by the pejorative term 'despotism' if it is rule over free men whose property rights are respected. The ruler's aim ought to be, and his situation gives good hope that it will be, 'the welfare of the state and the happiness of his subjects'.[174]

The teachings of Beck on certain issues are especially interesting. There are variations between the constitutions of different provinces of the Monarchy, which the ruler should respect.[175] He will do best to maintain the true religion, but he may tolerate others for reasons of state.[176] Torture, Beck says, is a disputed matter: it is considered by some to be actively pernicious; at least it should be used sparingly.[177]

Beck occasionally remarks that the age is growing more enlightened, for example in rejecting Machiavellism and revolution.[178] But he was writing in 1754–5, at an early stage in the diffusion of the Enlightenment. This is in any case clear from the works he cites. Reprinting of Pufendorf's works was about

[169] Benna, *Festschrift F. Loidl*, p. 195.
[170] The compilation forms the bulk of Conrad, *RuV*.
[171] Conrad, *RuV*, pp. 205–8. There are modern editions of *De jure naturae et gentium* and *De officio hominis et civis* (1673) in *The Classics of International Law*, ed. J. B. Scott. The former work (ed. W. Simms, Oxford, 1934) is accompanied by an English translation by C. H. and W. A. Oldfather; the latter (ed. W. Schücking, New York, 1927) is similarly accompanied by an English translation by F. G. Moore.
[172] Conrad, *RuV*, esp. p. 147 and n. 7.
[173] Conrad, *RuV*, p. 209: 'Wider alle Historie ist, was Locke, Du Gouvernement Civil, ch. VII, § 8, schreibt ...'
[174] Conrad, *RuV*, pp. 209, 218, 284, 288.   [175] Conrad, *RuV*, pp. 215–16, 243–4, 281, 297.
[176] Conrad, *RuV*, pp. 277–8.   [177] Conrad, *RuV*, p. 260.   [178] Conrad, *RuV*, p. 222.

to cease.[179] There is no sign in Beck's work of the *Encyclopédie*, the first two volumes of which were published in 1751. Of Voltaire's writings, only the *Siècle de Louis XIV* figures.[180] The school of French economists known as the 'physiocrats', which emerged only in the late fifties, is naturally absent.[181] One of the most recent and potentially the most subversive of the French works cited is Montesquieu's *De l'esprit des lois*, published in 1748 and permitted to circulate in the Monarchy only in 1753. But the numerous passages quoted with approval are not those which glorify representative government, although they do include some which stress the necessary variations in law and constitution between different countries and periods.[182] Joseph certainly did not receive, as Louis-Philippe claimed to have done two decades later, a 'democratic' education.[183]

There is a surprising number of references to English writers, especially Bacon, Hobbes and Pope.[184] English history often appears, particularly the wicked Cromwell.[185] Among Germans, Leibniz is unmentioned, while Frederick the Great's *Anti-Machiavel* figures prominently.[186] But of course nothing is cited more frequently than Pufendorf on the one hand and Roman writers, especially Cicero, Horace and Tacitus, on the other.

Although Beck represents natural law as a great discovery of the seventeenth century, which even the great Bacon had not recognised,[187] his compilation is not dominated by it as a manual prepared by Martini would have been. Beck was more concerned with the positive law than with what might be called ideal law, and after his more generalised sections on natural and international law he soon became caught up in the minutiae of the law of the Holy Roman Empire.[188]

After Joseph had been taken through this compendium, he went on to study documents prepared for him in 1759–60 about the constitutions of the Monarchy's various provinces. Bartenstein, in presenting these treatises, made some striking comments. First, he considered it important to set out the reciprocal advantages one province might get from another, and to make a comparison between their constitutions. Secondly,

---

179 L. Krieger, *The Politics of Discretion: Pufendorf and the Acceptance of Natural Law* (Chicago, 1965), pp. 262 and 303n.

180 E.g. Conrad, *RuV*, p. 170. Although there are many additions of uncertain later dates, the *Encyclopédie* and other works of Voltaire are nowhere mentioned. But Rousseau's *Émile* (1762) are Marmontel's *Bélisaire* (1767) are among the new citations.

181 Bernard (*Joseph II*, p. 19) has asserted that the physiocrats greatly influenced Beck.

182 Conrad, *RuV*, p. 218. Winter, *Josefinismus*, p. 41.

183 *Mémoires de Louis-Philippe, duc D'Orléans, écrits par lui-même* (Paris, 1973) vol. I, p. 3.

184 Conrad, *RuV*, *passim*.

185 E.g. Conrad, *RuV*, p. 202. A good many sections on English history were later added, including an account of Canute's encounter with the waves, and strictures on Henry VIII's gratuitous theological writings (pp. 283, 289).

186 E.g. Conrad, *RuV*, p. 163.   187 Conrad, *RuV*, p. 146.   188 Conrad, *RuV*, p. 15.

I have thought it right in respect of every province specially to indicate what has been observed to be useful or harmful to the state over more than forty-five years, partly because this knowledge seems to me the most valuable for a ruler and partly because for me no ground exists for harbouring any fondness or dislike for one or the other *Erbland*, so that I remark on the relevant good points and weaknesses of each place as a true and practical cosmopolite in deed and not only in words.[189]

Thirdly,

I am totally unwilling to argue in favour of an unrestricted oppressive despotism. For fifty years my motto has been: *Peragit tranquilla potestas, quod violenta nequit.* For what is rushed through in haste and, still more, what is imposed, never works well . . .

Estates must be permitted to put before the Court, with due reference, their proposals for meeting the needs of their provinces, and 'the mild Austrian government, which can never be too highly praised, does not permit that they should be blamed for it'. Sometimes it is the advisers of the monarch who are mistaken or self-interested; sometimes it is the Estates. In exceptional cases the Court must arbitrate, after taking the best and most experienced advice, for the wellbeing of the whole state. 'I have believed that in this way royal power should be reconciled with the privileges and liberties of the Estates.'[190] Such was the spirit in which Joseph was taught about the constitutions of the province he was to rule, and the methods by which they should be governed.

What Joseph was told about religion is of particular interest. 'Bigotry and superstition,' wrote Beck, 'astrology, soothsaying and witchcraft are enemies of God's honour.' But, the passage continues, atheism and freethinking can hardly even be contemplated.[191] That Joseph, as part of his study of Italian, should have read some of the works of Muratori is of significance here. This author was famous for his politico-religious as well as his vast historical writings. In the former, such as *Della carità cristiana* (1723, dedicated to Charles VI), *Della regolata divozione de' cristiani* (1747) and *Della pubblica felicità* (1749), he argued in favour of simple worship, the abandonment of all recent liturgical and doctrinal innovations, limitation of the number of monks and so forth. Hence his views were often considered 'Jansenist', that is, sympathetic to the French religious movement, Puritanical and anti-Jesuit, condemned by the bull *Unigenitus* of 1713. He further asserted the right and duty of the ruler to reform the church within his territories. These books had a wide influence in the Monarchy, were approved by cardinal Migazzi, archbishop of Vienna from 1757, and may be said to have set the tone of the 'reforming' or 'enlightened' Catholicism of the second half of the eighteenth century in the Habsburg lands. It is presumed that these are the works of Muratori which Joseph studied.[192]

---

[189] Conrad, *RuV*, p. 114.   [190] Conrad, *RuV*, pp. 116–17.   [191] Conrad, *RuV*, p. 157.
[192] See, on the importance of Muratori and his influence, Wandruszka, *L. II.*, vol. 1, pp. 26–8 and *Österreich und Italien*, esp. pp. 35–7; E. Zlabinger, *L.A. Muratori und Österreich*

This is not absolutely proven. But we know precisely what Joseph was taught by Beck about canon law and by Bartenstein about the position of religion in the Monarchy.[193] Beck's most interesting emphasis is on the concept of national or state churches – such as the French, Spanish, Sicilian, Venetian and also the German – existing within the whole Roman Catholic body. He allows a place for consultation between the ruler and the bishops over the better ordering of such churches. Bartenstein's account of the religious situation in the various provinces of the Monarchy, composed between 1755 and 1757, includes a valuable historical retrospect and embodies a most revealing approach to domestic ecclesiastical problems. He traces and deprecates the forcible reconversion of Bohemia after the battle of the White Mountain. He condemns the persecution instituted by the archbishop of Salzburg in the early eighteenth century against the Protestants of his lands, which led to mass emigration, with resulting economic loss to the state. The Monarchy's policy, of transplanting dissidents from predominantly Catholic provinces to others where Protestantism is tolerated, is much to be preferred. Bartenstein is not in favour of introducing general and open toleration even for the benefit of trade and industry. He is less liberal in this matter than Beck. His remedies for heresy are the provision of orthodox books in place of unorthodox, the establishment of more parishes and schools, the improvement of the education of the clergy, and missionary work. As in secular matters, he stresses differences between the provinces. In the 'German hereditary lands' he acknowledges that the clergy contribute more than their fair share to the state and in general perform their spiritual functions well. But, like Maria Theresa in the passage quoted above, he emphasises the unsatisfactoriness of the position in Hungary, where the untaxed upper clergy are monstrously rich and the lower desperately poor, so that parochial provision is exceptionally bad and needs special attention. It is an extraordinary fact, however, that Bartenstein, although he was president of the new religious commission, had been kept in ignorance of some of the empress's schemes to extract funds for reform from the clergy and of her secret approaches to the pope about them. So Joseph too may have remained unaware of this initiative.

In answer, then, to the first two questions posed above, the heir to the Monarchy was taught that it was vital to the wellbeing of his subjects that he should himself effectively rule, and that his aim must always be the further-

(Innsbruck, 1970); G. Holzknecht, *Ursprung und Herkunft der Reformideen Kaiser Josefs II. auf kirchlichem Gebiete* (Innsbruck, 1914); Garms-Cornides, *WBGN* (1976); Hersche, *Spätjansenismus*; and more generally, Chadwick, *Popes and Revolution*, pp. 27–30, 392–402; F. Venturi, 'History and reform in the middle of the eighteenth century' in *The Diversity of History: Essays in Honour of Sir Herbert Butterfield*, ed. J. H. Elliott and H. G. Koenigsberger (London, 1970), pp. 223–44; Venturi, *Settecento riformatore*, vol. 1.
[193] For the whole paragraph, Benna in *Festschrift F. Loidl*. Also Reinhardt, *ZKG* (1966).

ance of 'the general good' or 'the general best'.[194] He was responsible to no earthly power, only to God. He should concern himself with the reform of the church within his dominions. It would be desirable that he should be less trammelled than his predecessors by constitutional provisions of an antiquated character, especially in the Empire. Representative assemblies were less likely to promote the general welfare than an absolute sovereign. But of course oaths sworn to uphold constitutions ought to be observed, and the ruler ought always to act according to the law and to respect the views of the Estates. On this basis, and provided that the property of his subjects was respected, his rule would not be despotic.

This teaching is 'enlightened' in a sense, but only in a restricted sense. It was virtually untouched by many tendencies commonly associated with Enlightenment, or connoted by the word. It owed little to the French thinkers whose names and writings are usually placed in the forefront of the Enlightenment, partly because during Joseph's formative years many of their greatest works were very new or had yet to be written, but partly also because some were ignored and the principal exception, *De l'esprit des lois*, was presented in a particular light. Beck's citations from Locke, Pope and Wollaston were even less representative. The main effective influence was Pufendorf, a Protestant, a rationalist and a reformer, but a writer old-fashioned even in the German context of the 1750s. Christian Wolff, the populariser of the philosophy of Leibniz and often called 'the father of the German Enlightenment', was nearly fifty years junior to Pufendorf. He accepted a form of contract theory, praised aspects of representative government, and even allowed subjects some right of resistance to an absolute ruler who defied the constitution. His works were important in the education of Frederick the Great, were already being introduced into the curriculum of progressive monastic schools in Austria, and were used by Martini in teaching Leopold II;[195] but they scarcely figure in Beck's compendium. Perhaps the most prominent writer of the Enlightenment to play a significant role in Joseph's education, apart from Montesquieu, was the Italian Muratori. In this exceptional case the archduke had been encouraged to read something by a modern author in the original language. But Muratori, benevolent, tolerant and enlightened though he was, remained a loyal Roman Catholic priest, essentially concerned to reform the church from within – remote from any idea of rejecting its fundamental doctrines. The authorities used by Beck and Bartenstein in their compilations on ecclesiastical questions were more orthodox still.[196]

---

[194] I know of no study of this frequently encountered concept.
[195] L. Krieger, *The German Idea of Freedom* (Chicago, 1972), pp. 66–7; F. Hertz, *The Development of the German Public Mind*, vol. II (London, 1962), ch. 14; H. von Voltelini, 'Die naturrechtlichen Lehren und die Reformen des 18. Jahrhunderts', *HZ*, CV (1910), 65–104; Sturmberger, *MÖIG* (1939); Wandruszka, *L. II*, vol. I, pp. 90–2.
[196] Benna, *Festschrift F. Loidl*, p. 194.

In relation to this history of Catholic Reform in the Monarchy, as well as to the influence of the French Enlightenment, the precise dates of Joseph's education are critical. It was not until 1759 that the Jesuits' virtual monopolies of university teaching and censorship were broken. Only in that same year did Migazzi succeed in inducing the censorship, over Jesuit opposition, to allow into the Monarchy a German translation of Muratori's *Della regolata divozione*.[197] In other words, nearly the whole of Joseph's education took place before reform in this field got under way. Almost immediately afterwards, what he had been taught came to seem distinctly old-fashioned.

As we have seen, another available form of 'Enlightenment' was played down in Joseph's education – his mother's ecclesiastical plans, and her assault on the privileges of nobles and Estates. It can plausibly be questioned whether Bartenstein even understood the full significance of Haugwitz's reforms. Anyway, they were under a cloud in the late 1750s.[198] But their neglect in the scheme for training the heir to the Monarchy underlines the limitations both of the 'enlightened' and the 'despotic' elements in his training.

THE EFFECT ON JOSEPH OF HIS EDUCATION AND UPBRINGING

The prince de Ligne, one of Joseph's closest friends, wrote of his education: 'it had been, like that of many sovereigns, neglected by dint of being fussed over; they are taught everything except what they ought to know'.[199] The archduke was kept too long in isolation from affairs and contemporaries; his time was so well filled that he can have had little opportunity for unauthorised reading; and his teaching in some areas, especially in history, was over-elaborate. Perhaps the very idea of educating a prince for kingship is foolish. Knowledge of people and experience of the world are what rulers need above all else. But enough has already been said to disprove the commonly accepted view, deriving from the memoirs of Caroline Pichler, that all his teachers were stupid and restrictive; that 'the prince, with his dominating spirit and his aspiring genius, saw himself surrounded and, what was worse, subjected to men whom he easily far outshone'; or the still more preposterous notion that he was 'an autodidact'.[200] Much of what he had been taught was to be directly useful to him, for example the accounts of the constitutions of the Empire and of the various provinces of the Monarchy, the languages he learned, and the military lore; and in these areas he was well grounded. Ligne admitted that he

---

[197] Klingenstein, *Staatsverwaltung und kirchliche Autorität*, esp. pp. 107–11.
[198] Hrazky, *MÖSA* (1958), p. 239; and see ch. 4 below.
[199] *Mémoires et mélanges historiques et littéraires, par le prince de Ligne* (5 vols., Paris, 1827–8), vol. I, p. 240. See Plate 20b.
[200] Pichler, *Denkwürdigkeiten*, vol. I, p. 121. E. Winter, 'Josef II.', *Der Bindenschild*, III (1946), 11, and P. P. Bernard, 'The origins of Josephinism: two studies', *Colorado College Studies*, VII (1964), 3, both speak of J. as an autodidact.

spoke four languages fluently, and two passably.[201] Moreover prince Albert, who as his brother-in-law came to know him intimately, wrote that

he had developed a manner of reasoning derived from the lessons he had received during his education in peripatetic philosophy, by means of which he was able to uphold by sophistical arguments the most fallacious principles, in such a way that he discomfited all who lacked logical training and very solid princples and tried to combat his reasoning.[202]

Here is a remarkable testimony both to the impress left by Joseph's education, and to its old-fashioned character. To Albert what stands out is the emperor's Jesuitical training!

It was only very rarely that Joseph later referred to his early life or gave credit to any teacher or writer. But it was reported on good authority in 1769 that he had explained his ignorance of Ariosto's poetry by saying that his mother had excluded it from his studies as improper.[203] He made a point of attending Batthyány's funeral, and did not take an opportunity to criticise him when talking to Catherine the Great.[204] He paid for the solemn funeral of his philosophy tutor, Father Frantz. This is especially striking, since Frantz, though a progressive Jesuit, had been removed by Maria Theresa from the education commission just after he had taken part in teaching Joseph, had later failed as a headmaster and died after the suppression of his Order.[205] The emperor can hardly have believed his own studies and tutors to have been unsatisfactory, since he asserted, when discussing his daughter's, that 'education does everything'.[206] Further, he took an obsessive interest in the education of his brother's children, particularly the future Francis II; and his attitude closely resembled the approach of his own mentors, even in details: he employed an ex-Jesuit, he spared the boy study of poetry, and he stressed the value of history and logic.[207]

His failure to acknowledge many debts to teachers and authors no doubt stems partly from his pride and partly from his habit of looking to the future

201 Ligne, *Mémoires*, vol. I, p. 242. The four are obviously German, French, Italian and Latin. Presumably Czech was one of the passables, but I do not know which was the other.

202 Albert's memoirs, quoted in Arneth, *GMT* VII, p. 532.

203 Report of 3 May 1769 on HHSA FA Hofreisen 1. J. did write in the margin of a similar report of 22 March 'non e vero', but I take that denial to refer to the supplementary phrase there attributed to him: 'perche voi altri Signori non sapete, che Mamma rigorosa abbiamo noi altri'.

204 K-M VII, pp. 122–3; D. Maroger (ed.), *The Memoirs of Catherine the Great*, transl. M. Budberg (London, 1955), p. 179.

205 Wurzbach IV, p. 343. See the references in n. 113; Hersche, *Spätjansenismus*, p. 68; and p. 456 below.

206 J. to M.T., 24 Feb. 1766 (HHSA FA Sbde 55).

207 On J.'s preoccupation with his brother's children's education, and for the details of Francis II's, see Wandruszka, *L. II.*, vol. I, pp. 396–7 and vol. II pp. 43–4 etc.; C. Wolfsgruber, *Franz I.*, *Kaiser von Österreich* (2 vols., Vienna, 1899); W. C. Langsam, *Francis the Good: The Education of an Emperor 1768–1792* (New York, 1949); Hersche, *Spätjansenismus*, p. 148.

rather than to the past. But it must be ascribable also to the manner of his education. It was often remarked that he had a superficial command of almost every subject, but knew none really deeply.[208] He once even said so of himself.[209] This is an occupational weakness of sovereigns, and it is exactly what one would expect from someone taught out of compendia composed to order. Joseph had rarely read the books themselves. What he had studied were extracts and summaries, digests and selections.

There were areas, it is true, in which the teaching he received left little trace on him. When he wrote his first political memorandum early in 1761, he paraded a good deal of knowledge about the reign of Charles VI.[210] But subsequently he made few historical references, and those mostly contemptuous. The emphasis on historical study was one of the more advanced aspects of his education. Joseph drew from it only the lesson that the experience of the past was irrelevant to the problems of the present.[211] Similarly, he showed notoriously scant respect for survivals from the past, whether tangible objects or customs and traditions. The time-honoured variations between the provinces of the Monarchy merely annoyed him. Soon after his education was finished, in the *Rêveries* composed in 1763, he utterly rejected the prudent maxims of Bartenstein about the rights of Estates and the sanctity of constitutions.[212]

In religious matters, we can recognise his mentors' influence in his lifelong concern for the erection of new parishes, for purer worship and for the improved education of the clergy. Much of his legislation in these fields and about monasteries and charity can be, and was, supported from the works of Muratori. One of his decrees prescribed the use of the German translation of *Della carità cristiana*.[213] But he was to go beyond his teachers in extending toleration, even to the Jews, and in the scale of his assault on the contemplative Orders. However, some of those who have suggested that he entirely abandoned his early attitudes on these questions and became a thorough *philosophe* have demonstrably been deceived by the false Constantinople letters.[214] His views developed, but not to the point of condoning the more radical manifestations of the Enlightenment.

In the last analysis, though, the deepest marks left on him by his upbringing seem to have been those made by certain attitudes of his parents. In these cases there is observable in him an explosive mixture of emotional responses, part attraction, part repulsion.

---

[208] E.g. by Albert (Arneth, *GMT* VII, p. 532) and by the British Ambassador, Lord Stormont (to Suffolk, 19 Oct. 1771, PRO SP 80/210): 'He has great Quickness and Penetration . . . without having much of that Knowledge that is got from Study and abstruse Speculation.'
[209] J. to M.T., 9 Dec. 1773 (Arneth, *MTuJ* II, p. 25). [210] Arneth, *MTuJ* I, p. 2.
[211] See below, pp. 106–8.
[212] See below, pp. 98–101. [213] Zlabinger, *Muratori und Österreich*, p. 109.
[214] E.g. *ibid.*, pp. 149–50.

As with Court ceremonies, he rebelled aginst the pattern of his parents' recreations. As soon as he could, he banned the gambling card-games which both Maria Theresa and Francis loved. He thought his father had squandered his wealth in playing faro and other games for high stakes.[215] Joseph also crusaded to exterminate the wild boars which his father had preserved to hunt.[216]

Religion is a difficult case. Here he was ultimately to differ violently from his mother on toleration and many other issues. She considered him to be highly disrespectful toward the church and very neglectful of religious observance.[217] But his attitude to ritual, for example, had something in common with his father's approach, and a little even with his mother's. Whatever Francis felt bound to do publicly, his private piety, as revealed in his writings, virtually ignored Mariolatry and indeed the whole range of baroque rites, and in many respects appears almost Protestant.[218] Even Maria Theresa's interest in plans for lavish altar-pieces seems to have been confined to the question whether they would be easy to dust.[219] Amid the ostentation of Schönbrunn palace, the chapel is unexpectedly plain. Some of Joseph's activity in this field was to do little more than translate his parents', and particularly his father's, private opinions into public law. But he was less obviously devout than they, and became ever more impatient with the sheer amount of time his mother spent on prayer and worship, especially in her later years.[220]

In another area of vital importance the views and aims of his parents, reinforced by the education they prescribed, seem on the surface at least to have determined his attitudes. The emperor and empress, breaking with Habsburg tradition, had their elder sons Joseph and Charles trained as soldiers from an early age. Charles died in 1761 and the next in line, Leopold, who was then enlisted in the cause, never took to military life.[221] But with Joseph the plan seemed to be a complete success. He liked drawing and planning fortifications, reading works on the art of war and lives of great commanders, drilling troops, going on manoeuvres and wearing uniform.[222] He asked, but was not permitted, to go to the war in 1758.[223] Later, he

---

[215] On the level of Francis's gambling, Arneth, *GMT* VII, pp. 150, 517. On J.'s actions see below, p. 159.

[216] See below, p. 158.

[217] M.T. to marquise d'Herzelles, 1 Mar. 1771 (Baron Kervyn de Lettenhove, 'Lettres inédites de Marie-Thérèse et de Joseph II', *MARB in-8o*, xx (1868), 23–5). As often, M.T. did not give the full date. In such cases I accept the editor's date unless otherwise stated.

[218] Wandruszka, *MÖSA* (1959). See Plate 4a.

[219] I owe this point to my friend Dr G. Kelényi.

[220] See below, pp. 157–8, 204–5, 216.   [221] Wandruszka, *L. II.*, vol. 1, pp. 74, 316.

[222] See below, pp. 173, 184–5, 290–1, 318. I also owe to Dr Kelényi knowledge of fortification drawings made by J. (in the Albertina, Vienna: Architektur Zeichnungen, Mappe 95, Umschlag 2, Nr. 15, 16). See Plate 22b.

[223] Arneth, *GMT* V, pp. 353, 506.

thought it his right and duty, like Frederick the Great, to command the Monarchy's army in person.[224]

A strong element in this predilection is Joseph's relish for the relative simplicity of military life.[225] It was a way of escape from the traditional Court formality he hated. But it was perhaps most important that here was an aspect of his upbringing which did fit in with his mother's great programme of reform and the instructions given in her political testament. She there described the improvement of the army as the goal to which all her measures were directed, with a view to the recovery of Silesia and the humiliation of Prussia. The only document which she appended to her political testament was 'a two-volume manual on military discipline, drill and regulations'.[226] She sought to make military service prestigious, more agreeable and better rewarded.[227] She once said that military affairs were the only aspect of her duties which gave her pleasure.[228]

No doubt Batthyány's appointment as Joseph's *Ajo* is largely explicable on this basis, though Maria Theresa seems never to have said so. But this is what she wrote when giving instructions to Leopold's *Ajo*, count Thurn, in 1761. She wanted the boy taught

the science of arms, as the only way in which a prince of his birth can become useful to the Monarchy, shine in the world and make himself especially loved by me. It is a point about which I feel very strongly, and which has caused me to prefer a soldier for the task entrusted to you.[229]

She later cherished the absurd hope that her youngest son, Max Franz, might grow up into another prince Eugene.[230]

Ironically, just after Joseph was introduced into the Monarchy's decision-making processes, her attitude changed. She came to accept the hopelessness of trying to humble Prussia, the inevitability of Austrian defeat in any major war, and the need for retrenchment and recovery both for their own sake and for the security of the Monarchy.[231] Joseph's military interests were still of essential value in this context; and his approach was less aggressive than has been generally supposed.[232] But in so far as during her later years he worked for the expansion of the army, and for a forward policy against her now more pacific and defensive outlook, it was as the representative – indeed the deliberate creation – of her early years of embattled *revanchisme*.

Historians have not appreciated this point. Nor have they taken much account of the tension apparent in Joseph's personality between his public postures as a military man and his private doubts, apprehensions and

[224] See below, pp. 288, 415.   [225] Arneth, *GMT* VII, p. 185. Cf. pp. 172–3 below.
[226] Macartney, *Habsburg and Hohenzollern Dynasties*, pp. 106, 126–7.
[227] Much on this theme can be found in C. Duffy, *The Army of Maria Theresa* (London, 1977).
[228] Arneth, *GMT* VII, p. 213.   [229] Arneth, *MTKuF* IV, p. 21.
[230] Arneth, *MTKuF* II, p. 321.
[231] See below, pp. 110, 185, 290, 398.   [232] See below, pp. 290–4, 302–5.

hesitations. During the War of the Bavarian Succession in 1778–9 the reality of the relationship between mother and son was to be exposed. Though Joseph had helped to push her into war, she had to sustain his morale, even his courage, at a crucial moment during the actual fighting.[233] She had brought him up not so much as a loved son, but as the destined heir, who could carry further, unhandicapped by woman's weakness, the mission of re-establishing the power of the Monarchy, leading its troops into battle to defeat Prussia. Joseph tried to live up to this expectation, even in the face of her later discouragement of the original plan, and despite her frantic attempts to keep him out of danger. That he could never succeed as a general is easily explicable not only in military and political but also in psychological terms.

So the significance of Joseph's education and upbringing is equivocal. A largely conservative programme of study did not prevent the emergence of a radical. The attempt to teach wisdom and humility through historical awareness was a failure. On the other hand, the archduke had been well trained in some of the technical skills of his trade, and his opinions and manner of thinking owed much to his teachers. Perhaps the most important direct effect of his education arose from the unanimous conviction of his mentors that he must be taught entirely differently from a subject, and in virtual seclusion.[234] Although Joseph tried to escape from his personal isolation and was always begging to be treated as a man and not an emperor,[235] he clearly could never forget his unique position and responsibilities, and until the final *débâcle* believed himself to be bound, and uniquely fitted, to rule in fact as well as in name. He said once: 'There are ten or a dozen of us who decide the fate of men in Europe. Six or seven are entirely ignorant, and let things take their course. The others strive to understand and control. It is a question which is the better approach.'[236] But there was never any doubt that Joseph would belong to the group of rulers who tried to direct events. This attitude, which the accident of his birth in any case encouraged him to take, his education and upbringing certainly strengthened. Generally, though, in order to account for his adult personality and views, many other factors have to be brought into consideration: the impact on him of Court life; his relationship with his parents and particularly with his overpowering mother; the influence of certain associates, such as his first wife, marshal Lacy and Kaunitz; his experience as a member after 1761 of the *Staatsrat*, as co-regent after 1765, as soldier and as traveller; and finally an innate individuality that led him to respond to some people and circumstances, and to react against others. He was himself a living refutation of his own maxim that 'education does everything'.

233 See below, pp. 404–6.   234 Conrad, *RuV*, pp. 50, 86 etc.
235 E.g. J. to M.T., 24 Feb. 1766 (HHSA FA Sbde 55).
236 Pietro Verri's account in his diary (July 1769) in F. Valsecchi, *L'assolutismo illuminato in Austria e in Lombardia*, vol. II (Bologna, 1934), p. 303.

CHAPTER 3

Marriages, 1760–1767

'In the last years of the war,' wrote Joseph himself in 1765, 'emerging from the discipline of studies, I married, and was employed soon afterwards in attending the councils of the different departments, held in my presence.'[1] During his lengthy formal education he had been kept isolated not only from knowledge of business of state but also from private friendships outside the family circle. Now he was catapulted into adulthood both as councillor and husband.

His first marriage took place in the Augustinerkirche, the church of the Hofburg, on 6 October 1760. The bride was the Infanta Isabella of Parma. As shown in Figure 2, her father Philip was a Spanish prince, whose elder brother had become king Charles III of Spain in 1759. Isabella had been born in Spain and brought up there until she was seven.[2] But it was not the Spanish connexion which made her an attractive match for the heir to the Monarchy. Indeed, this was a positive embarrassment. Maria Theresa had virtually promised in the early fifties that Joseph would marry the eldest daughter of Charles III, who at that time was king of Naples. Just before Charles inherited the Spanish throne and moved to Spain, he was informed that the Court of Vienna had changed its mind: his niece, not his daughter, would be Joseph's bride. Maria Theresa sugared the pill by putting forward her second son, Charles, as a match for one of the king's daughters, with the prospect of an independent Tuscany to rule over after Francis Stephen's death. But offence had inevitably been given in Naples and Spain.[3] What attracted Maria Theresa to the marriage between Joseph and Isabella was the bride's French descent and associations. Her mother was Louise Elizabeth, eldest and favourite daughter of Louis XV. When Isabella had left Spain in 1748, she and her mother had moved in the first instance to Versailles, and many months

---

[1] Memorandum of 1765 (Arneth, *MTuJ* III, p. 336).
[2] Hrazky, *MÖSA* (1959), 174–6; Arneth, *GMT* VI, p. 191.
[3] Arneth, *GMT* V pp. 451–6; Lippert, *M.T. und Maria Antonia von Sachsen*, pp. 59–60 (M.T. to Maria Antonia, 12 Nov. 1759).

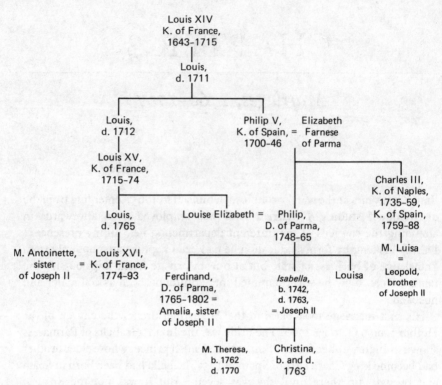

Figure 2. Genealogical table of the family of Isabella of Parma.

passed before they went on to Parma.[4] By the late fifties the duchy was heavily dependent on France: in 1759 Louise Elizabeth was back at Versailles and in Parma the duke appointed a notable prime minister of French extraction and reformist views, Guillaume Du Tillot.[5] The match between Joseph and Isabella was intended to renew the Austro-French alliance made in 1756.[6]

The arrangements are of interest not only because of their importance for Joseph himself but also because of the light they throw on the assumptions and practice of eighteenth-century dynasticism and on the situation of the Monarchy at this moment. King Charles was told that, on seeing pictures of the rival princesses, Joseph had immediately conceived a decisive preference for Isabella. This was not true, although Charles's eldest daughter was plain and was believed to be in poor health.

[4] Some information on the duchess of Parma and her daughter can be gleaned from C. Stryiénski, *Mesdames de France, filles de Louis XV* (Paris, 1911), ch. 2.
[5] U. Benassi wrote a long series of excellent articles on 'Guglielmo du Tillot, un ministro riformatore del secolo XVIII', *ASPP*, new series, XV–XVI (1915–16) and XIX–XXV (1919–25). The rise of Du Tillot is described in vol. XVI, esp. pp. 193–213, 334–68. See Venturi, *Settecento riformatore*, vol. II, pp. 214–16.
[6] Hrazky, *MÖSA* (1959), 175, 177; Arneth, *GMT* V, p. 451.

Placet [wrote the empress on the despatch concerned], because a better excuse could not be found than blaming it on my son's preference for the Infanta of Parma. But it cannot be laid to his charge, since he is a well-brought-up son; and I acquiesce in it as a measure of state, which we and the whole Conference concurred in.

She would not sanction the supplementary lies in Kaunitz's draft about 'the innumerable means tried to change this Most Serene Prince's mind, but all to no avail'.[7] In fact Joseph had professed complete indifference, and obedience to the will of his parents and Providence. 'I'm concerned', he said, 'neither about looks, good humour nor other charms.'[8]

Maria Theresa's true motive lay in the signs that French support for the Monarchy in the war against Prussia was flagging. She would take almost any step to keep alive the hope of inflicting a crushing defeat on Frederick. She was even induced to send a present to Madame de Pompadour, Louis XV's reigning mistress, at a cost of over 30,000 florins – though she drew the line at writing a letter to go with it. The arrangement with France was embodied in two treaties, one of them 'secret', which were agreed in the last days of 1758 but signed and dated 30 March 1759. On paper the terms were not especially favourable to Maria Theresa. France gave up the commitment of previous agreements that she would not make peace until Silesia had been recovered for the Monarchy, though she undertook to go on working to that end. While the empress withdrew her earlier offer of compensation for France in the southern Netherlands, she abandoned certain of her own claims previously acknowledged by France in Italy. From the Austrian point of view, the most vital provisions were those ensuring that France would continue to supply 100,000 men for the war in Germany, together with substantial subsidies. Kaunitz asserted that the Monarchy gained more than France from the agreements; and Arneth took the same view, on the ground that, whereas the alliance had hitherto been based on unrealistic expectations, it was now being renewed 'on the foundation of practical experience'.[9]

By the time the marriage took place, the war was going even worse for Maria Theresa. As we shall see, it was now questionable whether the Monarchy's administration and finances were equal to continuing it. But no expense was spared to make the wedding celebrations splendid. Prince Joseph Wenzel von Liechtenstein was sent with a vast train to collect Isabella from Parma. When she made her ceremonial entry into Vienna, nearly a hundred coaches-and-six formed part of the procession. Balls, operas and dinners were given without stint. Notwithstanding a recent order that silver plate should be melted down

---

[7] Arneth, *GMT* v, pp. 456, 538. Other documents are printed in K-M v, pp. 233–5, 237–52, 263–6.

[8] F. Zweybrück (ed.), 'Briefe der Kaiserin Maria Theresia und Joseph II. und Berichte des Obersthofmeisters Grafen Anton Salm 17. März 1760 bis 16. Jänner 1765', *AÖG*, LXXVI (1890), 115–16 (J. to Salm, 10 and 17 Sep. 1760).

[9] Arneth, *GMT* v, pp. 457–63, 538–41.

into coin to help pay for the army, the Court displayed at the splendid formal meals its new service of gold. The celebrations were recorded in a series of paintings which still hang at Schönbrunn. It seemed to observers that the war had been simply put out of mind; and Maria Theresa said that she had forgotten for a moment, in the happiness of motherhood, that she was the king.[10] The cost was put at three million florins.[11]

All this Machiavellian diplomacy and baroque ceremony had the uncovenanted result of bringing to Vienna one of the most remarkable princesses in history. She had barely three more years to live, but during that time her talents and personality enchanted the imperial family. Maria Theresa called her life 'angelic'.[12] Prince Albert wrote of her:

This truly astonishing woman, who was still less than twenty years old, was not only endowed with all the admirable qualities of the heart, but she possessed also all the information and talents which could be hoped for in the most accomplished of young men ... The careful education which she had received ... had given her understanding not only in fields necessary to a lady of her rank but also in the abstract parts of mathematics and even in tactics. She combined with this some special talents, such as for music – she played the violin perfectly – and for drawing and painting, and for certain crafts, in which she would direct the workmen whom she employed; and she wrote with facility and an uncommon wit. She had not, it is true, beauty which could shine beside that of her sisters-in-law. She was also too reserved in her speech, and her features revealed, despite all the effort she made to hide it, a tendency to sombre thoughts.[13]

Something of her personality can still be recaptured by the reader of her surviving writings. Here is a passage from a paper written for her sister-in-law, Marie Christine, 'on the fate of princesses', discussing whether they are better-off married or single:

What should the daughter of a great prince expect? Her fate is unquestionably most unhappy. Born the slave of the people's prejudices, she finds herself subjected to this weight of honours, these innumerable etiquettes attached to greatness ... The rank she holds, far from procuring her the least advantage, deprives her of the greatest pleasure of life, which is given to everyone [else], of company ... Obliged to live in the middle of the great world, she has, so to speak, neither acquaintances nor friends.

This is not all. In the end the effort is made to establish her. There she is, condemned to abandon everything, her family, her country – and for whom? For an unknown person, whose character and manner of thinking she does not know ... sacrifice to a supposed public good, but in fact rather to the wretched policy of a minister who can find no other way for the two dynasties to form an alliance which he pronounces indissoluble – and which, immediately it seems advantageous, is broken off ...[14]

[10] Arneth, GMT VI, pp. 189–91, 461; Lippert, M.T. und Maria Antonia von Sachsen, p. 92 (M.T. to Maria Antonia, 9 Oct. 1760). See Plate 4b.
[11] PRO SP 80/200: Stormont to Sandwich, 7 April 1764.
[12] Arneth, GMT VII, p. 62 (to Kaunitz, 26 Nov. 1763).
[13] This paragraph from Albert's memoirs is printed in Arneth, GMT VII, p. 500.
[14] Hrazky, MÖSA (1959), 199–200.

Some of her writings are entirely serious, such as a piece on trade, 'Reflections on education' and some Christian meditations which were published after her death.[15] On 'the true philosopher' she writes:

I have developed the habit of considering what affects me personally without any emotion ...

The principles that a philosopher sets up for himself vary according to each one's character, but all agree in the following: indifference to all the chances of life; parade of fine sentiments, both in their talks and their writings; and for foundation, absolute disinterestedness, which makes them love the good for itself alone, and eschew ostentation and praise, which they mistrust – if one wishes to believe them.

But she finds that, in common with all self-styled philosophers, she is actuated in practice by *amour-propre* and, far from being indifferent, is fanatical about things and people dear to her.[16]

She also wrote 'On fashionable philosophy'. Unfortunately, only the table of contents seems to survive. Presumably she is discussing the brand of philosophy associated with the French *philosophes*, who of course rejected the Christianised Stoicism she tried to follow. She had had excellent opportunities to judge the new tendency, because her father had brought to Parma in 1758 the radical *philosophe*, Condillac, to tutor her brother. Her table of contents reads as follows:

1. the Principles are varied
2. the Principles are extreme
3. the Principles are false
4. the Principles are dangerous
5. the Attitudes are not consistent
6. the Attitudes are culpable
7. There is, however, some good in them
8. This is what leads them astray
9. This is what gives them their reputation
10. What use ought to be made both of the good and the bad that they contain.[17]

---

[15] Arneth, *GMT* VII, pp. 39–40, 499–500; Hrazky, *MÖSA* (1959), esp. 185–6.
[16] Hrazky, *MÖSA* (1959), 194.
[17] Baguenault de Puchesse, *Condillac* (Paris, 1910), p. 112. The MSS of Isabella's surviving works should be in HHSA FA Sbde 68, where the table of contents, but not the text, of 'De la philosophie à la mode' is to be found. Since Hrazky did not print it, it was presumably already missing when he wrote.

    Hrazky also devotes a paragraph (p. 182) to an essay called *Observations sur les prussiens*, which Isabella is supposed to have copied out. He refers not to the original, but to the summary in A. Wolf, *Marie Christine, Erzherzogin von Oesterreich* (2 vols., Vienna, 1863), vol. I, pp. 15–19. I could not find this document in HHSA FA Sbde 68. On the other hand, there is an essay with this title in HHSA NL, Karton 2, which must be the piece in question – though the covering letter with it (dated Königsberg, 1 Jan. 1763) suggests a different origin from that which Wolf (vol. I, p. 15) proposed ('Sie scheint 1760 oder 1761 von einem Staatsmann verfasst zu sein'). I am at a loss to explain its significance for Isabella or for J. Its criticisms of Frederick seem rather wild. Cf. Arneth, *GMT* VII, pp. 39–40.

Yet amid all this earnestness, she composed a 'treatise on men', half-seriously questioning their superiority, and 'The adventures of thoughtlessness, dedicated to perpetual motion', a whimsical autobiography, intended to be seen by Maria Theresa as well as by Marie Christine, in which she described the rumpus she made as a child, the ornaments she broke, her fondness for somersaults, the falls she had, her rudeness to her hairdresser, and how she had loved France but hated Italy. She had therefore taken to science and become a philosopher, and had been delighted at the chance to come to Vienna.[18]

This *jeu d'esprit* testifies to the happy relationship she had established with the empress. But the apprehensions she had expressed in writing about 'the fate of princesses' were justified, at least in part, by the attitude of her husband. His first surviving letters date from the months before his wedding. Writing to count Salm, the head of his household, he talked to 'the new estate which I'm going to enter into, which is difficult for anyone, but especially delicate for me, for the reasons you're aware of'. These reasons are presumably those set out in his next letter:

I shall certainly do all I can to deserve her respect and her confidence. As for love, you know that I don't go in for making myself pleasant or for flirting, and that it's quite against my nature. Please, if you get the opportunity, forewarn her, so that she doesn't expect to find in me a beautifully groomed young man who will say a thousand pretty nothings to her, but a man determined to show her from the start all the consideration and attentions that she could wish for. That's what I believe to be my duty which, come what may, I shall certainly fulfil. But one method, and perhaps the only one, of capturing my heart is [this:] if she has the kindness to place her confidence in me, and to ask my advice from time to time, which I shall always give her most sincerely and as best I can, without flippancy. For when something matters so much to you as this, there is certainly no place for joking. *Dixi*.

His feelings about his wedding cut across his burning desire to take part in the war.

I've always predicted that, so long as they won't let me go, the war won't come to an end. You will say, 'That's a really silly utterance from a lover who is to be married in three weeks.' But my ambition, the service of the empress and the welfare of her peoples would make me leave for the front, if permission was granted, from the altar itself. But before leaving, still at the altar, I should kiss and embrace the princess and go off to the army content. Reading this, you'll think it's easy to see that I'm still a month short of marrying, and that when the time comes, I shall not think so much like Alexander. That may be, for I've never yet felt the charms of love, which will perhaps transform me, as has happened to so many people much wiser than myself.

As the moment approached, he became ever more fearful. The prospect of marriage, he said, frightened him much more than that of going into battle. If he was a private citizen, he would back out, 'but as a victim of the state I

[18] Hrazky, *MÖSA* (1959), 194–5, 202–6.

sacrifice myself, hoping that God will accept this obedience in good part and will reward me for it, if not in this world, at least in the next'.[19] Joseph was later to become notorious for his reluctance to remarry, and his mother compared his attitude before his second marriage to his hesitations before his first.[20] But if these letters read a little strangely, they are callow rather than callous. The humour is gentle, the self-deprecation attractive, the yearning for companionship endearing. It is hardly surprising that he should have felt some anxiety about marrying someone he had never seen, and that he should have found it difficult to reconcile his marital obligations with his political and military vocation. His awareness of these tensions made him and Isabella kindred spirits. But he was too inhibited and immature to give full satisfaction to such a rich and complex personality as his first wife.

She appears to have liked all the imperial family except the eldest archduchess, the crippled Marianne, whom she considered a spiteful 'false friend'. But her deepest affection was reserved for Marie Christine, 'adorable and adored sister', 'the most adorable of all creatures', 'my angel', 'divinity', whom she was 'very inclined . . . to suffocate by kisses', whom she burned to see during every short period of separation. When they had a row, she could not sleep. When she was in spiritual retreat for three days, she could think of nothing but her sister-in-law, and could bring herself to recognise the perfection of God only because he had created, and must therefore be superior to, 'so fine a piece of work' as Marie Christine.[21]

Two hundred of Isabella's letters were preserved by her loved one.[22] One of their dominant themes is her desire for death. The most striking letter in this vein, from the end of 1762, runs:

I am very pleased with my sister[-in-law] Joanna, and I even begin to hope that she will not die . . . Why am I not in her place? Death is a good thing . . . I have never reflected so seriously about it in my life as at this time . . . God sees my heart. He knows the desire that I have and have always had to serve him well. He sees that I am guilty of much more by thoughtlessness than by intention . . . The only pain that I can scarcely overcome is regret at leaving you . . . What have I to do in the world? I am useful in it for nothing, I only do harm. The longer I live, the more I meet and create obstacles to my salvation. So, if it were permitted to allow oneself to die, I should be very tempted to do so.[23]

'A secret voice' warned her she would not live long, and she was glad. She set about writing pen-portraits of the emperor, the empress and Joseph so that Marie Christine should know how to take her place in Maria Theresa's affections without offending the other two.[24]

---

[19] J. to Salm, 17 Mar., 10, 20 and 28 Sep. 1760 (Zweybrück, *AÖG* (1890), 114–18).
[20] M.T. to Salm, 29 Mar. 1764 (*ibid.*, 125).
[21] Hrazky, *MÖSA* (1959), 195–9, 210, 217, 220, 222, 237 etc.
[22] Those that survive are printed in *ibid.*, 207–39.
[23] *Ibid.*, 233–4.   [24] *Ibid.*, 228; Arneth, *GMT* VII, pp. 48–59. See pp. 78–9, 82 below.

All the same, she could show a great zest for life. In a letter to Marie Christine she mocked herself for

the confusion which reigns in a certain drawer which lives in my room, where are to be found together and without rhyme or reason a political tract, a pile of letters, a comic opera, a vaudeville, a treatise on education, a clavier part, some moral reflections. A sermon jostles a treatise on all types of foolishness, prayers are mixed up in a paper devoted to declaring my love to you, letters from the emperor muddled up with letters of a hundred persons who are indifferent to me, and with those letters which are so dear to me and constitute the sweetness of my life. Here is a picture of what's in my head: some philosophy, some morality, some stories, some meditations, some songs, some history, some physics, some logic, some metaphysics, some outbursts of feeling for you. In short, you can call it the shop most fully stocked with disorder and reason . . .[25]

She laughed at herself too for using paper so economically and over her efforts in the hunting-field – yet she had hit four boars with four shots.[26] She deliberately underplayed her talents. As she said, she kept much of her learning to herself, hating to appear pedantic and knowing how few people would appreciate her airing it.[27] But it shines forth sometimes in her correspondence with Marie Christine, as when she discussed with great intelligence the difficulties of adapting clavier music for the violin.[28]

From 1761 onwards a new source of information about the Court becomes available to us in the diary of count Karl von Zinzendorf, written up daily for more than fifty years. Less than a month after Isabella's death, he heard the great ladies of the Court talking about her:

She was so affected by the death of her mother [at the end of 1759, from smallpox, at Versailles] that she knelt and prayed to God to tell her how long she had to live. At that moment she claims to have heard four strokes. Immediately she said she would live only four days; when they had gone by, four weeks; then four months; finally when all these had passed, she maintained that she wouldn't reach her twenty-second year. She decided to become a nun, but when the archduke asked for her hand, her confessor persuaded her to accept the match, adding that she was formed to make her subjects happy. When countess Erdödy arrived to escort her to Milan, she said to her, 'I think you will have a good mistress, but you will not have her four years'. She always held to this premonition, in the midst of her wedding ceremonies, in the midst of the Court. Sometimes she would be happy and mischievous, but suddenly she would become serious again, and begin to brood. This summer she and the archduchess Marie, her great friend, were discussing Their Majesties' burial-vault. [Marie] said that the archduke would make another for himself, his wife and their descendants. She replied: 'For myself, I shall go into the present one, and the archduke will go into the new one with another wife.' When the Court last left Schönbrunn, she lingered behind with archduchess Marie, and kept on saying, 'Ah, if only we could stay at Schönbrunn.' She

[25] Hrazky, *MÖSA* (1959), 221.
[26] *Ibid.*, 234–5 (hunting) and 237 (economy). Cf. L.K. to E.L., 9 Nov. 1762 (SOALpZ, LRRA, P. 16/18).
[27] Hrazky, *MÖSA* (1959), 191.   [28] *Ibid.*, 227.

frequently went back to her room, saying 'Goodbye, my room, goodbye my fine arm-chair, we shall not see each other again.' When, a few days before her death, her confessor brought her the last sacrament, she raised herself in bed on her elbow, as though in a trance, and then lay down again, saying 'Courage, my soul'. Her mother was rather melancholic, her father too; and it is said that the king of Spain has bouts of madness.[29]

Both her talents and her character made her an exciting but a disturbing personality.

Isabella's attributes, however remarkable in themselves, would be of little importance for this book if they had not influenced Joseph. The pair were married for just over three years before she died on 27 November 1763. They had one daughter, Maria Theresa, in 1762, who survived her mother; a second was born during Isabella's last illness and died the same day. But brief though the marriage was, Joseph never ceased to lament his first wife. Soon after her death, he wrote to his father-in-law:

I never feel more consoled than when I am alone in my room, looking at the portrait of my beloved wife and reading through her writings and works. Since I have spent the whole day with her, I often think I see her before me; I speak to her; and this illusion comforts me ... I have preserved all the slightest scraps of paper left by this adorable woman ... I want to be able always to show the whole world what a companion I possessed in her and how much she deserves to be mourned ... I defy anyone to find a better marriage ...[30]

This was not just flowery language evoked by bereavement. During her lifetime he had written, in one of the very few letters of his surviving from the period, that he found it hard to be separated from her even briefly at a public entertainment.[31] Although she died of smallpox, and it was the usual practice to keep other members of the family away from victims of this disease, Joseph insisted on visiting her throughout the illness.[32] When he was crowned king of the Romans in 1764, he wrote that he could hardly bear the ceremonies in his loneliness.[33] He declared that he would never remarry because it would be impossible to find a second wife to equal his first.[34] He said he missed her acutely when it came to planning his daughter's education, a subject on which Isabella had left a treatise.[35]

[29] HHSA TZ, 10 Dec. 1763. See Plate 21a.
[30] E. Bicchieri, 'Lettere famigliari dell' Imperator Giuseppe II a Don Filippo e Don Ferdinando, Duchi di Parma (1760–1767)', *AMMP*, IV (1868), 112 (J. to Philip of Parma, 11 Dec. 1763).
[31] Arneth, *MTuJ* I, p. 16 (J. to M.T., 30 May 1761).
[32] Bicchieri, *AMMP* (1868), 111 (J. to Philip of Parma, 29 Nov. 1763); Salm to M.T., 25 Nov. 1763 (Zweybrück, *AÖG* (1890), 121).
[33] Bicchieri, *AMMP* (1868), 115 (J. to Philip of Parma, 27 Mar. 1764); Arneth, *MTuJ* I, p. 43 (J. to M.T., 24 Mar. 1763) etc. Cf. p. 115.
[34] Arneth, *GMT* VII, p. 89.
[35] HHSA FA Sbde 55, 24 Feb. 1766, memo. of J.'s on his daughter's education; HHSA FA Sbde 68, part of Isabella's 'Reflections sur l'éducation'; Hrazky, *MÖSA* (1959), 185–6; Bicchieri, *AMMP* (1868), 112.

Edward Crankshaw has claimed that he protested too much, that his love and his subsequent grief must be regarded as self-conscious poses rather than genuine emotions.[36] This is a very difficult line to draw. There are certainly several indications that Joseph was, and was thought, unfeeling even at this time. He once told his mother that he was finding his wife 'more agreeable than ever' because of her good public manner.[37] His father reminded him after her death that he had found her in some respects amazingly childish.[38] Zinzendorf, newly arrived at the Court, noted in his diary: 'I have studied the archduke. It doesn't appear that he will ever be as human as his august parents. He has a very haughty manner, and had such a serious and indifferent expression when he assisted his wife.'[39] Albert wrote that Isabella had been prevented from loving Joseph by discovering 'the hardness . . . in the depth of his character'.[40] She herself remarks clinically that his grief at her death would probably become violent.[41]

Most telling of all is the anticipation of Crankshaw's words by countess Leopoldine Kaunitz. From the early sixties she corresponded uninhibitedly with her sister, princess Eleonore Liechtenstein, whenever they were apart; and the letters survive.[42] The sisters, both in their twenties, were daughters of the prince of Öttingen-Spielberg in south Germany, and therefore born princesses; they were close relatives of countess Paar, the empress's mistress of the robes; Eleonore was married to a prince from a family much favoured by Maria Theresa, and Leopoldine was the chancellor's daughter-in-law. They belonged to the very select group with whom the imperial family mixed most freely. Princes and princesses of the Empire ranked halfway between sovereigns and ordinary nobles. Eleonore's brothers-in-law were the prince de Ligne, the young Kaunitz, a Khevenhüller, a Waldstein, a Kinsky and a Pálffy.[43] The sisters were in as good a position as anyone other than a Habsburg to observe the heir to the throne of the Monarchy. When his remarriage was being arranged at the end of 1764, they discussed his character. Eleonore described him as 'impenetrable'. Leopoldine called him 'cold', and went on: he 'looks at all women as one looks at statues. I'm terrified when I think that he has not yet been in love'. A fortnight later she elaborated:

I think that he is all the more difficult to get to know since he doesn't yet know himself. He's a machine that seems to me as yet quite unformed. He's heard people talk of crushes, love, affairs, but I don't think he is experienced in any of them. I don't know

---

[36] Crankshaw, *Maria Theresa*, p. 284.   [37] Arneth, *MTuJ* I, pp. 13–14 (3 Apr. 1761).
[38] Francis to J., 28 Jan. 1764 (HHSA FA Sbde 26).   [39] HHSA TZ, 3 May 1761.
[40] Quoted in Arneth, *GMT* VII, p. 503.
[41] Arneth, *GMT* VII, p. 54.
[42] The letters, now in the Žitenice section of the Litoměřice state archives in Czechoslovakia, were last used by A. Wolf for his *Fürstin Eleonore Liechtenstein* (Vienna, 1875). I am grateful to Dr Leopold Auer for advice about access to this collection.
[43] See esp. *ibid.* and J. von Falke, *Geschichte des fürstlichen Hauses Liechtenstein* (3 vols., Vienna, 1868–82), vol. III, esp. Beilage IV.

what may happen in future, but I imagine that either he'll never love or he'll love wildly. So long as the empress is alive, things will stay much the same.[44]

On the other hand, one of the Schönborn ladies, no less a member of the charmed circle than Leopoldine and Eleonore, told in Zinzendorf's presence a rather different story. She

claimed that [Isabella] lived an extremely restricted life and felt the constraint . . . They took away from her one of her confidential maidservants, which annoyed her very much. When a man was killed behind her carriage during the hunt, she showed not the slightest compassion. She didn't love the archduke, who loved her greatly. However, she formed his heart.[45]

The archduchess herself assumed that his friendship, if not his love, could be won provided that his respect was first gained.[46] The fact that he so rarely displayed emotion seems to argue for the genuineness of his open feelings about his wife rather than against it. If this was play-acting, it was so well and long sustained that it must have become second nature. It seems entirely to be expected that a young prince, kept until the age of nineteen from all close friendships, at times overwhelmed but often neglected by his parents, schooled to withdraw into himself and suppress his feelings, should delight in the company of the first person with whom he could live on terms of intimacy, 'my only friend',[47] especially when she was so exotic, mercurial and intelligent as Isabella. Maybe he was not head-over-heels in love. He certainly behaved awkwardly to her. But he was surely very fond of her.

A second complaint of Crankshaw's, however, is more justified. Joseph's expressions of grief are indeed self-centred.

Unhappy Joseph, I see my child perish in my arms, my wife expire, father and mother overcome with grief, all my family in despair, my dear father-in-law so emotionally afflicted, all Vienna in tears, all Europe sorrowing; and after this frightful spectacle I am still living! . . . What a loss for humanity is such a princess! what damage it does to the whole state, the whole family and unhappy me![48]

One can only comment in mitigation that the widower had reason to feel bitter, and that the religion in which he believed – and Isabella's own attitude – forbade him to imagine that she would be happier with him on earth than with God in heaven.

Her relationship with Marie Christine is difficult to reconcile with this picture of marital bliss. It is obvious that Isabella was passionately fond of her sister-in-law, and she sometimes contrasted these feelings with her attitude to Joseph. One of her letters in this vein conjures up a poignant vignette of a great

---

44 E.L. to L.K., 29 Nov.; L.K. to E.L., 4 and 18 Dec. 1764 (SOALpZ, LRRA P. 16/18).
45 HHSA TZ, 23 Feb. 1764.
46 Arneth, *GMT* VII, p. 59.
47 Bicchieri, *AMMP* (1868), 111 (J. to Philip of Parma, 29 Nov. 1763).
48 Bicchieri, *AMMP* (1868), 112–13 (J. to Philip of Parma, 11 Dec. 1763).

moment in history. On 5 October 1762 the whole Court attended the first performance of Gluck's opera *Orfeo*. That it was ever written must owe something to Isabella. The Court of Parma had been notable for its championship of 'French' as opposed to 'Italian' opera. The marriage ceremonies before she left Italy had been accompanied by the production of an opera-ballet in the French style by Traetta, *Le feste d'Imeneo*. This was presumably the 'opera' she sent to Joseph before they were married.[49] As soon as she reached Vienna, he had a work commissioned from this composer for the next carnival there. Traetta's arrival, and the interest in French opera which it encouraged, assisted Gluck's development towards the composition of *Orfeo*, the most challenging of all his works, with its mere three soloists and its self-consciously simple arias – a landmark in the history of music and of classicism. For the Court of Vienna its first performance was a family occasion, in honour of the emperor's name-day.[50] For Isabella herself, it was not only a musical experience and a family celebration, it was also an emotional trauma:

I was very wise yesterday at the opera, I occupied myself only with the beauty of the music and with some trouble-free braiding. In one black moment it was very hot. You perhaps know that, in order that you should not be able to accuse me of infidelity, I was between the archduke and my brother[-in-law] Leopold. I confess to you that I should not have been able to bear anyone else there. For I should have thought all the time: what has become of my dear Eurydice? and I should have wept as much as Orpheus at the very idea that you are mortal.[51]

So she identified herself not with the dying Eurydice but with Orpheus, though his part was sung not, as is usual nowadays, by a woman, but by a *castrato*.[52]

Even this incident, though, shows that Isabella could manage her relationship with Marie Christine without disturbing her association with Joseph. She spent most of her time with him, and snatched spells with her sister-in-law only when he was at meetings of the *Staatsrat*, out riding or hunting.[53] The three of them made music together, Isabella on her violin, Marie Christine on the clavier and Joseph singing or on the cello.[54] Isabella mediated between the other two when there was a row.

---

[49] Zweybrück, *AÖG* (1890), 117. On another operatic initiative of Isabella's, G. Zechmeister, *Die Wiener Theater nächst der Burg und nächst dem Kärntnerthor von 1747 bis 1776* (Vienna, 1971), p. 224.

[50] On music at Parma and its influence, A. Yorke-Long, *Music at Court* (London, 1954), esp. pp. 21–33; ed. E. Wellesz and F. Sternfeld (eds.), *The Age of Enlightenment, 1745–1790* (Oxford, 1973) (*New Oxford History of Music*, vol. VII), esp. pp. 38–45, 226–30.

[51] Hrazky, *MÖSA* (1959), 231 (Isabella to M.C., 6 Oct. 1762).

[52] P. Howard, *C.W. von Gluck: 'Orfeo'* (Cambridge, 1981), p. 30. Wangermann in Dickens, *The Courts of Europe*, p. 296, claims that *Orfeo* was not appreciated by the Court. This evidence, Zinzendorf's diary and the letters of E.L. to L.K. belie this statement.

[53] Hrazky, *MÖSA* (1959), e.g. 222, 230, 239. See Plate 3a.   [54] Arneth, GMT VII, p. 60.

You remember what happened yesterday [she wrote to Marie Christine]. It could have repercussions if you keep your word [(?) not to speak to Joseph]. I have convinced the archduke he was in the wrong, though the truth is it is six of one and half-a-dozen of the other; but he doesn't know that. I beg you then, when you see him, to act absolutely as you normally do. If he is cold towards you, pretend not to notice. If the subject of the incident in question comes up, make him a sort of joking excuse. Not that I'm planning to prove to him by this that he was right. I shall use it on the contrary to make him more conscious of his fault, and to make you more worthy in his estimation. If he teases you again, don't try to conceal anything, try to give in to him or laugh about it. I shall take pains to stress anything you do of this kind and to represent it to him as a merit in you, which will not fail to redouble his friendship for you. Forgive me for saying all this. It all comes from my friendship. I beg you to pay attention to it. Believe me that it is only for our mutual satisfaction that I speak. Adieu, I embrace you with all my heart and await your reply as a criminal does the sentence, for you know that I am infatuated with you.

Note that there must be no question, so far as he is concerned, that I have written to you today.[55]

Evidently Isabella concealed successfully from her husband any qualifications in her love for him.[56] Once when he had been briefly ill, she even wrote to Marie Christine: 'strong though my love is for you, I felt yesterday that the archduke comes first'.[57] But after Isabella's death, Maria Theresa made the most strenuous efforts to carry out her wishes and keep her more compromising papers out of Joseph's hands.[58] Some of Joseph's attitudes seem to derive from or to have been strengthened by Isabella's influence: his hatred of etiquette and ceremonial, his attempt to practise the Stoicism or indifference which they called 'philosophy', his interest in opera and some of his views about it, his yearning for companionship and his passion for intellectual conversation at intimate social gatherings – in contemporary terminology, coteries. Presumably they concurred in the views put forward in her essay on trade, which urged the importance for the Monarchy of obtaining a share in the commerce of the East.[59] Her piety chimed in with his: although she was strict in her observance, she once wrote, 'it's not a question of prayers; do your duty, that is the true devotion'.[60] Joseph, as well as others, must have been influenced by her insistence on taking a non-Jesuit confessor, the first for more than a century at the Court of Vienna.[61]

Isabella's papers and correspondence reveal more about Joseph and his

[55] Hrazky, *MÖSA* (1959), 229–30.
[56] See the letters in Bicchieri, *AMMP* (1868), 111–20; Arneth, *GMT* VII, p. 503 (from Albert's memoirs).
[57] Hrazky, *MÖSA* (1959), 211.
[58] Zweybrück, *MÖSA* (1890), 122–3, for M.T.'s efforts; but his editorial remarks are well wide of the mark (113). M.C. certainly retained possession of Isabella's passionate letters until after J.'s death.
[59] Arneth, *GMT* VII, p. 39.   [60] Hrazky, *MÖSA* (1959), 224.
[61] Hersche, *Spätjansenismus*, pp. 134–5.

family at this time than any other source. A good picture of the prince himself
emerges from her notes for Marie Christine, entitled 'Some questions to make
clearer how to win the archduke's heart'. In her answers to these rhetorical
questions, she first lays down that he should not be contradicted. Secondly,
however, he must be told the truth, 'but gently, in few words and never in
front of others'. As for his mockery of his sisters, the only thing to do is to
ignore it; his whole object is to annoy. It is sometimes worth flattering him,
but if it is tried too often he will become suspicious. Finally, she makes the
remark that he has not enough emotion in his heart to become one's friend at
once; his respect must be won first.[62]

For all her gifts and charm, Isabella showed herself detached and pitiless
enough here. But Joseph would surely have become a more balanced and
sympathetic person if she had survived to support and manipulate him all his
life. Moreover, if she had lived, her political intelligence would inevitably
have influenced his policy and therefore the history of the Monarchy.

Whatever Joseph was feeling after Isabella's death, his parents and politicians
had no doubt that he must remarry. The first discussion of the question even
antedated the tragedy.[63] After lengthy argument and negotiation, he eventually married at Schönbrunn on 23 January 1765, amid suitable festivities,
Josepha, sister of the elector of Bavaria, daughter of the anti-Habsburg
emperor Charles VII and of Joseph I's younger daughter.[64] The background
to this wedding further illustrates dynastic attitudes in this period, and the
whole episode illuminates aspects of Joseph's situation and character.

It is again necessary to take issue with Edward Crankshaw. He asserts that
no power on earth could have forced Joseph to marry again if he had been
utterly determined not to.[65] How valid this assertion is can be assessed from a
letter, hitherto virtually unknown, written to him by his father on 28 January
1764. Francis was replying to a lost letter from Joseph. The emperor sternly
criticises the style, the insubordination, the inconsistency and indeed almost
all the arguments of his son's letter. The only point he concedes to Joseph is
that a woman who had survived smallpox would be a safer bet as a wife than
someone who had never caught the disease. Francis simply declines to discuss
the pros and cons of marriage for his son: a prince who is not actually 'afflicted'
ought to have a wife, and that is that. Joseph had evidently said that it would
be 'useless' for his father to advise him to marry again. Francis retorts that he
does not expect any advice of his to be described as 'useless'; Joseph cannot

[62] Arneth, *GMT* VII, pp. 58–9.
[63] Lippert, *M.T. und Maria Antonia von Sachsen*, p. 209n; Arneth, *GMT* VII, p. 142.
[64] Arneth, *GMT* VII, p. 103. A Gluck operetta, *Il parnas(s)o confuso*, was performed, with four of J.'s sisters and Leopold taking part (Zechmeister, *Die Wiener Theater*, p. 266). See Plate 7 and Figure 1.
[65] Crankshaw, *Maria Theresa*, pp. 284–5.

have meant to write in this way. The prince has too high an opinion of himself and of his own ideas. The emperor and empress hope to persuade, but they have the power to exact obedience.[66]

This letter not only shows Francis, at least ostensibly, exerting more personal control over Joseph than has been suspected, but it also demonstrates that he and Maria Theresa between them virtually ordered Joseph to remarry. However hard it is to credit such a picture from the standpoint of the late twentieth century, there can be no doubt that the prince, though of age, though a widower, though about to be elected and crowned king of the Romans, was treated by his parents as a child and a subject who must obey them, and himself acknowledged his subordination in the last resort. What reads like rhetoric in Joseph's letters to Maria Theresa, when he talks of obliging her and submitting to her wishes,[67] or in one of his letters to Isabella's father – when he says he has been 'reduced' to remarriage 'not by reasons of state, for I would rebut them all, but by reasons of affection' for his parents[68] – was the scarcely varnished truth.

Khevenhüller, not usually sympathetic to Joseph or critical of the emperor and empress, wrote:

As far back as the return from Frankfurt [April 1764] both Most Serene Parents had compelled His Highness their noble Son to decide on a second marriage; and in fact the first proposal was the most suitable, to give him as his wife the Spanish Infanta, especially as the ceremonial engagement by proxy [with Joseph's brother, Leopold] had only taken place at the end of February and could therefore be quite easily reorganised and changed. But matters were not handled intelligently enough and the first grief of the prince was not sufficiently respected, with the result that he gave a negative answer, which – if they had been willing to wait only a couple of days (as I know on good authority) – would have turned out entirely satisfactory and affirmative.[69]

Even Khevenhüller was not fully informed. At the very beginning of January Zinzendorf heard that Joseph had

expatiated on the unfortunate necessity of his remarrying to secure the succession. He said . . . 'But what is this succession? Will you guarantee that the child I shall have will be as worthy of it as my brother [Leopold]? And I mean that quite seriously.' At this,

---

66 HHSA FA Sbde 26. This is presumably the memorandum to which Arneth briefly refers in *GMT* VII, p. 509, dating it 24 Jan. 1764.

67 Arneth, *MTuJ* I, pp. 19–127 consists of letters from J. to M.T. between 13 March and 2 May 1764, in which there are many expressions of this kind, e.g. p. 32: 'comme je ne puis me marier que pour l'amour de vous', translated (with the wrong emphasis, it seems to me) by Crankshaw as 'Unless to prove my love for you, dear mother, I shall never marry again' (*Maria Theresa*, p. 285). It is more natural to read: 'As I can bring myself to marry only out of love for you.'

68 Bicchieri, *AMMP* (1868), 118 (J. to Philip of Parma, 23 Aug. 1764).

69 K-M VI, p. 63 (5 Oct. 1764). He must, I think, have got his dates wrong. This episode must have taken place before the trip to Frankfurt. See Arneth, *MTuJ* I, pp. 111–14 and nn.

archduke Leopold made him a very fair reply, and added: 'Since you offer me a Crown that I shall never accept, I offer you in return my wife.'[70]

Joseph had answered that he was reluctant to steal Leopold's promised bride. It was in any case doubtful whether the king of Spain, already once slighted in this matter, would have agreed to the switch.[71]

Joseph continued to make difficulties, repeatedly throwing back at his mother the memory of his first wife's excellence, stressing how hard it was for him to acquiesce in his parents' wishes, and urging delay.[72] He proposed that the attempt should be made to procure as his bride Isabella's younger sister, Louise, since she would be likely to come nearest to his first wife in character and attainments. Though she was only 14 years old, Maria Theresa brought herself to write to Charles III of Spain, to one of whose sons Louise was promised, to ask him to release her to Joseph. But the king predictably refused.[73] Then Joseph declared that, since there was no princess in the field in whom he had the slightest personal interest, the choice should lie with his mother.[74]

At least half-a-dozen other possible brides were considered. Some were rejected for having too many bastards in their family tree, others because they were Protestant. A Portuguese was ruled out, because her country was England's ally and such a match would endanger Kaunitz's foreign policy.[75] Josepha of Bavaria, who was ultimately chosen, had none of these drawbacks. But nor had the candidate favoured by the empress: Kunigunde, youngest child of Augustus III, the late elector of Saxony and king of Poland, and of the elder daughter of Joseph I. Writing to Isabella's father in September 1764, Joseph explained the position:

Princess Kunigunde of Saxony, according to Their Majesties who have looked at her in detail, has a mature, solid and virtuous character without the brilliance of mind to which I was accustomed; she is not lacking in good sense, and is very sweet and well adapted to a large family. These qualities must satisfy a man marrying out of duty, who seeks only a companion who will not disturb his peace. But no one praises her appearance. Though I am sufficiently philosophical to overlook that, Their Majesties nevertheless, with excessive delicacy and tenderness, are good enough to want to show her to me before coming to any decision. So I go on the 6th of next month with my brother to Prague, and from there I expect to proceed to Töplitz, where I shall see the electress and the princess of Saxony. As I must judge only by the exterior, I expect to be

---

[70] HHSA TZ, 6 Jan. 1764.   [71] Arneth, *GMT* VII, pp. 142–4, 516–17.

[72] Arneth, *MTuJ* I, e.g. pp. 51, 87, 97.

[73] The marriage negotiations are described in Arneth, *GMT* VII, pp. 87–104. The letters to and from Charles III are printed in Arneth, *MTuJ* I, pp. 123–6nn, and M.T.'s memo. on pp. 111–14nn. For the whole question, see Figures 1 and 2.

[74] Arneth, *GMT* VII, pp. 99, 510.

[75] K-M VI, pp. 64 (5 Oct. 1764) and 333–9 (K.'s memo. of 20 Sep. 1764); Arneth, *GMT* VII, pp. 98–9, and VIII, pp. 5–9, where a similar memo. (dated 14 Nov. 1764 on p. 537) is summarised. See also letters of E.L. and L.K. between Sep. and Dec. 1764 (SOALpZ, LRRA P. 16/18).

there only twenty-four hours: there will be decided whether I can forgive her appearance on account of her merits or whether, finding her disagreeable, I cannot bring myself to it.[76]

Six weeks later, Joseph reported to his father-in-law again:

On returning from Töplitz I could only present to Their Majesties the picture of a princess endowed with virtues and good sense, but utterly devoid of what might be called charms. I was nevertheless ready to make the complete sacrifice. Parents too kind to require it wished otherwise, and persuaded me to go and see the Bavarian. Although with regret, I nevertheless submitted ... I went to Straubing; after three days' stay, I returned to bring my report to Their Majesties. Her twenty-six years; the fact that she has not had smallpox, a disease of which I have a frightful memory; a short, fat figure; no youthfulness; a common face; on it, some little pimples with red spots; bad teeth: all these things could hardly tempt me to return to a state in which I had enjoyed their opposite. I explained this to Their Majesties, and begged them to make up my mind for me in this difficult situation. After many prayers they had the goodness to tell me that the whole public, I cannot tell why, was in favour of the second [princess]; and that, since I was indifferent, they believed the Bavarian preferable ...[77]

Maria Theresa told Marie Christine:

You have a sister-in-law and I a daughter-in-law; alas! it is princess Josepha. Against my conviction, against my heart, I have had myself to help my poor son decide. He wouldn't give up the point, either on his own or in front of the Emp. and Kaunitz, that I must give the word, that he was doing it only for me. You can guess what a state he has put me in ... The worst of it is that one must appear happy and pleased, which in fact I ought to be on account of my son's behaviour, but my heart is not in agreement with my reason, I find it difficult to calm myself, although I've had the whole night to myself.[78]

Why did the empress act in this way? As to the desirability that Joseph should marry somebody, she and her husband were conscious that they were getting old and that the succession was precarious. Everyone expected him to remarry. 'The general good and that of my House' required it. So did 'Morality'.[79] His parents were obviously appalled by Joseph's suggestion that he could perfectly well obtain physical satisfaction without being married.[80] They must have become further agitated by his flirtations. A countess Tarouca married hastily in April to escape his attentions. Princess Liechtenstein reported on 22 November that a 'countess Waldstein' 'appeared to want to

---

[76] Bicchieri, *AMMP* (1868), 120 (J. to Philip of Parma, 28 Sep. 1764).

[77] Bicchieri, *AMMP* (1868), 121 (J. to Philip of Parma, 13 Nov. 1764). J. was twenty-three, Josepha actually twenty-five.

[78] Arneth, *GMT* VII, pp. 510–11.

[79] Bicchieri, *AMMP* (1868), 122n (Francis to Philip of Parma, 24 Jan. 1765). M.T. speaks of the ages of herself and Francis in Arneth, *MTKuF* IV, p. 271 (to Pergen, 7 Mar. 1763).

[80] In the emperor's letter of 28 Jan. 1764 he sternly rejected this suggestion.

make a conquest of him', and a week later that he had spent an hour-and-a-half charming a countess Paar; 'I've never yet seen him so smitten.'[81]

As to the attempt to secure Louise of Parma, this was a great concession on Maria Theresa's part, to try to please Joseph and make him happy, despite the fact that the youth of the intended bride would have kept the succession long in doubt. After the failure of this scheme, expected by the empress, the choice was soon narrowed down to German princesses. Maria Theresa said she saw advantages in the future emperor having a German wife; she mentioned it as a merit that the two possibles shared a grandfather; and they 'had had a Christian education' – that is, they were Roman Catholics.[82] They came from 'the best houses' in Germany, which made it possible to refute Joseph's gibe that, by marrying a German princess, he would acquire relatives so poor as to be starving and in need of subsidies.[83]

So far as the final decision to prefer Josepha to Kunigunde is concerned, much was admitted to favour the latter. She had survived smallpox. She was related to the Bourbons, and both France and Spain pressed her case. Maria Antonia of Saxony, correspondent of Maria Theresa, promoted her sister-in-law Kunigunde rather than her sister Josepha. The empress felt gratitude to the Saxon house for their loyalty during the Seven Years War; and if Kunigunde married Joseph, Maria Theresa would be able to achieve another of her aims, that Marie Christine should marry Albert, Kunigunde's brother, in a double match. That the decision turned in favour of Josepha clearly depended on political considerations, especially the prospect that the Habsburgs would thereby gain weight in the Empire, and ultimately obtain some Saxon lands in Bohemia.[84] It was an important point for Kaunitz that the succession to Bavaria was uncertain since the reigning elector and his cousin were the only surviving males of their line, and childless. But he seems not to have argued this case to Maria Theresa until after the decision had been taken.[85] The empress and the chancellor were not alone in their calculations. Princess Liechtenstein believed that Josepha was more attractive than Kunigunde, that 'the common people' favoured the Bavarian match, and that 'if the good God still intends to favour the House of Austria a little, He will bring about this marriage; for if [the Monarchy] remains as it is, it is bound to decline in relation to everyone else'.[86]

[81] K-M VI, p. 29. E.L. to L.K., 22 and 29 Nov. 1764 (SOALpZ LRRA, P. 16/18).
[82] Arneth, *MTuJ* I, pp. 111–12n. For all these family ramifications see Figure 1.
[83] Francis gets very cross at this remark of J.'s in his letter of 28 Jan. 1764 (HHSA FA Sbde 26).
[84] Arneth, *GMT* VII, pp. 99–100; Lippert, *M.T. und Maria Antonia von Sachsen*, pp. 213–14 (Maria Antonia to M.T., Feb. 1764); K-M VI pp. 340–2 (Colloredo's view); Beer, *AÖG* (1872), 63–74 (memo. of 27 Sep. 1764). See ch. 13 below for the later stages of the Bavarian question.
[85] K-M VI, pp. 342–4 (K.'s *Denkschrift* of [?] Dec. 1764).
[86] E.L. to L.K., 11 Sep. 1764 (SOALpZ, LRRA P. 16/18). She soon admitted her mistake, e.g. to L.K., 14 Sep. 1765 (*ibid.*, P. 16/19).

The marriage was a disaster. Four weeks after the wedding, Joseph wrote as follows to Philip of Parma:

Weighed down by what are called pleasure and amusements, I scarcely have time to write to you. But I find time all the same, because it is almost my only genuine Carnival to converse with such a dear friend, the respected father of my dearest late wife, who reigns more than ever over my heart. What a contrast! And how little I knew myself! In anticipation I thought I would be strong enough to blot out all comparisons, and to be oblivious of the terrible difference I should find. But human weakness has won, and I cannot conceal from you that I am in a most disturbed state! I have an irreproachable wife who loves me, and whom I esteem for her good qualities; but, being accustomed to adoring my wife, I suffer for her because I do not love her. This natural affection cannot be attained by reasoning; and to play the comedy is so out of my nature that I should seem quite extravagant if I behaved unnaturally ... I shall continue still in my straightforward way; and she will have in me, if not a loving husband, at least a friend, who will recognise her good qualities and treat her with all possible consideration.[87]

Maria Theresa wrote a fortnight later:

The fact is that my son is to be pitied. She is neither pretty nor agreeable. I want to believe that she is good. But, if it goes on [i.e. if she does turn out to be pregnant], we could not thank God enough that at least she brings us an heir – provided that it is a prince.[88]

Josepha's state of health led her and others to suppose that she was pregnant for much of the two years of her marriage. In October 1765, in sentences delicately omitted by Arneth from the published version of a letter to his brother Leopold, Joseph reported the position: 'As for my empress, there is no change. She has no illness but considerable disturbance. She may be pregnant though without the slightest swelling. I just don't understand it, and console myself with the happy life I lead as a bachelor husband.'[89] Next month he wrote: 'I live almost as a bachelor, getting up at 6 o'clock in the morning, going to bed about 11, seeing my wife only at table and touching her only in bed.'[90]

Khevenhüller recorded a talk with Maria Theresa in January 1766 about Joseph's 'unfortunately ever more obvious alienation from his wife'. The English Ambassador heard that the emperor had spoken of his 'Bed of Thorns'.[91] From Troppau, in Austrian Silesia, Joseph wrote to his mother in July:

[87] Bicchieri, *AMMP* (1868), 122 (J. to Philip of Parma, 19 Feb. 1765).
[88] Arneth, *MTKuF* IV, p. 457 (M.T. to countess Enzenberg, 6 Mar. 1765).
[89] HHSA FA Sbde 7 (J. to L., 4 Oct. 1765, section not printed in Arneth, *MTuJ* I). Cf. K-M VI, pp. 88, 98–100, 136.
[90] HHSA FA Sbde 7 (J. to L., 14 Nov. 1765, section not printed in Arneth, *MTuJ* I). This remark makes it difficult to credit the gibe often attributed to J. that, if he could find a spot on Josepha's body without a pimple, he would try to have a child by her (e.g. Crankshaw, *Maria Theresa*, p. 287).
[91] K-M VI, p. 164; PRO SP 80/203 (Stormont to Grafton, cypher, 'Most secret', 14 Jan. 1766).

I venture to enclose a letter for my wife; I would prefer, and would be less embarrassed, to write to the Great Mogul, for she is not satisfied with respectful sentiments and she has already criticised me for them. Ask yourself, dear mother, what can I write to her and where the devil would you expect me to go and dredge up any other feeling? Forgive the expression, which is simply the truth! This letter merely acknowledges hers, assures her I am well, am having a good trip, wishes her the same and assures her that I have the honour to be at the foot of the page her humble husband.[92]

In October Josepha's mistress of the household retired, because she could 'no longer bear to contemplate the *tableau de ce mauvais ménage*'. Apparently the poor young wife made matters worse for herself by telling her troubles to her servants.[93] When she contracted smallpox in May 1767, according to Albert, Maria Theresa caught it also, because, 'anxious to hide how little special fondness she had for her daughter-in-law, [she] had made the effort, not without repugnance, to embrace her when they parted'. Joseph's mother offered some defence of her son at this time, saying that as reigning emperor he could hardly behave to his empress as he had to his first wife.[94] When Josepha died on 28 May 1767, Khevenhüller wrote of her:

It is certain that, if ever the emperor could have become accustomed to her appearance and her certainly none too refined manners, and had not required of her an understanding as brilliant as his first wife had, she would have been worthy of his love in return for her own almost excessive tenderness for him and her entirely blind acceptance of his wishes; as he himself half acknowledges, since in the first reaction to receiving the news of her death he let fall to some of his intimates some remarks which imply some regrets for the coldness he has shown her.[95]

He brought himself to tell his sister-in-law, amid his customary protestations of frankness, that his wife had been 'for so many reasons worthy of respect'.[96]

Maria Theresa always regretted the choice she had made, and later obtained for Kunigunde a consolation prize: she became abbess of Essen in 1776.[97] Joseph's behaviour to Josepha was callous – though hardly worse than that of Frederick the Great and his brother Henry to their unfortunate wives. But if individuals are to be blamed rather than the conventions of the day, then Maria Theresa and Francis come out of this cheerless episode no better than their son. Their attitude smacks of hypocrisy. She, after all, had been allowed

[92] Arneth, *MTuJ* I, pp. 187–8.   [93] K-M VI, pp. 206–7.
[94] Lippert, *M.T. und Maria Antonia von Sachsen*, p. 257n (from Albert's memoirs). Cf. K-M VI, p. 237 (22 May 1767).
[95] K-M VI, pp. 240–1.
[96] Lippert, *M.T. und Maria Antonia von Sachsen*, p.483 (J. to Maria Antonia, 28 May 1767). M.C. is supposed to have said that if she was treated as Joseph treated Josepha she would go and hang herself from a tree at Schönbrunn (Wolf, *Marie Christine*, vol. I, p. 37); but I do not know the evidence for the remark.
[97] See M.T. to Maria Beatrix, 16 June 1777 (Arneth, *MTKuF* III, p. 282 and n.) and to Ferdinand, 12 June 1777 (*ibid.*, II, pp. 88–9); Lippert, *M.T. und Maria Antonia von Sachsen*, pp. 239–40 and nn., 444–7; below, pp. 428–9.

to set diplomacy at defiance and marry the man of her choice, and Francis had written very strongly against enforced marriages in his will.[98] It cannot cause surprise that Joseph felt aggrieved.

[98] See above, p. 23, and K-M VI, p. 398.

CHAPTER 4

Introduction to government, 1760–1765

Six weeks after Joseph's marriage with Isabella, the main departments of the central administration began to hold sessions in his apartments under his presidency. First, on 21 November 1760, came the Hungarian Court Chancellery (*Ungarische Hofkanzlei*), which directed Hungarian affairs from Vienna. On the 24th arrived the *Directorium in publicis et cameralibus*, the main product of Haugwitz's reforms, which administered Bohemia (including Moravia) and most of the Austrian lands and handled their revenues; on the 26th the *Ministerialbancohofdeputation* or *Banco*, which managed the Vienna city bank; two days later, the *Oberste Justizstelle*, effectively both the department of justice and the supreme court of appeal for Austria and Bohemia; on 3 December the *Directorium in commercialibus*, concerned with promoting trade and industry in the same areas; on the 6th the *Siebenbürgische Hofkanzlei*, which ran the affairs of Transylvania; and on the 10th the *Hofkammer*, which presided over the collection and the management of the revenues of the Monarchy's provinces other than those controlled by the *Directorium*. Meetings of this sort continued for some months, generally on Mondays and Wednesdays.[1]

Joseph wrote five years later of these sessions:

There were then eight different [departments], which took turns to meet in my presence. I certainly saw the faces and wigs of each of the individual members, but I learned nothing else. In any case, our system was then already very disorientated. The erection of the *Staatsrat* [Council of State] raised expectations of great change. So nobody looked to large questions, and mere trivia were discussed in my presence, without my discovering either the strengths or the weaknesses of the old system. A year passed in this way listening to trifles, which I am thankful to God I have forgotten. I did not work hard, since I had no occasion to indulge my desire for fame, and so I was merely a spectator.[2]

---

[1] Benna, *MÖSA* (1967), 118n. Zinzendorf (HHSA TZ) mentions such meetings of the 'Conseil de Commerce' on 9 and 11 Feb. 1761.

[2] Arneth, *MTuJ* III, p. 336. The eighth department referred to by Joseph must have been the *Hofkriegsrat*. Kaunitz made the *total* number eighteen in a *Votum* of 17 Nov. 1761 (Arneth, *GMT* VII, pp. 23–4, 497–8; F. Walter, *VKNGÖ*, xxix (Vienna, 1934), 104).

It was not only the prospect of great changes impending that made these meetings unsatisfactory, but also the fact that they were artificially contrived for Joseph's benefit. The agenda was doctored beforehand, precisely in order to eliminate 'trivialities and day-to-day matters' unworthy of his notice! The discussion, voting and minutes were planned in advance. Even the member-ship of the bodies was modified, both to reduce the size of the gatherings and to spare Joseph the peril and embarrassment of hearing a non-Catholic take part in policy-making.[3]

THE FOUNDATION OF THE *STAATSRAT*

It was a desperate moment in the history of the Monarchy. Although the French alliance had been patched up, and large Russian contingents had joined the Austrian army during the recent campaigns, Frederick the Great had nonetheless plucked victory out of apparently hopeless weakness, both at Liegnitz in August 1760 and again at Torgau in November.[4] Kaunitz had been urging since early in the war that only radical reform could save the state. For one thing, he believed that Maria Theresa could no longer dominate affairs as she once had, a view which she herself accepted. His memorandum of 9 December 1760, the culmination of a series, declared: 'The majority of the administrative departments are in the greatest disarray.' They dispute among themselves, show a lack of zeal, intelligence, principles and system, proceed

item by item, day by day, with no co-ordination or co-operation; in consequence, every day a mass of things is done to the disadvantage of the state, and a mass of other things is omitted which would be to its advantage; but the worst of it is that it can scarcely be otherwise, since there is no one in the position either to minimise the evil or to maximise the good, no one is entrusted with this task in virtue of his office, and no one, even if he wanted, could undertake it, because he would lack the necessary ideas and the necessary authority.

Hence the Monarchy is near-bankrupt, 'at the mercy of its enemies', and on the verge of descending to the rank of a second-class Power.

Kaunitz's 'first of all remedies – I will say rather, the only one which will make possible the discovery of all the others – will be the creation of this entity which Your Majesty has hitherto lacked, which can embrace the idea of the totality, watch over everything'. A prime minister will not do; nor will the existing Conference. There is 'only one sole and unique means ... the establishment of a fixed, permanent advisory council', whose task will be to propose to the sovereign how to co-ordinate and reform every aspect of

[3] Conrad, *RuV*, pp. 118–21. But C. Freiherr von Hock, *Der österreichische Staatsrath* (Vienna, 1879), p. 13, mentions an important decision reached at one of these meetings.
[4] Arneth, *GMT* VI, chs. 7 and 8.

domestic administration.[5] Maria Theresa wrote on this memorandum: 'The picture is in no way overdrawn. Our present situation is extremely critical. But with the aid of this council of state and of him who has proposed it I am confident I shall stave off the ruin of the state.' She described it a few days later as 'the salvation of my *Erbländer* [hereditary lands],[6] bringing peace to my mind and conscience'. Although there were some difficulties about its terms of reference and its membership, the council of state was established quickly and held its first meeting on 26 January 1761.

It was to be a purely advisory body; hence it could not give orders to any active department of administration. Maria Theresa was in no way bound by its advice. Its members were to be debarred from administrative posts, to ensure that they looked to the 'totality'. But an exception was made for Kaunitz on the grounds that his department was concerned with foreign, not domestic, affairs and that it was necessary to keep 'the principles in domestic matters ... always analogous and conformable with the system of foreign policy'. Although the *Staatsrat* was thought of as a council for internal questions, it was required to look out for territories to which the Monarchy might advance claims, avowedly following the example of Prussia. Hungary and Transylvania were at first excluded from its competence. So were the Netherlands and the Italian provinces, although they were in a sense represented by Kaunitz himself, who since 1757 had directed their government through the *Staatskanzlei*.

As originally established, the *Staatsrat* had six members and a secretary. Haugwitz gave up the headship of his great creation of 1749, the *Directorium*, and field-marshal count Daun his command of the army in the field and his post in the war department to join the new body and become 'Ministers of State in German internal affairs' (*Staatsminister in deutsch-inländischen Geschäften*). They and Kaunitz were associated with a fourth member of the nobility proper (*Herrenstand*) in this category, count Blümegen, formerly in charge of the administration of Moravia. Two representatives of the *Ritterstand*, Stupan and Borié, were added. They received the less grandiloquent title of 'state councillor' (*Staatsrat*), were paid less, and did more work. The secretary was called König. The council often met under the presidency of Maria Theresa or Francis Stephen.

This new council was seen by others, as it was obviously intended by Kaunitz, to be the instrument whereby, though not styled prime minister, he

---

[5] The complete memo. is in Walter, *VKNGÖ*, XXIX, 3–10. For the whole question of the foundation, membership and terms of reference of the *Staatsrat*, as dealt with in the next few paragraphs, see Arneth, *GMT* VII, 10–18; Walter, *VKNGÖ*, XXIX, 1–26 (documents) and XXXII, 270–8; Walter, 'Kaunitz' Eintritt in die innere Politik', *MÖIG*, XLVI (1932), 37–79; Hock, *Staatsrath*, ch. 1.

[6] For the term *Erbländer* See p. 52, n. 137. On this occasion M.T. presumably meant 'the Austrian and Bohemian lands'.

would dominate all aspects of the Monarchy's government. It marked his official 'entry into domestic policy-making'. The absorption by the *Staatskanzlei* in 1757 of the hitherto separate agencies which had controlled the Netherlands and the Italian provinces from Vienna had given him an opportunity to direct the domestic administration of two important areas. During the war he had taken an ever-growing part in military affairs. He had actually once descended on the army in the field, and had taken charge of the correspondence between the empress and her generals, bypassing the officially responsible departments.[7] The foundation of the *Staatsrat* indicated Maria Theresa's acceptance of Kaunitz's pretensions in these fields. It also announced the partial eclipse of Haugwitz and his system – despite her assertions in her political testaments that she would always be true, as her successors ought to be, both to the system and its architect. The appointment of Haugwitz to the *Staatsrat* was seen as a relegation. So was that of Daun, whose conduct of the campaign of 1760 was considered lamentable. The first problem Kaunitz posed to the new council was to establish the 'principles on which the whole system of the state and its internal constitution are to be built'. It was clear that Haugwitz would have to take part in dismantling his own cherished creation.

The Monarchy was so nearly bankrupt that the size of the army had to be reduced. The system of 1749 could no longer be regarded as a success. Most of the principal officials now wanted it changed. The attack centred on the *Directorium*, which had proved unsatisfactory as a tax-gathering and money-providing agency under the stress of war. After many months of paper warfare, in December 1761 Kaunitz's proposals won the day. The *Directorium* was deprived of its financial responsibilities, and it became merely the Austro-Bohemian Court Chancellery (*böhmisch-österreichische Hofkanzlei*). Its lost functions were distributed between the existing *Hofkammer*, a newly independent *Kommerzienrat* (board of trade) and three new agencies: the *ständische Credits-Deputation* (Estates credit commission), which existed to raise and guarantee loans on the credit of all the Estates of the central lands, acting jointly; the *Generalkassa* to receive and pay monies; and the *Hofrechenkammer* (exchequer), to keep accounts and pay out money. On the basis of these changes the Monarchy's finances were reorganised. But Haugwitz's great principle of administrative unification appeared to be seriously weakened.

However, there was another side to the matter. In the first place, Haugwitz and Kaunitz were firmly agreed on most important questions. They joined in

---

[7] For K.'s earlier activity in internal affairs: Walter, *MÖIG* (1932), 38–9; G. Klingenstein, 'Institutionelle Aspekte der österreichischen Aussenpolitik im 18. Jahrhundert' in *Diplomatie und Aussenpolitik Österreichs* (Vienna, 1977), pp. 89–90; documents for the 1757 change in Kallbrunner and Winkler, *VKNGÖ*, xviii, 422–3.

successfully resisting a threat of genuine reaction from those who wished to restore the provincial Estates to the position they had enjoyed before the reforms of 1749. Both of them supported the maintenance of the separation between justice and administration, the limitations of nobles' privileges, and the union of Austria and Bohemia. Moreover, in some respects the *Staatsrat* stood for an extension of Haugwitz's principles. Its mandate required it to consider every aspect of internal affairs, including for instance the relevant military and religious questions, so far as they concerned the central lands; and it was only a matter of months before Hungarian and Transylvanian business was in practice annexed, whereas Haugwitz's 'administrative unification' had been confined to Austria and Bohemia. Moreover, he had more supporters on the *Staatsrat* than Kaunitz had, and the veteran reformer soon became 'the soul' of the new body. If financial and strictly administrative arrangements were no longer of Haugwitz's devising, he can have felt no difficulty about working for the greater centralisation and uniformity in policy and government which the *Staatsrat* was designed to promote.[8]

This new council was a remarkable institution. It was highly unusual among major advisory bodies in including, at least in principle, no departmental heads.[9] Its procedure was as follows: on each problem that came to it, every member was supposed to give a written opinion or *Votum*, starting with the junior. If serious disagreement appeared, the roll was circulated again for further comments. Disputed questions were discussed at the twice-weekly meetings, but there was no requirement or expectation that the *Staatsrat* should give collective advice. The sovereign attended as she wished, and when present sometimes gave decisions then and there. Otherwise, having considered the *Vota* and any discussion, she settled the matter as she thought fit.

The members of the Council worked hard, because every issue, however apparently trivial, could be said to need consideration in relation to the 'totality'. Its procedure certainly generated vast quantities of paper. Yet its advice often seemed to have little effect. But its significance was that, for the first time, it brought together a group of experienced, able and influential persons other than the sovereign and co-regent, whose business it was to concern themselves with the entire gamut of domestic affairs for nearly the whole Monarchy, and further, that here was a body in which the lesser

---

[8] Walter, *MÖIG* (1932), 'Der letzte grosse Versuch einer Verwaltungsreform unter Maria Theresia (1764/65)', XLVII (1933), 427–69 and *VKNGÖ*, XXXII, chs. 5–7, discusses the dispute between Haugwitz and Kaunitz. Documents in *VKNGÖ*, XXIX, 84–124. Cf. Arneth, *GMT* VII, ch. 1; Schünemann, *MÖIG* (1933), 15–16; and A. Beer, 'Die Staatsschulden und die Ordnung des Staatshaushaltes unter Maria Theresia', *AÖG*, LXXXII (1895), esp. 6–15, 116–24. Macartney, *Habsburg and Hohenzollern Dynasties*, pp. 117–22, 131–2, for M.T.'s political testament.

[9] Daun became president of the *Hofkriegsrat* in 1762, while remaining an active member of the *Staatsrat*. According to Blümegen (HHSA TZ, 20 Aug. 1762), he was sent papers only about military questions. There were a few other later exceptions to this principle.

nobility – in other words, those who had risen to eminence in the service of the state on account of their personal merit – were guaranteed a powerful position. For all its limitations, it fulfilled, at least to some degree, the expectations of its inventor. It renewed the drive for reform in the crisis of the early sixties, and helped to prevent the triumph of inertia during the period of Joseph's co-regency.[10]

JOSEPH'S FIRST MEMORANDUM

At an early stage in the debates about the reform of the entire system of government, Maria Theresa put to Joseph some questions, in answer to which he wrote his first extant memorandum, dated 3 April 1761. Most of it is addressed to the general issue whether it is wise to change a system at the height of a war, with special reference to the possibility of reducing the size of the army or cutting down its cost. But he begins, as we have seen, by asserting his total ignorance of both the old and the new systems. What he is about to say, he goes on, a Capuchin monk is as well equipped to write as he.

The question how many troops we ought to maintain in peacetime to ensure the safety of the state seems to me quite beside the point, since the more we have the better. A reform in the situation in which we find ourselves, it seems to me, would be our ruin ... We should recall the example, still quite recent but very striking, of the emperor Charles VI who, one year after dismissing a good part of his army, was attacked from all sides and lost, through his own fault and that of his bad councillors, the kingdoms of Naples and Sicily. The emperor Charles VI was infinitely more powerful than Your Majesty. He had, in addition to what we now possess, Naples, Sicily and the whole of Silesia; his territories were not exhausted, since they had enjoyed a very long peace; he had generals of great reputation and vast experience; his enemies were not very numerous. He hardly needed to fear anyone save the Turks and the French ... even the king of Prussia was then regarded only as a minor power ... But when I think of our present situation, the mere word reform makes me tremble. If we cannot compel the king of Prussia to evacuate Saxony – as seems to be the case, since 500,000 men have already worked at it to no avail for five years – what sort of peace can we hope for? Undoubtedly the most advantageous we can get will merely restrict him to the same frontiers as those he had before this war. But what will thereafter protect us from the insults of this enemy, as redoubtable as he is implacable? Our alliances? Certainly not ...
The king of Prussia has just proved to all Europe what he did not himself believe

10 Walter, who was the first to make fully plain the significance of Haugwitz's reforms, was inclined to undervalue the *Staatsrat*. For more positive evaluations see Schünemann, *MÖIG* (1933); Haussherr, *Verwaltungseinheit und Ressorttrennung*, ch. 5; G. Ember, 'Der österreichische Staatsrat und die ungarische Verfassung, 1761–1768', *Acta historica*, VI (1959), 105–53, 331–71 and (1960), 149–82; and K-H. Osterloh, *Joseph von Sonnenfels und die österreichische Reformbewegung im Zeitalter des aufgeklärten Absolutismus* (Lübeck and Hamburg, 1970), pp. 23–8. On the end of the *Directorium*, J. Prokeš, 'Boj o Haugvicovo "Directorium in publicis et cameralibus" r. 1761', *Věstník královské české společnosti nauk – třída filosoficko-historicko jazykozpytná* (1926), no. 4, 1–74.

[possible], that on his own he is in a position not only to oppose the united forces [of France, Russia, Sweden, the Empire and ourselves], but even to constrain them to seek an unfavourable peace . . .

Here we are then at the mercy of the king of Prussia and of the Turks! . . . What would we do if, for example, we had [the Turks] at Buda in June . . .? We should have to weigh the kingdoms of Hungary and Bohemia against one another and choose which it would be least bad to lose . . . Your Majesty can reckon that, once peace has been made, if there is ever a war with the Turks . . . you will have the king of Prussia on your hands as well. Should one think of reforming the army in this state of affairs? But, supposing that we have nothing to fear from the Turks, will the French alliance be eternal? May not some storm blow up in Italy or the Low Countries? If Bohemia and Moravia are at the disposal of the king of Prussia, Croatia and the Banat at the Turks', would not Tuscany be equally agreeable to the king of Naples, Lombardy to the king of Sardinia, and the Netherlands to the French and the Dutch? . . .

However terrifying this picture, I believe it to be accurate, and I find no other means of countering the evils with which we are threatened than the maintenance of such a number of troops as can make an impression on our neighbours. We are in debt up to our eyes, and the state is exhausted, it is true, but . . . to allow ourselves to perish through retrenchment . . . is the very worst economy.

He goes on, after all, to name a figure below which the army cannot safely be allowed to fall – 200,000 men – and then to suggest reforms which would not involve limiting its size and effectiveness. Commerce and agriculture should be favoured, luxury and superfluous expense reduced, and the finances better ordered – obvious generalised aims which it was going to be difficult to achieve in the short time available to meet the crisis of 1761. More specifically, useless government posts should be reformed away; twenty persons should not be employed to do the work of eight; people should not be paid for doing nothing; and bad servants should not be compensated when they were removed. Here was a direct criticism of Maria Theresa's lavishness with pensions, and of her generosity as an employer, which she regarded not only as a means of attracting and keeping good subordinates but also as a long-standing and laudable custom of the dynasty. Perhaps Joseph was even indirectly questioning the cost of establishing the *Staatsrat*, which, given his mother's principles, involved no one in loss of emolument and secured to several officials substantial gains.[11]

Most of the memorandum is devoted to detailed proposals for reducing the cost of the army. Instead of gathering taxes from all the provinces to Vienna, then disbursing them to soldiers scattered all over the Monarchy, Joseph suggested that each province should be required to raise a certain number of

[11] On M.T.'s lavishness: Arneth, *GMT* VII, pp. 17–18; Macartney, *Habsburg and Hohenzollern Dynasties*, p. 108; H. Wagner, 'Royal graces and legal claims: the pension payments of Maria Theresa and their withdrawal by Joseph II' in S. B. Winters and J. Held, *Intellectual and Social Developments in the Habsburg Empire from Maria Theresa to World War I* (Boulder, 1975), pp. 5–29.

regiments, if necessary supplementing local recruits from Germany. These units would in peacetime remain in their regions, would be maintained locally, and could be employed in rotation on the land or in other useful civilian activities – thus relieving the central exchequer. In some cases at least, the nobles would have to apply to the military for labour for their estates. Similarly, peasants could be encouraged to breed horses, which, if they proved to be of sufficient quality, would be taken for the cavalry, but if not, left for agriculture. This plan to domesticate the army should apply over the whole Monarchy, even Tuscany: 'everything is the state's; that word embraces everything, hence everyone must work together for its advantage'. Finally, Joseph offered his assistance to his mother, whose dedication to the good of the state he praised, in any capacity whatever.[12]

This document shows many of Joseph's attitudes already well formed. He is rigidly economical. He begrudges officials their salaries and pensions, and believes the bureaucracy is too large. He asserts the unity of the provinces of the Monarchy – even including Tuscany, his father's duchy, already offered as an independent secundogeniture for his eldest brother.[13] He compliments his mother, but does not conceal his disapproval of her generosity or his conviction that during her reign the Monarchy has been brought low. The desire to base army units in the areas from which they had been recruited remained always one of his pet schemes. It is interesting that he envisages some interference by the state between the lords and their serfs.[14] Most striking of all, he shows himself notably respectful towards the Turks, so much so that he is terrified at the prospect of a war on two fronts, and is therefore convinced that an enormous army is required merely to preserve the frontiers of 1748. He is concerned with defence, not with aggrandisement.

JOSEPH'S *RÊVERIES*

Faced with this strident manifesto, Maria Theresa in May 1761 introduced Joseph to the *Staatsrat*. His status as a member is unclear. His participation, and his access to documents, appear to have been restricted by his mother, at least at first.[15] But he seems to have attended regularly, and it is in the context

---

[12] Arneth, *MTuJ* I, pp. 1–12.   [13] Arneth, *GMT* VI, pp. 360–1.

[14] Only W. E. Wright, *Serf, Seigneur and Sovereign: Agrarian Reform in Eighteenth-Century Bohemia* (Minneapolis, 1966), p. 43, seems to have noticed the significance of this passage. But I wonder whether it has the wide-ranging application he attributes to it. It is brief and unemphatic if what it is proposing is the complete supersession of *Robot* (i.e. labour service which the peasant was obliged to do for his lord) by military labour provided by the state in return for money paid by the lords.

[15] May 1761 is Arneth's date (*GMT* VII, p. 32), which seems correct, although many administrative historians give different dates, e.g. Benna, *MÖSA* (1967) 118–19 (Aug. 1761); Schünemann, *MÖIG* (1933), 19 (1762). But cf. K. Schünemann, *Österreichs Bevölkerungspolitik unter Maria Theresia* (Berlin, [1935]), p. 27 (1761). See Ember, *Acta Historica* (1959), 125, 144. In a letter to M.T. of 14 Jul. 1762 (ÖNB Handschriften 4/57/21) he says that on his return to Vienna

of his early experience of this body that another of his memoranda – as remarkable as any he ever wrote – ought to be considered. This is the document entitled by the prince himself *Rêveries*, which dates from 1763, probably from May or June. Although Arneth summarised it, it was not published in full, analysed or correctly dated until 1980.[16] Indeed, some historians have confused it with the document just discussed.[17] In it Joseph puts forward two basic aims: to create in the Monarchy, first, 'the absolute power to be in a position to do all possible good to the state, and [, secondly,] the means to maintain this state without foreign aid'.

By the latter phrase he understands financial independence. He believes that the most important measure to this end would be the reduction of the rate of interest on the state debt, vastly inflated during the war. This will 'strike hard at the most useless appurtenances of the state, which are the people who live off their capital'. He would announce the reduction of the interest-rate offered by the state from the present normal 6 per cent to 3 per cent. Those who considered the new rate too low would be able to withdraw their money, but only when their turn came to be paid out of a sinking fund to be established for the purpose.

The reduction of the interest-rate had long been under discussion, but so drastic a repudiation of obligations could hardly have succeeded. It is difficult to see how the state could have enforced what would surely have been, as Joseph realised, necessary corollaries: the control of interest-rates at home, and the prohibition of any investment abroad. But he still devoted some of his memorandum to considering how the state might best use the savings made in this process, together with others arising from a reduction in the number of officials and in the level of their salaries, plus the additional revenue from proposed new taxes. He wanted some for the army, some for trade and manufactures, and some for 'a sacrosanct fund, which could not be touched except in time of war', and would pay the costs of a first campaign.

His proposals for securing 'the absolute power to be in a position to do all possible good to the state', though in some ways unpractical, are of immense interest. His essential, breath-taking aim is 'to humble and impoverish the grandees, for I do not believe it is very beneficial that there should be little kings and great subjects who live at their ease, not caring what becomes of the

'je viendrai si V.M. le permet d'abord au conseil d'Etat'. Zinzendorf (HHSA TZ, 20 Aug. 1762) reported Blümegen saying 'Que c'est l'Imp. [i.e. M.T.] qui communique a l'archiduc tout ce qu'elle juge a propos des papiers qui passent par le *StaatsRath*.'

[16] On this document and its date see my article in *MÖSA* (1980). Dr P. G. M. Dickson's forthcoming account of the financial discussions of 1763 (in *Finance and Government under M.T.*) strengthens my view that the *Rêveries* belong to that debate, but inclines me to think May or June more likely than April, which I plumped for in my article (p. 150). Arneth, *GMT* VII, pp. 65–9.

[17] See Fejtö, *J. II*, p. 79; Bernard, *J. II*, pp. 20–1, and *Joseph II and Bavaria* (The Hague, 1965), p. 5.

state'. Every subject owes service to the state, which maintains him, protects him and secures him his rights. The service he owes is what the state, 'of which the sovereign is the spokesman', asks of him, not what it suits him to offer.

This smacks of despotism, but without an absolute power . . . to be in a position to do all the good which one is prevented from doing by the rules, statutes and oaths which the provinces believe to be their *palladium*, and which, sanely considered, turn only to their disadvantage, it is not possible for a state to be happy or for a sovereign to be able to do great things. I believe it to be fundamental that, in order to direct the great machine, a single head, even though mediocre, is worth more than ten able men who have to agree among themselves in all their operations. God keep me from wanting to break sworn oaths, but I believe we must work to convert the provinces and make them see how useful the *despotisme lié*, which I propose, would be to them. To this end I should aim to make an agreement with the provinces, asking them [to yield to me] for ten years full power to do everything, without consulting them, for their good . . . As soon as I have obtained that, it is the nobles I shall attack.

He will abolish all their tax immunities. Ordinary subjects will benefit, but in return will be required to accommodate troops, with the objects outlined in his previous memorandum.

Since the revenues of the nobles will be reduced, the Court will become less brilliant. But

internal strength, good laws, firm administration of justice, well-ordered finances, an impressive army, flourishing industries, respect for the sovereign, will better distinguish one of the great Courts of Europe than festivities, gala days, rich clothes, diamonds, gilded halls, gold plate, sledge races etc.

The impoverishment of the nobles would make young gentlemen who might under existing arrangements become wastrels work for their living in the service of the Monarchy.

If people knew that the only way to live in comfortable circumstances would be to rise by hard work in the service [of the state], and that only genuine merit, regardless of recommendations, family, or even merit of one's ancestors,

could achieve this result, everyone would work hard. 'What geniuses will not emerge, who are now lost in obscurity either through laziness or because they are oppressed by nobles!' But in Joseph's system there would not only be better, there would also be fewer, employees than at present; and their scales of payment would be lower.

To get a gentleman to serve the state, even very feebly, you have to pay him lavishly in gold; to get a chief to be willing to lend his name to an office without doing any work, to sit down for three hours three times a week, to set his secretaries writing, costs ten or twelve thousand florins. If he had no need of rich clothes, if his wife and daughters had no need of diamonds, and he didn't require six horses, he would be quite happy with 4000. So that a councillor shall set his clerks writing, go to the Prater, to the German comedy and to some taverns, he must be paid 6000 florins or at least 4000 . . . But who is it that does the work at the moment? It is the poorest officials, who have only 4 or 500 florins.

As for the supreme direction, all that is needed is 'a head to take decisions, but informed by a council like the *Staatsrat*'. Only two of the existing departments are well organised, the council of war and the supreme council of justice. These can be exempted from the control of the council of state, since the military knows best how to run its own affairs, and the ruler should not interfere in judicial matters. There should be one chancellery for the hereditary lands, under Hatzfeld. Not only Hungary, but also the Netherlands and Lombardy, should fall within the purview of the *Staatsrat*. Kaunitz is 'too busy to be able to do more than brush the surface [of the affairs of the detached provinces] once a month, and the sovereign knows less about them than about the government of France'. However, Joseph appears to think that Kaunitz may be left in charge of foreign affairs, so long as he is better controlled. All aspects of finance should be dealt with by one department, under Chotek; but a department of commerce, subordinate to the financial department, should be headed by Zinzendorf.[18]

Under his new system, the *Staatsrat* would have to be expanded in order to be able to deal with the business of Hungary, the Netherlands and Lombardy. To cut down the amount of paperwork, it should meet daily from nine till midday. Trifling matters should be left to the departments concerned. 'The decision should not be written on the protocol itself, but on a detached sheet, so that one can add or subtract whatever one wants.'

Joseph devoted particular attention to the affairs of Hungary and Transylvania. In the case of Hungary, he wrote:

I would judge that, before we can reasonably expect anything more from this country, we must work to make it happy. To achieve this, we must reform their internal system, enable them to sell their products, promote trade. Above all, we must work to increase population and to educate youth, and to convert the reasonable old men by proving to them that it is for their good that we are working. We must be especially careful to create no suspicion that we want to infringe their privileges, although in private we feel no respect for them at all. But we must never allow this to appear except when we are sure of achieving the result we aim at.

It is said that Hungarian trade would be prejudicial to the Austrian provinces. But if Hungary contributed [taxes] as they do, of which I don't despair in the long run, it would be another Peru discovered. But in order to achieve that, we must ask absolutely nothing by way of increased taxes at the first diet, because the small amount we should obtain would prevent us making internal arrangements, since feelings would have been roused; and while gaining one million, we should lose the chance of enjoying six or seven in a few years' time.

The great nobility ought to be kept quiet either by honours or by fear. The lesser

---

[18] He must mean by 'Choteck' Rudolf (and not Johann) Chotek, and by 'Sinzendorff' Ludwig (and not Karl) von Zinzendorf (and not Sinzendorff).

nobles should be supported against the great, and won over by appointing them to all types of offices, which the sovereign ought to keep within her control. The serfs should be upheld against the tyrannical domination of the nobles; if they had the opportunity to sell their produce, my aims would be readily achieved.

Joseph's remarks on Transylvania were provoked by specific difficulties arising from an attempt to erect a 'military frontier' there and to exact higher taxes.[19]

I must state my opinion that, if the matter had been put on a different footing from the start, both here and there, it would now have been concluded. But ... we must now force the issue, since I don't know anything more harmful, and more dangerous in its consequences for all our plans, than to reveal to subjects that, if they don't like something which the sovereign asks, even though it is just, they can stop it. I certainly regret all violence and bloodshed, but this is of too great importance for future generations for us not to decide to insist on it, since it is just, whatever it costs.

He thinks in fact that firmness will achieve success more easily than has been supposed.

Towards the end of this document Joseph reiterates his main point. If his proposals are adopted, he says, the Monarchy will be 'in the most brilliant condition. Some individuals, and particularly the grandees, will suffer. But for serious illnesses one has to take an emetic.' This is the moment to act, when everyone knows that the situation of the state requires strong measures.

As for the humbling of the nobles, which I think the most useful and necessary, it is something one hardly dares speak about to oneself. But we must have it in view in all our actions. Even the council of state should know nothing of it. But the sovereign's decisions should follow from it.

Many features of the *Rêveries* derive directly from the prince's recent experience on the *Staatsrat*. Unlike the other members, he seems not to have been expected to compose fully argued *Vota* as a matter of course. When his view is recorded on the roll, it is in very few words, supporting one or other of the opinions already submitted.[20] The document under discussion may be regarded as an unusually long *Votum*, arising out of the financial debate of 1763 but going beyond it, and written for Maria Theresa only. Indeed Joseph refers in it to 'the other *votants*'.

---

[19] There is a little on Transylvania in Arneth, *GMT* VII, p. 216 and X, pp. 131–3. Some documents in Ember, *Acta Historica* (1959–60), e.g. 121, 136. But a pretty full story can be gathered from M. Bernath, 'Die Errichtung der siebenbürgischen Militärgrenze und die Wiener Rumänenpolitik in der frühjosephinischen Zeit', *Südost-Forschungen*, XIX (1960), 164–92; C. Göllner, *Die siebenbürgische Militärgrenze*, Buchreihe der südostdeutschen Historischen Kommission (Munich, 1974) and Schuller, *Brukenthal*, vol. I, esp. pp. 126–48.

[20] See examples in Ember, *Acta Historica* (1959), 125, 137, 142, 144, and Schünemann, *Österreichs Bevölkerungspolitik*, p. 27n (a *Votum* of 1761 in which J. complains of bureaucratic delays). In HHSA FA Sbde 4 there are two unpublished documents in J.'s hand which look like *Vota* from this period. One concerns the *oberste Justizstelle*, the other the *Hofkriegsrat*. Perhaps he was required to submit any extended statement of views directly to his mother.

For this period the archives of the *Staatsrat* have perished. But the indexes survive, together with notes and transcripts of certain portions, among them some concerning Hungarian questions between 1761 and 1768. These fortunate survivals make it perfectly clear that, almost from its inception, despite protests from the officials involved, and notwithstanding its ostensible terms of reference, the *Staatsrat* gave the most serious consideration to Hungarian affairs. The notes also reveal some of the background to Joseph's thinking in the *Rêveries*. A particularly instructive exchange of views took place in late August 1761. The members speak of their ignorance and incomprehension, as Germans, of the Hungarian constitution; of the obstructiveness and ill-will of the Hungarian Court Chancellery; even of the inhabitants' 'nationalism'. They condemn the constitution in so far as they understand it. The state of the relations between lords and serfs, they agree, is intolerable. Nowhere else are the peasants so burdened and the lords so repressive. Because of the nobles' tax exemptions, guaranteed by Maria Theresa in 1741, the country does not contribute fairly to the state's revenues or to the costs of the war. The peasants bear the whole burden of taxation and services; and, in contrast to other provinces of the Monarchy, the charge is laid on the individual serf and not on the land. Somehow the whole system must be changed. Then, says Kaunitz, the power of the dynasty will be doubled.

Some members of the *Staatsrat* believe that the government can hope for assistance from a Hungarian diet. Others believe it would be unwise to risk summoning it. Kaunitz optimistically cites what has been achieved in another country tenacious of its medieval privileges, Belgium, where the Estates of Flanders have agreed to give the sovereign a fixed income. No one thinks it prudent to challenge the Hungarian constitution openly. All of them recommend that the regime should base itself first on its undoubted prerogatives, in church matters and in appointments. Much may also be done on the ground that historically, while many Hungarian laws have been made with the diet's consent, others have simply been enacted by the sovereign. Borié, in general the bitterest critic of the Hungarian magnates, argues for the establishment on royal lands of better conditions for the peasantry, as an example to other landlords. He also wants Hungarian industries encouraged; but the other members dread the effects of the resulting competition on the provinces of the Monarchy. Joseph agrees with Kaunitz who, except over manufactures, has concurred with Borié.[21]

Joseph's discussions of Transylvanian affairs, the bureaucracy, tax questions including nobles' exemption, and the problem of the debt must also

---

[21] Ember, *Acta Historica* (1959), 130–7. On commercial questions there is much information about Hungary's place in the discussions of the *Staatsrat* in F. Eckhart, *A bécsi udvar gazdasági politikája magyarországon Mária Terézia korában* (Budapest, 1922, with a German summary). Dr P. G. M. Dickson generously lent me his copy of this work.

derive from experience on the *Staatsrat*.[22] But the crucial point is that, on all these topics, he goes further than the ministers. Mixed with and arising out of Joseph's consideration of the state's immediate problems are large general principles, guides to action over the long term. Maria Theresa, who was not shocked by the opinions of Borié and Kaunitz, and who had accepted from Haugwitz talk of 'God-pleasing equality',[23] seems to have been horrified by this document. As Joseph in effect requested, its very existence appears to have been kept secret. As late as 1778 Leopold confided to his coded diary:

> The empress gave me a document written by the emperor when he first married, containing his ideas at that date on the government of the state and its system. This is confused and unsystematic, but includes very strong and violent principles of arbitrary despotism, involving the removal of all privileges of the Estates, even those that have been guaranteed by promises and oaths.[24]

Neither Maria Theresa nor her ministers would go so far as that, or dream of attacking the whole basis of the aristocracy.

Where Joseph picked up his extreme opinions it is impossible to be sure. Beck had impressed upon him that sovereign power was essential to a state, which in any case was the rationale of the whole governmental system of the Monarchy. But there is no trace, in the numerous treatises prepared for his instruction by his mentors, of an attack on aristocratic privilege. So far as local privileges are concerned, Bartenstein, as we have seen, had ensured that despotic notions were kept out of the accounts compiled for the archduke of the various provinces of the Monarchy. Other rulers of the period took a quite different line from that of the *Rêveries*. Frederick the Great had written in his political testament of 1752: 'An object of policy for the sovereign of this state is to preserve the noble class.'[25] Some of Joseph's views must have developed out of opinions expressed on the *Staatsrat*. Haugwitz would be the most plausible influence in this direction, especially since Joseph later praised his system with surprising warmth.[26] The idea that the provincial Estates should surrender their powers to the central government for a period of ten years is only an extension of what Haugwitz had proposed and carried through in the forties. It is remarkable too how many echoes of Maria Theresa's political testaments, documents which Joseph may not have seen but which Haugwitz had inspired, can be found in the *Rêveries*. Writing of the 'vaunted privileges' of

---

[22] References for Transylvania in n.19 above. On finance, Walter's writings already cited, and Beer, *AÖG* (1895), esp. 9–15, 121–2, 124. See the agenda for 1761–5 reproduced in K-M VI, pp. 555–82.
[23] E.g. Haugwitz's memo. quoted in Walter, *VKNGÖ*, XXXII, 134.
[24] Wandruszka, *L. II.*, vol. I, 329–40, 438. See Beales, *MÖSA* (1980), 143–6, arguing that Arneth was wrong to conclude that the *Rêveries* were known to ministers.
[25] See above, pp. 58–60, 62 for this aspect of Joseph's education. For Frederick's political testament, Macartney, *Habsburg and Hohenzollern Dynasties*, esp. p. 332.
[26] See below, p. 210.

the provinces, she had declared that 'the maintenance of them is rightly to be understood only as applying to those ancient customs which are good, not to the bad'; and she took pride in having enforced her will on Carinthia, 'after failing to bring the Estates to any kind of reason, . . . *jure regio*', that is, by her royal prerogative.[27] The empress seems to have lost during the Seven Years War much of her zeal for radical reform. The failure to recover Silesia called into question the whole effort to establish Haugwitz's system. The war coincided with her change of life and with a shift in her religious position.[28] As with the conflict between mother and son over military strength and territorial aggrandisement, so in their disputes over domestic policy, Joseph often took the stand of the young Maria Theresa in arguing against the old. But still it remains true that some of the views he expressed in the *Rêveries* – his approach to the Hungarian problem, his stress on purity of administration and his fundamental critique of aristocracy – were, by any contemporary criterion, revolutionary.

It is strange that he makes no reference whatever to the religious and ecclesiastical questions with which his name is universally associated. In detail, he later changed his mind, at least in his public utterances, about Kaunitz's domestic administration. But many of the opinions he expressed on other matters in the document remained characteristic of him throughout his life. He always disdained Court pomp, ceremony and luxury. His zeal for economy and his Puritan rigour about patronage and salaries never left him. The reduction of the rate of interest on the state debt was the cause to which he was to devote the vast fortune he inherited from his father – though the scheme adopted was less drastic than the one proposed here.

A crucial question now arises. Should the revolutionary aims, the desire to humble and impoverish the nobles, and the wish to set aside provincial constitutions, also be seen as part of a continuing political programme, now stated for the first time, but never abandoned until the final *débâcle*? It is obviously of vital importance for any study of Joseph to decide how much significance to attach to his statement that these objects must at all times be pursued, but must never be avowed.

Historians have given this document virtually no attention. But they have shown tremendous interest in another piece of writing with a similar title, the *Rêveries politiques* which Frederick the Great appended to his political testament of 1752. Comparison between the two is instructive.

In his *Rêveries politiques* Frederick set out various possible annexations which Prussia might hope to make in the future, peacefully for preference, but if necessary by war, and if convenient by breaking treaties. When these passages were discovered in the archives in the late nineteenth century, the

[27] Macartney, *Habsburg and Hohenzollern Dynasties*, pp. 109–123.
[28] See Hersche, *Spätjansenismus*, esp. pp. 136–42.

German government would not permit their publication, since their cynicism would have shocked liberals and their revelation of Frederick's schemes would have cast doubt on the mythology of national unification. After the First World War the ban was lifted, and the *Rêveries politiques* were printed in 1920. A debate ensued on the morality of Frederick's attitudes, and the significance of his views. This turned to some extent on the precise meaning of this title. Were these far-reaching ideas to be regarded as fantasies, speculations, pipedreams, or as realistic future plans which Frederick seriously hoped to implement?

He began his discussion by contrasting the 'solid', which he had already treated, with the 'chimerical', on which he was about to embark. But soon he was talking of

the spacious field of chimerical projects, which may sometimes become real if one does not lose sight of them, and if successive generations, marching towards the same goal, are sufficiently skilled to hide their designs deeply from the curious and penetrating eyes of the European Powers.

Before long, still under the same heading, he was proposing 'the means of acquiring' the territories concerned, and producing a detailed plan of campaign for the conquest of Saxony. While he always recognised that elements of the future were unpredictable, he believed that rational calculation could prepare for most eventualities. In his *Rêveries politiques* he was manifestly discussing serious possibilities and, in some cases at least, matured plans. This interpretation gains force from the fact that in the eighteenth century the word *rêveries* meant 'reflexions', 'meditations', 'musings', rather than 'fantasies' or 'pipedreams'.

Joseph cannot possibly have known of these thoughts of his great rival. But the same considerations apply to both sets of *Rêveries*. Indeed the two documents illuminate each other. Both of them must be understood as carefully calculated, though secret, plans for a future which their authors hoped would not be distant.[29] The parallel between them can be still further extended. The Austro-Hungarian 'Establishment' of the 1870s and 1880s suppressed certain passages of Joseph's *Rêveries*, those in which they considered 'the lion's claws showed themselves too savagely' against the aristocracy.[30]

[29] The standard edition of the political testaments of Frederick II is G.B. Volz (ed.), *Die politischen Testamente Friedrich's des Grossen* (Berlin, 1920) (Ergänzungsband of the *Politische Correspondenz Friedrichs des Grossen*). I have used Macartney's translation where appropriate (*Habsburg and Hohenzollern Dynasties*, pp. 340–6). There is an excellent discussion of the problem and the historiography of the *Rêveries politiques* in E. Bosbach, *Die 'Rêveries Politiques' in Friedrichs des Grossen Politischem Testament von 1752*, Kölner historische Abhandlungen 3 (Cologne, 1960). See esp. ch. 8. Macartney unfortunately uses the title 'pipedreams'. The best-known published *Rêveries* of this period, those of marshal de Saxe (1732), contain very little in the way of speculation about the future; they amount virtually to *Memoirs* or reflections on the art of war.

[30] Beales, *MÖSA* (1980), 143, 146–7.

Frederick, of course, was writing for posterity as a king of twelve years standing with great achievements behind him. Joseph was no doubt looking to his own reign after his mother's death, but he had to submit his ideas to her as the effective ruler of the Monarchy at the moment, and he was wholly inexperienced. However, it reflects the permanent and fundamental difference in the approach of the two men that Frederick's talk should be of aggrandisement through war, and Joseph's of reform through despotism. Even before he came to the throne, Frederick had seen expansion as his goal.[31]

Maria Theresa must have firmly told her son to jettison such notions. He claimed in his next major memorandum, of 1765: 'I have abandoned my *rêveries*.'[32] But he probably never lost sight of the basic aims first stated in the *Rêveries*. His attitude to Hungary, for example, seems never to have wavered. Although he appears less consistent about the aristocracy, it may be that he always longed for the day when he could attack them – as he finally did during his sole reign.[33]

JOSEPH'S GOVERNMENTAL ACTIVITY, 1761–5

In the same memorandum of 1765 Joseph looked back on his first four years on the *Staatsrat*, and especially on the discussions which led to the remodelling of the administration:

Being a young man without experience or great application, I expected to find myself among Solons or Lycurguses and to hear nothing but oracles. From the first months the new system was in the making. The great arguments and the frequent discussions which took place in this connexion were for me so sublime that, since I did not understand either their force or their significance, but only the words, I was so ill-advised as to think about other things, when I ought to have been absorbing and savouring all the twists they were giving to reason and the mind of Man, as well as the perfection and high intelligence they were attributing to humanity. I became a financier the moment the issues were simplified and the basis of a distinction was made between a full purse, a man whose business it is to fill it and another who keeps an exact account of how it is emptied.[34]

I verily believed, when I was picturing in my imagination the safe deposits from six different places being brought together into one vault, with a president whose only task was the direction of all the departments, and finally another who would control the whole, that I was almost as wise as a Colbert.

So I went overboard for these new ideas, without pausing to consider what my colleagues were intoning about emperors Ferdinand and Leopold. I was just astonished that people had lived so long in this crass ignorance, and I regarded everything that had previously been done as though it was a creation of the Iroquois Indians.

[31] In the letter to Natzmer of Feb. 1731 (Bosbach, *Die 'Rêveries Politiques'*, pp. 17–20).
[32] Arneth, *MTuJ* III, p. 335; Arneth, *GMT* VII, pp. 194–5.
[33] Mitrofanov II, ch. 7.
[34] Joseph evidently refers to the *Generalkassa*, the *Hofkammer* and the *Hofrechenkammer* respectively.

It took another year to explain our ideas to everyone, and I could not understand how something which had appeared so simple to me, and which I had grasped without thinking in five minutes, did not effect a lodging in the minds of our officials. After this year of lessons, and after everyone had learned them, I recognised that, if men had been created according to the system, it would have worked, but that the system had not been tailored to fit humanity and its weaknesses.[35]

Joseph goes on to refer to the renewed debates on the administrative system which began in 1763 and occupied much of 1764 and 1765. After the introduction of the changes promoted by the *Staatsrat* in 1761, it had soon become apparent that, whatever had been gained, a good deal had been lost. The creation of three new agencies, and the division between them and two old or remodelled agencies of the work withdrawn from the *Directorium*, had cost money and wasted time. Haugwitz understandably wished to revert to the arrangements of 1749, but most of Maria Theresa's advisers still thought they had been unsatisfactory. In Joseph's words, 'We changed over again, and made a compromise.' In the summer of 1765, after long and inconclusive discussions, the empress decided to give the *Hofkammer* extended competence, and put count Hatzfeld at the head of both *Hofkammer* and *Banco*. The *Kommerzienrat* was associated with the Austro-Bohemian Chancellery, and the *Generalkassa* disappeared. Haugwitz and his system had won a partial victory and Kaunitz had suffered a reverse.[36]

Few passages of Joseph's own writing are more telling than the two paragraphs in which he commented on this reaction and his part in it:

My pride was well and truly punished for my having so hastily taken sides in this business. I came to see that I had accepted in five minutes what, after prolonged reflection, I could no longer contemplate. From this moment I became circumspect, and took good care not to land myself in such embarrassment again.

Since that time I have been an atheist where financial dogmas are concerned. I see several religions and believe none of them. I was converted from that of my predecessors by incontrovertible arguments, or at least arguments I could not answer. I see that the modern dogma is contrary to daily practice, and that its most zealous promoters are beginning to waver. Given my limitations, when these financial gentlemen browbeat me with powerful speeches, I have no idea how to reply, but I do not believe what they tell me. It seems to me that I am a good Capuchin father who might be discussing first principles with Voltaire. The latter would silence him, but the Capuchin would be right all the same. So, from all that I have seen and heard, I have learned nothing except to fear intelligence and all its subtleties. I recognise no argument which comes from the ancient Greeks or the modern French. Propositions derived from the past century and from a hundred years' usage do not persuade me. The Austrian Monarchy is like no other, and the year 1765 cannot be compared with any one of its predecessors since the birth of Jesus Christ. Let us act then according to what good sense and reflection prescribe to us, and we shall have done enough if we

---

[35] Arneth, *MTuJ* III, pp. 336–7.
[36] Walter, *MÖIG* (1933) and *VKNGÖ*, XXXII, chs. 6–7; documents in *VKNGÖ*, XXIX, 203–59.

make judgements and carry them out by the light of the talents the Creator has given us. But once we have decided, there must be firmness, and no hesitation.[37]

Although the context is financial, this seems to be a general declaration of independence from all theory, all precedent and all history – except only the Christian religion. That Joseph should mention the ancient Greeks and the modern French, and in particular Voltaire, suggests that he had expanded his cultural awareness since the end of his formal education. But they are mentioned only to be rejected as guides. It would be absurd to claim that he was henceforth a pure pragmatist. On the other hand, in the face of this eloquent renunciation of ideology, it is difficult to support the widespread view that he was rigidly doctrinaire, or 'the Enlightenment enthroned'.[38] It is also impossible to maintain, in the light of these remarks, that he was completely unaware of the dangers of hasty action. Further, he shows himself here, no doubt uncharacteristically, capable of laughing at himself, and of admitting that he has made mistakes. The *Staatsrat*, whatever its deficiencies as an organ to save the Monarchy, had evidently contributed notably to the education of the heir to the throne.

This of course was also true in a more limited sense. By virtue of his involvement in the business of the *Staatsrat*, he could learn almost all that the government knew about the provinces and become familiar with most current domestic problems. When he was present at its meetings and both his parents were absent, it seems that he presided, at least nominally.[39] His participation in other aspects of government appears to have increased, especially after his coronation as king of the Romans. At the end of April 1764 he took part in a meeting of the Conference on Polish affairs.[40] Later in the year he accompanied his parents to the Hungarian diet at Pressburg, where his pessimism in the *Rêveries* proved well justified. A small additional sum was granted, but the magnates would not hear of any restriction either of their taxation privileges or of their rights over their serfs.[41]

To make a full assessment of Joseph's actual influence on policy during these years is impossible. The evidence does not exist. His opportunities of talking to his mother in private ought to have given his opinions a weight denied to those of ordinary councillors. But he was not successful in preventing the reduction of the army in 1761.[42] On the other hand, his account of the changes in the financial administration indicates that he felt

---

[37] Arneth, *MTuJ* III, pp. 337–8.
[38] E.g. Macartney, *M.T. and the House of Austria*, pp. 107–8; quotation from E. N. Williams, *The Ancien Régime in Europe* (Harmondsworth, 1972), p. 460.
[39] This was proposed at the first meeting of the *Staatsrat* by K., and accepted by M.T., to come into effect when the empress should decide to call J. to the meetings. (Walter, *VKNGÖ*, XXIX, 20).
[40] Arneth, *GMT* VIII, pp. 52, 545.   [41] Arneth, *GMT* VII, ch. 4.
[42] E. Kotasek, *Feldmarschall Graf Lacy* (Horn, 1956), pp. 60–2.

some responsibility for the decisions of the same year in this field. Although his father was the chief family influence at this period, on at least one occasion Joseph's view is known to have counted even when the emperor's was already in play. The empress told Kaunitz in November 1762: 'I warn you that we must take advantage of the favourable disposition of the master, which may yet change again. But today he seems to want the end [of the war] like me, as does my son.'[43]

It has been assumed that the *Rêveries*, because 'unrealistic', had no impact whatsoever on policy.[44] But no attempt has been made to relate the document to the financial and administrative developments of 1763–5.[45] Certainly the more far-reaching aims were quite unacceptable to Maria Theresa. But it was her normal reaction to Joseph's diatribes to concede some lesser points. He was, after all, the heir to the throne, about to become king of the Romans, and a member of the *Staatsrat*. It is at least suggestive that, soon after his scheme to reduce the state debt had been put forward, Francis Stephen was put in charge of a more realistic plan with the same object, and that, again soon after Joseph had demanded the amalgamation of the financial departments, nearly two years' discussion of administrative reform centred on this proposal.[46]

---

[43] Arneth, *GMT* VI, p. 489. In his letter to M.T. of 14 July 1762 (ÖNB Handschriften 4/57/21) he advises against peace, having apparently been told by M.T. it is necessary.
[44] Arneth, *GMT* VII, p. 67.
[45] Neither in his articles nor in his contributions to *VKNGÖ* did Walter consider the *Rêveries*.
[46] These suggestions are developed in my article in *MÖSA* (1980).

CHAPTER 5

King of the Romans and Holy Roman Emperor,
1764–1780

Peace was made between Prussia and the Monarchy at Hubertusburg in February 1763. The basis of the settlement was the *status quo* before the war. Kaunitz's great contrivance, the Diplomatic Revolution, had definitively failed to wrest Silesia back from Prussia. Maria Theresa now saw that aim as a 'chimera'.[1] But she obtained one advantage from the peace: Frederick promised his vote to Joseph as king of the Romans or emperor.[2]

While an emperor was alive, it was possible for the nine electors to elect a king of the Romans, who would then automatically become emperor on the death of the incumbent, thus avoiding an interregnum. In the early fifties a long bout of negotiations had been devoted to an attempt to procure the election of Joseph as king. But these efforts had failed, essentially because they were the result of an English initiative designed to refurbish the Anglo-Austrian alliance, while the secret policy of the Monarchy already envisaged an understanding with France.[3] With the end of the Seven Years War Maria Theresa became concerned to secure the dynasty's future in the Empire, and to extract at least this benefit from the pacification of Germany.[4]

It took roughly a year to get Joseph elected. Prussia proved on the whole a reliable supporter; and the only elector to make significant difficulties was the elector Palatine, who had to be sweetened by Maria Theresa's renunciation of certain remote Habsburg claims to some of his territories. In the end, despite many proposals to the contrary, the conditions to which the new king had to submit in his *Wahlkapitulation* (election charter) were the same as his father had tolerated in 1745.[5]

[1] Arneth, *GMT* VI, p. 476 (M.T. to Starhemberg, 22 Mar. 1762).
[2] On the peace see Arneth, *GMT* VI, ch. 17.
[3] See R. Browning, 'The Duke of Newcastle and the Imperial election plan, 1749–1754', *Journal of British Studies*, VII (1967), 28–47 and the earlier literature there cited; and, for a less rosy picture of the policy of Newcastle, D. B. Horn, 'The Duke of Newcastle and the origins of the Diplomatic Revolution' in *The Diversity of History*, ed. Elliott and Koenigsberger, pp. 247–68. Cf. Klingenstein, *Diplomatie und Aussenpolitik*, p. 78.
[4] See her letter to Pergen of 7 Mar. 1763 (Arneth, *MTKuF* IV, pp. 271–5).
[5] Arneth, *GMT* VII, pp. 70–83, 86–7. Professor H. P. Liebel kindly sent me a copy of her article, 'The election of Joseph II and the challenge to Imperial unity in Germany, 1763–64', *Canadian Journal of History*, XV (1980), 371–97.

Before the election had been concluded, Joseph, his father and Leopold set out on 12 March 1764 for Frankfurt, where imperial coronations took place. Such was the scale of the suite that at every posting station 450 horses had been ordered. It took twelve days for them to cover the 400 miles to the outskirts of the city. They then waited five days until the election itself occurred and they could make a formal entry into Frankfurt.[6]

Goethe, who was living in the city and whose father was one of its officials, kept a diary of the proceedings as he saw and heard about them, which formed the basis of his famous and marvellous description in *Dichtung und Wahrheit*, his autobiography. He wrote the chapter concerned in 1811, and many of its reflections belong to the time of composition rather than to the period of the events described. He over-emphasised in retrospect his youthful enthusiasm for the Empire as a focus of German national feeling. The romantic relish with which he describes the traditions, symbolism and even the apparent absurdities of the coronation belongs to the early nineteenth century rather than to the 1760s, and owes much to the nostalgia evoked by recalling a system which had been abolished in the 1800s. But the details of Goethe's picture are almost always accurate, and it is presented in such a way as to bring into relief the complexities, incongruities and antiquarianism of the old constitution and to reveal the historical significance not only of the coronation but of the Empire itself. It is far too long to reproduce complete, but some of its central passages are so vivid and intelligent that they demand quotation.[7]

While the election was being organised, Goethe was impressed by the extravagant suites of the electors' ambassadors, which filled the city to overflowing. He notes that by far the most popular was baron Plotho, the representative of Frederick the Great, hero of this Protestant community as of most Germans outside the Roman Catholic states.[8] The elaborate formalities affected Goethe profoundly:

On the one hand these things gave me much pleasure, as all that took place . . . always had a hidden meaning; and such symbolic ceremonies momentarily gave a renewed appearance of life to the old Empire of Germany, almost choked to death by so many parchments, papers and books. But on the other hand I could not suppress a secret regret . . . that several Powers were here balancing and opposing each other, and were agreed only in so far as they were scheming to limit the new ruler even more than the

---

[6] Arneth, *GMT* VII, pp. 82–6; K-M VI, pp. 5–15.
[7] I have learned much from the editorial apparatus in *Goethes Werke*, vols. IX (Hamburg, 1961) and X (Hamburg, 1960).

The translation published as *The Autobiography of Johann Wolfgang von Goethe* (London, 1971) is useful, but it dates back to the 1840s and is not only stilted and literal, but sometimes inaccurate. In some passages I have been helped by the translation of E. Wilkins and E. Kaiser (J. W. von Goethe, *Truth and Fantasy from my Life*, ed. J. M. Cohen (London, 1949)). I owe this reference to Professor H. B. Nisbet.
[8] *Goethes Werke*, vol. IX, pp. 182–3.

old one . . . On this occasion they were more watchful than usual, because they were beginning to fear Joseph the Second, his vehemence and probable plans . . .

Goethe exaggerated in 1811 the fears aroused by Joseph in 1764. Little was known of the young archduke when he came to Frankfurt to be crowned king; and hard-headed rulers and politicians were well aware that the powers of the emperor were insufficient to enable him to take decisive action in that capacity. Francis's *Wahlkapitulation* was quite restrictive enough.

When the emperor and his son made their ceremonial entry, wrote Goethe:

What was bound to be particularly pleasing to a Frankfurter was that on this occasion, in the presence of so many sovereigns and their representatives, the imperial city of Frankfurt also appeared as a little sovereign; for her equerry opened the procession; chargers with armorial trappings . . . followed him; then came attendants and officials, drummers and trumpeters, and deputies of the council, accompanied by the clerks of the council, in the city livery, on foot. Immediately behind these were the three companies of citizen cavalry . . . We rejoiced in our participation in this honour, and in the hundred-thousandth part of a sovereignty which now appeared in its full brilliancy. The varied suites of the hereditary imperial marshal, and of the envoys deputed by the six temporal electors, marched after these step by step. None of them consisted of less than twenty attendants and two state carriages . . . Now the retinue of the spiritual electors filed by, endlessly – their servants and domestic officers seemed innumerable: the elector of Cologne and the elector of Trier had more than twenty state carriages, and the elector of Mainz just as many . . .

Then the train of his imperial majesty, as was fitting, surpassed all the rest. The riding-masters, the led horses, the equipages, the saddle-cloths and caparisons, attracted every eye; and the sixteen six-horse gala wagons of the imperial chamberlains, privy councillors, high chamberlain, high stewards and high equerry concluded with great pomp this division of the procession which, in spite of its magnificence and extent, was still only to be the vanguard . . .

Immediately behind the elector of Mainz, ten imperial footmen, forty-one lackeys and eight *heyducks* [Hungarian attendants] announced Their Majesties. The most magnificent state carriage, ornamented with paintings, lacquer, carved work and gilding, covered . . inside with red embroidered velvet, even had an undivided back window of plate glass, and so allowed us an excellent view of the emperor and the king . . . in all their glory . . .

The strange coachmen and outriders . . . looked as if they had come from some other nation or even from another world, with their long black and yellow velvet coats, and their caps with large plumes of feathers after the fashion of the imperial Court . . . The Swiss guard on both sides of the carriage; the hereditary marshal holding the Saxon sword upwards in his right hand; the field-marshals, as leaders of the imperial guard, riding behind the carriage; the imperial pages in a body; and finally, the imperial horse-guard itself, in black velvet frocks with all the seams edged with gold, under which were red coats and leather-coloured camisoles also richly decked with gold . . .

Impressed though he was by all this display, Goethe remarked on a certain lack of consistency about the ceremonies:

We ... were always noticing something which did not quite satisfy our eyes or our imagination. The Spanish mantles, the huge plumed hats of the ambassadors ... had indeed a truly antique look; but on the other hand there was a great deal half-new or entirely modern, so that the whole affair took on a motley, unsatisfactory, often tasteless appearance ...

Five days later came the climax:

The coronation day dawned at last on 3 April 1764: the weather was fine, and everybody was out and about. I ... had ... a good place in ... [the cathedral square] itself ... There was the newly erected fountain, with two large tubs to left and right, into which the double eagle on the pedestal was to pour from its two beaks white wine on one side, and red wine on the other. There, gathered into a heap, lay the oats:[9] here stood the large wooden hut in which for several days we had seen the whole fat ox being roasted ...

[Later] the hereditary treasurer ... mounted a fine steed, from the sides of whose saddle were suspended, instead of holsters, a couple of splendid bags ... Plunging his hands into these pockets, he liberally scattered, right and left, gold and silver coins, which ... glittered merrily in the air like metallic rain ... The crowd tumbled over each other, struggling violently for pieces which might have reached the ground ...

Goethe captured the difference in attitude of the emperor and the king, reflected in their dress:

Both Their Majesties approached ... The emperor's domestic robes, of purple-coloured silk richly adorned with pearls and stones, as well as his crown, sceptre and imperial orb, struck the eye with good effect. For all in them was new, and the imitation of the antique was tasteful. He moved, too, quite easily in his attire; and his true-hearted, dignified face indicated at once the emperor and the father. The young king, on the other hand, in his monstrous garments, with the crown jewels of Charlemagne, dragged himself along as if in disguise; so that he himself, when he caught his father's eye, could not refrain from laughing. The crown, which it had been necessary to pad out a great deal, projected from his head like an overhanging roof. The dalmatic and the stole, though they had been well fitted and taken in, looked far from impressive. The sceptre and imperial orb excited some admiration; but to achieve a more regal effect, one would rather have seen a man of larger physique invested and adorned with these robes ...

Finally, Goethe obtained unauthorised entry to the state banquet, an official providing him with a spare silver vessel to carry.

At the far end of the hall, immediately by the windows, raised on the dais and under canopies, sat the emperor and the king in their robes; but their crowns and sceptres lay at some distance behind them on gold cushions. The three spiritual electors had taken their places on a lower dais, with their sideboards behind them ... This upper part of the hall was imposing and cheerful to behold, and excited the remark that the spiritual power likes to stay on good terms with the ruler as long as possible. By contrast, the sideboards and tables of all the temporal electors, magnificently ornamented but

---

[9] A symbolic offering for the imperial horses.

without occupants, made one think of the bad relations which had developed over centuries between them and the head of the Empire. Their ambassadors had already withdrawn to eat in an ante-room; and if most of the hall assumed a sort of spectral appearance, with so many invisible guests being so magnificently attended, a large unoccupied table in the middle was still more depressing to look upon; for there also, all the places were empty, because all those who had the right to sit there had kept away to avoid any loss of face [in disputes over precedence] . . .[10]

Joseph's own reactions to these events are given in daily letters to his mother while he was away from Vienna, and in a few letters to his father-in-law. He had described the coronation beforehand, to the latter admittedly, as 'this disagreeable and useless function'.[11] He complained during the journey about the formalities, the disputes over protocol, some 'pretty grotesque cere-monies', bad roads, poor lodgings and vapid conversation. He was character-istically captious about many of those who were presented to him, especially the men.

The duke of Ossuna has this instant left me . . . he's a terrible sight . . . his speech is incomprehensible . . . The elector of Trier . . . is sad and gloomy, of few words and, so far as I can see, not very thrilled with his position. The prelate of Salmansweiler has just left me; he has heightened his wig, which makes him look very grotesque.[12]

As for the women,

Among those we saw, the most beautiful were the princess of Nassau Usingen and Mademoiselle de Franckenstein. The first has a very fine figure, fine eyes, a round face, very nice hair and very good teeth, but she is not a child; she must be a woman of twenty-eight. She much resembles Madame Durazzo, but blonde. She speaks well and knows how to ogle. The second is a little small, with very nice eyes, a face genuinely like the Virgin in paintings, but with rather a wide mouth and less neck than my sister Antoinette; when she speaks she is more gracious, but she holds herself badly. For intelligence I think Madame de Wartensleben takes the prize . . . Your Majesty will gather from this description . . . that . . . animated by your orders and requests, I have talked nineteen to the dozen.[13]

At the coronation service itself, which lasted several hours, he found the crown and the robes heavy, and was very hot. 'The dinner was very long and stifling.' He reported a mishap in the streets, which Goethe passed over in silence:

[10] The quotations come from *Goethes Werke*, vol. IX, pp. 183, 191–3, 184, 199, 204–5, 203, 207. Cf. K-M VI, pp. 13–24. See Plate 6.
   The vestments worn by both father and son are still preserved in the Imperial Treasury in the Hofburg in Vienna. So are the Crown jewels, which of course date from a later period than the time of Charlemagne.
[11] J. to Philip of Parma, 11 Dec. 1763 (Bicchieri, *AMMP* (1868), 112).
[12] J. to M.T., 26 Mar. 1764 (Arneth, *MTuJ* I, p. 49).
[13] J. to M.T., 31 Mar. 1764 (*ibid.*, pp. 63–5, where the year is given as 1791, obviously in error).

I thought of Your Majesty, and how you would have screamed, seeing the scuffles that took place. The troops that were there hit out at the crowd unnecessarily and in a frightful fashion. But in the end the populace counter-attacked so effectively that the company of grenadiers was entirely dispersed and almost crushed with blows. Four or five persons perished, for in the end the troops opened fire, and a girl of nineteen was hit by a ball which sent her to the other world.

In the same letter, written on the day after the coronation, he made again the point which he most often stresses in this correspondence, that the loss of his wife had destroyed all possibility of his deriving any pleasure from the affair, and had placed him under special strain throughout the journey:

I cannot deny that the role I am playing is very hard; apart from all the difficulties and inconveniences associated with such ceremonies, there is into the bargain my legitimate grief, which does not leave me for an instant but if anything increases, although I hide it as much as possible, and my character which in any case does not at all relish high society; but I must set that aside, and, to do you honour, I am making and will make the most cruel efforts.[14]

However, Joseph spoke well of more individuals than his reputation for censoriousness would lead one to expect. 'The count of Ötting' proved 'very amiable' and fed them a very good dinner; the elector of Cologne was 'a man of intelligence who speaks well on all subjects, and bears in mind that he is [(?) a mere] count of Königsegg'.[15] What is more surprising is that Joseph should have followed up the remarks about his grief with these:

Yesterday's ceremony, I must confess, is superb and august. I tried to carry it off decently, but without embarrassment. His Majesty the Emperor has admitted to us that he could not keep back his tears; they say that the same thing happened to almost the whole congregation.

Princess Liechtenstein thought 'the king looked strikingly beautiful and acquitted himself with nobility and with charming grace'. Joseph expressed his gratitude to his mother for procuring him this honour, while protesting that 'a single look [from her] is worth more to me than all the kingdoms of the world'.[16]

After holding Court for a further week in Frankfurt, the emperor and the new king set off for Vienna. They varied the route, travelling for some days by boat down the Danube. But the weather was so bad and the navigation so incompetent – one day, dinner was delayed for some hours because a catering ship had run aground – that the principals eventually resorted to the roads for the last part of the journey to the abbey of Melk, where Maria Theresa had

---

[14] J. to M.T., 3 and 4 Apr. 1764 (Arneth, *MTuJ* I, pp. 74–6); J. to Philip of Parma, 5 Apr. 1764 (Bicchieri, *AAMP* (1868), 115).

[15] J. to M.T., 19 and 26 Mar. 1764 (Arneth, *MTuJ* I, pp. 33, 49).

[16] J. to M.T., 3 and 4 Apr. 1764 (*ibid.*, pp. 73–6); E.L. to L.K., 5 Apr. 1764 (SOALpZ, LRRA P. 16/18).

come to meet them. The return took almost a fortnight.[17] The whole business had cost over two million florins.[18]

All this pageantry aroused much enthusiasm in Germany. Especially in Roman Catholic areas, feelings of national identity focussed on the Empire; and many people hoped that the young king and future emperor would reform and strengthen the shadowy institutions of the *Reich*, giving Germany a greater measure of political unity. The most effective of the publicists in this vein was Friedrich Carl von Moser. He had written *The Master and the Servant* with an opposite moral in 1759. But he produced in 1765 *Of the German National Spirit*, in 1766 *What is Good in an Emperor, and What is Not Good in an Emperor?* and in 1767 *Patriotic Letters*, pamphlets in which, contrary to his earlier views and to what he admitted was the common opinion, he became the advocate of the emperor's rights as the best protection of the *Reich*, its institutions and its citizens: 'It is and remains a precious and eternal truth that Germany would be the most unhappy Empire in the world without a common overlord, and she is happy and powerful only in proportion as the head and members are justly harmonised one with another.'[19]

Another strand in German patriotic feeling, however, looked to the small states for national salvation. The best-known publicist of this school was Justus Möser, who found it possible to glorify the bizarre constitution of the state of Osnabrück. This was a prince-bishopric, held alternately by a Catholic and a Protestant. In 1764 it had acquired as its temporal and spiritual head Frederick, second son of George III of England and Hanover, who at the time of his election by the chapter was six months old. Möser's *Osnabrückische Geschichte* appeared in 1766.[20]

Most observers were simply sceptical that the Empire could ever now be made politically meaningful. Pufendorf, on whose views Joseph had been reared, had called its constitution 'monstrous' and 'irregular', because he could find no effective sovereign within it.[21] Frederick the Great had written in his political testament of 1752:

---

[17] Arneth, *GMT* VII, pp. 88, 94; K-M VI, pp. 24–8, esp. 25 (13 Apr. 1764).

[18] Cf. Arneth, *GMT* VII, p. 82, and H.L. Mikoletzky, *Österreich. Das grosse 18. Jahrhundert* (Vienna, 1967), p. 223.

[19] For the Empire in this period see K. O. Freiherr von Aretin, *Heiliges Römisches Reich, 1776–1806* (2 vols., Wiesbaden, 1967), esp. vol. I, ch. 1; H. Holborn, *A History of Modern Germany, 1648–1840* (London, 1965), esp. ch. 1; K. Epstein, *The Genesis of German Conservatism* (Princeton, 1966), esp. pp. 238–53; Blanning, *Reform and Revolution in Mainz*, esp. pt I; J. A. Vann and S. W. Rowan (eds.), *The Old Reich: Essays on German Political Institutions, 1495–1806* (Brussels, 1974); E. Bussi, *Il diritto pubblico del sacro romano impero alla fine del XVIII secolo* (2 vols., Padua, 1957 and Milan, 1959).

On Moser, Aretin, *Reich*, vol. I, pp. 17, 23; Epstein, *Conservatism*, pp. 244–5 and nn.; A. H. Loebl, 'Österreich und Preussen. 1766–1768', *AÖG*, XCII (1903), 456–78. I regret that J. Whaley's excellent *Religious Toleration and Social Change in Hamburg, 1529–1819* (Cambridge, 1985) appeared too late for me to use it here.

[20] Epstein, *Conservatism*, ch. 6; W. F. Sheldon, *The Intellectual Development of Justus Möser*, Osnabrücker Geschichtsquellen und Forschungen, (Osnabrück, 1970).

[21] Pufendorf, *De jure naturae et gentium* (ed. Scott), pp. 45–6.

It seems to me likely that the power of the emperors will continue to diminish, because the electors, now that they are powerful princes, can match imperial authority and power by uniting together and calling on the help of France . . .

I would not advise you [his heir] to aim at this supreme post . . . a king of Prussia should rather work to acquire a province than to decorate himself with a useless title.[22]

When the coronation took place, Voltaire's famous joke was still fresh, that the so-called Holy Roman Empire was 'neither holy, nor Roman nor an empire'.[23]

Within the borders of the Empire (see Map 1) were to be found over three hundred political units which, though technically subordinate to the emperor, were either themselves virtually sovereign states, or belonged to sovereign states whose territories extended beyond the *Reich*. The largest of these states were able to assert total sovereignty and, in the case of Prussia at least, to attain the position of a Great Power. Even the smallest paid little heed to the Empire, and then chiefly to the law courts which provided some scope for the peaceful settlement of disputes among the lesser states. The Diet or *Reichstag*, though now an assembly of representatives in continuous session, was no more than a talking shop and a sort of final court of appeal. The Protestant states were generally aligned against the Catholic. Parts of the Empire were non-German: Bohemia, Moravia, the southern Netherlands and, if it was proper to include them at all, portions of northern Italy. Perhaps the most concrete proof of the continuing political significance of the Empire was the imperial army, which was from time to time raised and put at the emperor's service by a group of states acting for the *Reich*. But Frederick the Great had routed this force with such contemptuous ease at the battle of Rossbach in 1757 that little confidence could be placed in its future usefulness.

In so far as a modern parallel exists with the Empire of the eighteenth century, the United Nations seems in many respects closer than any true federation. The member-states pursued their selfish interests almost without regard to the existence of the *Reich* – though of course the greater states could act more independently than the lesser. A good many persons were employed in imperial institutions, but more effort went into running them than the results seemed to warrant. Minor disputes might be settled peacefully through these bodies, but on what were seen as major questions members would go to war against each other with little compunction. The elaborate and hallowed structure of law which was supposed to govern relationships within the *Reich* offered endless opportunities for appeals to justice and opinion, and every state thought it worthwhile to woo support in the *Reichstag* and among other members; but the only advantage likely to accrue was moral.

However, this parallel, if pursued, brings out some of the strengths of the

---

[22] Bosbach, *Die 'Rêveries Politiques'*, pp. 147–8.
[23] The phrase comes from the *Essai sur les moeurs*, ch. 70 (ed. R. Pomeau (Paris, 1963) vol. 1, p. 683) and was apparently first added in the 1761 edition.

Empire. Within its borders, compact states scarcely existed. Virtually every ruler possessed lands detached from his main territory, and had to accept that other rulers held enclaves within it. Nearly all the states were landlocked, and the great rivers and roads passed through many jurisdictions. Hence each depended heavily on the goodwill of others, especially in such matters as trade, post and communications. It was to everyone's benefit to maintain imperial law in these fields.

Further, the *Reich* looked more significant to its southern and western than to its northern and eastern members (see Map 1). A series of large states controlled nearly all the land from the north down to the south-east: from north to south, three Protestant electorates, Hanover, Prussia and Saxony; then the two great Catholic states, the Monarchy and Bavaria. On the west, fragmentation reached its height. Moreover, here were concentrated what the Enlightenment saw as the greatest anomaly of the whole imperial structure, the ecclesiastical principalities.[24] In the western *Reich* most of the larger political units were prince-bishoprics: in the north Osnabrück, Münster, Hildesheim and Paderborn; along the Rhine the three archbishopric-electorates of Cologne, Trier and Mainz; and more than a dozen other sees ranging from Liège in the southern Netherlands to Würzburg and Bamberg in the centre, from Basle, Constance and Augsburg in the south to Salzburg and Passau bordering upper Austria. In each of these hybrid organisations the cathedral chapter elected an archbishop or bishop who was a secular ruler as well as a church dignitary. In many cases his diocese covered an area largely distinct from his state. As well as these bishoprics, a number of monasteries ranked as independent states.

Many implications followed from the existence of these ecclesiastical principalities. Enlightened and Protestant opinion was ready to abolish them, and their survival was evidently bound up with the survival of the *Reich*. They looked to Vienna as the capital of the German Counter-Reformation and of German Catholicism; they saw the emperor as their protector; and they seemed natural allies of the Monarchy against the Protestant bloc of the north and east. They were inclined to regard themselves as constituting the Empire *par excellence*. The elector of Mainz was *ex officio* arch-chancellor of the Empire, and as such necessarily involved in its administration.

In general, the existing German states accepted the existing imperial system. Interested Powers whose lands lay wholly or mainly outside the Empire also believed themselves to benefit from its maintenance, since they saw it as a means of neutralising Germany, or at least helping to preserve a balance of power within it. France especially considered the continuance of

---

[24] See for the ecclesiastical states esp. H. Raab, *Clemens Wenzeslaus von Sachsen und seine Zeit*, vol. I, pp. 9–21.

the *Reich* as vital to its own interests, and lavished money and diplomacy to attract support there.

It must seem surprising that Joseph should not have protested more seriously against having to undergo tiresome and antiquated formalities that involved his accepting a *Wahlkapitulation* under which he virtually renounced any sovereign rights as emperor. It appears, however, that at this period he did not fundamentally question the value of the imperial dignity to the house of Austria. His education had been heavily biased in the direction of preparing him for the role of emperor. Maria Theresa and Francis Stephen obviously had no doubt that the loss of the title to Bavaria in 1742 had been a disaster and that its recovery in 1745 and renewal in 1764 were of paramount importance to the Monarchy.[25] The reasons why Vienna cared so much about the Empire are best stated in a series of papers beginning with a questionnaire prepared, apparently under Joseph's auspices, in November 1766.[26] It was sent to Kaunitz and to two officials especially concerned with the affairs of the Empire: the imperial vice-chancellor, prince Rudolf Colloredo, head of the imperial bureaucracy in Vienna; and count Pergen, now a member of the *Staatsrat* but until recently the Monarchy's representative at the court of the elector of Mainz.[27]

The first question sets the tone of the whole:

1. In general, what sort of system to establish, in order somehow to take advantage of the favourable disposition of men's minds – a system which will involve this Monarchy ... in no damagingly high expenditure; which will raise imperial authority and make the states [*Stände*] see and acknowledge to the full that it is unavoidably necessary for their self-preservation; which will strengthen the devotion and sympathy of the well-disposed to the Archducal House ... [and] His Present Majesty ...; which will gradually lead the ill-disposed to a better way of thinking, and at least keep them from any too effective alliance among themselves, and especially with foreign Powers – until the domestic situation of this Monarchy permits the adoption of more positive measures; and, most important, will make it possible to present to everyone, whether well- or ill-disposed, the internal forces, constitution and power of this Monarchy and the true system of this Court (which exactly corresponds to them) as ... full of moderation and wholly without plans for aggrandisement, purely as a peace-loving defensive system?

It is impossible to tell what Joseph meant by the future 'adoption of more positive measures'. Perhaps he was thinking only of the proposals which he puts forward later in the same document. Some of these were in fact perfectly calculated to alarm the German states and give them a picture of his policy as aggressive and domineering. He asks, for example, what may be done to assist

[25] See Arneth, *GMT* VII, pp. 70–1, and *MTKuF* IV, pp. 271–83. Cf. pp. 25–7, 48 and 110 above.
[26] These questions are printed in K-M VI, pp. 479–82.
[27] It is curious that Aretin, *Reich*, vol. I, pp. 14, 188, 128, ascribes this exchange to 1764.

Catholic and other friendly states to enlarge their armies; how other Powers can be prevented from denuding the *Reich* of its inhabitants, even while the Monarchy is enabled to recruit there; how elections to archbishoprics, bishoprics and other spiritual and temporal positions in the *Reich* may be influenced so that the choice falls on those who are devoted to the imperial Court and well qualified to serve it as ambassadors and so on:

how commerce and coinage in the *Reich* may be put on such a footing that foreign Powers obtain from them the least, the states of the Empire on the other hand every possible, but above all this Monarchy the most and greatest, practical advantage?

Joseph asks

how the imperial feudal suzerainty in Germany and Italy might again be established, and all the powerful states brought to make proper feudal payments; how lapsed feudal rights and other encroachments might be recovered; and especially how the Republic of Genoa in Italy might be compelled to fulfil its duties as a vassal and observe its obligations to the emperor and the Empire.

Specific plans for aggrandisement, even through hereditary claims, scarcely appear. The successions to Bayreuth and Ansbach, Baden-Baden, Württemberg and Modena are mentioned. But Joseph writes rather of keeping them out of the hands of Prussia and her acolytes than of seizing them for the Monarchy. The only exception is Modena, where his brother Ferdinand was to marry the duke's heiress with the prospect of ultimate succession. However, Joseph's sixth question runs:

especially, how to behave towards the electorate of Bavaria and to draw that Court out of its recent lethargy and inaction, and to make it render itself useful to the emperor, the Empire and the Catholic religion; to bind it indissolubly to this august Court, to keep it from all further alliances with the Palatine electorate or still more with France, and first and foremost from all premature succession treaties; and particularly how to wean the Bavarian nation from its previous hereditary antipathy to the Austrian?

This question shows that he was aware of the Bavarian succession issue, but contains no hint of aggression on the subject. Of course he was still married to Josepha.

He stressed the importance of spreading dissension between Prussia and her allies, of dividing the Protestants, and of persuading the pope that the cause of Catholicism depended on the support of the Monarchy. Perhaps some gifted Protestant writers could be enlisted at moderate cost to generate trust and enthusiasm for himself and for the peaceful system of the Court of Vienna.

A few questions deal with entirely disinterested proposals for reform of the imperial courts. Otherwise, the document treats the Empire as little more than a convenient adjunct to the Monarchy, an aid to the domestic and especially to the foreign policy of the House of Habsburg. Joseph seems to have no doubt of the utility of his new position for the Monarchy. But he does not appear much concerned for the Empire in its own right.

Colloredo's lengthy memorandum in reply does little more than elaborate the possibilities, and suggest means of carrying out the plans implicit in Joseph's questions, while urging that the German states should be humoured by strict adherence on the emperor's part to the terms of his *Wahlkapitulation*.[28]

Pergen, however, appended to his answers a further document in which he offered replies to questions of his own, including these:

2nd: whether, and for what sort of reasons, [the imperial crown] ought to be regarded as of inestimable value to the August Archducal House? . . .
3rd: whether a Holy Roman Emperor could achieve anything great in the German Empire? . . .
4th: what essential advantages for his own House are to be obtained? . . .
5th: whether the possession of the imperial crown could be damaging?

He answers that the special privileges of the Habsburg lands within the Empire depend on the retention of the imperial crown by the dynasty; that the Monarchy has more friends among the German states because its ruler is the emperor; that the dignity enables its holder to recruit troops within Germany, to move his armies more freely through the country, to obtain military assistance from the states, to exact certain financial advantages and to augment the population of the Monarchy. He is the leader of the Catholic cause, which will be useful to him in a war against the Turks; and he has the prestige attaching to the first ruler of Christendom.

To be emperor could be disadvantageous only in the following circumstances:

if a ruling emperor showed signs of contempt for the German states, allowed indifference or neglect to appear in his treatment of affairs concerning the wellbeing of the *Reich*, gave ground for the suspicion that he was ready to misuse the power of his House to coerce states that did not wish to follow his advice, or evinced, by a notably high and despotic manner, warlike ambitions . . .

Then Prussia would be able to gather support from Catholic as well as Protestant states both inside and outside the *Reich*, to make the emperor detested and to do real damage to the Monarchy.

As for acquiring fame and respect in his capacity as emperor, there are plenty of abuses for him to remedy, in the administration of justice, feudal matters and the coinage, and he might aspire to mitigate the rivalry between religions. Thus he would have 'prepared the way to achieving greater things'.[29]

[28] For Colloredo's answers see K-M VI, pp. 482–502.
[29] Pergen's supplementary questions and answers are printed, together with an introduction which comments usefully on the whole exchange of views, in H. Voltelini, 'Eine Denkschrift

Kaunitz's reply was nearly as long as Colloredo's, but much more generalised.

At the start, the doubt must be settled whether it is worth the trouble to take on such a burden of government with the unremitting application that such a large, complicated and tottering machine as the present constitution of the *Reich* seems to require.

The revenues are only a shadow of what they once were. But all sorts of other advantages can come to the emperor from the Empire, of which Kaunitz gives a list much like Pergen's. None of them, however, will materialise unless, as Joseph has proposed, 'a genuine, well-founded system appropriate to the situation is laid down, and all measures conform to it'. 'Ruling without a system is like trusting a ship without rudder and compass to the winds and waves.'

The chancellor is now on his favourite ground. He lovingly develops an argument about the problems of system-making:

Most people hold ... that a political system ought to consist of nothing but the most refined maxims, the most subtle motives and the most secret devices.

This view seems to be founded chiefly on a kind of human pride, which despises the easy, straightforward and simple, and considers only the complex and artificial to be worthy of itself and its honour.

In fact, however, a genuine and well-based political system perfectly resembles a machine.

The simpler a machine is, and the fewer wheels it requires to effect the operation necessary to its purpose, the greater is its perfection.

A system depends above all on knowledge of the true end, the true means and the proper application of these means.

The end of Your Imperial Majesty's rule in the *Reich* is the true wellbeing of the Empire and the reconciliation of that prosperity with the prosperity of the august Archducal House.

Knowledge of the true means of achieving this double end and the proper applications of these means determines the system for governing the *Reich*, which is not to be confused with the *Reich*'s own system.

Kaunitz labours for some paragraphs more a series of Polonian distinctions between the useful and the harmful, the important and the unimportant, too much and too little, ideas and facts, before abruptly arriving at a general policy recommendation, which does not follow obviously from the long preamble:

Therefore compulsion, severity, haste, autocracy, oppression – in a word, the least shadow of a violent approach – must be kept far away from all decisions and enterprises of the imperial government. Instead, everything must be illuminated by the affection of the father of the *Reich*, trust, observance of the law, impartiality, patriotic spirit, majestic imperturbability, a true desire to succour the oppressed, comfort the weak, administer justice with the mildest hand, promote peace, avoid quarrels, give a

des Grafen Johann Anton Pergen über die Bedeutung der römischen Kaiserkrone für das Haus Österreich' in *GV*, pp. 152–68.

practical demonstration of the necessity of a head to the protection and peace of the whole, and draw ever closer the common bond between head and members.

After more high-sounding passages in a similar vein, Kaunitz reaches his sovereign remedy. As with the internal affairs of the Monarchy, 'no better, more reliable and in the nature of the case more suitable way exists to establish and carry through consistently a well-founded system . . . than the erection of a kind of council for the affairs of the *Reich*'.

Having at long last assigned to his proposed council – an imperial *Staatsrat* – the task of erecting the desired system for the Empire, Kaunitz settled down to answering the specific questions put by Joseph. The most interesting points he made concerned Bavaria. He acknowledged that Joseph's marriage with Josepha, though it had been envisaged as the best method of reconciling the two Powers, had totally failed in its object; and he referred to another memorandum he had prepared in which the question of the Bavarian succession was discussed. Kaunitz offered no criticism of any of the emperor's implied aims.[30]

This exchange of views took place in the course of (perhaps because of) a conflict between Joseph on the one hand, and his mother and Kaunitz on the other, over an imperial issue – by far the most serious such dispute during Joseph's co-regency. It is obvious that the interests of the emperor and those of the ruler of the Monarchy, if considered separately, would not always coincide. The emperor's bureaucracy for imperial affairs, the *Reichshofkanzlei* headed in Vienna by prince Colloredo, inevitably felt itself to be the rival of the Monarchy's administration under Kaunitz, and the two bodies often differed. Moreover, the emperor at his coronation swore to uphold decisions of the imperial courts, the most effective of which was the *Reichshofrat* or Aulic Council, based in Vienna. Nearly every imperial claim to authority and jurisdiction was disputed, but no question was more uncertain than that of imperial rights in Italy. All these aspects came together in the affair of San Remo.

For many centuries the Genoese republic had claimed and exercised sovereignty over San Remo, but in the 1750s some dissident inhabitants of the town appealed to the Aulic Council to intervene between them and the republic, on the ground that the emperor had rights of suzerainty there. The Aulic Council eventually took the case, and in 1764 upheld the emperor's claims. But Francis Stephen had been expected not to implement the decision, because the matter raised serious difficulties for the Monarchy. Genoa was a client-state of France, and the French were not prepared to see Genoese sovereignty impaired. Nor were they ready to allow the slightest assertion of imperial authority in Italy. From 1764 to 1767 inclusive, the correspondence

---

[30] Kaunitz's answers are printed in K-M VI , pp. 502–18. It seems from J. to L., 12 Dec. 1765 (Arneth, *MTuJ* I, p. 166) that J. had already thought of establishing such a council.

of the French envoys in Vienna is full of the issue. It was made clear to Austria
that the emperor must refrain from pressing his claims in San Remo if the
Monarchy wished to retain its alliance with France intact.[31]

Joseph, however, was less complaisant than his father, and brought fresh
zeal to the affairs of the Empire. Although Kaunitz kept on assuring the
French that nothing concrete would be done, Joseph let the laborious
processes of the Aulic Council grind on and eventually endorsed its judgement
in his favour. When the chancellor tried to commit him to moderation –
perhaps it was not accidental that the attempt was made while Joseph was
away on manoeuvres in Bohemia – this reply came back on 10 September
1766:

I have just read quickly Kaunitz's draft for the S. Remo affair. It seems to me that its
basis is inaction, which in my opinion has been wrongly adopted up to now. The
substance of the whole letter [is] verbiage; and the motive a puerile fear of displeasure,
[at once] very remote and certain to be without result.[32]

Next day he dictated a virulent memorandum:

Conviction, duty and necessity have decided me not to let the affair of San Remo lapse
again. Authentic documents show well enough the undoubted rights of the emperor
over this town. The enforcement of strict justice towards the weak and the oppressed,
without favour or political aims, is the duty of every honest spirit . . . I have said words
which I thought, think, and the meaning of which it was for me alone to interpret. This
verbosely written screed basically consists of nothing other than [the recommendation]
that the case should be dropped . . . If I allow my judgement to be declared, I approve
its being carried out . . .

Should I sacrifice duty, honour and reputation, which I have staked only in the most
crucial cases and in the most important matters of state; should I go back on my word,
which I gave not casually but after consideration, with an empty excuse that a child
would deride – and all for the sake of a particular friendship of Choiseul with Sorba, the
patriotism of a Grimaldi and concern for his convenience . . .?

In brief, this paper not only fails to state what I am going to do in this case, but it also
twists my words. In order that Her Majesty the Empress shall be brought into collision
with me and her sacred word be given in a matter where she cannot promise and I
cannot uphold her, there is to be no justice done in the case itself, and I am to appear
before foreign Courts as a phantom, of whom people would have it believed that he
intended something different from what the words he uttered meant, and as a proper
minister's puppet. I can therefore do nothing but send it back, reject it, disavow it;
and, best of all, just forget it.[33]

The empress acknowledged: 'It is your affair, it is a question of justice, I enter
into it only as a party to the peace of Aix[-la-Chapelle].' Kaunitz, not
surprisingly, was 'mortified', and on that account Maria Theresa took the

[31] The notes made available to me by Dr H. M. Scott are the basis of this section. The reference is
AAE CP (Autriche), 299–308. The San Remo affair is both complex and obscure, and deserves
study.
[32] Arneth, *MTuJ* I, pp. 193–4.   [33] *Ibid.*, pp. 194–6nn.

opportunity to write perhaps the most devastating of all her rebukes to her son, which it will be appropriate to consider in the content of the co-regency.[34] When Colloredo, Pergen and Kaunitz replied to Joseph's questions about the *Reich*, the dispute was still smouldering. The emperor appeared to be intent on sacrificing the interests of the Monarchy, as understood by the empress and the chancellor, to the interests of the Empire as he saw them. There were thus excellent reasons for Kaunitz's cautious generalisations and counsels of prudence, coupled of course with protestations of deference to Joseph's wishes. The chancellor had to spend much effort in the next few months reassuring France that the emperor's attitude over San Remo did not imply opposition to the French alliance: Joseph was only doing his duty; he was not coquettish enough for a mistress like France; there was no need 'to be frightened by phantoms, the results of ancient prejudices'. The French refused to be wooed, and placed troops at the disposal of Genoa in case the emperor tried to enforce the decree. In consequence, it was a dead letter.[35]

Joseph gave his own account of imperial affairs down to the spring of 1768 in a document referred to as the 'General picture of the affairs of the Monarchy'. This was composed in order to inform Leopold of the developments that had taken place in all departments since he had left for Tuscany in 1765, just after Francis Stephen had died and Joseph become emperor. Here I shall deal only with what Joseph has to say in connexion with the internal affairs of the *Reich*. But it should be made clear that he discusses them within the context of the foreign situation and policy of the Monarchy. The overriding aim, he insists, with a firmness which neither Maria Theresa nor Kaunitz could have bettered, is to preserve the peace, in order to give the Monarchy time to recover its strength and restore its finances after a crippling war.[36]

He first allows himself a short general introduction on the Empire:

Although I have been its head for more than two years, I should nevertheless find it impossible to explain to you in detail the system. It exists only in books, and I should defy even Montesquieu to define it as it is at present observed by the different princes

---

[34] *Ibid.*, p. 201 (M.T. to J., 14 Sep. 1766). See pp. 147–8 below.

[35] Arneth & Flammermont II, pp. 320–31; AAE CP (Autriche), 307, K. to Choiseul, 28 Jan. 1767; Durfort to Choiseul, 11 Feb. 1767.

[36] HHSA FA Sbde 88 contains two copies of most of this document (see p. 177, n. 136). The section on the Empire, translated into German from the original French, is printed by H. Conrad, 'Verfassung und politische Lage des Reiches in einer Denkschrift Josephs II. von 1767/68', in *Festschrift Nikolaus Grass*, ed. L. Carlen and F. Steinegger, 2 vols. (Innsbruck, 1974) vol. I, pp. 161–85. I owe the reference to this article to the late Prof. W. Ullmann.

The final form of the document must date from March–April 1768, since the election of the elector of Trier on 10 Feb. 1768 is referred to, and J.'s report on his visit to the Banat, which started in April, is not. The visit is mentioned in notes for a 'Supplement au Tableau General des Affaires de la Monarchie, fait en 1768' (also in HHSA FA Sbde 88). Cf. Conrad in *Festschrift Nikolaus Grass*, vol. I, p. 161n, and Arneth, *GMT* VII, p. 526; and see pp. 176–8, 273–7 below.

and states. Everyone thinks only of himself, and seems to have taken it as his rule to encroach on others. Each religion, each unit, every little individual has a way of looking at things which is appropriate to his petty policies, convenience or interest, and governs his actions only in accordance with principles which do not contribute to the general wellbeing. They recognise no chief except in name, and his authority as well as that of the laws has force only in so far as it suits them. Justice always gives way to politics; a wrongdoer, provided he is sustained by force, can go unpunished and be notorious without incurring disrepute ... The capitulations have in any case so restricted the imperial dignity and authority that not only is the emperor prevented from acting according to his good pleasure, but he cannot even work for the general good though the whole world recognises it.

The efforts of France and other Powers help to maintain the disunity of the Empire. 'The immediate [*unmittelbar*] nobility and some free cities are the most sincerely attached to the emperor; it is on account of their weakness that they need our support, but they are also of very little use.'

'It is impossible', Joseph continues, 'to undertake or to hope for anything great.' Plainly, he has rejected the enthusiastic approach of Pergen. The control exercised by Prussia directly over the Protestant states and through them indirectly over the whole Empire– a domination 'more imperious and despotic than the most powerful and absolute emperor could [wield]' – makes it impossible for even the best-intentioned emperor to achieve anything, at least until he has managed to correct the false views of the German rulers, their distrust of him and their suspicion that he intends to aggrandise the Monarchy at their expense.

This requires much time, trouble and patience, but above all skilful negotiators, intelligent and versed in the constitutions of the Empire and in the natural interests of each Court; instruments rather rare with us, and which it would be necessary to fashion as the first stage in this great work.

What, then, can 'an emperor zealous for the good of his country' try to do 'at the present juncture, and until such time as the state of affairs in the Empire and in Europe in general takes on a more promising appearance'? He can seek to gain confidence by straightforwardness and equity, and by not giving the slightest provocation, and try also

to preserve for as long as possible the sad relics of the old imperial authority, and to keep them from the total destruction which seems roughly to correspond with the intentions not only of foreign Powers but of the states of the Empire themselves, who are the most interested in conserving this species of anarchy.

What still remained of it in the preceding reigns was chiefly confined to the jurisdiction of the tribunals of the Empire, and to the feudal rights which the states, even the most powerful, used to recognise publicly and in the most solemn fashion by the investiture which they were obliged to obtain from the emperor. I found these two columns of the former majesty of the Empire in a very shaky condition, and this vast edifice, propped up by such feeble buttresses, on the point of crumbling. To prevent so imminent and fatal a collapse, we started with what was most pressing; and since, as you know, of the two great tribunals of the Empire, only the Aulic Council depends solely on the emperor (the Imperial Chamber [*Reichskammergericht*] at Wetzlar being almost entirely in the hands of the states), we took as our first concern the reform of the former of these tribunals, into which a great many abuses had entered, together with faults of substance and of personalities, which had caused it to lose almost completely the confidence of the states of the Empire ... and had supplied pretexts ... for these frequent *Rekurse* to the Diet, a method newly invented to avoid all the judgements, even the most just, of the tribunals of the Empire.

Constitutionally, the *Reichshofrat* lapsed at the death of an emperor. Joseph ordered it to continue its work on a provisional basis until he could decide how best to reform it. He re-established it in April 1766, but at that time some of the changes which he most desired, involving longer sittings, were so strongly opposed by the members that he abandoned them, while publicly expressing his 'displeasure' that the Council's zeal for justice, 'if not extinct, was now much blunted'.[37] Even so, he could say to Leopold that the relevant 'ordinance, which is printed and in the hands of the whole world, has had a good reception in the Empire and ... has to some degree restored confidence'. He got his way on the disputed questions by a decree of 21 October 1767,[38] to which he refers in the following passage:

Disinterestedness being the foundation of a supreme department of justice, I have just forbidden very solemnly all presents, under whatever name, even if hitherto custom-ary, and I have declared that those who contravene this decree will have verdicts in their favour set aside. To speed up the litigation, the tribunal sits an extra day a week, and even has one session a week after dinner; and every day the Council has to sit an hour longer than previously.

Joseph next discussed the reform of the *Reichskammergericht*. His father had proposed in 1764 that a 'visitation' of the Chamber should be arranged. No such enquiry had been instituted since the 1710s, when, according to Joseph, the effort of many years had yielded meagre results. He renewed his father's proposal, and the machinery was set in motion.[39] But it was obstructed by concerted opposition from the Protestant states, whose object seemed to be

[37] For this row see K-M VI, pp. 174–5, 432–41; O. von Gschliesser, *VKNGÖ*, vol. XXXIII: *Der Reichshofrat* (Vienna, 1942; facsimile edn 1970), pp. 469–72; L. Gross, *Die Geschichte der deutschen Reichshofkanzlei von 1559 bis 1806*, Inventare des Wiener HHSA, I (Vienna, 1933), p. 87. See n. 39.

[38] This decree, which seems to have escaped the attention of the editor of K-M and of the authors referred to in the previous note, and therefore of Aretin (*Reich*, vol. I, p. 101), is mentioned by A. Wolf and H. von Zwiedineck-Südenhorst, *Oesterreich unter Maria Theresia, Josef II. und Leopold II.*, ed. W. Oncken, *Allgemeine Geschichte*, III.9 (Berlin, 1884), p. 128. Portions of it, and other interesting material on the reform of the *Reichshofrat*, of which he was a member, were printed by F. C. von Moser in his *Patriotisches Archiv für Deutschland*, VIII (1788), 77–108 and X (1789), 345–418.

[39] R. Smend, *Das Reichskammergericht*, Quellen und Studien zur Verfassungsgeschichte des Deutschen Reiches in Mittelalter und Neuzeit, ed. K. Zeumer, Band IV, Heft 3 (Weimar, 1911), pp. 232–40, is the authority.

to worsen the evil, and to annihilate completely, or at least to weaken as much as possible, the authority so necessary for the preservation of a tribunal which is the only protection remaining to most of them against the oppression of some of their co-states.

He could report no progress, and was beginning to wonder whether to give up the visitation altogether, 'which costs a lot without any return'.

So far as both tribunals were concerned, he was keenly aware of the uselessness of their passing judgements if powerful parties paid no attention to them, and claimed to spend much time and trouble trying to get the decisions implemented. He mentioned also attempts he was making to meet complaints from the Protestants that they were treated less favourably than the Catholics in imperial matters.

Strangely, he did not refer to another reform of some importance which had provoked opposition from other Powers and from the elector of Mainz as arch-chancellor of the Empire. In January 1767 Joseph established the Conference for the Affairs of the *Reich* which Kaunitz considered so necessary, consisting of Colloredo, Pergen and Borié. The objection to this change – and other administrative arrangements made by the new emperor – was that it restricted the influence of Colloredo and the *Reichshofkanzlei* in particular, and in general of those whose main concern was with the Empire rather than with the Monarchy. Choiseul, the French prime minister, described it wildly as 'the most pernicious gathering imaginable'.[40]

On another issue Joseph made a characteristic pronouncement:

Being an enemy . . . of all the minutiae of useless ceremony and Asiatic pomp, which is no longer appropriate in the century and the circumstances in which we find ourselves, I have already declared to the electors that I will in no way stand on it, and that, so long as they will recognise and actually swear the oath as vassals, it will not matter to me in the slightest whether I see their representatives upright or kneeling, whether they kiss the pommel of the sword or not.

After running through the individual states of major significance, Joseph summed up as follows:

You see . . . that the picture I drew for you at the beginning . . . was not exaggerated, and that it is only by a miracle, or rather by the mutual jealousy of foreign Powers, that an entity so irregular still survives. The best remedy for so many disorders would be a satisfactory 'perpetual Capitulation', which has already once been mooted at the Diet, and of which there already exists a well-developed draft that, without prejudicing the

Epstein, *Conservatism*, p. 241, may mislead students by his statement that Smend deals only with early history. In fact his volume, though described as vol. I (and no more appeared), deals with the history of the Court down to 1806.

Conversely, Epstein in the same place describes Gschliesser on the *Reichshofrat* as definitive, when it consists only of a slim general introduction followed by a series of biographical entries on each of the members of the tribunal, dressed up as a coherent account.

On the *Reichskammergericht* see also Aretin, *Reich*, vol. I, pp. 98–102.

[40] Gross, *Reichshofkanzlei*, pp. 87–92, 184–7. AAE CP (Autriche), 307: Choiseul to Durfort, 27 Feb. 1767.

reasonable liberty of the states, at least gives the emperor the power that he needs to maintain the laws and good order, and to sustain the weak against the oppression of the powerful. But this is not a note to strike in the present critical circumstances.

All that can be done at the moment, he concludes, is to try to persuade the states that one means well and has no desire for aggrandisement.

Questions concerning the internal affairs of the Empire soon became secondary to issues more naturally regarded as aspects of the Monarchy's foreign policy, principally the problem of the Bavarian succession and the campaign to procure the election of Joseph's youngest brother, Max Franz, as coadjutor or successor-designate to the electorate of Cologne. These topics will be discussed later. But it is convenient here to carry the account of the domestic (excluding the ecclesiastical) affairs of the *Reich* down to 1780.

The reform of the *Reichshofrat* seems to have borne fruit. Litigation proceeded more quickly, and the tribunal became more popular. The number of cases dealt with each year rose from 2088 in 1767 to 3388 in 1779. So effective were Joseph's efforts to ensure that this overwhelmingly Catholic body should treat Protestants fairly that the Catholics began to complain of discrimination against themselves.[41] The tribunal appears in many instances to have successfully upheld the claims of subjects and Estates against princes. In particular Joseph insisted on backing its decision in favour of the Estates of Württemberg and against its extravagant ruler, duke Charles Eugene, who eventually gave way.[42]

It was another story with the visitation of the *Reichskammergericht*. Goethe again comes to our aid here. In 1772 he observed for some months the visitatorial proceedings at Wetzlar, as part of his training in the law. He had no doubt that the tribunal needed reform, and especially that it was under-staffed. But he viewed Joseph's intervention, at least in retrospect, from the standpoint of the states:

Without asking whether it was his imperial right, without seeing his way to a successful outcome, he proposed the visitation and hastened its opening. For 160 years no regular visitation had taken place: a monstrous chaos of papers had mounted up and increased every year, since the seventeen assessors were not even able to despatch the current business. Twenty thousand cases had piled up; sixty could be disposed of every year, and every year double that number was initiated. In addition, it was by no means a small number of 'revisions' that awaited the attention of the visitors; it was estimated at fifty thousand ... But the most critical matter of all was the personal delinquency of some assessors ...

[41] Gschliesser, *Reichshofrat*, pp. 38–9, 64.
[42] Aretin, *Reich*, vol. I, pp. 30–1. For this and the next few paragraphs see F. Hertz, 'Die Rechtssprechung der höchsten Reichsgerichte im römisch-deutschen Reich', *MÖIG*, LXIX (1961), 331–58. On the extraordinary case of Württemberg, from two utterly different standpoints, Yorke-Long, *Music at Court*, ch. 2; F. L. Carsten, *Princes and Parliaments in Germany* (Oxford, 1959), pp. 133–48. See now J. A. Vann, *The Making of a State: Württemberg, 1593–1793* (London, 1984), ch. 7.

Worthy German industriousness, which was more directed to the collection and elaboration of details than to results, found here an inexhaustible impulse to ever renewed activity . . .

Here was the Holy Roman Empire once more assembled, not for mere outward show, but for the most fundamental business. But even here I thought of that half-empty banqueting hall on coronation day, where the bidden stayed away, because they were too proud. Here, indeed, they had come; but even worse symptoms were to be seen. The want of coherence in the whole, the mutual opposition of the parts, were continually apparent; and it was no secret that princes had privately confided to each other the intention to see whether something could not on this occasion be wrung from the sovereign . . .[43]

Goethe's figures may be wrong – an even higher total of cases pending, sixty thousand, is commonly given.[44] Otherwise his picture is only too accurate. The visitation proceedings lasted nine years. Joseph tried to implement the resulting recommendation to increase the number of assessors, but this took a further seven years, and even then the money to pay them was not forthcoming. Despite the fantastic backlog of work, the *Reichskammergericht*, when it resumed operations, found itself so little respected that the number of cases brought before it – in any case much smaller than came to the *Reichshofrat* – fell steadily, and the new assessors often had nothing to do![45] The emperor's initiative had received publicity in the lengthy writings of the visitation period as an instance of high-handedness rather than as an example of benevolence, and the main German rulers evidently took great offence at it.[46]

Apart from legal reforms, the relations between emperor and Empire were largely a matter of propaganda. Moser came to Vienna in 1766, and wrote *What is Good in an Emperor . . .?* and subsequent imperialist tracts as a secret pensioner of Joseph's, to the tune of 2000 florins a year. But even this exceptional extravagance was said by Colloredo to be unproductive, since the identity of the author and the nature of his connexion with the emperor were guessed; and, though virtually every German writer of the period earned his living in the service of some government, to work for Joseph was represented as peculiarly dishonourable and unpatriotic.[47]

An imperial prerogative which it is relevant to discuss here is the *Bücherregal*, which amounted to a general oversight of publications throughout the *Reich*. Prior censorship – the scrutiny and perhaps the modification or banning of printed materials before they were even published – was carried

---

[43] *Goethes Werke*, vol. IX, pp. 530–1(*Dichtung und Wahrheit*, book 12).
[44] Epstein, *Conservatism*, p. 241.
[45] Aretin, *Reich*, vol. I, pp. 101–2; Smend, *Reichskammergericht*, pp. 237–40.
[46] See, e.g. Suffolk to Keith, cypher, 16 Aug. 1774 (PRO SP 80/216) encl. Alvensleben to Suffolk, 11 Aug.; Keith to Suffolk, cypher, 21 Jan., 18 Feb., 1 Mar., 4 Mar. 1775 (SP 80/217). M. Walker, *Johann Jakob Moser and the Holy Roman Empire of the German Nation* (Chapel Hill, 1981), pp. 317–23.
[47] Gschliesser, *Reichshofrat*, pp. 475–8; K-M VI, pp. 177, 493; Sheldon, *Möser*, p. 66.

out by all the states of the Empire more or less effectively and strictly. The emperor could do little more than watch over this process, though he sometimes supplemented the efforts of the lesser governments. His main opportunities for action lay, first, in his undoubted right to grant to an author, publisher or printer the 'sole' privilege of reprinting some work, and secondly, in the control he exercised, jointly with the pope's representative, over the commission which regulated the great book fair at Frankfurt.

So far as the privilege of reprinting was concerned, it was sought after – and paid for – because it offered the beneficiary some protection, over large areas of the *Reich*, against pirated editions. But the safeguards were incomplete, since the big states like Prussia – and the Monarchy itself – also dealt in these grants, and it was obviously difficult to enforce them over the whole of Germany.

As for the commission at Frankfurt, it was effective to a point. Goethe describes the burning of a book at the order of the censors, the impact the event had on him and the desire it evoked in him to get hold of the condemned text.[48] The rival fair at Leipzig, safe within the borders of Saxony, prospered at the expense of Frankfurt's because its rulers were less restrictive. But when in 1774 a small state set up another competitor at Hanau, the emperor's power was sufficient to stifle the enterprise within a year. Moreover, he promoted editions published in the Monarchy in rivalry to Leipzig's.

At the beginning of his reign, Joseph's henchmen at Frankfurt were banning, among other works, the complete writings of Montaigne and Voltaire, Bayle's *Dictionnaire* and Montesquieu's *Esprit des lois*. The emperor was so zealous in maintaining his rights that he was rebuked by the *Reichshofrat* for acting without its co-operation, which was constitutionally required. It was presumably due at least in part to Joseph's own attitude that the censor became more liberal as time went on. In 1780 he appointed a Protestant book commissar in Frankfurt, severing the link with the church. It is interesting that one of the motives of liberalisation was apparently to keep his imperial prerogative respected.[49]

As has been said, Joseph wished to revive the practice whereby German rulers were invested with their lands by the emperor or his representative, a tradition which had lost much of its force since the sixteenth century, especially during the reign of the weak Bavarian, Charles VII (1742–5). The acceptance of investiture not only amounted to an acknowledegment of the emperor's suzerainty, it also involved making substantial payments to imperial agents and agencies. Joseph had some success with the lesser princes,

[48] *Goethes Werke*, vol. IX, pp. 150–1.
[49] For this whole section see the interesting study by U. Eisenhardt, *Die kaiserliche Aufsicht über Buchdruck, Buchhandel und Presse im Heiligen Römischen Reich Deutscher Nation (1496–1806)* (Karlsruhe, 1970); also F. Lehne, 'Zur Rechtsgeschichte der kaiserlichen Druckprivilegien', *MÖIG*, LIII (1939), esp. pp. 396–7, 407.

particularly the bishops and other clergy, partly by suing them in the imperial courts. But the last investiture of an elector had taken place in 1748, and the major rulers were not to be tempted by Joseph's mitigation of the ceremonial. In fact his pressure on them in this matter only increased their exasperation with his rule.[50]

There was not much prospect of Joseph increasing his power as emperor. But on balance, his early reforms, associated with an ostentatiously pacific policy, appear to have enhanced his reputation. It is notable that in 1769 Klopstock, an already famous German poet residing at a safe distance in Copenhagen, should have dedicated to Joseph his *Hermannsschlacht*, a glorification of the struggle of the Germans against the invading Romans.[51] Even in 1778 Herder's *To the Emperor* begged him to 'give us what we thirst after, a German fatherland, and a law and a beautiful language and sincere religion'. The fact that Joseph had founded two years earlier a German national theatre in Vienna helps to account for this fantasy. But his policy in the Bavarian question destroyed his benevolent image in the Empire.[52]

In considering Joseph's attitude to imperial matters, it is important to realise that the German state that claimed the widest privileges against the Empire was none other than the Monarchy. Austria itself was exempt from the usual imperial investiture. Vienna ran its own post, refusing to allow the imperial post to participate except in outlying territories. No ruler was more jealous than Maria Theresa of the right not to be judged by the imperial courts. The same applied to the imperial censorship and printing privileges.[53]

The empress had played a large part in procuring her son's election as king of the Romans. Just after he succeeded his father as emperor, while protesting that she normally held aloof from imperial affairs, she actively promoted Joseph's reform of the two tribunals. She even exchanged roles with him, telling Pergen in Mainz: 'all these great changes can be done only at a stroke; if there is too much deliberation, they do not come off'.[54] But as early as November 1765 she was saying that Joseph was in control in the *Reich*, and later she remarked that he would not listen to others on imperial matters.[55]

---

[50] J.-F. Noël, 'Zur Geschichte der Reichsbelehnungen im 18. Jhdt.', *MÖSA*, XXI (1968), 106–22; and e.g., Keith to Suffolk, private and confidential, cypher, 12 Dec. 1774 (PRO SP 80/216).

[51] *Goethes Werke*, vol. IX, p. 535. See the whole paragraph which begins by referring to the dedication to Joseph.

[52] Bruford, *Germany in the Eighteenth Century*, pp. 198–9. See pp. 230–6 and ch. 13 below. I am grateful to Professor E. Wangermann for sending me his article, 'Deutscher Patriotismus und österreichischer Reformabsolutismus im Zeitalter Josephs II.', *WBGN*, IX (1982), 60–72.

[53] Benna, *MÖSA* (1971), 5–7; Mechtler, 'Der Kampf zwischen Reichspost und Hofpost', *MÖIG*, LIII (1939), 411–22; references in n. 49 above.

[54] Arneth, *MTKuF* IV, p. 289 (13 Nov. 1765).

[55] M.T. to Pergen, 13 Nov. 1765 (Arneth, *MTKuF* IV, p. 289); M.T. to K. (perhaps 1767, as Arneth says, or conceivably from the time of the row over San Remo in the previous autumn), *ibid*. IV, p. 156.

The San Remo affair showed how seriously the interests of Emperor and Monarchy could clash. Thereafter, although the emperor's assertions of his imperial rights, by offending states inside and outside the *Reich*, continued to embarrass the makers of the Monarchy's foreign policy, in general Joseph treated the interests of the Empire as subordinate. His declining concern with imperial matters is reflected in the fact that he never attended the Conference on *Reich* affairs, established after so much paper warfare in 1767, and allowed it to lapse when two of its members moved to other duties in 1772. Whereas he considered it essential to travel all over the Monarchy, and to visit other European states, he showed no desire whatever to see the lands of the Empire.[56]

[56] Gross, *Reichshofkanzlei*, p. 186. For J.'s travel plans, see below, pp. 251–2.
    This account is based mainly on published sources, and I have not ventured on the massive *Reich* documentation in the HHSA. There must be much scope here for further research.
    Mr T. Krause kindly read this chapter for me.

CHAPTER 6

Mother, son and minister:
the early years of the co-regency, 1765–1768

Francis Stephen died at the age of only fifty-six on 18 August 1765. His end came suddenly and without warning. The Court was at Innsbruck for the wedding of Leopold with the king of Spain's daughter, Maria Luisa. The emperor had been to the theatre, where he had sat through 'a serious play of Goldoni's, *Il tutore*, and the ballet of *Iphigénie*, as long as it is sad'. On his way to his rooms, he collapsed. Joseph was at hand, prevented his father from falling, and helped to carry him into a servant's room and lay him on the bed. But by the time confessor, doctor and surgeon could arrive, Francis was dead.[1]

In making the necessary arrangements after the emperor's death, wrote Khevenhüller, 'the present young lord [Joseph] came to our aid with great fortitude and prudence, although (as I cannot deny him my faithful witness) he was most profoundly affected'. Maria Theresa was shattered, and thought of abdicating. Kaunitz dissuaded her, but she still talked of 'never again appearing before the world'. The court went into deepest mourning.[2]

After lengthy searches, Joseph eventually found his father's will in the Vienna town house. It contained numerous specific bequests, some of them designed to secure to his family a private fortune. But its essential point was that the heir to the rest of the vast inheritance should be the eldest son living at the time of the emperor's death, provided that he was of age. So, to his mother's consternation, Joseph became master of something like twenty million florins in bonds and money alone, together with land worth thirteen million.[3]

---

[1] K-M VI, pp. 123–6. The composer of the ballet was Gassmann (Zechmeister, *Die Wiener Theater*, p. 269).

[2] K-M VI, pp. 126–39, esp. 126 (18 Aug. 1765) and 139 (7 Sept.); Beer, *JLuK*, pp. 432, 501 (letters of M.T. to K., quoted on pp. 140, 144–5 below).

[3] The finding of the will in K-M VI, p. 139; text pp. 396–402 (an extraordinary example of French well written but crazily, though phonetically, spelled). Mikoletzky, *Franz I. und der Ursprung des Familienvermögens*. The total figure is hard to be sure about. I am working on J.'s figure of eighteen million, plus perhaps two million in Tuscany. Dr P. G. M. Dickson has helped me greatly here, and his account, when published, will clarify matters. See pp. 151–3, 162 below. M.T.'s displeasure in a letter to K., preserved with J. to K., 9 Sept. 1765 (in HHSA FA Sbde 70).

On 17 September Maria Theresa declared him co-regent, expecting, she said, that the same advantages would accrue from the appointment as in his father's case 'to our peace of mind, to the benefit of our dynasty and to the welfare of all true subjects'. She added that she made this arrangement 'without however surrendering the whole or any part of our personal sovereignty over our states, which will continue to be kept together, and moreover without the least actual or apparent breach of the Pragmatic Sanction'. Joseph accepted in these terms:

We, Joseph the Second, by God's grace elected Roman Emperor, perpetual enlarger of the Empire, King in Germany, heir to the kingdoms of Hungary, Bohemia, Dalmatia, Croatia, Slavonia, etc., Archduke of Austria, Duke of Burgundy, Lorraine and Bar, Grand Duke of Tuscany etc., ... most thankfully accept the transfer thus signified to us of the joint administration and joint rule of the aforesaid united hereditary kingdoms and lands, and likewise we shall always direct our whole care and all our most strenuous efforts ... to fulfil so far as possible the great expectation of Her Royal and Imperial Apostolic Majesty our most beloved lady mother that her hard task of ruling will thereby be eased.

We further bind ourselves in the strongest possible manner by means of the present ceremonial renunciations ... to everything which is included and stated in the above-mentioned document about the undiminished force of the Pragmatic Sanction, and especially about the express reservation of the sole and single inherent and continuing sovereignty over the hereditary kingdoms and lands to our dearest lady mother's Imperial and Royal Apostolic Majesty, against which ... the co-regency ... cannot weigh in the slightest, and to derogate from which is utterly remote from our intentions.[4]

At the same time Maria Theresa gave to Joseph the general control over the army which Francis, at least nominally, had previously exercised.[5]

Joseph thus acquired vast duties – potentially. But except in his capacities as emperor and heir to his father, he owed his position solely to his mother's grants, and was in law completely subject to her ultimate authority. She could give him as co-regent almost everything, or relatively little, to do; but in neither case did she have to accord him any power. They were not, as is sometimes said,[6] both co-regents. He was the co-regent; she was the ruler. He pointed out the difficulties inherent in such an arrangement, but was persuaded to acquiesce in it.[7]

Historians have scarcely stopped to enquire why Joseph was made co-regent.[8] There are obvious simple explanations such as were included in the official deed of appointment: Maria Theresa was used to being assisted by a co-regent; she was ageing and grief-stricken, had seriously considered abdi-

[4] K-M VI, pp. 394–5. A separate act was necessary for Hungary.
[5] Arneth, *GMT* VII, pp. 184–5.
[6] E.g. E. Hubert, 'Joseph II', in *Cambridge Modern History*, vol. VI (Cambridge, 1909), p. 627.
[7] See pp. 199–200, 219–20 below.
[8] I know only of the two pages in Reinöhl, *MÖIG* Ergänzungsband (1929), pp. 659–61.

cation and intended to remain in seclusion; she needed support more than ever. No doubt, so far as they went, these reasons were genuine. But we know that the issue was discussed on a quite different basis, at Maria Theresa's request, by certain officials; and it is reasonable to infer that other considerations, too delicate to be more than hinted at, played a part.

When Francis had been made co-regent, the main political purpose in view had been to help secure for him the imperial crown. In 1765 the problem of the *Reich* arose again, though in a rather different form. It was an accepted element in the imperial constitution that the emperor must himself possess enough land to maintain the integrity of the Empire and resist the Turks. In 1740 it had been hoped to enable Francis to meet this criterion by giving him a title of sorts to all the Habsburg lands – namely, the co-regency. In 1765 Joseph possessed in his own right even less than his father had in 1740, since he had just signed away his rights to Tuscany in favour of Leopold. Of the lands Joseph had inherited directly from his father, the duchy of Teschen was soon to be surrendered to Albert and Marie Christine, and even the tiny county of Falkenstein on the French border was administered as part of the Monarchy. Although he had now succeeded as emperor, it was agreed that he must be supplied with the territorial power to validate his position. Maria Theresa consulted old Bartenstein, who had been her principal adviser in 1740, and also his son, now an imperial official.[9] Both declared that either Joseph must be ceded a portion of the Monarchy as his own, or he must be made co-regent. The latter was clearly more desirable, since it would not breach the Pragmatic Sanction or divide the Monarchy's army, and would expose Joseph only to 'those counsels which are directed towards the advantage of the lands of the Monarchy and the interest of the dynasty that is bound up with them'.

A possible objection to appointing him co-regent was that Hungary might resist it, as had happened in the case of Francis in 1741, when the diet had taken the opportunity to tie his hands for the future. The Bartensteins saw no need to consult the diet this time. Fortunately, it was not in session. Maria Theresa could merely, by her prerogative, declare Joseph co-regent.

Behind the arguments about his status as emperor, and behind his mother's relief when Kaunitz undertook to bring about the co-regency,[10] can surely be discerned more serious anxieties. The emperor was the senior crowned head of Europe; in principle he conducted his own foreign policy; he had his own bureaucracy, Court and courts; he possessed a variety of minor powers and rights which, used against the Monarchy, could be highly inconvenient; in

---

[9] The advice of the two Bartensteins is printed in K-M VI, pp. 381–95. Quotation from p. 387. On Falkenstein, K. Oberdorffer, 'Die Reichsgrafschaft Falkenstein' in *Vorderösterreich*, ed. F. Metz (2nd edn, Freiburg, 1967), pp. 565–78.

[10] See below, p. 140.

certain circumstances he could raise an imperial army, which he had the right to command. Clearly, immense harm could be done to the Monarchy by a wilful emperor acting independently. If it was felt necessary to make Joseph co-regent in order to satisfy the imperial constitution, the appointment could be at least equally valuable in restricting his freedom of action as emperor, and harnessing his policies, rights, powers and prestige in that capacity to the service of the Monarchy. Maria Theresa and her chancellor had good reason to expect squalls ahead, and the establishment of the co-regency ought to limit the damage they would do.

To a considerable degree, then, Joseph owed the co-regency to the fact that he was emperor. The question at once arose: what power was he to be allowed as co-regent within the Monarchy? The French envoy expressed the general opinion when he said: 'we have seen from the way things have gone on up to now that the title of co-regent carries with it no share of authority'.[11] But he exaggerated; and old Bartenstein thought Joseph ought to be seen to exercise some power, for the sake of his standing in the Empire. Young Bartenstein ventured briefly beyond his proper sphere to touch on the problems that the co-regency might create for the government of the Monarchy. If, he said, Maria Theresa found herself differing from her co-regent, she could always ask the opinion of the *Staatsrat*; its members had been carefully chosen in the past and could be equally carefully selected in future; no one could blame her for accepting the majority view of the *Staatsrat* even if it went against her son's. So the council of state could be seen as a means of nullifying the opportunities ostensibly given to Joseph by the co-regency, at any rate in domestic affairs.[12]

A further consideration was mentioned by the Sardinian ambassador and by him alone:

I am convinced [he wrote] that this princess ... will not delay in having him declared co-regent, a step useful for the internal constitution of the different provinces and absolutely necessary for external relations, since [otherwise] for example, the Austrian armies could no longer be reckoned imperial or enjoy the prerogatives which belong to them in that capacity.[13]

Ambassadors quite often get the wrong end of the stick. But it does seem possible that Joseph's position as head of the Monarchy's army was materially strengthened by his being both co-regent and emperor: enabling him perhaps as emperor to claim for all the Monarchy's troops passage across Germany, and to recruit in the Empire for the army of Maria Theresa. This is a most obscure but clearly important question, worthy of further study.[14]

[11] Chatelet to Praslin, 18 Aug. 1765 (AAE CP (Autriche), 303).   [12] K-M VI, pp. 386–7.
[13] Canale, 16 Sep. 1765 (Ada Ruata, *Luigi Malabaila di Canale: reflessioni della cultura illuministica in un diplomatico piemontese* (Turin, 1968), pp. 160–1). I am grateful to Dr J. Black for calling my attention to this book.
[14] Bussi, *Il diritto pubblico del sacro romano impero*, throws no light on this point.

The co-regency was to last fifteen years, but it is convenient in this chapter to discuss just the first two-and-a-half. This short period saw many features that endured through the whole phase become established, but nonetheless had a character of its own.[15] Joseph, fresh to his tasks, laid down, in the fullest memoranda he ever composed, his views on most aspects of policy. His role as co-regent, which ostensibly imposed on him the duty to involve himself in all the affairs of the Monarchy but allowed him final responsibility in none, might have been especially designed to encourage such productions; but it was naturally in the early stages that he felt most inclined to generalisation. At the same time, while several of the notable ministers of Maria Theresa's prime died, Kaunitz attained a status so special that he ranks as a third force with mother and son throughout the co-regency. The Vienna government was at its most pacific, conscious of the need for recuperation after the Seven Years War. Joseph had not yet embarked on his great programme of travel, and was rather more deferential towards his mother than he later became. After the quarrel over San Remo in 1766–7, he seems never again to have insisted on acting in his capacity as emperor against the perceived interests of the Monarchy.

Further, it was a time, if not of crisis, certainly of growing anxiety about the succession. Joseph had had only a daughter by his first wife. His marriage to Josepha soon went sour; her run of false pregnancies diminished hopes of an heir; in May 1767 she died of smallpox. Joseph refused to contemplate a third marriage. The other adult son, Leopold, took what was considered a long time to produce his first child; it was a daughter. Only with the birth of his son Francis on 12 February 1768 did the prospect of succession in the male line become hopeful. Both Maria Theresa and Joseph, as we shall see, treated this event as a landmark in the fortunes of the dynasty.[16]

During the same epidemic of smallpox that carried off the emperor's wife, his sister Josepha also died, his sister Elizabeth lost her renowned beauty, and Maria Theresa herself was despaired of.[17] But she recovered, and this remission appeared to her to be providential. Often in the later years of her reign she declared that it was only the fact that God had preserved her from death which had persuaded her to take up again the full burden of ruling.[18] She made a partial return to the social and ceremonial life of the Court; and though she threatened more than once to abdicate, her sense of duty, fortified by what she believed to be God's will, always kept her to her task. This change

[15] Much of the evidence for this and the next few paragraphs will appear only in later chapters.
[16] Arneth, *GMT* VII, pp. 457–8. For concern in Vienna about the succession, Langlois to Grafton, 14 May 1766, cypher (PRO SP 80/203), and a number of other despatches in the same series. See M.T. to Maria Beatrix, 7 Feb. 1767, Arneth, *MTKuF* III, p. 85.
[17] Arneth, *GMT* VII, pp. 325–34.
[18] For example, M.T. to Ferdinand, 1 Oct. 1771 (Arneth, *MTKuF* I, p. 71); K-M VII, pp. 62–3. Cf. Durand to Choiseul, 22 Aug. 1770 (AAE CP (Autriche), 313). See below, pp. 206, 350–1.

of attitude is another factor that marks off the rest of her reign from the two years immediately following her husband's death, when she remained in deepest mourning and seclusion, seriously intending to go into retirement sooner rather than later.

THE TRIUMVIRATE

From the start, Joseph worked hard, with evident zest. Within a month of his father's death he described his day as follows:

I am overwhelmed by business and audiences. I get up at half-past six, go to Mass and at eight o'clock begin sitting at my table where, with my new secretary Roeder, I deal with imperial ... affairs ... At about ten the [late emperor's] treasurers Simon and Ditelbach come ... Then the ministers or other gentlemen begin to appear. At about half-past twelve I take my morning's report to the empress. At one o'clock, the hour for going to dinner, according to laudable custom, prince Kaunitz arrives. We have a little conversation, sometimes of an hour and a half, then we go and dine ... Every afternoon, as soon as I've put down my spoon, I go to rummage and search among his late Majesty's effects.[19]

Two months later, when that particular task had been completed and he was co-regent, he spoke of holding meetings two or three times a week about the finances and of studying, between four and nine o'clock every day, the revenues and expenditure of the Monarchy, in order to try to balance them.[20] He complained that he sometimes had to give sixty audiences a day.[21] 'I have a hundred thousand projects in my head', he told Leopold, almost in the words of Gilbert's Mikado, 'as many good as bad. I'll let you know about some of them when they are sorted out a little.'[22] It will become apparent later in this chapter that he remained extremely critical of his mother's regime.

Soon after her bereavement, Maria Theresa spoke of herself as 'half-dead'; 'I do not know myself any more, for I live like the animals, without spirit and reason. I forget everything. I get up at five, go to bed late, and do nothing all day. My situation is cruel.'[23] 'The sun itself seems black to me.' 'What remains to me and what I await with impatience is my bier ... which will reunite me with the only person whom my heart has acknowledged in this world, and who was the aim and object of all my actions and all my love. Imagine the void I feel ...'[24]

Her sense of loneliness was renewed as several of her faithful ministers followed Francis to the grave. Haugwitz, his influence newly restored, died

---

[19] J. to L., 12 Sep. 1765 (Arneth, *MTuJ* I, pp. 128–9).
[20] J. to L., 14 Nov. 1765 (*ibid.*, pp. 154–5).
[21] J. to L., 14 Nov. 1765, portion not quoted by Arneth (HHSA FA Sbde 7).
[22] J. to L., 4 Oct. 1765, portion not quoted by Arneth (HHSA FA Sbde 7).
[23] M.T. to Silva-Tarouca, undated (Karajan, *Feierliche Sitzungsberichte KAW* (1859), 58, 60).
[24] M.T. to countess Enzenberg, 9 Nov. 1765 and 12 Feb. 1766 (Arneth, *GMT* VII, pp. 521–2).

within a fortnight of her husband.[25] In February 1766 her most notable general, marshal Daun, the army's representative on the *Staatsrat*, also died.

> The good God [she wrote] takes away from me the two men who possessed, and justly, my entire confidence ... both Christians and zealous and devoted, my true friends who told me the truth roundly, to whom I could open my heart without restraint. This resource too is now lost to me ... This [desolation] has an effect on all my senses: memory, hearing, sight, judgement. I'm beginning to lose them all. Discouragement is now much more pervasive.

But she went on: 'I have not thought of finding solace in any other way than by plunging myself more deeply than ever into work, wishing to numb myself and leaving myself no time to contemplate or feel my condition.'[26] She was only forty-eight when Francis died. For all her sorrow, she showed herself still strong and active enough to maintain her control of affairs. But she now rarely showed the desire or the energy to promote wide-ranging reform herself.

Her decision to declare Joseph co-regent was made in consultation with Kaunitz. While still at Innsbruck on 28 August 1765 she wrote to the chancellor:

> I am most obliged to you for all the services and advice you have rendered and given to me during the life of our incomparable master. I have always benefited from them and have them very deeply engraved in my heart. I shall likewise follow with complete confidence the advice you give me about my unhappy future. It is in accordance with your counsel that I allow myself to be dragged back to Vienna to take care of nine orphans ... Their good father idolised them and could not refuse them anything. I shall not be able to follow the same line. God knows how long my miserable life will last ... Their fate must be decided this winter. I count on you. I shall do nothing without your advice ... I shall gladly give you the credit of establishing them as well as our system of state.
>
> What you said about the co-regency comforts me infinitely, and I count on your working to bring it about. Do not leave my son alone. I see that he is flattered and happy when he is speaking to you. But he is also used to being sought after, and likes it. You may neglect me instead. I shall thank you for it, because I could never have the slightest doubt of your attachment to me.[27]

Kaunitz's position had sometimes irritated even the complaisant Francis.[28] It was now in some ways even enhanced. One of Maria Theresa's characteristics was her exceptional readiness to give her confidence to tried servants. This letter shows that in the case of Kaunitz she went to extraordinary lengths. In urging him to cultivate Joseph, she must have expected that sometimes the result would be that they would work together against her. When it happened,

---

[25] K-M VI, p. 134 (30 Aug. 1765).
[26] M.T. to countess Enzenberg, 12 Feb. 1766 (Arneth, *GMT* VII, p. 525). Old Bartenstein died in 1767.
[27] Beer, *JLuK*, pp. 432–3.
[28] Arneth, *GMT* VII, pp. 152–6, describes a specially serious row of 1761 over finance.

she in fact disliked it. But ordinarily she could rely on the chancellor to find ways of neutralising Joseph. For this purpose she wrote the minister letters behind the co-regent's back, sometimes giving Kaunitz information she withheld from her son.[29]

Her attitude is the more remarkable in that she knew Kaunitz was slow in the despatch of business – and getting slower.[30] She could show irritation at his unwillingness to visit her.[31] As we shall see, she was exasperated by his behaviour when he proposed to resign in 1766.[32] She can hardly have relished his unpunctuality. Although she must have realised that his frequent absences from official religious ceremonies reflected a lack of piety, she accepted his excuses.[33] His foreign policy was unpopular, and the Seven Years War had not seen it triumph.[34] But if her opinion of his competence had become poorer, nothing shook her fundamental trust in him.

Ordinary mortals had to put up with even more than she did from Kaunitz. His vanity and eccentricity pass belief. He prided himself, even into his seventies, on his horsemanship.[35] The prince de Ligne said of him:

The exactness of his pronunciation in four languages which he knew perfectly made his conversation imposing rather than attractive. Thinking about it, one realised that he had no wit, no imagination; but through believing he was the leading man in the world, he had almost become so.[36]

A traveller wrote:

He is remarkably cold and inattentive to strangers, sometimes scarcely deigning to speak to them ... The common hour of dining at Vienna is half-past two, and nobody dines after three; but the ... day I first dined there, the company were assembled at half-past five, and it was past seven before he made his appearance, and he never thought of making any apology.[37]

He showed off at table his various orders set in diamonds, presented by his grateful sovereigns. After dinner he went through an elaborate procedure, offensive even to eighteenth-century manners, of publicly cleaning his teeth.[38] His daughter-in-law thought he was the most eccentric man she had ever seen;

---

[29] Cf. her letters to K. in Beer, *JLuK*, pp. 513–14, and a good many others in HHSA FA Sbde 70.

[30] M.T. to Ulfeld, 18 May 1762 (Arneth, *MTKuF* IV, p. 200); M.T. to countess Enzenberg, 9 Aug. 1766 (Arneth, *GMT* VII, p. 543). Her criticism of K. is a commonplace of British representatives' despatches.

[31] Langlois to Conway, cypher, 6 Aug. 1766 (PRO SP 80/203).   [32] See below, pp. 144–5.

[33] Cf. M.T. to K., 31 Mar. 1774 (Beer, *JLuK*, p. vii n), where she ostensibly accepts K.'s excuse of his health for not attending Maundy Thursday services, while hoping 'for my consolation ... and for the public' that he'll manage it next year. K. had sent her a ticket of confession!

[34] Cf. Arneth, *GMT* VII, pp. 287–8.   [35] Arneth, *GMT* IX, p. 323. See Plate 12.

[36] Ligne, *Fragments*, vol. I, pp. 239–40.

[37] G. Smyth (ed.), *Memoirs and Correspondence of Sir Robert Murray Keith* (2 vols., London, 1849), vol. II, p. 197.

[38] Wraxall, *Memoirs*, vol. II, pp. 485–6. He thinks K.'s behaviour even worse than Charles XII's, who only spread his butter with his thumbs.

'no one knows better than I', she said, 'that you have to have a cast-iron stomach with my father-in-law'.[39] He spoke a good deal of the frailty of his health. When Maria Theresa was preparing to appoint him chancellor in the early 1750s, he would promise only to set the new system in motion, claiming that he would not be able to stand more than two or three years of high office.[40] After her attack of smallpox in 1767, he issued this circular:

To all those who have some friendship for me

At the time of the frightful malady which some years ago threatened the precious life of our august empress, as a result of my personal attachment to this great princess, I was so keenly affected by the thought of this illness that since then I have not been able to hear its name without shuddering, to the point that I am at once seized with shortness of breath and a general trembling which give me inconceivable pain. And I earnestly beg you for this reason,

1. never to speak in my presence of the malady in question, nor of anything in the slightest degree connected with it.

And so

2. when you are reading to me anything whatever, printed or in manuscript, please be most careful never to read out, but to omit as you read, sections which concern this matter or might be connected with it.[41]

His self-assurance was astonishing. He fought for thirty-six years to maintain the French alliance he had made, never showing the slightest doubt that he had been right to advocate it and never hesitating to repeat the same arguments in its favour with remorseless logic.[42] He was no less insistent on the merits of his other brainchild, the *Staatsrat*: he attributed the disasters of 1740 to the absence of such a body, and saw it as a panacea for the weaknesses of the Monarchy.[43]

No one, however, could doubt his ability. Successive British envoys in Vienna, though they deplored his policy, acknowledged his talent. The English traveller, Wraxall, briefed by them, said of him: 'Endowed with uncommon penetration, he seizes with facility the difficulties of any affair; and never was a head better organized, nor more capable of uniting precision with dispatch, in the transaction of public business.'[44] He was a most unusual minister in the consistency of his aims and in the elaboration and clarity with which he regularly expressed them – he claimed to apply geometrical

---

[39] L.K. to E.L., [?]14/17 Mar. 1767 and 23 Jan. 1770 (SOALpZ, LRRA P. 16/21–2). Eleonore thought K. far worse: frightening, totally unreliable and often thoroughly disagreeable (e.g. 6, 9, and 20 Apr. 1767, *ibid.*, P. 16/21). In the face of this kind of evidence, I cannot accept F. A. J. Szabo's claim that it was only K.'s enemies who spread tales about him ('Staatskanzler Fürst Kaunitz und die Aufklärungspolitik Österreichs' in *MTIZ*, pp. 41–2).

[40] Klingenstein, *Aufstieg des Hauses Kaunitz*, pp. 291–4.   [41] Arneth, *GMT* VII, pp. 547–8.

[42] See Beer, *AÖG* (1872), 1–98 and vol. II of this work.

[43] See, e.g., his memorandum of 1766 (Beer, *AÖG* (1872), esp. 114–58).

[44] For the whole paragraph see Wraxall, *Memoirs*, vol. II, last chapter (quotation from p. 488) and the despatches of Stormont, Keith and their substitutes in PRO SP 80/199. See Plate 21b.

reasoning to politics.[45] There is real intellectual pleasure to be derived from reading his more spacious state papers, partly because they sometimes wander so far from practical politics. It is often doubted by historians that ministers, especially those successfully concerned with foreign affairs, can follow steady policies. The great Lord Salisbury affected to believe that 'Governments can do so little nowadays ... It is all pure drifting. As we go down stream, we can occasionally fend off a collision; but where are we going?'[46] This attitude stands in complete contrast to Kaunitz's. He could be, or tried to be, opportunistic in seizing his moment; he liked to appear subtle and mysterious in the day-to-day conduct of diplomacy. But for forty years he pursued the same clear and lucidly expounded foreign policy. The British envoys praised not only his talent but also his moderation and prudence and, in essentials, his straight forwardness.

He was admitted to be incorruptible. He did not trouble to flatter the empress with regular attentions, or to defer much to her principles in religion and morality. With her, he played 'hard to get'. When necessary, he displayed great skill at Court intrigue – or political infighting. But the main method by which he sought to secure his power and further his policies was by filling as many posts as possible with his clients. By 1765 he had already succeeded with most diplomatic appointments, but in the internal departments he was only beginning to obtain places for supporters like Pergen and the Zinzendorfs.[47]

Many of his skills and qualities, together with an inexhaustible capacity for beautifully turned, slowly unfolding flattery, are exemplified during the serio-comic affair of his resignation in 1766. It also reveals the balance of power within the triumvirate. Maria Theresa had decided to recall prince Starhemberg, the ambassador in Paris, ostensibly to assist Kaunitz in his work and to fill Haugwitz's place on the *Staatsrat*. This clearly constituted a threat to the chancellor's position, despite all the empress's assurances to the contrary.[48] It so happened that Kaunitz's principal assistants in both the Belgian and Italian departments died within six days of one another in the spring of 1766. He took the opportunity to request that he be relieved of all his offices, which, he said, in the circumstances his 'infirmities' would no longer permit him to manage properly.

His lengthy letter of 4 June began typically with the assertion that 'what is necessary is a stable and solid plan for the future'. He has always been convinced, he goes on, that 'nothing is more pernicious than half-measures'.

[45] See e.g. pp. 122–3, 295. Cf. Klingenstein, *Aufstieg des Hauses Kaunitz*, pp. 170–1.

[46] R. Taylor, *Lord Salisbury* (London, 1975), p. 145.

[47] Cobenzl's memoirs discuss this (Arneth, 'Graf Philipp Cobenzl und seine Memoiren', *AÖG*, LXVII (1886), 104–8).

[48] There is much to this effect in Langlois's despatches for 1766 (PRO SP 80/203). Cf. the Venetian ambassador (Arneth, *GMT* VII, p. 544) and K-M VI, pp. 196–7 (20 Aug. 1766).

M.T. had gratuitously consulted Starhemberg on internal affairs in 1764 (Walter, *MÖIG* (1933), 440–2).

The best course would be to replace him here and now by Starhemberg, who might even prove superior to Kaunitz himself. In double harness, 'with all imaginable philosophy on both sides', disagreements and faction would be unavoidable. But Kaunitz does not wish to be thought falsely modest:

I will honestly admit that I have had the happiness of rendering to Your Majesty and to the state very great and very signal services; that I do not think there has ever existed or perhaps ever will exist a minister who has served his master with more fidelity and more attachment to his person; and that I hope that in the twenty-five years during which I have had the honour to serve Your Majesty she has never found in me blameworthy ambition or a spirit of domination or hatred or enmity or a spirit of persecution or of intrigue, or interested views, or plans to enrich and aggrandise myself or my family at the expense of the state.

It is through the happiness of not having had any of these faults, together with that of having always been honoured with Your Majesty's confidence, that I have always, during the whole of my troubled ministry, found ... the composure and the inexhaustible courage necessary to face all the setbacks I have suffered and so many extremely critical situations in which not only myself but the state has found itself. I am perfectly aware, however, that since I owe my good qualities to God alone, there is nothing about them in which I can take pride, and it is for this reason that I have dared to acknowledge them.

He asserts that 'all his departments have attained to a degree of perfection which perhaps has never yet existed in the world'. He is

delighted that, instead of the decayed state in which most of the affairs of the Monarchy, external as well as internal, were thirteen years ago, I have the satisfaction of leaving them in such a state of improvement of every sort that, if it is sustained and perfected in the future, as I do not doubt it will be, in the same way that it already today exacts the just admiration of all Europe, it will transmit the glory of Your Majesty's reign to all the centuries to come.[49]

Maria Theresa replied with an irresistible emotional appeal, a classic example of her management of men:

You have caused me to spend twenty-four very bitter hours, since I did not wish to act on my first feeling ... After ripe reflection, as sovereign and your friend, I return this paper to you and wish never to know anything of its content, since I cannot as sovereign permit you [to take] such a step, while at the same time offering you every necessary assistance and every consideration that may conserve your precious life. It was for this reason that I recalled your two pupils Starhemberg and Pergen to help us, and in order to have some people to be trained in accordance with our principles ...

She then brings up the problem of her son, conspicuously unmentioned by Kaunitz – her emotion getting the better of her grammar:

You saw that my first care in the frightful position in which I found myself, there was nothing I was more concerned about than to establish your credit with my son as firmly as with me. I have completely succeeded in this. I must tell you that he had not been

    [49] K. to M.T., 4 June 1766 (Beer, *JLuK*, pp. 489–500).

well disposed, and it was this which caused the early rows. And now you want to leave me, you who preached to me at such length about not giving up the reins of government, was it to leave me in the lurch after ten months without any good reason?

She demands to know what the real motives of his resignation are. Is it something she has done?

How unhappy we are if we can have no true friend! I thought I had one, I was calm and happy, imagine my disillusionment. With another, I venture to assert, you would run many risks. But with me, who have had only too long to get to know men, I am indulgent and kind, I can even assure you that I am not capable of any rancour and that I can entirely forget things . . . Let us die with our swords in our hands, or both go and hide in the gloomy mountains of the Tyrol to finish our days in obscurity, abandoned by everyone else and the universe.[50]

Kaunitz gave in, but in a manner which Maria Theresa found grudging. He insisted that Starhemberg be nominated his successor, in which case he agreed to stay on as 'chief chancellor' (*oberster Kanzler*) for up to two years to train him. Joseph, away in Bohemia, was now mobilised to put further pressure on Kaunitz:

One thing [wrote the emperor] . . . you will not refuse to the state and the country which admires you or to your sovereign who loves you, is to pledge your judgement, the discernment which always seizes the truth in every matter and enables you always to find the best course for the state and for her, not for two years but for ever. Nothing could be more just than that the detail or routine of your departments should be entrusted to others. But the ruling spirit must always be yours. It is the clarity of your ideas that we cannot do without, and which will never be weakened by age or ill-health to the point when it becomes useless. So, my dear prince, shed all routine. Neither read nor write, but think for the good of the state and for the service of the masters who love you . . . You know me well enough to know that I think as I speak.

Kaunitz responded:

I am so filled with admiration, and at the same time so touched, by everything which we received yesterday from Your Majesty that my heart could not hold all the emotions which he has made it feel if they had to be kept shut up within it. Your Majesty, who happily unites the qualities of a great man with those of a good prince, will on this account not therefore disapprove if the servant who is the most tenderly and sincerely attached to his person ventures to open his heart to him . . . I admired – with that sweet satisfaction which we feel when we have the pleasure of seeing great qualities revealed in those to whom we are attached in our hearts – the sagacity, the rare discernment and the incomparable judgement with which Your Majesty saw and at once adopted the best of the possible courses on the matter of the letter addressed to marshal Lacy, and I had no less opportunity to admire his judgement in seizing, so to speak, in a moment all the advantages of a plan which anyone other than the incomparable son of the august Maria Theresa would certainly not have appreciated unless after a long period of meditation. I have known during my life few men endowed, even at an advanced age,

[50] M.T. to K., 5 or 6 June 1766 (*ibid.*, pp. 501–3).

with the rare qualities of mind and heart that Providence has brought together in Your Majesty, and I have known no one of his age in this class, whether at home or abroad. This is an avowal which the truth, and the joy I feel, extract from me. I congratulate the country and humanity on it, and I venture to trust that Your Majesty will not regard it as flattery on my part.

Nevertheless, he still insisted on resigning within two years, and now demanded that the story of the transaction, and a promise that he would be released, should be published to the Monarchy's envoys and officials, foreign Powers and the public.[51]

Meanwhile, Starhemberg, resting at Spa on his way from Paris to Vienna, prudently informed both Maria Theresa and Kaunitz that he was convinced the great plan could not work, that a chancellor working under a chief chancellor would not command the confidence of the envoys or ministers of other states. Joseph went to dine with Kaunitz at his country seat at Austerlitz to discuss the whole project. The emperor was strongly opposed to the public announcement desired by the minister. A multilateral exchange of notes took place.

Finally, late in August it was agreed that Starhemberg and Pergen should simply become members of the *Staatsrat* without other offices, learning from Kaunitz and helping him where possible. An announcement was made, but to the Monarchy's chief officials and envoys only; and Maria Theresa supplied Kaunitz with a private note in these terms: 'I grant you, since you wish it so, your complete resignation at the end of two years from now, assuming that the state of your health does not permit you then to carry the burden of the business which you have conducted with as much rectitude as zeal.'[52]

This dispute had become public knowledge at an early stage. The reports of the British representative in Vienna add one or two touches to the picture. Starhemberg had been generally suspected of intriguing for power, and his sister on his behalf. It was suggested also that the discontent then affecting Lombardy, and perhaps malversation on the part of Kaunitz's two late assistants, had caused Maria Theresa to criticise his administration there and in Belgium. As to Kaunitz's resignation,

opinions are much divided; his Enemies say, that the Reason of the Ill Health, that he alleges, is only a Pretence to cover the Diminution, he perceives of his Credit & Influence, as well as the Apprehension, he has, that he shall find himself much more thwarted by the present Emperor, than by the last.[53]

51 J. to K., 16 June 1766 (*ibid.*, pp. 507–8); K. to J., 20 June (*ibid.*, pp. 508–12).
52 The quotation (M.T. to K., 19 Aug. 1766) from *ibid.*, p. 514; other correspondence *ibid.*, pp. 512–16; Arneth, *GMT* VII pp. 540–4; Arneth, *MTuJ* I, pp. 190–1; K-M VI, pp. 446–57.
53 Langlois to Grafton, cypher, 14 May; Langlois to Conway, part cypher, 2 July, and cypher, separate, 30 July (all 1766, PRO SP 80/203).

Certainly, he had kept 'the Power of his Employment, [but] thrown the Drudgery into other Hands'.[54] But the secret of the whole affair seems to have been revealed by Maria Theresa, admittedly as late as 1772, in a conversation which Khevenhüller recorded:

HM ... complained, as indeed frequently happens, about this minister's daily increasing weaknesses and extravagances, but always with the same rider, that she could find no one to replace him in this sphere so long as the emperor remained ill-disposed towards the prince of Starhemberg, although she would have hoped to bring him round in the end ...[55]

In the upshot the chancellor had evidently established his power on a much firmer footing, outmanoeuvring the empress by resigning when Starhemberg was in limbo and Joseph absent, and securing the emperor by standing forth as the alternative to Starhemberg. Although the latter soon acquired the office of 'directing minister' of the *Staatsrat*, that is, in internal affairs, Kaunitz retained control of foreign policy, with Pergen as his assistant in this sphere.

It is against this background that the row between mother and son over San Remo, already mentioned,[56] has to be considered. Joseph's violent rejection of Kaunitz's draft, quoted in the previous chapter, was written scarcely a fortnight after the resignation incident had been closed.

I must tell you [wrote Maria Theresa] that the German note was drafted in a manner which has given me pain, that you can think like this and find satisfaction in ironically withering and humiliating others. I must tell you that it is quite the opposite of what I have done all my life ...

Imagine my situation with Kaunitz! I must do him the justice of saying that he was mortified and remarked only: 'I did not think I had deserved these reproaches.' What will Starhemberg think when he sees how you are thinking? And what strikes me most, it is not a first reaction; it is twenty-four hours after receiving the despatches, in other words after mature reflection, that you have enjoyed yourself putting the dagger into the heart, ironically and with reproaches too extreme for people whom you yourself believe to be the best and whom you have striven to keep. How I fear that you will never find friends who will be attached to Joseph – by which you set such store. For it is not the emperor or the co-regent from whom these biting, ironical, mischievous shafts come, it is from the heart of Joseph, and this is what alarms me, and this is what will bring ill fortune into your life, dragging the Monarchy and all of us with you ...

After pointing out that the great hero, Frederick the Great, had by his similar behaviour lost all friends, and making further defence of the official, she resumed the attack:

54 Stormont to Conway, 24 Oct. 1767, cypher (PRO SP 80/204).
55 K-M VII, pp. 128–9 (20 May 1772). Arneth's invaluable account (*GMT* VII, pp. 287–318) is decidedly ingenuous in its appraisal of motives. It was clear to M.T. at the time that K.'s principal feeling was jealousy of Starhemberg (K-M VI, pp. 196–7).
  Some additional light is thrown on the episode by letters in Arneth & Flammermont II, pp. 217–19, which suggest that all concerned were playing double games. Starhemberg evidently wanted control of foreign rather than domestic affairs.
56 See pp. 123–5 above.

Your heart is not yet bad, but it will become so. It is more than time that you ceased to relish all these *bons mots*, these witty remarks which only result in wounding and ridiculing others, alienating all honest men, and hence [encourage you] to believe that none of the human race deserves respect and love, since by your own conduct you have separated yourself from all that is good and have only kept and opened the door to knaves, copying and flattering your talents.

After all this long sermon, which you will forgive since it arises from the excessive tenderness of my heart for you and my lands, I am going to put to you a comparison with all your talents and charms. You are a coquet of wit, you run after it wherever you think you'll find it, without discrimination. A *bon mot*, a phrase, that is what interests you, whether found in a book or in someone's mouth, you apply it at the first opportunity, without considering whether it is appropriate – almost like [archduchess] Elizabeth with her beauty, happy and asking nothing more so long as she gives pleasure, whether to a Swiss [guardsman] or a prince.

In conclusion I take you . . . and kiss you tenderly . . .[57]

When Joseph received this diatribe, he claimed just to have sealed for the post a letter containing these words:

I dare to assure [Your Majesty] with all the frankness she has come to expect of me, and with the small ration of compliments that I put into my speeches, that [while on my travels] I miss terribly the happy hour before dinner which I spend nearly every day at her feet, and that despite all the noise outside and the novelty of things I nevertheless often think, not that I am a marshal, but that I am your son. This glorious title which sets before me all my duties, my model, includes and is worth more than all the others.

In answer to Maria Theresa's strictures, he added a postscript:

Moved by her benevolence which beats me with such sweet rods, wielded by this incomparable mother's heart, I very humbly kiss her hands. Do not suppose that this will have no effect. A heart like mine, a spirit equally responsive, is more touched by the embrace with which you honour a son whom you for the moment believe unworthy than by the most frightful punishment or threat that could have followed it. My eyes are full of tears of gratitude, and I promise you to avoid henceforth all that can give the least pain, even if I have to sacrifice an opportunity of shining.

I must admit that I thought this note, though in every point true, would not be made available to all the ministers, especially not to [Kaunitz], but that will certainly teach me a lesson for another time.[58]

This, as we have seen, was a rare case, an imperial matter, in which the empress and the minister simply conceded to the emperor the point at issue – for the time being. She probably also expressed regret for having shown Kaunitz the offending letter.[59] Yet it was the occasion of Maria Theresa's strongest criticism of her son, and of Joseph's most servile flattery of his mother. One would be tempted to treat his loving remarks as ironical, if their

[57] M.T. to J., 14 Sep. 1766 (Arneth, *MTuJ* I, pp. 200–3).
[58] J. to M.T., 15 Sep. 1766 (Arneth, *MTuJ*, I, pp. 205–6).
[59] M.T. to K., undated (Arneth, *MTKuF* IV, p. 250), is likely to refer to this.

sincerity were not attested by the conspicuous devotion he showed to his mother at certain crises, particularly when she had smallpox in 1767. He then slept in the antechamber to her room, and when she received the last rites, came away from her with tears in his eyes

and did not take it amiss that I [Khevenhüller] and a pair of her old servants had in our first sorrow loudly lamented the expected loss of so great, able and good-hearted a monarch, which after all could not be quite indifferent to the ruler who would follow her; from which indeed I conclude that this young lord cannot have so hard and evil a heart and spirit as people attribute to him.[60]

Domineering, meddlesome, hypercritical and restrictive as his mother could be; hectoring, sarcastic, resentful and self-righteous as he often showed himself: he could not utterly reject her graciousness, charm, admiration and affection. No doubt she meant it when she said, as she frequently did, that she only continued to rule for love of him.[61] Both the angry, even hysterical, exchanges between mother and son, and the expressions of affection, have to be accepted as genuine. Despite all alarms they did contrive to work together – unlike successive princes of Wales with George I, George II and George III. Perhaps the nearest parallel is the relationship between the brothers prince Henry of Prussia and Frederick the Great, in which extreme personal bitterness proved compatible with close public collaboration.[62] But the mutual affection was decidedly stronger in the case of Joseph and Maria Theresa.

Something of the same duality is observable in the dealings between Maria Theresa and Kaunitz, and much more clearly between Joseph and Kaunitz. Again, the emperor, despite his frequent criticisms of the chancellor, remained committed to the view that the insufferable old minister was the state's best available servant. In this respect the empress had converted him from the views he had expressed in the *Rêveries*. He had brought himself to write to Kaunitz in October 1765: 'I am striving, and I shall strive, to model myself on your admirable principles and talents.'[63]

How far, in this complex situation, Joseph was able to exert political influence will emerge as different aspects of the Monarchy's affairs are discussed.

THE ROYAL FAMILY AND THE COURT

It is natural to consider next the 'affairs of the family and the Court',[64] since, though Kaunitz was much consulted about them, they were the particular concern of mother and son, and since the emperor was able to carry significant changes in this field even in the short period down to 1768.

---

60 K-M VI, pp. 242–3 (1 June 1767).
61 E.g. M.T. to J., 28 Jan. 1769 (Arneth, *MTuJ* I, p. 237).
62 C. W. Easum, *Prince Henry of Prussia* (Madison, 1942).
63 J. to K., 9 Oct. 1765 (HHSA FA Sbde 70). See above, pp. 100, 104 for the *Rêveries*.
64 Joseph's own heading in HHSA TG, f. 258.

Joseph's closest relationships within the family were with his mother, his first wife and his daughter. But next to them came Leopold. The two brothers, though six years apart in age, had evidently been close companions as children and young men. Maria Theresa complained in 1764 of their walking out together in the city, and in the next year remarked cryptically to Joseph that he had not always treated Leopold with 'the superiority and aloofness that Nature and your birth' warranted, and had often been 'rather his younger than his elder brother'.[65] It seems that after Leopold's departure for Tuscany on 30 August 1765, except during the brief periods when the brothers were together, they wrote to each other at least once a week for the rest of their lives. Many hundreds of these letters survive, all in French – the majority of them from Joseph, because Leopold kept the more systematic files.[66] There were reasons of state to justify this correspondence: Tuscany was a useful observation-post in Italy for the Vienna government; and, because Leopold was next in line of succession to Joseph, it was prudent to keep him informed about the affairs of the Monarchy.[67] A batch of despatches, reports and decrees usually accompanied Joseph's letters; and in 1768 the emperor sent to his brother the 'General picture of the affairs of the Monarchy', already mentioned.[68] Joseph also used the correspondence to obtain reliable information for himself, in cipher, so that he should not have to depend on what his mother and his ministers knew or wished to tell him.[69] But there was also friendship, at least on Joseph's side. The emperor concludes one of his early letters by saying, 'I embrace you with my whole heart and beg you to be persuaded that, though a hundred leagues distant, I love you and shall always esteem you beyond all expression.'[70] Despite the occasional contretemps, Joseph almost always maintained this tone of intimacy. He knew that his

---

[65] Wandruszka, *L. II.*, vol. 1, p. 102; Arneth, *MTuJ* 1, p. 160 (M.T. to J., [?] late Nov. 1765).

[66] Arneth published in his *MTuJ* a good proportion of J.'s surviving letters to L. for the period of the co-regency, although not, as he claimed, all which were of significance. He minimised the extent to which he omitted passages within the letters he published (*MTuJ* 1, p. xiv), and he rarely indicated omissions in his text. Quite a lot of criticism of M.T. and the Vienna government is cut out (cf. pp. 207–9, 214–16, 341–2, 355–6); and so are almost all remarks about sexual matters. Very few of L.'s replies were included.

Wandruszka says a little about Arneth's practice (*L. II.*, vol. 1, pp. 414, 421), and has published in the course of his biography many letters and portions of letters, especially from L., omitted by Arneth. Fejtö, *J. II*, printed others, but in modernised language and without giving references. However, there is valuable material still unpublished from this correspondence.

The originals are in HHSA FA Sbde 7 for this period. There are gaps, especially a blank from Mar. 1766 to Apr. 1768 and another from Dec. 1768 to Dec. 1770; but it seems to me likely that they result from losses, not (except when the brothers were together) from breaks in the correspondence. The enclosures are seldom preserved with the letters. Plate 22b is one example.

[67] Wandruszka, *L. II.*, vol. 1, pp. 176, 195.

[68] See pp. 125–9 above and pp. 176–8, 273–7 below.

[69] Wandruszka, *L. II.*, vol. 1, pp. 198, 421. Evidence for this is omitted by Arneth from *MTuJ*.

[70] J. to L., 26 Sep. 1765 (Arneth, *MTuJ* 1, p. 136).

brother was 'very suspicious and tries to disguise all his actions', but seems to have been unaware of the deep resentment which Leopold harboured against him and confided to his coded memoranda.[71] The emperor's letters to his brother generally appear sincere; but they were often hastily written and were obviously used as an opportunity for airing grievances in colourful language.

At first, the complaints are cautious. On 19 December 1765 Joseph reports: 'we continue to work at our affairs with plenty of diligence; but there should still be many more things done, and we employ only palliatives; the evil is still by no means attacked at source'. Most of the early letters consist mainly of descriptions of the two brothers' activities and plans. They exchange musical information. They do not fail to mention their ailments, more numerous as time goes on. Joseph discusses his sex-life, and grumbles to Leopold:

I've not heard the word except from Richi who is positive that your wife is pregnant. This is not fair, that the master should know nothing of the progress of the disciple. So I beg you, dear brother, just let me know whether my axioms have been true and good and whether you have found the practice as easy as the theory.[72]

Unfortunately, Francis's will was so drafted as to make a dispute between Joseph and Leopold inevitable. Written in 1751, this document assumed that Tuscany, though governed separately from the Monarchy, would be under the rule of his eldest son. But of course, as part of the marriage treaty for Leopold, he had been made Francis's successor as its grand duke; and Joseph had reluctantly signed away his rights to the duchy.[73] It was impossible to disturb this arrangement. However, Francis had explicitly stated in the will that the revenues of Tuscany were greater than its government required, and that the surplus should be applied to pay for his individual bequests. No one in Vienna doubted that it was Joseph's right to recover from Leopold the two million florins Francis had left in the Tuscan treasury.[74] But Leopold wished to use them for relief work after the recent famine and for the draining of the malarial swamps of the Maremma. Joseph's answer was that he was giving his father's entire fortune to the state, to relieve its debts; and that 'it matters more to the sovereign of Tuscany that a good and salutary financial operation should establish and support the Austrian Monarchy and put it in a position to protect him than a hundred drainings of the Maremma'. Joseph in the end

---

[71] See J. to M.T., 30 May 1769 (Arneth, *MTuJ* I, p. 282), and Wandruszka, *L. II.*, esp. vol. I, pp. 342–8. Cf. pp. 196, 423–4.

[72] These two quotations are omitted by Arneth. The date of the second is 19 Oct. 1765. HHSA FA Sbde 7.

[73] The will in K-M VI, pp. 396–402. On the marriage treaty and the renunciation, Arneth *GMT* VII, p. 144; K-M VI, pp. 70–1 (12 Jan. 1765); PRO SP 80/202, Stormont to Sandwich, 19 Jan. 1765.

[74] Francis's view: K-M VI, p. 400; the opinions of Viennese officials: *ibid.*, pp. 402–17; J. to K., 3 Nov. 1765 (HHSA FA Sbde 70) asking K.'s opinion. K-M says (VI, p. 164, 15 Jan. 1766) that Francis had intended to bring this money out of Tuscany himself.

extracted 1,200,000 florins, though he paid Leopold 4 per cent interest on the capital for life.[75]

Maria Theresa firmly supported Joseph in his view of his rights in the matter, but worked for a compromise. She deplored the manner of both brothers' letters. Joseph, she said of one draft, should resist the temptation to correct Leopold's style, and avoid displaying pride or rancour. He should not stress his position as the eldest son.

The end of the letter is too contradictory; you embrace him in order to humiliate him to the utmost extent because of the need he has of your friendship. It is true, and he can expect no more, that you are excusing him and doing him a good turn, but why make him feel it? One must do good and convince the world by doing it, but never say so. You kiss him while making him see the path of reason; it's stronger than what the braggart says in the comedy. Forgive me, I had to laugh, though it was scarcely what I wanted to do.

When Joseph said he was shocked by a letter of Leopold's, she refused to agree: 'To a young monarch, somewhat inflated by the flattery lavished on him and by his own natural gifts, everything is shocking, the least thing which he finds in his way or opposes him.' But she wrote crushingly enough herself to count Franz Thurn, whom she had sent to Florence with Leopold to guide him:

I cannot believe that you have known nothing . . . of the letters that have been written, which candidly have not been suitable. There is in them an arrogance and an impetuosity which are not reasonable and which, ten months ago when I saw my son seized with this frenzy, I attributed to the state of his health; but I tremble that it may be his character disclosing itself bit by bit . . . You have all forgotten that your establishment is entirely due to the generosity of the present emperor. Will or no will, you could never [otherwise] have hoped for a fate different from that of all the younger sons of our House: an apanage of 40,000 florins, while serving the eldest son all your life . . . You start pleading, haggling, looking for injustices; that has given offence, and I very much fear that this affair will create bitterness and coldness for a long time.[76]

It was not only Joseph who wrote devastating rebukes, and it was not only Joseph who received those of Maria Theresa. Poor Thurn died soon afterwards. But certainly the question rankled with Leopold, though it did not, at least on the surface, contaminate the brothers' later correspondence.[77]

Mother and son had agreed to establish out of the fortune of Francis, as his will had envisaged, a fund of over 8,000,000 florins for the provision of

---

[75] Arneth, *MTuJ* I, pp. 163–4 (J. to L., 5 Dec. 1765); Wandruszka, *L. II.*, vol. I, pp. 136–67.
[76] Arneth, *MTuJ* I, pp. 160–1 (M.T. to J., [?] late Nov. 1765); pp. 157–8 (M.T. to J., 26 Nov.); p. 161n (M.T. to Franz Thurn, 29 Nov.). Gooch, *Maria Theresa*, p. 20 has misunderstood this letter as a criticism of J. On M.T.'s earlier dissatisfaction with L., Wandruszka, *L. II.*, vol. I, pp. 101–5.
[77] On the death of Franz Thurn, Arneth, *GMT* VII, pp. 178–80; Wandruszka, *L. II.*, vol. I, pp. 153–4. On the brothers' relationship, *ibid.*, vol. I, pp. 164, 224.

dowries and so forth for the younger members of the family. The eldest sister, Marianne, who was intelligent but sickly, was made abbess of the imperial and royal convent for noble ladies in Prague, with the promise of 80,000 florins per annum.[78] Marie Christine, the next in line and her mother's favourite, was allowed to marry prince Albert of Saxony, whom she had come to love, although he was without lands. The pair were endowed by Maria Theresa to the tune of 4,000,000 florins, and Joseph assisted the process, with striking if uncharacteristic generosity, by transferring to them the duchy of Teschen, virtually the only land he possessed in his own right. Albert was to be governor (or *locum tenens*) of Hungary, with the reversion to the governorship of Belgium when the present incumbent, Francis's brother Charles, died. Joseph welcomed the whole arrangement with surprising enthusiasm:

For me, philosophical Joseph, nothing more agreeable could happen than to ensure for me such good company for my whole life; since I am unhappily without resources in my own house, this new family will be a great comfort to me, and I shall spend my moments of recreation there. I love the mistress and am a friend of the master of the house.[79]

Maria Theresa wrote to Kaunitz:

You sent my son back to me very quickly and quite decided. He couldn't wait for the moment when his sister was to be told. I summoned her; it was a touching scene, but the pleasure that I saw my son had in making them happy affected me more even than the satisfaction of arranging this marriage.[80]

One other member of his family gave Joseph happiness at this time: his little daughter, Maria Theresa, 'my second self'.[81] In February 1766 he took up with his mother the question of the young archduchess's education. His memorandum on the subject starts with a highly didactic and somewhat inconclusive discussion of what a princess needs in the way of education. Joseph seems unable to reconcile his two main points: first, that she must be well trained, so that she may command general respect and outshine potential mistresses in the eyes of her future husband; but secondly that she is very likely to marry a fool, since 'there are certainly ten of us to one agreeable

[78] In the end Marianne gave up the Prague position, and became abbess of Klagenfurt, with a smaller provision. See HHSA FA Sbde 10, 'Memoire sur la destination faite par S.M. L'Imp'ce de la Caisse particulierre et des fonds pour l'Etablissement de ses Enfans', in German.

[79] J. to L., 14 Nov. 1765 (Arneth, *MTuJ* I, pp. 152–4). Cf. J. to K., 10 Nov. 1765 (HHSA FA Sbde 70). Figures etc. from HHSA TG, ff. 258–9; K-M VI, p. 174; Mikoletzky, *Franz I. und der Ursprung des Familienvermögens*; Beer, *AÖG* (1895), esp. 134–5.

In Hungary, Belgium and Lombardy it was usual to appoint a member of the royal family as governor or viceroy, who was often referred to as Statthalter, lieutenant or, in Hungary, *locum tenens*.

[80] Arneth, *MTKuF* IV, p. 254 (M.T. to K., Nov. 1765). Cf. J. to K., 11 Nov. 1765 (Beer, *JLuK*, pp. 444–5).

[81] J. to M.T., 1 May 1769 (Arneth, *MTuJ* I, p. 265). See Plate 5a.

character. This arises from the educational prejudices and from the manner of life now existing almost universally in all Courts.' His recommendation is that his daughter should be entrusted to one thoroughly suitable governess, who should be permanent. She should preferably not be chosen from among the present Court ladies. His own choice would be the marquise d'Herzelles, who had previously struggled as governess with the wayward archduchess Elizabeth, but had abandoned the task and returned to her home in Belgium in 1763.

With apparent inconsequence, Joseph then launches into a tirade about the social life of the Court.

The Hofburg is an assemblage of a dozen old married ladies, three or four old maids, and twenty young girls, who are known as Ladies of the Court, seven archduchesses, an empress, two princes, [and] an emperor co-regent under the same roof – and yet no Society at all, or at least none that is rational or agreeable, since they all keep themselves to themselves. The gossiping and squabbling between one old woman and another, lady and lady, archduchess and archduchess, keep everyone at home, and 'What will people say?' prevents the most innocent gatherings or parties ... The intelligent, bored to death by the stupid women, eventually find an outlet for their intelligence, and then use it in unsuitable ways, whereas if they had the opportunity to deploy it in good company they would never contemplate such follies.

The remedies for this state of affairs are: to find more and better company, including men, for the archduchesses; to permit some of the ladies to receive without ceremony and with no account taken of rank or relationship; to rid the Court of several of the old women and 'these objects of pity who make others suffer and take the pleasure from all society'; to employ married women; and to let the ladies go out in less elaborate state and stay out later at night – till ten instead of eight.

At Schönbrunn, he unexpectedly adds, the gardens should be thrown open to anyone.

As for myself, [continued Joseph,] I can assure you that I shall always, without ulterior purpose, seek out the liveliest company and that in which I can learn the most, for it is certain that one can pick up and learn more in six months from associating with rational persons of intellect and culture than they themselves perhaps have learned in a very long time, since one extracts only the essence of the knowledge which they have acquired in several years of continuous labour.

Joseph wishes to be able to go out to good company in the evenings, not to formal assemblies but to private 'coteries'. Rather than hunt every day, 'shoot sparrows every day whatever the weather, and be dragged at walking pace through a town every day', it is more profitable to

frequent good society, get to know one's subjects, and amuse oneself – instead of with possessions and the chase – with our fellow-creatures, with men.

That the Emperor Rudolf didn't do it, that kings Frederick and Louis don't do it, does not mean that the Emperor Joseph ought not to do it. On the contrary, men of intellect, amiable and talented, like prince Kaunitz, Zinzendorf, O'Donnell, Mercy, do it. Consequently, Joseph the man, who wishes to be amiable, to possess intellect and talent, ought to do it. I infinitely prefer this last point of view, which is the way I look at myself, to all the titles of the world. And I shall not exchange my character as Joseph, good and zealous servant of his God, his sovereign and his state, throwing in certain of the pleasures of human life, for all the monarchies of Europe. It would be a sad situation if the status of Man were incompatible with that of Emperor.

Joseph here almost anticipates the egalitarianism of the *Magic Flute*: 'He is a prince. More than that – he is a man.' But having made his radical pronouncement, the emperor concludes, as usual, abjectly: 'I promise that even my conviction will never for a moment delay my blind submission.'[82]

No document shows better than this one the intensity of Joseph's revulsion from traditional Court life and against the restrictions imposed on him by the continuing authority of his mother as ruler and head of the family. The tone is almost that of teenage rebellion. But it is surely an extraordinary situation when the Holy Roman Emperor and co-regent has to submit arrangements for his daughter's education to his mother for approval, and has to write her a passionate memorandum pleading that he should be allowed to talk to whom he likes and to go out where and when he likes.[83] The connexion between the two subjects, tenuous in logic, is evidently close in Joseph's mind because the marquise d'Herzelles is a woman he admires, and whom he can imagine providing him, if she comes to Court, with some of the social opportunities he desires, as well as setting his daughter an appropriate example, 'more pleasant to copy than the disagreeable prudence of the moustachioed matrons of the Court'. 'If she [the marquise] is happy with complete trust and total freedom, both as to her servants and for herself, that is what she will get, because that is my system.' 'She will need to have dealings with no one save my august mother and myself: lodged next to my daughter, she will be quite separated from the rest of the bickering.'[84]

Maria Theresa agreed to the appointment, and the marquise was prevailed upon to return to Vienna. Two years later the old empress paid a formal visit to her granddaughter, was impressed, and complimented the governess. Joseph wrote to the marquise: 'I was right, then, to contend against all obstacles for this Flemish lady, while the whole terrifyingly respectable corps of Ayas and Grand Mistresses were expecting me simply to indicate my preference and choose one of their tone and type.' But Maria Theresa had taken care to give

---

[82] 24 Feb. 1766 (HHSA FA Sbde 55). W. H. Auden *et al.*, *The Great Operas of Mozart* (New York, 1962), p. 359. See Plate 5b.

[83] Karajan, *Feierliche Sitzungsberichte KAW* (1859), 66–8, prints letters showing that M.T. tried to restrict J. to what she considered suitable company.

[84] J. to his aunt, Anne Charlotte of Lorraine, abbess of Remiremont, 25 May 1766 (Kervyn de Lettenhove, *MARB in-8o* (1868), 55).

detailed instructions of a traditionalist character to guide the marquise in her task.[85]

However justified Joseph's strictures on the ladies of the Court may have been, it is not surprising that his dislike of them should have been reciprocated. Moreover, he notoriously enjoyed baiting his sisters. The archduchess Josepha, who died in the epidemic of 1767, must have been an exception, since Joseph was extremely fond of her. But when marriage plans for the archduchess Elizabeth fell through, her mother reported that 'she began to sob ... [saying] that all [the others] were established and she alone was left behind and destined to remain alone with the Emperor, which is what she will never do. We had great difficulty in silencing her.'[86]

During these years Joseph was nowhere more active and effective than in remodelling the ceremony and amusements of the Court, and to a lesser extent its administration. Here he had a freer hand than in most matters, for several reasons. First, some aspects of Court life were his affair alone: imperial etiquette; the pervasive ritual of the Order of the Golden Fleece of which he was the sovereign; and arrangements for hunting and shooting, since he was a man and the heir to his father's estates. Secondly, under the immediate impact of her husband's death, Maria Theresa herself felt disposed to limit pomp, frivolity and extravagance. She at first forbade her ladies to use rouge.[87] Thirdly, although Khevenhüller and other Court officials did their best to obstruct change, they possessed in their sphere nothing like the influence which, in questions concerning the Monarchy's public policy, the bureaucracy could exert.

The emperor hated the wearing of the Spanish mantle, according to Khevenhüller because with it he could not have his hair in a pigtail. Joseph himself wrote in the 'General picture':

Although the abolition of the mantle may appear of no importance, yet it seemed to me necessary, so that old prejudices might be entirely forgotten and totally eradicated, together with everything in matters of etiquette reminiscent of the past century.[88]

Court gala days were largely abolished, leaving New Year's Day as the only regular fête. The duration of mourning was halved. Joseph justified these measures chiefly on the ground that the previous arrangements had encouraged the import of foreign luxury goods. According to the French ambassa-

[85] J. to marquise d' Herzelles, 25 Apr. 1768 (Kervyn de Lettenhove, *MARB in-80* (1868), 15); M.T. to the marquise, 24 Oct. 1767 (*ibid.*, 11–13).
[86] M.T. to M.C. (Arneth, *GMT* VII, p. 540). On Josepha, Renier's despatch of 7 Oct. 1767, *ibid.*, pp. 548–9; E.L. to L.K., 29 Feb. 1768: 'plus qu'un gout ordinaire' (SOALpZ, LRRA P. 16/21).
[87] Arneth, *MTuJ* I, p. 140 (J. to L., 4 Oct. 1765) and n.
[88] From HHSA TG, ff. 261–2. See K-M VI, pp. 149–50 (31 Oct. 1765) and 522. Also H. Haupt, 'Die Aufhebung des Spanischen Mantelkleides durch Kaiser Joseph II.' in *ÖZKJ*, pp. 79–81. See Plate 20a.

dor, the public feared that the emperor's economical principles 'would progressively substitute a sad and too philosophical simplicity for the display appropriate to a great Court, and would eventually banish the amenities and pleasures necessary to the capital of a vast Empire'.[89]

Even more striking changes affected the Court's religious observances. At the end of 1765 Khevenhüller lamented that

this unhappy spirit of innovation, which appeared soon after the death of the late emperor Charles VI and has daily gathered strength, seems under the present reign to be going to gain complete control, so that, if it continues, we shall recognise scarcely any etiquette or order in the Court any more; for it has already now come to pass that, by superior order, the so-called Court Calendar, where all old Court devotions and old religious services were listed, has been more than half reformed and in the copies printed for the coming year the majority of the visits to churches have been omitted, as can at once be seen by comparing the old and the new Court Calendars.[90]

He was still further disturbed during Holy Week 1767:

On the 16th [April, Maundy Thursday] the [pre-]Easter communion was celebrated in the manner of last year, without distinctions of rank, but on this occasion also for the first time without the wearing of the mantle. The washing of the feet, although already announced and although everything had been prepared according to the old usage . . ., was suddenly abolished, and the chosen men and women received two ducats a head from charity.

No one could give me any reason for this further innovation, which naturally created an exceptional sensation, save that the emperor found it inconvenient and perhaps in some way dreaded it. It is certain that, when someone mentioned the matter to him in a friendly manner, he replied that people would inveigh against it for fourteen days but that then, as with other changes of the same kind, they would forget it. No doubt his lady mother, who is the only person who can get anywhere with this lord (who regards every old usage as idle prejudice), could have prevented this questionable innovation; but partly, as is well known, she inclines in the same direction herself, and partly she often lacks the necessary courage and firmness, from which he knows exactly how to win advantage . . .

On the 18th the visit to the Easter sepulchres was also abolished, although it could not have taken place in any case because of the rain.[91]

Joseph wrote in the 'General picture': 'Don't suppose on this account that we are any less devout . . . The fewer trappings associated with piety, the more solid it seems to be.'[92]

What was in question can be better appreciated with the aid of Zinzendorf's description of the old Maundy Thursday rite, as performed in 1762:

[89] On gala days, K-M VI, pp. 209–10, 215–16, 523; HHSA TG, ff. 260–1; Bérenger to Choiseul, 3 Dec. 1766 (AAE CP (Autriche), 306).
[90] K-M VI, p. 161 (31 Dec. 1765).   [91] *Ibid.*, pp. 231–2.   [92] HHSA TG, f. 263.

The emperor and the archdukes served the old men their food, but rather casually. When the earthenware plates had been removed from the table and put into each man's basket, the dessert was brought on, and then also put into their baskets. The table was moved away, a cloth was put over the old men's knees, and they each took off one shoe, partly on their own, partly with assistance. After bishop Marxer had been censed and the Gospel read, the emperor with a towel went down on his knees and kissed the feet of all of them, sliding on his knees from the first one to the last. Then the eleventh, called Strigauf [?], seventy-seven years old, delivered clearly and without embarrassment a harangue in an inflated style which had been written for him ... I didn't see any feet washed, so you could call it rather foot-kissing than foot-washing.[93]

The effect of these reforms of Joseph's was to shatter the mould that for centuries had fused royal and religious pomp and ceremony. The seventy-eight solemn services attended annually by the Court in various churches during the reign of Francis Stephen had been reduced to thirty-two by 1767, and by 1774 to twenty-two. Many of those that still continued were much curtailed.[94] The celebration of Maria Theresa's recovery from smallpox brought a momentary reaction: trumpets and drums, banned in 1752, were again permitted during the liturgy. Joseph said that if people wanted them, they should have them.[95] But another newly invented festivity symbolised changing attitudes. Until now Van Swieten had prevented any of the imperial family being inoculated against smallpox, believing the treatment harmful. But after the epidemic of 1767, Maria Theresa arranged for her children and sixty-five others to be inoculated by John Ingenhousz, sent out from England with a recommendation from George III. When the experiment succeeded, a feast was held at Schönbrunn on 5 October 1768, at which the royal family waited on the sixty-five.[96]

As for amusements, Joseph substantially reduced the number of horses in the imperial stables. This was economical, and anyway he himself took little interest in hunting. His particular penchant at this time was for the smaller-scale sport of coursing.[97] He set about exterminating the wild boars hitherto preserved as game, because they damaged crops. He proudly informed Leopold on 19 December 1765 that his sisters had already shot 1400 of them that year.[98] He opened to the public an old hunting reserve of the Court's on the edge of Vienna, the Prater, previously restricted to the nobility.

[93] HHSA TZ, 8 Apr. 1762.
[94] Kovács, *MÖSA* (1979), esp. pp. 128–9nn, 132n. See above, p. 36.
[95] C. Wolfsgruber, *Christoph Anton Kardinal Migazzi, Fürsterzbischof von Wien* (Saulgau, 1890), p. 463; K-M VI, p. 246.
[96] Arneth, *GMT* VII, pp. 335–6. Stormont to Weymouth, 2 Nov. 1768 (PRO SP 80/205).
[97] Cf. HHSA TG, ff. 265–6 and J.'s letters to L. in 1765, esp. 26 Sep. (Arneth, *MTuJ* I, pp. 134–6) and 19 Oct. (*ibid.*, pp. 145–6). Arneth omitted some passages on coursing, e.g. in the letters of 12 Sept. and 4 Oct. (HHSA FA Sbde 7).
[98] Arneth, *MTuJ* I, p. 168.

Every day [reported the Venetian ambassador] and especially on holidays, the crowd is so great that it has become a most attractive spectacle. Immediately by the entrance have been built on various sites a multiplicity of houses suitable to receive those who want to amuse themselves, and much food and drink is consumed to the profit of the royal treasury. The emperor, the empress, the archdukes and the archduchesses are happy to appear there, and so that everyone may enjoy complete and egalitarian liberty, it has been ordained that no one should make any sign of respect or obeisance at the appearance of the emperor and the imperial family. Such a concession, which creates an impression of democracy in a part of Vienna which is ruled despotically, has gained for him immense goodwill and applause.[99]

Life at Court and outside were both affected by the prohibition of gambling card-games, at first because of Francis's death, later by a permanent order to which Joseph attached great significance. His argument was that faro, Maria Theresa's favourite, and similar games of chance had caused the ruin of many individuals and injury to others. According to Khevenhüller Joseph did not know how to play any card-game properly, even innocent picquet; and the consequence of the prohibition was that at Court there was, 'so to speak, no kind of rallying-point for society'.[100]

The theatres of the capital depended heavily on Court patronage. During the lengthy mourning for Francis, public performances ceased altogether. The empress handed over to her son the making of future arrangements – or so she said. The main issue was whether to give any state subsidy or privilege to foster opera and drama, since without government help impresarios would face two particular difficulties. First, Kaunitz and the higher nobility attached immense importance to maintaining a French theatre company, which experience had shown was uneconomic. Secondly, the chances that theatres would make a profit had been reduced by the new prohibition on gambling. Hitherto, casinos established in the foyers had subsidised the other entertainments.

Joseph proved, as so often, to have a developed and dogmatic view:

I can only reiterate what I believe to be in every way glorious and appropriate to say: that, since the state regards [shows] as trifles, and sovereigns do not treat them as ceremonial occasions and attend them only for want of anything better, we should not contribute in any way ... to any shows that take place in this capital, but leave to entrepreneurs, the nobility and amateurs complete freedom to mount such performances within the limits imposed by public decency, making no exception from Punch-and-Judy shows to the plays of the Greeks, with free choice of language as of music ...

Then ... we shall have peace.

[99] Arneth, *GMT* VII, p. 527 (despatch of 3 May 1766). My 'egalitarian' is a translation of 'popolar'. See K-M VI, pp. 441–2.
[100] HHSA TG, f. 117; K-M VI, pp. 149 (28 Oct. 1765), 182 (8 May 1766) and 219 (13 Jan. 1767).

The emperor wished to entrust the direction of all public entertainments, on this basis, to one impresario, Afflisio.[101]

Maria Theresa was concerned above all to maintain control over any theatre established near the Court. She claimed that otherwise she would never be able to risk attending the performances. She resorted to the mediation of Kaunitz, to whom she sent several confidential and anguished notes on the subject.

> I am resisted to the uttermost in the affair of the theatre. You alone can rescue me. Prepare me a clause such as you spoke of yesterday: that the permission shall be null and void unless [Afflisio] maintains full decency in the show and in the persons involved, for whom he must answer. There is another point that you alone can carry for me: that you promise me to have nothing to do with these women and girls, and never to be seen in their homes.
>
> I am sure of you, but this example influences others . . . I require this sacrifice of you for my peace of mind, and that Afflisio shall never appear as director and never approach the emperor . . .

She would not allow Kaunitz to take public or official charge of any theatre, because that would be to associate his respected name with 'what is vilest in the Monarchy'. However, she did sign a contract with Afflisio. But the venture soon went bankrupt, and the impresario fled to Italy, where he was eventually sentenced to the galleys.[102]

Joseph tried to be exceedingly economical in his Court administration. Unlike his father, he did not keep a separate Court from Maria Theresa's. But initially, little was saved by amalgamating the two institutions, because it was considered necessary to provide for all those previously employed. However, the German Guard was rendered less expensive, and the Swiss Guard was replaced – as seemed, wrote Joseph in the 'General picture', 'more fitting for the House of Austria against whom they had once been rebels'.[103] Something therefore was achieved in this field, but there was good ground for the scepticism of the British representative:

> I have from time to time given Accounts of all the Emperor's Projects of Oeconomy, rather to show his Turn and Views, than as thinking they can produce any material Change in the State of the Finances of this Country; the Empress Queen's Liberality will dissipate faster, than he can save.[104]

---

[101] J.'s letter in Arneth, *GMT* IX, pp. 584–5 (dated in the original 9 Apr. 1767; HHSA FA Sbde 70). On the theatre question in general, the relevant volumes of the Austrian Academy's *Theatergeschichte Österreichs*: Zechmeister, *Die Wiener Theater* and O. Michtner, *Das alte Burgtheater als Opernbühne* (Vienna, 1970). In English, Wraxall, *Memoirs*, vol. II, pp. 442–3, and (of much wider interest than its title suggests) J. Rosselli, *The Opera Industry in Italy from Cimarosa to Verdi* (Cambridge, 1984).

[102] Arneth, *GMT* IX, pp. 269–76, 585; HHSA FA Sbde 70; Rosselli, *Opera Industry*, pp. 29, 185. Afflisio's name is spelt in several different ways.

[103] Arneth, *GMT* VII, p. 526.   [104] Langlois to Conway, 9 July 1766 (PRO SP 80/203).

Still, as a result of the changes made during these years, largely on Joseph's initiative, the Court had been transformed. Dr John Moore, who spent some time in Vienna during the 1770s, wrote: 'I had often heard of the scrupulous etiquette of the Imperial court, but have found everything directly opposite to that account.'[105]

JOSEPH AS HIS FATHER'S HEIR: THE ATTACK ON THE STATE DEBT

As his father's heir, Joseph had the opportunity to act independently and decisively in financial matters. Apart from helping to establish the fund to provide for his brothers and sisters, he devoted the whole of his father's fortune to the cause of reducing the state debt and shoring up the Monarchy's finances. In the 'General picture' Joseph described the financial position and gave his own estimate of the importance to the state of his munificence. It is interesting that he was judicious enough to give weight to views which he had earlier combated. The fact that his account is oversimplified and in some details inaccurate does not greatly reduce the historian's gratitude that it is so clear and free of technicalities.

At the end of the war, he begins,

the finances and revenues of the Monarchy were ... in the saddest state in the world ... It was only by incurring new debts that current expenditure could be met ... The loss of all credit ... by a bankruptcy was inevitable ... To obtain more money from the country by augmenting the Contribution was an impossibility, both because in the long run the provinces would not have been in a position to supply it, and because it would not therefore have been a genuine remedy, since it would have deprived the state beforehand of all conceivable recourse in a time of war ...

Other possible new impositions would have been too small for the purpose, and in any case harmful to trade.

So there was no other course open than to cut down expenses ... To procure for the state an annual saving proportionate to its needs, it was necessary either to reduce the military, or salaries, or to damage the credit of the Monarchy by a forced reduction of interest [rate].

But the army needed more than its 16,000,000 florins a year, not less; and its requirements had still not been satisfied by the additional 500,000 florins provided by the Hungarian diet in 1764. 'To reduce its cost was ... to lay ourselves open to dictation by our formidable neighbours.' To cut salaries seemed equally impossible. A variety of expedients was considered, such as inaugurating tontines,[106] expanding the issue of paper money initiated in 1762, or transferring money from the Netherlands.

---

[105] [J. Moore,] *A View of Society and Manners in France, Switzerland, and Germany* (2 vols., London, 1779), vol. II, p. 305.

[106] Annuities shared by subscribers to a loan, the last survivor taking all.

But all these projects would not have fulfilled the three great aims that the state must always promote, which are the provision of a formidable army, the maintenance of credit, and the increase of the wellbeing and domestic wealth of its subjects ...

It looked as though the debt, which amounted to nearly 300,000,000 florins, would never be reduced.

At this juncture, the sad event at Innsbruck, while most justly afflicting us, nonetheless came opportunely to save the state. Nearly 18,000,000 florins in papers and money were found in his late Majesty's strongboxes, not counting lands ... The plan was formed of saving the state 1 per cent interest per annum, by a voluntary reduction of the rate of interest from 5 and 6 per cent to 4 per cent. Loans were therefore raised in Holland, the southern Netherlands and Genoa, which, with the money in the strong boxes, took the total amount of cash to nearly 18,000,000 florins, with which we ventured to offer to all the Bank's creditors the repayment of their capital if they did not wish to allow their interest to be reduced to 4 per cent ... This plan had all imaginable success, and only 14,140,000 florins were repaid ... [Since new capital came in to the amount of] 5,940,000 florins, the whole conversion caused the Bank to repay only 8,200,000 florins ... It is noteworthy that this reduction of interest was achieved without employing the force or the power of the sovereign.

Overall, the state saved 870,000 florins a year. Further, he says, the whole economy benefited: the price of land rose, since the return on it was rendered by the conversion more nearly comparable with the return on state loans; and substantial amounts of capital were made available for worthwhile enterprises. Finally,

the equity and punctuality shown on this occasion to the state's creditors has so augmented our credit both internally and externally that our Bank in particular ... is certain of obtaining ... at reasonable rates as much money as it wishes ... and that [almost] all other public bonds ... now stand at par ...
  That is what has so far been done of importance in finance.

Joseph went on to describe what he regarded as minor activities, such as tax-farming, attempts to increase tax yields and efforts to improve accounting. On the last point, he has to confess that there still exists no accurate statement of the revenues and expenses of the Monarchy, though one is in preparation. He devotes considerable space to a campaign to modernise book-keeping in government offices. The double entry method was 'found too difficult by the *Hofrechenkammer* itself', although 'every scamp in the schools of the Piarists[107] masters it in six months'. So a less demanding procedure has been invented and introduced, called the *Cameral-fuss*. But this has so far produced only a mountain of paper, a doubling of the number of officials, and faulty returns. It is hoped, however, that in the end it will yield the desired results, and the Piarists are now helping by teaching this method. No doubt Joseph's

---

[107] A teaching order of recent foundation (1617).

jaundiced account of the impact of the reform is at least partly justified. It is a story that was to be many times repeated in this history of the Monarchy.

Finally, he referred to an attempt to introduce 'the *Erbsteuer* [inheritance tax] for the clergy regular as well as secular, and the Teutonic and Maltese Orders'. Agreement had not been reached, and so negotiations were proceeding with the papacy to try to obtain for the state, instead, a tenth of all the tithes paid to the clergy.[108] This issue was soon to become important in the story of church–state relations and Josephism.[109]

Joseph was surely justified in treating the debt conversion, made possible by his gift to the state, as the major financial development of the co-regency. It was not universally welcomed. The British representative thought it less completely successful than the emperor made out. The public burning of the superseded obligations gave the whole operation an antiquated and superstitious air.[110] It was criticised both because it dissipated Joseph's heritage and as a misuse of money in a time of international tension, heavy taxation, dearth and inflation.[111] But it must have contributed significantly to the unique achievement of two later years of the co-regency, 1775 and 1777, when the Monarchy's budget was actually balanced.[112]

Certainly, it was a completely convincing demonstration of Joseph's devotion to the state, and of his consistency – here was one of the two main aims of the *Rêveries* realised. Very few other rulers have been willing to surrender their private capital to public purposes. If the fortune had been left to Maria Theresa, she would surely have used it on her family, her favourites and her palaces. The contrast between father and son is blinding. In the previous year, Francis had managed to save over a million florins by economical use of the money provided by his wife and her subjects towards Joseph's coronation as king of the Romans. The Monarchy was already suffering from the financial crisis described in the 'General picture', and

---

[108] To this point, I have done little more than summarise the account in HHSA TG, ff. 47–69 (HHSA FA Sbde 88). Arneth, *GMT* VII, pp. 204–9, did the same, with less quotation and without acknowledgement.

   A memorandum by Hatzfeld, of 2 Jan. 1768 (also in HHSA FA Sbde 88) (partly published in Beer, *AÖG* (1895), 133–5) commented on J.'s original draft of this section; and it is clear that J. took some note of it in his final version. Lacy also commented (HHSA NL, Karton 3, Lacy to J., no. XLIV, n.d.).

   Little that has been published improves on J.'s account. See, however, Beer, *AÖG* (1895), 18–32, 124–35, and Mikoletzky, *Österreich. Das grosse 18. Jahrhundert*, pp. 215–21 and the literature there cited. He evaluates the '*Kameral-Rechnungs-Fuss*' more positively than Joseph did. Dr P. G. M. Dickson's *Finance and Government under M.T.* will establish the matter on a new footing, and his advice has saved me from many errors in this section.

[109] See below, pp. 444, 448.

[110] E.g. Langlois to Grafton, 23 Apr. 1766 and to Conway, 4 June 1766 (PRO SP 80/203).

[111] E.L. to L.K., 26 Oct. 1765 (SOALpZ, LRRA P. 16/19); Lacy to J., no. XLII, n.d. but must be Apr. 67 (HHSA NL, Karton 3); Arneth, *GMT* VII, pp. 527–8. Bernard, *J. II*, pp. 33–4, treats J.'s action as a mistake on economic grounds.

[112] Arneth, *GMT* IX, pp. 442–3.

Francis was in charge of efforts to restore the situation. But he paid this profit into his private fortune.[113]

THE MEMORANDUM OF 1765

Sometime between the death of his father and the end of 1765, Joseph wrote for his mother a 'Memorandum on the defects of the present system and the most effectual means of remedying them'. Arneth published this document in the original French, though curiously without its proper title.[114] It has been briefly discussed by many historians. In English the principal account comes from G. P. Gooch, who in his *Maria Theresa and Other Studies* translated portions of it, summarised more and commented on the whole. 'This massive disquisition', he wrote, 'ranks with the two Political Testaments of Frederick the Great among the classical utterances of the era of the Philosophical Despots.'[115] There remains much to be said about it. It has never been seriously studied as a manifesto of enlightened despotism. Nor has it been sufficiently recognised as an early statement of a wide range of policies which Joseph pursued for the rest of his life.

It deals with domestic affairs only, does not refer to the state debt and says little about the Court. In other words, it relates to those aspects of internal policy in which the co-regent could do nothing except by persuading his mother to endorse his plans. It falls between the *Rêveries* of 1763 and the 'General picture' of 1768 not just in date but also in scale and approach. It contains roughly 10,000 words, as against about 3,500 in the *Rêveries* and about 40,000 in the 'General picture'. It is more comprehensive and in some respects less extreme than the *Rêveries*. As compared with the 'General picture', it is a more personal statement, concerned with what Joseph as an individual would like changed, whereas the later treatise deals, for the most part objectively, with what the government has done and is likely soon to do.

The format is interesting, because characteristic. It is not exactly muddled,

---

113 Mikoletzky, *Österreich, Das grosse 18. Jahrhundert*, p. 223.

Beer, *AÖG* (1895), 18–19, points out that J. did not propose the debt conversion out of the blue. But he does not mention the *Rêveries*, which show that J. himself was concerned with the question earlier. M.T.'s letter of 24 Aug. 1765, with which he seeks to show that she took the initiative, was written before she knew that J. was named sole heir in her husband's will. In the event it was J. who was in the position to decide.

114 Arneth, *MTuJ* III, pp. 335–61. In HHSA FA Sbde 87 is a copy, corrected by Joseph, with the title 'Memoire sur les defauts du sisteme actuel et sur les moyens les plus efficaces pour y remédier'. Arneth's version includes the corrections. The archivist was evidently right who wrote on it that J. originally dictated it.

K-M VI, pp. 467–8, publishes a document from the same source which the editor, Schlitter, suggests was notes for the memorandum. I doubt this. Certainly, the memorandum departs radically from the 'notes', and also fails to cover some of the twenty-four points listed. The piece begins: 'Comandes sans voire qu'ils s'executent ont un manque de force ou de volonte.'

115 Gooch, *M.T.*, pp. 21–9.

but it is badly organised: the effect is of ideas tumbling out in haste and some disorder. Five separate numerical classifications and sub-classifications are employed, one of them running to seventeen heads; but they do not always correspond with the divisions of the argument. General points are mixed up with what seem like petty details, such as a proposal that owners of diamonds should be required to register them. It was evidently dictated. The style, like Joseph's conversation, is at times 'somewhat dry and laconic'.[116] But some passages are powerful and eloquent.

I have already quoted from the section in which the emperor, after describing his apprenticeship on the *Staatsrat* during the discussion of changes in the financial administration, announced his rejection of all theoretical systems in politics.[117] He then went on to consider the administration as a whole, acknowledging that here he lacked detailed knowledge and so could deal only in general principles. 'There is no minister in the state, other than prince Kaunitz, who can claim to have rendered any service in recent years. All the rest of the good that has been done, sparse enough in any case, the state owes to the prudent collaboration of twelve persons at least.' In general, he goes on, committees are thoroughly unsatisfactory. They lead to compromises, which 'certainly incorporate the essence of the two [or more] views, but miss the purpose'.

Another great evil of the Monarchy is the mutual distrust between the administrative heads and their subordinates. The former fear that they may have to discipline the latter, who of course wish to safeguard themselves at all costs. The result is that no constructive work is done, and 'among the hundred reams of paper consumed every week in the ministries of Vienna there are only four pages of intelligence, novelties or original ideas'. 'I do not think that so many requests and enquiries have been made in [any previous] century as in the last three years, and yet we know less [than before].' Vast sums are wasted on administration in order to save a few florins. Drastic action is necessary if ruin is to be avoided.

The members of the *Staatsrat* have worked like supermen, especially in using up paper. But they cannot hope to achieve much, because they lack the necessary information and because the council's basis is defective: 'Can it be described as anything more than a council which watches over the finances and the Chancellery of Austria and Bohemia?' 'Henceforward every council held should be a gathering of ministers from the various departments.' If they disagree, they should come and put their points of view to the emperor, who will settle the dispute. 'By this means all committees and multiple memoranda would be cut out.' To save more money and time, Joseph further proposed the amalgamation of several pairs of then distinct departments.

However, he continued, the important thing is not the administrative

[116] K-M VI, p. 138 (7 Sep. 1765).   [117] See pp. 107–8 above.

structure but the selection and treatment of officials. In choosing them he would consider nothing save their fitness for the precise task in question, and would take no account of 'age, ancestors, connexions, friendships, chastity or bigotry'. Elsewhere in the memorandum he stridently rules out any objection to *mésalliances*, and goes on:

We inherit from our parents at birth only animal life. Whether king, count, citizen or peasant, it makes not the slightest difference. Gifts of mind and spirit we receive from the Creator; vices or virtues come to us from good or bad education, and from the examples we see.

'In order to inspire people to serve the state', every soldier and official of the government or Court should take precedence over every other person.

Joseph would brief his officials as follows:

I entrust to you this department. You will govern it in my name, but with the same authority as if I were doing it myself ... I shall never listen to anyone with an axe to grind, or to menials, so long as you serve me well. But ... since I give complete liberty to the whole universe to bring me their complaints, and [since I] have their truth rigorously examined, as soon as I see in you partiality or weakness, you will be reproached. If you have not the capacity, it is my fault as much as yours for having chosen you, and you will be transferred as befits your talents ... But let me never find in you faults of malice or against justice, interested views or deceit. Be assured that the purest blood running in your veins, fifty years service, your whole family or connexions, and anyone dear to me, would not stop me for an instant from punishing you for just one of these faults in the most ignominious, the most painful and the most public fashion in the face of all Europe.

The emperor next states some general principles 'which in all the detailed affairs of our Monarchy ought to be kept in view, in order to attain the great aim'. The ruler, though he should not interfere in the day-to-day administration of justice, must maintain its impartiality and prevent delays. He must also ensure that 'simplicity and clarity' characterise legislation. But

I consider the principal aim, in accordance with which not only the government in general but also the financial and military administrations ought to regulate their actions, to be population, that is the conservation and the augmentation of [the number of] subjects.

There will then be more men to defend the state and overawe other Powers, and the country will be richer both by increased taxes and higher consumption. Immigrants of both sexes and all ages should be welcomed.

After population come internal trade and industry, which should be encouraged by the abolition of restrictions and monopolies, especially with a view to increasing the state's revenue. Nobles should be applauded, not blamed, if they engage in commerce. Exports are beneficial, because they bring silver into the country. Imports, except for spices, should simply be forbidden.

It is very important that 'impositions should be equal, that the lord, the citizen and the peasant should contribute in just proportions'. But the sovereign should reduce his expenditure as much as possible.

His inviolable maxim ought always to be that his person and his happiness and true pleasure cannot be separated from the good of the Monarchy. How could he think himself rich if he had money in his coffers but the provinces were depopulated and impoverished? The proposition that two and two make four is not more true than the statement that a hundred florins in a hundred different purses are worth more and are more useful than a thousand [*sic*] florins in one.

'I could never regard it as just to flay two hundred good peasants in order to overpay an idle lord.'

As to the relations between the central government and the provinces,

To cut short all these immense correspondences ... I would lay down that at the beginning of every year the chiefs of each province ... [viz. Bohemia, Moravia, Austria, the Littoral, the Tyrol, Hungary, Transylvania and the military frontier], one civil and one military, should come to the capital, bringing an exact account of everything that has passed under all heads in the previous year ...

After they have been thoroughly examined by the sovereign and the councils, they should be sent back to get on with their tasks, according to their instructions, for a further year. Any appointments vacated during the year would remain unfilled until the annual visit to Vienna. 'As there are eight chiefs, and all of them coming with their ideas at the same time would throw the departments into disorder, I would assign each of them a different month in which his political year would begin.'

Joseph then starts on a series of 'detached ideas' under seventeen headings. The first five chiefly concern education and related religious questions.

Education is much neglected here. Parents ... think they have achieved everything, and have produced a great man for the state, when their son serves Mass, tells his rosary, confesses every fortnight, and reads nothing but what the limited outlook of his priest leads him to believe is permitted.

This attitude would be admirable 'if our state were a monastery, and our neighbours Carthusians'.

One major source of weakness in the Monarchy's schools and universities is that they are located in big towns, where there is too much dissipation and distraction. Moreover, the professors are too well paid. All young nobles ought to serve for at least three years in the army at their own charge, or else be ineligible for any government post or honour.

Monasteries are too thriving for the good of the state. They entice too many people to take vows before they are old enough to know their minds, thus depriving the state of the services of men of genius. 'I should ordain, whatever the pope and all the monks in the universe might say, that none of my subjects could embrace any ecclesiastical condition before the age ... of twenty-five completed years.' Further,

> I should have all existing foundations examined by an impartial commission. In the places where the intentions of the founder were being disregarded, I should reform them and employ them for pious purposes which would be at the same time useful to the state, such as the education of children who, while becoming Christians, would become good subjects.

Monasteries which had become too large would be reduced in size, and their surplus inmates would be sent to minister in areas short of clergy.

Under a later heading, where the advantages of persuading foreigners to live in the Monarchy are proclaimed, Joseph returns to his attack on the present religious position. How can people be expected to come and live under Habsburg rule when 'they have to change their morals and their libraries at the frontier'? A ruler has no business to try converting foreigners. In any case, forcible conversion is morally valueless. Except in extreme cases non-Catholics, if suitable on other grounds, should be employed by the state as readily as Catholics. 'For the service of God is inseparable from that of the state, and he wishes us to employ those to whom he has given talents and the capacity for business, leaving to his divine mercy the reward of the good souls and the punishment of the bad.'

Similarly, the censorship system is both ineffective and damaging. All prohibited books can in fact be purchased in Vienna 'at double cost'. But the prohibitions unnecessarily restrict citizens, and discourage foreigners from entering the Monarchy.

> I believe that, in everything that can be called trivial or a matter of private taste, full liberty should be left to men, while requiring first and foremost that in all matters of concern to the state they should submit blindly and look at things from the same point of view as the sovereign decrees. To this end, the liberty innate in Man should be accorded to him so far as possible, and the sovereign should not even want to know everything that is going on, for he is not obliged to try to punish people himself when there is no accuser, or to prevent evil of which he knows nothing.

Luxurious living of all kinds should be discouraged. The prohibition of imports from abroad will diminish the possibilities of expenditure on rich materials for clothes. Soldiers should always appear in uniform. Officials should wear black except on the one gala day which Joseph will allow at Court. At table, French wine and cooking should cease to be fashionable, and only one course should be served.

He naturally devotes considerable space to his particular charge, the army. Here he reiterates many of the ideas found in his first memorandum of 1761, for example that troops should be quartered in their provinces, be encouraged to marry and also to do useful work of all kinds. Recruits should be sought abroad with the utmost vigour. Promotion should be strictly by merit. Old soldiers should be employed in all possible walks of life, to save the state paying them a pension. In particular, the police should become their preserve.

He is passionately anxious to travel.

I consider it an absolute necessity for a sovereign, and it is indispensably necessary, whether politically, civilly or militarily, that one should see for oneself what is going on. It is not that I am arrogant enough to believe that all defects will be remedied by my presence and inspection. But ... although we see things half-disguised and looking their best, nevertheless, if we return several times, we see differences, hear complaints, get to know subjects [suitable] to be employed later ... see the lie of the land ... and judge more or less the capacity and zeal of our ministers.

He does not wish to travel in state at great cost. The monarch

ought to adopt the style of a private person, so that he does not do more harm to his peoples by his travels than the good they could derive from his presence [among them]. It is given only to the great to change their condition, they can become small and private when they like; others, by contrast, whatever they may want, will always remain private persons.

His peroration again praised Kaunitz and his department. Maria Theresa's own courage and fortitude are made grounds for hope that she will adopt his proposals. These stand or fall together, and 'great things must be done at a stroke'. 'The aim of every provision is directed to the whole, every action is related to the universal point of view which alone the sovereign and the most loyal servants must recognise and pursue.' If he is forced, like 'a modern apostle, to proselytise and win everyone round to my faith', it will 'arouse my yearning for fame, the only motive other than duty which governs my actions and would make me gladly risk my neck'. At this stage in his life Joseph is still thoroughly optimistic:

Everything in the world can be good if one removes its defects and strengthens its merits. The greatest of all prejudices, and the least pardonable, is not to dare to attack and break them. Much courage and still more patriotism are needed to be an innovator in this century ... We shall give an account one day of the good that we should have sought and attained.

But of course, if she rejects his advice and tells him to follow 'the more enlightened ideas of others', he will cheerfully do her bidding.[118]

As we have seen,[119] Joseph claimed to have abandoned his *Rêveries*, and in some respects the claim seems justified. Though the memorandum of 1765

---

[118] It has not seemed right to clutter up the last few pages with detailed footnote references to so comparatively short a document as the memorandum of 1765. In general, I have followed Joseph's order. See Arneth, *MTuJ* III, pp. 335–61.

[119] See p. 106 above. The mentions of *rêveries* in the memorandum of 1765 are on pp. 335 and 360 of Arneth, *MTuJ* III.

makes no allowances for the autonomy and variety of the provinces, it says nothing either about the withdrawal or flouting of their privileges. Even the Hungarian constitution goes unscathed. Population growth, not the humbling of the nobility, is now singled out as the ruler's first concern. Joseph's declaration of financial atheism, with its apparently general implications, appears to show that he has become less doctrinaire and has learned a lesson in pragmatism; and he excuses on the ground of his ignorance and inexperience the theoretical tone of his other remarks. He now praises Kaunitz, whom he had earlier criticised. He has become disenchanted with the *Staatsrat*. However, he allowed himself to refer even in this memorandum to 'my detached points of *rêveries*'. The criticism of the nobility, who are said not to know the meaning of patriotism, is as violent as before, though less central. Moreover, some of the new ideas in the memorandum seem to be potentially as alarming as those that have been discarded from the *Rêveries*: the ecclesiastical schemes are very advanced for a Catholic state.

It is again impossible to know at all precisely how Joseph arrived at these views. The only thinker mentioned in the whole piece is Voltaire, expressly so that his influence can be repudiated. But the populationist theory, that an increase in the number of inhabitants will infallibly bring greater wealth and strength to the state, was a commonplace of eighteenth-century political thinking, especially in the German-speaking lands. Maria Theresa herself accepted it, so long as it did not involve the issue of monastic professions and religious celibacy. It was restated by Joseph von Sonnenfels, professor of political science at the University of Vienna, in the first volume of his *Foundations of the Study of Politics, Commerce and Finance*, which appeared in the same year as Joseph wrote his memorandum and had been composed under the direct supervision of the *Staatsrat*.[120]

Restriction of imports was also a commonplace aim, long advocated by statesmen and political writers. It was especially respectable in Vienna just at this moment, when the government was trying to restore the Monarchy's industry after the ravages of war. However, to argue for the mere limitation of imports, in cases where the products concerned were available internally or else not strictly needed, was more usual and more realistic than to propose total exclusion. The emperor's view here was old-fashioned, and his continued inclination to it for the rest of his life brought him into conflict with the growing number of proponents of freer trade between states. In particular, his

---

[120] See R. A. Kann, *A Study in Austrian Intellectual History* (New York, 1973), pp. 175–8; Schünemann, *Österreichs Bevölkerungspolitik*, esp. pp. 7–10.

   K. in his comments on J.'s memorandum seems clear that J. is associating his attack on the monasteries with the population question (Beer, *AÖG* (1872), 107). J.'s wording does not seem to require this interpretation, though it would be up-to-date and like Sonnenfels's theory. J. is explicitly concerned only with keeping potential servants of the state, and persons unsuitable to be monks and nuns, out of the cloister (Arneth, *MTuJ* III, p. 350).

extremism on this issue separated him from the new school of French economists, known as the 'physiocrats', who are often supposed to have influenced him.[121]

His emphasis in the memorandum on the equality of men at birth, and on the overwhelming influence of education thereafter, is a common enough attitude for the eighteenth century, and had been present in Beck's compendium.[122] On the other hand, as in the *Rêveries*, he showed himself exceptionally radical in his stated determination to disregard aristocratic birth and connexions in making appointments, and to tax nobles equally with other subjects. But although he expresses sympathy with peasants, he makes no specific proposal to ease their lot, as he had in the first memorandum of 1761.

Much of the memorandum amounts to a barely concealed critique of his mother's methods and opinions. This is true of her religious attitudes, as we shall see later.[123] The existing administrative system, officials and practices are openly condemned. Implicitly, so is the manner of appointing civil servants and army officers, and the way they are managed. Too many noblemen are employed, they are paid too much, pensions are too freely given.

It is right that a sovereign should be generous, even in accordance with his whim; but it is of his own money, set aside for his pleasures, that he is master, not of responsible offices and employments in the state, nor of raising or creating salaries charged to an appropriated fund. By handing out tasks without the strictest observance of merit he sins against his duty and against justice, which gives to every subject, if he has the appropriate merit and talent, the *jus quaesitum*. I would rather make a gift of 50,000 florins to an officer than promote him on some pretext in our present system – and the same with civil employments.[124]

As he showed in his application of his father's fortune, Joseph made exceptionally clear distinctions between the public and the private capacities of the monarch, between state and family considerations. He extended these distinctions, where applicable, to other persons. There was nothing he was more anxious to eradicate than 'interested views' among officials, especially if they involved the exploitation of office for private gain. He disapproved of fees and perquisites, and favoured salaries. He proved a determined opponent of the long-accepted method of promoting industry in under-developed provinces of the Monarchy, whereby the officials concerned had been encouraged to take up shares in the new enterprises, so that public and private

---

[121] Schünemann, *MÖIG* (1933), esp. 19–20. Cf. Eckhart, *A bécsi udvar gazdasági politikája*, esp. pp. 356–8; and, on the trade war after 1763, Loebl, *AÖG* (1903), 376–7.

[122] Conrad, *RuV*, pp. 191, 271–3.   [123] See pp. 445–7 below.

[124] Arneth, *MTuJ* III, p. 357. On pensions and the difference between M.T. and J. in these matters, see Wagner in Winters and Held, *Intellectual and Social Developments*. Dr R. F. Tuck has very kindly informed me that *jus quaesitum* classically means a sought-after legal decision, and that the reference here seems to be to *Digest* I.1.10, in spirit rather than in letter. J. must mean 'the rights he has earned'.

profit would go hand in hand. He objected on the same grounds to tax-farming.[125]

His attitude to travel corresponds to this conception of the monarch's role. The journeys, he says,

should be arranged with the needful economy, and divested of the old prejudices which deluded sovereigns into believing that they were governing gloriously and themselves holding the reins of government when they had seen and learned nothing except through others' eyes and reports, and that a monarch was doing enough when he was playing his role of phantom of glory.

He considers it positively beneficial that the ruler should travel incognito.[126] Similarly, he should behave when at home as the first servant of the state, the chief functionary, and not as the godlike fount of honours, pageantry and largesse.

A trivial example will highlight the difference of attitude between mother and son. The Belgian prince de Ligne, serving in the Monarchy's army, recalled in his memoirs that, furious at not being at once appointed on the death of his father to command the family regiment and to a Knighthood of the Golden Fleece, he had written to the appropriate official, using the phrase: 'Born in a land where there are no slaves, I shall be in a position to take my small merit and fortune elsewhere.' When this insubordination became known to Maria Theresa and Joseph, they called a 'council of war'. The emperor wanted to take the initiative and dismiss the prince forthwith. Another member wanted him imprisoned. But a third, marshal Lacy, made the courtier's suggestion which the empress adopted: for three months she would refuse to speak to Ligne, or to look at him when he kissed hands. The prince claimed that on one occasion during the period of this cruel sentence he had caught her laughing.[127]

What Joseph has to say about clothes – and even about diamonds – is in fact highly significant for his view of monarchy. The Spanish mantle was objectionable not only because it was antiquated, and irretrievably associated with the old quasi-religious Court ceremonies, but also because it was costly, and to wear it was a matter of privilege. In Europe generally, and for ordinary Court occasions even in Vienna, the *habit habillé* had superseded it. This was the elaborate and colourful dress characteristic of eighteenth-century portraits, which Francis generally wore, and which most people can be seen wearing in pictures of Court festivities. Joseph disapproved of this style too. As he said, it depended on French manufactures; and the French Court adhered to it long after most others for that reason. With the diamonds and jewellery that often decorated it, it could be so costly that only the very richest

---

[125] Schünemann, *MÖIG* (1933), 25–30. See below, pp. 249, 266, 268.
[126] Arneth, *MTuJ* III, p. 359.
[127] Ligne, *Fragments*, vol. I, pp. 65–6.

1　Joseph in Hungarian costume, *c.* 1747. Oil, M. van Meytens, KHM, Gemäldegalerie, Inv. No. 7059.

2 The imperial family in formal splendour at Schönbrunn, *c.* 1754. Left-hand group, left to right: Francis, Marianne, Marie Christine. Centre: Amalia, Johanna, Josepha and Carolina, with Ferdinand in the cradle. Right-hand group, left to right: behind, Joseph, Elizabeth, Charles, Maria Theresa; in front, Leopold. Oil, school of Meytens, KHM, Gemäldegalerie, Inv. No. 7458.

3 (*Opposite*) In contrast, two pastel studies by Marie Christine, which hang at Schönbrunn (Terrassenkabinett, Inv. Nos. I.20.545 and 7521), showing the private life of the imperial family: (a) Joseph at the bedside of Isabella soon after the birth of their daughter, Maria Theresa, Mar. 1762. Top left, Marie Christine herself;

a

b

(b) Christmas-present giving, 1762. Francis seated in dressing-gown, Maria Theresa behind, Marie Christine on the left. The children, left to right, are Ferdinand, Marie Antoinette and Max Franz.

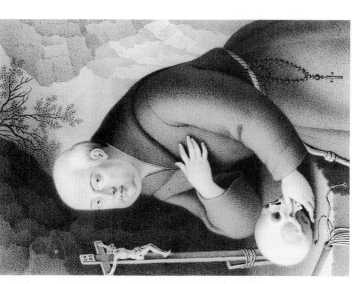

4a This extraordinary miniature is Francis's own portrait of himself as a Franciscan monk, further evidence of his religious preoccupations. Präsidentschaftskanzlei, Hofburg, Vienna. Bildarchiv, ÖNB, 167.180.

4b Isabella of Parma, Joseph's first wife. Engraving by J. G. Haid, 1760, from a portrait sent from Parma. British Museum, Prints and Drawings, C229, PORT 14, BB.30–80.

5a Joseph's daughter, Maria Theresa, c. 1765. Oil, school of Meytens, KHM, Gemäldegalerie, Inv. No. 2066.

5b The marquise d'Herzelles (1728–93), governess of Joseph's daughter. Oil, [?]Meytens, marquis de Trazegnies, Château de Corroy, Belgium.

6   Coronation banquet of Joseph as king of the Romans in the Römer, Frankfurt, 3 Apr.
1764. As Goethe described, most of the tables are deserted. Oil, school of Meytens,
Schönbrunn, Inv. No. 19.335.

7   The performance of *Il parnasso confuso* (music by Gluck, libretto by Metastasio) in the *Anticamera*, now called *Zeremoniensaal*, at Schönbrunn on 24 Jan. 1765, for the marriage celebrations of Joseph and his second wife, Josepha of Bavaria. Joseph is in the front row, extreme left; Josepha sits behind him. The singers are archduchesses Amalia, Carolina, Elizabeth and Josepha; the continuo player is Leopold. Oil, J. F. Greipel, Präsidentschaftskanzlei, Hofburg, KHM, Inv. No. 6826.

a

b

8 The costly magnificence of Schönbrunn: (a) Bellotto's oil painting of count Kinsky arriving in the entrance courtyard of the palace on 16 Aug. 1759, bringing the news of the Austro-Russian victory over the Prussians at Kunersdorf four days previously. KHM, Gemäldegalerie, Inv. No. 1666. (b) The *Vieux-Laque-Zimmer* at Schönbrunn, fitted up by F. I. Canevale in 1767–70. The portraits of Francis and of Joseph and Leopold are by Batoni.

a

b

9   In contrast, the Augarten: (a) Joseph's summer house, built by F. I. Canevale, first used in 1780, extended in 1783. Österreichisches Bundesdenkmalamt, Vienna, 7433. (b) Entrance to the park, engraving, J. Ziegler, 1782. The new gateway erected when Joseph opened the Augarten to the public in 1775 stands in front of the enormous hedge on the left. The old palace is on the extreme right. Historisches Museum der Stadt Wien, Inv. No. 64289.

10 Idealised bust of Joseph, *c.* 1765, F. X. Messerschmidt, KHM, Sammlung für Plastik und Kunstgewerbe, Inv. No. 5476. The style of this splendid piece is still baroque.

11   Double portrait of Joseph and Leopold, done for Maria Theresa in Rome, 1769, oil, P. Batoni, KHM, Inv. No. 1628. The volumes are Montesquieu's *De l'esprit des lois*.

12 Count (after 1764 prince) Wenzel Anton Kaunitz(-Rietberg) (1711–94), *Staatskanzler*
1753–94, on horseback. Charcoal, J. H. Schmuzer, 1784, Graphische Sammlung
Albertina, Vienna, Dt. Sch. Bd. 62.

could afford it. From Joseph's point of view, the people who should cut the most notable figure at Court should be those who served the state best, whether in civil or military employment. The model here was the Court of Prussia, where Frederick the Great had always appeared in uniform and encouraged others to do so. With Joseph, a stronger egalitarian sentiment intensified his dislike of rich clothes. For those without military uniform, he preferred the *frac*, the plain black coat, to the *habit habillé*. To try to move straight from the Spanish mantle to uniform and the *frac* was like leaping overnight from morning dress to jeans.[128]

At one extreme among monarchs was the Holy Roman Emperor, unable to achieve anything significant in the way of political action, a nominal lord over ungovernable vassals, but crowned with medieval religious pomp and expected to take pride in his largely symbolic status. In the other half of the spectrum, certainly, came Maria Theresa, an absolute ruler working long hours for the state and the general good. But she still retained many of the ceremonial and religious trappings of kingship, showed some respect for provincial constitutions, and felt few or no qualms about indulging personal caprice and pursuing family advantage. Almost at the far end came Joseph in this memorandum – and as ruler of the Monarchy – shedding all he could of pomp and mystical aura, cold-shouldering his family, working and travelling frantically to make his lands one, uniform and prosperous, a soldier-bureau-crat governing in accordance with strict principles of public policy. Virtually the only relics of feudal and divine-right monarchy in his conception of his task were his insistence on being available to every subject in person – a medieval rather than a modern aim – and, of course, the inescapably hereditary basis of his rule. That Joseph was only too conscious of his royal position is clear from his remark that, while the great may become small, private men must always so remain. He does not appear to have confronted the paradox inherent in the notion that a ruler chosen by the accident of birth, governing territories originally brought together only by dynastic ties, should strive to unify them on rational, egalitarian principles.

As well as this major inconsistency, he allowed certain other obvious confusions to mar his memorandum. He had not entirely shed all respect for aristocratic birth, since he blamed the heads of departments for preferring to employ

careerists [*gens de fortune*], whom they can treat despotically, and who help them to cover up their ignorance and blunders, rather than persons of good family, by whom they fear they would be found out; and from this lack of [suitable] subordinates arises the embarrassment and misfortune in which the state finds itself.[129]

[128] See P. Mansel, 'Monarchy, uniform and the *Frac*, 1760–1830', *Past and Present*, 96 (1982), 103–32. It would obviously be possible to make much more use of the example of J. II than Mansel is able to do. See Plates 11, 20a, 24.

[129] Arneth, *MTuJ* III, pp. 358–9.

It seems perverse to wish to free internal trade, and cripple external, both on principle. There is an inherent paradox in 'according' to men 'their innate liberty'. But if this is not enlightened despotism or absolutism, the concept has no meaning. And its expression in this memorandum – together with the very phrase *despotisme lié* of the *Rêveries* – antedate the classical theoretical discussion of *despotisme légal* in Le Mercier de la Rivière's *L'Ordre naturel et essentiel des sociétés politiques* of 1767.[130]

A comparison has been proposed between the memorandum and Frederick the Great's political testaments. It is not possible to treat them as if they were on exactly the same footing. Frederick devotes much space to foreign policy, Joseph none. Frederick is writing, on the strength of great experience and success, for his heir; Joseph, innocent and untried, is addressing his still dominant mother. The political testaments wholly lack the adolescent dogmatism and passion of the memorandum. But the documents are comparable in that they both contain considered statements on the role of the monarch and on domestic policy.

Here there are many points of similarity, as well as revealing differences. Frederick and Joseph are agreed in their dedication to the state. Each believes that as the sovereign he is uniquely qualified to govern it and to decide what is best for it. Both are prejudiced against committees, concerned to augment the population, anxious to improve education, ready to let justice take its course, opposed to the granting of lavish pensions, and interested in maintaining a large army well integrated with society. But Frederick of course is the friend of the aristocracy, and Joseph their foe. The Prussian takes a more reasonable line on the prohibition of imports. He does not make a point of receiving the petition of every subject personally. Though anti-religious, he is untroubled about the position of the churches in his dominions; indeed he acknowledges that the Lutherans are ideal subjects. Incidentally, he describes Maria Theresa's council as the best in Europe. But the essential difference is that Frederick is describing a system with which in large measure he is now content. Joseph, by contrast, wishes to transform the Monarchy.[131]

Maria Theresa submitted the memorandum to Kaunitz for comment, and it is instructive to see how he fulfilled this rather delicate assignment. Needless to say, he was more measured and verbose than Joseph, while covering less ground.[132] But after some initial flattery he seized on some of the emperor's more obviously impractical proposals. In the course of a striking, lengthy and

130 See e.g. M. S. Anderson, *Historians and Eighteenth-Century Europe, 1715–1789* (Oxford, 1979), pp. 119–21.
131 Volz, *Die politischen Testamente*. Macartney's version in *Habsburg and Hohenzollern Dynasties* contains too little of the domestic sections of Frederick's testaments to be adequate in this field.
132 Beer, *AÖG* (1872), 98–158. There are several copies of K.'s memorandum in HHSA FA Sbde 87. It is dated 18 Feb. 1766. Lacy also commented briefly, at J.'s request (HHSA NL, Karton 3, Lacy to J., n.d.).

largely irrelevant discussion of public education for all classes, he rebuts the notion that universities should be moved out of cities. The students need to acquire good manners and urbanity, and towns are the places in which to acquire these qualities.

By way of applauding Joseph's emphasis on population, Kaunitz reaches the question of monasteries, on which he assembles 'the arguments that the most enlightened statesman and the greatest enemy of the monks might advance against the administration of the regular orders and especially of the mendicants', and then proceeds to refute them. This extremely interesting discussion will be considered when ecclesiastical matters are reviewed in a later chapter.[133]

Kaunitz next takes issue with Joseph's contention that the police should be run by the military. He neatly points out that the emperor himself condemns the suffocating effect of the present system on the willingness of subordinates to take initiatives in civil matters. In the army, however, orders have to be obeyed, and there is no room for independent action by junior ranks. The military, therefore, on Joseph's own showing, are unsuitable in the civil role of police. In general, the chancellor urges that the Monarchy should not be placed, like Prussia, under the domination of the army.

As for the encouragement of industry, and particularly the abolition of monopolies, there are difficulties about making a drastic change of policy, since state contracts would then have to be dishonoured. The complete prohibition of imports cannot be lightly undertaken, certainly not without enquiry into the Monarchy's needs. Even an embargo on rich foreign cloth is of dubious merit, 'as all prohibition is odious'.

I believe that, since it is important not to extend constraint to trifling objects, and since even superficial comfort affects foreign opinion about the wealth and strength of a state, everyone should be left free to wear what he thinks fit, especially so long as the [materials] have been made in the country.

For the same reasons, Kaunitz would not institute a register of diamonds.

Having disposed of these lesser points, the chancellor launches into an elaborate defence of the *Staatsrat* and the existing administrative system. He begins with a highly critical account of the position of 1740. After praise for Haugwitz's reforms, he then explains that they were never perfected in time to cope with the expenditure of the Seven Years War. But

our present [system of] government is founded on the most incontestable principles of the art of ruling, recognised as such by all the most enlightened nations of Europe, and it is regulated and suited to the system and the particular constitution of the different provinces and Estates of the Monarchy.

---

[133] See below, pp. 446–7.

It is only necessary to compare it, and the personnel operating it, with the state of affairs at the beginning of the reign, or even in the 1750s, to be persuaded of the improvement achieved. There are many complaints against it, and no doubt these contain some justice. But there is no better system in Europe, or imaginable, so far as its essential elements are concerned. Joseph's particular proposals for union between departments are not prudent. While the departments must be left as much initiative as possible,

everything which involves legislation, for example, and everything which can have an impact on the Universality, could never be abandoned to the arbitrary judgement of a particular chief, who is not, as the sovereign and his council are, in a position to be able to grasp the idea of the Totality . . .

Kaunitz disposes of Joseph's scheme for calling the heads of the provincial departments to Vienna, each for a month. It will be much more helpful to send out some minister every two years from the capital, to see for himself how well the government's directives are being obeyed in the provinces. The provincial chiefs – and here, as often, Kaunitz cites the example of the Italian and Belgian departments which he himself conducts – should, instead of travelling to Vienna, make an annual report in writing.

The chancellor left few of Joseph's wilder schemes and inconsistencies untouched. But he did not of course venture to make the general point that the emperor shows himself conspicuously innocent and inept wherever dealings with people are concerned. The idea of summoning the provincial chiefs, one each month, seems especially naive; and the ferocity of his remarks about officials who offend against his principles is ominous. The casual reference to a civil and a military head in each province reflects one of Joseph's assumptions, which in the end was to contribute, by creating obvious difficulties of mutual co-operation between the two, to the success of opposition to his rule. Although experience had already made him intellectually aware that paper projects were not always adaptable to the attitudes of the officials who would have to work them, he hardly began to understand the difficulties. This was the cardinal failure of his upbringing: for all his theoretical protestations and good intentions, despite his affability and accessibility, he could not enter into the minds of subordinates. For Maria Theresa they were individuals, fallible, self-regarding and lovable; for Joseph they were cogs in the state machine.

'THE GENERAL PICTURE OF THE AFFAIRS OF THE MONARCHY': CIVIL MATTERS

When on 16 February 1768 Maria Theresa heard that Leopold had a son, she was so overjoyed that, abandoning the seclusion of a widow and the decorum of an empress, she rushed from the Hofburg to the theatre and gave the news to her family and then to the audience in person.[134] As for Joseph, the event strengthened him in his resolution not to remarry. He could now thankfully acknowledge the promise of a secure succession in his brother's line. He wrote to Leopold later in the year:

Excellent populator, dear brother, how much I owe you! Your wife is pregnant yet again. As well as being a service which you render to the state, it imposes on me an eternal obligation. Continue, dear brother, and do not slacken your efforts. Boldly present as many children to the Monarchy as you can. If they are like you, there will never be too many of them.[135]

In the end Leopold had twelve legitimate sons, ten of whom reached manhood.

It was evidently in the hope that Leopold would fulfil his role that Joseph in 1767 began compiling the 'General picture of the affairs of the Monarchy'. The document was completed and sent off in the spring of 1768.[136] His covering letter (in French, like the document itself) ran:

As it is equally useful to the Monarchy and to you, dear brother, who concern it so nearly, that you should be aware of its present situation and the arrangements which have been made since your departure, their purpose, the reason for everything, where we have succeeded completely, and where we have only laid the foundations of future success: I wish to outline for you as shortly as possible in these pages the position of the Monarchy at the time of your departure, how it has changed, and how it now stands, whether militarily or as regards finance, commerce, police and the general welfare, relations with foreign Courts or external policy; and finally some Court arrangements. These constitute the different sections of this document.

This lengthy and factual survey is so well organised and soberly written, especially by comparison with the memorandum of 1765, that it is at first sight difficult to believe that the emperor could have drafted it. On the other hand, his personal views frequently obtrude and his style is often unmistakable. We know that he submitted his original versions of the financial and military sections to Hatzfeld and Lacy, the ministers concerned, and incorporated some of their suggestions.[137] This must have been the procedure with other parts of the document. But the 'General picture' clearly embodies Joseph's

---

[134] Arneth, *GMT* VII, p. 458 has the date of the reception of the news wrong. See Langlois to Weymouth, 17 Feb. 1768 (PRO SP 80/205) and the supplement to the *Gazette de Vienne* of the same date, enclosed with it.

For M.T.'s anticipation, see Arneth, *MTKuF* III, p. 85 (7 Feb. 1767, M.T. to Maria Beatrix).

[135] J. to L., 8 Sep. 1768 (not in Arneth) (HHSA FA Sbde 7).

[136] See p. 125, n. 36 for the dating of this document, which I refer to as HHSA TG in these notes.

I found it in HHSA FA Sbde 88, in sections. It is easy from internal evidence to make up the complete 'General picture' in the original order. Cf. Conrad, *Festschrift Nikolaus Grass*, vol. I, p. 162n. I have numbered the folios myself, since they bear no numbers in the original. The Xerox copy I have used will be deposited in the Seeley Historical Library, Cambridge.

It is clear that J. was working on the piece in 1767 (see Conrad's article, p. 161n and the comment on the financial section by Hatzfeld, also in HHSA FA Sbde 88, date 2 Jan. 1768).

[137] See p. 163, n. 108 above.

own understanding of affairs and betrays his approach to them, even though he does not give full rein to his personal bias on all issues. As such it represents as full, careful, informed and frank an appraisal of the condition and politics of a state, from a ruler's point of view, as exists for any country at any period. For the biographer of Joseph, it is pure gold. Unfortunately, except for short sections on the Empire and the papacy, and a few brief quotations on other topics, this great treatise has not been published.[138]

The portions dealing with the Empire, finances and 'affairs of the family and the Court' have already been considered. The sections on foreign affairs, which amount to about half the whole, will be analysed later, though it is important to emphasise here that they are wholly pacific and that Joseph's declared anxiety is to put the Monarchy in a position to defend itself, not to attack other states.[139] At this point it is convenient to discuss the domestic part of the document, especially those aspects of it not so far covered.

Joseph's attitude in this document is much more pragmatic than in his earlier memoranda. There is little trace of his animus against the nobility, the existing administrative system seldom attracts his sarcasm, and religious questions do not figure prominently. On the other hand he does allow his opinion of the old etiquette to appear; and except when dealing with the outlying provinces, Lombardy and the southern Netherlands, he treats the Monarchy for nearly all purposes as a unit, and largely discounts provincial variations and privileges. Although there is no evidence that Leopold had seen the memorandum of 1765, and although we know that he had not yet been shown the *Rêveries*,[140] some passages in the 'General picture' read like progress reports on the fate of Joseph's earlier proposals. But many new topics are considered, and some new radical attitudes emerge.

So far as administration is concerned, Joseph gives an instructive picture of how business was conducted. It seems that the emperor had abandoned the drastic notions of the memorandum of 1765 and, after some changes had been made in procedure, had accepted the arguments of Kaunitz about the *Staatsrat* and its efficacy:

Our internal system . . . and the manner of doing business is still more or less the same, except that Her Majesty sees, jointly with me, every Tuesday, the ministers and heads of the different supreme departments, who are the president of the supreme council of justice, the head of the present chancery of Transylvania, the president of the Chamber and the Bank, the grand chancellor of Austria and Bohemia, . . . the chancellor of Hungary, and finally the president of the *Hofrechenkammer*. The president of war has no fixed day. All these ministers bring their reports or papers, giving explanations by

---

138 The section on the Empire has been published by Conrad in *Festschrift Nikolaus Grass*, vol. I, pp. 161–85. Arneth (*GMT* IX, pp. 550–1) printed a short section on the papacy, dated straightforwardly to Mar. 1768. He also paraphrased sections, sometimes without acknowledgement (e.g. *GMT* VII, pp. 204–9).

139 See pp. 273–7 below.   140 See p. 103 above.

word of mouth as requested, and they also send their packets daily during the rest of the week to Her Majesty or myself. Her Majesty, having looked at the contents, decides at once, or keeps the papers, or has them circulated to the *Staatsrat*, as she thinks fit. Councils held in her presence no longer exist, and all major questions, or those requiring detailed knowledge, are dealt with in 'mixed commissions' of the *Staatsrat* and the relevant departments. By this means the admirable establishment of the *Staatsrat*, which, while relieving the sovereign, at the same time eases her conscience, has been yet further perfected ... All [members], without exception, work unremittingly, and it only remains to be desired that they could be relieved ... by distinguishing the important from the less important issues. We are now working on that; and since no new thing is ever perfect, this too will achieve a greater degree of perfection in time.[141]

Joseph then moved on immediately to the military. But here it is more satisfactory to deal with civil matters first. On 'commerce', the 'General picture' has little progress to record. While the emperor begins by saying that the best hope of restoring the country after the depredations of war must lie in improving its trade, industry and agriculture, he is forced to acknowledge that the Monarchy is in a weak position in all these branches. Internal communications are bad; the only port accessible to most of the Monarchy is Trieste, whose development has been disappointing and in some respects inefficiently managed; it is difficult to attract foreign workmen; there is not enough money available for major works. All that can be said is that efforts are being made in many fields. Textile manufactures, cotton, wool and silk are all being fostered. Thousands of mulberry trees have been distributed *gratis*. After debate, competing foreign manufactures have been prohibited, although 'several [officials] wished to prove that the section most worthy of attention in a state, namely the cultivators, would suffer' because they would consequently lose markets for their exports abroad. But Joseph believes that the import controls have not in fact damaged agricultural producers. Attempts are being made at drainage works and at river, road and port improvements; and various proposals have been considered for the establishment of trading companies. But 'the establishment of a good tariff is the true key and the cornerstone of trade', and work is in progress on this front also.[142]

In so far as anything had been achieved in 'commerce', Joseph had had a large hand in it. He had presided in 1767 over a special committee to consider the question of import restrictions – which had led to their mitigation. He also took a great interest in the scheme for a new tariff. He had now abandoned the notion of banning all imports, and was talking of excluding only those which competed with domestic products.[143] But before any of these changes is taken too seriously, we should notice the lofty cynicism of the British representative in Vienna about the Monarchy's economic policy-making. He had advised his

[141] HHSA TG, ff. 2–4.   [142] *Ibid.*, ff. 70–83.
[143] Schünemann, *MÖIG* (1933), 20; Arneth, *GMT* IX, pp. 449–54.

government in 1764 not to worry too much about recent drastic prohibitions on the import of manufactures. They will soon be found unworkable, he said, and so will be quickly countermanded.[144] He was proved right.

Under the heading 'Justice, police and welfare of the lands in general', Joseph has little to report about 'justice'. No 'cardinal' law has been changed. He has not himself seen the new criminal law code, which the government hopes soon to introduce; it is now being translated into the various languages of the Monarchy. 'Police' too is virtually unaltered. The emperor includes here various measures for keeping down food prices, such as government purchase of grain to be marketed cheaply; but he admits that their effects have been slight. Most agricultural improvement comes under this rubric. Encouragement is being given to the growing of clover, sainfoin, potatoes and other new crops. It is hoped to conserve the forests by converting some manufactures to the use of coal, instead of wood, for heating. Several orphanages have been founded, in which the children are taught useful skills, like weaving, as part of their education. Further,

to use the unproductive hands of many beggars and unemployed, two houses have been established, one here and one in Hungary, where people gathered off the streets who are in a state to work are compelled to it, in return for a small payment, which they have to supplement by their earnings . . . [Incidentally, in this way] the city of Vienna and the country is purged of vagabonds and harmful beggars.

Vienna is growing, land in the city is short, and rents are rising. So permissions have been requested for building on the glacis.

But since this would have ruined the fortifications which, though poor, are still of some consequence, and there is still much land not built over in the space between the lines, this is to be made available first; and by leaving the gates open day and night, as we now do, we connect, so to speak, the town to the suburbs.

Some houses have been purchased with which to make a new and better customs house.

To show you that we have not forgotten the public's pleasures, we have granted a licence for animal fights, which are put on fifteen times a year during the summer and are much appreciated . . . They used to take place, but had for some years been banned.

The emperor's enlightenment cannot be said to have extended to sympathy with the sufferings of beasts.

In the university,

the Jesuits have been deprived of a Chair of Theology to which they had had a prescriptive right, because their moral teaching has been found unsuitable. It has been

---

[144] Stormont to Sandwich, 7 Apr. 1764, cypher (PRO SP 80/200). What J. says in HHSA TG, f. 79, bears this out.

divided between two professors, one brought expressly from Italy. That of canon law has been given to a secular.

Amid this hotch-potch of topics, the most interesting discussion concerns the relations between lords and peasants, especially in Hungary, and between the four 'nations' in Transylvania. Here Joseph does consider the affairs of individual provinces, and shows displeased awareness of their privileges and peculiarities. He starts from the point that, to enable peasants in general to continue to pay their taxes, it is necessary to ease their lot. So their complaints against their lords are being seriously considered. Action has been taken to curb the unjust demands of Silesian landowners. 'But it is principally in Hungary that these remedies have been needed.' The official attempt to discover the true position 'encountered, as you can imagine, great difficulties, in a country so infatuated with liberty, which carries ancient privileges, even if harmful, to the point of preserving abuses'. After the government failed at the diet of 1764 to obtain any guarantees from the lords, the situation worsened. Some peasants took to the woods, refused to obey their lords, and sent emissaries to Vienna. 'To avoid the violence, which the lords so ardently desired, against persons whose crimes were unknown, Her Majesty sent a commission of a military character to examine their complaints and return them to their villages in obedience.' The commission found that the peasants had been badly, even cruelly, treated. Maria Theresa felt obliged in conscience to help them. Anyway, they are 'the most useful and the only tax-paying part of the kingdom'. The fundamental laws of the kingdom, which Joseph says he refrains from citing lest he appear to be pedantic, authorise her to act 'as king of this country, as sovereign of her other states, as mother of her peoples'. But all ordinary procedures would have been slow and would have been frustrated by the lords. So three commissions were sent into the worst-affected counties, which reported to the Hungarian chancellery and to the *Staatsrat*. The government then laid down norms of peasant service, varying according to the wealth of the various villages. These regulations are being applied with justice and firmness. Her Majesty has thus become 'the first to dare to show the Hungarian nobility that, to do good and mete out justice, she fears no opposition'.

She has not only taken the most glorious step of her reign, but at the same time consolidated for ever her Contribution. She has got to the bottom of the matter, she can judge the strength of the peasant and the nobility, and finally this has laid the first stone of many still more useful arrangements to be made in future.

Joseph reports that, after the death of the primate of Hungary in 1765, his office has been kept vacant, and its revenues applied to pious uses, such as the endowment of several Croatian benefices. The palatine or viceroy of Hungary had also died in 1765; his office too is to remain unfilled, because only a diet can elect to it, 'which, at the present moment, and until the urbarial arrangement[145] and the planned judicial arrangements have been firmly established, will not be advisable'.

Transylvania, says Joseph at the end of this section,

is composed of four nations, Hungarians, Szekels, Saxons and Vlachs: the last being serfs and in a very impoverished condition; the Szekels being sufficiently burdened; and the Saxons on the other hand, the most opulent portion, mainly consisting of all the citizens of the towns, being the most tenderly treated in tax-paying. There is at present an idea of equalising these nations and, while relieving the last group, perhaps obtaining greater profit from the third.[146]

In these fields of 'justice, police and the welfare of the lands in general', it is particularly difficult to gauge Joseph's influence. Since he remarks that he has not even seen the draft of the new criminal law code, it is evident that in this particular area he was not being much consulted.[147] In Hungarian affairs, he must have welcomed the extension of central intervention and of the *Staatsrat*'s involvement, even if his own inclination would doubtless have been to avoid seeking 'pedantic' justification in the fundamental laws of the kingdom. Other members of the *Staatsrat* and Maria Theresa herself shared his passionate concern for the welfare of the serfs. She spoke of the 'cruelties' of the lords to 'these poor people', and complained bitterly against the great and favoured Hungarian noble families, the Batthyánys and Esterházys, who were among the most blameworthy.[148] We know that the emperor had urged his mother in 1761 to regulate peasant services,[149] but the initiative was not his alone.

Although in the administration of the Monarchy Belgium and Lombardy were considered inseparable from the department of foreign relations, and Joseph in the 'General picture' respected this view, it is appropriate to consider their internal affairs here. He starts by remarking on the flourishing state of the southern Netherlands, despite the fact that their taxes have recently been increased in order to provide more money for the Vienna government. Since the provinces are indefensible if attacked by France, and safe so long as the French alliance subsists, 'our first consideration ought . . . to be . . not their state of defence and the military, but . . . finance and trade'. If their debt can be paid off, enormous advantage may accrue to the Monarchy from their surplus revenues.

Joseph rejoices in the fact that, although France is Belgium's neighbour, there have been no repercussions in the Austrian Netherlands from the religious controversies across the border, associated with the works of

---

[145] *Urbarium* was the name given to a set of regulations about peasants' services and lords' rights.
[146] The section of HHSA TG on 'justice, police and welfare' runs from f. 84 to f. 117.
[147] Clearly K. too had been left in ignorance, since he reacted to its publication by proposing its suspension and alteration: Hock, *Staatsrath*, pp. 42–3.
[148] Arneth, *GMT* VII, pp. 257–9, 267–9; X, pp. 111–14.   [149] See p. 97 and n. above.

Jansenius. This happy state of affairs arises from the imposition of silence on all such issues.

In Lombardy, taxation has borne much more heavily. One possible means of easing the burden is 'to assess and abolish the excess wealth which the clergy and the religious orders had been allowed there'. 'The requirement to sell their property and to receive no novices beyond a certain number are the remedies which have just been applied by the latest ordinances, with which the Court of Rome is not at all pleased.'[150]

Since Kaunitz jealously controlled the administration of these provinces, it is unlikely that Joseph was able to influence it at this period. But in conjunction with other evidence, the 'General picture' shows Joseph to have made a difference to some, though not all, aspects of the Monarchy's internal policy in civil matters, even in the short period between his nomination as co-regent and the spring of 1768.

MILITARY AFFAIRS AND THE 'GENERAL PICTURE'

Military matters naturally took up much space in the 'General picture'. Not only were they Joseph's particular province after 1765, but they had the first place in the Monarchy's domestic policy and in the minds of Maria Theresa and her collaborators. The chief spur to Haugwitz's reforms had been the ambition to create an army of a size to compete with the forces of Prussia and her allies. The unsatisfactory outcome of the Seven Years War had led, despite the desperate financial situation, to an agreement in 1763 to increase the peacetime military budget. Roughly 17,000,000 florins were made available annually, that is, half of the Monarchy's total revenue.[151] At the same time marshal Daun, first as commander-in-chief during the war, then as *Staatsminister*, finally as president of the *Hofkriegsrat* as well as *Staatsminister* (1762–6), was trying to carry through a radical programme of army reform. A general staff had been established in 1758; in 1762 the *Hofkriegsrat* was put into the hands of generals rather than of civilians; then, just after Joseph took charge in 1765, three inspector-generals were appointed to oversee the main branches of the army. Plans were being prepared for introducing conscription and the canton system. Daun's right-hand man in all these efforts was general count Maurice Lacy.[152]

Joseph had argued in his first memorandum of 1761, like Lacy and other generals, against the army reduction of 1761. In the *Rêveries* he had advocated making a large financial provision for the army in peacetime, not merely a sum

[150] HHSA TG, ff. 198–211.
[151] I am relying here on Dr P. G. M. Dickson's unpublished account.
[152] Kotasek, *Lacy* pp. 24–70; Duffy, *Army of M.T.*, pp. 23, 135–6; HHSA NL, Karton 3, Lacy to [?]M.T., 17 June 1765, urging her not to give him all the credit for the canton and conscription plans, but to acknowledge Daun's part; Arneth, *GMT* vii, pp. 183–6.

of 17,000,000 to be spent annually, but a further 5,000,000 to be saved each year so that money would not be lacking if war broke out. In the first document and in the memorandum of 1765 he supported the introduction of conscription and the canton system. It is impossible to tell how far these interventions affected policy. But in this field of activity, exceptionally, his views resembled those of the principal officials. His dealings with Daun appear to have been amicable and fruitful.[153]

All the same, his position as head of the army must have been strengthened by the death of this famous and experienced soldier, his nominal subordinate, in February 1766. Maria Theresa allowed her son to choose Daun's successor. On Joseph's recommendation Lacy was appointed field-marshal and president of the *Hofkriegsrat*. Both Daun and the empress would have made the same choice.[154]

Lacy's appointment caused great irritation. He was a foreigner: of Irish extraction, he had been born in Russia, where his father had made a notable military career. The new marshal was junior to many generals who considered themselves equally competent. Princess Eleonore Liechtenstein, married to one of them, thought Lacy 'a horrible man'. The new president's zeal for economy, efficiency and professionalism was bound to offend the old guard.[155]

Joseph must already have known Lacy well, as their first exchange of notes after his appointment shows. The marshal asked whether, like Daun, he could be a member of the *Staatsrat* as well as president of the *Hofkriegsrat*. Joseph replied that it was against the rules and that, though the rules were bad ones, it would be better to let matters ride until people came to recognise

> the bad composition of the whole machine. Yet more confusion will clarify their minds. To overwhelm them with muddles, and to reduce them to the point when they don't know what's to be done, are better ways of curing and convincing them than the best-posed dilemmas. This is between ourselves.

Perhaps the emperor's motives included unwillingness to have a rival spokesman for the army on the *Staatsrat*. But he liked – indeed revered – Lacy, describing him as 'my teacher in the business of glory, whom I regard also as a true friend of Joseph rather than of the vain titles of the emperor'.[156]

As Maria Theresa had planned should happen, her son had developed a

---

[153] See above, pp. 95–8, 168–9; Beales, *MÖSA* (1980), 159; and Arneth, *GMT* VII, pp. 185–6.

[154] *Ibid.*, pp. 212–13.

[155] Arneth, *GMT* VII, pp. 213–14; E.L. to L.K., [?] 13 Feb. 1766 and 13 Dec. 1771 (SOALpZ, LRRA P. 16/19 and 22); Kotasek, *Lacy*, pp. 2–4, 71.

[156] J. to Lacy, 8 Feb. 1766 and 11 Apr. 1767: HHSA NL, Karton 2. For other expressions of J.'s admiration for Lacy see Kotasek, *Lacy*, pp. 246–9 (but, as always in her book, without any references) and P. P. Bernard, 'The emperor's friend: Joseph II and field marshal Lacy', *EEQ*, x (1976), 401–8 (but using, I think, only portions of NL). I am most grateful to Prof. Bernard for sending me a copy of this article.

passion for military affairs, which his new duties and opportunities intensified.

He enjoys [wrote the Venetian ambassador] talking not only with the officers, but even with the common soldiers. He turns out for the military parade almost every day. He is happy discussing everything to do with the conduct of war, and is careful to keep his body accustomed to exertion and exercise in order to preserve his fitness and so nourish the martial spirit that is showing itself in his character.[157]

In the summer of 1766 he made first an exhausting tour of the battlefields of the Seven Years War, and then went off again on manoeuvres in order, as he said, that the generals should be able to instruct him in the art of war. He also helped to decide a long-vexed question about where to site a major fortress.[158]

Maria Theresa claimed to have surrendered the whole direction of the army to Joseph.[159] This was simply untrue. It was not until 1772 that the emperor ventured to ask whether he might see all the correspondence of the *Hofkriegsrat*, and even then the request caused embarrassment.[160] The empress regularly corresponded with Lacy behind her son's back, and she and the marshal devoted much ingenuity to covering their tracks.[161] But Joseph had to be treated as the official head. An incident at the end of 1766 illustrates the position. Lacy had prepared a statement of what needed to be done before an army could be put into the field. He submitted it first to the empress, asking her whether he should even show it to Joseph. She thanked him for

this admirable but also frightening survey. Everything that is pointed out is incontestably true ... Nothing is so necessary as to take measures against the misfortunes that threaten us, but where are we to find the funds for all that? I've been thinking about it the whole night, and I see no remedy, if you can't suggest one. You are the only man who can grasp the scale of the enterprise ... With your aid I am still hopeful of recovering my old [courage] – or rather the courage that I had in my youth, which has been destroyed by the defeats and the cruel losses of all kinds that I have suffered ... Give this paper to my son and indicate to me what is needed, and I shall willingly and as a duty support the only man in my Monarchy and perhaps in Europe who can undertake and carry through this task.[162]

That was at the end of November. A month later, Joseph weighed in with a memorandum entitled *Si vis pacem para bellum*. This document restated, with new supporting detail, many of his arguments of 1761, but it also echoed Lacy. With only 100,000 men under arms, he says, the Monarchy 'is in no state to resist its neighbours'. Joseph foresees that

---

157 Renier, 3 May 1766 (Arneth, *GMT* VII, p. 531).   158 *Ibid.*, pp. 217–22.
159 M.T. to Silva-Tarouca, Feb. 1766 (Karajan, *Feierliche Sitzungsberichte KAW* (1859), 69).
160 J. to Lacy, 26 Jan. 1772; M.T. to Lacy, 1 Feb: HHSA NL, Karton 2.
161 This is a repeated theme of HHSA NL. Cf. p. 223 below. Bernard's emphasis on J.'s concern for secrecy (*EEQ* (1976), 404) must arise from confusing the handwritings of J. and M.T.
162 Arneth, *GMT* VII, p. 530. He states (p. 222) that J. had commissioned the document.

it is probable that the Austrian Monarchy will once again, before the end of time, face a war, and in consequence we must make all arrangements, even if only for the sake of our great-grandchildren, so that it can defend itself worthily.

To this end we must choose, here and now, suitable places for fortresses; we must train men to replace the dead; secure horses both for fighting and to transport everything needful; have weapons to fire; and finally be sure of having bread for the men and oats for the horses.

The emperor believes that any future war will be 'very bloody and keen, because the desire to fight over trifles has disappeared in Europe'. The early campaigns will decide the conflict, because they will be so costly that thereafter neither side will be able to mobilise the resources to turn the scale.

From this axiom it follows that we ought to increase our army by 65,000 men and 14,000 cavalry horses, have nearly 3000 carriages made, have 1900 mules or pack-horses, 14,000 artillery and supply horses, 3000 pontoon horses, ... 100,000 new firearms and an incalculable quantity of bullets, bombs and powder in proportion, so that we can act immediately and defend ourselves, without the [aid of the] army of the Empire, the French, the Swedes or the Russians, against a force which, when it had to fight against all of us at once, reduced us to within an ace of disaster, and caused us to finish the war scarcely able to defend our frontiers.

He goes on to propound his favourite scheme of combining the duties of the soldier and the citizen by causing them to live and work side by side, by allowing the soldier to marry, and by employing and educating his family. The Monarchy should be divided up into cantons, each of which would be responsible for recruiting and supplying a regiment. Only then can the army, as he demands, be put on a war footing in peacetime.

It will cost something, but will repay the outlay with interest. Perhaps it will be possible to accomplish this great object with a few million florins, from which I exclude the fortresses and the first purchase of equipment, which will be expensive.

No effort should be spared to this great end. 'A state in this situation will have credit and political weight in [pursuing] its just aims.'[163]

Kaunitz replied to this in all senses extravagant document. It is impossible and unthinkable, he said, to maintain an army as big as those of all conceivable enemies put together. Superiority in generalship, not mere numbers, had saved Frederick. It would be ruinous to try to keep up a war footing in peacetime, since the state would have to use up its capital and would be unable to improve conditions for its subjects. Anyway, the division between civil and military is positively beneficial. But some additional money for the army could be made available from the Belgian treasury and French subsidy payments.[164]

[163] The memorandum is printed in K-M VI, pp. 458–67. There is in HHSA FA Sbde 87 a draft, heavily annotated in J.'s hand, from which Schlitter's version in K-M seems to derive. It is dated 28 Dec. 1766, is in French, and is entitled 'Si vis pacem para bellum ou Memoire sur les preparatifs de guerre indispensablement necessaires pour la Conservation de la paix'.
[164] Printed by Schlitter in K-M VI, pp. 468–75. An original is in HHSA FA Sbde 88. It is in German and dated 24 Jan. 1767.

Maria Theresa, while supporting some of Lacy's and Joseph's demands, indicated that she agreed with much that Kaunitz had said. She did not think the people would put up with the full range of her son's proposals:

It is well known how resentfully and unwillingly our peasants enter the army, and how they detest priests, lords and officials. Such deeply engrained prejudices cannot be removed at a stroke. It will need much patience and time.

She feared Joseph's scheme would lead to mass emigration. Much could be done, she thought, through the present system if the soldier were permitted to marry and his children were provided for. But Lacy continued to press the case that he and Joseph had argued, while Kaunitz as steadily opposed it. Maria Theresa remitted the whole vexed question of cantons to a committee, under the emperor, of Starhemberg, Lacy and Blümegen.[165] At the end of 1767, the chancellor asked her to suppress one of his memoranda in this field, for fear of crossing the emperor. 'I follow your advice', she replied, 'to reserve the matter until another time, since I perceive only too well the discouragement of [my son], all the more as I feel it myself.'[166]

The major issues were still being disputed when Joseph wrote the 'General picture'. But he could report some progress.[167] Soldiers had been permitted, in certain circumstances, to marry. Veterans capable of serving had been brought back into active military duties, and others had been declared fit enough to earn their living; only the genuinely incapacitated now received pensions in idleness. Steps had been taken to tighten army administration and make it more economical. As Joseph had proposed in the memorandum of 1765, the commissariat department had been amalgamated with the war department.

Effective recruitment abroad had nearly raised the army to its official peacetime establishment. There were more horses, guns, carriages and other equipment available. Drill and uniforms were better standardised. A beginning had been made in improving certain crucial fortresses. The general staff was engaged in providing maps of the Monarchy's terrain, and would soon be free for wider tasks. All these improvements depended on the somewhat increased financial allocation now received by the army.

Joseph devoted several pages to the various frontier districts in which settlement was encouraged for both military and civil purposes. To take a recently established example,

The colonisation carried out in the Banat ought to be very useful, though it is as yet very far from reaching its perfection. For, as well as serving to populate and cultivate the country, it serves at the same time to guarantee it against invasion and to form a

---

165 See K-M VI, pp. 475–7 for M.T.'s memorandum. Arneth, *GMT* IX, ch. 16; HHSA NL, Karton 5.
166 Arneth, *GMT* VII, p. 228.   167 The military section of HHSA TG is ff. 5–46.

strict cordon against the plague on the Turkish border, and links up the frontier militia of Slavonia to that of Transylvania.

But in Carlstadt and Varasdin, districts of Croatia, there is a great shortage of men, and yet not enough spare land to give to new recruits. A commission has found out that the clergy have too much property, and it is hoped to recover some from them by a strict land survey. However, there is always difficulty in preventing the emigration of these settlers to less regimented countries.

The most radical passage in the military section of the 'General picture' marks an important shift in Joseph's views on the assimilation of civil and military, soldiers and peasants. He has been discussing the need in the existing situation to attract recruits from abroad. They keep the army up to strength, and so allow subjects of the Monarchy to stay at home and cultivate the land.

But to speak strictly, it is less an advantage for the state than an evil necessary for its defence that we make use in this way of these strangers. They are good for being killed in war in preference to subjects, but they are a heavy burden on the latter in peacetime.

They cost a lot, and they 'make almost a profession of desertion'. It would really be better to dispense with them.

And the means to do so would be to conscript men, horses and all the internal resources of the Monarchy, to cultivate them and multiply them by favouring their propagation, and to try by establishing cantons to form all subjects into as many soldiers ready to defend the country well in time of war, who in time of peace, if one may so express oneself, would form an equally useful army of cultivators and artisans. By this method the need for foreign recruits would simply disappear, the money they cost would remain in the country, and bad mercenaries, loafers and vagabonds would be replaced by good citizens or subjects with an interest ... in serving their sovereign well.

Joseph always mentions, when listing his and the state's broad aims, among others, the 'general welfare', 'the advantage of all and of each one in particular'.[168] But in the 'General picture' his chief concern is clearly to strengthen the army and to raise revenue sufficient to maintain it. Those aims are stated first, and the 'general welfare' seems to come a poor third. His earlier memoranda, as we have seen, had gone further, and advocated what looked like the militarisation of the civil government of the Monarchy. Both Kaunitz and Maria Theresa had condemned these proposals, as damaging to the wealth and comfort of individual subjects.[169] Joseph here suppresses these schemes, but his new proposal of a form of conscription, to create a citizen army, tends in the same direction. This 'militarism', even if its motives were purely defensive, seems distasteful.[170]

I have already quoted, at the beginning of this book, the passage in which,

---

[168] *Ibid.*, f. 84.   [169] See above, pp. 175, 186–7.
[170] Cf. Macartney, *Habsburg Empire*, p. 130.

writing to Leopold in July 1768, Joseph dedicated himself to the service of the state. The letter continued with his own answer to this criticism:

Nothing appears to me petty or trifling in this imposing task, every aspect interests me equally. I am no more attached to the military than to finance. If I could be persuaded that the reduction of the army could be a real advantage, I would disband them this very day and make them labourers. But our circumstances are very far from permitting us to do anything like that. We must therefore try always to combine the necessary security with the country's welfare, and ensure that the former protects the latter as cheaply as possible.

This, dear brother, is high-flown reasoning, but it comes out because my head is continuously full of it.[171]

The British ambassador, Lord Stormont, in reply to the suggestion that Joseph was an aggressive militarist, made the same point. The emperor, he said, wants to find out about his territories, 'and without neglecting other Objects to direct his principal Attention to the improving and perfecting their Military Establishment, as thinking *That* in the situation of his Dominions the most necessary Bulwark'.[172]

It was when discussing Prussia, later in the 'General picture', that Joseph completed the argument. He claimed, even though many of his own military proposals had been rejected, that 'all our political actions and internal arrangements have to be, and are, consequent on the manner in which this formidable enemy and neighbour thinks and acts'. He concedes, just as Kaunitz and Maria Theresa would have wished, that Frederick's 'purely military government so [enervates] his provinces that he cannot extract further resources from them when war comes'. But he nonetheless rates the Prussian threat as very grave:

The Prussian Monarchy, given its situation, given the means by which it has been aggrandised, but especially given the outlook, principles, strength and reputation of the king, its chief and sole director ... is our most powerful, natural and, so to speak, our only truly daunting enemy. Since glory is his sole aim – regardless of all other considerations, even good faith – he seizes every opportunity. Besotted by his luck, genius and resources, which have already extricated him from several false moves during the last war, he dares everything. Hence his neighbours can feel safe only if they have themselves a sufficient force capable of resisting him.[173]

Prussia and Russia were allies, and the Turks were still seen as the inveterate enemy of the Habsburgs. The Monarchy's land frontier was enormously long. There was reason to fear war on two, if not three, fronts. No conceivable army could be too large to cope with such a situation. Kaunitz, on the other hand, contended that a good system of alliances could offer security

---

[171] Arneth, *MTuJ* I, pp. 225–6. (J. to L., 25 July 1768).
[172] Stormont to Rochford, 1 Dec. 1768, 'Most secret', 'By Garstin' (PRO SP 80/205).
[173] HHSA TG, ff. 145–6, 149.

to the Monarchy without a large increase in the size and cost of the army, but in the circumstances his argument rang hollow.[174] It was Joseph's particular charge, as head of the military branch, to wrestle with this problem. He would have been irresponsible not to regard the Monarchy's weakness as serious, and not to try to remedy it.

The 'General picture' reveals Joseph in a very different light from the *Rêveries* and the memorandum of 1765. There are passages in which his long-term radical aspirations emerge. But for the most part he appears as the spokesman of the Monarchy's agreed policy, even though he has contributed to it only as one influence among many. This is a side of Joseph that has to be taken into account. In the memorandum he had criticised the regime fundamentally. He had told Lacy of his desire to wreck the existing constitution of the *Staatsrat*. During the row over San Remo, he had furiously denounced Kaunitz and other officials. But in between – that is, for most of the time – he showed himself ready to work as Maria Theresa's assistant, and as a colleague with Kaunitz and the rest. He acquiesced in the continuance of the old system of administration, modified only in small ways. Committees he chaired put forward recommendations he had opposed. He accepted decisions of the *Staatsrat* which he had combated. He would defend and even applaud the compromises so made.

He does not, of course, appear as enlightened in this document as in some others. He takes no opportunity to attack superstition. The nearest approach he makes is his remark: 'now that the centuries are more enlightened, the Court of Rome has no longer much influence in Europe's political activity'.[175] As compared with the memorandum of 1765, the 'General picture' says little against the present condition of the church. Liberty is mentioned once, in reference to Hungary, but only to be criticised. Even the aristocracy comes off lightly.

What stands out from the 'General picture' is the sense of responsibility Joseph displays for the Monarchy and its subjects, associated with a detailed mastery of its affairs. It is indicative that much of what he wrote constitutes as good an account of the topic in question as any historian has provided. In this document the emperor expresses himself with uncommon clarity and organises his material admirably. Lacy was as good at flattery as Kaunitz, though briefer. But perhaps the marshal's praise of the 'General picture' may be allowed a certain justice: he said it showed 'the industrious, vigilant and sagacious spirit characteristic of Your Majesty, which will one day command the admiration of the universe'.[176] Here Joseph stands forth not as a wild, unpractical zealot, nor as a ruthless despot, but as a reforming statesman

---

[174] Memo. of Kaunitz, 27 July 1767 (HHSA NL, Karton 5).   [175] HHSA TG, f. 189.
[176] Lacy to J., n.d. but obviously 1767 (HHSA NL, Karton 3).

working conscientiously, knowledgeably and rationally, within the existing system, to strengthen the state and to benefit its people.[177]

---

[177] ÖNB MS Ser. n. 1796, entitled 'Esprit de Ciceron sur le gouvernement', is tentatively ascribed to J., because it at least purports to be written in Vienna by a prominent personage to his brother, about to go to a post in Italy (sc. Leopold). It is dated 16 Mar. 1766. H. Liebel, 'Enlightened despotism and the crisis of society in Germany', *Enlightenment Essays*, I (1970), 151–68, accepts the attribution to J. If it were his, I should have to revise my account of his views and writings in this chapter. But the date does not fit, and internal evidence makes it impossible for this interesting essay to have been written by J. However, I have to thank Professor Liebel for giving me a copy of the German version of her article which contains valuable material.

CHAPTER 7

The later years of the co-regency, 1768–1780: the royal family and the central administration

INTRODUCTION

Against all expectation, rule by triumvirate continued until Maria Theresa's death in harness on 29 November 1780. Though she was always talking of abdication and in 1773 actually offered it, it never happened. Kaunitz too stayed on, despite his stipulations of 1766 and many later threats; his three formal resignations of 1773, 1776 and 1779 were all rejected. Joseph, though he several times asked to be relieved of the co-regency and in 1778 came near to abandoning it, in fact retained it.[1] Superficially, therefore, this was a period of remarkable political continuity for the Monarchy, and the situation appears scarcely different from that of the years 1765 to 1768.

It is true that much was unchanged. It can properly be said of the whole co-regency that the empress exerted the ultimate authority, relying heavily on the advice of her chancellor, while the emperor struggled to make what impression he could on this formidable combination. But it is also clear that, in general, Maria Theresa's and Kaunitz's activity and influence were diminishing and Joseph's were increasing. This was not, however, a steady development affecting equally all aspects of policy and administration. On the contrary, each of the principals had his or her moments of triumph, now in one sphere, now in another.

After her nearly fatal illness of 1767, the empress staged something of a comeback. She always wore mourning. But she can be found attending the German comedy, allowing masked balls to be revived, mounting elaborate entertainments for her children's marriages and for visiting relatives, and even planning a great excursion to Gorizia in 1776.[2] The famous prohibition on the

---

[1] See for the main episodes pp. 198–201, 205–6, 219–26, 350–4, 407, 426–7, 470. I know of no satisfactory discussion of the balance of power between empress and co-regent. Some of the most important letters bearing on it are collected in T. G. von Karajan, 'Maria Theresia und Joseph II. während der Mitregentschaft', *Feierliche Sitzungsberichte KAW* (1865).

[2] E.g. for the German comedy, J. to L., 7 Jan. 1771 (not printed by Arneth; HHSA FA Sbde 7); for the masked ball, J. to L., 10 Dec. 1772 (Arneth, *MTuJ* I, p. 390); for the planned journey to Gorizia, Arneth, *MTuJ* II, pp. 106–13 and *MTKuF* III, pp. 226–9. K-M VII and VIII, *passim*, as well as Arneth, *MTuJ*, *passim*, for the family entertainments.

wearing of rouge was withdrawn in 1770.[3] But she devoted several hours daily
to Masses and pious exercises, with extra sessions during the penitential
seasons, and she went into retreat for the whole of each August, the month of
her husband's death.[4] After much fuss, the trip to Gorizia was called off. So in
fact she scarcely travelled further than the forty miles to Pressburg, the capital
of Hungary, where she would go to stay with Marie Christine.[5] Her health
deteriorated, though not steadily – she felt and seemed better in the middle
and late seventies than during a bad spell in 1771. By the end, however, her
'extraordinary Corpulency' and shortness of breath made it necessary to install
a lift if she was to reach the upper floors of Schönbrunn; and she found it
difficult even to walk about the garden.[6] Until her last week of life she worked
hard at state business, and made the final decisions except where she had
explicitly delegated them. Some of her most remarkable initiatives date from
1776–9. But she, Joseph and Leopold all agreed that her capacity to control
the government machine, and to settle the issues placed before her, had
dwindled. Her main interests now seemed personal, in her family, her friends
and her servants.[7]

Kaunitz grew ever slower and more eccentric. In 1768 he was excused from
commenting on internal affairs as a member of the *Staatsrat* – except in cases
that appeared to him especially significant. This, together with the elevation of
Starhemberg, seemed to threaten the chancellor's pre-eminence.[8] He came
less and less to Court.[9] In certain respects his position was weakened by the
intervention of the emperor. But Kaunitz remained dominant in almost all
questions of foreign affairs, and made many successful forays on the domestic
front. As we shall see, Starhemberg gave up the struggle to displace him in
1770; Kaunitz routed his rivals in a confrontation of 1773; and in church
reform his role was always central.[10]

In 1771, when Joseph attained the age of thirty, Maria Theresa became

---

[3] E.L. to L.K., 9 Dec. 1770 (SOALpZ, LRRA P. 16/22).

[4] Wraxall, *Memoirs*, vol. II, p. 328, says M.T. spent five hours a day on religious devotions. She
certainly made August into a period of retreat. K-M gives much information in this field, as
does Arneth, *MTKuF* III, M.T.'s correspondence with Maria Beatrix.

[5] For journeys to Pressburg, K-M VI–VII; for the Gorizia cancellation, J. to L., 24 Apr. 1776
(Arneth, *MTuJ* II, pp. 112–13).

[6] Ernest to Suffolk, secret, cypher, 6 Apr. 1776 (PRO SP 80/218); Glaser, *Schönbrunner Chronik*,
p. 42; Wraxall, *Memoirs*, vol. II, p. 312 etc.; earlier, 27 Nov. 1768, M.T. to Maria Beatrix
(Arneth, *MTKuF* III, p. 99). On her improved health after 1771, e.g. M.T.'s letters to
Herzelles (Kervyn de Lettenhove, *MARB in-8o* (1868), 43, 48–9).

[7] For M.T. on her own inadequacies, and J. on the same subject, see this whole chapter. For
L.'s view, Wandruszka, *L. II.*, vol. I, pp. 332–42.

[8] Walter, *VKNGÖ*, XXIX, 34 and n., 39.

[9] Wraxall, *Memoirs*, vol. II, p. 475, says K. visited M.T. about once a fortnight. This is perhaps
generous. But K. used, e.g., to go to Laxenburg with the Court in June. However, he very
seldom attended the *Staatsrat*, the Conference was very rarely summoned, and K. kept his own
court in the evenings. So his private interviews with M.T. were a high proportion of his total
appearances.

[10] See pp. 207, 219–26, and ch. 14.

fifty-four and Kaunitz sixty. The emperor certainly had the advantages of youth, enthusiasm and energy. He pressed incessantly for decisions and reforms, and throughout made sober efforts to achieve improvements by ordinary administrative processes. In the years 1771–3 he went further, and presented a series of wild demands for violent change – barely concealed attempts to usurp control of the whole government machine. But his mother and the chancellor succeeded in frustrating these more radical schemes, and from 1774 the emperor appears to have accepted that he could not hope to achieve fundamental reform while Maria Theresa remained capable of ruling.

THE ROYAL FAMILY

As in the years 1765 to 1768, so also during the remainder of the co-regency it is impossible to disentangle the personal from the official relationships of mother, minister and son. The intensity of feeling involved will be better understood if something is first said about Maria Theresa's dealings with her whole family.

She was a devoted but a highly self-conscious mother; and she did not forget that she was also a ruler and the head of her House. She drew up for each child, as it left the nest, elaborate instructions on religious observance, health precautions, diet and the duties of his or her station. These were some of the empress's precepts: Lent and other penitential seasons must be strictly kept, and Francis's death solemnly remembered; confession and communion must be regular; only approved books are to be read, and decorous clothes worn; wives must obey their husbands; nudes in paintings ought to be covered up.[11] She wrote to each child at least once a week. As well as combating and lecturing Joseph, she blamed Leopold for his coldness and reserve, Ferdinand for not organising his time better, Amalia for her poor French and haughty airs, and Marie Antoinette for her laziness, frivolity, extravagance and failure to take every possible opportunity to conceive an heir. The empress's married daughters and daughters-in-law received a stream of advice about conduct towards husbands, pregnancies, miscarriages, babies and their weaning. She confessed that she was 'insatiable in the matter of grandchildren'. She criticised the political activities of Amalia, Carolina and Marie Antoinette.[12] She not only gave advice. She saw herself as entitled to exercise authority over all her children, even if they happened to be emperor, grand duke, queen of Naples or queen of France. No wonder that Marie Antoinette told Mercy: 'I

---

[11] These documents are scattered through Arneth, *MTKuF*. Marie Antoinette's is in Arneth & Geffroy I, pp. 1–6. Wandruszka has discussed L.'s in *L. II.*, vol. I, pp. 110–19.

[12] The correspondence is in Arneth, *MTKuF* and (for M.A.) in Arneth & Geffroy; but the latter must be supplemented by Christoph, *MTuMA* (see Introduction p. 10), where the intimate passages are reinstated, though unfortunately the letters are all translated into German.

love the empress, but I'm afraid of her, although from afar; even when writing to her I'm never at my ease with her.'[13]

She was at once indiscreet and secretive. She made damaging comments about one member of the family to another. The following examples come from her correspondence with Maria Beatrix of Modena, her son Ferdinand's wife. The empress wrote in 1768, before the wedding, that he

will not have Leopold's great diligence, but more graces, and will care more for pleasures, if the emperor doesn't make him, as he puts it, a philosopher – which I'm not worried about because I see no attraction in this so-called philosophy which consists of forming no attachments and enjoying nothing, whether shows, hunting, cards, dancing or conversation.

She later declared that she had given up hope that the *ménage* of her daughter Amalia in Parma would return to reason. Leopold, she said, is more agreeable than he appears at first sight; he is not very good to his wife; she 'is an angel who has no will of her own, which is to be admired rather than imitated'.[14] She would tell almost anyone the story of her disputes with Joseph – old friends, her ladies, ambassadors, junior as well as senior officials.

Her letters, vigorous, direct, compelling, breathe warmth and frankness. Yet she regularly set spies on to her children. Marie Antoinette was closely watched during her last years in Vienna; and when she reached Paris, the ambassador reported on her with the aid of observers carefully placed in her entourage.[15] Officials were instructed to send the empress accounts of Leopold's and Ferdinand's behaviour as rulers.[16] Joseph was spied on during his visits to Italy and France.[17] Sometimes he or Leopold was sent to report on another child.[18] The British envoy was quite right when he wrote: 'It has been a Characteristical Mark of the Empress Queen's Conduct through Life, to be Suspicious, & close towards Her nearest Relations, and frequently too unreserved towards menial Attendants.' His deputy had been equally justified in saying that, as she grew older, she became ever more wilful, irritable, 'suspicious and cavilling'.[19] The emperor once put the position to Leopold with unexpected psychological insight: 'so far as your children, your health and your *ménage* are concerned, you can be quite sure that the empress is

13 Mercy to M.T., 16 Jan. 1773 (Arneth & Geffroy I, p. 404).
14 M.T. to Maria Beatrix, 27 Nov. 1768, 5 Nov. 1772, 8 July 1776 (Arneth, *MTKuF* III, pp. 99, 148, 237–8).
15 M.T. to Maria Carolina of Naples, 9 Aug. 1767 (Arneth, *MTKuF* III, p. 31); Arneth & Geffroy, *passim*.
16 See the instructions to the Thurns (Arneth, *MTKuF* IV, pp. 17–35) about L. and to Rosenberg (*ibid.*, pp. 80–6) about Ferdinand.
17 See the letters and reports in HHSA FA Hofreisen 1, and Mercy's reports in Arneth & Geffroy III.
18 See pp. 255, 260–1 below for J.'s trip to Naples. The visit to France was partly to observe Marie Antoinette. For L.'s mission to Naples, Wandruszka, *L. II.*, vol. 1, pp. 203–18.
19 Keith to Suffolk, by Sir Thomas Clarges, 12 Apr. 1776; Ernest to Suffolk, most secret and confidential, cypher, 31 Jan. 1776 (PRO SP 80/218).

perfectly satisfied and happy, that is to say, as far as the petulance and suspicion which constitute her style of loving allow'.[20]

Joseph in his turn made increasingly uninhibited criticisms of his mother to his cronies and in his letters to his brother. The emperor too cultivated his own sources of information. As we have seen, Leopold was one of them. Maria Theresa had the effrontery to complain of Joseph's activities to Maria Beatrix:

As for myself, I am neither inquisitive nor demanding. My children must acknowledge this ...

I cannot refrain from letting you know that there is a mass of letters here telling of the inner life and conduct of your Court. If I knew someone, I would get in touch with him. But it is the emperor, and some low persons in town, who know the smallest details ... a post before I do ... I suspect servants in the stables or elsewhere, who came from here, writing home. But what shakes me a little is that it is the same with the affairs of Milan.[21]

The empress, Joseph and Leopold all suspected that Ferdinand was having their letters opened.[22] When Leopold came to Vienna in 1778, he wrote a secret account of the 'State of the family' in which he showed dislike, distrust and jealousy of every one of his relatives.[23] Against this background of maternal possessiveness and interference, general prying and backbiting, it is no wonder that the squabbles between Maria Theresa and Joseph were so bitter.

Feelings were intensified by their differing views about the role of the monarch. Maria Theresa belonged to the tradition of Louis XIV, that sovereigns should be extravagant, ostentatious and formal. She continued to spend large sums on numerous royal residences. She had palaces erected for Ferdinand and his wife in Monza, Mantua and Milan, where also the Scala opera house was rebuilt. Works were carried out for other members of the family in Prague, Buda, Pressburg, Schlosshof and Brussels. Though 'rather thinly modelled, quiet and somewhat impersonal', the new palaces and wings were indubitably large; and their internal decoration was lavish and pretty. The empress also built a religious house for noble ladies at Innsbruck in memory of her husband. At Schönbrunn the *Vieux-Laque-Zimmer* received its lacquers; the ground floor was remodelled to create the *Berglzimmer*, a suite that she could enjoy on hot days without climbing stairs; the *Gloriette* was constructed on the hill to commemorate the victories of the Seven Years War; and a 'Roman ruin' was simulated in the park.[24]

---

[20] J. to L., 31 Aug. 1775 (not in Arneth, *MTuJ*; quoted by Schüller, 'J II.', p. 53).

[21] M.T. to Maria Beatrix, 6 Apr. 1772 (Arneth, *MTKuF* III, pp. 134–5). See also same to same, 9 Dec. 1776 (*ibid.*, p. 258). See p. 150 above.

[22] Wandruszka, *L. II.*, vol. I, pp. 353–441.   [23] *Ibid.*, pp. 332–55. Cf. pp. 423–4.

[24] These remarks are largely based on guide-books and personal observation. On Schönbrunn, Glaser, *Schönbrunner Chronik*, pp. 72, 83, 94–5, and E. Neubauer, 'Die Gartenarchitektur der theresiansichen Schlösser' in *MTIZ*, pp. 363–9. On the work at Innsbruck and part of the work at Prague, cf. I. Gampl, *Adelige Damenstifte: Untersuchung zur Entstehung adeliger*

Joseph had little sympathy with any of this activity.[25] He thought that even great rulers should be content with modest homes and an economical Court. Younger sons and daughters should be allowed neither political influence nor social importance. He hated the grandeur and exclusiveness of Schönbrunn, where his mother invariably spent most of the summer and autumn. By 1771 he no longer slept there but turned up only for dinner.[26] In 1780 he moved into a house he had ordered for himself in the Augarten, a royal park near the Prater. This retreat was no bigger, and much plainer and less ostentatious, than a Victorian suburban villa.[27] Other monarchs of the period claimed to seek simplicity, like Marie Antoinette in her dairy. But her milk-pails were of gold. Even Frederick the Great built opulent palaces. Joseph totally rejected the grand tradition.

His attitude to his individual subjects was still more unconventional. He regularly visited, without warning or ceremony, the houses and the theatre-boxes of the more civilised aristocrats, paying special attention to the wives. Maria Theresa no doubt considered the freedom of his conversation danger-ous to state security, but she was much more exercised about the risk of sexual immorality.[28] More generally, Joseph made a point of allowing all subjects of whatever social standing to bring their troubles to him. When he was in Vienna, they came to the Hofburg, and the corridor where they waited, the *Controleurgang*, became legendary. The enlightened Leopold strongly disap-proved. Joseph, he wrote,

likes nobody and thinks only of himself and receives no one except in the corridor, where his servants bring [visitors] under the eyes of all the lowest, most dishonourable and most disreputable persons. All those who pass by see there every day the most indecent pimps and prostitutes, since he can't resist these base and squalid women, whom he pays very well. He readily believes these humble people, and what they tell

---

Damenstifte in Österreich, Wiener rechtsgeschichtliche Arbeiten, vol. v (Vienna, 1960). On the Scala and other work at Milan: L. Patetta (ed.), *L'idea della magnificenza civile: Architettura a Milano, 1770–1848* (Milan, 1978) and F. Haskell, 'The age of romanticism: 1750–1860' in *The Italian World*, ed. J. J. Norwich (London, 1983), p. 202, from which I take the quotation. On the work of one of the two chief Court architects, the pioneering study of G. Kelényi, *Franz Anton Hillebrandt* (Budapest, 1976). I am particularly grateful to Dr Kelényi for presenting me with a copy of this book. See Plates 8a, 18a and 18b.

[25] E.g., in her correspondence with Ferdinand, M.T. is always blaming J. for obstructing the progress of the plans and building of the Italian palaces (Arneth, *MTKuF* 1). More generally, see pp. 172–3.

[26] J. to L., 14 Dec. 1770 (wrongly dated 18), Arneth, *MTuJ* 1, p. 319; 21 Apr. 1771, *ibid.*, pp. 337–8; 19 Sept. 1771, not printed by Arneth (HHSA FA Sbde 7): 'ne restant a Schönbrunn que pour diner couchant, et etant, tout le reste du temps, en Ville'. Also M.T. to Herzelles, 9 July 1771 (Kervyn de Lettenhove, *MARB in-8o* (1868), 30).

[27] K-M VIII, p. 194. J. to K., 21 Sep. 1780: HHSA FA Sbde 70. See Plate 9a.

[28] See J.'s defensive remarks in HHSA FA Sbde 55, the memo. on his daughter's education; M.T. to Herzelles, letters of 1771 (Kervyn de Lettenhove, *MARB in-8o* (1868), pp. 21–32); Wandruszka, *L. II.*, vol. 1, p. 244.

him puts him in a position to take action against everyone with all kinds of despotic measures.[29]

Having already opened the Prater to the public, he did the same with the nearby Augarten in 1775. He had had this park remodelled under the inspiration of London's Vauxhall Gardens. Many amusements were provided, and social rank was ignored. So that the largest area possible could be accessible when Joseph was not in residence, it was made easy to remove the protecting fences round his house. On the gateway he inscribed: 'Pleasure-ground dedicated to the People, from one who esteems them'.[30] Leopold tells us that the empress was delighted when Joseph won popular applause – until people started saying they wished he was already in charge.[31]

Relations between the emperor and his mother were often poor and sometimes appalling. But their more bitter disagreements fill a disproportion-ately large place in the archives and therefore in the history-books. Some happier incidents should be borne in mind when reading the rest of this chapter. In October 1770 Zinzendorf, acting as chamberlain, heard the imperial family, dining with the empress in the next room, 'extremely cheerful, making a great noise ... The empress, the emperor, the grand duchess, prince Albert were laughing a lot.'[32] At Schönbrunn two years later, the emperor, the duke of Braganza and count Rosenberg 'sang, or more accurately miaowed. They performed in the empress's presence the *Stabat* of Pergolesi ... then some *grandes messes*, some *Misereres* and no doubt a *Dies irae* or two as well.'[33] During one of Maria Theresa's journeys to Pressburg in 1775, she and her party had to abandon her boat and send to Vienna for assistance. Joseph himself drove over, taking with him his own dinner as a picnic, and rescued them. The empress was so pleased that she had the event publicised in the *Wiener Diarium*.[34]

THE CO-REGENT'S REBELLION: DISPUTES OVER THE CENTRAL ADMINISTRATION, 1769–74

In this section the nature of the relationship, political and personal, between sovereign, co-regent and ministers will be illustrated, with special reference to the major disputes concerning the central administration of the Monarchy.

After the alarms of 1766,[35] the first major row known to us took place in January 1769. By this time the emperor had become rather more influential,

[29] *Ibid.*, vol. I, p. 344.
[30] K-M VIII, pp. 76, 234; F. Nicolai, *Beschreibung einer Reise durch Deutschland und die Schweiz, im Jahre 1781* (8 vols., Berlin, 1783–7), vol. III, pp. 12–16. See Plate 9b.
[31] Wandruszka, *L. II.*, vol. I, pp. 335–6.   [32] HHSA TZ, 15 Oct. 1770.
[33] L.K. to E.L., 27 Sep. 1772 (SOALpZ, LRRA P. 16/23).
[34] Arneth, *MTuJ* II, pp. 80–1 (J. to L., 9 Aug. 1775).   [35] See pp. 143–8 above.

partly as a result of his inspection tour to the Banat in 1768 and of his growing involvement in foreign policy. This was his opening salvo:

The new arrangements made for the *Staatsrat*, which at the same time affect my own position, are of such a nature as to require an explanation [between us]. From now on [the record of] all business at the *Staatsrat* is to be signed by whichever of us is present, or jointly by both of us. This novelty requires me to reiterate the same representations that I made once before about the military department which it was proposed to give to me exclusively ... In the nature of the case, my opinion, my way of thinking cannot and ought not to appear anywhere save at the feet of my august mother. I am nothing, and in affairs [of state] not even a thinking being, except in so far as I have to carry out her orders and reveal to her all I know. If under the vain title of co-regent there is any idea of implying something else, I hereby declare, with the sincerity I profess and the firmness I glory in, that I shall never be brought to consent to it, and that nothing will shake me, since I am firm in this principle, on which my present tranquillity and happiness as well as my future reputation and fame depend. Signatures are so contrary to monarchical laws, of which the essence is one head ... that I see no alternative but to excuse myself and to refuse absolutely to sign.

He goes on to propose two formulae which he considers satisfactory for use with his signature, since they would specifically indicate his subordinate status.[36]

Biographers have described the personal dispute between mother and son, using their published letters. They have concluded that Joseph was making a fuss about nothing, giving unnecessary pain to his poor old mother. They have neglected the ostensible cause of the quarrel, the new arrangements for the *Staatsrat*.[37] Administrative historians, on the other hand, have explained the changes made in the procedure of the *Staatsrat* on the basis of material, now mostly destroyed, from the archives of that body. But they have paid no attention to its implications for Joseph and the co-regency.[38] No writer has brought the two sets of issues and documents together. When this is done, it becomes clear that, however tiresome and self-righteous the emperor showed himself to be, he had a serious point. He had mentioned in the 'General picture' that by 1768 the *Staatsrat* as such no longer held meetings in the presence of Maria Theresa but that consideration was being given to ways of improving the conduct of its business. On 16 December, after the customary months of paper warfare, the empress issued an instruction designed to achieve this end. It provided, among other changes, for a revival of the practice of holding meetings of the *Staatsrat* in the presence of the ruler or the co-regent or both. Since the object of these exceptional gatherings was to reach

---

36 J. to M.T., 19 Jan. 1769 (Arneth, *MTuJ* I, pp. 233–4).
37 Even Arneth, *GMT* VII, pp. 236–40.
38 E.g. Walter *VKNGÖ*, XXXII, 431–2 does not mention the provisions about the co-regent to be found in the document he prints in XXIX, 37.

decisions on specially thorny questions, a real difficulty could arise for the
co-regent if he found himself present without his mother.[39]

Maria Theresa proposed a concession, while pulling out all the emotional
stops:

> If you choose rather to continue on the old footing, as operated until 5 January this
> year, I should prefer it, although I should not obtain the relief which I had hoped to get
> from it. But you [surely] would not force me to procure a change in a solemn agreement
> so dear to my heart [the co-regency], which was the work of my love on 21 November
> 1740 and renewed on 19 September 1765, the most cruel day of my life. Only the hope
> of finding in you a son worthy of such a father, and of being able to be useful to you, has
> sustained me so far and will sustain me in future, for I do not wish to survive a moment
> without being convinced of your love as well as of your esteem and confidence.

In his reply Joseph called his mother his benefactor and friend, 'the only one
. . . on the whole earth', for whom he would willingly sacrifice everything. But
he still begged to be allowed this one boon, 'which for you is of no consequence
and for me of the greatest'. The empress tried another tack:

> I know that you are very good at talking and writing. I hope all the more that your heart
> feels [what you say], but your obstinacy and prejudices will bring misfortune on you, as
> at present they do on me . . . Only God knows what I suffer. Yes, I am your friend and a
> passionate friend, who has to do her duty, and could not yield in the slightest against
> her conviction and experience.

She sent Starhemberg, the newly created 'directing minister' of the *Staatsrat*,
to see Joseph and find out what was really the matter. The emperor assured
him that he was by no means displeased with the conduct of affairs. So the
empress claimed she could not identify his problem. Her son returned to the
charge in a letter which is certainly hard to follow, and which she said she
could not understand after three readings. Finally, they compromised, and
agreed to go back to the old system until they could jointly devise a better.[40]

Both sides had worked themselves into a state of high agitation. For several
days they had discussed the matter only by letter. Although the changes in the
arrangements of the *Staatsrat* increased the awkwardness of the co-regent's
position, they scarcely seem to justify such a confrontation. But the deepest
feelings of both mother and son were engaged: her love for her husband and
her son, her pride in her rule, her desire both to use and to curb the co-regent;
his emotional ties with his mother, cutting across his absolutist convictions,
his resentment at his subordination, his zeal for the welfare of the state and his
yearning for fame. Perhaps he was obliquely protesting against the elevation of
Starhemberg, or trying to override her objections to his programme of travel.
It seems inconceivable that he could seriously have expected to obtain a major
modification of the terms of the co-regency. It may well be that Maria
Theresa, having stood firm there, conceded points to him elsewhere. This was

---

[39] HHSA TG, f. 3; Walter, *VKNGÖ*, XXIX, 34–9.   [40] Arneth, *MTuJ* I, pp. 234–42.

her usual tactic.[41] But the main result of this, Joseph's first direct challenge to the co-regency, was a widening of the rift between mother and son.

During much of the rest of 1769, the emperor was away in Italy or meeting Frederick the Great in Silesia. But in January 1770 he was at home when a different type of family crisis occurred. His seven-year-old daughter, Maria Theresa, Isabella's child, fell ill of a 'pleuretick fever'. Her namesake and grandmother wrote to Lacy:

It is the poor father who attends his daughter, even at night. I am as worried about him as her. This affection of callousness is not sustained on this occasion. The child scarcely knows me, so I cannot be a consolation to her. My son loves everything which belongs to him only, unshared . . .

The little princess quickly got worse and, after receiving her first and last communion in public, died on the 23rd. When Khevenhüller had to disturb Joseph in order to make the arrangements for the funeral, the emperor, with tears in his eyes, told him 'he had lost, so to speak, his only consolation and pleasure'. Maria Theresa approached Lacy again:

After this cruel blow, take care of my son. Try to see him every day, even twice a day, so that he may share his grief with you whom he knows to be his friend. No one can distract him better than you with your business, the only sort where he does not find fault.[42]

In his desolation Joseph wrote highly emotional letters to his daughter's governess, the marquise d'Herzelles. Biographers of the emperor have scarcely used them, although they have been in print for over a century. They are so important, and yet so mystifying, that they must be quoted here at some length.[43]

Madame,

If decency permitted, it would be with you alone that I would be pouring out the sorrow which . . . pierces my soul. I have ceased to be a father: it is more than I can bear. Despite being resigned to it, I cannot stop myself thinking and saying every moment: 'O my God, restore to me my daughter, restore her to me.' I hear her voice, I see her. I was dazed when the terrible blow fell. Only after I had got back to my room did I feel the full horror of it, and I shall go on feeling it all the rest of my life, since I shall miss her in everything. But now that I have, I believe, fulfilled all the duties of a father – and a good father – one [duty] remains which I hear my daughter imposing on me: that of rendering thanks to you. Madame, where would you wish me to begin? All your trouble and care have been beyond price. But [she] would never forgive me if I did

41 See Kervyn de Lettenhove, *MARB in-8o* (1868), 26, for one example.
42 Langlois to Rochford, 17 and 24 Jan. 1770 (PRO SP 80/207); Arneth, *GMT* VII, pp. 340–1, 550; K-M VII, pp. 2–4, 199–200; M.T. to Lacy, 23 and 24 Jan. 1770 (HHSA FA Sbde 72); M.T. to Maria Beatrix, 23 Jan. 1770 (Arneth, *MTKuF* III, p. 107).
43 Until p. 208, all quotations and information come from Kervyn de Lettenhove, *MARB in-8o*, (1868) unless otherwise stated. I am greatly indebted to the present marquis de Trazegnies, her descendant, for sending me copies of his articles, notes on the family archives and slides of portraits, and also for his advice and encouragement.

not at least try to induce you to accept the enclosed offering as a memento of all that I owe you and a pledge of all that I should like to do for you. If in addition the sincere respect and true friendship that I have sworn to you can in some way discharge [my obligation], you can be sure it will be unshakeable. I venture to ask only one favour from you, which is that no one shall ever know anything about it and that even between ourselves – since I am counting on our weeping and talking again together about this dear child – there will never be any mention of it, or you will at once cause me to regret fulfilling this duty. I beg you to urge the same absolute silence on Mlle Chanclos, for whom I also enclose a letter; it is for me a point of importance. As my daughter's sole heir, I have just given orders ... that I should keep only her diamonds. [You are to have everything else.] One thing that I would ask you to let me have is her white dimity dressing-gown, embroidered with flowers, and some of her writings. I have her mother's, I shall keep them together. Have pity on a friend in despair, and be sure that I can hardly wait for the moment when I come to see you ...

Your true friend and servant,

Joseph

This unhappy 23 January, which has overturned our
happy and so successful household, 1770.

We do not possess the marquise's side of the correspondence. But evidently she replied at once, commiserating with the emperor and raising the question of her accommodation. He wrote her two short letters during the next twenty-four hours, mainly concerned with this matter. In the first he remarked, 'I fear for you too, since I almost dare to say that we are mutually necessary to one another.' In the second he stressed how much he wished to see her, adding that Maria Theresa had even agreed that the marquise could already receive visits in her new quarters. In another letter on the 25th he begged her to conserve her health 'for the sake of a friend who genuinely has now only you to rely on and work for'.

The *dénouement* came on the following day. Joseph wrote:

In reply to your letter, I have the honour to thank you, dear friend, for the discretion you have generously shown in denying knowledge of what I am so anxious should remain secret. But I have to warn you that HM the empress put the same questions to me as you say the public is asking, and she pressed me so hard that in the end I was forced, and thought it best, to reveal the secret. She strongly approved and promised me the most absolute discretion. I warn you only so that if she speaks to you about it, which I don't expect will happen, you will know you are not obliged to deny it to her on her own. What a consolation, though, for an unfortunate [like myself] to have you! Forgive me if I come and present my sad countenance to you even more often. Although your resolve to go away is cruel for me, since I lose a dear, charming and useful friend, all the same I understand your situation and ask only one thing: to [let me pay your removal expenses].

The marquise departed almost at once.

The obvious problem is: what was this offering – in French, *obligation* – that the emperor made to the marquise? It is natural to wonder, with the editor of the letters, whether he had proposed marriage. There seems no prospect of establishing the truth with certainty: very little of her correspondence survives; incredibly, the relationship between her and Joseph seems not to have been discussed by any contemporary.[44] What we know of it before 1770 is this. In 1766 the emperor, then married to Josepha, had specifically named the marquise as his chosen governess for his daughter, in a context implying strongly that he saw her also as an asset to his own social life. She was evidently a beauty.[45] She arrived in Vienna late in 1767, by which time Joseph was again a widower. Almost as soon as she arrived, he arranged for the promotion of her brother to lieutenant-colonel, saying that 'the legitimate feeling of gratitude makes me do things for a woman which no one else has been able to make me do'. Writing from the Banat in the following April, he spoke of their relationship in connexion with other people's marriages, but made a now impenetrable distinction: 'The two good husbands who are with us receive from their wives letter upon letter, always enclosing some little present ... Let's leave them to it; the laugh is on our side.' He had strong views about arranged royal marriages and declared after Josepha's death that he would never marry again; but in the memorandum of 1765 he had defended *mésalliances* and argued that wives of whatever social origins should rank with their husbands.[46] Maria Theresa alleged as one reason for discouraging him from visiting Italy in 1768 that, with his views on marriage, he would constitute a threat to Leopold's *ménage*.[47] The emperor was at this time obsessed by what he saw as the problem of his relations with women.[48]

The fact that the marquise was twelve years older than Joseph would help to account for the lack of gossip about their relationship. But it also makes the notion that he wanted to marry her seem less plausible. That he asked her to stay in Vienna and act as his hostess appears much more probable. That the *obligation* was a ring or an offer of marriage – presumably morganatic – is possible but unlikely. It seems surprising that Maria Theresa should have approved either arrangement; but her words in a letter to the marquise of March 1771, 'the blame falls on you', imply that it was the governess and not the empress who rejected Joseph's scheme, whatever it was.

Almost a year after the marquise had left Vienna, in January 1771, Maria Theresa sent her a letter in which she revealed her anguish about Joseph. The frankness of this document would be inexplicable if Herzelles had not become intimate with both mother and son. The empress begins by recalling the tragedy of his daughter's death:

[44] Perhaps the reference in Ligne, *Mémoires*, vol. 1, p. 64, is to Herzelles: J. is said to have told Catherine the Great that Ligne had prevented him succeeding with an angelic marquise.
[45] J.'s memo. on his daughter's education (HHSA FA Sbde 55). See Plate 5b.
[46] See pp. 165–6 above. Cf. p. 211 below.
[47] Wandruszka, *L. II.*, vol. 1, p. 244.   [48] See pp. 322–3.

I have good reason to say that this was the moment of the total change in my son's heart. From the time of his daughter's illness he began to separate himself from me, and this has continued more and more, so that we are now reduced, solely in order to preserve appearances, never to seeing each other except at dinner. I have indicated my feelings about this on three different occasions, but nothing has had any effect. On the contrary, it has led to scenes that I don't want to remember. So I am reduced to playing the part of the empress Josepha. Indifference, if nothing more, is plain. Judge the suffering of my heart, which lived only for this adored son. It is bitterer than death. His temper gets worse every day, and deceit is not unknown. I beg you to burn this letter ... I beg you to make no use of it, even with the emperor. There is nothing to be gained, but everything to be lost ... [Perhaps] the bitterness I subsist on will count in my favour in the other world, and will bring my worse than sad life to an earlier end.

It is evident and understandable that Joseph became further alienated after his daughter's death. There was a story that he blamed it on Van Swieten, whose views on inoculation had already contributed to the loss of both the emperor's wives.[49] Since the doctor was the empress's *protégé*, this would have involved blaming her as well. The marquise's departure made the blow of his daughter's death still more traumatic, by depriving him of what remained of his home life. Even if Maria Theresa had not precisely caused Herzelles to leave, it can hardly have escaped Joseph that the marquise seemed more attached to the empress than to himself.

In March 1771 Maria Theresa wrote again to Herzelles at still greater length and even more harrowingly, in reply to a lost letter which must have embodied some justification of Joseph. The empress was suffering from a stiff right arm, erysipelas and shortness of breath.

I am glad of these ailments [she wrote] and I confess that I welcome their onset. I can find solace only in death itself, trusting in the mercy of God; to hope for comfort here would be vain ... I try to do penance and look to his salvation, and I confess that this last makes me tremble, since I am too much troubled and discouraged and my obligations are too great. There is no longer any hope of putting the clock back. The matter is settled, and by now is a question both of custom and preference. I am the only person in the way and so I am a nuisance and a burden. I think that in the beginning his heart did not enter into it. But it is now a matter of pride to keep it up. I will tell you just one anecdote. Father Höller having died, I took care just to mention the word 'confessor'. At the same time van Swieten was also [ill]. So I said that I would take Störck and Kestler for myself if my illness worsened. From that moment he found both of them out of the question for himself, and even said, with a certain air of freedom and decision, that he had no need either of a doctor or a confessor.

Maria Theresa has tried reasoning with him, but so far without success.

How am I to have it out in a friendly fashion with my son? He carefully avoids all opportunities of seeing me, or at least of being alone with me ... He knows he has behaved badly to me; he doesn't want to admit it, so he avoids me. This has got to the

49 Arneth, *GMT* VII, p. 550 (the Venetian ambassador). Princess Liechtenstein thought the same thing (to L.K., 21 Jan. 1770: SOALpZ, LRRA P. 16/22).

point that, now that we have cards on Mondays, Wednesdays and Saturdays in Lent, as you advised me, countess Thurn doing the honours and very well, that works admirably, for everyone plays or chats as he prefers in the lower apartments, and the emperor does the same, but always in the room where I am not. That's nothing. But I see him only at 7.30 in the evening, when cards begin, since we now dine apart, because of the fast. A further point: without asking van Swieten or any doctor, he has on his own authority dispensed himself from [the observance of] Lent, and he wouldn't even have the nuncio asked, as is usual, but only the parish priest. Van Swieten said to him that he had not obtained permission. He laughed at him. One dare not talk in his presence about religion, the clergy, the authority of the church. His maxims are enough to make one's hair stand on end. Unhappily he trumpets these fine principles with which he is imbued in every theatre-box, and everyone is aware of it, more even than I am. On this point, he adopts an astonishingly decided and partisan attitude. But it is rather to oppose me, since, as is my duty, I have stood firmer on this point than on any others. His confessions are rare; his prayers scarcely edifying; he seldom hears a complete Mass, and often misses it; no spiritual reading or conversation . . .

More generally,

it is only necessary that something should have been done in our day or our parents' for it to be ridiculed and despised, in affairs [of state] as well as in ordinary life. In order to avoid disputes and quarrels which yield no result, I keep silent about everything and I swallow the poison, the most fatal that is known. So I cannot achieve anything beneficial, being obstructed and deceived, and often the best plans are diverted into bad courses.

Mixed up among these personal laments were criticisms of Joseph's attitudes in policy disputes, especially over the Russo-Turkish war. But it is plain that her son's moral and religious behaviour troubled the empress as much as any political disagreements. Her abdication, 'which used to be a question of preference, has now become a necessity'. Otherwise she will go mad.

In her next letter, however, a month later, the empress was able to announce an improvement, which had comforted her more even than his birth. He had appointed a confessor, admittedly a parish priest, and had made his first general confession for six years. Her son had told her: 'I've been working on it for two days and, even though I've been writing very small in the Jesuit manner, I've filled thirteen pages.' He had attended the Holy Week services with devotion. He had been pleasant to her, though 'always embarrassed'.

After this, in the few remaining letters which survive, Maria Theresa could report only a worsening situation. She disapproves of the company Joseph keeps and of the servants he employs. 'You know him, he is charming when he wants to be; he charms everyone. It is only within his family that he is not like that.' Their disagreements are public knowledge, and she no longer has the health and courage to impose her will in affairs of state.

These letters to Herzelles were highly personal and secret, intended to be burned. But the empress said much the same to Khevenhüller. She spoke of Joseph as her 'family cross'. She often talked of abdication. In one of these conversations, which took place at almost exactly the same time as Maria Theresa was writing her bitterest letter to the marquise, Khevenhüller, to bolster the empress's morale,

frequently used the following arguments: that, since God, Who knows all and Who decrees nothing save for His greater honour and glory, by what seemed like a miracle preserved her in her bad attack of smallpox ..., He will also continue to ease the burden of governing by His divine consolations; that people are studiously trying to make her sick of ruling, in order to take the sceptre entirely out of her hands and to get her out of the way altogether, either by a premature abdication or by some other method of taking the main business of government away from her, with which she would be only too ready to comply, in order to obtain complete control of affairs for themselves and to appear more notable before the world under a young, undoubtedly able, but still insufficiently experienced master; that therefore she, as a godly woman, is bound in conscience, out of love for her lands and so that religion should not suffer a fatal blow from the freethinking maxims which are daily gaining ground and from the growing indifferentism, so to speak to stand in the breach and to sacrifice the peace she seeks to these Christian objects.[50]

It is impossible to be sure whether Khevenhüller, in attributing these machinations to others than Joseph himself, was saying what he really believed, or rather shrank from making explicit accusations against the emperor. But it was not difficult to imagine Hatzfeld, for example, harbouring such plans.[51] Of Joseph's cronies, count Nostitz was generally distrusted and suspected.[52] Maria Theresa herself told Herzelles that she believed unknown advisers were leading her son into evil paths. At the least, an atmosphere of faction and insecurity prevailed at Court, since the empress was obviously unwell and was always talking of abdication, and Joseph's ambition was plain enough. The elder Zinzendorf let fall a remark that hints at enmities of longer standing: 'the empress [he said] had an obligation to him for not having got up to any dirty tricks with the emperor during her illness'.[53]

Overall, however, she was manifestly unfair to her son in the denunciations she sent to the marquise. They almost seem calculated to alienate his friend from him. It may be that this was the period of his greatest sexual laxity and religious rebellion. But his attitude to his aged Jesuit confessor was not the product of libertinism, moral or intellectual. Joseph was taking sides in a

[50] K-M VII, pp. 49, 62–3 (27 Feb. 1771, the quotation), 76.
[51] This statement is supported implicitly, though not I think explicitly, by the reports of the British representatives in Vienna during 1771 (PRO SP 80/209 and 210). Lacy seems also cast for the role, but his relationship with M.T., as shown in HHSA NL, was so close that the notion seems absurd.
[52] This assertion, though I am sure it is justified, is none too easy to document. But see letters of M.T. and Lacy, Dec. 1770, on Nostitz (HHSA NL, Karton 6).
[53] HHSA TZ, 17 Oct. 1770. Cf. M.T. to Lacy, 1 Oct. 1771 (Plate 22a).

current theological debate about how frequently confessions should be made, whether Jesuits ought to be appointed Court confessors and whether the parish priest should not act instead.[54] Further, Maria Theresa gave Herzelles a highly tendentious account of her son's part in framing foreign policy and of his relations with Kaunitz. She said his 'desire to make a name for himself' had led him to work for war and, failing that, for the establishment of a camp in Hungary to threaten the Russians; and that 'Kaunitz, whom the emperor doesn't like and often gets impatient with, goes along with him to avoid bother'. As we shall see, there was much more to it than that. Maria Theresa's restrictiveness, misrepresentations and emotional blackmail, as revealed in these letters to the marquise, go far to account for the violence of Joseph's struggle for independence.

His confidant was Leopold. From the letters between them, which survive in large numbers from late 1770 onwards, it is possible to reconstruct the emperor's side of the argument. In a letter to the marquise, the empress blamed Joseph for the objectionable features of the military promotion of New Year 1771. But he informed Leopold that she had forced him to sign it against his will, and now 'tells everyone that I alone am the cause'. In the same letter he complains that what he considers would be a fatal attack on Russia is being contemplated. Later, he fumes because no action is being taken about the grain shortage in Bohemia. 'We're going to try to put things in order, but it's like drinking the ocean achieving something here.' Next month: 'I often envy Job on his dunghill. At least he could scratch himself peacefully.'[55]

As always, the *Staatsrat* figured prominently in the disputes. Early in 1770 Starhemberg had seized the opportunity of a vacancy in the coveted post of minister in Belgium to throw up his task as directing minister in internal affairs. He was replaced, in effect if not in title, by Blümegen. Borié, one of the more active original members of the *Staatsrat*, was then sent as the Monarchy's representative to the *Reich*. Of the newer appointments, neither Pergen nor Rosenberg was expected to play a full part, and the illness of Stupan left decisions in the hands of a rump, or in effect of Blümegen. Moreover, resolutions were being drafted before the emperor or the empress knew anything about them. Joseph, who was evidently 'under-employed', pointed this out, and in April 1771 Maria Theresa allowed him to intervene, as he told Leopold, to

correlate all resolutions with the *Vota*, put in my grain of salt and explain my opinion and reasons, when they are different, which I do not doubt will happen very frequently, draft other resolutions, finally take them to HM.

Since at this moment it is only the empress, Kaunitz and I who see the whole, and the

[54] I owe this point to discussions with Dr E. Duffy and Dr N. Hope.

[55] J. to L., 10 Jan. 1771 (Arneth, *MTuJ* I, p. 332); 24 Jan. (p. 329); 7 Feb. (not printed by Arneth; HHSA FA Sbde 7); 21 Feb. (p. 333).

other two let me make proposals and minutes on my own, I have to draft all the decisions and to follow the golden mean, not too much, not too little, nor too great expense, but yet enough to be prepared for all contingencies.

This heavy labour, he went on, made his presence necessary in the city every morning, and so excused him from being at Schönbrunn.[56]

Very soon another new departure was made. Hatzfeld, already head of two financial departments, had been arguing that they should be united not only with the *Hofrechenkammer* but with the Austro-Bohemian Chancellery. This would of course have revived Haugwitz's system in a new and more formidable guise. Joseph seems to have supported this proposal for further concentration of power in the central administration. In June 1771 Maria Theresa went so far as to appoint Hatzfeld Austro-Bohemian Chancellor. Since the *Kommerzienrat* remained subordinate to the Chancellery, Hatzfeld had now secured for himself the direction of four departments. However, on the advice of the *Staatsrat*, she denied him the control of the *Hofrechenkammer* and also refused to admit him to the *Staatsrat* itself. This reunion of the financial with the general administration of the central lands of the Monarchy, although it was personal to Hatzfeld rather than a genuine integration, constituted a further advance for Joseph's views and influence as opposed to Kaunitz's.[57]

There followed a summer of discontent, when at times he and Binder, Kaunitz's assistant in foreign affairs, were the only members of the *Staatsrat* in town, to deal with what Joseph saw as the ultimate crisis of the Monarchy. In one of several diatribes to Leopold he wrote:

Things are bad in every way, both ... in internal and in external affairs. No system. No plan. Inaction, dilatoriness, confusion. The result will undoubtedly be that the Turks will make a shameful peace, everyone [else] will gain but we shall get nothing. Bohemia is practically ruined. Famine has existed there, exists there, and will exist there still more cruelly this winter, for no precautions are being taken. No one knows what's happening: a change of system begun and not finished; intrigue and cabals, and therefore complete stagnation of business, which will result in the death of the state. This is the melancholy picture which at thirty years of age, filled with the desire to act and with love for my country, I not only have to observe, but even am unhappy enough to appear, through no fault of my own, responsible for.[58]

---

[56] J. to L., 18 and 21 Apr. 1771 (Arneth, *MTuJ* I pp. 335–8); Arneth, *GMT* IX, pp. 296–7; Schünemann, *MÖIG* (1933), 38 and n. On Starhemberg, E.L. to L.K., 5 and 13 Feb. 1770 (SOALpZ, LRRA P. 16/22); M.T. to Mercy, 20 Dec. 1773 (Arneth & Geffroy II, p. 86).

[57] Walter, *VKNGÖ*, XXXII, 437–9; XXIX, 315–16.

[58] J. to L., 19 Sep. 1771. Cf. J. to L., 30 May and 3 June 1771. None of them printed by Arneth (HHSA FA Sbde 7). Fejtö, *J. II*, pp. 132–3 has a version of part of the letter of 19 Sep.
     Arneth's failure to print these pieces belies his statement that he omitted only what was unimportant from the letters of J. to L. and convicts him of a readiness to gloss over the weaknesses and disputes that M.T. tolerated in the administration. See also nn. 26, 55, 59, 60, 64, 66, 70.

Later the emperor speaks of continuing 'paralytic lethargy and languor'. He has submitted some proposals to his mother 'with frankness and force', which she has merely put to a committee, 'a remedy as futile as it is frivolous'.[59]

He went to Bohemia at the beginning of October. From Prague he despatched radical recommendations for improving the situation there. But on his return to Vienna in mid-November, he found that orders given before he left had still had no impact, and that he had to 'nag, write and preach for hours' to get anything whatever done. 'O poor Monarchy, how you are treated!'[60]

He now delivered to the empress, under the guise of further instalments of his report on Bohemia, a general critique of the administration of the whole Monarchy. This document deserves comparison with the *Rêveries*, the memorandum of 1765 and the 'General picture'. One historian, Schlitter, called it 'the most important memorandum ever composed by Joseph II; for it touched on all the reforms which were taken in hand by the people's emperor after Maria Theresa's death'.[61] But it is difficult to award the palm to any one of these utterances. Rather, each represents the emperor's views in a different context and therefore with a different emphasis. In this document Joseph naturally writes more than elsewhere about local government. He makes his most passionate statement in support of the canton system and the militarisation of civil administration. On the basis of his Bohemian experience, he is more specific than before about the evils of serfdom and abuses in the church, and his advocacy of educational reform is more informed and elaborate. But nearly all the main points have appeared in previous documents. On the other hand, he says little here about central-government finance or about economic policy, and nothing about foreign affairs. As with the *Rêveries* and the memorandum of 1765, the tone of this piece is excited, the style (this time in German) is elliptical, ideas tumble over one another, and the organisation into numbered sections does not correspond well with

---

[59] J. to L., 25 Sep.1771 (Arneth, *MTuJ* I, pp. 344–5, prints most of it, but omits the point that M.T. has again delayed J.'s departure for Bohemia; see ch. 11 below). The proposals must be about an *Urbarium* for Bohemia.

[60] J. to M.T., 27 Oct. 1771 (Arneth, *MTuJ* I, pp. 347–8); and J. to L., November 1771, part printed by Arneth, *MTuJ* I, p. 349, but without any indication of what is omitted. After 'ma bonne part', where Arneth puts a full stop, J. goes on 'de Capellacio'. Then the text in Arneth is correct, though tidied up, until 'commencées', when J. writes, with unusually eccentric spelling: 'au pauvre monarchie comme tu est traité'. (Cf. Fejtö, *J. II*, p. 133.)

See Arneth, *GMT* IX, pp. 342–82 and X, pp. 41–59 for the whole Bohemian affair: but he omits much (see n. 58).

[61] K-M VII, p. 373. The whole document, i.e. the 'anderte Abtheilung', of the Bohemian report, takes up pp. 373–98. A similar document in ÖNB (ser. n. 1622), whose title is 'Seiner Majestät des Kaisers Entwurf und Anzeige von denen Mängeln in den österreichischen Staaten und wie solchen abzuhelfen', seems to me like a better-organised version of the *Relation*, compiled by officials. Cf. pp. 343–6, 452–5.

the divisions of the rather confusing argument. But the document makes up in stridency and forcefulness what it lacks in orderliness.

I shall discuss several aspects of this memorandum elsewhere. Here I shall confine myself to its proposals for reforming the central administration. These were the focus of interest in another confrontation between mother and son, because Joseph's recommendations amounted to a bid for personal power.

The emperor started with a surprisingly generous appreciation of Haugwitz's system. He did not, he said, approve of the principle of a Contribution; but he must acknowledge that it had kept the state afloat for twenty-three years. In other respects Haugwitz's principles were admirable. Unhappily, incompetence and selfish interests had reduced the system's effectiveness. Worse than this:

since the war the whole internal constitution of the state has never been on a solid basis, and still less on a permanent one, for a year together. Continual alterations, incessant intrigues; administrative fragmentation at one moment, centralisation at another; now a batch of departments was created, now their abolition was ordered; first, ministers' hands were tied, then they were given unrestricted power. In short, when people observed the prevailing doubt and indecision, they all trimmed their sails to the wind and set about ... procuring for themselves and their friends and clients advantages, titles, salary, pensions and other delights, without giving a thought to the general benefit, relying on YM's indulgence. YM's ministers and advisers, none excepted, very often went along with this, partly because they considered it proper, partly because it answered their own purposes.

No official who failed in his duty had anything worse to fear than retirement on full pay, suitably honoured. So administrative confusion daily grew, and the state treasury dwindled.

YM's departments, ministers and advisers ascribe all mistakes to the provinces, which blame the departments and ultimately the *Staatsrat*, which [in turn] shuffles the responsibility on to the departments. In this vortex of folly the only sufferer is the peasant and worthy citizen, who gets no benefit from all the intrigues and is ever more repressed and tormented, since their result is that the state's requirements increase and the landlord tries to improve his income, so that he can live luxuriously and keep advantages which in many cases have had to be bought, not by promoting manufactures, but by harassment and bullying.

None of the departments, not even the *Staatsrat*, adheres to its brief. Officials in the various ministries correspond with each other more or less secretly, in order to frustrate any attempts at reform from above. There is no one in a position to uncover all these abuses. The memoranda on which legislation and government instructions are based are compiled in Vienna in ignorance of what is going on in the provinces they will affect. In consequence, the resulting directives are often impossible to carry out, or simply absurd.

What is the remedy? It is exceptionally difficult, since it consists in YM according unlimited confidence to an honourable, disinterested and no less discerning, industrious person, feared by both great and small, who is in a position to act fairly in all parts of the Monarchy without prejudice of any kind, and to unite all parts in the common cause and direct them together for the good of the whole. In my opinion nothing will improve unless such a person is chosen, who under YM's eyes and orders will control the *Staatsrat*, the chiefs and ministers, the departments, and through them the provinces in all aspects. His selection is certainly not easy. But even a half-suitable person, uniting all departments under him, will be better than the continual discord, disputes and doubts which are now rampant. He must have the fullest knowledge of military, financial and political matters, and even foreign affairs also. YM would have to promise absolutely to give not even the smallest order except to him and through him, because, since he will certainly be a thorn in everyone else's flesh, his whole position, and the very possibility of his carrying out YM's intentions, will depend entirely on the unshakeable trust that YM shows in him, of which there must be no doubt even in petty matters.

Only such an appointment will make possible the complete remodelling of the administration in the interests of the whole Monarchy. 'Until now we have always set up departments and commissions at the centre, without having proper control over the parts and [their] actual working.' 'But first and foremost it is necessary to know what is happening in the provinces, how they are organised, and whether and how the orders given are carried out.'

After lengthy discussion of reforms in provincial government, followed by a section on religious and ecclesiastical questions, Joseph returns to the central administration, with a passage strongly reminiscent of the memorandum of 1765. He denounces the education received by officials, and castigates again their idleness, self-interest and love of unearned honours. Joseph would take no account of birth. All would have to work their way up from the bottom, even the sons of princes. Civil servants would take the same oaths as soldiers. Only those who served the state would be well received at Court; and their wives, whatever their origins, would take rank with them. Officials would have no security of tenure, no absolute right to a pension. Unless all these measures are taken, and 'virtue, love of the fatherland, assiduity and the fear of inevitable punishment implanted, I despair of all improvement, and the so-called indulgence of the House of Austria will always constitute the tyranny of the Austrian provinces. Ten unworthy men gain, and millions of people languish.'

Twelve headings follow, under which the emperor considers the economy, taxation, the army and serfdom. He then reverts again to the question of centralisation, this time in relation to the provinces rather than to the administration as such. Each *Land* (or province) ought to look to 'the best of the whole state', gladly making sacrifices for the general good. Joseph would divide the Monarchy (excluding Lombardy and Belgium) into only five districts: Austria, Inner Austria, Bohemia with Moravia and Silesia, Hungary with Croatia, and Transylvania. All important questions would be settled by special conferences in Vienna. But this would not suffice to 'arouse brotherly love' among all the Estates. The emperor suggests – ingeniously if insensitively – that in each province three deputies from other regions, approved and appointed by the ruler, should watch over and report on the administration, and co-ordinate action with their own provinces. For example, in Hungary the empress should nominate, say, an Austrian, a Bohemian or a Moravian, and a Transylvanian. They would sit on the governor's council but be independent of his administration, and would report to Vienna and to their own provinces. Not only would each *Land* thus learn about the constitution and condition of the others, but the ruler would be informed of the true state of affairs and so be able to control the situation.

Finally comes a variant of his usual submissive last paragraph. His remarks, he says, are hasty, rough and condensed. He trusts that they will be taken, not as questioning Maria Theresa's good intentions, but as an honest expression of his good will.

I write without prejudice, in no spirit of innovation or criticism. My only guides have been YM – to whom I have always, from the time of my birth, felt true filial devotion – and love of the fatherland. How happy I should be if I could remove all YM's doubts on the first count, and if my efforts could be useful on the second ... I want and intend only the good.

If he can be persuaded that other means than those he has proposed can succeed, then they will become his own aims, and he will not spare himself in promoting them.

I am not so vainglorious as to want to be the only person who promotes and upholds the good for YM and the fatherland. Let whoever seeks it do it. I shall always most fervently rejoice if YM's service is advanced, abuses abolished, the provinces in a state of greater felicity, and if I see the whole Monarchy preserved from extinction for many years more.

Maria Theresa received this manifesto with exceptional tact and sympathy. She called his journey to Bohemia 'a truly glorious episode for you here and in the next world'. The purity of his intentions could not be doubted. But nor could hers. 'God, who alone knows the depths of my soul, sees that I never had any other aim than the public good, even at the expense of my own and of that of you all.' How, then, does it come about that she and Joseph are so continuously at odds?

You will please me, my dear son, by revealing to me how this unfortunate situation has arisen, by helping me with advice and action. I am beginning to lose my courage. You are full of it, you are beginning your career ... I want to share with you the overwhelming [problems] of our situation. My experience may be useful to you by way of advice, but not in order to stop you carrying out what, after careful consideration, you consider desirable. Let us then lay down principles for our own harmony and behaviour, to make our peoples happier than they are. To achieve that, we must be in agreement, with the most perfect sincerity, confidence and consistency. Everything else depends on this.

Tell me honestly, in writing or by word of mouth, as I have always begged you to do, my defects, my weaknesses. I shall do the same, but let no one apart from us believe or suspect that we have different opinions. In the first year, 1766, everything went well; it is only since then that things have gone differently, and it is because we have both forgotten this principle. You are so good at devising principles. Undertake this task, my dear son, for the public good and peace between us. Let us prescribe for ourselves maxims and rules . . .

I should be entirely overwhelmed if I had not a son such as you, granted me by Providence; and as long as you do not fall into vice, and keep faith and trust in the sacred law, I can only hope that you will be the saviour of your peoples. This prospect stirs me to do everything I can to assist you.[62]

Joseph responded to the spirit of this appeal. He acknowledged that what he had proposed was appropriate only to a situation of the direst need, when business was virtually at a standstill. If that was not the case, then only interim measures could be taken. He proposed the amalgamation of departments as opportunity arose, and a ministerial reshuffle, especially affecting the *Staatsrat*. He made no mention of Kaunitz or foreign policy.

It was the *Staatsrat* which concerned him most. He wished to change its membership, and in particular to remove Blümegen, who stood for provincialism, and whom 'he considered too timid and submissive to Mama'. He should be replaced by the centralising finance minister, Hatzfeld, 'to whom all parts of the Monarchy are equal'. The emperor also wished to get rid of Binder, and proposed two new names, those of Kressel and Festetics, a Hungarian. He wanted Blümegen transferred to the headship of the Austro-Bohemian Chancellery. Hatzfeld's financial departments would be given separate chiefs again, but the Chancellery under Blümegen would resume responsibility for the Contribution.[63]

Maria Theresa at once accepted these nominations, declaring that her principal object was to maintain the system of 1748. But both Blümegen and Hatzfeld raised objections. The former did not wish to leave the *Staatsrat*. The latter was reluctant to give up the powerful position he had won, by dint of much lobbying, only a few months before. Moreover, he disapproved of Joseph's proposed reallocation of financial responsibilities. Asked to choose between the two men, the emperor chose Hatzfeld, but had to accept a modified scheme of reorganisation. Hatzfeld was told that he was to become

[62] M.T. to J., Nov. 1771 (Arneth, *MTuJ* I, pp. 350–2).
[63] J. to M.T., 27 Nov. 1771 (*ibid.* I, pp. 352–6); K-M VII, p. 106; Schünemann, *MÖIG* (1933), 37–8.

the 'minister in chief' whom the state required, in charge of 'the supervision, direction and co-operation of all parts, provinces and branches of the Monarchy for the general best' through the *Staatsrat*. Joseph said Hatzfeld would be 'after himself, co-regent'. However, it was decided not to declare openly that Hungary and Transylvania would now be treated like the other provinces. So Hatzfeld's post was defined as Starhemberg's had been; and Festetics was not appointed to the *Staatsrat*, to avoid advertising the extent to which it concerned itself with Hungarian affairs. Löhr, who was nominated instead, was Borié's nephew but also the brother-in-law of Maria Theresa's closest personal servant, 'la Gutenberg'. Pergen as well as Binder, both *protégés* of Kaunitz, ceased to be effective members of the *Staatsrat*. Kollowrat became head of the *Hofkammer*, still united with the *Banco*.

It well illustrates the difficulties Joseph encountered in putting his aims into practice that this very appointment of Hatzfeld, for which the emperor had specifically asked, though it furthered one sort of centralisation, meant that financial administration was again divided. Moreover, Hatzfeld himself, and other people too, saw his change of office as a demotion, even a vote of no-confidence; and it is clear that they had some justification, since doubts had arisen about his health and Joseph had uncovered in Bohemia what he considered to be maladministration in Hatzfeld's departments. Nor was Hatzfeld the emperor's lackey; as over this reorganisation, he had no hesitation in maintaining with tenacity views known to be opposed to Joseph's. It would be hard to find a better demonstration of the obstacles which the characters, attitudes and limitations of individuals placed in the way of the emperor's paper schemes.[64]

All the same, in the struggle for power at the top, these changes constituted a notable victory for Joseph. His mother was heard to complain that she no longer possessed enough influence to risk dabbling in the domestic affairs of the women of Vienna; she had given everything over to her son; and she told Lacy that Blümegen was 'the sacrifice for the public welfare of my states'. On the other hand, she assured Zinzendorf that she was 'relieved to see the

---

[64] Arneth, *MTuJ*, I, pp. 357–8, and J. to L., 19 Dec. 1771, not printed by Arneth (HHSA FA Sbde 7): 'le conseiller löhr, beau frere de la Gutenberg que S.M. a choisi pour conseiller; c'est un jeune homme, qu'à peine on conait', K-M VII, pp. 105–8. Arneth, *GMT* IX, pp. 297–305 and X, pp. 58–9. Walter, *VKNGÖ*, XXXII, 437–42 and XXIX, 42–7. E.L. to L.K., 8 and 16 Dec. 1771 (SOALpZ, LRRA P. 16/22). HHSA TZ, esp. 3 and 15 Dec. 1771.

Arneth (*GMT* IX, pp. 304–5) surmises that Hatzfeld objected to the extension of the *Staatsrat*'s competence to the Hungarian lands etc. and asserts (X, p. 58) that his power was confined to the *Erbländer*. This seems impossible in view of the documentation in Walter, *VKNGÖ*, XXIX, 44–5nn, which shows that the *Staatsrat* had already been given explicit duties towards the Hungarian lands in the late 1760s. See also Ember, *Acta historica* (1959). As the question of Festetics's appointment suggests, it was probably more a matter of ostensible than real restriction of the *Staatsrat* and its directing minister. Hatzfeld's main grumble was at the renewed separation of the financial departments. On Festetics see J. Bölöny, 'Maria Theresias vertrauter Ratgeber: Paul Festetics' in *MTIZ*, pp. 105–12.

anarchy which had lasted seven months brought to an end'. Kaunitz announced that he would take no further part in the internal business of the *Staatsrat*, with which he had never wanted to be involved in the first place. Princess Liechtenstein, usually so hostile towards the chancellor, thought he was showing himself to be 'a great man, and I regard it as a very bad mark against the emperor that he gives him so little credit'. Joseph in fact was riding high, because of the impression made by his visit to Bohemia. 'Everyone', reported the princess again, 'is enthusiastic about the emperor. It's no longer permissible to take a different view. His penetration and his application alike are unimaginable ... He has displayed the greatest generosity and human-ity.'[65] For the moment he seemed to have the game in his hands.

Despite this success, Joseph continued to complain to his brother about the conduct of affairs. Within a few days he was writing:

You wouldn't believe what goes on here. Indeed, to watch it is enough to turn one into a madman or a hermit ... The empress is worse than ever about maintaining her petty secrecies. Underlings have more ears than ever, and she is swayed now by one party, now by another.[66]

In June 1772, as his earlier memorandum was being smothered in committees, he made a new appeal to his mother to accept his proposal and appoint a single man, 'a dictator', as the only means of preserving the Monarchy from the catastrophe with which it was threatened by the famine in Bohemia. 'His character must comprise patriotism, fearlessness, industry, insight, and a philosophy which makes him subordinate his life, his reputation, even Your Majesty's favour, to the general best, which he keeps before his eyes.'[67] But Maria Theresa was persuaded neither of the seriousness of the danger nor of the appropriateness of the remedy proposed. In October Joseph wrote an even more than usually exasperated letter to Leopold:

When I am asked my advice on the 150,000 trifles with which the *Staatsrat* wears itself out every year, I always reply that, so long as the basis is not altered, all subsidiary [changes] are useless; and it is as though I had to advise a pagan whether it would be better for the salvation of his soul to worship Jupiter, the moon or Fitzliputzli. I should of course say that, so long as he did not become a Christian, he would never attain salvation, and that as between a number of bad alternatives it was a matter of indifference which one he chose.[68]

---

[65] HHSA TZ, 11 and 15 Dec. 1771; E.L. to L.K., 4 and 16 Dec. 1771 (SOALpZ, LRRA P. 16/22); M.T. to Lacy, 14 Dec. 1771 (HHSA NL, Karton 2); Durand to D'Aiguillon, 25 Dec. 1771 (AAE CP (Autriche), 317).

[66] J. to L., 19 Dec. 1771, not printed by Arneth (HHSA FA Sbde 7). Cf. other letters in the same file also omitted by Arneth, of 16 Jan., 11 May, 25 May and 11 June 1772. Fejtö, *J. II*, prints modified portions on pp. 134–5.

[67] Summarised in Schünemann, *MÖIG* (1933), 41–3.

[68] J. to L., 29 Oct. 1772 (Arneth, *MTuJ* I, p. 383). Arneth's 'Junon' reads 'la lune' in the original.

Matters came to another crisis at the end of 1773. This time Kaunitz was directly involved. His activity was now largely confined to foreign affairs. During the Russo-Turkish War of 1768–74, the members of the triumvirate were often at loggerheads, and Maria Theresa combated Kaunitz's policies, when they seemed to her bellicose or faithless, almost as strongly as she opposed Joseph's. On the other hand, she quite often deputed the chancellor to frustrate or placate the emperor. Occasionally, she and her son allied against the minister. More commonly, the two men appeared to be in league with each other.[69] But Joseph's opinion of Kaunitz was falling. Two quotations will illustrate his most critical mood. In January 1772 he told his brother:

We are sleeping the deepest of sleeps. Prince Kaunitz goes to the play and the riding-school every day. I also. HM prays and gives audiences, and we talk no more about the reply that has to be made [about proposals for partitions of Poland etc.] than about anything else. If I press, I am told that the prince doesn't want to be hurried, that all geniuses are like that. So, by dint of genius, and waiting on moments of inspiration, we are losing time, opportunities are missed, and in the end we shall find ourselves, as they say, up the creek without a paddle.

In September 1773 he went further:

I don't believe that even among the Iroquois and the Hottentots such ridiculous things occur . . . as here, and especially in the famous departments and in the *Staatskanzlei* of prince Kaunitz. You could write comedies about it which would seem incredible to anyone who did not know the facts and to posterity. Suppose I were to tell you that they don't even know the names of the rivers; that until I myself had told them and made them see it, they thought that the Bug flowed into the Dniester and not into the Vistula; finally that they thought an area 20 leagues by 5 a trifle because it looked so small on a general map. But I'll stop, for I may say that my heart bleeds to see the fatherland in such hands . . .[70]

Joseph's proposals of December 1771 and June 1772, that Maria Theresa should appoint one man to control and reform the entire administration, had threatened Kaunitz's whole position, in foreign as well as domestic affairs. But in the changes which Maria Theresa had actually accepted, only internal departments had been affected. So the chancellor had preserved his dominance over foreign policy – and over Italy and the Netherlands. However, he had lost much ground in domestic matters generally. Not only had he ceased to deal with them at the *Staatsrat*, but he failed to prevent the further amalgamation of the financial departments desired by Hatzfeld and Joseph.

---

[69] See ch. 9 below.
[70] J. to L., 26 Jan. 1772, wholly omitted by Arneth, and 23 Sep. 1773, partly printed in *MTuJ* II, pp. 17–18, but omitting the quoted portion without the slightest indication (HHSA FA Sbde 7).
     The phrase 'up the creek without a paddle' is an attempt to translate 'la fourche au cu'.

The battle swung to and fro, but Kaunitz suffered another notable defeat when the *Hofrechenkammer* lost its independence early in 1773.[71]

Any attack on the *Staatsrat*, even the mere suggestion that its procedures should be modified, was liable to be taken by Kaunitz as a criticism and a threat to his position. He worked hard to keep heads of departments, other than himself, out of the council – a principle respected in the arrangements of December 1771. He naturally rejected any idea that it should be controlled by a prime minister or a dictator.[72]

A new round of discussions about the *Staatsrat* began in the spring of 1773. The chancellor presented a memorandum of 240 pages on the improvement of the internal system. He wickedly claimed to the empress that he had 'drawn [it] in large part from the various writings of the Emperor's Majesty ... put in a new order'. Since Joseph had received it with a show of gratitude, both Kaunitz and Maria Theresa at first spoke of the emperor's having approved the document.[73] But in fact Joseph was in one of his most excitedly critical moods. He wrote to his brother:

The uncertainties here have now reached an incredible point; I swear to you that I am quite disgusted. Every day there are more memoranda, but nothing is done. I assure you that I am always at work every morning till five or six in the evening, except for a quarter of an hour when I eat on my own, and all the same nothing is done. Petty reasons, intrigues which have been deceiving me for a long time, hold up and prevent everything, and in the meantime everything goes to the devil. Let us change places, my friend. On my word, I yield to you, without mess of pottage, my rights as eldest son, for I am in a black melancholy and without hope for the future, for affairs of all kinds are going from bad to worse in such a way that there is no longer a prospect of making progress or even of daring to hope that one will ever be able to achieve anything good in life. Goodbye my reputation and pride! I take part against my will in this destruction, and my patriotic heart is lacerated by it.

In another letter he gave his honest reaction to Kaunitz's 240 sides. He has had to refute it: 'it contains a quantity of maxims and commonplaces'. He has also criticised the chancellor's plans for the internal government of newly annexed Galicia. 'I do not think that this will have been well received, but it is a tissue of theoretical ideas about which the only thing that one can find to say is that they cannot possibly be carried out in practice.'

---

[71] On K. and internal affairs and esp. the arrangement of the departments, see Walter, *VKNGÖ*, XXXII, 439, 457; Stormont to Suffolk, 19 Oct. 1771, particular, by Langlois, tells how K. made a point of attending the *Staatsrat* when Hatzfeld's proposals for amalgamation were being debated, and characterised them as 'an arbitrary tyrannical System'; Arneth, *GMT* IX, pp. 440–2.
The *Kommerzienrat* was abolished in 1776. See below, p. 366.

[72] Walter, *VKNGÖ*, XXXII, 438–9. See above, pp. 91–2.

[73] Walter, *VKNGÖ*, XXIX, 73–5 and XXXII, 454–5; Arneth, *GMT* IX, pp. 306–8 (the vast memo., evidently the work of Binder, was dated 14 Apr. 1773). Walter, *VKNGÖ*, XXXII, 454n, thinks the joke about J.'s writings is against K.

A few days later, Joseph submitted his own plans to his mother. He had summarised them for Leopold:

I am in the process of composing four documents for HM which will be accompanied by a note explaining the reasons and the need for the changes I propose. They are: [first,] an account of the defects to be found in the *Staatsrat*, and remedies by which it may be perfected if she wishes to keep it; then the plan showing how she could change the *Staatsrat* into a true cabinet for internal affairs, and associate with it another cabinet for foreign policy to direct and speed up the *Staatskanzlei*, get rid of all private correspondence, and oversee the whole from a true centre.

Next there are minute provisions for the secretariats required by these schemes, including 'the details of the Netherlands and Italy'. Fourth comes a project to simplify the provincial and central administration. Finally he has added recommendations about the family fund and the fund administered by Mayer, from which were drawn the large amounts Maria Theresa spent on pensions and other largesse to servants and favourites.[74]

The actual documents are even more highly spiced than this summary. His covering note started with compliments to the empress on the success she had enjoyed. 'Caution, natural mother-wit and knowledge of all ... internal circumstances' tempted him to remain silent, to take no trouble and to avoid risking her displeasure. But his 'conviction of the true best' has persuaded him to speak out. There is no adequate central authority in the Monarchy. Instead of a prime minister or dictator, he now suggests 'directing cabinets' for foreign and domestic affairs. In particular, enormous benefits would accrue from employing 'trusted and able men, who out of duty and in their manner of thought would be far removed from all feminine meddling and partisanship'.

If YM would only experiment with allowing business which Nature has made masculine in character to be transacted by men, YM would notice the same difference as I would if girls and women had been supplied to me as soldiers, foresters, hunters etc. How difficult it must be for YM, remote from all reliable assistants, either reading everything yourself, or through others' reading often missing precisely the most important and crucial point; for only a man versed in affairs can get at the essence of the thing and single out those points on which judgement is most vital in coming to decisions.

Although the emperor submitted alternative schemes for improving the *Staatsrat* if it was to be retained, his cherished proposal was for the establishment of these cabinets in its place. It was his most revolutionary to date, a frontal attack both on his mother's petticoat government and on Kaunitz's management of foreign affairs.[75]

Maria Theresa's standpoint emerges from her comments to the chancellor

---

[74] J. to L., April 1773, misdated 1772, and 22 Apr. 1773 (Arneth, *MTuJ* II, pp. 5–7); Wagner in Winters and Held, *Intellectual and Social Developments*, pp. 5–29.
[75] Walter, *VKNGÖ*, XXIX, 48–73, quotations from pp. 49 and 52.

on his vast memorandum. This was 'another great service' to add to all the others he had rendered, 'which are known best to me'. His ideas ought to be adopted by all officials. They held out to her the 'hope, with his help, of achieving what is necessary for the state and of somewhat restoring my so much oppressed spirits'. 'I regard it as like my own testament.'

But if it doesn't succeed, then I must tell him that I can no longer endure this burden, and after fifty-six years devoted to the world, I shall finally devote my last moments completely to the rest and retreat I need.[76]

By this time Joseph was travelling in Transylvania. He went on to Galicia, which was being administered by the *Staatskanzlei*. There he both uncovered abuses in the civil government and persuaded himself that certain disputed frontier areas must be secured to the Monarchy. On both scores he blamed Kaunitz for inefficiency, dilatoriness and lack of zeal. After the emperor's return to Vienna in September, relations between the two men worsened. In November the chancellor was forced to surrender control over the internal government of the province.[77] Finally, on 7 December Kaunitz offered his resignation. The occasion he picked was a difference with Joseph over the frontier with Poland. But it cannot be doubted that he had been affronted by the emperor's proposals to subject the *Staatskanzlei* to the control of a cabinet and to interfere with his direction of Belgian and Milanese affairs, as well as by the humiliations Joseph had inflicted on him in the affairs of Galicia.[78]

Maria Theresa replied to him:

Your letter has neither surprised nor astonished me, but it has seriously grieved me. I have been expecting it for some time . . . I neither can nor will accept what you request, and so wish to know nothing of it, but I count on you . . . not to abandon me in my cruel situation. Let us see if there are still ways of saving the state . . . and if there are not, let us leave together, but not otherwise.

As in 1766, she threatened abdication if Kaunitz would not stay. But this time she was wholly sympathetic with her chancellor. In effect, they were conspiring together against Joseph to keep her on the throne and in control.

Joseph counter-attacked with an explicit request to be relieved of the co-regency. On 9 December, after an interview with her, he wrote her a formal letter of self-justification. He had always 'foreseen that, given my situation and perhaps my manner of thought, I could not play the role of my late august father'. He had tried keeping out of the way, by travel and by living apart from his mother. He had made the best he could of the dual arrangement of which he disapproved in principle. Yet his mother 'has often done everything imaginable to make me forget who I am, and to put people in doubt about my

[76] Walter, *VKNGÖ*, XXIX, 73–4 and 73n.
[77] On Galicia, Arneth, *GMT* VIII, pp. 414–26, 492–3, and ch. 12 below.
[78] For the row of Dec. 1773 the essential letters of M.T., J. and K. in Arneth, *MTuJ*, II, pp. 21–9 and nn.

position'. If he has offended her by telling her how badly the Monarchy is administered, it is only out of duty to the state that he has done so. He does not forget who she is. But 'Who am I?'

She thinks me something quite different from what I can and must be. She does me an injustice if she thinks I am ambitious or anxious to command. I wish with my whole heart that I did not even have to dread the prospect. That is true, God is my witness! She is blind about me if she thinks me a mass of talents and genius, capable of directing great affairs. On my honour, I am far removed from this, by nature lazy, lacking in application, superficial, frivolous. I must say, to my shame, that I have perhaps more froth than substance, and that, except for my zeal and my firmness when the good of the state and its service are involved, there is nothing very solid about me.

He is simply one among her advisers. If only she would always take decisions, and take them for herself, nothing would go wrong. Her experienced ministers of course deserve more attention than he. But just 'as we can have only opinions and not wishes, she can have only wishes and not an opinion'. 'If his character has alienated from her men a hundred times more useful and capable' than he, then he begs her to permit him to resign the co-regency. 'None of my predecessors, my contemporaries, my colleagues as heirs presumptive [sic] are employed, why must I be? Let her leave me to my imperial business, my books and my honest amusements.' The last thing he wants is to be a cause of trouble to her, whom alone in the world, with the state, he loves.

Maria Theresa responded to this mawkish *cri de coeur* with another. His letter has allowed her to begin 'to live again with a sort of confidence', now that his 'heart returns to me'.

I am ready to hand over everything to you, keeping back nothing for myself, to withdraw even, either here or elsewhere, but you have so often assured me that you cannot tolerate this idea. I propose it to you once more, as the only thing which could give me peace and comfort. If it is important to you to preserve me, this is the only way. Never fear any regret on my part. I have seen only too much of what the world is like; I shall leave it with the greatest alacrity. Two things stop me: your opposition and the state of our affairs, which I find in such a bad condition that I should not like to burden you with them on your own against your will.

She desperately needs his advice. Her 'faculties, sight, hearing, quickness, are rapidly deteriorating'.

Your and Kaunitz's abandoning me, the death of all my intimate advisers, irreligion, the depravity of morals, the jargon that people talk nowadays which I have difficulty in understanding, all these add up to sufficient reason why I should be overwhelmed.

So she would like Joseph to make whatever arrangements he thinks fit to improve the *Staatsrat*, but without change of personnel or of the departments. 'I cannot watch the state perish on account of my unhappy situation; I cannot win through except by your aid. I promise you my entire confidence, and I require of you that you tell me at once if you find me at fault.'

You used to love the state; you kept yourself for it alone; what has happened to this proper ambition? I have often lamented that your dedication was tearing you away from the bosom of your family and from your happiness … So give your help to a mother who for thirty years has had no object in life but you, who lives on desolate, and will die so if she sees all the care and trouble of her love set at naught.

Neither Maria Theresa nor Joseph ever wrote more significant letters than these. At this moment and in these two documents the fundamentals of the relationship between mother and son during the co-regency stand revealed. We have seen the emperor apparently straining both to revolutionise and to dominate the state by reducing his mother to a cipher – 'putting me into care', she called it[79] – or compelling her abdication. In this cause he has enlisted every argument. He has maintained that the Monarchy is on the point of destruction. He has detected every possible defect in its administration, which he has blamed on her ministers, her companions, her methods, her expenditure, her prejudices, even her sex. In this latest letter he has gone so far as to hint at a lack of respect for his complaisant father. He has revealed deep frustration and bitterness at his situation – a grown man, a soldier and an emperor subordinated to a widow and her women. Constructively, he has displayed a fearless radicalism in proposing reforms, and what seemed like an insatiable ambition to seize the reins of government and win fame for himself. He has ridiculed the proceedings of Kaunitz, and his conduct during 1773 suggests an intention to force the chancellor's resignation as well as his mother's abdication.

Yet Maria Theresa's letter leaves no doubt that he has refused offers she has made to abdicate. The two documents, taken together, show that in their interview she must have talked him round to the position that, since he will not himself assume the government, it is his patriotic as well as his filial duty to assist her to rule, and to accept Kaunitz as her minister, and hence that, out of all Joseph's wide-ranging schemes, the only one which can be contemplated is a little administrative reform, mildly tinkering with the constitution of the *Staatsrat*. This harmless change she has magnanimously placed entirely in Joseph's hands, having made sure that its scope will be so restricted that it will make little difference and Kaunitz cannot be seriously offended by it. On the same day Joseph wrote to Kaunitz begging him to continue in office. This is a masterpiece of her art, a blend of emotional blackmail and political cunning such as only Elizabeth I of England could have matched.

What are we to make of Joseph's hesitation, and his protestations of inadequacy? They are hard indeed to reconcile with the confident criticisms

[79] M.T. to Lacy, 3 Jan. 1774 in Arneth, *GMT* IX, p. 632.

and strident demands of his earlier letters. One vital factor must have been the absence of support for his views among prominent officials. If he had become sole ruler at this moment, he could hardly have hoped for Kaunitz's assistance, except on stringent terms. When Maria Theresa told Lacy, who was in the south of France, about the crisis, she asked:

by whom can Kaunitz be replaced? In my confidence by no one; but certainly Starhemberg would have been the most suitable chancellor. But since he is detested by the master, he cannot be put forward. Mercy will not accept it, and he is at least as fussy about his health and convenience as Kaunitz.[80]

She must have threatened her son yet again with Starhemberg if Joseph would not climb down and urge Kaunitz to withdraw his resignation. The administration was full of the old chancellor's *protégés*, such as Mercy; it was doubtful how loyally they would have served Joseph if he had driven Kaunitz out of office. The emperor had no respect for another possible candidate, Blümegen. Hatzfeld, in commenting on Joseph's proposals to set up directing cabinets, had stressed the advantages for the general welfare of a splendid Court and a rich aristocracy, and the importance of maintaining the nobility.[81] He would hardly have served the emperor's purpose.

Lacy was the obvious man to replace Kaunitz. Joseph had meekly accepted him as his teacher in military matters, and they had worked together for seven years to carry the plan for conscription and cantons. After arduous battles within the army and the administration, they had attained a large measure of success. Lacy could report in March 1772 that the conscription, or census, had been completed in the central provinces. Every house now bore a number, and the allocation of regiments to their recruitment districts could begin. Other reforms too had been introduced, such as new drill and exercise manuals, and improvements in the arrangements for supplying the army with horses, carts, equipment and food. The thrust towards professionalisation continued: wealthy nobles were no longer allowed much independence in managing the regiments they had raised, and could no longer count on automatic promotion to the highest ranks.[82] Foreign envoys marvelled at the results achieved, and even Frederick the Great admired the exercises he saw at Neustadt.[83]

[80] M.T. to Lacy, 20 Dec. 1773, *ibid*, p. 630. She sounded out Mercy on the same day (Arneth & Geffroy II, pp. 86–7).

[81] Summarised in Arneth, *GMT* IX, pp. 310–11. On J. and Blümegen, p. 213 above.

[82] Kotasek, *Lacy*, esp. pp. 80–3, 92–5, 97–100; Duffy, *Army of M.T.*, esp. pp. 32–3, 52, 103–4. The *Kriegsarchiv* in Vienna notoriously contains immense quantities of evidence for military development in this period. I did not dare venture into it, lest I should never re-emerge and this book never appear. My knowledge comes from secondary works, the archives of the central government, HHSA NL and occasional references in other sources.

[83] Arneth, *Relationen*, pp. 315–17; Durand to D'Aiguillon, 21 Dec. 1771 (AAE CP (Autriche), 317), enclosing *tabelles* showing the resources of the Monarchy which were also sent home by the British and Venetian, and no doubt other, envoys (PRO SP 80/210; Biblioteca Marciana, Venice, MSS It. VII, 1883, ff. 244–94). Duffy, *Army of M.T.*, p. 209. See pp. 284–5 below.

Yet in October 1773 the marshal was given permission to take an extended holiday in France for the sake of his health. This journey provoked massive speculation both at home and abroad.[84] Unpublished documents, however, make the true position reasonably clear. He claimed that his work-load was too great. He was coughing up blood. He had himself bled. But his doctors would not declare that a trip abroad was essential. His desire to travel was plainly not a product of ill health alone.[85] It was also a matter of disputes and misunderstandings with Joseph. As early as December 1770, Lacy had complained of his lack of credit with the emperor. Maria Theresa had replied that hers was infinitely lower. Early in 1772 Joseph, saying he was often 'under-employed and at a loss to pass his time at all usefully', asked to see all the minutes of the *Hofkriegsrat*, while protesting that he had no intention of challenging them or delaying the orders based on them. In order to maintain her personal influence in military affairs, the empress resorted to ever more elaborate ploys and subterfuges in her contacts with Lacy, borrowing documents from him for a couple of hours, returning his letters to him, urging him to burn all hers, telling him what to say to the emperor, letting the marshal know exactly how much she had told Joseph, writing 'ostensible' letters for Lacy to show to her son, and paying secret pensions to officers whom the emperor refused to promote.[86] Lacy's situation, despite his great skill as administrator and courtier, must have grown progressively more difficult. In April 1773 Joseph and he disagreed seriously about the peacetime deployment of the army and about promotions.[87] In July, when the emperor was in Galicia, Lacy asked for a short leave, on grounds of health. Joseph refused, or was taken to have done so. He claimed some letters had gone astray. At the end of August he was telling Lacy not to take their differences of opinion tragically. Later, when Lacy was bled, the emperor was thought to have agreed with unflattering alacrity that the services of the marshal could be dispensed with while he travelled abroad to recuperate. Joseph was not only 'feeling the yoke' that Lacy tried to impose on him; the emperor's friendships with Nostitz and the Liechtensteins threatened the marshal's authority over the army. Lacy was a fanatical worker, dictatorial and sensitive to criticism, a man of independent means rendered wealthier by the generosity of the empress. He told his *amie* or

[84] E.g. Keith to Suffolk, esp. 13 Oct. 1773, secret, cypher (PRO SP 80/214), in which J. is said to have criticised Lacy's administration in reference to the state of the magazines; the correspondence of E.L. and L.K. (SOALpZ, LRRA P. 16/23); Mercy to M.T., 12 Nov. 1773 (Arneth & Geffroy II, p. 76).

[85] Arneth, *GMT* IX, ch. 16 and nn., prints many of the letters from HHSA NL, but his conclusions are, as usual, anodyne. See for Lacy's actual state of health, HHSA NL, Karton 8, documents of July 1773, and Karton 4, of Sep. (esp. immense *apostille* of M.T. on Lacy's of 9 Sep.); HHSA FA Sbde 72; E.L. to L.K., 13 Oct. 1773 (SOALpZ, LRRA P. 16/23).

[86] HHSA NL, Karton 6, Lacy to M.T., 21 and 22 Dec. 1770, with her *apostilles*; Karton 2, J. to Lacy, 26 Jan. 1772 and M.T. to Lacy, 1 Feb., 23 and 25 Aug. 1772; Karton 7, M.T. to Lacy, 16 Mar. 1771 and 9 Feb. 1772; Karton 4, M.T. to Lacy, 3 Jan. 1774. See Plate 22a.

[87] J. to L., 22 Apr. 1773 (Arneth, *MTuJ* II, p. 6).

mistress, princess Francis Liechtenstein, that he was 'cutting the thread of a thorny career'.[88]

Just after Lacy's departure, the emperor visited the chancellor at Austerlitz. The young countess Kaunitz described to her sister one of the conversations between the two great men. 'A propos of nothing in particular', Kaunitz embarked on a long disquisition arguing that it was the mark of lesser men always to look for weaknesses in others.

The emperor muttered a few monosyllables, claimed it was *amour-propre*, the desire to show off one's cleverness. But my father-in-law maintained in a headmasterly tone that it was worse than that, it was the sign of a narrow mind, of an enemy of the good, of a fool, of crass inexperience . . . I should have liked the ground to swallow me up.

Joseph's treatment of Lacy had terrified other officials – though many soldiers were glad enough to see the marshal go. But Kaunitz had seen his opportunity. As we shall see, in 1771 Lacy had contracted a diplomatic illness to frustrate the chancellor's foreign policy. This time they were on the same side. With the marshal abroad and discontented, there was no one left in high office to whom the emperor could turn for support.[89] Maria Theresa evidently rubbed in the point as well, since in his letter of 9 December Joseph spoke of having 'alienated from her men a hundred times more useful and capable' than himself.[90]

In fact, his political failure was more fundamental still. He was no match for his mother, partly because he would not, or could not, use all available methods. In his mother's manoeuvrings very few holds were barred. True, the Court of Vienna remained civilised: she did not resort to corporal punishment and imprisonment, as Peter the Great and Frederick William I had with their recalcitrant sons. She never dreamed of disturbing the line of succession to the throne. But she played mercilessly on her son's emotions; she used her own as weapons in foreign as well as domestic policy; and while retaining her absolute power, she wished Joseph to give her the advice she wanted to hear, render her any assistance she might request in detail, and accept full responsibility for her policies. Although she asserted that he had complete charge of the army, she used every device to interfere in military affairs behind his back, and to keep Lacy her servant rather than his. Joseph, on the other hand, respected certain rules of the game. He did not go round about. He made frontal attacks in private letters and memoranda to his mother. If they obtained wider currency, it was with her consent. He gossiped about their disputes, but he was always saying he would have nothing to do with Court intrigue, and he seems to have

[88] See HHSA NL, Karton 8, documents of July 1773; Karton 4; J. to Lacy, 27 Aug. (HHSA FA Sbde 72); E.L. to L.K., quoting Lacy's *amie*, 19 and 30 Oct., L.K. to E.L., 8, 13 and 16 Oct. 1773. (SOALpZ, LRRA P. 17/23). I call her 'princess Francis' because, though her Christian name was Leopoldine, she was universally known as 'Françoise' or *die Franzin*, and I wish to distinguish her from E.L. and L.K.
[89] L.K. to E.L., 13 and 20 Oct. 1773 (*ibid.*). See pp. 291–2.   [90] See p. 220 above.

meant it.[91] As we shall see, his private friendships sometimes affected his public stance; but he was ashamed of the fact.[92] By contrast, those ambitious for office knew very well that one of the ways to Maria Theresa's notice was through the favour of her ladies-in-waiting, and particularly 'la Gutenberg'.[93] The empress openly and avowedly used her charm, pensions, gifts, offices and backstairs intrigue to maintain the loyalty of her servants. She wrote of her 'clique' in Belgium, which included Starhemberg.[94] Joseph, it must be admitted, talked once of his 'tools', whom he was 'keeping in reserve' for better times.[95] But he refrained from trying to create a party within the administration to work against his mother's and Kaunitz's *protégés*. His principles of administrative purity and economy prevented his wooing followers by largesse. He adhered also to the principle of absolutism or monarchy. Just as he would not accept any measure of independence as co-regent, because that would derogate from the sovereign's authority, so he would not obstruct or undermine his mother's ministers while they repre-sented the ruler's will. If these self-denying ordinances were merits in a son and a co-regent, they were defects in a politician.[96]

Even so, if he had possessed the overweening self-confidence and total impracticality with which he is often credited, he could evidently have accepted his mother's offer to abdicate, and seized power. One must conclude that, when it came to the crunch, he genuinely felt unsure of himself. In his letter declining her offer, he protested too much, as usual. But he was not at bottom the self-sufficient, imperturbable Stoic he pretended to be. Nor was he a man of level temper. He overworked himself, he was lonely, he was already perhaps unwell. If he had little heart, he had strong emotions. His letters often sound almost, sometimes quite, hysterical. When his mother was there, taking the ultimate responsibility, as she always had as long as he could remember, he could indulge his feelings about the Monarchy, the co-regency and his personal situation without having to face up to their implications. She was a bulwark on which he needed to lean even while he was pummelling it with his fists. According to Leopold, Joseph feared that foreign Powers would hold it against him if he drove her into retirement. Similar points can be made about his relationship with Kaunitz. Frederick the Great had observed that Joseph treated the chancellor like a father.[97] The emperor had to acknowledge his talents and international standing, even while scoffing at his eccentricities and deficiencies. In default of Lacy, Joseph needed Kaunitz as much as he

---

91 HHSA TZ contains a number of such statements. Cf. Schüller, 'J. II.', pp. 54–5, 57.
92 See below, pp. 333–4.
93 Arneth, *AÖG* (1886), esp. 106–7 (Cobenzl's memoirs). This whole document is most revealing on the power relations within the Court and administration at Vienna.
94 In an undated letter, evidently of early 1774, to Lacy (HHSA NL, Karton 2).
95 Arneth, *AÖG* (1886), 127.
96 Schüller, 'J. II.', ch. 2, esp. pp. 48–9, 53–4, is very persuasive on J.'s refusal to create a party.
97 Frederick to prince Henry, 13 Sep. 1770 (*PC* xxx, pp. 130–1).

needed his mother. In the last resort he lacked the audacity and nerve to take charge and try to carry through his programme without their co-operation.[98]

This was the only occasion when at one and the same time Kaunitz resigned, Maria Theresa offered to abdicate and Joseph asked to be relieved of the co-regency. It was in another respect a very different affair from the chancellor's resignation of 1766 or the emperor's refusal to sign documents in 1769: Joseph's standing had in the meantime risen far higher. But his mother and her minister had still routed him. Although all the same problems persisted as long as the triumvirate lasted, and although each personage more than once renewed his threat to retire, it seems right to regard the confront-ation of December 1773 as decisive, as establishing where the balance of power fell and as setting the pattern for the remainder of the co-regency. It was the last moment during Maria Theresa's reign when Joseph demanded full power, and when the complete remodelling of the central administration was seri-ously considered.

THE LAST PHASE, 1774–80

The story of these bids for power, as personal disputes, is widely known through the work of Arneth. But their constitutional and administrative implications are not well understood, especially so far as the crisis of 1773 is concerned. To do justice to this theme would require massive research. But the upshot of the clash of 9 December 1773, spelled out in detailed discussions and regulations over the next six months, seems to have been to inaugurate a new phase of the co-regency, distinct like the years 1765–8 from the period of confrontations in between. Joseph acquired a new or modified role which, though far from satisfying him, kept him occupied, useful and reasonably co-operative.

His direct executive responsibility remained the army. Lacy stayed abroad for more than six months. During this time both Maria Theresa and her son wrote him a stream of flattering and confidential letters. The emperor, she said, had never been 'so consistent as in his actions relative to your absence. He refuses to permit any change in your arrangements.'[99] Joseph kept on sending to the marshal documents from the *Hofkriegsrat*, asking his opinion about them, and discussing with him the arrangements for taking over the Jesuits' building. 'We were made for one another', he wrote. He was 'a friend ... who sincerely respects and loves you, and who would not tell you so if he did not'.[100] But the empress, without informing her son, had promised Lacy

---

[98] Wandruszka, *L. II.*, vol. 1, p. 364. Cf. J. to Lacy, 16 July 1773: 'je me crois propre a etre employé, mais pour cette grande direction je vous avoue que j'en tremble et que sans complimens j'y sens toute mon insuffisance' (HHSA FA Sbde 72).

[99] M.T. to Lacy, 3 Jan. 1774 (Arneth, *GMT* IX, p. 631).

[100] J. to Lacy, 14 Oct. 1773 (*ibid.*, p. 628) and 18 Jan. 1774 (HHSA NL, Karton 4).

that, if after some months of rest he was still inclined to resign as president of the war council, she would let him. Eventually in May 1774 Joseph faced up to the fact that the marshal intended to retire.

However much pain it gives me to see my life made gloomy by exceptional ill fortune, I nonetheless confine myself to expressing the hope that, although I no longer have the best president of war, good management and a quiet manner of life will at least preserve to me for many years a useful friend, who is not only willing to offer his life to help me to win glory on the day of battle, but will also assist me with his good advice and his talents to win it during the sad days which I spend, worn out by my responsibilities, working for the general good.[101]

Empress and emperor resorted to a variant of the device used earlier with Kaunitz. Lacy would at last become a member of the *Staatsrat*, but without the full burden of duties normally associated with membership. He would continue to advise the two rulers on military matters while a new president of the *Hofkriegsrat* was found in marshal Hadik.[102]

With the change of personnel, a review of military policy was undertaken. In a memorandum from this period, drawing on the advice both of Lacy and Hadik, Joseph declared that enormous progress had been made, but it was not nearly enough. The Monarchy was, if anything, less well protected than it had been in 1763. 'Its frontiers have been extended, but not secured.' It has aroused distrust, which is especially dangerous for such a fragmented and ill-defended state. Prussia and Russia have both become stronger. More expenditure is necessary, to make possible an increase in the army. Conscription should be introduced as soon as possible into the Tyrol, Galicia, Transylvania, 'yes, even into Hungary'. This is the only means to create a big enough army while at the same time, through the canton system, enabling soldiers to contribute to the local economy. Maria Theresa warmly welcomed Joseph's memorandum, but in fact worked against many of its proposals. The emperor therefore achieved limited success before 1780.[103]

Other than in military affairs, it was only in connexion with the *Staatsrat* that he was accorded a well-defined role in domestic administration. As compared with the revolutionary and self-glorifying schemes he had proposed between 1771 and 1773, the changes made in 1774 in the statute governing the work of the *Staatsrat* certainly deserve to be classified as 'tinkering'. However, they were not merely of lasting importance in the history of that body,

[101] J. to Lacy, 1 May 1774 (Arneth, *GMT* IX, pp. 635–6). Cf. M.T. to Lacy, 2 May (*ibid.*, p. 635).

[102] Arneth, *GMT* IX, p. 535. See p. 184 above.

[103] *Ibid.*, pp. 535–42. J.'s memo., entitled 'Uber die allgemeine Verfassung des Militär Staats', must have been written earlier than the date, 27 Mar. 1775, inscribed on it (HHSA FA Sbde 5); it is partly printed in E. Benedikt, *Kaiser Joseph II., 1741–1790* (Vienna, 1936), pp. 257–63. Cf. M.T. to Lacy, 3 Jan. 1774 on the Tyrol militia (Arneth, *GMT* IX, p. 633). Other similar comments of later date in HHSA NL, Karton 4.

surviving well into the nineteenth century;[104] they were also of great significance for the last years of the co-regency.

After the high drama of 9 December 1773, it took some months to arrive at a
modus vivendi. The empress wrote to Lacy on 20 December:

I'm going to make one final attempt more to get the emperor to work within the
system ... He grumbles only too often about his critical situation, and that he would
like to be prime minister. There's nothing I should like better, and I shall insist that he
organise business himself, as and with whom he wishes. We shall see what emerges. I
have no great hopes, but I shall try. There would be nothing for me to do but give in
and cheerfully align myself with you two [(?)Lacy and Kaunitz] if I did not love my
states and did not believe that I ought to try everything else before taking this
course.[105]

This statement seems the key to what happened. The new statute for the
Staatsrat, dated 12 May 1774, gave Joseph a specific new role. First, the office
of the council was relocated along the *Controleurgang.*

Secondly, it is my firm intention that all and every instruction and decision issued
concerning internal affairs shall without exception pass through the *Staatsrat* office ...
to the heads of the departments ... so that the *Staatsrat* may keep cognisance of
everything ...

All the papers laid before the *Staatsrat* are to be listed daily, put together with
the empress's decisions, and passed to the emperor. He is to collect the *Vota* of
the members and the other papers that must be submitted to her for
decision.[106] She had formally declared that a 'directing cabinet', such as he
had asked for, could not be created.[107] But the arrangements for recording
royal decisions were improved by measures like making a ledger of copies of
Handbillets.[108]

By these reforms Kaunitz's control of foreign policy, and of the affairs of
Lombardy and Belgium, was unaffected; Maria Theresa retained her ultimate
authority; she could still use 'private letters' unbeknown to Joseph; the
Staatsrat remained an advisory body without direct executive responsibilities,
including by now several only half-active members; and its relationship with
the affairs of Hungary was still undefined. But from Joseph's point of view,
many valuable changes had been made. Within the stated limitations, all

---

[104] Hock, *Staatsrath,* p. 41.   [105] Arneth, *GMT* IX, p. 631.

[106] Walter, *VKNGÖ,* XXIV, 80–2; a summary in more modern German is in Hock, *Staatsrath,*
pp. 40–1, but not making clear the role of the emperor.

[107] M.T. to J., 12 Mar. 1774 (Arneth, *MTuJ* II, pp. 32–3).

[108] This is an obscure matter. See Reinöhl in Bittner, *Gesamtinventar HHSA,* vol. V, pp. 156,
162. I believe that (contrary to what is said on p. 156) the series starting in 1774 included some
of M.T.'s *Handbillets.*

   HHSA TZ, 25 Feb. 1776, records J. attempting to take the opportunity of the death of
Nény, M.T.'s secretary of cabinet, to make a further reform.

executive decisions had now to be properly recorded and made known to the *Staatsrat* and therefore to him. If the council still lacked explicit executive responsibilities, it was now an integral link in the chain of command. If he himself was not prime minister – he used to say he was 'one of Her Majesty's ministers'[109] – he had a precisely stated and vital set of duties to perform. They were the duties of a secretary or civil servant of the highest class, rather than of a responsible minister. But they were time-consuming: Maria Theresa frequently stated that she could not cope with them, as was her duty according to the regulations, when Joseph was absent.[110] And they gave access to most, though not all, government papers.

The emperor found the job worth doing, usually. During the confrontation of 1773–4 he had begun to talk again of paying a visit to France. This was a long-cherished project, made more immediate by the prospect of meeting Lacy there. It also offered an opportunity for Joseph to escape from the constraints, not to say humiliations, of Vienna. It is significant that, after the changes of 1774, he repeatedly postponed the journey. On the first occasion he seemed to have a convincing excuse, the death of Louis XV in May 1774. But the decision to stay at home had been taken earlier. For the next three years Joseph generally wished to remain in Vienna for the sake of influencing some important decision, often relating to the affairs of Bohemia.[111] Between September 1773 and April 1777 he made only one extended journey, to Croatia in the summer of 1775. The pattern of the last three years of the co-regency was to be different: the visit to France in 1777 was followed in the next year by a long campaign in Bohemia, in 1779 by a trip to Bavaria and in 1780 by the immense expedition to Russia. Over the same period foreign policy rather than domestic took priority, both for him and for the Monarchy.[112] But while he was in Vienna after 1773 he was kept fully, and fairly contentedly, occupied with organising the work of the *Staatsrat*.

Maria Theresa used to say in her last years that she had given over 'the task' (*la besogne*) entirely to her son. She clearly intended to imply that he now carried the full responsibility.[113] This was quite untrue. In so far as the statement was justified, it referred to his work with the *Staatsrat*. As in 1771, he was devoting his time to greasing the wheels of a machine in which he professed no confidence, to adjusting details and perfecting routine. The co-regency itself had been intended to confine the eagle. By imposing on him this *besogne* as well, the empress had succeeded in chaining him, for much of the time, to a desk.

[109] E.g. J. de Witte (ed.), *Journal de l'abbé de Véri* (2 vols., Paris, n.d.), vol. II, p. 48.
[110] E.g. Arneth, *MTuJ* II, pp. 32–3. Walter, *VKNGÖ*, XXIX, 80.
[111] Cf. K-M VIII, pp. 18–19.   [112] See below, ch. 13.
[113] E.g. to L., 12 Mar. 1778 (Arneth, *MTKuF* I, p. 38).

THREE EXAMPLES

In later chapters this picture will be filled out with accounts of Joseph's travels and matters affecting particular provinces, of foreign policy, of his more private life and of the development of Josephism. It is convenient to consider here three lesser topics, the theatre, the abolition of judicial torture, and commercial questions. All these cases reveal much about his role during the co-regency – and also about the colour of his Enlightenment.

The theatre

The Viennese theatre was one of the areas of state responsibility which Maria Theresa claimed to have given over to her son. His initial programme, as we have seen, envisaged finding an entrepreneur to whom complete freedom would be accorded both in managing the playhouses and in choosing the entertainments, but to whom nothing would be paid. The empress had insisted on imposing a moral censorship on both scripts and personnel, but otherwise the emperor had had his way. Afflisio had been appointed as the impresario.[114]

There were two theatres in the old city of Vienna where serious drama was performed, the Burgtheater adjacent to the royal palace and the theatre by the Kärntnertor. Although they attracted and needed a public following as well as a Court audience, and prominent citizens put up substantial sums of money to maintain them, the theatres remained royal property and the government did not dream of abandoning all control over them. Hence it faced continual problems – anything but the 'peace' that Joseph had predicted. There arose both financial difficulties and the inevitable personal disputes.[115] In addition, the development of the theatre was at this period a subject of public concern and controversy to an extent never matched before or since. It was the focus of a classic debate on the language, literature, education, culture and nationhood of Germans both within and outside the Monarchy. The domination of Continental culture by French writers and their language was now being seriously challenged, especially by Germans and the German language. This movement became important in Vienna with the foundation there in 1761 of a German Society dedicated to popularising German literature and purifying the language; and in the next year the first Austrian weeklies appeared, with similar aims.[116] Sonnenfels soon emerged as the most important Viennese advocate of Germanising the stage. Somewhat paradoxically, he wished to eliminate the traditional vernacular comedy of Austria, *Hanswurst*, a version of Punch-and-Judy with actors, because the language was impure, the

---

[114] See pp. 159–60.   [115] By far the fullest account is in Zechmeister, *Die Wiener Theater*.
[116] See in general Réau, *L'Europe française*, book III; Bruford, *Germany in the Eighteenth Century*, esp. pt IV, ch. 2; Arneth, *GMT* IX, pp. 268–9.

plot frivolous and the performances extempore. He therefore fell in with Maria Theresa's desire for strict censorship of the theatre, and helped to operate it.[117] Gebler, as well as sitting on the *Staatsrat*, wrote plays in German, of which the most famous is *Thamos, King of Egypt* (1774), because music was composed for it by Mozart. He corresponded regularly with Nicolai, the greatest north German promoter of national literature, editor of the *Allgemeine deutsche Bibliothek* of Berlin. But the vernacular writer whose plays commanded the widest respect was Lessing, a radical Protestant of wide-ranging genius, whose tragedy, *Emilia Galotti*, was produced with success in Vienna in 1772, the year of its completion.[118] From the point of view of the enthusiasts in the cause, to establish a German dramatic tradition of high quality would make a crucial contribution to national education and culture. During the sixties and seventies this movement gained strength in Vienna, isolating the French theatre as an aristocratic toy.

In the early years of the co-regency Joseph intervened in the management of the theatres only at moments of crisis. When Afflisio gave up the struggle to make his enterprise pay, the emperor arranged for count Koháry to replace him in 1770. At this point Kaunitz tried to induce the empress to give private financial aid to the French company, and she tried to persuade her son to acquiesce. But in a conversation which she ensured was heard by two witnesses, he remained adamant, speaking 'very well and forcefully, without any lack of respect', but declaring 'he will never set foot in the theatre again, that I had surrendered control to him'. She had to yield; no subsidy from the government, private or public, was offered to the French troupe, and they left Vienna early in 1772. Koháry was losing money fast, and in the same year his lease of the theatres was taken over by a committee of his creditors.[119]

Kaunitz and the higher aristocracy were infuriated by Joseph's attitude towards the French theatre. They were further annoyed by his treatment of the ballet-master, Noverre. This man had a European reputation, which he enhanced during seven years' work in Vienna, where he produced a vast number of ballets, ranging from pantomimes to French classics, with great success. Early in 1774 he left with his dancers for Italy. Countess Kaunitz thought his loss was as discreditable to the emperor as the nearly contemporary departure of Lacy. Joseph said the great ladies of society would 'talk of it despairingly for three days' and then forget it. But at the theatre six weeks

---

[117] Kann, *Austrian Intellectual History*, esp. pp. 151–3, 200–24, 236–44; Zechmeister, *Die Wiener Theater*, pp. 49–64.

[118] The best source on Gebler, containing also much of interest on Lessing's fame in Vienna, is R.M. Werner (ed.), *Aus dem Josephinischen Wien: Geblers und Nicolais Briefwechsel während der Jahre 1771–1786* (Berlin, 1888). On Lessing see also the works cited in n. 117 and P.A. Scholes (ed.), *An Eighteenth-Century Musical Tour in Central Europe and the Netherlands*, vol. II (London, 1959), pp. 73–5 (Burney's).

[119] Zechmeister, *Die Wiener Theater*, pp. 70–1, 85, 91–3; Arneth, *GMT* IX, pp. 273–5, 586.

later he was subjected to a public demonstration in Noverre's favour. These ballets clearly had much wider appeal than plays in French.[120]

Between March 1775 and March 1776 the emperor schemed successfully to abrogate the existing agreement with Koháry's representatives and to put the management of the capital's theatres on an entirely new basis.[121] When the Court's supervisor of musical entertainments or *Musikgraf*, count Sporck, was posted to Galicia, Joseph transferred the duties to old Khevenhüller, supposedly as a temporary expedient. This was in March 1775. The emperor was travelling in Croatia and neighbouring lands from the middle of April until 1 July. On 20 July he sent Khevenhüller an instruction in his most withering and autocratic style:

Since the management of the theatres misuses its position to debase every kind of show, going far beyond all the contracts it has signed and the supplementary licences it has received, and I am not inclined in the long run to tolerate this scandal, especially since the whole public is discontented about it, you will inform [the management] by decree in the usual manner that it must either take such steps immediately as will place *opera buffa*, the ballets and the German troupe on an advantageous footing, or at least give the firmest assurances and submit arrangements and regulations to that end, certainly within three months, so that one can feel confidence that all three types of performance will without fail be placed on an entirely new footing, and in particular that the truly indecent ballets in the German theatre will be completely altered and improved, and also [that] the mostly worthless singers of both sexes in the *opera buffa* will be replaced with the best from abroad. Otherwise, the terms of the contract will be declared null and void, and on 1 November, without any compensation other than the return of the wardrobe and scenery that belongs to them, the whole enterprise will be terminated and the shows will be organised in a different fashion.[122]

Joseph rejected all the management's counter-proposals, but the change of administration was delayed while the status of the contract was considered by the courts. The Lower Austrian government and the *Staatsrat* were both consulted about the plan. During the winter a season of French theatre funded by a consortium of aristocrats came to an early and ignominious end.[123] Until the middle of March 1776 the emperor talked of appointing a fresh impresario, but on 16 March he sent Khevenhüller twelve questions which in fact amounted to the statement of a quite novel policy. Although the answers were

[120] Zechmeister, *Die Wiener Theater*, esp. pp. 292–5, 324–38; L.K. to E.L. 8 Oct. 1773 (SOALpZ, LRRA P. 16/23); J. to L., 13 Dec. 1773 and 17 Feb. 1774 (Arneth, *MTuJ* II, pp. 30–1); Eva König to Lessing, 26 Mar. 1774 (A. Schöne (ed.), *Briefwechsel zwischen Lessing und seiner Frau* (Leipzig, 1885), p. 352). Cf. K-M VIII, p. 72.

[121] The following account is largely based on F. Hadamowsky, *Die Josefinische Theaterreform und das Spieljahr 1776/77 des Burgtheaters. Eine Dokumentation*, Quellen zur Theatergeschichte 2 (Vienna, 1978), which for the origins of the Nationaltheater largely supersedes R. Payer von Thurn, *Joseph II. als Theaterdirektor* (Vienna, 1920). See also Zechmeister, *Die Wiener Theater*, pp. 93–101; Michtner, *Das alte Burgtheater*, esp. introduction.

[122] Hadamowsky, *Die Josefinische Theaterreform*, p. 3.

[123] Zechmeister, *Die Wiener Theater*, pp. 73–7, 359–60; K-M VIII, pp. 107–8; see p. 334.

to be supplied only 'after ripe consideration', the new system was actually put into effect a week later – officially as an interim measure.[124]

No overall management was appointed. All the existing singers, dancers, musicians, officials and copyists were sacked – except the German troupe. From now on, the Burgtheater was to become the home of the German players and would be called the Nationaltheater. In order to foster vernacular drama, the Court guaranteed the German players' wages for a trial period of one year; and Joseph offered prizes for German playwrights and sent a talent-scout into the Empire to seek out distinguished actors. When the German troupe was not using the Nationaltheater, and in the Kärntnertortheater, anyone who could find the money could hire the building and mount any production he pleased – subject to the approval of the censors. No restriction would be placed on the founding and running of new theatres elsewhere in the city and its suburbs.[125]

People at first simply could not believe that this degree of freedom had been accorded. The German party was exultant. As early as May 1776, Gebler told Nicolai:

We now have three troupes of players in the suburbs, and soon a fourth will be coming – regrettably, they all have to perform *censored plays* – and as well as the national stage in the imperial palace, Noverre gives ballets four times a week in the ... city theatre, involving sixty dancers and accompanied by a German opera company summoned from Brünn. This last goes back at the end of May, and then Italian operas will probably commence ...

If Your Excellency sets beside these plays two grand firework displays ..., then the animal-baiting, and the two public parks holding many thousands of people, the so-called Prater and the delightful Augarten, must you not acknowledge that we have an embarrassing choice of entertainment? ... Every patriot must rejoice that our German *Joseph* has designated the national stage as his *Court theatre*. He will certainly employ no Frenchmen until German plays are performed at Versailles.

The supposedly temporary arrangement lasted in essentials well into Joseph's sole reign, and in many respects beyond it. The German national theatre made such good profits that the government was happy to continue guaranteeing the players' wages. Brockmann, considered the best German actor of his day, was attracted to Vienna, and in June 1779 Gebler could report: 'Our theatre is in the most flourishing condition ... Equally remarkable is the progress of the German opera. It yields nothing to any Italian Court theatre in the integrity and beauty of the music ... We lack nothing save Noverre's ballets.'[126]

Gebler described only one side of the coin. The loss both of the French theatre and of Noverre's ballets was to be regretted. Wraxall thought Joseph

124 Hadamowsky, *Die Josefinische Theaterreform*, pp. xv, 13–17.
125 As well as *ibid.*, pp. xv–xxi, *passim*: D. Hadamczik, *Friedrich Ludwig Schröder in der Geschichte des Burgtheaters* (Berlin, 1961), esp. (on prizes) pp. 63–6.
126 Gebler to Nicolai, 26 May 1776 and 15 June 1779 (Werner, *Aus dem Josephinischen Wien*, pp. 786–7, 97); Hadamowsky, *Die Josefinische Theaterreform*, pp. xx, xxiii.

had ruined the Italian opera. Not only did the German company find itself short of good plays, it could not man the Nationaltheater when it was performing at Schönbrunn or Laxenburg; hence its seasons in Vienna were sometimes brief. Censorship, even when the emperor wielded it personally, could be fatuous. Perhaps to please his mother, he banned a German version of *Romeo and Juliet* together with all pieces 'in which funerals, churchyards, graves and such sad incidents occur'.[127] But his reform had unquestionably made Vienna the capital of the German stage – at a time when Frederick the Great would patronise only French players. This was the justification for remarks like that of Le Bret, a prominent populariser and translator of Enlightened writings: 'How benignly', he wrote in 1778, 'the Philosopher on the Viennese throne smiles on the Muses.'[128]

Joseph's actions after 1775 conflicted with his original line of 1767 in that he now took part in the running of one of the theatres and risked the government's money in backing the German troupe. But his direct involvement, even any personal contact with the actors, had at first been ruled out by Maria Theresa's scruples.[129] It seems not unlikely that he was all along working towards a position in which he could impose a programme of reform and join in carrying it through. It is striking that three out of four signatories to a plan for giving Germany a national theatre based in Vienna, submitted to the emperor in 1769, should have taken active roles in the direction of the new venture of 1776.[130] His refusal to assist the French company or the Noverre ballet had ensured the departure of both, leaving the way clear for the triumph of the German company.

His initiative must have owed something to Gebler's views and support on the *Staatsrat*, to meeting Lessing in Vienna in April 1775,[131] and to Sonnenfels's campaign. But Joseph's attitude was individual. He did not share the intellectuals' highbrow hostility to *Hanswurst*. He used the argument of economy as well as more elevated reasons for preferring the German players to the French theatre company and the Italian opera. Khevenhüller claimed that the emperor had no great opinion of shows of any sort, and valued the theatre as a place to go in the evenings where he could gossip with his female friends.[132] But this remark was made at the height of his infatuation with

---

[127] Wraxall, *Memoirs*, vol. II, p. 494; Hadamowsky, *Die Josefinische Theaterreform*, pp. xxi–xxiii; Hadamczik, *F.L. Schröder*, p. 54.

[128] On Frederick and the stage, Payer von Thurn, *J. II. also Theaterdirektor*, pp. 3–5; J.F. Le Bret to Bertolà, 7 Jan. 1778 in *Erfahrene und erfundene Landschaft: ... Bertolàs Deutschlandbild und die Begründung der Rheinromantik*, ed. J.U. Fechner (Opladen, 1974).

[129] Arneth, *GMT* IX, p. 585.

[130] Hadamowsky, *Die Josefinische Theaterreform*, pp. xvii–xviii.

[131] Zechmeister, *Die Wiener Theater*, esp. pp. 93–4; Werner, *Aus dem Josefinischen Wien*, pp. 67–8; Arneth, *GMT*, IX, pp. 267–8.

[132] See above, p. 159; Hadamowsky, *Die Josefinische Theaterreform*, p. xvii; K-M VIII, p. 124 (20 Apr. 1772).

Eleonore Liechtenstein, and it is plain from his correspondence that he felt some interest in what was staged. As early as January 1771 he told Leopold: 'the empress was at the German comedy yesterday and saw the ballet *Diane*. A miracle has occurred: they performed a translation of Diderot's *Le Père de famille*, and they played it superbly.'[133] He would discuss the calibre of singers and actors, and criticise the ballet. He saw *Emilia Galotti* twice in 1772 and remarked to Gebler that he had never before laughed so much at a tragedy.[134] This is a typical, rather forced *bon mot* which can be read as naive and also sarcastic, but actually makes a good point since the scene depicting the prince's frivolous approach to his weighty duties is genuinely amusing. Later, when Joseph was helping to manage the national theatre, he naturally mentioned productions more frequently. The reform he imposed had a number of characteristic features. It accorded a surprising degree of freedom not only to entrepreneurs at large but also to the German players, who in principle ran their own affairs and decided what to perform.[135] Yet the intervention of the state, in this case of the emperor, had been essential to establishing the freedom and operated continuously to sustain the favoured company. As Gebler indicated, Joseph's policy towards the theatre corresponded with his policy on the royal parks: in both cases the intention was to free a form of public entertainment from Court and aristocratic control and open it to the people at large. Similarly, his hostility to France was visible in his diplomatic as well as his theatrical activity.

His mother evidently acquiesced in his measures with reluctance. No doubt the failure of three successive managements made it difficult for her to argue for another experiment on the same lines. She must have found it easier to ratify a scheme that was introduced under the aegis of Khevenhüller and continued after his death in May 1776 by Rosenberg, who seems to have placed more emphasis than Joseph did on the purification of stage morality.[136] But her basic attitude is well illustrated by her reaction to a suggestion of Lacy's in May 1775, that she should engage a French troupe to help entertain archduke Ferdinand and his wife on their forthcoming visit to Vienna. Joseph was away on his travels, but she replied that she dared not take it upon herself to do this: 'you know the sensitivity of the emperor on this subject'.[137] She had said she had handed over the matter to him; in the end she would have to let

133 J. to L., 7 Jan. 1771 (HHSA FA Sbde 7, not in Arneth). The translation was Lessing's. Cf. Zechmeister, *Die Wiener Theater*, p. 179. For other references see Arneth, *MTuJ* II, pp. 70, 127; III, pp. 204, 237.
134 Eva König to Lessing, 15 July 1772 (Schöne, *Briefwechsel*, p. 270).
135 Hadamowsky, *Die Josefinische Theaterreform*, pp. xvii–xviii, xxv–xxvi.
136 *Ibid.*, pp. xix, xxii. It seems to me doubtful that M.T. had much say in the decisions she is here recorded as ratifying, despite Hadamowksy's assertion that she sympathised with them. In *Theatergeschichte* the view that she was extremely economical seems to be canonical (*ibid.*, p. xi; Michtner, *Das alte Burgtheater*, p. 13; Zechmeister, *Die Wiener Theater*, esp. pp. 32–4).
137 M.T. *apostille* on Lacy to M.T. of 16 May 1775 (HHSA NL, Karton 2).

him do more or less what he wanted. Here was a sphere of action, like Court ceremonial and the army, in which he did not have to accept the ordinary restraints of the co-regency but could enact his programme of reform during his mother's lifetime.

The abolition of torture

In 1776 torture as part of the judicial process was abolished in the central lands of the Monarchy. In the story of this reform Joseph was allowed by his mother to play a unique and curious role.

When Maria Theresa came to the throne, torture was still commonly employed in most European legal systems to try to compel accused persons to incriminate themselves and others, and also in the punishment of those found guilty of serious crimes. However, well-known writers like Thomasius had already pronounced against it, and Frederick the Great soon abolished it in Prussia.[138] The campaign of Enlightened writers against torture, with which they usually associated the death penalty, intensified in the sixties. The case of the critics was strengthened by the fate of the French Protestant, Jean Calas, who in 1762 was wrongfully convicted, after torture, of murdering his son, and then executed by breaking on the wheel. Voltaire's crusade to quash this judgement, which attracted huge publicity, was mainly directed against the religious intolerance displayed by the court, but also castigated the cruelty of the law and its methods.[139] In 1764 Cesare Beccaria, a Milanese subject of Maria Theresa, published – though anonymously and outside her dominions – the classic attack on both torture and the death penalty, *Dei delitti e delle pene* (*Crimes and Punishments*).[140] In the late sixties Sonnenfels argued in his lectures and writings against the use of torture except in extreme cases, and also against capital punishment for any but the most serious crimes.[141] But in 1769 a new criminal code for the Monarchy was promulgated, nicknamed the *Nemesis theresiana*, which not only reiterated nearly all the old provisions allowing torture and prescribing the death penalty, but contained gruesome pictures showing how torturers and executioners operated.[142]

This production had been intended as a codification, not a reform. But its

[138] Kann, *Austrian Intellectual History*, p. 186n; W. Hubatsch, *Frederick the Great* (London, 1973), pp. 41, 211.
[139] See D.D. Bien, *The Calas Affair* (Princeton, 1960).
[140] On Beccaria, esp. Venturi, *Utopia and Reform*, ch. 4.
[141] For Sonnenfels's role, Kann, *Austrian Intellectual History*, pp. 181–9; Osterloh, *Sonnenfels*, pp. 165–9.
[142] Except where otherwise illustrated, the rest of the section on torture derives from Arneth, *GMT* IX, pp. 202–15 and Hock, *Staatsrath*, pp. 42–8. The quotations are fuller in Hock. Cf. K-M VIII, pp. 126–7. Attempts to abolish torture in Belgium and Italy were unsuccessful under M.T.: W.W. Davis, *Joseph II: An Imperial Reformer for the Austrian Netherlands* (The Hague, 1974), pp. 57–8; Arneth, *GMT* X, p. 194. Mr T. Krause and Mr H. Scheuch kindly helped me with this section.

appearance helped to provoke further debate on the subject, beginning with a fierce protest from Kaunitz against a compilation likely 'to serve in our enlightened times as an object of ridicule rather than as a model of severity'. As often during the empress's later years, the honours went now to one side, now to the other. Sonnenfels, bitterly attacked by conservatives like Migazzi for criticising the established order, was upheld at the end of 1769, told in August 1772 to keep silence, vindicated in December, and then in October 1775 reprimanded for having allowed an official document he had written to be published. But opinion was moving in his direction. The *Staatsrat* majority was on his side, as was the jurist, Martini; and in 1773 the medical faculty of the University of Vienna petitioned against the use of prolonged torture. Maria Theresa agreed to abolish it, and set in train consultations about wider reform. The provincial governments of Upper and Lower Austria, Bohemia and Moravia, and the *Oberste Justizstelle* (the supreme court) reported in favour of the existing system, but the majority of the *Staatsrat* declared for the abolition of torture. A compromise was agreed, which left those accused of some especially heinous crimes still at risk.

Before this decision was announced, the co-regent, just back from Croatia and fresh from excoriating the theatre management, took the opportunity to comment on the question as it arose in the papers of the *Staatsrat*. He had been taught as a boy that the use of torture was of doubtful value. Even before the publication of *Dei delitti e delle pene*, he had told his mother that he was opposed to capital punishment. But he had been allowed no part in the preparation and publication of the *Nemesis theresiana*,[143] and his main contribution to legal reform so far had been to uphold at critical moments Sonnenfels's right to state his views publicly. On 12 August 1775 Joseph wrote:

I must avow that I am convinced the abolition of torture is not merely a just and harmless measure, but a necessary one. I should have no hesitation in agreeing to its being eliminated from the *Nemesis theresiana*. But I must at the same time draw attention to another matter necessarily related to it, namely that the death penalty should at the same time be much restricted, and not carried out except on those caught *in flagrante delicto* or on undoubted and confessed criminals. All others ought to be sentenced to non-capital punishments. Certainly it will be necessary to devise new types of labour for them, and the convicts must be treated quite differently, since they are now better off than if they were free.

However, he was ready to accept the compromise if his more radical proposal failed. Maria Theresa now minuted:

I request the emperor, who has studied law, and whose sense of justice, insight and humanity I rely on, to decide this affair without my advice, since I do not understand it and could only accept the majority view. This does not exclude the possibility of consulting one or two foreign lawyers if the emperor still has any doubts.

[143] See p. 180 and J. to M.T., 8 Apr. 1764 (Arneth, *MTuJ* I, p. 91).

This gentle zephyr took the wind out of Joseph's sails. He asked the advice of no foreigners; but, quite contrary to his principles, he embarked on an elaborate series of discussions involving a committee composed equally of representatives from the *Staatsrat* and the *Oberste Justizstelle*. Predictably, they were deadlocked. Only an opinion from Blümegen, the Austro-Bohemian chancellor, produced a majority for the emperor's view. The abolition of torture was duly enacted, 'after the example already set in many states, . . . in all my German hereditary lands including the Banat and Galicia' on 2 January 1776. The decree went on to order consideration of means by which capital punishment might be much restricted. The main problem was seen to be the absence of houses of correction in which those convicted of serious crimes could be punished with sufficient severity. Joseph himself added to the decree the clause: 'whereby the often repeated sight of such convicts may intimidate and deter the public more than the death penalty [does], and in such a way that Society may also gain some advantage from the labour of such criminals'.

Although the enquiries about capital punishment had yielded little by the end of Maria Theresa's reign, the emperor's view on torture had triumphed. Yet he had declined his mother's invitation to settle the question on his own without further ado. Perhaps he felt rather less sure of his opinion than he sounded when pressing it on her as a mere adviser; or he was in the mood to act as a judicious chairman ready to give weight to the arguments of all the relevant departments. In either event he was belying his reputation for autocratic haste.

Commercial questions

If this book were to give to economic questions proportionally as much space as Joseph spent time on them, they would have to bulk very large. Some account has already been given of his general approach to them in the 1760s, and they figure in later sections that are devoted to particular provinces.[144] But something should be said here about Joseph's administrative role in the endless and bitter disputes over the Monarchy's tariff policy, which culminated in the establishment of a new system in 1775.

Work on a new scheme of customs duties had already begun when the emperor wrote the 'General picture'. The official in charge from 1768 was Philipp Cobenzl, who was instructed to apply to the whole Monarchy his experience of Belgian practice. So far as external trade was concerned, 'it was necessary to devise an entirely new tariff, determined by the interests of national trade and industry, in place of the old one, whose only object was to supply certain sums to the royal treasury'. Internally, the movement of goods

144 See pp. 249, 266–8, 346–57, 363, 366.

and people was obstructed by a profusion of customs barriers.[145] Countess Kaunitz complained in 1770 that a peasant or trader taking produce to market came first to a barrier where he had to pay

a passage-toll; at the second step there is a road-toll; at the third step there's a horse-toll. Finally, having paid each of these tolls at least twice and often three or four times, he reaches the gates of the town. There he must pay the sales-tax on everything he's carrying. What profit is there left for him to make? Everything has already been taken by the customs! And what is he to live on?[146]

But a strong party within the administration fought against any radical change, among them Hatzfeld. The *Kommerzienrat* naturally favoured the continuing involvement of the government in economic enterprise, since that was the *raison d'être* of the department. Blümegen may be cited as a moderate representative of those who were chiefly interested in maintaining the privileges of their own provinces. On the other hand, many powerful figures, influenced to some extent by the thought of the physiocrats, supported free trade in principle, though making a variety of exceptions; this group included Kaunitz, the two Zinzendorfs, Kressel and Cobenzl. Maria Theresa herself could say 'no one doubted our commercial principles were bad'. Feelings ran so high that the elder Zinzendorf and Hatzfeld were not on speaking terms; and the younger Zinzendorf and Cobenzl exploited the issue in their rivalry for higher office. The latter established himself as the emperor's man and, after a period of eclipse, was restored to favour in May 1774 and enabled to carry through a modified version of his original proposal.[147]

Karl Zinzendorf, as one of Joseph's chamberlains and an official in a minor commercial department, had many dealings and conversations with him on economic questions. The emperor told him, for example, that the Bohemian famine was caused by the export of grain from Hungary; that the growth of Hungarian industry would harm the German provinces; and that 'it was only possible to apply general principles by acquiring local knowledge'. In October 1773 Zinzendorf

finished reading the 154 questions that the emperor has put to ... count Pergen. They demonstrate a great breadth of knowledge of detail, but at the same time an almost total absence of principles. HM appears to have the following principles. *Lucri bonus odor*. First extract money, then make your peoples happy. First a number of indirect taxes, then the land-tax. The tobacco-tax is a useful impost. The present arrangement of the hereditary provinces is excellent. At the end, however, HM declares that he desires no

145 See p. 179 above. Arneth, *AÖG* (1886), 101–2, 104–8 (Cobenzl's memoirs). Cf. Arneth, *GMT* IX, pp. 453–4, 457.
146 L.K. to E.L., 21 Dec. 1770 (SOALpZ, LRRA P. 16/22). I would not like to go bail for my translation of the names of the taxes. Leopoldine is being unwittingly unfair in this letter, since she blames M.T. and J. for maintaining these imposts, which they were trying to remove.
147 Schünemann, *MÖIG* (1933), 45–7; Arneth, *GMT* IX, pp. 454–7; Arneth, *AÖG* (1886), 104–6, 108, 113–18; HHSA TZ, *passim* and 15 Dec. 1771.

kind of tax that can harm agriculture, industry. He proves to be very well instructed in the maxims that are at present employed, and very ignorant of every kind of principle.

But in February 1774 Zinzendorf found that Joseph had at least a very decided view, that 'the provinces of this Monarchy ought to be self-sufficient', so that external trade should be severely restricted, while internal impediments to commerce should be abolished.[148]

Zinzendorf stood for the primacy of economic theory, Joseph for the primacy of politics. This was how the emperor argued in his *Votum* of 11 February to which Zinzendorf was referring:

The Monarchy is not small. Nearly 13 [*sic*] million people live in it; they have a surplus output of the products essential both for food and for the coarser types of clothing. From abroad they need nothing save the usual spices, finer sorts of clothes and luxury goods. Therefore, in my opinion, all the hereditary lands should be regarded as one; and we ought first of all to try to police the frontiers ... so that, as far as possible, we prevent the import of foreign produce and wares that are available in one of our provinces. For example, Hungary, Transylvania, Galicia would have to take our cloths and linens ... If 2 or 3 million would thereby suffer some hardship but 10 million would gain by it, we should not mind, since the greater benefit should take precedence over the lesser evil, and the greater number over the smaller.[149]

This ruthless, centralising, illiberal approach evoked much opposition. Kressel and Kaunitz condemned the very idea of autarky. Much anxiety was expressed at the cost of policing the frontier and at the loss of revenue from internal customs. So long as Hungary had a fundamentally different constitution from the central lands, and paid less in direct taxation, it was held necessary to maintain the customs barrier between them. But with that vast exception, in the final decree of July 1775 the barriers to internal trade were mostly swept away. So far as foreign trade was concerned, the export of raw materials was freely permitted; it was laid down as an 'immutable guideline' that 'henceforth freedom is to be taken as the rule, prohibition as the exception'; and import controls were replaced by low tariffs. To make up for some of the lost revenue, certain imports like sugar were placed in the hands of monopolists and heavily taxed. It was frankly declared that

since agriculture, especially in a state like ours, which has so much land and so few manufactures, always takes precedence over industries, therefore everything that detracts from agriculture, even if industries were thereby to obtain some real advantage, is to be regarded as generally harmful to the state.[150]

Joseph had certainly played a part in securing a new system, and his attitudes had much influenced it in relation to internal trade. But he had not succeeded in inspiring others with his vision of 'the Monarchy freeing itself

---

[148] HHSA TZ, 27 Feb. and 27 Oct. 1773, 27 Feb. and 1 Mar. 1774.
[149] Schünemann, *MÖIG* (1933), 47–8.
[150] *Ibid.*, pp. 50–1; Hock, *Staatsrath*, pp. 93–4; Arneth, *GMT* IX, pp. 457–8.

entirely from dependence on foreigners, and 13 million people standing together as one man, protecting, feeding and clothing each other without external assistance'.[151] Although this ideal evidently meant much to him, he seems to have avoided confrontations with his mother on these issues, and instead to have schemed, negotiated, attended committees, immersed himself in detail and listened to advice over many years, ultimately accepting with a good grace a solution very different from what he had himself advocated.

[151] Schünemann, *MÖIG* (1933), 48.

CHAPTER 8

Early travels: the Banat and Italy, 1768–1769

Among the characteristic features of Joseph [wrote Wraxall,] must be accounted his passion for travelling; scarcely any Prince of whom we read, having so minutely examined his own dominions. Adrian, in antiquity, and Charles the Fifth, in modern ages, whose whole reigns were a perpetual journey, can alone be compared in this point of view, to the present Emperor. He has visited nearly all the Courts of Italy ... traversed the whole kingdom of France ... Every part of Bohemia, Hungary, and Transylvania, he has rode over ... nor has he omitted to inspect the Sclavonian frontier, as far as Semlin; and to go in a boat upon the Danube, to the walls, and quite under the cannon of Belgrade.[1]

These remarks date from 1779, after which Joseph revisited France, Italy and the eastern lands of the Monarchy, went to Belgium and Holland, and undertook his two longest journeys to Russia. In addition, he attended at least one military camp in nearly every year, and fought in two major campaigns. Altogether, he spent about a quarter of his time travelling, and covered well over 30,000 miles.[2] Map 2 shows the routes of his major expeditions down to 1780.

In its sheer scale this activity was almost unparalleled in history. The only ruler contemporary with Joseph who made a point of foreign travel was Gustavus III of Sweden, but he showed little interest in visiting his own provinces.[3] Frederick the Great of course conducted many campaigns, and he also undertook inspection-tours of his lands, but he scarcely went abroad.[4] Catherine the Great, born and brought up in Germany, stayed in Russia once she had reached it, and made only a rather limited effort to get to know her

[1] Wraxall, *Memoirs*, vol. II, pp. 457–8.
[2] There is a useful account of the travels in *ÖZKJ*, pp. 82–4 (by W. May) and in the next few articles, and excellent maps on pp. 712–15. A full chronology, with a few scraps of additional material of interest, can be found in P. von Radics, 'Die Reisen Kaiser Joseph II. und ihre Bedeutung für Oesterreich-Ungarn, besonders vom volkswirthschaftlichen Standpunkt', *Oesterreichisch-Ungarische Revue*, neue Folge, VIII (1889–90), 241–68, and IX (1890), 1–44.
[3] R. Nisbet Bain, *Gustavus III and his Contemporaries* (2 vols., London, 1894), esp. vol. I, pp. 53–9, 200–4, 260–8. Gustavus's journeys seem to have been less well planned than J.'s, but more affected by etiquette.
[4] Hubatsch, *Frederick the Great*, pp. 43–55, 74, 95, 136.

adopted country by ceremonial progresses.[5] At the extreme were the cases of George III and Louis XVI, who seldom strayed far from the palaces near their capitals. In the entire eighteenth century, though George I and George II used to travel to their electorate of Hanover, no British monarch set foot in Ireland, Scotland or Wales.[6] Maria Theresa herself had toured Hungary and visited Tuscany before she became ruler of the Monarchy, and saw her husband crowned at Frankfurt in 1745. But after the fatal journey to Innsbruck in 1765 she never travelled more than fifty miles from Vienna.[7]

Much-travelled sovereigns of earlier ages, like the Angevin kings of England and the emperors Hadrian and Charles V, had generally been constrained to move about their territories by pressing civil or military business, and had done so with ceremony. The manner and motives of Joseph's journeyings were wholly different. Precedents for some aspects of his practice could be found in Frederick's informal domestic tours, in Peter the Great's incognito visits to western Europe in search of enlightenment, and in Charles XII of Sweden's incognito visit to Vienna. Both Charles and Frederick insisted on travelling rough, and inuring themselves to the hardships of campaigning.[8] Joseph must have been well aware of all these examples. But no single ruler laid down the pattern that he followed, and none has imitated him since.

Contemporaries and historians have all noticed and on the whole applauded Joseph's enthusiasm for travel. Biographers in particular have reason to be grateful when their subjects go abroad, because visitors attract descriptions, and anyway it is instructive to see how people behave in unfamiliar situations. The emperor put historians further in his debt by writing accounts – admittedly both unromantic and hypercritical – of all his expeditions. But no one seems to have appreciated the full significance of Joseph's journeys. They have been treated as little more than an amiable personal eccentricity. But in fact the way in which he travelled represented an assertion of principles, his motives went far beyond simple curiosity, and the results of his tours were important enough to deserve a place in any history of the Monarchy. This was especially true for the period of the co-regency.[9]

<hr/>

[5] I. de Madariaga, *Russia in the Age of Catherine the Great* (London, 1981), pp. 62, 370–3.

[6] J. H. Plumb, *The First Four Georges* (London, 1974), p. 202; Padover, *Louis XVI*, pp. 127–9.

[7] See above, pp. 92–3. The places she visited in Hungary, like Pressburg and the Esterházy palace at Fertöd, were in the far west, on the Austrian border.

[8] For Frederick, Hubatsch, *Frederick the Great*. For Peter, V. Klyuchevsky, *Peter the Great* (London, 1958), pp. 23–30. For Charles XII, R. Hatton, *Charles XII* (London, 1968), esp. pp. 384–9.

[9] See G. Klingenstein, 'Rom und der Kirchenstaat im Jahre 1767', *Quellen und Forschungen aus italienischen Archiven und Bibliotheken herausgegeben vom Deutschen Historischen Institut in Rom*, LI (1971), 466–90, for some reflections on the wider significance of J.'s travels. A general estimate of his domestic journeys is attempted in H. Rumpel, 'Die Reisen Kaiser Joseph II. nach Galizien', Erlangen University PhD thesis (1946). I am most grateful to Prof. Klingenstein for supplying me with a copy of this dissertation.

Map 2. Joseph's major journeys during the reign of Maria Theresa. Minor detours have had to be ignored, and it has been necessary to omit many lesser journeys within the Monarchy, most but not all of them to military camps. The maps in *ÖZKJ*, pp. 710–13 have been used as a basis, but this map incorporates substantial corrections to the routes there shown of the journeys of 1773 and 1777.

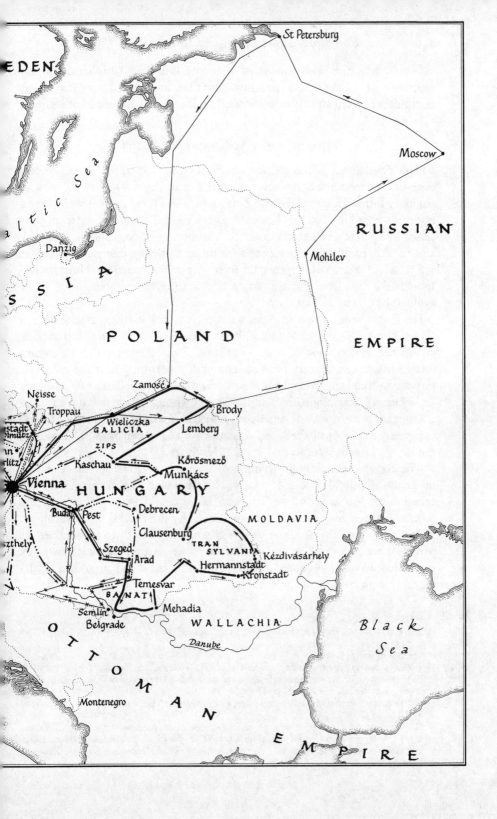

I shall take the opportunity, as I pursue him round his lands, to say something about the various provinces and their treatment during this phase, not limiting myself strictly to discussing his visits and their immediate effects.

THE JOURNEY TO THE BANAT, 1768

Joseph proclaimed in the memorandum of 1765 that travel was absolutely essential for monarchs. He never departed from this view, and was always planning future journeys. He told Zinzendorf melodramatically that he kept a horse ready saddled, so that he could go at a moment's notice wherever duty called him.[10] He insisted too that travel for him must be economical of time and money, to make it efficient as a means of gathering information. Before 1765, he had taken part in formal Court progresses to Frankfurt, Hungary and Innsbruck. But, from the time when he became emperor and co-regent, he avoided all ceremonial journeys.[11]

His first serious foray as emperor was the visit to the battlefields of the Seven Years War in Saxony, Bohemia, Silesia and Moravia in 1766. His reports about fortifications won Kaunitz's applause,[12] but the trip had little significance outside the military context. His first opportunity to make a general inspection-tour came when he was authorised to go to the Banat of Temesvar. This journey was originally planned for the spring of 1767, but had to be postponed because of the smallpox epidemic in the royal family. Joseph eventually left in April 1768, and was away for nearly two months. As well as the Banat, he saw Slavonia and parts of Hungary.[13]

The Banat – a mainly low-lying area on the north bank of the Danube, nowadays divided between Hungary, Romania and Yugoslavia – had been ceded to the Monarchy by the Turks at the peace of Passarowitz in 1718. Its economy was managed directly from Vienna by the *Banco*, the government department that controlled the Vienna city bank.[14] The district contained no private property, no nobles and no Estates. When acquired, it had been thinly populated and had produced little. The government had promoted settlement, though by Roman Catholics only.[15]

---

[10] HHSA TZ, 22 Mar. 1776.
[11] See, e.g., K-M VII, p. 31–2 (30 June and 4 July 1770). Cf. J. to L., 6 July 1768 (Arneth, *MTuJ* I, p. 223).
[12] See above, pp. 145, 185.
[13] J.'s own papers on the journey are in HHSA FA Hofreisen 2, fasz. 2. I have found S. Neidenbach, 'Die Reisen Kaiser Josephs II. ins Banat', University of Vienna PhD thesis (1967), very useful. See Arneth, *GMT* VII, p. 462.
[14] On the administration of the Banat, Walter, *VKNGÖ*, XXXII, pp. 85–8, 230–8; Schünemann, *MÖIG* (1933), esp. 24–6.
[15] K. Schünemann, 'Die Einstellung der theresianischen Impopulation (1770/1771)', *Jahrbuch des Wiener Ungarischen Historischen Instituts*, I (1931), 177–213; K. A. Roider, Jr, 'Nationalism and colonization in the Banat of Temesvár, 1718–1778' in *Nation and Ideology: Essays in*

Attempts had been made to establish industry and develop trade. The state took some of the profits, and so did individual officials, who had been encouraged to invest in the enterprise. These features made the Banat unique in the Monarchy. In the early sixties its administration became a vexed question. On the one hand the *Banco* and its local representatives were engaged in a running dispute with the provincial officials and with a semi-independent *Impopulations-Commission*. On the other, the *Hofkriegsrat* was trying to erect a more regular and effective military-frontier organisation than had previously existed there. In the background lurked the further difficulty that Hungary claimed the Banat, and Maria Theresa had accepted the claim in principle. Two committees of enquiry had already been sent to the province, and had made opposite recommendations.[16] Since Joseph was seeking every opportunity for travel and political action, and since the issues were partly military, Maria Theresa could hardly refuse to let him go and see what he could do in this tangled situation. In any case, there can have been few officials anxious to travel to this remote and disease-ridden area in order to concoct a third contentious report on the squabbles of the local bureaucracy.

Joseph conducted this visit on the lines which he invariably followed on later journeys within the Monarchy.[17] He first informed himself about the province. In this case it was necessary to prepare a new systematic account, since none had been written for his instruction earlier. Full orders were sent to the local administration. No formal receptions were to be arranged. Every subject, however humble, provided that he gave his name, was to be allowed to approach the emperor and to present a petition. Accommodation must be adequate but not sumptuous or formal. The main objects of his visit would be, first, military – to see the frontiers, fortresses, barracks and communications; secondly, economic – to inspect mines and factories; and thirdly, administrative – to spend a few days in the provincial capital, Temesvar, talking with officials and observing the workings of the government.

His retinue was rather larger than one might expect from his insistence on economy and simplicity. In the first coach travelled Joseph and his brother-in-law, prince Albert; in the second marshal Lacy, counts Karl Johann Dietrichstein and Joseph Colloredo; in the third baron Laudon and counts Nostitz and Miltitz. Altogether thirteen vehicles and seventy-six horses were taken, to carry personal servants, a doctor, a surgeon, a chaplain, two cooks, two under-cooks and six postillions. For a later journey on a slightly smaller scale,

Honour of Wayne S. Vucinich, ed. I. Banac, J. G. Ackerman and R. Szporluk (New York, 1981), pp. 88–9; Schünemann, *Österreichs Bevölkerungspolitik*, p. 73.
16 For this paragraph, in addition to the works by Neidenbach and Schünemann (nn. 13 and 15) see J. H. Schwicker, *Geschichte der österreichischen Militärgrenze* (Vienna, 1883), pp. 122–30; Arneth, *GMT* x, pp. 121–9.
17 Details in this and the following paragraphs from HHSA FA Hofreisen 2, fasz. 2, from Neidenbach, 'Reisen Josephs II. ins Banat', esp. pp. 12–20, 36–7, 112–13, 123, and from Rumpel, 'Reisen Kaiser Joseph II. nach Galizien'.

the following were among the items of food ordered to be available every night: 70 lb of beef, a whole calf, twenty-four chickens, 6 lb of butter, 6 lb of animal fat and forty eggs. This provision was presumably comparable to what a noble household on the move might require. It was far less than was necessary for royal progresses.

Joseph did not get all his orders obeyed. Whatever he said, special preparations were often made to receive him. The party was amused to see fowls picking in unthreshed straw with which cottages had been too hastily thatched. Some local officials tried to stop petitions being presented to him. Some subjects thought it prudent to take to the woods. The detailed cooking directions given for later tours suggest that the food was unsatisfactory on early journeys. But these shortcomings did not prevent Joseph procuring most of the information he wanted.

When he was on the road, Joseph travelled hard and fast. He would start at four o'clock in the morning and go on till nightfall. He often left his coach in order to ride, and he liked to reckon up the time he spent in the saddle: on this journey of 55 days, it was 249 hours and 50 minutes. When he reached an administrative centre, he settled down to an almost continuous round of visits, audiences and discussions with officials, into which he somehow had to fit writing letters to his mother and brother and dealing with papers sent from Vienna. He allowed himself only brief meals, probably in the company of one or two of his fellow-travellers, but liked eight hours' sleep. Every night he wrote down or dictated some notes on the day's work.

After returning to Vienna, he produced both a travel diary and a report or *Relation* on what he had seen, with recommendations for improvements. In his report he took account of the hundreds of petitions he had received, but he also carried them with him back to the capital and insisted that they were studied there by officials.

His *Relation* on the Banat displays many of the characteristics to be found in his other travel reports. It is extremely censorious. He complains about the state of the hospital, the prisons, the fortresses, the cordon, the barracks and the roads, about the faulty plan of the new villages and the unsuitable site of the old capital. He found the clergy, both Catholic and Orthodox, ignorant and superstitious. The government might as well still be Turkish. It possessed no population figures, not even a full account of the province. It was too bad to be worth the trouble of describing: 'every step misconceived, every order ineffectual'. He scarcely brought himself to praise a single official. Corruption, he claimed, was virtually universal.[18]

He denounced with special vigour the practice of shipping annually from Vienna to the Banat about 200 'undesirables' – vagabonds, subversives,

[18] For this paragraph, Neidenbach, 'Reisen Josephs II. ins Banat', pp. 28–37, quotation from p. 31.

poachers and prostitutes – supposedly to increase the population of the province while cleansing the capital of crime. Many of those transported, he pointed out, had been proved guilty of nothing. Since the public was never told exactly what kinds of delinquents were at risk, the scheme could not, as was claimed for it, act as an effective deterrent. When the victims reached the Banat, they could seldom find a livelihood, and the unhealthy climate killed many of them off. The net effect was to make the province unattractive to more promising settlers, who were naturally reluctant to associate themselves with a penal colony.[19]

He recommended, with even more force and greater justification than usual, a clean sweep. He considered economic management from Vienna fundamentally unsound. Officials, however well intentioned, whose personal fortune was bound up in the projects they were administering, could not give wholly disinterested advice. Moreover,

it is as indisputable in theory as it is shown to be in daily practice that lands under the state's own direction are never run well or for the benefit of the subjects and, despite the money they yield, never prosper so much as those that are in private hands.

He thought the effort that had gone into populating the province would have been better directed towards improving it and educating its inhabitants. The provincial government ought to be established on an ordinary footing, which would not only produce better results but also bring the Banat into conformity with the rest of the Monarchy. Joseph proposed the adoption there of the constitution of docile Moravia. Once the land had been properly surveyed, it ought to be sold off in relatively small lots to private individuals, without distinction of class, nation or religion. It would then be possible to establish Estates representing the property-owners, which would work with the bureaucracy to levy taxes and 'care for the general best'.[20]

If this radical plan did not find favour, then Joseph recommended as an alternative that the whole province be made a military frontier under the *Hofkriegsrat*. If that too was unacceptable, he suggested drastic changes within the existing pattern of administration. He did not discuss the question of annexation to Hungary.[21]

None of Joseph's reports had a greater impact. Kaunitz told Maria Theresa:

It is no flattery, but a true index of my inner feelings, [to say] that I marvel at HM the emperor's travel report on Banat and Slavonia. A commission composed of diverse members would never in so short a time have so thoroughly grasped the whole issue in its context and in its different aspects, distinguished [what is] good from abuses,

[19] Schünemann, *Österreichs Bevölkerungspolitik*, pp. 78–88.
[20] Neidenbach, 'Reisen Josephs II. ins Banat', pp. 40–62; Schünemann, *MÖIG* (1933), 23–33, quotations from pp. 30, 31; Roider in Banac *et al.*, *Nation and Ideology*, pp. 95–7.
[21] Arneth, *GMT* x, p. 124.

advanced solid proposals for improvement and made available on the basis of its work such a vast amount of clear information.

The empress herself declared that the *Relation* could not be improved upon, and that it brought her special consolation as mother and as queen.[22]

All the same, its proposals aroused strong opposition. Among the bureaucracy there was a great weight of traditionalist and mercantilist opinion to be shifted. Borié on the *Staatsrat*, acknowledging his personal interest as owner of shares in the Banat trading company, defended the operations of the *Banco*. Maria Theresa herself fought particularly hard to retain the practice of transporting Viennese undesirables. But in the end, over the period of a decade during which he visited the Banat twice more, Joseph got most of his main recommendations accepted. The financial involvement of officials was brought to an end. The province was surveyed, and land sales began. Eventually Maria Theresa allowed transportation to be discontinued for a trial period of two years; it was not resumed. The regular military frontier was established, but only in a portion of the province. In 1778 the main part of the Banat was assimilated to the rest of the Monarchy, and was provided with Estates and a nobility, though in a manner different from that originally envisaged by the emperor. Urged on by prince Albert as viceroy, and remembering her promises, Maria Theresa annexed it to Hungary. Joseph accepted this solution.[23]

Of course it was not entirely Joseph's doing that so many of his paper recommendations were eventually carried out. The government in Vienna knew before he went to the Banat that something was rotten in its administration and that changes would have to be made. On certain issues the emperor received strong support from the *Staatsrat*, for example over transportation. But many officials disagreed with him when he criticised the role of the bureaucracy in the economic exploitation of the province and when he urged that state land should be sold off to private individuals. Despite her fulsome praise of the *Relation*, Maria Theresa stubbornly defended the transportation system and showed little enthusiasm for any of her son's proposals when it came down to detail. In some matters no one in Vienna could hope to control events. No sooner had it been decided to stop the indiscriminate advertising for colonists than famine in central Europe led to a quite unplanned and unmanageable immigration in 1770–2.[24] But in so far as changes at the centre affected the situation in the province, Joseph's part in getting them accepted must have been crucial, and his substantial success must have depended on his

[22] Schünemann, *MÖIG* (1933), 23.
[23] Neidenbach, 'Reisen Josephs II. ins Banat', pp. 91–115; Schünemann, *Österreichs Bevölkerungspolitik*, pp. 87–8; Schünemann, *MÖIG* (1933), 27–33, 44; Arneth, *GMT* x, pp. 125–8.
[24] Schünemann, *Jahrbuch des Wiener Ungarischen Historischen Instituts* (1931), esp. 169–76, 192, 213.

almost unique first-hand knowledge, acquired through travel. It was a territory, he wrote, 'so remote from the centre that it is almost forgotten'.[25]

Johann Friedel, in his *Briefe aus Wien* of 1783, also drew on personal experience in Temesvar, where he had been brought up. He wrote that 'people did not say much about this journey' to a land not of palaces but of straw huts. Philosophers knew nothing of it. But it was far more significant than the famous visit to France of 1777. 'It was one of the most glorious things that Joseph did. He killed the Lernaean hydra.'[26] Yet some historians describe administrative development in the Banat without referring to this indecorous interruption of the bureaucratic process.[27]

JOSEPH'S PLAN OF TRAVEL, 1768

Fresh from his tour of the Banat, the emperor prepared a paper for his mother setting out his proposals for future journeys.[28] It breathes dedication, energy and impatience. On the general issue,

If travel is useful to any thinking person, it is much more so to a sovereign and to a man who, rejecting all pleasure, concentrates solely on utility. One's own observations, if associated with some capacity to make just comparisons, are very useful. One sees what is good and imitates it; one sees the bad and avoids it. In the absence of unnecessary comforts the expense ceases to be heavy. As an enemy of all formality, not entering into society nor seeking it in anyone's house, one ceases to be a burden, and no question of ceremonial arises ... Everything depends on the strict and fair observance [of this principle]. What is done for each has to be done for all. Whether it is possible to resist all importunities depends on you. I guarantee my own firmness. The utility of travel

---

[25] J. to L., 11 June 1768 (Arneth, *MTuJ* I, p. 220).

[26] J. Friedel, *Briefe aus Wien verschiedenen Inhalts an einen Freund in Berlin* (3rd edn, Leipzig, 1784), pp. 24–33, quotations from p. 32. This is a dangerous source to rely on, but in this case the Temesvar connexion seems to justify it. See Wurzbach IV, p. 357. G. Gugitz, 'Johann Friedel', *Jahrbuch der Grillparzer-Gesellschaft*, xv (1905), 186–250, does not succeed in throwing light on his subject's connexion with the Banat.

[27] Of the historians cited in the footnotes to this section, Schwicker and Walter ignore the journey. So does E. Lesky in her work on the plague cordon (e.g. 'Österreichisches Gesundheitswesen im Zeitalter des Absolutismus', *AÖG*, cxxii (1959), esp. pp. 63–4), where she attributes the changes officially sponsored by J. to the influence of an expert operating in Transylvania, called Chenot. However, J. thought him a 'sulky ignoramus' (*ein ignoranter Maulmacher*): Schuller, *Brukenthal*, vol. I, p. 297. Roider in Banac *et al.*, *Nation and Ideology*, p. 93, stresses the impact on J. of the unhealthy conditions he saw in the Banat.

[28] In HHSA FA Hofreisen I, fasz. 4, the memorandum on travel appears in three versions. One, of only four (though large and closely written) sides, is entirely in J.'s hand. Another, formally written out by an official but corrected in J.'s hand, has twenty-eight sides. The third seems preliminary to the formal version. All major points are found in all versions.

I have quoted and summarised from J.'s own autograph, though that may well never have been submitted to M.T. The main differences between the autograph and the formal version are that the latter includes detailed itineraries; it is more fussy about the timing of the journeys; and it is even more emphatic about the utility of travel, denied only by 'limited minds' and 'timid spirits'.

seems to me so incontestable that ... nothing can stop it but a vulgar prejudice, especially in my present situation.

He has four lengthy journeys in mind, which will enable him to visit all the remaining provinces of the Monarchy: one to Belgium, taking in the detached territories in south-west Germany; a second to southern Austria and Italy, including Tuscany to see his brother; a third to Croatia and the Littoral; the last to Hungary and Transylvania. The order, he says, matters little, but one of the journeys ought to be undertaken in each of the next four years, since the long-term future is unpredictable, whereas at the moment peace reigns, his health is good and it makes little difference whether he stays in Vienna or not.

On all the journeys he will look at both civil and military aspects, but the emphasis will vary according to the province. In Belgium and Germany – and, by implication, in Italy – military matters will take second place. He singles out as objects of special interest not only fortresses, battlefields and frontiers, but also rivers, the sea, ports, forges, mines and factories. He will visit his troops, and stay in the provincial capitals long enough to find out what is going on and to get to know the officials.

A few remarks creep in about seeing neighbouring countries. On the Belgian trip he would inevitably approach very near to Holland. 'In the strictest incognito, a tour of fourteen days in this land would enable me to admire its singular beauties, make me appreciate the worth of liberty and give me a tincture of commercial and naval affairs.' *En route* to Belgium he might proceed through the electorate of Bavaria, on his return through that of Cologne. About Italy he is less demanding. He says that, after seeing his brother in Florence, he will return across the Alps straight away 'if it is not thought that the sight of Rome can be as useful as it is interesting'. He mentions passing through Venice and, in another version of the paper, visiting Naples. But it is interesting that he does not assume he will automatically be allowed to undertake the journey to the major Italian cities for which he had obtained but not used permission both in 1767 and earlier in 1768.[29]

Much is left unsaid in this document. Joseph does not spell out that travel enables him to escape from the detested formality of the Court, to get away from his mother and to relieve his inner loneliness in the company of his cronies. As Maria Theresa recognised, he could not stand Vienna indefinitely.[30] The visit to Frederick the Great, though already mooted, is not mentioned. He does not refer to journeys to Switzerland, France, Russia and Britain, though he must surely have already contemplated them. Above all, he

[29] K-M VI, p. 270 (6 Oct. 1767); J. to L., 6 Jul. 1768 (Arneth, *MTuJ* I, p. 223); Arneth, *GMT* VII, p. 463; Klingenstein, *Quellen und Forschungen* (1971).

[30] M.T. to Lacy, [?]9 Sep. 1773: 'que je sais mauvais grée a l'Emp: par l'antipathie ou plutot l'ennuis qui le tourmente toujours ici'. And [?]4 Apr. 1774: 'mon fils at bien besoing de s'eloigner d'ici on parle de voyage de laxembourg' (HHSA NL, Karton 4). Cf. Keith to Suffolk, 'private and confidential, by Pisani', 8 June 1774 (PRO SP 80/215).

gives no hint that he intends using his travels for political purposes and to enhance his own influence. He says nothing about looking out for possible frontier adjustments or annexations, about uncovering defects in provincial administration with a view to reform, or about detecting abuses in the church in order to eradicate them. But his behaviour during his journeys proves that he had all these things in mind.

The empress seems never to have replied formally to this submission. She eventually permitted Joseph to travel to most of the places he proposed in the manner he desired. But her persistent obstruction delayed his plans. His absence, she complained, made her job harder. She explained once that it had not been possible, while he was far away, to give him information about a hurried negotiation. 'If you had been here with me, everything would have been better, and this is your [proper] place and not in the Carpathian mountains.'[31] She sometimes pleaded her ill-health or the difficult situation.[32] In reality she disliked every aspect of the programme. First, it was physically dangerous. As well as risking his health, Joseph alarmed her by going about with no attendants.[33] She was worried by accidents, as when his boat nearly capsized under the walls of Belgrade.[34] 'The emperor's journey [to Galicia] will take ten years off my life . . . He tires himself out and he'll feel the effects. In a few years he'll be old and broken.'[35] She saw France as especially perilous morally, and Protestant countries religiously. 'This dreadful Switzerland' was 'the refuge of all extremists and criminals; we have a couple of women there whom I hope you will not see.'[36]

I have never approved of all these jaunts, from which I've never seen any good come, only disadvantages. But I dislike the trip to Paris and London even more, since I find it truly inconceivable that an emperor of thirty-three should run about like a youth of eighteen.[37]

In the last year of her life, when he was in Russia and talking of visiting England, she complained about both, seizing on the Gordon riots as ammunition:

This [present] journey gives me a great deal of worry, and still more another [planned expedition] that will carry my anxieties to the highest point, especially after the terrible disturbance that has just taken place, unheard of among civilised Powers. That is [the

[31] M.T. to J., 20 June 1773 (Arneth, *MTuJ* II, p. 10). Cf. M.T. to Maria Beatrix, 6 Jan. 1777: Arneth, *MTKuF* III, p. 262; Arneth, *GMT* X, p. 706.
[32] E.g. M.T. to Ferd., Apr. 1774: Arneth, *MTKuF* I, p. 271: 'Les affaires des Russes, des Turcs et même de Pologne exigent sa présence ici . . . je serais plus embarrassée, s'il était en France.'
[33] M.T. to Ferd., 14 May 1772 (Arneth, *MTKuF* I, p. 123).
[34] J. to L., 24 June 1768 (Arneth, *MTuJ* I, p. 261).
[35] M.T. to Beatrix, 20 June 1773 (Arneth, *MTKuF* III, p. 160).
[36] M.T. to J., 5 Jul. 1777 (Arneth, *MTuJ* II, pp. 146–7).
[37] M.T. to Lacy, [?]4 Apr. 1774 (HHSA NL, Karton 4).

result of] this liberty, this unique legislation, that are so much extolled! Without religion and discipline, nothing can stand.[38]

As for his manner of travel, she naturally disliked his fondness for secret departures and surprise arrivals.[39] Her ideal of monarchy involved ceremony and ostentation, condescension and deference. 'The emperor receives no one, he is unique, but I cannot approve.'[40] To appear incognito, she said, offends decency, because of 'the ineffaceable character of royal princes'.[41] 'A country and its inhabitants need to feel the influence of the presence of princes, and that can be done only through personal contacts.'[42] To Joseph's annoyance, she allowed her youngest son, Max Franz, to travel widely at an early age, without 'an aim', and receiving a round of fêtes and receptions.[43]

Although she seldom spelled it out, she evidently also feared the political impact of Joseph's journeys. In the case of Bohemia in 1771, though it was the risk to his health that she spoke about, her persistent obstruction of his inspection-tour showed clearly enough that she dreaded both his interference on the spot and his returning home fortified by first-hand knowledge to assist his campaign for drastic reforms. She doubted whether any good could come of the visits to France and Russia.[44] She finally put her cards on the table when discussing the latter with count Mercy, her ambassador in France: 'Since the situation is past remedy, it would not do to make my dislike of it obvious, but there can be no doubt, seeing what the results of all these journeys have been for me, that they are [directed] against me.'[45]

However, she had given orders that reliable persons should be sent into the provinces every year, to report to the *Staatsrat* on the work of the officials and the condition of the people. If count Karl Zinzendorf could travel for years together at government expense, why not her son? And just occasionally she acknowledged with maternal pride the success of Joseph's methods. For example, she wrote in 1773:

I have very good news of the emperor . . . from Fogaras [in Transylvania]. The people are mad about him, they've never seen an emperor, and one so friendly and democratic; and, what astonishes them still more, so frugal, never holding banquets. That seems to them incredible.[46]

[38] See below, pp. 431–8 and Arneth, *GMT* x, p. 758.
[39] E.g. K-M VIII, p. 83 (8 June 1775); M.T. to Maria Beatrix, 24 Mar. 1777 (Arneth, *MTKuF* III, p. 270).
[40] M.T. to Beatrix, 22 June 1775 (Arneth, *MTKuF* III, p. 193).
[41] M.T. to Beatrix, 23 Aug. 1779 (Arneth, *MTKuF* III, p. 379).
[42] M.T. to Beatrix, 25 Jan. 1773 (Arneth, *MTKuF* III, p. 154).
[43] See memo. by J., dated 22 July 1775 (HHSA FA Hofreisen 2, fasz. 11), headed 'Reise Project von Erzh. Max.', printed in Arneth, *MTuJ* II, pp. 72–6.
[44] See below, pp. 369, 433.   [45] M.T. to Mercy, 2 Apr. 1780 (Arneth & Geffroy III, p. 417).
[46] Hock, *Staatsrath*, p. 27. In HHSA TZ there are many references to J. taking an interest in Zinzendorf's travels.
    M.T. to Ferd., 10 June 1773 (Arneth, *MTKuF* I, p. 211). Cf. her compliment to J. on the Bohemian journey: Arneth, *MTuJ* I, p. 350 (Nov. 1771).

In the end Joseph fulfilled all the plans announced in the memorandum of 1768, though it took him ten years longer than he had originally hoped. Only in 1781, after Maria Theresa's death, did he finally get to the Netherlands. But in the meantime he had fitted in several journeys he had not at first proposed, to Galicia, France and Switzerland, and Russia. Unfortunately he never managed to see England.

THE ITALIAN JOURNEY, 1769

It was the Italian journey that was permitted first. Joseph had intended to accompany his sister Josepha on her way to become queen of Naples in the autumn of 1767, but she had caught smallpox and died.[47] In the following year he had actually preferred to visit the Banat rather than Italy, letting Leopold do the honours for Maria Carolina, the substitute queen of Naples. The emperor wrote to his brother:

You are wallowing in pleasures, I am pacing over deserts ... I have often thought to myself that I would not have exchanged my Wallachian hut [with you], for there I was my own master and peaceful, whereas I imagine that you will have many trials to endure.[48]

But on 3 March 1769 he left Vienna for Rome and was away for five months. He did not, after all, dally in southern Austria. He visited all the larger mainland capitals of Italy except Genoa, which his mother excluded as unfriendly.[49] In most of the states, of course, he counted as a foreign ruler. But he came to Milan as co-regent.

Joseph's journeys usually had some special justification as well as the obvious general motives. In this case the reasons are complex and, in part, disputed. The Turks had asked that, because of their war with Russia, he should not travel to Croatia in 1769. Maria Theresa said that one of her grounds for allowing him to go to Italy instead was the hope that he might be sufficiently attracted by a Modenese or Piedmontese princess to agree to marry again. Another was that Rome was dragging its feet over granting a papal dispensation that was needed to make possible the marriage arranged between the duke of Parma and the emperor's sister, Amalia. The empress also wanted him to see how Maria Carolina was getting on with the boorish king of Naples.[50] On Joseph's side, he particularly desired to visit Lombardy and study its government. He had just been disputing with his mother about the co-regency, and was complaining of boredom in Vienna. He relished an

---

[47] See n. 29 above.
[48] J. to L., 11 June 1768 (Arneth, *MTuJ* I, p. 220). Cf. letter of 6 July on p. 223.
[49] Arneth, *GMT* VII, pp. 461–71, for the visit to independent Italian states. On Genoa, pp. 469–70; the San Remo affair was still festering.
[50] M.T. to Rosenberg (late Feb. 1769): Arneth, *MTKuF* IV, pp. 65–7.

opportunity to tell his woes to his brother, whom he had not seen for more than three years, and for whom he prepared a Supplement to the 'General picture' just before he left. The precise timing of the journey must have been influenced by the sudden death of pope Clement XIII on 2 February. He was regarded in Vienna as an enemy. With him out of the way and a papal election in progress, there would be no local sovereign in Rome to complicate protocol for the emperor, and the Holy Week ceremonies would be less grandiose than usual.[51]

This was a time of crisis for the papacy. In the late fifties and throughout the sixties the demand had been growing for the suppression of the Jesuits. By the beginning of 1769 they had been expelled from Portugal, Spain, France and Naples, accused of every sort of economic, political and moral malpractice. All these states were determined to secure the election of a pope who would dissolve the Society. In most Catholic countries, including Milan, legislation had recently been enacted to restrict the power of the papacy, the independence of the church, the extension of ecclesiastical wealth and so on. The duchy of Parma had introduced in January 1768 a particularly strong measure against papal jurisdiction within its territory. In reply Clement reasserted the vast powers claimed by the papacy since the Middle Ages over secular rulers. He declared the measure null, and excommunicated the duke and his officials. This presumption was too much for the Bourbon relatives of the duke of Parma. France, Spain and Naples demanded the withdrawal of the condemnation and of the ancient bull *In coena domini* which justified it. France and Naples occupied the pope's outlying possessions of Avignon and Benevento. Maria Theresa too was indignant at this treatment of a secular ruler who was Joseph's brother-in-law and the destined husband of her daughter Amalia. But her response was more moderate. Her opposition prevented an armed attack by Parma on the territory of the papal state.[52] So the situation in Italy was both critical and exciting when Joseph set out for Rome – much more so than when he had first planned this journey.

People naturally jumped to the conclusion that the emperor was intending to intervene in the conclave, at which the ruler of the Monarchy was recognised to possess a veto, perhaps in order to promote the election of a pope who would suppress the Jesuits. Lacy wrote to him:

51 On these motives, Arneth, *GMT* VII, pp. 463–4; Wandruszka, *L. II.*, vol. I, pp. 244–5; Stormont to Rochford, 1 Mar. 1769, 'by Roworth' (PRO SP 80/206); Klingenstein, *Quellen und Forschungen* (1971), esp. 467, 486–90. There is a very full study of the visit to Rome by I. P. Dengel, 'Der Aufenthalt Kaiser Josephs II. in Rom im Jahre 1769', *Jahrbuch der österreichischen Leogesellschaft* (1926), 36–97; on the motives of J. see 39–41. For the Supplement, see p. 125, n. 36.

52 On M.T.'s attitude Arneth, *GMT* IX, pp. 18–26, 549–50; Maass, *Josephinismus*, vol. I, pp. 74–8, 267–77. On the situation in Italy, Venturi, *Settecento riformatore*, vol. II; Benassi, *ASPP* (1925), esp. 72–8. Generally, Chadwick, *Popes and Revolution*, pp. 345–68; Fig. 2.

Provided that YM causes the anti-Jesuit party to triumph at the conclave, we shall have gained enough in securing the immediate prospect of seeing YM's treasuries enriched by the immense spoils of the religious usurers of the Society of Jesus who swarm in your states. This, Sire, is not all. These ecclesiastical bankers have also very fine and very large buildings in every town of your Monarchy, especially in Prague and Vienna.

Such edifices, he goes on, are exactly what the army needs, and the one in Vienna would make perfect offices for the *Hofkriegsrat*.[53] As we shall see, Lacy misjudged the emperor's position. But in giving permission for the journey, Maria Theresa could not help recognising Joseph as a semi-official emissary of her policy at this important moment.[54]

The journey was arranged at only a few days' notice.[55] But before he left, Joseph read a report on the papal state prepared for the abandoned visit of 1767.[56] He also compiled a 'list of things to see', which included modern and ancient buildings, paintings, statues, gardens, battlefields, public works and charitable institutions in all parts of Italy.[57] The list is lengthy, eclectic and demanding.

Especially full accounts survive of this journey. This is partly because Italy was freer and contained more writers than the Monarchy. But it looks as though Maria Theresa took special pains in this case to have her son's activities monitored and his words overheard. In the archives at Vienna are to be found competing descriptions by various hands of all the main incidents of the tour. Some of this information came from private letters intercepted and opened by the censorship. A few of the documents have brief annotations in the emperor's handwriting: 'true', 'true for the most part', 'it is not true'.[58]

---

[53] Lacy to J., [?]1 Mar. 1769 (HHSA NL, Karton 3). It is striking that Lacy should write like this so early. His wish was duly realised when the Jesuit building on Am Hof in Vienna became the offices of the *Hofkriegsrat* after the suppression of the Order. See below, pp. 460–4.

[54] On the more general problem of motives, Arneth is bland, and I am sure Klingenstein is right to argue, against him and Wandruszka, that the visit had political significance (see references in n. 51 above). But I think he cared more about the sights than she allows (see his remarks on St Peter's); it seems to me that Arneth's evidence about the forbidden visit to Genoa and the letter to Rosenberg make it clear that M.T. was in control of the whole journey; and the account of the papal state by Brunati, which Klingenstein most usefully publishes, cannot have had the importance in shaping J.'s views which she ascribes to it. Cf. the portion of HHSA TG on the papal state, reproduced in Arneth, *GMT* IX, pp. 550–1. I do not see how M.T. could have let J. go to Rome during the conclave without expecting to take advantage of his presence there. See references in n. 51 and Arneth, *GMT* IX, ch. 2.

[55] E.g., J. to Lacy, 28 Feb. 1769, asking for plans and descriptions of Italian battles and campaigns to be drawn in the strictest secrecy from the archive of the *Hofkriegsrat* (HHSA NL, Karton 6).

[56] Klingenstein, *Quellen und Forschungen* (1971), 468–9 and *passim*.

[57] HHSA FA Hofreisen 1, fasz. 2B: 'Table des choses a voire' ([?] in J.'s hand).

[58] HHSA FA Hofreisen 1, fasz. 2; and some documents in Hofreisen 2 may relate to this Italian journey.

Most of the material for the next few paragraphs comes from Hofreisen 1, fasz. 2. See also Arneth, *MTuJ* I, pp. 243–300, and Dengel, *Jahrbuch der österreichischen Leogesellschaft* (1926).

On intercepts, some of Alessandro Verri's letters from Rome to his brother Pietro in Milan are to be found in the Hofreisen file. E.g. 1 Apr. 1769: E. Greppi and A. Giulini (eds.),

Joseph set out with the utmost secrecy. His departure was not officially announced for several days.[59] He took his customary small suite, though on this occasion Lacy did not accompany him. He tried to observe many of the same rules he had established for travel within the Monarchy. There were to be no official welcomes; he would not stay in royal palaces; he would not give or accept dinners or presents. But journeys partly outside the Monarchy necessarily took on a somewhat different character from purely internal journeys. He could not hope to control the situation in other states as he and his military henchmen did at home. Heads of state received him, their subjects flocked to see him, and his actions and words became the property of Europe. Furthermore, it seems to have been only for journeys that took him outside the Monarchy that he compiled lists of non-military sights to see.[60]

He travelled from Vienna, with only the briefest stops, for thirteen solid days and three nights, arriving in Rome without warning on 15 March in the company only of Dietrichstein, having left the rest of the suite behind. On the road, while his horses were changed at Forli in the Romagna, he had an encounter that became famous. Covered with mud, he accosted and talked for half-an-hour with

count Papini, walking up and down under a portico. The gentleman asked him about the Jesuits of Germany. The emperor replied that they behave very well there; they are learned and zealous – adding other praises – and concluding that what has happened to them elsewhere wouldn't happen in Germany. Hearing these praises, the count supposed that this was a young man educated in the *Theresianum*, who spoke out of loyalty. He questioned him about it. 'No', [the emperor] replied, 'I was educated at home, and I said that out of simple regard for the truth.' He [the count] asked him how the affair of the bull *In coena Domini* was proceeding in Germany. He replied that it had never been accepted or rejected in Germany, and so things were still on the old footing. The count then gave him some good advice. 'My son', he said to him, repeating the phrase several times, 'My son, you're a handsome youth, and well-heeled. Watch out for Roman women. They're artful. You might get into danger.' 'I'm not afraid of Roman women', [the emperor] said. 'I'm going to Rome to see whether anything now remains of the spirit of Scipio, Fabius and Metellus.'[61]

When count Papini discovered who his acquaintance was, he wrote an apologetic letter, to which Joseph replied warmly. The emperor's letter was published all over Europe.[62]

Carteggio di Pietro e di Alessandro Verri (Milan, 1910–39), vol. II, pp. 225–6. I was greatly assisted in using this elusive work by Prof. G. Becattini and by Dr A. Abrami-Calcagni of the Biblioteca nazionale, Florence.
[59] Stormont to Rochford, 4 and 13 Mar. 1769 (PRO SP 80/206). J. called it 'un secret secretissime' to Lacy on 28 Feb. (see n. 55 above).
[60] HHSA FA Hofreisen 10 (France, 1777); 11 (Russia, 1780) and Belgium (1781).
[61] This comes from one of the two accounts in HHSA FA Hofreisen 1. I have used the other account for some of the circumstantial detail. For the *Theresianum* see p. 455 below.
[62] HHSA FA Sbde 26 has J.'s original of [?]1 Jan. 1770. A version is to be found, for example, in the *Annual Register* for 1770, p. [85]. Cf. Greppi and Giulini, *Carteggio di P. e di A. Verri*, vol. III, letters of 31 Jan. (Pietro) and 7 Feb. (Alessandro) 1770.

He spent a fortnight in Rome, in the company of Leopold, and managed to see a high proportion of the sights he had listed beforehand. Five hours looking round St Peter's proved too short; he said it required months. But he showed particular enthusiasm for hospitals, workshops, colleges and other 'useful' buildings. He walked through the city almost unattended, with crowds following him everywhere. He appeared at various receptions, talking pleasantly, though telling his mother in his letters how bored he had been. Occasionally he turned his back on the perpetrator of a tactless remark. Otherwise, he gave continual 'proofs of his clemency to every class of person'. Pompeo Batoni, abandoning the British tourists who provided most of his sitters, painted the well-known portrait of the two brothers, with a panorama of Rome in the background and Montesquieu's *L'Esprit des lois* on the table beside them.[63]

Joseph ostentatiously displayed 'heroic piety', praying for longer than expected, refusing special treatment in churches, and kneeling when religious processions passed by. If asked for political views, he announced that 'the emperor and his will had remained in Vienna'. But he teased the general of the Jesuits about their wealth 'from the Indies'. He also took the opportunity to visit the conclave, and to pass on to the cardinals the attitude of the Vienna government to the election: Maria Theresa would not actively promote the suppression of the Jesuits, but she would not oppose it; she did not intend to veto any candidate; she merely hoped that the next pope would be both experienced and godly.

She had found herself in a difficulty before and after Joseph's departure in trying to nominate an appropriate cardinal to represent her interests at the conclave. She and Kaunitz had lost confidence in her ambassador to Rome, cardinal Albani. Cardinal Migazzi, the archbishop of Vienna, who expected to be charged with this duty, had recently begun to obstruct their ecclesiastical policies and could not be trusted to carry out their wishes. The next best candidate fell ill. In the end, the authority was sent to Joseph in Rome with the name left blank for him to fill in as he thought best.[64] By the time he left the city, however, the conclave had made little progress towards an election.

Politically, it could be said that the emperor's presence in Rome had in a general way strengthened the Monarchy's influence. But it could hardly be maintained that he had achieved anything concrete unless, perhaps, by winning the goodwill of the next pope, he had hastened the grant of Amalia's

---

[63] Plates 8b, 11. On the portrait, Wandruszka, *L. II.*, vol. 1, pp. 246–7. The catalogue of the 1982 exhibition at Kenwood, *Pompeo Batoni and his British Patrons*, throws only indirect light on the portrait of J. and L. At least it can safely be affirmed that *L'Esprit des lois* must have been specially chosen as a prop for these sitters. Dengel, *Jahrbuch der österreichischen Leogesellschaft* (1926), pp. 69, 87–8 and nn.

[64] As well as *ibid.* and the material in HHSA FA Hofreisen 1, Arneth, *GMT* IX, pp. 4–6, 30–40; Wolfsgruber, *Migazzi*, esp. p. 227. See pp. 442, 450 below.

dispensation. Maria Theresa was willing to sanction a medal celebrating the visit, but doubtful whether the papal election should feature on it, since the resulting new pope, Clement XIV, was an unknown quantity. In truth, Joseph could not have changed the course of affairs unless he had departed from his mother's passive policy, which he scrupulously refrained from doing. She had promised to support a candidate for the papacy agreeable to the Bourbon Powers; that was the real meaning of her pious assertions about not interfering and not excluding anyone, and wanting only a good shepherd of the flock. Her stance on the Jesuit question was designed to salve her conscience and to placate both friends and enemies of the Society at home, while not displeasing her allies or encouraging a confrontation between them and the papacy. Kaunitz had to confess to count Firmian, his minister in Lombardy, that the Monarchy had played an inglorious part at the conclave. They could not, he had the effrontery to add, kick the papacy when it was down.[65]

In Joseph's life, however, this visit was a landmark. It was bound to make a sensation that the 'Roman emperor' should come to Rome, the first to set foot there since Charles V – and the more so because he behaved with startling informality and because a conclave was in progress. The occasion was celebrated in numerous poems, pamphlets and memorials.[66] It established the more attractive side of Joseph's image in the minds of a European public: energetic, well-informed, enquiring, affable, courteous, unassuming, a lover of simplicity, a respectful son of his mother and a devout critic of the Church. When he moved on to Naples he was dubbed 'the Christian hero', 'the Catholic Marcus Aurelius'. 'If he is better than Trajan, may he be more fortunate than Caesar.'[67]

He stayed nine days in Naples, sightseeing and taking part in the Court routine of king Ferdinand and his queen. At the end he wrote a lengthy account of his sister's situation for his mother. This is the most domestic of all his writings, revealing much about his own attitudes in its comments on the Neapolitan Court.[68] He admired the conduct of the queen in establishing her influence and maintaining her self-respect under the most trying circumstances. The king, though amiable, had received little education, disapproved

---

[65] On the dispensation, J. to M.T., 22 May 1769 (Arneth, *MTuJ* I, p. 273). On the medal, Arneth, *GMT* IX, p. 42. On Vienna's policy in general, *ibid.*, pp. 33–42; Wolfsgruber, *Migazzi*, pp. 226–8; K. to Firmian, 3 July 1769 in F. Maass, 'Vorbereitung und Anfänge des Josefinismus im amtlichen Schriftwechsel des Staatskanzlers ... mit ... Firmian, 1763 bis 1770', *MÖSA*, (1948) 439–41.

[66] See ÖNB Handschriften Ser. n. 3419 as well as the material in HHSA FA Hofreisen I and in Dengel, *Jahrbuch der österreichischen Leogesellschaft* (1926).

[67] Quotations from HHSA FA Hofreisen I, reports of 4 and 8 May.

[68] This is in HHSA FA Hofreisen I, fasz. 2B, in French and dated Florence, 21 Apr. 1769. It is extensively quoted and summarised in H. Acton, *The Bourbons of Naples, 1734–1825* (London, 1956), pp. 135–49.

of reading, was scarcely capable of connected discussion, and never wrote anything down except lists of the nicknames he had given his servants. 'He has no inkling that a sovereign has special duties and is bound to render an account to God of the welfare of the kingdom.' He resented the influence of Spain and disliked the Spanish etiquette, but had no idea of doing anything about them. His notions of religion and morality were primitive to a degree. 'He knew that the devil was black and angels were white; he believed in ghosts and spirits, and that St Januarius was a superlative saint.' What he liked was horseplay and practical joking, endless contrived hunting, badinage and games with his attendants, slapping ladies' bottoms. Joseph humoured him by carrying him pick-a-back 'for an age'. Ferdinand's personal habits were disgusting, though 'at least he does not stink'. He liked to call the emperor 'Don Pepe' and 'mad rascal'. Joseph summed up: 'I was nine days playing the courtier. I swear I've never come across a harder job than that.'

According to the British envoy, Sir William Hamilton, there was another side to the story:

Joseph, who held his brother-in-law's understanding in great contempt, endeavoured to assume over him the sort of superiority, arrogated by a strong over a weak mind. But Ferdinand, though confessedly his inferior in cultivation and refinement, was by no means disposed to adopt his political opinions or ideas. He even manifested, in various conversations and on many occasions, that, defective as his education had been, he possessed as much plain sense, and even acute discernment, as the Emperor, or his brother Leopold ... Joseph did not, indeed, inspire any very high admiration by his deportment or general conduct, while he remained at Naples. He was irritable, and even irascible, where he should have shown good humour or command of temper.[69]

It does not take long to tell the rest of the story of Joseph's visits to independent Italian states. In Florence he prolonged his stay in order to keep his brother company while he was recuperating from inoculation against smallpox. Leopold was following the example and taking the advice of the emperor and his mother, who had had themselves inoculated after the fatal epidemic of 1767.[70] In Bologna Joseph showed great interest in a collection of wax anatomical models, a recently developed form of teaching aid for surgical students. In Modena and Turin he met the princesses that Maria Theresa had in mind for him, but reiterated his determination to remain single.[71] In Parma

[69] N. W. Wraxall, *Historical Memoirs of my Own Time*, ed. R. Askham (London, 1904), p. 152. The authority given is a conversation with Hamilton, ten years after the event. Although Hamilton's despatches (PRO SP 93/24) do not contain these criticisms of J., Wraxall's version sounds convincing. See p. 310 and n. 20 below.
[70] Arneth, *GMT* VII, pp. 335–7, 468; Wandruszka, *L. II.*, vol. I, p. 247; J. to M.T., 16 and 22 May 1769 (Arneth, *MTuJ* I, pp. 270–5). See p. 158 above.
[71] Arneth, *GMT* VII, pp. 467–8; Arneth, *MTuJ* I, pp. 267–9 (J.to M.T., 16 May 1769) and 294–6 (16 June). HHSA FA Hofreisen I (15–16 May). On the Turin visit, G. Claretta, 'L'imperatore Giuseppe II a Torino nel giugno di 1769. Memorie anedottiche', 5th series, VI (1890), 386–425.

he made the acquaintance of the duke, who had been educated by *philosophes* including Condillac.

His looks are quite good, but his figure poor, very fat and squat. He is lame in the left leg ... He is extremely well brought up, very inexperienced, very knowledgeable, but seems to have no genius and little intelligence, is as tiresome as it is possible to be, leaning on my arm and never leaving me alone for a step. So I can assure YM that, if the king of Naples had been educated like this, it would have succeeded infinitely better than with the duke, and that I would much prefer to spend eight days with the king than with him.

However, he saw no reason why Amalia, 'if she is wise', should not be perfectly happy in Parma.[72]

In Venice, finally, he caused the fantastic celebrations prepared for him to be countermanded. But he found time for sightseeing, for attending and admiring a session of the Council of Forty, for visiting eighty-three noble ladies in their boxes at the theatre, and for a long interview with the former Venetian ambassador in Vienna and chief architect of the Republic's foreign policy, Andrea Tron. They talked of the inevitable competition between the ports of Venice and Trieste, the emperor asserting the old mercantilist doctrine that each state must wish to attract as much gold as possible to itself and that it could do so only by impoverishing other states. But he praised the Republic's recent ecclesiastical legislation, and gave the impression that he was well disposed towards her.[73]

Between his visits to Florence and Venice, the emperor spent six weeks in the Monarchy's Italian territories, the duchies of Milan and Mantua. As elsewhere in the peninsula, he saw the sights, admiring many of the buildings. Crowds followed him, to his expressed annoyance.[74] He appeared incognito at a few receptions. He attended plays and operas, taking the opportunity to meet notables informally in their boxes.

One celebrity he encountered was Pasquale Paoli, who, after ruling Corsica for fourteen years in rebellion against Genoa, was at last expelled from the island by a French army in June 1769. Joseph had spoken privately in favour of Paoli's cause, and just before the final *débâcle* Maria Theresa had written to her son suggesting that the defeated patriot might be taken into her army. The emperor replied:

---

[72] J. to M.T., 16 May 1769 (Arneth, *MTuJ* I, pp. 266–7, 269). On the duke's education, Venturi, *Settecento riformatore*, vol. II, pp. 218–19.

[73] See Plate 14a. There is virtually nothing in HHSA FA Hofreisen on the visit to Venice. See ASV Corti Senato I (Secreta) Fᵃ 334–5. The *relazione* of Tron (28 July 1769) is summarised in S. Romanin, *Storia documentata della Repubblica di Venezia* (10 vols., Venice, 1853–61), vol. VIII, pp. 188–94, and G. Tabacco, *Andrea Tron (1712–1785) e la Crisi dell' Aristocrezia senatoria a Venezia* (Trieste, 1957), pp. 147n, 163–4.

I am very grateful to Dr N. S. Davidson for supplying me with microfilm of the relevant files from the Archivio di Stato in Venice.

[74] Firmian's report to M.T. (Valsecchi, *L'assolutismo illuminato*, vol. II, p. 315).

This man has no military aptitude. He is not even personally brave. He is a rebel chieftain who has acquired his reputation through the enthusiasm and fanaticism with which he was able to inspire his nation by telling it a thousand lies, and still more by the negligence of those whose duty it was to act against him. I would strongly advise YM to expel him from your states if he came, rather than ask him to enter them.[75]

There speaks not only the son who invariably reacted against his mother's suggestions, but also the autocratic opponent of revolutionaries and the hidebound professional soldier. However, a few days later Paoli landed in Tuscany and had friendly interviews with Leopold, who enquired of Vienna whether the Corsican might be allowed asylum in Tuscany. Kaunitz, having consulted the empress about this 'delicate proposition', replied on 3 July that Paoli could be unofficially promised asylum on the understanding that, if France made serious protests, he must leave as though of his own free will.[76] A fortnight later Paoli left Tuscany *en route* for England. He passed through Mantua when Joseph was there, and the two men talked together. Apparently the emperor afterwards told Leopold he was satisfied with Paoli. Much myth and mystery surrounds the meeting, but it seems entirely plausible that Paoli should have been provoked to remark to the emperor, as the story goes: 'Where there is freedom there is a fatherland, where there is no freedom there is no fatherland.'[77]

'My work begins here', said Joseph when he reached Austrian territory.[78] In Lombardy he was not primarily concerned with the sights, but with the government in all its aspects. The situation, of course, was utterly different from that in the Banat. Compared with almost every other part of the Monarchy, the Italian lands, with one-and-a-quarter million inhabitants, were

[75] J. to M.T., 8 June 1769 (Arneth, *MTuJ* I, pp. 291–2).
   For J.'s earlier sympathy with Paoli's cause, J. to L., 15 Sep. 1768 (*ibid.*, p. 232).
[76] Letters from and concerning Paoli during these months are published (ed. N. Tommaseo) in *ASI*, XI (1846) and 5th series, VI (1890), 266–306; and in *BSSHNC*, ed. Perelli, the third series published in 1890 and the fifth in 1899. The editing of the latter is shocking, and the periodical is a bibliographical quagmire. K.'s letter is on p. 301 of *ASI* (1890) and on p. 174 of *BSSHNC* (1890), p. 174. See also W. S. Lewis, W. H. Smith and G. L. Lam, *Horace Walpole's Correspondence with Sir Horace Mann*, vol. VII (London, 1967), pp. 130, 136–7.
   No sign of Paoli in Wandruska, *L. II*.
[77] I have so far failed to find any direct evidence from either J. or Paoli that they even met. Some of the primary and secondary sources referred to in the literature on the meeting are plainly unreliable. For example, Bettinelli in *BSSHNC*, I (1881–2), 299–304 is in a ghastly muddle as to where and when the meeting(s) might have taken place. The best evidence I have found is in Mann's letters (Lewis *et al.*, *Horace Walpole's Correspondence*, p. 137n, Mann to Weymouth, 5 Aug. 1769). See also P. to A. Verri, 22 July 1769 (Greppi and Giulini, *Carteggio di P. e di A. Verri*, vol. II, p. 369).
   On what is supposed to have passed between J. and Paoli, F. Venturi, *Italy and the Enlightenment* (London, 1972), p. 146, and O. Chadwick, 'The Italian Enlightenment' in Porter and Teich, *The Enlightenment in National Context*, pp. 99–100 (see also n. 22 on p. 237 of the book).
   A. Verri, by 11 Nov. 1769, had heard that J. was dissatisfied with Paoli (Greppi and Giulini, *Carteggio di P. e di A. Verri*, vol. III, pp. 115–16).
[78] J. to M.T., 30 May 1769 (Arneth, *MTuJ* I, p. 284).

highly civilised, wealthy, densely populated and urbanised. Traditional liberties were guarded by ancient institutions of which the most prestigious was the aristocratic Senate of Milan, which possessed an ill-defined mixture of legislative and judicial powers. But something like a renaissance had recently stirred the intellectual life of educated and aristocratic circles. Its most notable product, marquis Cesare Beccaria's *Dei delitti e delle pene*, advocating the abolition of torture and the death penalty, had acquired European fame since its publication at Florence in 1764. From 1764 to 1766 counts Alessandro and Pietro Verri had run in Milan 'the liveliest periodical of the Italian Enlightenment', *Il Caffè*. Links were close between progressive writers and the government. Pietro Verri had a prominent place in the financial administration of the province.[79] Moreover, after 1757 the Italian lands were ruled from Vienna by Kaunitz himself. He carried through in Lombardy a programme of reforms, some based on existing practice in Austria and Bohemia, but others more novel and later extended to other parts of the Monarchy. In 1760 a new, more reliable and equitable tax-survey had finally been completed, under which the clergy and nobility were made to pay a share. But the taxes were still collected by a group of 'farmers' whose activities and wealth were much resented. Subsequent administrative changes included the establishment in 1765 of the so-called *Giunta economale*, whose task was to tighten the screw on the church, allowing the clergy independence only in matters purely spiritual. Its secret instructions of 1768 embodied a radical anti-papal programme.[80] As Joseph recognised in his *Relation*, with uncharacteristic effusiveness and generosity,

Your Majesty, who since [the beginning of] her reign has, so to speak, given a new impulsion to the whole Monarchy, who has made it think, and dragged it out of the stupidity in which ancient prejudices were keeping it, has not forgotten Lombardy and the numerous abuses gradually introduced there by the old Spanish government, ... abuses that merited the reform she applied to them ...

I have seen with my own eyes – and I am certainly not a flatterer, particularly at a moment when, knowing Your Majesty's desire to know the truth, I should regard myself as responsible to the Supreme Being if I gave even a veiled, let alone a falsified, account – ... that all the principles that Your Majesty has laid down in her royal orders, especially in the last few years, are fair, just and well founded. Foreigner, inhabitant, educated or uneducated, everyone agrees ...

[79] On the condition of Austrian Lombardy, Valsecchi, *L'assolutismo illuminato*, vol. II; Fondazione Treccani, *Storia di Milano*, vol. XII (Milan, 1959); Capra's section on 'Il Settecento' in D. Sella and C. Capra, *Il Ducato di Milano dal 1535 al 1796* (Turin, 1984); Arneth, *GMT* x, ch. 6; Venturi, *Settecento reformatore*, vol. I, ch. 9 and vol. II, ch. 5; S. Woolf, *A History of Italy, 1700–1860* (London, 1979), pp. 81–91, 98–104. See above, p. 236 and n.

[80] As well as the works cited in the previous note, D. M. Klang, *Tax Reform in Eighteenth Century Lombardy* (New York, 1977); Maass, *Josephinismus*, vol. I and *MÖSA* (1948), 289–441; F. Diaz, 'Toscana e Lombardia nell'età di Maria Teresa: modelli di sviluppo del riformismo absburgico in Italia', *Studi settecenteschi*, I (1981), 7–34. I should like to thank Prof. V. Becagli for sending me a copy of this article and for much other assistance. See ch. 14 below.

He made a point of praising Kaunitz too.[81]

The emperor inspected fortresses, barracks and soldiers, sometimes drilling the troops. He scrutinised the charitable institutions behind their imposing façades and found, for example, that the University of Pavia possessed 'neither a book nor instruments'.[82] But he devoted most time to studying the working of the central administration. During three weeks in Milan he attended a meeting of some council almost every day after early Mass, fifteen meetings in all.[83]

Joseph kept a diary, made notes and wrote a *Relation*, as always. But for this visit, unusually, we have two complementary sources: a report to Maria Theresa from the minister plenipotentiary, count Karl Firmian, who was a sufficiently trusted councillor of the empress to venture some respectful criticisms of her son's behaviour; and letters from Pietro Verri describing some of the meetings that both he and the emperor attended.[84] So it is possible to give a fuller picture of his governmental activity in Milan than anywhere else on his travels.

When he first arrived in Milan, in plain military dress without decorations, Joseph seemed ill at ease and stilted in his politeness. A contretemps occurred almost at once. The royal figurehead in the province, called the viceroy or *Statthalter*, was the duke of Modena. 'The duke', wrote Verri, 'tried to accompany [the emperor] at the start of the visit, but he pointed to count Firmian and said, *I have my companion*, and [the duke] departed like lightning.' Joseph considered the old man a preposterous figure from the past and had made it clear enough that he disliked being bothered by him. The duke said he thought Joseph 'believed he had laid himself out to be polite in dealing with him, but he feared the public would not take that kind of politeness in that way'. The emperor disapproved of princely viceroys who tried to play a positive role. He also thought the old man corrupt. Further, there were family embarrassments. The duke's granddaughter and heiress, Maria Beatrix, was engaged to marry Joseph's brother Ferdinand, who would eventually succeed both as duke of Modena and as viceroy of Milan and Mantua. But if the emperor had said the word, he could have had her for his own wife. However, he admired her mind and conduct more than

---

[81] One copy of this *Relation* is in HHSA FA Sbde 88, another in ÖNB Handschriften Ser. n. 1612, a third in HHSA FA Hofreisen 1, fasz. 2B. It is summarised in Arneth, *GMT* x, pp. 171–5.

[82] Valsecchi, *L'assolutismo illuminato*, vol. II, pp. 322–3 (J.'s diary, 8 June 1769).

[83] Arneth, *GMT* x, pp. 164–70, 776.

[84] Most of these documents except the *Relation* are printed in Valsecchi, *L'assolutismo illuminato*, vol. II, pp. 291–330. Arneth, *GMT* VII, pp. 470–2 and x, ch. 6 and notes thereon, prints many extracts from these sources, except for the Verri letters. There is additional information in HHSA FA Hofreisen 1, fasz. 2A and 2B; in Arneth, *MTuJ* 1, pp. 284–92, 297–300; and in Greppi and Giulini, *Carteggio di P. e di A. Verri*, vol. II.

her looks. After this experience of Joseph she 'seemed more attached to Ferdinand'.[85]

The emperor got on better with the officials at the council meetings. He opened the proceedings with the words: 'Gentlemen, I am a pupil, you must instruct me.' The purpose of the sessions was 'to give HM an idea of our system'. They were not designed to decide anything, however small. But there was much disagreement, even with views expressed by Joseph. 'His M.ty tolerates contradiction to an astonishing degree, for I never once caught a hint of impatience from him in almost twelve hours of observation.' Verri thought this especially creditable since he considered that most of his colleagues talked far too much anyway. Firmian reported:

Everyone was struck by the clarity of his ideas, the soundness of his reasoning, the penetration of his mind and the readiness of his grasp. He always spoke with the greatest respect of Your Sacred Majesty, on every subject he said that he hadn't come to decide anything, but only to inform himself and to put himself in the position to make a faithful and exact report on Lombardy, Your Majesty's province. In all these committees he adopted the right method for getting to the bottom of problems, he wanted to know what was the old form of the state, then ... the present system introduced by order of Your Sacred Majesty: he brought up questions that compelled everyone to come to his opinion; he conciliated opposing views; he approved and controverted various opinions from time to time, but always with the best grace in the world and the greatest affability. I can confidently say, without fear of being accused of flattery, that he got up from each session at least as well informed about the subject as the best-informed minister.

Verri thought Joseph disguised very well his feelings about particular officials, but made his attitude on issues of principle pretty clear. He argued strongly for the end of all protection in the grain trade, and also for the abolition of the tax-farming system – in both cases against the views of most councillors. Verri entirely agreed with him about the tax-farm, but was less sure about his other economic ideas, for example:

that the chief concern should be to protect the inhabitants of the countryside; it doesn't matter much if the cost of living is high in the cities so long as it isn't in the fields. Population is best not huddled together, but spread as uniformly as possible over the face of the earth. He prefers numerous small manufacturing units in many houses to vast, elaborate firms contained in one building. It seems that he aims at making a large number of men happy rather than limiting wealth to a few. All his speeches breathe goodness, beneficence, paternal care for the people.[86]

Joseph's private opinion of the council of finances makes an interesting comparison:

[85] Arneth, *GMT* VII, pp. 471–2; Valsecchi, *L'assolutismo illuminato*, vol. II, pp. 292, 315–16, 323; J. to M.T., 6 June 1769 (Arneth, *MTuJ* I, p. 290); HHSA FA Hofreisen I, fasz. 2A.
[86] Valsecchi, *L'assolutismo illuminato*, vol. II, pp. 292–7, 307; Greppi and Giulini, *Carteggio di P. e di A. Verri*, vol. II, esp. pp. 334–9.

[It] seems to me to consist of innovators and of people not very well informed, especially in legal affairs ... The president seems well-educated but superficial, like Lothringer, Neny and la Tour. They are hard foreigners who show no consideration. Montani, Verri and particularly Pellegrini are more moderate and have infinitely more knowledge, especially the last ... I do not understand what good this council will be able to do, and it costs a lot and is disliked.[87]

It was surprising enough that the emperor should prove so informal, so reasonable and so approachable at committee meetings. It was 'extraordinary and unnecessary' that he should positively request his subjects, whatever their station in life, to call on him and present petitions.[88] Firmian told Maria Theresa:

Every day after the meetings the emperor gave public audiences, which always lasted until 3 o'clock and sometimes until 3.30, after which the emperor sat down at table. Everyone without exception was admitted to these audiences. The number was incredible. Nearly 5000 petitions were presented to the emperor. HM was gracious enough to entrust them to me, with the order that a short summary should be prepared of them, and a short reply to each. We are working at this as diligently as possible. I have orders to send them on to him at Vienna, so that he can present them to YM.

... One of the most remarkable was that submitted by the *Congregazione dello Stato*, which the emperor allowed to be read in his presence at one of the early meetings ... All these strong complaints embodied in this document manifestly tend to overturn good order, to nullify the tax-survey bit by bit, to weaken the sovereign authority ...

Almost all the complaints are either without any foundation, or of such a nature that they could easily be put right if people would take the trouble to ask for the redress of grievances, with full details. But people fight shy of detail, they like complaining, it has been the custom in this country since the rule of Charles V. People believe that someone who speaks up and complains excites pity. I'm sure that, the more these grievances are redressed, especially when not genuine, the more the complaints will increase ...

One of the petitioners had been caught out forging a letter from Firmian, and was imprisoned. The minister was convinced that many of the complaints had been orchestrated by a few trouble-makers. But he took comfort from the belief that 'the emperor has found out for himself that the nation is naturally given to griping, that it doesn't like its abuses, which it calls its rights, being tampered with'.[89]

Joseph, however, though no doubt sceptical about some petitions, attached immense importance to them. He insisted that all of them – except begging letters, which he burned – should be treated seriously.[90] In his *Relation* he wrote:

[87] Valsecchi, *L'assolutismo illuminato*, vol. II, p. 328 (J.'s diary, 11 July).
[88] Langlois to Rochford, 14 June 1769 (PRO SP 80/206).
[89] Valsecchi, *L'assolutismo illuminato*, vol. II, pp. 311–13.
[90] J. to M.T., 4 June 1769 (Arneth *MTuJ* I, pp. 285–6).

This tax-farm is in truth the object that the whole land views with horror. Great and small, there is only one opinion about it, and more than 4000 memorials that I have received, of which certainly three-quarters concern complaints against the farm, prove it.

He considered it positively desirable that subjects should be able to go behind the back of the provincial government and state their case direct to Vienna.[91] He never fully trusted officials.

His *Relation* was accompanied by thirty-nine supporting papers that he had commissioned or obtained while in Italy. Much of it concerned the tax-farm. Clearly Joseph felt about the farmers somewhat as he felt about the bureaucratic shareholders in the Banat. He was consistently hostile to any system under which individuals profited personally from public duties, other than through fixed salaries and pensions. He had found powerful support for this approach in the petitions of the inhabitants. He claimed that the regulations controlling trade and manufacturers in the interests of the farm were so restrictive and complex that 'ten innocents are harassed to find one guilty'.[92]

On other matters Joseph urged on his mother points of view which often, though not always, amounted to criticisms of her administration. As Verri expected, the emperor argued that the grain trade ought to be quite untrammelled. He was appalled by the variety of weights and measures found in one small territory. Whereas the government disliked the ancient Senate, the highest judicial body of the province, Joseph considered that, properly reformed, its position should be strengthened. Only on ecclesiastical questions did he come close to approving Kaunitz's policies. Joseph endorsed the efforts of the *Giunta economale* to limit the wealth and numbers of religious institutions, though it was 'doubtless viewed with horror both at the Court of Rome and therefore by all the clergy'. But he thought it had behaved too violently towards the Charterhouse at Pavia, and ought to soften its methods.[93]

In two ciphered passages of letters to his brother, Pietro Verri described what he believed to be the emperor's true situation and intentions.

Caesar can do nothing, as I'll show. While he's here, despatches keep on coming in. One prescribes the reciprocal lowering of tariffs between Germany and ourselves, of which a few days ago Joseph was expressing disapproval. Another praises Greppi, [the friend of the tax-farmers,] whom he considers at fault. Redaelli, who denounced the farm to Vienna, has been imprisoned, though he was daily in Caesar's antechamber . . . Caesar has done nothing that suggests he commands; he listens to everything and decides nothing.

On the other hand,

91 Italian *Relation* (HHSA FA Sbde 88), ff. 10v, 20v–21r.   92 *Ibid.*, f. 13v.
93 *Ibid.*, ff. 8v–9r, 16v–19r.

This journey of Caesar's has been undertaken in order to discover, in maladministration and especially in the favour shown to the farmers, weapons with which to fight Kaunitz. The empress, jealous of her authority, will find that the minister, precisely because he is ill-regarded by her son, must be upheld.[94]

The first piece of analysis is certainly correct: while in Lombardy, Joseph was permitted to find facts and make recommendations, but had absolutely no delegated power to take decisions. The second, if perhaps exaggerated, came very near the bone.

It is doubtful how far Joseph was familiar with the internal affairs of Lombardy before he visited it. When he insisted that the secret instructions to the *Giunta economale* be read out to him, and highly approved of them, it sounds almost as though he was hearing them for the first time.[95] But there was much pretence in the very nature of these sessions intended to give information to the already knowledgeable co-regent. He certainly learned much, from officials and petitioners, that he could not have known before. More important, until he went to Milan, it was especially difficult for him to influence the affairs of the province, since they were controlled by Kaunitz and excluded from the competence of the *Staatsrat*. The visit and the *Relation* arising from it gave the emperor unquestioned standing in the matter. Kaunitz hastened to come round to his view about the farm, and it was abolished at the end of 1770.[96]

During 1771, in preparation for the arrival of Ferdinand as viceroy, plans were being made to reorganise the administration in Milan. Firmian, Verri and other local officials deliberated about it, then came to Vienna to consult Kaunitz and his colleagues, and eventually made proposals. Joseph wrote to Leopold in August 1771:

The arrangements about the departments at Milan, which have been considered and discussed for three months, have finally appeared. They are a mass of verbiage. It's the most complicated system I've ever seen in my life. Imagine: nine departments or *aulae separatae*, three of justice, four of finance and commerce, a council of government, and one for ecclesiastical matters. I expressed my view at great length. HM and prince Kaunitz were sympathetic. I've reduced all these elements to three, that is, justice, finance . . . and the accounts department . . .[97]

Difficulties continued over personalities and with Ferdinand, but in September a scheme essentially like Joseph's was carried into effect. In fact, the nine

---

[94] Letters of 8 July and 1 July 1769 (Greppi and Giulini, *Carteggio di P. e di A. Verri*, vol. II, pp. 352–3, 341).
[95] Valsecchi, *L'assolutismo illuminato*, vol. II, p. 309 (Firmian's report).
[96] Arneth, *GMT* x, pp. 191, 782.
[97] J. to L., 8 Aug. 1771 (HHSA FA Sbde 7, not printed by Arneth (!)). See also J. to L., 12 Aug., 19 Sep. and 23 Sep., all omitted by Arneth.
  K.'s response to the Italian *Relation* is in ÖNB Handschriften Ser. n. 1612.

bodies were reduced to five: the *Giunta economale* and a commission on trade remained independent.

It would be natural to suppose that the emperor had exaggerated his part in this coup if Verri had not given him full credit for it in a most circumstantial account written at the time. He describes how Kaunitz's officials both in Vienna and Milan cooked up the initial scheme, which the chancellor idly endorsed. Verri alone opposed it, as too complex, and in particular because it divided the Senate into two chambers, civil and criminal, thus destroying its ancient form and authority. He approached Joseph who, according to Verri, although successful in getting the tax-farm abolished, had failed in an attempt to get Firmian moved, and felt he had to tread very warily. At first he would not see Verri alone, then said that nothing could be done unless Maria Theresa formally asked his opinion. At last she did so, not wishing

to ignore her son when it was a question of founding a new system of finance, something he had recommended in a province he had visited and got to know. So she let him see all the papers. The emperor stayed up the whole night studying them and writing his opinion. He reorganised everything from its foundations. He rejected the principle of establishing so many departments as bad in policy, especially in a small province. Their multiple jurisdictions would cut across each other, slow down the conduct of business, be the despair of those who had to deal with them, and cause those seeking justice or assistance to be shunted indefinitely from one tribunal to another without obtaining what they need. He proposed as a principle that all affairs involving justice and jurisprudence should go to the Senate, whether concerning commerce, *Regalie* or contraband. Then all merely administrative matters to go before the *Magistrato camerale*. The accounts department would be composed of a president and some accountants to audit the accounts of every office . . .
The empress . . . adopted Caesar's plan.[98]

Soon after the decision in principle to accept his scheme, he went to Bohemia. During his absence, modifications were made, and people were appointed of whom he disapproved. But here was an encounter he had won – a fact of which he showed himself both conscious and proud. Among the by-products of the reform was a reduction in the power of Firmian; and it was laid down that Ferdinand as viceroy should possess little independence. In the words of professor Valsecchi, the greatest authority on these matters, 'Absolutism . . . desires a government at Milan, not a governor; Joseph II is preparing docile instruments for future reforms.'[99] But he wished to limit the power of the bureaucracy not only against Vienna but also against the locally recruited aristocratic institutions. Verri called Joseph 'a firm friend of the Senate'.[100]

[98] Letter or memorandum, presumably of late 1771, in Greppi and Giulini, *Carteggio di P. e di A. Verri*, vol. III, pp. 311–42; more accessibly but less correctly in C. Casati (ed.), *Lettere e scritti inediti di Pietro e di Alessandro Verri* (4 vols., Milan, 1881), pp. 139–86, quotation from pp. 171–2.
[99] Valsecchi, *L'assolutismo illuminato*, vol. II, pp. 185–94, quotation from p. 194.
[100] Casati, *Lettere e scritti*, p. 175.

That the emperor was able to make these changes was a direct product of his travelling. Only his Italian visit had given him standing in the matter, and provided him with the knowledge and contacts to bring his influence effectively to bear. The new system was cheaper and simpler than that proposed by the officials. It also vindicated the symbolism of the Batoni portrait. Here was the emperor, following Montesquieu, asserting the principle of the separation of powers.

It was even suggested that his activity in Milan had led to reforms in other states. The British representative in Venice reported home in September 1769 that a new magistracy was being established on the Terraferma to remedy abuses in its government. He claimed that the step would never have been taken but for Joseph's long visit rousing

them from their indifference; the accurate informations he took of everything relative to this Country: the pleasure he was observed to express in regard to the fineness of the climate, & fertility of the soil; the antient claims on great part of their State, lately reviv'd by the publication of a treatise in Germany, investigating that jealous subject; the vicinity of Trieste, said to be the Emperor's favourite place, with Istria on the one side, & Friuli on the other; the apprehensions they are under, after the death of the Emp. Queen, from that active & enterprizing Prince.[101]

[101] Richie to Weymouth, 1 Sep. 1769 (PRO SP 99/74).

CHAPTER 9

Foreign policy during the co-regency:
I. The eastern question, 1765–1776

Almost every historian has condemned Joseph's foreign policy as exceptionally aggressive. In the 1850s Sybel called him

an unscrupulous conqueror, [who] engages in quarrels along the whole line of his
extensive frontiers, never allows a weaker neighbour to rest, or knows how to be at
peace with a stronger; and at last fills half the world with the tumult of his arms.[1]

In the 1880s Sorel asserted that the emperor aimed at the partition of Poland,
'the annihilation, or at least the dismemberment, of Prussia', 'the dismemberment of the Venetian republic', the annexation of Bavaria and, in conjunction
with Catherine II, 'the conquest of the Ottoman Empire'.[2] Even the most
sober and scholarly twentieth-century historians speak of his desire for
aggrandisement, his 'restless imperialist ambitions' and his 'hunger for
territorial expansion'.[3] Crankshaw writes:

he harboured dreams of glory: unlike any of his Habsburg ancestors for centuries past,
he thought in terms of territorial aggrandisement through war and was determined to
prove himself as a brilliant commander in the field.[4]

Padover described his foreign policy as 'violent and crude, worthy of a
medieval robber baron'.[5] E. N. Williams may stand as the representative of
those who believe that all the emperor's internal reforms 'were designed
ultimately to make larger revenues and more powerful armies available for the
pursuit of an aggressive foreign policy'.[6]

It is generally argued that, while it was during his sole reign that Joseph's
aggressiveness ran wild, his aims during the co-regency had been the same.

[1] H. von Sybel, *History of the French Revolution* (English translation of the 3rd German edition),
vol. 1 (London, 1867), p. 195.
[2] A. Sorel, *Europe and the French Revolution*, trans. and ed. A. Cobban and J. W. Hunt (London,
1969), esp. pp. 479–84.
[3] E.g. Mitrofanov 1, p. 117; Macartney, *Habsburg Empire*, pp. 130–2; L. Gershoy, *From
Despotism to Revolution, 1763–1789* (New York, 1944), p. 181; M. S. Anderson in *NCMH* VIII,
p. 272.
[4] E. Crankshaw, *The Habsburgs* (London, 1971), p. 190.
[5] Padover, *Revolutionary Emperor*, p. 232.
[6] E. N. Williams, *The Ancien Régime in Europe* (Harmondsworth, 1972), p. 457.

Then, however, the story goes, he had been held in check by the pacific attitude of Maria Theresa and by the moderating influence of Kaunitz.[7]

In his first memorandum of 1761, however, we have seen that he had expressed his dread of a war on more than one front. In the paper of 1766 entitled *Si vis pacem para bellum*, he had not only repeated this point; he had doubted the Monarchy's capacity to survive unaided against Prussia alone.[8] Before considering his part in the making of foreign policy during the co-regency, it is natural to look at what he has to say on external affairs in the 'General picture', which embodies his fullest discussion of these matters, and in particular to see whether his views appear any more aggressive in that document than in his earlier writings.

FOREIGN POLICY IN THE 'GENERAL PICTURE'

Joseph starts from the 'exhaustion and weakness' of the Monarchy at the end of the Seven Years War, and the slowness of its recovery. It must therefore 'have as its first object in all its political actions the preservation of peace'. To this end a good system of foreign policy must be associated with 'internal arrangements which inspire respect, but not alarm, in our neighbours'. To avoid war, it is necessary to 'maintain a certain political leverage, and to speak in a tone neither too feeble nor too imperious'. It would be equally inappropriate to be without allies, and to try too hard to attract some. So the present policy is 'to be on good terms with everyone, to form no new connexions, and to keep up the old ones, never to forget our natural enemy', to act straightforwardly and amicably with our allies, but not to submit blindly to their views. The ministry has conducted itself wisely, moderately and consistently; and so far peace has been preserved.

The French alliance 'still subsists with the same sincerity and cordiality on both sides'. The main reason why it has brought greater advantages than the old connexion with the maritime Powers is this:

So long as we were allied with the latter, we were exposed to three powerful enemies, namely the kings of Prussia, France and Spain, all three of whom were interested in making conquests, attacked us in three different areas and compelled us to divide our forces. When we concentrated them, as is natural, towards the centre, our distant provinces were at once delivered to the mercy of our enemies. The peace treaties were always to our disadvantage. England had even stated perfectly clearly that she would never contribute to humble our greatest enemy.

If the Monarchy had maintained this alliance, it would infallibly have lost Belgium and Lombardy, while receiving from England nothing but cavalier treatment and fitful subsidies.

[7] E.g. *ibid.*, pp. 457–9, 479; Padover, *Revolutionary Emperor*, ch. 5; Blanning, *J. II*, pp. 82–5; Macartney, *M.T. and the House of Austria*, pp. 140–7.
[8] See above, pp. 95–6, 186.

By contrast, our present alliance secures our distant provinces. Thus covered, we can concentrate our forces against our first enemy, the king of Prussia. We have only him to fear, and he alone could be in the position to make conquests from us. By the weight France has [with Turkey] we are also secured on that side.

France even sends sizeable subsidies.[9] The alliance is 'one of the greatest *coups d'état* a minister has ever made'. It is to be cemented by a marriage between Louis XV's heir and Joseph's sister, Marie Antoinette.

Between 1765 and 1768 the only general developments of any significance have been negative. The Monarchy has declined an alliance with Spain, not wishing to provoke the formation of a rival league. An Austrian proposal, that in any war between France and England the neutrality of the Monarchy should be recognised, has failed through French coolness.[10]

This somewhat complacent picture of the Monarchy's international position and of the advantages accruing to it from the French alliance is partially corrected in Joseph's subsequent remarks, which are arranged by country. In his general discussion of the French alliance, Joseph had merely summarised the main arguments Kaunitz always advanced in its favour, while duly praising his achievement in making it. But under 'France' he mentioned certain difficulties in the relationship between the two Powers. She had shown herself extremely jealous of any rapprochement between the Monarchy and any other state, except her ally Spain.

In the affairs of the *Reich* we can by no means hope for much co-operation on the part of France; for, imbued with ancient prejudices, ... [her ministers think] that the first principle of French policy is to restrict the emperor's power.[11]

Under 'Empire' Joseph returns to the theme, listing as France's main client states in Germany Bavaria, the Palatinate, Zweibrücken and Württemberg.[12] This point contradicts one of Kaunitz's arguments for the French alliance, which he claimed neutralised the opposition to the emperor in the *Reich*.[13]

Successive British envoys in Vienna believed that Joseph had opposed the formation of the French alliance, continued to dislike it, and only awaited the opportunity to restore the old system.[14] The 'General picture' affords no evidence in support of this comforting illusion. The emperor acknowledges that since the end of the war there has been no reason to complain of Britain's

---

[9] This rather surprising remark seems to be explained by P. P. Bernard, 'Kaunitz and Austria's secret fund', *EEQ* XVI (1982), 129–36. I am most grateful to Prof. Bernard for sending me a copy of this article.

[10] HHSA TG, ff. 118–28, deals with 'affaires étrangeres et sisteme politique'.

[11] HHSA TG, ff. 128–33.

[12] HHSA TG, ff. 213–14.   [13] See K.'s memo. of 27 Sep. 1764 in Beer, *AÖG* (1872), 63–74.

[14] E.g. Keith (senior) to Holderness, 15 May and 20 Sep. 1756, cited in Coxe, *House of Austria*, vol. II, p. 390; Stormont to Grafton, 14 Sep. 1765, separate, cypher (PRO SP 80/202); Keith to Stormont, 1 July 1781, private and confidential, cypher (PRO FO 7/2).

behaviour to Austria. However, difficulties at home and in America make Britain no longer either formidable as an enemy or valuable as an ally.[15]

I quoted in a previous chapter the more violent of Joseph's comments in the 'General picture' about Prussia.[16] He also makes some surprisingly sympathetic remarks. 'If ever we could persuade [Frederick] that we have genuinely forgotten the conquest of Silesia, perhaps it would not be impossible to contract with him some solid and useful agreements, especially on subjects of mutual interest.' Frederick has his own problems: the war did not go well for him, his country too is exhausted, the succession itself seems in doubt. Joseph believes that his present intention is to maintain peace, and that he seeks no further territorial gains.[17] This is an early instance of an attitude which the emperor was often to express, usually in opposition to Kaunitz. But when Joseph was writing, as we shall see, the chancellor was himself working for a rapprochement with Prussia over Poland. The bland words of the 'General picture' gloss over a lively debate on this issue within the Vienna government.[18]

The emperor's comments on Russia and Turkey modify his statements on the uniqueness of the Prussian threat to the Monarchy. Russia, he says, protected from most of her potential enemies by convenient natural or (in the case of Poland) political barriers, well supplied with cannon fodder and raw materials, and despotically governed, is 'undoubtedly the most formidable Power in Europe', especially under the rule of so intelligent, bold and rational an empress as Catherine II. 'Imbued with a rather romantic spirit, glory and the perpetuation of her name seem to be the principal aims of her actions, rather than the solid good of her state and its peoples.'

There is no question that Russia was always one of our most natural allies, given the situation of our states, which is such that we have nothing to get embroiled about, [which] makes our enemies common, and in consequence puts us in a position to assist each other.

However, this alliance, surprisingly, has been broken. The whim of Peter III in 1762 had led to the Russian army changing sides; Catherine has remained the friend of Prussia. So the Vienna government makes every effort to please her, to avoid

exposing all our provinces at the same time, and making of her the most dangerous enemy for our Monarchy, though we always regard our allying with Russia as not only possible but also very desirable, since, if she were sincerely connected with us, that would be the true way of making peace permanent, by jointly restraining both the Turks and the king of Prussia, our common enemies, from any infringement.

---

[15] HHSA TG, ff. 138–43.   [16] See pp. 189–90 above.   [17] HHSA TG, ff. 145–53.
[18] Arneth, *GMT* VIII, pp. 138–53. See below, p. 280.

Joseph believes that in time she will revert to an Austrian alliance, since the Monarchy is potentially her most dangerous enemy.[19]

As for the Turks, they

are and will always be considered by us a very dangerous neighbour, whose power, and the great extent of their country, together with their religion, courage and attitudes, can turn them in a trice into a powerful enemy who cannot gain except from us, whereas we cannot gain anything from them in return. A Turkish war, therefore, will always be avoided by us with the greatest possible care. Even if it is successful, the money and the number of men it costs, especially through sickness, make it always very damaging, without taking into account all the provinces which are devastated, and the depopulation and infertility of those which can be conquered.

But the emperor believes that at present the Turks want peace.[20]

Poland is now dominated by Russia, which seeks still greater influence and perhaps some annexations there. The country is so anarchic and feeble that it cannot rank as a fully independent Power, and can do the Monarchy neither good nor harm, except as a buffer state against Russia and shelter against the Turks. In order to reconcile Vienna's desire to please Catherine II with its wish to maintain an independent Poland, a very moderate policy has been followed, and Russian plans will be tolerated, 'provided that no partition is made, that the Polish constitution remains more or less in the same state of inertia, and that Russian troops, . . . once affairs have been settled, do not stay in the country'.[21]

In the East, then, Joseph discloses no interest in aggrandisement. Given his later policies, his assertion that no worthwhile gain can be made from Turkey is particularly notable. Moreover, he shows surprising respect for Turkish military power. But he does declare the aim which in the long run he was able to achieve, the making of an Austro-Russian alliance. At this stage, as we shall see, his inclination towards Russia and against Turkey separated him from both Maria Theresa and Kaunitz.[22]

Although I considered earlier Joseph's approach to the Empire, I then omitted discussion of his attitude to particular German states. His most interesting points, in view of his later actions, concern Bavaria. He condemns the elector for his laziness, his subservience to France and his support of the Protestant party in the *Reich*, and mentions the 'pitiable' state of the country's finances. But the emperor says nothing about the Bavarian succession. He hopes for the sympathy of Saxony, which has every reason to oppose Prussia. He regrets the strongly Protestant and anti-imperial stance of the electorate of Hanover, ruled by king George III of England. He makes no allusion whatever to any possible annexations by the Monarchy.[23]

---

[19] HHSA TG, ff. 153–67.   [20] HHSA TG, ff. 177–80.
[21] HHSA TG, ff. 157–8, 167–71.
[22] See below, pp. 280–1.
[23] HHSA TG, ff. 235–44 deals with the lay electors. See pp. 125–9 above.

His remarks on the Italian states are more notable. He speaks of the 'smallness' of the Monarchy's possessions in Lombardy.[24] In commenting on Venice, he says that she 'has always been considered by us as grounding her policies on aggrandisement at our expense'. She also does her best to restrict the trade of Trieste. However, like all the other states of the peninsula, Venice now has to face the fact that the French alliance 'secures the tranquillity of Italy'. Sardinia has been more disconcerted by the Austro-French alliance than any other Power, since it was the essence of her policy to play off the Bourbons against the Habsburgs. But like Venice, Sardinia makes a show of cordiality towards the Monarchy. Naples, whose young king is about to marry Joseph's sister Carolina, is subservient to Spain. Parma, where another sister, Amalia, is to become the ruler's wife, is subordinate to France and Spain. Modena, by contrast, where Joseph's brother Ferdinand is to marry the duke's heiress, 'has thrown herself completely into our arms'. Behind these statements it might be thought that a desire for new annexations in Italy could be discerned.[25]

Except perhaps in these comments on Italy, the emperor shows no sign of a desire for aggrandisement, still less of having made any plans to achieve it. His whole approach is moderate, prudent and pacific. The fact that he hardly alludes to the important debates on foreign policy which were proceeding within the Vienna government while he was writing the 'General picture', and that he repeatedly refers to his hopes for a Russian alliance at a moment when Kaunitz was thoroughly alarmed at Catherine II's expansionism in Poland, seems to prove that he was trying to detach himself from the immediate problems of 1768 and to explain to Leopold his own view of the Monarchy's fundamental aims. The chancellor had obviously influenced the document,[26] but Joseph had stamped his own approach on it. It is impressive, therefore, that in this lengthy discussion of foreign affairs he displays neither the radicalism and self-assertion evident in his consideration of internal problems, nor the aggressiveness and expansionism with which he is so often credited.

THE POLISH QUESTION: INTRODUCTION

If all aspects of the Monarchy's foreign policy were to be fully treated, even only as they concerned Joseph, several volumes would have to be devoted to these matters alone. It will be necessary here to restrict attention to the main

---

[24] HHSA TG, f. 207.
[25] HHSA TG, ff. 181–97 deals with the Italian states, other than Lombardy, which is considered under a different heading (ff. 207–10), and Tuscany, which Joseph does not presume to discuss.
[26] Arneth cites (*GMT* VII, p. 526) a letter from J. to K. about the memorandum for L., which shows at least that K. knew all about it. Comparison with K.'s own memoranda (e.g. in Beer, *AÖG* (1872)) proves that the 'General picture' is not the chancellor's own work. On the other

issues, and those which best reveal the emperor's role and attitudes: within the co-regency, first and foremost, the eastern question, involving the Russo-Turkish war of 1768–74, the two meetings with Frederick the Great, the first partition of Poland in 1772 and the annexation of the Bukovina in 1775; the war of the Bavarian succession of 1778–9; the efforts to secure the election of Joseph's youngest brother, Max Franz, as coadjutor to the archbishop of Cologne; and the origins of the Russian alliance. In this chapter the eastern question will be considered. Maps 1 and 3 will help to clarify the story.

No issue is more important to an assessment of the emperor's approach to foreign affairs than the eastern question in all its ramifications, and especially the first partition of Poland. By this measure the Monarchy gained easily the largest accession of territory which it was to obtain during his lifetime, 'the kingdom of Galicia and Lodomeria'. His attitude during the long period of at least twelve years, from 1763 to 1775, when the situation of Poland and related matters were the chief preoccupation of the Monarchy's foreign policy, should provide a crucial test of his 'aggressiveness' and 'expansionism'.

The partition of Poland is a large, much-studied and controversial subject. The account which follows focusses on Joseph's role, and on this score alone is novel. But I have found myself in addition compelled to disagree with some of the opinions of previous writers on wider aspects of the Monarchy's eastern policy in these years.

Although large both in area and population, Poland had declined to a condition of internal anarchy and external impotence by the mid eighteenth century. The nobility obstructed their elected kings in any attempts to strengthen the power and increase the revenue of the government. The derisory army consisted of less than 20,000 men. The country was literally at the mercy of its well-armed neighbours, Russia, Prussia and the Monarchy.[27]

This situation became more obvious and serious when in 1762 Russia and

---

hand, J.'s muted style in the foreign affairs section suggests that he had modified it to take account of criticism from K.

[27] On Poland and the partition in general see the chapters by M. S. Anderson and L. R. Lewitter in *NCMH*, vol. IX; A. Sorel, *La Question d'orient au XVIIIe siècle* (Paris, 1880); H. H. Kaplan, *The First Partition of Poland* (New York and London, 1962) (but see J. Topolski, 'Reflections on the first partition of Poland', *Acta poloniae historica*, XXVII (1973), 89–104); B. Leśnodorski, 'Les Partages de Pologne', *Acta poloniae historica*, VIII (1963); Easum, *Prince Henry of Prussia*, ch. XVIII; the early part of R. H. Lord, *The Second Partition of Poland* (Cambridge, Mass., 1915); D. McKay and H. M. Scott, *The Rise of the Great Powers, 1648–1815* (London, 1983), esp. pp. 215–28; Madariaga, *Catherine the Great*, pt IV. Documents in K. Lutostański, *Les Partages de la Pologne et la lutte pour l'indépendance* (Lausanne and Paris, 1918).

I have learned a lot from two theses and their authors: G. T. Lukowski, 'The *Szlachta* and the Confederacy of Radom, 1764–1767/68: a study of the Polish nobility', Cambridge University PhD, 1976, and H. M. Scott, 'Anglo-Austrian relations after the Seven Years War: Lord Stormont in Vienna, 1763–1772', University of London PhD, 1977. Dr Scott generously gave me a copy of his book and read this chapter in typescript. I am very grateful for his comments.

Prussia joined forces. Augustus III, king of Poland and elector of Saxony, died in the following year, and Frederick supported Catherine's candidate at the subsequent royal election. Under Russian pressure, which included the occupation of much of the country, Stanislaus Augustus Poniatowski, a Polish noble, formerly her lover, was duly chosen to be king. Catherine maintained her troops in Poland after the coronation, in order to impose constitutional changes that would establish her as the permanent overlord of the country. Publicly at least, Frederick seconded her, and they made a formal alliance in 1764.

In Vienna, Russian domination of Poland was regarded as a major threat to the Monarchy and to the balance of power, a threat that would be enhanced by the annexations on the part of Prussia which were expected to accompany it. Kaunitz became progressively more alarmed as Russia imposed her yoke ever more firmly on Poland, and was strongly pressed by France to act against her. But for several years he could see no way of checking her, and so submitted with the best grace he could muster. The Monarchy was acknowledged to be in no condition to fight a war.[28]

An Austro-Prussian alliance would probably have restrained Catherine without the use of force. But when Frederick first hinted at such an agreement, early in 1766, Kaunitz declined the overture as premature and

---

[28] A. Beer, *Die erste Theilung Polens* (3 vols., Vienna, 1873) remains the standard work concentrating on the Austrian side, and is especially valuable for the appendix of documents in vol. II and the documents of which vol. III consists. However, about half of Arneth, *GMT* VIII is devoted to the same subject, and corrects many points of detail in Beer, while putting forward an interpretation more sympathetic to Austria and especially to M.T. Both Arneth and Beer are corrected in E. Reimann, *Neuere Geschichte des preussischen Staates*, vol. II (Gotha, 1888), esp. pp. 682–98. Beer is one of the very small number of authors who has suggested that J. was not indiscriminately aggressive, and in so doing he naturally slighted M.T. and K. Arneth makes a good case for dissociating M.T. from any desire for war or partition, but in my opinion fails to show that J. was consistently more aggressive and grasping than K. The most pertinent twentieth-century contribution is S. K. Padover's PhD thesis, 'Prince Kaunitz and the first partition of Poland', University of Chicago, 1932, which is attractively written and based on material in the Vienna archives. Padover makes some valid, but other less acceptable, points against Beer, while relying more heavily than he acknowledges on the documents Beer published. He pays little attention to the disputes between K., M.T. and J. His inclination to laconic, breezy and thinly supported judgements is exaggerated in the published summary of the thesis, 'Prince Kaunitz and the First Partition of Poland', *SR* XIII (1934–5), 384–98. I am most grateful to Dr H. M. Scott for lending me his microfilm of Padover's thesis. Roider, *Austria's Eastern Question*, chs. 7–8, is invaluable on Austro–Turkish relations.

It is plain that Austrian policy in the Polish question ought to be looked at again, esp. since Kaplan, *Partition*, is inadequately informed about it. I have of course not been able to undertake this formidable task in the context of a biography of J. But as well as the published material, I have used unpublished letters of J. to L. and K., and the reports of the British envoys in Vienna.

So far as the election of Stanislaus Augustus is concerned, I cannot regard Loebl's (*AÖG* (1903), 371–3) and Padover's ('Kaunitz' (thesis), pp. 21–2) criticism of K.'s acquiescence as realistic. See H. M. Scott, 'France and the Polish throne, 1763–1764', *SR* LIII (1975), 370–88. In general, however, Loebl's article is of great value. No other historian in the field has used such a wide range of sources; and some of his discussion is highly original and intelligent, and of wider interest than his ostensible subject.

suspect. The king then suggested a 'surprise' meeting between himself and the emperor during the latter's tour of battlefields that summer. Both Kaunitz and Joseph reacted uncertainly. When it came to the point, the emperor was without clear instructions from his mother. He therefore responded coolly, and Frederick left the district. Maria Theresa, still dreading the effect this wicked enemy might have on her son, was thankful. She was also, rather unfairly, amused that 'these princes, having forsworn all etiquette and ceremonial, took offence . . . over which should approach or invite the other, and so . . . missed what they very much desired'.[29]

Russian activity in Poland steadily increased, and early in 1768 Kaunitz came round to proposing to the empress that an agreement should be sought with Prussia to counteract it. The chancellor now accepted, or was ready to argue, that Frederick wished for peace; the king should be sweetened by an assurance that the Monarchy no longer aimed at the recovery of Silesia. Evidently Maria Theresa refused to sanction the plan at this stage. But in August Kaunitz tried again, alarmed by the news that war between Russia and Turkey was imminent. He now pressed hard for a meeting between Frederick and Joseph, with the specific aim of obtaining a mutual agreement to be neutral. This project had no immediate result, apparently because Joseph took umbrage at the chancellor's tone. Kaunitz wrote to Maria Theresa that his two letters to the emperor 'had had the misfortune to seem to him an instruction. All this confirms me more and more in the opinion that I have always held, that I am not formed to serve another master than Your Majesty.'[30]

THE MONARCHY AND THE RUSSO-TURKISH WAR, 1768–70

In October 1768 Turkey, egged on by France, presented an ultimatum to Russia demanding that she at once promise to withdraw her troops from Poland. When she refused, Turkey declared war. This step of course greatly widened the area of disturbance in eastern Europe. In Vienna it was feared that the conflict would spread, and also give occasion for Russian and perhaps Prussian aggrandisement. Kaunitz now unveiled one of his most far-reaching schemes. On 3 December, relying on some hints from Constantinople, he suggested that the Turks might be put up to propose a treaty between Prussia, Austria and themselves under which Russian influence would be checked,

[29] Beer, *Theilung*, vol. I, pp. 271–83; Arneth, *GMT* VIII, ch. 5; Beer, 'Die Zusammenkünfte Josefs II. und Friedrichs II. zu Neisse und Neustadt' *AÖG*, XLVII (1871), 385–96, 433–8 (documents); Arneth, *MTuJ* I, pp. 180–7; Loebl, *AÖG* (1903), 391–406.

[30] Beer, *Theilung*, vol. I, pp. 283–6 and vol. III, pp. 1–5 (K.'s memo. of 4 Jan. 1768); Beer, *AÖG* (1871), 396–404, 439–46 (documents); Arneth, *GMT* VIII, pp. 138–45; Loebl, *AÖG* (1903), pp. 448–50; E. Reimann, 'Friedrich der Grosse und Kaunitz im Jahre 1768', *HZ* XLII (1879), 193–212. I omit from the text three relevant but subsidiary issues: the succession in Prussia, the Confederation of Bar, and disputes in the Empire.

Silesia be recovered for the Monarchy, and Courland and perhaps Polish Prussia be presented to Prussia. He compared this proposition in importance to his original recommendation of a French alliance, and claimed that, though it might at first sight appear chimerical or even laughable, it was perfectly practicable, because it corresponded to the interests of all parties.

Joseph wrote a note on this plan. He cast all manner of doubts on it: the Turks probably cannot be trusted; they are unlikely to welcome Austrian aggrandisement; Prussia will hardly regard any territory except Saxony as a fair exchange for Silesia; and other Powers may oppose the scheme. But after these very sane and apparently annihilating objections, he described the project as 'worthy of the genius and zeal of the author, which have no parallel'. However, he thought it would be wise to arrange for the Turks to hear of it through a private channel which could if necessary be disavowed. Maria Theresa at first agreed, but later decided, in the emperor's words to Kaunitz, that 'the scheme ... should be buried in oblivion' and 'have no other result than to confirm me more and more in the perfect esteem which I have pledged to you'.[31]

Arneth gave a lead to subsequent historians in arguing that the emperor must really have favoured such a grand annexationist plan.[32] But Joseph's praise of Kaunitz can only have been ironic flattery intended to console the chancellor for the defeat of his cherished but absurd proposal. This was a case in which the emperor, using his private influence over his mother, got the better of the minister. No doubt it was easy to persuade her that the plan was preposterous. After all, even the famous French alliance had failed in its aim of recovering Silesia. Maria Theresa was evidently determined to embark on no more vast and costly schemes with uncertain prospects. But it is noticeable that, while this grand design for Austrian aggrandisement and Polish partition did not originate from Joseph, and though he had criticised it as impracticable, he showed no repugnance to it in principle. In other words, his approach was now less innocent than it had appeared to be in the 'General picture'.

It was very soon after this, in February 1769, that Joseph made notes for a Supplement to the 'General picture'. He now wrote of 'the great risk we have run, and still run, of losing this unique barrier which we have against Russia', namely Poland. Moreover,

Russia, as its power grows, will become formidable to the whole of Europe, and we especially shall always have much to fear, and little to hope except that, pushed back behind her old frontiers, she will revert to us and again seek our alliance.

31 Beer, *Theilung*, vol. I, pp. 286–99 and vol. III, pp. 262–75 (documents, incl. J.'s note (*pace* Beer's heading) on pp. 272–5); Arneth, *GMT* VIII, pp. 144–53; Loebl, *AÖG* (1903), 448–56; Reimann, *HZ* (1879), 202–7; Roider, *Austria's Eastern Question*, pp. 111–12.
32 Arneth, *GMT* VIII, p. 152.

The respect he had shown in the 'General picture' for the Turks' military strength was already giving way to uncertainty whether they would successfully combat Russia. But his anxiety to maintain the integrity of Poland had only grown.[33]

After the outbreak of war between Russia and Turkey, the Monarchy strengthened early in 1769 the cordon on its eastern borders. This raises a murky question, into which it is necessary to enter because Austrian action in this context brought the partition of Poland nearer and because the emperor has been held responsible.[34]

The line chosen for the cordon was evidently generous to the Monarchy, and in some cases intentionally so. It may be significant that one of Joseph's notes for the Supplement to the 'General picture' runs: 'Progress of colonisation in the Banat. Necessity to increase it in order to strengthen and extend our cordon there.'[35] But the force of the word translated as 'extend' is doubtful. The most important case of deliberate encroachment concerned the area known to western historians as Zips. This district was in the possession of Poland because it had been mortgaged to her by Hungary in 1412; but it had never been actually ceded. It was almost completely surrounded by Hungarian territory. Maria Theresa and her predecessors had repeatedly promised to act on demands from Hungarian diets that Zips should be recovered.[36] Well-informed observers took this claim into consideration when discussing the Polish question in the middle sixties.[37] When in 1767–8 Russian interference in Polish affairs provoked opposition leading to civil war, a real risk developed that Hungary would be drawn into conflict by way of Zips, and the king of Poland himself proposed that the Monarchy's troops should occupy the district, in order to frustrate the efforts of his opponents to take advantage of its situation. But Kaunitz would not use the argument of the king's request, since to have done so would have weakened Hungary's claim to sovereignty and would have violated the neutrality that Maria Theresa had promised to observe in the affairs of Poland.[38] There were other pressures involved. Local

[33] The notes for a 'Supplement au tableau general des affaires de la Monarchie, fait en 1768' (see p. 125, n. 36 above) are concerned with the remainder of that year and the very beginning of 1769, and must have been composed in February 1769 since the death of pope Clement XIII (2 Feb. 1769) is the latest event mentioned in them. If, as seems likely, the Supplement was never completed, it was presumably because J. left for his hastily arranged visit to Italy and his brother on 3 March 1769. See pp. 255–9.
     Quotations from ff. 27 and 29 of the notes for the 'Supplement'.
[34] On the general issue Arneth, *GMT* VIII, pp. 170–2, 295; Beer, *Theilung*, vol. II, p. 48; Kaplan, *Partition*, p. 111 (inaccurate).
[35] HHSA 'Supplement', f. 3.
[36] Arneth, *GMT* VIII, p. 295; H. Glassl, 'Der Rechtsstreit um die Zips vor ihrer Rückgliederung an Ungarn', *Ungarn-Jahrbuch* I (1969), 24–5.
[37] Loebl, *AÖG* (1903), 372; and cf. 417, and the rather inconclusive references there given to Frederick the Great's correspondence.
[38] Arneth, *GMT* VIII, pp. 171–2.

Hungarian landlords and the local administration had been urging action. Lacy wanted the district occupied,[39] no doubt influenced by the soldiers on the spot. The whole issue was complicated by the fact that the cordon had a second purpose, sometimes seen as the more important, namely to keep out the plague, which had recently broken out in Poland. Joseph himself took a direct interest in this aspect, as well as in the military side, after his visit to the Banat in the spring of 1768.[40] For whatever complex of reasons, Kaunitz gave orders in July 1768 that Zips should somehow be taken over, but ostensibly on local initiative.[41] When the cordon was advanced early in 1769, the district was included within it. While the rights of Poland were publicly acknowledged, Kaunitz explicitly recommended an assertion of the Monarchy's sovereignty.[42] How far Joseph was involved is impossible to say. The orders were sent to him for approval while he was travelling in Italy.[43] But it seems plain that at this stage all the principals in Vienna agreed with the men on the spot that the occupation was desirable.

In the summer of 1770 the Austrian cordon was further extended to include a small additional tract of Poland to which Hungarian claims had just been unearthed locally. The orders were given by Maria Theresa in the middle of July. Kaunitz had opposed the step, but some members of the *Staatsrat* had recommended that the Monarchy should seize this unique opportunity for aggrandisement when Poland was helpless. They had also suggested that the responsibility should be officially shifted on to the local administration, which could stress the risk from the plague. The army officers chiefly concerned on the spot, Török and Seeger, had urged the occupation with arguments about 'natural frontiers' and the requirements of defence. Probably more important, Joseph, during his Hungarian journey in company with Lacy, visited the district on 9 June. He declared in his diary of the trip: 'So far as the frontiers are concerned, we should be completely within our rights ... To redeem the thirteen towns would be very useful. They yield 15,000 ducats ...; the

---

[39] P. Skwarzyński, Review of Kaplan, *First Partition of Poland*, SR XLII (1963–4), 221–5; Glassl, *Ungarn-Jahrbuch* (1969), 36–7.

[40] The plague cordon is considered rather summarily in G. E. Rothenberg, 'The Austrian sanitary cordon and the control of the bubonic plague: 1710–1871', *Journal of the History of Medicine and Allied Sciences*, XXVIII (1973), 15–23; more fully in Lesky, *AÖG* (1959), esp. 59–67. But the Zips affair is not mentioned in these articles. See F. X. Linzbauer, *Codex sanitario-medicinalis* (3 vols., Budapest, 1852–61), vol. II, pp. 461–2: a decree of 25 July 1768 and a *Handbillet* to Lacy of 10 Jun. 1768 involving the military in drawing the sanitary cordon. I owe thanks to Professor D. Kosáry for this reference. Glassl, *Ungarn-Jahrbuch* (1969), esp. 24, 36. Cf. above, p. 248 on J. and the Banat.

[41] Padover, 'Kaunitz' (thesis), pp. 27–8. Glassl, *Ungarn-Jahrbuch* (1969), 36.

[42] Arneth, *GMT* VIII, p. 172; Stormont to Rochford, 12 Apr. 1769 (PRO SP 80/206); Glassl, *Ungarn-Jahrbuch* (1969), 37.

[43] Arneth, *GMT* VIII, p. 565 dates the orders to Apr. 1769. I assume it is to these that M.T. refers in a note to Lacy of 22 Apr: 'der kayser aprobirt all dise Vorrückungs Veränderungen die vorgeschlagen werden' (HHSA NL, Karton 6).

inhabitants themselves assured me that they would be pleased to see it.'[44] Clearly, Joseph and Lacy and those on the spot prevailed over Kaunitz. But Maria Theresa still wrote in October, 'I have a very poor opinion of our titles', and Kaunitz agreed.[45] However, at first the newly occupied district was not declared annexed. Then in November its administrator, Török, described it on his seal as 'reincorporated'. This seems consistent with the orders given in July, but was taken as a novel assertion of sovereignty by both Frederick and Catherine, and alarmed Maria Theresa and Kaunitz. Whether Joseph had any part in this incident seems undiscoverable.[46] In the Zips affair as a whole, he had evidently favoured a forward policy, but in common with many others.

Meanwhile, Kaunitz had been pursuing his scheme for a meeting between Frederick and the emperor. The chancellor won over both Maria Theresa and Joseph, and the two rulers finally met at Neisse in Silesia from 25 to 28 August 1769. It was a highly interesting occasion, about which participants and observers wrote copiously. But so far as politics was concerned, little of substance was achieved. The emperor had been supplied with elaborate instructions by the chancellor. As directed, he renounced any desire to recover Silesia, agreed that the Russian domination of Poland was most disturbing, stressed that Vienna wished to avoid war, and encouraged Frederick in his own pacific statements. Some other anticipated topics never came up for discussion: Joseph was spared stating a view on the Bavarian succession or asserting, as instructed, that the reconquest of Belgrade would not be worth the cost involved. All that was committed to paper was a joint declaration of neutrality in any war between France and England. Although Joseph agreed to a modification of the draft which Kaunitz had supplied, the chancellor persuaded himself that the document was still harmless; and he was able to congratulate Maria Theresa on the distrust which the emperor had come to entertain of the underlying motives of the inveterate enemy. Both sides considered the interview held out hopes of closer co-operation; but Prussia rather than the Monarchy benefited, since the meeting helped to encourage Catherine to renew her alliance with Frederick.[47] However, it is significant that Joseph's love of travel, his desire to make the personal acquaintance of

---

[44] HHSA FA Hofreisen 2. I do not think this reference has been previously noticed.

[45] Arneth, *GMT* VIII, pp. 299, 588.

[46] For the paragraph Arneth, *GMT* VIII, pp. 296–303, 587–90; Beer, *Theilung*, vol. II, pp. 48–50, 327; Kotasek, *Lacy*, pp. 138–9; Kaplan, *Partition*, pp. 126–7; Glassl, *Ungarn-Jahrbuch* (1969), 39–50.
    Arneth concludes that J. must have been responsible for the adoption of the offending title by the administrator (*GMT* VIII, p. 299). But direct evidence seems to be lacking.
    A comprehensive edict about the sanitary cordon for Hungary had been issued on 14 Dec. 1769 (Linzbauer, *Codex*, vol. II, pp. 499–508).

[47] Beer, *AÖG* (1871), 400–20, 446–71 (documents); Arneth, *GMT* VIII, ch. 7 and pp. 192–5; Arneth, *MTuJ* I, pp. 300–15. Cf. Padover, 'Kaunitz' (thesis), p. 42, where K.'s attitude to the neutrality declaration seems to be misunderstood. See Plate 15a.

other rulers, and his affability, had been channelled into the service of Kaunitz's policies.

For the next year and more, the Vienna government devoted most of its effort in foreign policy to various projects of mediation between Russia and Turkey, involving negotiations not only with Prussia but also with France and England. These plans were in general supported by Joseph and Kaunitz, but disliked by Maria Theresa.[48]

The official standpoint of Austria during this period was that she hoped to keep out of the war herself, and devoutly wished for its end; but she would not be able to approve terms of peace which left Catherine with more than small gains. As we have seen, Joseph regretted and Kaunitz dreaded the aggrandisement of Russia. They both attached great importance to keeping her at a distance. So they wished to preserve not only Poland, but also the semi-independent Turkish principalities of Moldavia and Wallachia, as buffer-states. They were even reluctant to see Catherine's troops established on the Black Sea coast, or her ships permitted to sail freely on the sea itself, and talked of the Khanate of the Crimea as yet another buffer-state which it was important to the Monarchy's interests to keep under Turkish suzerainty.

During 1770 Russia made matters worse by conquering most of Moldavia and Wallachia, and by driving the Turks from most of the northern shores of the Black Sea. The Ottoman Empire now seemed riper for partition than Poland. But Vienna continued to insist that Russia's gains must be limited. If Catherine would not make a reasonable peace and achieved still greater successes in the war – certainly if she threatened to destroy the Ottoman Empire altogether, and perhaps if her troops merely crossed the Danube – then Austria, it was said, would feel compelled to intervene by force. It was commonly also stated that alternatively, though only if absolutely necessary, large Russian gains might be acceptable on condition that the Monarchy was 'compensated' to preserve the balance of power.[49]

Another meeting between the emperor and the king of Prussia took place at Neustadt in Moravia from 3 to 7 September 1770. Vienna hoped to concert with Frederick a plan of mediation. On this occasion Kaunitz accompanied Joseph, and did almost all the talking – more than Frederick liked. The emperor was left to show off his troops in torrential rain. The encounter had even less tangible effect than the previous one, but Maria Theresa later

---

[48] Beer, *Theilung*, vol. I, ch. 8; Arneth, *GMT* VIII, and esp. ch. 8 and pp. 232–41; Stormont to Rochford, 14 Feb. 1770, private, cypher, and 7 Apr. 1770, private (PRO SP 80/207).

[49] As well as the references in the previous note, see the statements to the British envoys by K. (Stormont to Rochford, 10 Feb. 1770, cypher, PRO SP 80/207) and M.T. (same to same, 9 June 1770, private, cypher, *ibid.*, and Stormont to Halifax, 1 July 1771, private, by Rev. Mr Shuttleworth, PRO SP 80/209).

On the question of the Khanate of the Crimea, there is a valuable book in English: A. W. Fisher, *The Russian Annexation of the Crimea, 1772–1783* (Cambridge, 1970).

concluded that 'this pompous interview' had helped Frederick to inveigle her into the policy which led to partition.[50]

By the end of 1770 Catherine had made it plain that she would not accept peaceful mediation on any terms so far tabled. Kaunitz now argued that the time had come when the Monarchy must take up arms against the Russian menace. Catherine appeared to insist that she should retain control of Poland and obtain possession of some Black Sea ports, while at least the Crimea and perhaps also Moldavia and Wallachia should become 'independent'. These changes, Kaunitz maintained, must be prevented, because they would too greatly disturb the European balance of power, to the special disadvantage of the Monarchy. It was to be hoped that Prussia would join with Austria in opposing them. If so, a force should be sent into Poland to 'restore order' there, and should then proceed eastwards to impose mediation on Russia by threatening her army from the rear. The unfortunate Turks would be expected to bear the expenses of the operation, and would cede at least a portion of Wallachia to the Monarchy as a token of their gratitude. The king of Poland, equally grateful for his deliverance from Russian vassalage, would yield up Courland to Prussia and accept Hungarian claims to Zips and the other occupied districts. Kaunitz recognised that Frederick might well not agree to join in this expedition. If he would not, then perhaps he would be willing to remain neutral while Austria acted alone. In that case the Monarchy might still expect to receive its portion of Wallachia from the Turks as a reward.[51]

The debate on this proposal was fierce, since it was seen as deciding not merely the future policy, but perhaps also the fate, of the Monarchy. Joseph contributed at least four memoranda on the subject between 23 November 1770 and 27 February 1771. In the first he addressed himself to the question whether the Monarchy's resources would be equal to such enterprises as Kaunitz had in mind. He drew a frightening picture of the dangers and difficulties of a long march through Poland into Russia, and of the costs and internal dislocation that any such campaign would inevitably involve for the Monarchy. He concluded that it would be utterly irresponsible to act without the full co-operation of Prussia.[52] In a letter to Leopold in December, Joseph explained that he knew very well Frederick would never take part. He went on

50 Beer, *AÖG* (1871), 420–32, 495–527 (documents); Beer, *Theilung*, vol. I, ch. 8; Arneth, *GMT* VIII, ch. 8 and p. 601.
51 Beer, *Theilung*, vol. II, pp. 1–8; Arneth, *GMT* VIII, pp. 244–50.
52 Arneth, *GMT* VIII, pp. 242–4, for a summary of the memorandum of 23 Nov. 1770.

to relay Maria Theresa's decision, that a resolution drafted by himself should be the basis of instructions to the Austrian minister in Berlin. The emperor's idea was to let Russia and Turkey fight it out for another campaign, in the hope that Catherine's victories would cease. If not, and if her troops crossed the Danube, then the Monarchy would be compelled to act; and orders had been given to assemble 50,000 men and borrow four million florins, ready for that contingency. But the emperor said he did not expect it to arrive. He claimed that his mother

has to contend in these great and important decisions with the same spirit of indecision, which makes me useful sometimes; she has been entirely of my opinion in this affair, very much wishing, like me, not to get involved, and to let things sort themselves out . . .[53]

Since this decision did not prove to be final, Joseph wrote another memorandum on 14 January. He continued to insist that the Monarchy must not attempt to confront Russia either on its own, or just with the support of Turkey. But he now proposed throwing the whole decision into Frederick's hands, and telling the Turks so. If Prussia proved willing to help, the Monarchy would gain one way; if Prussia would not, the Turks would lose their trust in Frederick, and the Monarchy would gain another way. Meanwhile, troop movements and military preparations should be given 'an appearance of more publicity, without however showing too much ostentation'. He listed the appropriate military measures under thirteen heads. All this would 'keep Russia in uncertainty whether she would be attacked, Prussia in doubt whether she would be forced ... to declare for or against, and [Turkey] in hopes of being solidly supported'. If in the end the Ottoman Empire were destroyed or had to submit to a humiliating peace, the Monarchy would surely be able to seize and retain some eastern provinces in compensation for Russian expansion.[54]

Joseph wrote to his brother a few days later, as the disputes dragged on:

I leave you to judge how my zeal for the state's welfare suffers. I cannot give up my system; it seems to me good and safe from every point of view ... If the decision is for outright war [against Russia], I shall carry it out, but I shall protest in writing about all the unhappy results which I think will inevitably follow. If the intention is to do nothing at all, and leave everything to chance and display such great weakness, I tell

[53] J. to L., 14 Dec. 1770 (Arneth, *MTuJ* I, pp. 316–19) (for Arneth's own correction of the date from 18 Dec., see *GMT* VIII, p. 583).

[54] Beer, *Theilung*, vol. III, pp. 11–23. Cf. J. to L., 10 Jan. 1771 (Arneth, *MTuJ* I, pp. 321–3). It is extraordinary how accurately Stormont reported this dispute, esp. in his despatch to Rochford, secret, cypher, 'by a private conveyance', 2 Jan. 1771 (PRO SP 80/209), in which he quoted a phrase which J. was to use in his memo. of 14 Jan., that Bosnia and Serbia might be seized 'as a Deposit' ('en depôt'). However, Stormont thought this was being proposed by J. for immediate action, whereas the emperor suggested it only if Turkey was about to collapse. See p. 289 below.

you that I shall be obliged to make some demonstration, and let the public know thereby that I am no party to it.[55]

At the end of January Maria Theresa approved the notion of an approach to Prussia and Turkey, but not on the lines Joseph had proposed. The two Powers were to be informed, in rather different terms, that the Monarchy would go to war with Russia if the existence of the Ottoman Empire was threatened. The Turks were to be offered a defensive 'concert' under which they would pay subsidies to Austria and cede her some territory. Frederick was to be asked to promise neutrality in a personal letter. The empress accepted most of the thirteen points, including the despatch of troops to Hungary, but not the emperor's more adventurous plans for recruitment or his suggestion that the army be officially told that they were to expect marching orders shortly. She told Kaunitz: 'You will be displeased with me that I have accepted the emperor's advice not to go to war against Russia'; 'I trust you to see that these dispositions do not lead us to a war, but only to peace.'[56]

I have already quoted portions of her astonishing letter of 1 March 1771 to the marquise d'Herzelles, in which she denounced Joseph's attitude to herself and to religion. She went on to talk about foreign policy just as frankly:

This courier is proof that I cannot prevent evils. For a year I have stopped any intervention in the war. I am the first to admit that policy entered into it less than my fears of a war and of the consequences to be expected of it. Last year I won ..., [and trusted] that this winter we should have peace. But unhappily all [hope] has vanished, and here am I on my own in opposition to these longings to make a name for himself; and what I decide makes my situation worse. In the end I think I shall even be blamed for being jealous of his fame. I was induced to approve a camp in Hungary, of 30,000 men; that was three months ago, and only for the security of our frontiers. Little by little it has been pushed up to 60,000, always on specious grounds ... This courier bears marching orders for three regiments from the Netherlands ... I tried protesting and even delaying the orders for a month, but I had to give in against my better judgement, since the whole plan communicated to the Turks and the king of Prussia could not come into operation without all these troops here. I confess to you: this blow crushes me and it will show you that I am no longer of any use, save to serve as a cloak to the plans of others. Kaunitz, whom the emperor doesn't like, and often gets impatient with, goes along with all this to avoid bother, or even out of fear. The emperor knows this well, takes advantage of these weaknesses to attain his ends. I have no one else. Khevenhüller, Batthyány, Colloredo are no comfort to me; they no longer know what is going on. Opposed in this way, continually distressed, I succumb and in the end let things happen. I am fated to survive all my family; I am fated to recover from a mortal

---

[55] J. to L., 24 Jan. 1771 (Arneth, *MTuJ* I, p. 329).

[56] Beer, *Theilung*, vol. III, pp. 19–25 and (documents) pp. 327–9, 332–4 and vol. III, pp. 23–6; Arneth, *MTuJ* I, pp. 324–34; Arneth, *GMT* VIII, pp. 264–9, 584; K-M VII, pp. 62, 339–41 (for the last of the four memoranda of J.) and 68, 348–68 (for the instructions to the Austrian envoy in Russia, Lobkowitz, dated 22 Mar. 1771); Roider, *Austria's Eastern Question*, esp. pp. 115–20.

illness at the age of fifty in order to see the work of thirty-one years of rule and weariness and cares perish, to see the Monarchy collapse as well, to make all my subjects unhappy by war, plague and famine.[57]

Joseph had obviously given Leopold a false impression when he claimed in December that he and his mother were in full agreement. If at that stage both Maria Theresa and Joseph argued for a pacific policy, it was for quite different reasons. Later they disagreed violently. The empress felt sympathy with both sides in the war: with the Russians because they were Christian and victims of aggression; with the Turks because they had assisted her and the Monarchy – perhaps saved her throne – by their neutrality during the long struggle with Prussia. Basically, she wanted no war, no partitions, no military demonstrations – even, as she confessed, no foreign policy.[58]

However, she was simply not telling the truth when she suggested that Kaunitz and her son had been more or less agreed, with the emperor calling the tune. Joseph summed up his policy to Leopold in January:

I am for a thousand reasons of opinion that we ought never to wage war on our own against Russia, but that we ought to put ourselves into a condition to profit promptly and without risk from the Russians' moments of weakness, if any present themselves, or at least to take our quota, and if we cannot satisfactorily prevent their aggrandisement, at least to get an equivalent for it, advantageous for us.[59]

This statement corresponds with the advice he gave in his memoranda. Kaunitz, on the other hand, argued fanatically for war against Russia, even if the Monarchy had to fight single-handed. Khevenhüller, Maria Theresa and Joseph all agreed that the chancellor was in a wild mood – in the words of lord Stormont, the British ambassador, 'the Dupe of his own Ability, and Penetration'.[60] Stormont had excellent sources of information at this time: he had good relations with Lacy, and had acquired in countess Thurn a close friend, perhaps a mistress.[61] He informed London in January that Kaunitz had proposed 'a Plan of Operations' which 'carries strong marks of It's not having been drawn by a Military Man'.[62]

The role of Lacy in this business must have been crucial. Born in Russia,

57 Kervyn de Lettenhove, *MARB in-8o* (1868), 25–7.
58 Arneth, *GMT* VIII, pp. 252–67, is very severe on Beer for accepting J.'s statement that he and his mother were agreed, and in general criticises *Theilung*, vol. II, pp. 9–21 for indulgence towards J.'s attitudes. However, Arneth is unwilling to probe into the question of differences between J. and K. (cf. *GMT* VIII, pp. 277–9), or to give weight to the evidence that K. might be the more bellicose.
59 Arneth, *MTuJ* I, p. 328 (J. to L., 24 Jan. 1771).
60 K-M VII, pp. 58–9 (30 Jan. 1771), 128–9 (20 May 1772), 330–2 (ref. 5 Sep. 1770); Stormont to Halifax, 1 May 1771 (PRO SP 80/209).
61 L.K. to E.L., 10 Aug. 1772 (SOALpZ, LRRA P. 16/23): 'un ami comme Mylord, supposé même qu'il ne soit pas son amant'.
62 Stormont to Rochford, 2 Jan. 1771, cypher, 'secret, by a private conveyance' (PRO SP 80/209). See Stormont to Rochford, cypher, not numbered, 1 Dec. 1770, for his relationship with Lacy (PRO SP 80/208).

the son of a general in the Russian service, he was not merely sympathetic to his native country, he was convinced of its strength and impregnability. On seeing Joseph's first memorandum of 23 November, the marshal composed letters and a long paper of his own for both Maria Theresa and the emperor. He contended that war against Russia would be fatal. Instead, 'wouldn't it be possible for YM to join this triple alliance to crush the Turks in Europe and share the spoils between us, Russia, Prussia and Poland?' The empress replied: 'I think you're both inclined to go to war, though in different ways, and I, who have been too much buffeted by war, intend to have no more of it.' Lacy must not spur Joseph on to war. She would never fight against 'my Moslems'.[63] In February 1771 she used Lacy to tell the Russian ambassador of her regrets at the despatch of troops and of her peaceful intentions. But, she said, 'inviolable secrecy is necessary here'.[64]

So a policy was adopted that represented a compromise between the views of all four principals. The Monarchy aligned itself with the Turks against Russia, as Kaunitz insisted and as Maria Theresa, forced to make the choice, preferred. But she secured that the military demonstration, as eventually made, was understood by all four to be directed towards preserving peace; and she did everything she could to reassure the Russians, thus pleasing Lacy but weakening the deterrent effect of the troop movements to which Kaunitz and Joseph attached so much importance. Since the Turks were intended both to foot the bill for the demonstration and to provide the territorial compensation required by the Monarchy, Maria Theresa's financial worries were alleviated and Lacy's partition plans received some encouragement. The expected success of the demonstration would satisfy Joseph's desire for military glory without expenditure of blood or money.

Two reports from Stormont are exceptionally revealing in this context. The first, admittedly, dates from 1 December 1768. It represents the results of a careful enquiry as to whether Joseph was likely, when he succeeded his mother, to try to recover Silesia. The ambassador concluded that the emperor had no particular antipathy to Frederick and showed no tendency 'to encroach on others', although he would be 'incapable of bearing the least Encroachment, of brooking the slightest Injury'.

It is true that He directs His principal Attention to Military Affairs, and when He speaks upon those Subjects . . . it is in the Manner in which a Man speaks of a favourite Study; But then the Stile of his Conversation is not that of a young Prince who is waiting eagerly for an Opportunity of signalizing himself, but rather that of a Man who has thought deeply upon the Subject, is aware of the numberless Vicissitudes of War, of the Difficulty of acquiring and preserving Military Glory, and of the Hazard to which that of the ablest General stands exposed from numberless Events, which no

---

[63] HHSA NL, Kartons 2 and 3, Lacy to J. and M.T., 24 and 27 Nov. with M.T.'s *apostilles*. See Arneth, *GMT* VIII, pp. 252–3, 583.
[64] HHSA NL, Karton 7: M.T. to Lacy (24 Feb. 1771).

Human Prudence can controul. I myself have more than once heard Him upon this Topick.[65]

The second despatch, confirming the first, was written in October 1771. The Turkish 'concert' had been agreed in July.[66] Kaunitz now revived his plan of intervention against Russia. The emperor, reported Stormont, during his recent camp in Hungary, 'in his Moments of Gaiety', used to scoff at the current military preparations as too feeble to impose on other Powers, and diverted himself and others by imagining

the wildest and most extravagant Schemes, such as often occur to men who are not of the Profession, and who plan Marches and Counter-Marches without stirring out of their Closets. He more than once said, smiling, 'Gentlemen, you eat too much, you should accustom yourselves to spare Diet, for if we march you must expect to fast for weeks together.'

... A few days before the Emperor left Peste, a Courier arrived with a Project drawn by Prince Kaunitz, for the immediate March of the Army into Transilvania. His Imperial Majesty scouted this Project, as absurd and impracticable, and without further Discussion, broke up the Camp, a day or two sooner than he originally intended, and said to his Confidants, 'That is the best and only Answer to be given, to such wild and impracticable Schemes.'[67]

This story may not be accurate in every particular, but the attitude it ascribes to Joseph is authentic. He had written to his mother from the camp on 4 September, advising her on no account to send troops into Transylvania:

Against the Russians there is not and there never will be anything to be done without the king of Prussia. I see it more every day; it would be to sacrifice the army, your states and perhaps your power if such a war as I envisage, ruinous and fruitless, [took place] in Wallachia and at the same time in Bohemia and Moravia. I cannot abandon this conviction and I've always written in this sense ... Nevertheless, so far as I'm personally concerned, I'm ready to go, with perhaps more pleasure than I ought [to feel], to Bender, the Crimea and anywhere where I might find glory and follow my favourite profession.[68]

65 Stormont to Rochford, 1 Dec. 1768, 'most secret', 'by Garstin' (PRO SP 80/205).
66 Roider, *Austria's Eastern Question*, pp. 120–5; Arneth, *GMT* VIII, pp. 282–92; Beer, *Theilung*, vol. II, pp. 26–37. Anyone who supposes that M.T. was a model of matronly virtue even in diplomacy should read the reports of the British ambassador in which her lies about the Turkish alliance are recorded: Stormont to Suffolk, 18 Dec. 1771, 'private', 'from German Chancery' (PRO SP 80/210) and 29 Feb. 1772, 'private', cypher (PRO SP 80/211). In the latter despatch J. is also reported to have denied, on his word of honour, that any convention had been signed.
67 Stormont to Suffolk, 'private, by Langlois', 17 Oct. 1771 (PRO SP 80/210).
68 J. to M.T., 4 Sep. 1771 (Arneth, *MTKuF* I, p. 7). In Arneth, *GMT* VIII, pp. 291–2, 586, evidence is given that a plan favoured by K. for an advance into Transylvania was rejected, apparently just before J. left for the camp. But the letters of 2 Sep. and 4 Sep. from J. to M.T., written during the camp, are not cited in Arneth's *GMT* and were not published by him until 1881. However, Beer, *Theilung*, vol. II, pp. 98–104, also shows that such a scheme was being discussed after J. went to the camp. I don't know whether it was true that he broke it up early. The same story is in E.L. to L.K., 1 Oct. 1771 (SOALpZ, LRRA P. 16/22).

Lacy did not attend this camp at all, but set off to take a cure at Spa.[69] According to the Kaunitz household, this trip was a deliberate gesture to assure the Russians that they were safe from intervention by the Monarchy. The marshal had inspired Joseph with 'a kind of pusillanimity'. 'Posterity will discover the reasons which led to peace, and will be astonished that a politician counselled war as an indispensable measure and a soldier opposed it.'[70]

It is absolutely clear, then, that the emperor was not ready to seize every opportunity for war. The famine of 1771 in Bohemia certainly reduced the Monarchy's financial and military potential at a critical moment and strengthened Joseph's opposition to Kaunitz's schemes.[71] But his attitude had been much the same beforehand, and early in 1772 he was still urging that Vienna should encourage Turkey to go on fighting for yet another campaign. After this – but only after this – the belligerents might be so weakened that the Monarchy could safely intervene.[72] This approach is characteristic of him. His yearning to distinguish himself at the head of his troops in battle was offset by an acute awareness of the risks and uncertainties involved. He was cautious, not to say timorous, in committing himself to war against any strong Power. He was the sort of commander who wishes above all to build up and preserve his forces, who can never satisfy himself that they will be equal to the demands even of defence, let alone of aggression. He seems to have possessed only limited notions of grand strategy or of offensive tactics. Like modern military historians, Kaunitz believed that it was this kind of thinking, contrasting so sharply with the opportunism and vision of Frederick the Great, which had alone permitted Prussia to survive the Seven Years War.[73] No general in the Austrian service epitomised it better than Lacy, the mentor and confidant of Joseph. He was an indefatigable organiser but a hesitant campaigner – a theoretician of defence.[74] It was the emperor and Lacy who wanted the internal arrangements of the Monarchy subordinated to the requirements of a huge army; but all their emphasis was on defence. The chancellor, opposing them, considered a smaller force sufficient, though he devised far-reaching schemes for employing it in the service of an imaginative and aggressive foreign policy.

Joseph had played a more prominent part in the making of foreign policy

---

[69] K-M VII, p. 62.   [70] L.K. to E.L., 26 May 1772 (SOALpZ, LRRA P. 16/23).

[71] J. to M.T., 17 Oct. 1771 (Arneth, *MTuJ* I, p. 346). See below, pp. 341–2.

[72] Beer, *Theilung*, vol. III, pp. 39–42. Padover ('Kaunitz' (thesis), p. 93) misrepresents this document as a plea for Austria to fight.
     Cf. K-M VII, pp. 77–8 (8 June 1771): J. takes K-M.'s point that 'in our present internal confusion all warlike undertakings should be avoided', 'despite his predilection for the military'.

[73] K.'s memorandum of 24 Jan. 1767 (K-M VI, pp. 469–71). See the next note.

[74] Kotasek, *Lacy* is the best published source, despite the lack of footnotes. Cf. Duffy, *Army of M.T.*, esp. pp. 189–209, and H. Temperley, *Frederic the Great and Kaiser Joseph* (London, 1915), pp. 118–19.

during this dispute than at any previous period. His firm opinion on military questions could hardly be overruled. In this case he had taken a position between the indecision of his mother and the bellicosity of Kaunitz. It is necessary to stress this point, because nearly all historians have declined to accept it. Most of them simply cannot shake themselves free from the received wisdom that Joseph invariably wanted a fight and was always as grasping as anyone. Some have contended, in conformity with this view, that Kaunitz never really intended to involve the Monarchy in war with Russia, that he always really wanted to preserve peace, and that he was bluffing the emperor and empress in order to procure acceptance of a policy which would in turn bluff Frederick and Catherine. A Russian minister, Panin, supplies convenient evidence. He wrote:

Kaunitz ... wished to frighten Russia, but he has made a mistake. It is known that, sunk in the rut of his perfidies, devised the better to blind and deceive his own Court, he has understood neither the fundamental interests, nor the dignity of a Christian power.[75]

But if it is possible to believe that the chancellor's deception went so far that he argued with both Maria Theresa and Joseph for years on end in favour of military action which he did not actually desire, then he duped the two rulers completely. Both of them manifestly accepted that he wanted war, and that he must be dissuaded or else resisted. It seems to me that it is much more natural to assume that the chancellor meant what he said. I believe that such attitudes were characteristic of him. He showed on several other occasions a reckless readiness to involve the Monarchy in war: against Prussia in 1756 and against Turkey in 1783 and 1787. And whether or not he was bluffing in 1770–1, the emperor's opposition must be regarded as genuine.

It would be absurd, of course, to claim that Joseph was a pacifist, or much of a moralist, in foreign policy. He liked deploying his troops in circumstances he considered safe. He may have originated – he certainly promoted – the plan for an armed demonstration in Hungary. He looked forward to attacking the Turks as soon as they were on their knees. As we shall see, he took a special delight in forcing frontier adjustments on weaker neighbours. He felt no qualms about annexations in principle. His opposition to Kaunitz's policy stemmed from a calculation totally different from the chancellor's, but just as cynical. Joseph, evidently influenced by Lacy, was convinced that war single-handed against Russia would be fatal. Both men believed that portions of the Ottoman empire, especially Belgrade and Bosnia, would be truly valuable acquisitions for the Monarchy. Incidentally, to recover them would

---

[75] Panin to Galitzin, 6 Dec. 1771, quoted in Padover, 'Kaunitz' (thesis), p. 86. Padover and Kaplan are prime examples of historians convinced that Joseph was always more bellicose than anyone else.

be to avenge the humiliation of the last years of Charles VI.[76] The emperor had disagreed with Lacy about the details of the intervention, and was less committed to the side of Russia.[77] But all his initiatives in foreign policy during the Russo–Turkish war seem explicable on the assumption that what he most wanted was to ensure that the Monarchy should obtain its share in any partition of Turkey.

THE PARTITION OF POLAND

By the time the terms of the Austro–Turkish concert were agreed in July 1771, Prussia and Russia were secretly working for a partition of Poland. Both Powers had found means of suggesting that Austria might like to consider what available territories she would wish to claim if they decided on mutual aggrandisement as the only means of ending the war and the troubles in Poland. Emperor, empress and chancellor all still concurred that they would prefer a peace to be made between Russia and Turkey which would concede so little to Catherine that neither Prussia nor Austria could reasonably feel endangered and demand 'compensation'. But the triumvirate agreed on almost nothing else. Joseph and Kaunitz showed no great compunction in discussing numerous schemes of partition, whether of Turkey or of Poland or of both, perhaps involving also Silesia and Venice. Such arrangements would become 'necessary', they held, if Russia insisted on gains so large as to upset the balance of power to the Monarchy's serious disadvantage – in which case it was assumed that Frederick would insist on annexations still more damaging to Austria than those of Catherine. But emperor and minister had quite different priorities. Maria Theresa, on the other hand, was not only passionately opposed to any territory being seized from the Turks, allies to whom she felt obliged, but most reluctant to agree to any partition whatsoever. She took several steps against the advice of Joseph or Kaunitz, or both, in order to try to stave off this outcome. She modified the form of the Monarchy's claim to the occupied districts of Poland, and repeatedly offered to surrender them all, usually but not always excluding Zips itself, if Prussia and Russia would

---

[76] J. to Lacy, 7 Jan. 1784 (HHSA FA Sbde 72): 'Au reste je vous prie ... de vouloir concerter ... les moyens à employer pour continuer à nous maintenir à l'avenir dans la connoissance des objets principaux qui se passent sur les frontieres turques, et pour rester en disposition à pouvoir executer un jour, quand l'occasion s'en presentera, les grands desseins que nous avions formés et surtout ceux sur Belgrad.'
   In Aug.–Sep. 1772 count Dietrichstein, one of J.'s intimates, visited Frederick the Great to sound him out about possibilities of annexations. It would be interesting to know more of this initiative which, as Aretin (*Reich*, vol. I, p. 113n) points out, Arneth did not mention. Frederick concluded that the mission was from the emperor and Lacy rather than (as Aretin accepts) from M.T. and K. Frederick wrote to Solms at St Petersburg, 30 Aug. 1772: 'Je vois clairement que l'Empereur et Lacy ne sont pas contents de ce bout de la Pologne qu'ils obtiennent. Ils voudraient chasser le Turc de l'Europe' (*PC* XXXII, p. 435). See p. 390.
[77] Arneth, *GMT* VIII, pp. 279–80.

withdraw their own demands on Poland. She kept on reopening matters which the emperor and chancellor thought had been settled. She sometimes proposed compensating Poland as well as the three great Powers. Most infuriatingly, Joseph told Leopold in a wild letter of September 1771,

in a conversation she had with Rohde, the Prussian minister, she overturned our whole system – we who wanted to put pressure on Russia, perhaps ally with the Turks, threaten them with war etc. She strongly assured him that she would never want or permit war, that the possession of the Crimea seemed to her only a small point, that she didn't mind at all if Russia retained it . . .[78]

She hesitated even to demand parity in any partition.[79]

Joseph and Kaunitz differed at most stages, often violently. In January 1772 the emperor at first rejected the chancellor's plan of pacification through partition. He was still urging instead, as we have seen, that Russia and Turkey be allowed to fight it out, though he also wanted part of Poland occupied forthwith in order to assert the Monarchy's interest there in the event of partition.[80] Kaunitz replied so powerfully that Joseph, for once, actually conceded defeat and turned his attention to choosing between the various alternatives under discussion:

Although in my opinion it would still be desirable to cause the war to last longer, I must freely admit that the reasons for doing otherwise in the present situation, which prince Kaunitz mathematically sets out, are equally persuasive. So there remains only the question, which of the many plans is to be preferred: militarily, politically and financially nothing would suit us better than the Glatz and Neisse districts [of Silesia], but on no account Bayreuth and Ansbach. If this is reckoned impossible, which unhappily I have no doubt will be the case, the most useful of all would be Belgrade with the part of Bosnia up to the Golfo della Drina; remote from enemies, this would cover the whole Carlstadt district and Inner Austria against any possible Turkish attack.[81]

There was a moment when Maria Theresa and Kaunitz seemed agreed that Wallachia and parts of Moldavia and Bessarabia should be Austria's portion. Joseph then argued on military grounds for the extension of the Monarchy's frontiers to the rivers Pruth and Danube, but not beyond.[82]

---

[78] J. to L., 25 Sep. 1771 (Arneth, *MTuJ* I, pp. 344–5). Padover attaches immense importance to this gaffe or initiative of M.T.'s ('Kaunitz' (thesis), pp. 79–82, and his article, 'Prince Kaunitz' résumé of his eastern policy, 1763–1771', *JMH*, V (1933), 352–65). It seems to me that K.'s policy was defeated over a long period, by developments abroad and opposition and famine at home, rather than by this one admittedly spectacular intervention of M.T.'s. Even at this moment, the affair of the aborted camp contributed powerfully.

[79] For the whole paragraph Arneth, *GMT* VIII, ch. 12 and pp. 364–6; cf. Beer, *Theilung*, vol. II, ch. 11. Documents in *Theilung*, vol. II, pp. 329–32, 334–40, and vol. III, pp. 26–38. Arneth, *MTuJ* I, pp. 341–6, 362–3. Roider, *Austria's Eastern Question*, pp. 131–9.

[80] Beer, *Theilung*, vol. III, pp. 39–42 (memorandum of 19 Jan. 1772).

[81] J. to M.T., 21 Jan. 1772 (Arneth, *MTuJ* I, p. 361) (for Arneth's correction of the date from 22 Jan., see *GMT* VIII, p. 594). The Golfo della Drina is in modern Albania. See Maps 1 and 3.

[82] J.'s memorandum of 14 Feb. 1772 (Beer, *Theilung*, vol. II, pp. 343–4). Arneth, *GMT* VIII, pp. 361–4.

SWEDEN

St Petersburg

RUSSIAN

Baltic Sea

COURLAND

EAST
PRUSSIA

Danzig

Moscow

Smolensk

Mohilev

EMPIRE

PRUSSIA

Warsaw

POLAND

Schweidnitz

Neisse

Kiev

Glatz

Kosel

GALICIA

Lemberg

Neustadt

Bar

Zips

BUKOVINA

Danube

Vienna

(1770)

(1775)

HUNGARY

Buda

Bender

Cherson

TRAN-

MOLDAVIA

SYLVANIA

Trieste

CRIMEA

Fiume

Carlstadt

Old

Orsova

LITTLE WALLACHIA

Belgrade

WALLACHIA

Kutchuk-

Black Sea

BOSNIA

Kainardji

Adriatic Sea

SERBIA

BULGARIA

Gulf of
Drina

Naples

OTTOMAN

RUMELIA

Bosphorus

Constantinople

GREECE

EMPIRE

MOREA

Mediterranean   Sea

200 miles

300 km

Boundary of Ottoman Empire before war of 1768	The Monarchy in the 1760s
The Monarchy's gains during the 1770s	Russian gains, 1768–80
Boundary of Poland before war of 1768	Prussian gains, 1768–80

Map 3. The eastern question, 1768–1780.

When finally Maria Theresa, refusing to rob the Turks, was persuaded of the 'cruel necessity' of partitioning Poland, and Austria was required to stake her claims there, the emperor supplied maps of appropriate portions, after consultation with Lacy.[83] It was decided to demand in the first instance a very large area, with a view to obtaining ultimately what Joseph considered would be genuinely useful to the Monarchy, the salt-mines of Wieliczka, the town of Lemberg and means of access to the new provinces from upper Silesia. After Russia and Prussia had demurred at the scale of Austria's claims, the chancellor proposed to recede somewhat, but the emperor commented:

I could not possibly declare my agreement with the statement drafted by prince Kaunitz, either in substance or in form. Not for the former, since the proposals, especially the two last, seem to me entirely inadmissible; not for the latter, because nothing but childish fear, ignorance, doubt and weakness shine through it; and confidence in our two so recently reconciled friends cannot possibly go so far that we should expect to obtain our true advantage from them and their decisions.

Joseph carried with him first his mother, and then the chancellor, in ordering troops into the districts which he really prized.[84] At this stage of the proceedings, when war was unlikely to follow, the emperor was using his position as head of the army to stiffen the Monarchy's policy. No doubt this show of strength and determination helped to secure what he wanted.

Despite the fact that Austria's share was so large – greater both in area and population than Prussia's, greater in population than Russia's – the outcome caused little rejoicing in Vienna. Maria Theresa had resisted the partition as immoral and continued to call it unfortunate. She blamed herself for most of the decisions of the previous four years, and told the British ambassador that the reports about the condition of the annexed territories were so depressing that she could not bear to read any more of them.[85] Kaunitz, whom she strongly criticised for his part in the business,[86] had certainly worked for some sort of partition, at least as one policy option, long before either she or Joseph was ready to take it seriously. The chancellor evidently congratulated

---

Kaplan's quotation from J. that the scheme would be 'detrimental, unjust and unfeasible' (*Partition*, p. 166) comes from this document, but does not refer (as he claims) to the policy of partitioning Poland, only to the particular scheme for Moldavia, Wallachia and Bessarabia, just proposed by K. and M.T.

83 J. to K., 10 Mar. and 23 June 1772 (HHSA FA Sbde 70).
84 Arneth, *GMT* VIII, pp. 380–3. See also *ibid.*, pp. 384–6, for another dispute, in which K. and J. settled matters between them. Cf. documents in Beer, *Theilung*, vol. II, pp. 344–7 and vol. III, pp. 49–50.
85 A powerful critique of the whole proceedings by M.T. was printed by Arneth, *GMT* VIII, pp. 601–2; the date is early in 1772. Cf. her letter to K. of 22 Jan. 1772, published in Arneth, *MTuJ* I, pp. 362–3, with the wrong addressee and date (see Arneth, *GMT* VIII, p. 594). Stormont to Suffolk, separate, 5 Dec. 1772 (PRO SP 80/212).
86 The comments in *GMT* VIII, pp. 601–2 amount to criticism of K. rather than of J. See K-M VII, pp. 128–9 (20 May 1772).

himself on the result. But even he admitted to Stormont that the thing was *louche*.[87]

Joseph too apologised for it, in a remarkable audience he gave to Stormont at the end of 1772. It was the only occasion in seven years when he allowed such a lengthy political conversation to take place between them. He avowed, 'with an Hesitation and Embarras that is not usual to Him', 'the Anxiety he was under, lest the Polish Business should give the World a false Opinion of His Character'. He knew it looked 'ignominious'.

He added, that one of the Advantages Private Men had over Sovereigns was, that their Duty was generally so clear, that they could not mistake it, and the Line so distinctly marked that they could always follow it, if they pleased; but the Case is very different with Us, added He, We are too often in Situations where there is a number of Considerations to be attended to, a variety of weighty urgent and seemingly opposite Duties, which it is hard to reconcile. In such Cases . . . it is difficult if not impossible, to hit upon any Determination that is free from Objections . . . He then repeated, that what He had done, or rather approved, for he was not an Actor but a Counsellor, was from a Conviction of the absolute Necessity of it, and said, He should be very sorry if the World put a false Construction upon it, and considered Him as a Man of loose and unsettled Principles. That *that* was far from being the Case, that he meant to be a truly honest Man, both in Public and in Private Life, and was convinced that Honesty was the wisest and soundest Policy, and though it might make you lose some seeming momentary Advantages, which less scrupulous Men would seize, you were always a gainer in the End.[88]

This pronouncement is matched by an entry in Khevenhüller's diary for 23 August 1772. The old great chamberlain, having made the point to the emperor that Kaunitz now conducted foreign policy without telling the members of the Conference what was happening, went on:

there seem to me, in relation to this proposed partition, of which all the newspapers are full, to be two difficulties and flaws, one *moral*, since I cannot easily see by what right and authority we can seek to aggrandise ourselves at the expense of a friendly nation, which in a sense can be said to be allied with us by the old Holy League, a matter on which no doubt Their Majesties have consulted their confessors; secondly a *political*, since we are in fact ourselves assisting the aggrandisement of our strongest and our natural enemy. The emperor sought to excuse the decision taken to share the cake, by the course of events and the alternating threats and friendly offers made to us. However, since this lord has a natural straightforwardness, I could easily tell that my first objection went home and that he is well aware of the hollowness of the pretended rights of convenience and of the strongest. Hence the motive that seems to him plausible (which in my opinion would ultimately be the most appropriate ground to take if there is to be an official statement) is that the kingdom of Hungary should bring forward the withholding over more than three centuries of about 100,000 gulden a year

---

[87] Beer, *Theilung*, vol. II, p. 198; Arneth, *GMT* VIII, p. 390; Stormont to Suffolk, private, 26 Nov. 1772 (PRO SP 80/212). Kaplan, *Partition*, gives K. credit for the most skilful conduct of the affair.

[88] Stormont to Suffolk, 2 Dec. 1772, 'secret' (PRO SP 80/212).

in respect of the mortgaged Zipser district, and further the revenues extracted from this mortgage for so many years by the Poles, which, if one also counts interest at the highest rate, would come to some millions; we are then entitled to this sum in gold or, failing that, to its equivalent in land.[89]

When Kaunitz devised a manifesto, this extraordinary argument was not included. But Joseph wrote:

I have carefully read and re-read it; and, if it is possible to find any other reasons than the convenience of the king of Prussia, the need Russia had of him and of peace, and the absolute necessity we were in to expand so that we should not become too inferior to the others, you have certainly found them.[90]

From these three statements it is clear that the emperor did not relish the outcome. He evidently felt some glimmering of moral scruple. He obviously thought that the Monarchy had come off worst. He regretted what he saw as the necessity to be inconsistent and dishonest. On the other hand, he did not in the circumstances apologise for Austria's aggrandisement; and he certainly betrayed no awareness of the insult done to the Polish national consciousness.

His attitude on this last issue was generally shared. The notion that the partition of Poland was a great crime against national feeling did not become widespread until much later. In other states the main complaints had been levelled not so much against the outcome as against the secrecy of the negotiations and the accompanying duplicity. But both Maria Theresa and Joseph proved right in their fears that the Monarchy's participation had shattered its carefully cultivated image as an innocent Power, bent only on defending itself.[91] The British Secretary of State wrote in the following year to his new envoy in Vienna, Sir Robert Murray Keith:

After all, singular as the Conduct of Russia may have been, it is not more so, nor more liable to censure, than that of the Court where you reside, which, so long habituated to a more civilized System, & so well informed of her own Interests, has, in direct Opposition, both to the one & the other, & at the Expence of political Independence & publick Honor, blindly laboured to aggrandize a Rival Power, &, at the same Time, to establish, in Europe, *le Droit de plus fort.*[92]

This reaction was not entirely fair. Despite the business of Zips and the other districts claimed for Hungary, the main initiatives had come from other Powers: from Frederick, with his settled plans to annex north-western Poland, revealed in his political testaments; and from Catherine, whose troops

---

[89] K-M VII, pp. 140–1 (23 Aug. 1772). I have taken the passage out of indirect speech.
    M.T. did indeed consult her confessor (see Lewitter, *NCMH*, vol. VIII, p. 338).
[90] J. to K., 23 July 1772 (Arneth, *GMT* VIII, p. 605).
[91] For J.'s fears, Stormont to Suffolk, 2 Dec. 1772 (see n. 88 above). For M.T.'s her letter to K. of 22 Jan. 1772 and her memo., both cited in n. 85 above.
[92] Suffolk, letter to Keith, 11 June 1773, secret, by Blackmore (PRO SP 80/213).
    See D. B. Horn, *British Public Opinion and the First Partition of Poland* (London, 1945); Arneth, *GMT* VIII, pp. 427–39; and the final pages of the present chapter, and nn. 107–13.

had for many years occupied much of the country with a view to making it a client state of Russia for ever. The Monarchy had lagged behind, all of its leaders genuinely reluctant to see Poland partitioned.[93]

So far as Joseph himself was concerned, although he had been much more ready than Maria Theresa, he had been decidedly less willing than Kaunitz, to settle for partition. The disputes in Vienna had been so continuous and had resulted in so many compromises that each of the three principals could plausibly disclaim responsibility for the policy ultimately adopted. The emperor had characteristically argued in January 1771 that his 'system' must be accepted in its entirety and that any attempt to combine it with the approaches of Maria Theresa or Kaunitz would amount to rejecting it.[94] In logic he was right. But, having asserted himself as never before, he had at least succeeded in deflecting the Monarchy's policy at the end of 1770 and in 1771. Thereafter Kaunitz appears to have resumed his old dominance. It looks as though it was only when the army might be involved that the emperor was certain to be listened to. At least once in 1772, an important step was taken by the empress and her minister without consulting Joseph.[95] So Joseph was justified in his claim that he had not been the principal influence in shaping the foreign policy of the Monarchy during the crisis that culminated in partition.

THE GALICIAN FRONTIER AND THE ANNEXATION OF THE BUKOVINA

In common with all the principal rulers and statesmen of the time – even, under protest, Maria Theresa – Joseph saw annexations as a natural aim of states. Although down to 1771 he hardly seems to have envisaged that the Monarchy could obtain territorial gains from the eastern imbroglio, during the partition year he had weighed all the plans and possibilities, and established, as we have seen, an order of priority among them.[96] After the partition had been agreed in principle, he became obsessively active in discussions about the details of the new Galician frontier, and also about possible annexations from Turkey. Although Vienna had never implemented the 'concert' with the Turks, Kaunitz expected to be able to extract some territory from them when they made peace with Russia.

The chancellor proposed early in 1773 that six million florins should be offered to the sultan in return for 'little Wallachia'. The emperor's reaction illustrates his thinking on such matters. He considers the possible advantages

---

[93] Kaplan in *Partition* places great weight on the Zips affair as having set the bad example of Polish annexations to the other Powers. Frederick and Catherine certainly used it as a pretext. But in general Arneth's criticism of the viewpoint revived by Kaplan stands (*GMT* VIII, pp. 391–4). See Topolski, *Acta poloniae historica* (1973), pp. 89–104.

[94] E.g. J. to L., 24 Jan. 1771 (Arneth, *MTuJ* I, pp. 328–9).

[95] See Arneth, *GMT* VIII, pp. 454–5, 612.

[96] See p. 295 above.

13 Joseph, rather implausibly, ready to accompany his two unmarried sisters, Marianne and Elizabeth, in a vocal duet. Oil, J. Hauzinger, 1770s, KHM, Gemäldegalerie, Inv. No. 8856.

a

Exemple majestueux d'examiner tout et d'encourager les
Sujets, Diligence, donné par l'Empeur Ioseph II.
le 19. Aout 1769. en Moravie.

b

14   Joseph on his travels: (a) A bullfight staged for Joseph in the Roman amphitheatre at
Verona, 21 July 1769. Engraving, V. Comendú, British Museum, Prints and Drawings,
F/H 1769: 1871-12-9-1441. (b) One of many prints showing Joseph himself driving the
plough at Slavikovice in Moravia on 19 Aug. 1769. The monument on the left is the one
subsequently erected by prince J. W. Liechtenstein. Engraving, J. B. Bergmüller,
Albertina, Inv. No. Hist. Bl. Joseph II/1769.

a

b

15   Joseph on his travels: (a) The meeting of Joseph and Frederick the Great at Neisse, 25 Aug. 1769. Lithograph by Paalzow after a drawing by G. Opiz, Historisches Museum der Stadt Wien, Inv. No. 85383. (b) Joseph hearing Mass said by Abbot Gerbert of St Blasien in Freiburg minster, 20 July 1777. Alabaster, J. Hör, St Paul im Lavanttal, Stiftssammlungen. Österreichisches Bundesdenkmalamt, Vienna, N 32775.

a

b

18 Palace-building in Maria Theresa's later years: (a) Elevation of the new royal palace in Buda, as designed by F. A. Hillebrandt, completed 1770. Albertina, Architekturzeichnungen, Mappe 90, Umschlag 18, No. 1, No. 7183. (b) 'The New Royal and Ducal Theatre of Milan', now called 'La Scala'. After a fire of 1771 it was rebuilt, partly at the state's expense, by G. Piermarini between 1776 and 1778. Joseph had battled with his mother to keep down the cost of the scheme. Engraving, D. Aspari, Bildarchiv, ÖNB, 197.891.

19 (*Opposite*) Early neo-classical building in the Monarchy: (a) The façade of the cathedral of Vác, Hungary. This astonishing design was carried out for bishop Migazzi (who was also archbishop of Vienna) during the 1770s by F. I. Canevale. (b) The scheme prepared by P. M. d'Ixnard after a fire in 1768 for the abbey of St Blasien. It was not fully executed, but the church was completed in 1783. Salzmann, 1772, Generallandesarchiv, Karlsruhe, GLA G/Salzmann Mappe 2.

a

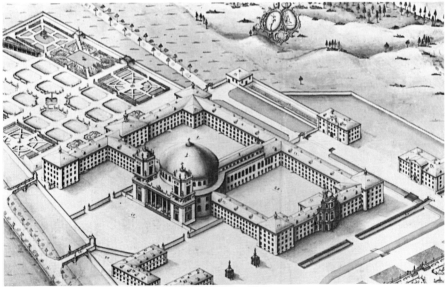

b

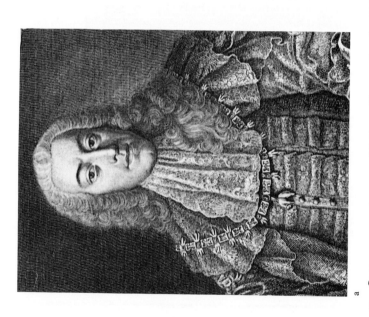

a   b

20   Contemporary observers: (a) Count (from 1764 prince) Johann Joseph Khevenhüller(-Metsch) (1706–76), a Court official, eventually the equivalent of great chamberlain, whose diaries survive for the years 1742–9, 1752–5, 1758–9, 1764–7 and 1770–6. He is wearing the Spanish mantle. Engraving, I. W. Windter. E. H. L. Jennings Portrait Collection, Cambridge University Library. (b) Charles Joseph, prince de Ligne (1735–1814). He saw a great deal of Joseph both at Court and in the army for over forty years, and his extensive writings are highly informative about the emperor. Oil, Le Clercq, 1785–9, Château de Beloeil, Belgium.

a

b

21 Contemporary observers: (a) Count Karl von Zinzendorf (1739–1813), who came to Vienna in 1761 and soon entered the Austrian government's service. His MS diary, written up each day, records many dealings with Joseph and opinions about him. Engraving, Bildarchiv, ÖNB, Inv. No. 34439. (b) Sir Nathaniel William Wraxall (1751–1831), whose *Memoirs of the Courts of Berlin, Dresden, Warsaw, and Vienna, in the Years 1777, 1778, and 1779* gives a full and lively account of the Austrian Court at the end of the co-regency. Engraving, T. Cheesman, British Museum, Prints and Drawings, C.III, PORT 4, A.2–91.

a

b

22 Letters of Maria Theresa and Joseph (HHSA): (a) M.T. to Lacy at Spa, 1 Oct. 1771. As always after 1765, the notepaper has a mourning band. The photographer's skill has made the letter look presentable, but it was folded small and badly blotted. She speaks of the row over Ayasasa's visit to Belgium, saying she has not told Joseph. But she is 'more content with the emperor. The essence is good, but these surroundings are bad, and he's not diligent enough and, to our misfortune, has too much capacity.' NL, Karton 2, Konv. III/1–2, Handbillette 1758–92, fol. 177r. (b) J. to Leopold, 1 Oct. 1780. J. often doodled in a small way on his letters, but this time he seems to have drawn a rough plan of the proposed new fortress at Pless, the site of which he was about to inspect. L. had just declined to accompany J. on a visit to Belgium. FA Sbde 7, Reise nach Flandern, fol. 93r.

23   Maria Theresa's last day, 29 Nov. 1780. Joseph kneels beside her. To her left stands Elizabeth, to her right provost Müller (her confessor), Max Franz, Doctor Störck, Albert, Marianne and Marie Christine. Engraving, H. Löschenkohl, British Museum, Prints and Drawings, F/H 1780: 1925–7–15–159.

24   Joseph, *c*. 1780. As usual after 1765, he is in uniform. The inscription refers to his visit to the newly annexed Innviertel. Oil, F. Streicher, Benedictine abbey of Michaelbeuren (vicarage of Perwang).

under four headings: first, the 'numerical' or financial, that is, human and animal population; secondly, the military, including possibilities for recruiting and defence, and connexion with the rest of the Monarchy; thirdly, the commercial, namely trade, manufactures and communications; and fourthly, the political, concerning both the inner strength of the Monarchy and its relations with other states. He concludes that little Wallachia qualifies under none of these headings as 'a useful annexation and *arrondissement*'.[97] At that juncture Joseph was overborne in Vienna. But the offer was never actually put to the Turks, because a Russian ultimatum disrupted the negotiations.[98]

The emperor spent the summer of 1773 visiting the eastern provinces of the Monarchy, including those newly annexed from Poland. He lighted on a portion of nominally Turkish territory which, though at present a 'real desert', could be 'a most useful object', because it would improve communications between Galicia and Transylvania.[99] This district became known as the Bukovina. Joseph also hoped to extract from the Turks Old Orsowa, just west of Little Wallachia.[100] In 1774 Russia imposed a humiliating peace on Turkey at Kutchuk-Kainardji, under which she obtained access to the Black Sea, while the Crimea became 'independent' of Constantinople and therefore dependent on St Petersburg. She restored Moldavia and Wallachia, though under conditions that gave her rights of interference in the two provinces.[101] The Bukovina was now effectively under Russian rather than Turkish control. To strengthen Austria's claim to a share in the spoils, her troops occupied part of Moldavia. Maria Theresa asserted that 'we are completely in the wrong', and that Kaunitz was simply doing the emperor's bidding, in demanding the cession of the Bukovina. But in fact the chancellor considered the province a valuable strategic acquisition, and worked ruthlessly to secure it. In 1775 it was surrendered to the Monarchy and placed under military administration. Orsowa, however, remained in Turkish hands.[102]

---

[97] Beer, *Theilung*, vol. III, pp. 51–5 (21 Feb. 1773).

[98] Arneth, *GMT* VIII, pp. 456–7, 612, correcting Beer, *Theilung*, vol. II, p. 255.

[99] J. to M.T., 19 June 1773 (Arneth, *GMT* VIII, pp. 613–14; not in *MTuJ*). J. to Lacy, 10 Aug. 1773 (HHSA FA Sbde 72) is less enthusiastic: 'un arrondissement de ce coté nous conviendroit guerre surtout, si il devoit couter chere'.

[100] J. to M.T., [?] June 1773 (Arneth, *MTuJ* II, p. 8).

[101] Arneth, *GMT* VIII, ch. 15; Beer, *Theilung*, vol. II, ch. 14; M. S. Anderson, *The Eastern Question, 1774–1923* (London, 1966), introduction.

[102] M.T. to Mercy, 4 Feb. 1775 (Arneth, *GMT* VIII, p. 489). On the whole question, Arneth, *GMT* VIII, ch. 16; Beer, *Theilung*, vol. II, pp. 269–75; Roider, *Austria's Eastern Question*, pp. 140–50. See also R. F. Kaindl, 'Kaiser Josef II. in seinem Verhältnisse zur Bukowina', *Jahrbuch des Bukowiner Landesmuseums*, II (1896), esp. 1–6; J. Polek, 'Joseph's II. Reisen nach Galizien und der Bukowina und ihre Bedeutung für letztere Provinz', *ibid.*, I (1895), esp. 32–4. On K.'s attitude H. L. Dyck, 'Pondering the Russian fact: Kaunitz and the Catherinian Empire in the 1770s', *Canadian Slavonic Papers*, XXII (1980), 461. The anonymous *Rapt de la Bukovine d'après des documents authentiques* (Paris, 1875) shows from K.'s correspondence with Thugut in Constantinople how ruthlessly Vienna bullied the Turks over the Bukovina.

On the same journey in 1773 the emperor had also taken a fancy to a tract of still Polish territory. 'I cannot conceal from you', he wrote to Lacy, 'that the land contained behind the Sbrutz is infinitely more beautiful and fertile. This little river makes a very good natural frontier, and we must try at all costs to find a way of keeping it.'[103] The partition treaty designated as the boundary in this north-eastern area of Galicia the river 'Podorze', which did not exist. It became disputed whether the Sbrutz or the next river to the west, the Sereth, should be taken as the frontier. In a long 'Note' Joseph contended that the Sbrutz must have been meant.[104] When Kaunitz refused to pursue this claim as ruthlessly as the emperor wished, Joseph accused the chancellor of cowardice. Kaunitz resigned; Joseph joined Maria Theresa in begging him to stay on. The chancellor acquiesced, and implemented the emperor's policy.[105] When further problems arose, Joseph proposed that, unless this portion could be obtained, the whole province should be surrendered and the other Powers should be required to abandon their own shares, abrogating the entire partition. Eventually Austria had to make some concessions, but the Sbrutz duly became her boundary.[106]

In these petty disputes Kaunitz had shown himself fastidiously reluctant to press extreme demands in the north-east, although he had urged the purchase of little Wallachia and recognised the value of the Bukovina. Maria Theresa had washed her hands of the business, except at one or two moments of crisis between chancellor and emperor. Joseph had successfully insisted that a strong line should be taken, and had achieved some of his objects. But in these cases, it should be noted, he was working on a small scale, using his position as head of the army and his experience as a traveller; and there was no serious risk of involving the Monarchy in war.

JOSEPH'S REPUTATION FOR EXPANSIONISM

For Joseph the Polish question constituted his apprenticeship in *Realpolitik*. Partly because of his attitude and actions, and partly because measures were ascribed to him which he had not in fact proposed, he acquired during this crisis an unenviable reputation for expansionism. The most extreme denunciation came from the comte de Guibert, a highly intelligent and radical writer on military matters who in 1773 had an audience with Joseph, just returned from Galicia:

---

[103] J. to Lacy, 16 Aug. 1773 (Arneth, *GMT* VIII, p. 609). Cf. J. to Lacy, 28 Aug. 1773 (HHSA FA Sbde 72).
[104] Beer, *Theilung*, vol. III, pp. 57–64 (26 Aug. 1773).
[105] Arneth, *GMT* VIII, pp. 493–5, 617–18. See pp. 219–21 above.
[106] For the whole question, Arneth, *GMT* VIII, pp. 423–6 and ch. 17; Beer, *Theilung*, vol. II, ch. 15 and (documents) pp. 348–9 and vol. III, pp. 51–75; H. Glassl, *Das österreichische Einrichtungswerk in Galizien (1772–1790)* (Wiesbaden, 1975), pp. 68–9, 77–8.

He won [his mother] over to the infamous line taken by . . . Vienna in not going to the help of the Turks after receiving 18 million from them, in the abominable partition of Poland: in the same way he will carry the day again to get war declared against the Turks, or at least to make himself the armed mediator of a peace between them and the Russians. Since he controls the army, he has already taken all possible preparatory measures . . . The moment he thinks he can aggrandise himself by a warlike move, he will cause hostilities to break out on the cordon and land his mother, despite herself, in a course of action repugnant to her scruples, which damages her alliance with us . . .

Guibert was uncertain whether Joseph would turn out to have a taste for war and talent for command. But

the brilliance of the king of Prussia's reign has persuaded him that the whole strength of a state lies in the military; so, to augment his troops in order to extend his possessions, and to extend his possessions so that they can sustain the increase in troops, have become the foundation of his system.

His subjects dread his accession to full power. 'They feel threatened by a military regime, an iron sceptre, the abolition of their privileges.' More than that, the whole of Europe has reason to fear him. His plans of aggrandisement and 'the appearance he gives of prodigious military strength' will force all other states to arm if they wish to avoid partition or subjugation. Prussia and the Monarchy together will cause 'an absolute revolution in European politics, in the system of all governments, with the general adoption of the military regime as their basis . . . I see Europe becoming again the prey of another kind of barbarians, more enlightened but not less destructive.'[107]

This prophecy was not published until 1803, but opinions like it, if rather less apocalyptic, gained strength after the outbreak of another frontier dispute with which as head of the army Joseph was naturally identified. In 1773–4 Austrian troops in Dalmatia violated the boundary with Venice. The Venetians, already thoroughly alarmed by the partition of Poland and the encroachments of the Monarchy on the territory of the Ottoman empire, feared invasion. The British envoy in Venice wrote home:

I will not pretend to say how far a reasonable Jealousy, or rather Fear, may incline this Republic to anticipate these Misfortunes, but too many Circumstances seem to shew that they are at least strongly threatened by [the Austrians]. Perhaps they will not happen during the present Administration at Vienna, as the Designs meditated in Dalmatia seem rather a Scheme of the Emperor's . . .[108]

When Joseph visited Venice in the following year, he passed the matter off lightly and it was amicably arranged. Perhaps he was justified in blaming the men on the spot. Certainly it is difficult to associate with a plot of Machiavell-

---

107 *Journal d'un voyage en Allemagne, fait en 1773, par G. A. H. Guibert* (Paris, 1803), vol. II, pp. 252–3, 256–8, 260–2. I have not seen the MSS, if indeed it exists. But it seems plausible that the original, dating from 1773, has been faithfully reproduced.
108 Strange to Rochford, 22 Sep. 1774 (PRO SP 99/77).

ian sophistication incidents like the burning of forests and the seizure of pasture grounds, still less the detention by the Venetian governor of an Austrian officer's wife.[109] But even outside the Republic the dispute was taken as further evidence of the emperor's greed for aggrandisement.

Frederick the Great, both before and after this affair, harped on the Monarchy's, and especially Joseph's, yearning for Venice as well as for Bavaria and portions of the Ottoman Empire.[110] The German princes were being alienated by what they saw as the interfering and arrogant attempts of the emperor to carry constitutional reforms in the *Reich*: George III as elector of Hanover was one who became strongly hostile to Joseph.[111] Keith wrote from Vienna on 4 January 1775:

That the Emperor has it in his Character, as well as in the Plan of his future Reign, to extend the Limits, and at the same time the Power, of the Monarchy He is born to govern, may be easily, and, in all Probability, justly admitted.[112]

But the most violent denunciations came from statesmen of France, his nominal ally, whose queen was his sister, Marie Antoinette. The comte de Vergennes, made foreign minister when Louis XVI came to the throne in 1774, warned his master against the emperor, and especially against the dangers that might threaten Europe after the death of Maria Theresa. Vergennes claimed, for example, that Joseph wished to impose unification on the *Reich*. When Louis demurred, the minister wrote:

It is possible, as Your Majesty remarks, that I depict the consequences that might follow the death of the empress-queen in too dark colours. But, Sire, the character of the emperor is adventurous and ambitious; he admires the king of Prussia, perhaps without liking him, and some incidents give ground for the fear that [Joseph] is no more delicate than [Frederick] about the means [he adopts]. His finances and his army are in pretty good order. All this may well give cause for apprehension.

Joseph apparently told the French ambassador in Vienna in 1775 that 'it seemed to him impossible not to cherish always enough aims to keep one busy, since he believed that everyone should always be thinking about increasing his possessions'. After receiving the report of this conversation, Louis himself put pen to paper, expressing indignation at the emperor's behaviour to the Turks and the Venetians and calling him 'a usurper, an ambitious and despotic

---

109 This episode is little known. For details see PRO SP 99/77 and also 80/213–16. It is outlined in Tabacco, *Andrea Tron*, p. 97. On pp. 95–6 the impact of the partition of Poland is stressed.
　　J.'s pacific interview with Tron in 1775 is described in the latter's *relazione* (Biblioteca Marciana, Venice, MS It. VII, 1987 (8480), ff. 95–102). Dr N. S. Davidson very kindly obtained for me a microfilm of this report.

110 See for example *PC* XXXII, pp. 440, 472, 479–80 (all of Sep. 1772).

111 See pp. 130, 276 above. Keith's despatches contain a good deal about Hanover's attitude to Vienna, chiefly as seen by Kaunitz and Joseph (e.g. Keith to Suffolk, cypher, private and confidential, not numbered, 30 July and 7 Aug. 1774 and Suffolk to Keith, cypher, 16 Aug. and 2 Sep. 1774, PRO SP 80/216).

112 Keith to Suffolk, 4 Jan. 1775, cypher (PRO SP 80/217).

character', who accepted 'the right of the strongest'. Vergennes replied echoing these views, which he had helped to implant in the king's mind, adding: 'It is Your Majesty's mission ... to erect a dam against this torrent which threatens to burst its banks.'[113]

Maria Theresa had indulged her conscience, and sometimes frustrated Kaunitz and Joseph, by ostentatiously dissociating herself from some of her government's actions. In so doing she had encouraged observers to form an unfair impression of the balance of influence in Vienna. In fact she still took the final decisions, and when she allowed herself to be overborne, it was more often by the cunning flattery and specious logic of Kaunitz than by the cutting criticism and passionate zeal of Joseph. The chancellor was grasping enough in his own way, and sometimes more bellicose than the emperor. In any case Joseph derived his general approach to foreign policy as much from Kaunitz as from anyone – though the influence of Lacy was important. But most outsiders attributed the resumed expansionism of the Monarchy simply to the efforts of Joseph.

---

[113] All these quotations come from the lively article by A. Tratchevsky, 'La France et l'Allemagne sous Louis XVI', *RH* XIV (1880), 266, 270–1. See also G. Fagniez, 'La Politique de Vergennes et la diplomatie de Breteuil', *ibid.*, CXXXIX (1922), esp. 5–8; Arneth & Geffroy II, p. 292n; C. A. Rauscher, 'Die Aussenpolitik Kaiser Josephs II. (1780–1790) und ihre internationale Zusammenhänge im Spiegel der französischen Botschaftsberichte', University of Vienna PhD, 1951.

    I am uneasy about some of the remarks attributed by the French ambassador, Breteuil, to J. They certainly have a quite different ring from those passed on by Stormont and Keith. Fejtö, *J. II*, pp. 183–4, expresses the same doubt.

CHAPTER 10

The man

Joseph loved to distinguish the emperor or co-regent from 'the man' or 'Joseph'. Sometimes he used the distinction in a normal way, as when conveying both personal and royal approval of a minister.[1] Superficially, this usage corresponded with Maria Theresa's. But the parallel was not exact, since she openly accompanied her private gratitude with public largesse, whereas Joseph maintained that personal considerations should play no part in government patronage;[2] and he could not match the warmth of the concern that she displayed for the state's servants as individuals.

More often, he used the distinction in a special sense, almost peculiar to himself. According to the Scottish traveller, Dr John Moore, Joseph said:

It would be hard indeed, if, because I have the ill fortune to be an Emperor, I should be deprived of the pleasures of social life, which are so much to my taste. All the grimace and parade to which people are accustomed from their cradle, have not made me so vain, as to imagine that I am in any essential quality superior to other men; and if I had any tendency to such an opinion, the surest way to get rid of it, is the method I take, of mixing in society, where I have daily occasions of finding myself inferior in talents to those I meet with.[3]

But since he was always asserting that his life was dedicated to ruling, that he was therefore thankful to be untrammelled by marriage, and that he could not even feel well unless the Monarchy was in good shape,[4] it is apparent that he did not expect to secure for himself much of a private life. He stressed the utility as well as the pleasure of going into society, emphasising how much he could learn from the conversation of the eminent. When he travelled, he claimed it was chiefly to instruct himself.[5] As we shall see, certain personal friendships mattered greatly to him; and he set much store by his little refuge in the Augarten. But his insistence that he be treated as a man rather than an emperor related less to his private than to his public life. He wanted to behave and be received, in the very act of fulfilling what he considered to be essential

---

[1] See pp. 155, 184.
[2] E.g. M.T. to Lacy, 13 May 1773 (Arneth, *GMT* IX, p. 625). See p. 171. Cf. p. 334.
[3] Moore, *View of Society*, vol. II, p. 388.   [4] See pp. 3, 322–3, 331.   [5] See pp. 154, 251–2.

royal duties, as if he was not in fact the emperor and co-regent. He desired to work nearly full-time as a ruler, but without the usual trappings: to be a soldier sovereign, a bureaucrat monarch, a citizen king.

Even in so far as he allowed rein to his personal predilections, they mostly, because of his position, acquired public significance and became entangled with official motives. For example, his liking for military life and his hatred of Court ceremony were subsumed into a political and religious programme that coloured the history of the Monarchy over a long period; and his approach to the visual arts, music and drama, reinforcing other tendencies, greatly influenced the cultural development of his territories.[6]

To present a chapter on 'the man' is therefore doubly unsatisfactory. In the first place, it is hard to find aspects of his life and activity that were genuinely and purely private. Secondly, the whole book is about him; and his administrative and military work, his relations with his family and the chief ministers, and his travels all illustrate his personality and were affected by it. But as Maria Theresa used to complain, he behaved in one way where she was concerned, and in quite another way elsewhere.[7] In this chapter I shall attempt to paint a portrait of Joseph and his personal relationships, as seen outside the royal family.

AS OTHERS SAW HIM

He was nearly five feet six inches tall, about the average for his day.[8] His stern regimen ensured that, unlike both his parents, he never ran to fat, and he would return from his more arduous journeys so thin that his mother was shocked.[9] If he was not notably handsome, he was reasonably good-looking – remarkably so for a Habsburg. His most striking feature was his blue eyes.[10]

Everyone who met him remarked on the simplicity of his dress, which was nearly always plain uniform without decorations. But his manner aroused even more comment. Stormont, who saw much of him in society, reported in October 1771:

He has great Quickness and Penetration, and its natural Consequence clear, easy Elocution; without having much of that Knowledge that is got from Study and abstruse Speculation, He has, what is infinitely preferable, a sound, ready & (if I may use the expression) Practical Understanding ...

[6] See e.g. pp. 154–8, 172–3, 231–6, 345–6.

[7] See M.T. to Herzelles, esp. 9 July and 16 Dec. 1771: Kervyn de Lettenhove, *MARB in-8o* (1868), 30–1.

[8] I accept J.'s own evidence (Acton, *Bourbons of Naples*, p. 138). Cf. Wraxall, *Memoirs*, vol. II, p. 429, saying J. was rather above the middle height; Moore, *View of Society*, vol. II, p. 382, 'of a middle size'; Hamilton, 'rather low in Stature' (to Weymouth, 4 Apr. 1769, PRO SP 93/24).

[9] E.g. M.T. to Ferdinand, 13 Sep. 1773 (Arneth, *MTKuF* I, p. 228).

[10] See above, pp. 20–1. The best single description of J. is probably that of Wraxall, *Memoirs*, vol. II, esp. pp. 386–468. Wolf and Zwiedineck-Südenhorst, *Österreich unter M.T., J. II. und L. II.*, p. 214. See Plates 11, 13 and 24.

He . . . has the truest & most unaffected Simplicity of manners. He often runs about with a single Servant behind Him; likes to converse with men of all Ranks, puts those He talks to, quite at their Ease; loves easy, familiar Conversation, as much as He hates to talk in a Circle; visits the Ladies in their boxes at the Theatre, converses with them, & with the Men He happens find there, in the easiest & most agreeable manner; avoids Topics He does not chuse to speak upon, particularly Politics, at least whenever I have seen him; but talks on various Subjects as They arise, with the utmost openness and frankness, and has, in his whole Language, Air & Carriage, the most extraordinary Condescension; but, at the same time, has that Dignity about Him, that, even in the most familiar moments, no one can forget the Respect due to Him; Due, I had almost said, to the Man; still more than to the Crown he wears.[11]

A year later, after 'the only Political Conversation I ever had with the Emperor', Stormont wrote of his 'naturalness & Perspicuity, and strong manly Sense'.

He has too, a Sort of peculiar Life and Vivacity, which it is very difficult to describe, and which renders his Conversation, singularly animated and pleasing. He never loses himself, never wanders, but yet, though he is talking with ever so much Earnestness, He will all at once fly from the Subject for a Moment to throw out any Idea, gay or serious, that happens to come across Him: of this our Conversation furnished several Instances. I will just mention one. [Speaking of the partition of Poland, he said:] 'There's nothing, my Lord, like being in a good, safe Island.'[12]

A sympathetic picture of Joseph can usually be matched by a hostile one. By contrast with British observers, Frenchmen, during this period of Franco-Austrian alliance, commonly saw the worst in everything Austrian. No doubt the emperor's informality and pragmatism approached nearer to British than to French ideals. Guibert, after an hour-and-half's conversation with Joseph in 1773, felt both weary and jaundiced. The emperor, he wrote

speaks with facility, sometimes even with a sort of eloquence. But you soon perceive the lack of education: you see that these are parrot phrases; or you know that they come from other people with whom he's talked on the same subject; you do not pick up or take away any flash of wit, any idea. You come to realise that he lacks discernment; that he's irremediably superficial; that he doesn't grasp things . . . During the conversation he said some indiscreet things, even some things that were out of place; but most conspicuously, some [that were] obscure, empty and commonplace. Every minute he would use the phrase 'a young man, a man who needed to learn'. He was forgetting that at the age of thirty-three a man has no right to call himself a young man, especially when he's a sovereign. After describing the way in which he passes his days, he finally said: 'this is how I try to fill my time, and when I've been faithful to my scheme, I say to myself happily in the evening, "Joseph, go to bed."' And as he uttered this common expression, he smacked himself lightly on the cheek, so vulgarly that I shall never forget it.[13]

---

[11] Stormont to Suffolk, 19 Oct. 1771, 'particular' (PRO SP 80/210).
[12] Stormont to Suffolk, 2 Dec. 1772, 'secret' (PRO SP 80/212).
[13] Guibert, *Journal*, vol. II, pp. 247–9. See below, p. 315, for another example of J. apostrophising himself.

Wraxall drew his more favourable portrait of the emperor six years later, at the end of the co-regency:

[His] countenance is full of meaning and intelligence. I have rarely seen a more speaking physiognomy; and it is impossible to look at him, without conceiving a favourable idea of his understanding. His eye, which is quick, sparkles with animation . . . An air of mind, which is spread over his features, pleases and prejudices in his favour.

But by this time both Joseph's appearance and his manner had deteriorated. 'So bald is he now become at only thirty-eight, that on the crown of his head, scarcely any covering remains; and in order to conceal the defect, he wears a false toupee.' In his audiences 'he may be reproached . . . with frequently anticipating the answers of the persons with whom he converses. A mixture of vanity and of impetuosity conduce to this defect. While he talks, especially if he is eager, he always plays with the money in his pocket.'[14] The prince de Ligne, who knew Joseph well for forty years, mentioned other eccentricities. The emperor kept in his pocket some large cards so that he could easily make notes or write messages. He would take a visitor by the elbow and then seem to repent of it. He would break off a conversation to put a log on the fire, to pick up the tongs or to look out of the window. In the company of women he would perform all the duties of a waiter.[15]

This 'extraordinary Condescension' – or, as Guibert thought it, vulgarity – could go further still. Ligne said: 'It often happened that I annoyed the emperor Joseph. But there were many ways of handling such a nice man who possessed such superior qualities, I . . . two or three times told him some harsh truths in the presence of all those who made up society.' If the emperor was contradicted, he might show a moment's irritation. Then he would rub his hands and resume amicable conversation.[16] Ligne, of course, had a specially favoured position, being a prince of the Empire and one of Joseph's army comrades. But humbler mortals too remarked on his reasonableness. Karl von Zinzendorf, for most of this period an imperial chamberlain and a lowly official, was impressed not only by his master's civility and graciousness but also by his receptivity. In June 1771 'the emperor called me into his study and made me read a plan for commercial reforms, very badly written and thoroughly pernicious. I told him my frank opinion of it. He came out again in order to discuss it with us.'[17] Even the empress acknowledged: 'the emperor likes the truth, provided that it is put to him in a certain fashion, without muttering'.[18]

[14] Wraxall, *Memoirs*, vol. II, pp. 430, 445.   [15] Ligne, *Mémoires*, vol. I, pp. 240–3.
[16] Ligne, *Fragments*, vol. I, p. 122. Dittersdorf exactly captures this reaction of J.'s in recounting their meeting in 1786 (K. D. von Dittersdorf, *Lebensbeschreibung*, ed. E. Schmitz (Regensburg, 1940), pp. 211–12).
[17] HHSA TZ, 26 June 1771. Cf. 9 Jan. and 27 Feb. 1771, 24 May 1772, 2 May 1774, 16 Apr. 1775, 7 Jan. 1776 etc.
[18] M.T. to Rosenberg, Feb. 1769 (Arneth, *MTKuF* IV, p. 66).

All these statements betray a lurking unease about Joseph's temper. Others were more explicit. Binder told Zinzendorf: 'You must ... speak to the emperor in such a way that he may give the impression of always taking the decision himself. Count Hatzfeld often sees the resolutions he has drafted, completely crossed out.'[19] During Joseph's visit to Naples in 1769 Sir William Hamilton 'accompanied him to the summit of Vesuvius, and with concern saw him break his cane over the shoulders of the guide, Bartolomeo, for some slight offence he had given His Imperial Majesty'.[20] But these pieces of evidence are put into a rather different light by comments made during the same visit by Leopoldine Kaunitz, whose husband was then Austrian ambassador to Naples. She tells her sister that she has observed in Joseph good qualities she had no idea he possessed. The empress had never allowed it to be known that he was 'always kind and never familiar'. 'He shows consideration for servants such as many private persons don't show.'

From this time, I cannot thank God enough that we have a prince who thinks as he does. I acknowledge that there is much eccentricity – perhaps as much as in my dear father-in-law – but all his ideas are just and good in tendency. He wills and desires the good, and to help him obtain it he has much – very much – talent.[21]

Challenged by her sister, the countess reiterated her opinion:

I saw the emperor here, I assure you I took immense trouble to find in him traces of the character that is described to us, and I swear to you that I found him on every possible occasion the most humane, the most straightforward, the most honourable man in the world.

She was quite certain that he behaved exceptionally well towards his servants.

But ... it is true that he's determined to be properly served, and that deceit, dishonesty, tale-bearing, excessive delicacy and exaggerated deference can put him in a frightful rage ... I think ... that the majority of our great aristocratic lords will not be treated as well as they would like; but so far as injustice is concerned, he will do it to no one, he will be the father of the poor – not of the layabouts, but of the common people. He will always put the general good before his whims and fancies, but he will require others to think the same, and if they refuse, he will act on their behalf and they will call him hard because they are too tender towards themselves.[22]

No one else who knew him well spoke quite so favourably of him as she did. It was poor recompense – but alas! typical of him – that he should have said of her to Leopold: 'I find her as ugly as she is insufferable.'[23]

---

[19] HHSA TZ, 26 May 1776.
[20] Wraxall, *Historical Memoirs*, p. 152. This is a continuation of the passage quoted on p. 261 and discussed in n. 69 above.
[21] L.K. to E.L., 9 Apr. 1769 (SOALpZ, LRRA P. 16/21).
[22] L.K. to E.L., 10 Feb. 1770 (*ibid.*, P. 16/22). In fact, M.T. in her instructions for Max Franz wrote an encomium on J.'s behaviour to his servants (Arneth, *GMT* VII, p. 573).
[23] 17 Nov. 1772 (Arneth, *MTuJ* I, p. 387).

Frederick told one of his ministers after meeting the emperor in 1769: he 'is frank and full of candour'.[24] Wraxall, by contrast, declared him 'a profound dissembler, rarely or never speaking his real sentiments on any point of moment'.[25] Guibert took a more convincing position than either: 'since he talks a great deal, he keeps on laying bare his principles'.[26] Frederick confirmed this judgement after mature reflexion, in his *Memoirs of 1763 to 1775*: 'This young prince affected a frankness that seemed natural to him ...; but what indicated his character more than anything ... were some remarks that escaped him despite himself, and revealed the boundless ambition that consumed him.'[27] He certainly guarded himself against revealing state secrets. In the *Rêveries* he envisaged keeping his fundamental purposes hidden.[28] He paid consciously hypocritical compliments to Catherine II.[29] His stories, like most people's, no doubt sometimes improved in the telling, as perhaps in his more violent diatribes to Leopold about his mother and Kaunitz. But the fact that he often responded to importunate enquiries by turning his back[30] strongly suggests that he found dissimulation difficult. As Stormont indicated, he was reluctant to talk politics to ambassadors, lest he give himself away.[31] When asked about the interception of despatches, which was generally a taboo subject, he was unusually, if not completely, honest: he admitted that the practice existed but said it yielded little information and was justifiable only in wartime.[32] His spontaneous letters to Leopold contrasted sharply with the canny replies.[33] He found it, in fact, easier to be open than deceitful. As countess Kaunitz said, 'while others torture themselves to seem or become good, the emperor strains to appear wicked'.[34] The chief deception he practised – as all monarchs surely must – was to be polite and friendly, nearly all the time, to people he despised and disliked, like poor countess Kaunitz.

Many observers accused Joseph, if not of dishonesty, of affectation. His grief at his first wife's death had seemed forced, his ideas about love

---

[24] F. to Finckenstein, 7 Sep. 1769 (*PC*, vol. XXIX, p. 69).
[25] Wraxall, *Memoirs*, vol. II, p. 446.
[26] Guibert, *Journal*, vol. II, p. 253.
[27] J. D. E. Preuss (ed.), *Oeuvres de Frédéric le Grand* (31 vols., Berlin, 1846–57), vol. VI, p. 25.
[28] See p. 101.
[29] See pp. 436, 438. In a letter to Lacy, 22 Aug. 1773, he scoffs at the performance of the Russian troops he has just seen, but tells Lacy to compliment the Russian ambassador on it: 'cella ne pourra faire que du bien' (HHSA FA Sbde 72).
[30] See p. 259.
[31] See not only Stormont's remark quoted above (p. 308) but also Keith to Stormont, e.g. 16 May and 1 July 1781 (PRO FO 7/1), on the difficulty of obtaining information once J. had become sole ruler.
[32] De Witte, *Journal de l'abbé de Véri*, vol. II, p. 47. See F. Stix, 'Zur Geschichte und Organisation der Wiener Geheimen Ziffernkanzlei', *MÖIG* LI (1937), pp. 131–60.
[33] See pp. 150–1, 423–4.
[34] L.K. to E.L., 16 Oct. 1773, taking up a similar remark in E.L.'s letter of 13 Oct. (SOALpZ, LRRA P. 16/23). Cf. K-M's remarks, quoted p. 298 above.

counterfeit. Frederick has just been quoted on his affected frankness, countess Kaunitz on his spurious wickedness.[35] Guibert not only considered his conversation second-hand, but said of his manner of travel:

> He made his latest journey with only four or five people in his suite; lodging in hotels, often sleeping on straw, eating very badly, riding peasants' horses . . .; in all this he shows affectation, meanness, he glories in it; he told everyone about it on his return.[36]

Others beside Guibert stressed his imitation of Frederick.[37] According to Verri, he 'tries so hard to be affable that I fear at bottom he isn't'; 'Caesar's charm, I think, is borrowed; perhaps his information is too; he makes every effort to be democratic.'[38] His hatred of ceremony was thought self-conscious. Leopold claimed he 'says and does everything in order to be praised and talked about'.[39] The testimony is strong – though not universal – that his public personality seemed false. It was not the fault of the artists who painted him, usually for public exhibition and in more formal dress than he liked to wear, that they generally made him look cold and constrained. Only Liotard succeeded in capturing something of his private liveliness.[40]

A defence was supplied by Dr Moore: 'If the whole tenor of any person's words and actions is to be considered an affectation, I do not know by what means we are to get to the bottom of his real character.'[41] So far as some of Joseph's stances are concerned, this argument seems at first sight conclusive. He was utterly consistent in his grief for his first wife, in his manner of travel, in his dislike of ceremony and in his zeal for economy. He scarcely wavered in his military predilections. But he was excessively self-conscious about his views and principles, always narcissistically preening himself on them. To some degree Joseph himself justified his critics in a disarming letter to Leopold: 'I am a charlatan of reason and modesty. I overdo it a bit in these respects so that I seem simple, natural, thoughtful even to excess; and this is what has won me approval.'[42] He evidently did not realise what a poor actor he was.

It is not hard to identify the origin of this almost adolescent insecurity. Maria Theresa too used to scoff at her son's persona, but, herself 'an actress all her life', she clearly had much to do with its artificiality.[43] George III's

---

[35] See p. 311.   [36] Guibert, *Journal*, vol. II, p. 254.

[37] M.T. for example (see p. 147). The overriding importance of Frederick's influence on J.'s and Lacy's army policies was stressed by 'Cogniazzo', the mysterious author of *Freymüthiger Beytrag zur Geschichte des österreichischen Militairdienstes* (Frankfurt, 1780) and *Geständnisse eines Oestreichischen Veterans* (4 parts, Breslau, 1788–91).

[38] P. to A. Verri, 1 and 8 July 1769 (both in cipher), Greppi and Giulini, *Carteggio di P. e di A. Verri*, vol. II, pp. 341, 352.

[39] E.g. Moore, *View of Society*, vol. II, p. 391; Wandruszka, *L. II*, vol. I, p. 342.

[40] See Frontispiece and Plates 10, 11, 13 and 24. On J.'s portraits, H. Egger in *ÖZKf*, pp. 274–8. On Liotard, W. Koschatzky in *MTIZ*, pp. 308–19.

[41] *View of Society*, vol. II, p. 391.   [42] J. to L., 10 July 1777 (Arneth, *MTuf* II, p. 148).

[43] E.g. M.T. to Herzelles, 2 July 1772: Kervyn de Lettenhove, *MARB in-8o* (1868), 33; E.L. to L.K., 16 Oct. 1778 (SOALpZ, LRRA P. 17/24).

mother, it was said, kept urging him to 'be a king'. Joseph's made greater demands still. He must prove not only a worthy emperor, but also a submissive co-regent, a great yet pacific general, and a moral paragon. Khevenhüller reported a discussion with Joseph in 1772 that illustrates the pressure that was put on him and felt by him. The chamberlain had been sent by Maria Theresa to settle differences with her son over the Court's forth-coming visit to Laxenburg.

The conversation ... turned on the way in which great men are trammelled, and the difficulties they have in getting to know their servants, since everyone tries to dissemble in their presence; and although we were not fully in agreement on the first point, since it is very well known that this young lord much dislikes accepting constraints, still he had to agree with me that he was bound in many circumstances to accept them of his own free will and for good reason. Moreover, I must acknowledge to his praise that he listens to the truth, and that it is very evident that he never stops working on himself, so that there is good ground for hope that, with the Grace of God, he will become in his time a great Christian ruler.[44]

How far he sought popularity is a difficult issue. Contemporary remarks on this subject can be misleading. 'Popolare' in Italian, 'populaire' in French and other such adjectives, which were often applied to his conduct, have pejorative connotations reflecting noble disdain at ungentlemanly behaviour; they seldom relate to what we call popularity.[45] Joseph's readiness to be affable to everyone, to eliminate the cost and complexity of traditional dress and etiquette, to behave in a way that put relatively humble members of society at their ease, to throw open the royal parks, to go behind the backs of lords and officials and receive the complaints and petitions of the poorest – all this represented for many observers treason not just to monarchy, but to the entire aristocratic order. Such critics refused to entertain the possibility that an emperor might genuinely sympathise, and think it his duty to sympathise, with the lower classes. This incomprehension is evident in Guibert, and also in Verri, Firmian and Leopold.[46] It was a further black mark against Joseph that, while he was mean in his own pleasures and towards the already wealthy, he was generous in rewarding hard cases and those who did him small services on his travels.[47] He never dreamed of asking the advice and opinion of the people as a body; he made no public speeches; and he shrugged off public criticism, speaking savagely of journalists and pamphleteers.[48] When asked

---

44 K-M VII, pp. 142–3 (30 Aug. 1772).
45 I have translated them as 'egalitarian' and 'democratic' on pp. 159, 254, 312. Guibert uses both *populaire* and *trivial* in this sense; I have translated them as 'common' and 'vulgarly' (see p. 308).
46 See pp. 197–8, 267, 308, 312.
47 L.K. to E.L., 9 Apr. 1769 (SOALpZ, LRRA P. 16/21); Dengel, *Jahrbuch der österreichischen Leogesellschaft* (1926), p. 87; Wandruszka, *L. II.*, vol. I, p. 344; Rumpel, 'Reisen Kaiser J. II. nach Galizien', p. 8; Wraxall, *Memoirs*, vol. II, pp. 461–2.
48 See p. 5. J. to L., 6 Mar. 1775: 'je suis de l'avis qu'il faut laisser dire tranquillement tout le monde ce qu'ils veulent, pourvu qu'ils nous laissent faire ce que nous voulons' (Arneth, *MTuJ*

about 'the tribute of public applause', he said 'he himself had sometimes been
applauded ... when he didn't deserve to be, and vice versa. We must do good
according to our own views.' But he displayed some pleasure in what we call
popularity; he sometimes appealed to public opinion in writing; and he tried
to find out what impression he had made during his journeys, 'as a guide to my
future conduct'.[49]

There was something forced about his relationship with ordinary people.
He was not one of those very rare monarchs like Peter the Great and Henry IV
who could throw off his royalty and talk naturally with all his subjects.
However unsatisfactory his education and reading, he was an intellectual. His
fastidiousness had blenched at the coarseness even of the king of Naples.[50] But
nonetheless it was his own special eccentricity, for which he had no obvious
model – and it is striking that it was regarded as so eccentric – to be accessible
to all petitioners and, worse still, to act on their petitions.[51]

He loved telling his visitors and correspondents how busy he was, though
sometimes it was with what he considered useless formal engagements.[52] Yet
he often felt under-employed, especially when in Vienna. He might then
complain to his mother and perhaps be given something more to do, as with
the *Staatsrat* in 1771 and 1774 or with the *Hofkriegsrat* in 1772.[53] Or he might
go on a journey, when his days would certainly be filled with hectic travel,
sightseeing, inspections, audiences and committees.[54] It is impossible to
accept the view, quite common at the time, that he shunned hard work.[55] He
would not interrupt his performance of his duties to have a decent or even a
punctual dinner. He found it difficult to get secretaries who could write as fast
as he wanted to dictate.[56] What he chafed at was slow, meticulous work,
especially when it allowed him no chance to show initiative. But he revelled in
activity he regarded as useful to the state. He wrote to Lacy:

II, p. 57). I guess that the 'libelle fait en Angleterre' to which J. here refers was G. Pansmouser
([?] J. Lind), *Le Partage de la Pologne, en sept dialogues* (London, [1774]). See Horn, *British
Opinion and the Partition of Poland*, pp. 29–31; Beales, *HJ* (1975), 489.

[49] P. Verri's diary of J.'s visit to Milan (Valsecchi, *L'assolutismo illuminato*, vol. II, p. 304). J. to
L., 1 Aug. 1773 (Arneth, *MTuJ* II, p. 16). See p. 4 above for the 'pastoral letter' published
in 1783.

[50] See pp. 260–1.

[51] See pp. 267–8. Although Frederick the Great made much of inspection-tours and insisted on
incognito, lack of ceremony and limited expenditure during his travels, he did not make
himself available to receive petitions from all and sundry. (Cf. Hubatsch, *Frederick the Great*,
esp. pp. 43–55; an eye-witness account in P. Paret (ed.), *Frederick the Great: A Profile*
(London, 1972), pp. 79–98.) However, Charles Eugene of Württemberg did (see J. A. Vann,
The Making of a State: Württemberg, 1593–1793 (London, 1984), p. 263).

[52] See pp. 139, 392n.   [53] See pp. 207–8, 223, 228–9.   [54] E.g. pp. 248, 265–8, 361.

[55] E.g. Guibert, *Journal*, vol. II, p. 255: 'il n'aime pas le travail, excepté celui ayant rapport au
militaire'. L., having first said J. was casual about all business except military affairs, then said
J. left even them to Lacy (Wandruszka, *L. II.*, vol. I, pp. 342–3).

[56] K-M VII, p. 137 (2 Dec. 1772).

The continuous application you have practised all your life saps your health. I see myself going the same way, more or less. But one must achieve something sometime, come what may. The future is so uncertain that only a fool neglects to take advantage of the present. This argument can be used by the lazy on behalf of their system, but I apply it to mine: do all the good one can, acquire all imaginable knowledge and reputation, and it's always prudent to play for high stakes because, since one doesn't know how long the game will last, it's better to risk making a great gain or losing altogether than to proceed cautiously and find oneself on the point of finishing one's career just at the moment of achievement. God knows whether the things that are going right today, if I put them off, will go so well tomorrow.[57]

He longed for fame; but he also sought an outlet for his energies, and a refuge from inner unhappiness and frustration, in frantic administration.

His claim that his health was being undermined by his activity seemed justified. Already in 1771 he had a boil that prevented him riding, and the first of many recorded attacks of piles.[58] Two years later, Khevenhüller thought that Joseph had himself bled too often for a man of only thirty-two.[59] At the end of the decade, according to Wraxall:

the Emperor ... is affected with an aneurism in his leg. When he is heated, the pulsation of the artery is so strong, that I am assured it may be perceptibly felt with the finger, through the thickest stocking ... He has another extraordinary source of disease: it is an excrescence, of the nature of a wen, on the crown of his head, which naturally increases in size, and may become dangerous in process of time.[60]

In this period, however, illness rarely prevented him from travelling, working or taking recreation.

Guibert wrote that Joseph's work in Vienna

fills his morning, which he begins very early ..., with the result that in the afternoon, since he is incapable of occupying his mind with anything instructive or interesting, he is consumed with boredom. He doesn't know what to do with himself; he gets into his barouche, goes to the public parks, to the theatre even though he doesn't like it, into private houses ... until ten o'clock when he returns home, going to bed early, never taking supper.[61]

The emperor certainly appeared restless, but he commonly worked longer hours than Guibert said, fitting in a daily visit to his mother, and he usually found enough recreation as well. He took a good deal of exercise, riding regularly, hunting or shooting quite often, and playing tennis.[62] In the

[57] J. to Lacy, 2 July 1773 (HHSA FA Sbde 72). I wonder whether this passage was construed by Lacy (or even intended) as a refusal of the leave for which he had asked. See p. 223 above.
[58] J. to L., 8 Aug. 1771 (HHSA FA Sbde 7, not in Arneth, *MTuJ*).
[59] K-M VII, p. 162 (25 Apr. 1773).
[60] Wraxall, *Memoirs*, vol. II, p. 431.
[61] Guibert, *Journal*, vol. II, p. 256. The timetable is largely borne out by other accounts, e.g. J. to L., 22 Dec. 1774 (Arneth, *MTuJ* II, p. 52), though J. includes his visit to M.T. and, after dinner, some work on state papers or some music.
[62] In addition to J.'s correspondence Wraxall, *Memoirs*, vol. II, p. 434.

evening he was frequently to be seen at the opera or the play. If he spent much of the performance talking to ladies or to Kaunitz in their boxes, this was normal contemporary behaviour;[63] it did not mean that he lacked interest in the productions. On the contrary, as we have seen, he had decided views about them and therefore influenced the development of the theatre.[64] He would sometimes attend balls, though he very rarely danced and refused to wear a mask – except, perversely, once when it was optional.[65]

He hardly alludes in his surviving correspondence to purely instrumental music or to his own playing. But several independent witnesses tell us that he regularly, even daily, set aside time for it.[66] Dr Charles Burney, the English musical historian and traveller, wrote in 1772: 'The whole imperial family is musical; the Emperor perhaps just enough for a sovereign prince, that is, with sufficient hand, both on the violoncello and harpsichord, to amuse himself; and sufficient judgment to hear, understand, and receive delight from others.'[67] Joseph accompanied his sisters' singing, and thought himself skilled enough to assist their musical education. He occasionally sang himself in family concerts.[68] But his favourite instrument was the cello, which he frequently played with some of the musicians in his employment. Joseph was thought to be over-influenced by the opinions and jealousies of these men, especially of Kreibich, their leader, who was an enemy of Haydn.[69] But in 1768 the emperor tried, though without success, to secure the performance in Vienna of an opera he had encouraged the young Mozart to write, *La finta semplice*; and five years later Joseph attended rehearsals of Dittersdorf's oratorio, *Esther*, and preferred it to the rival work of a composer he employed

---

[63] E.g. HHSA TZ, 29 Dec. 1770: 'l'Empereur fut chez lui [Kaunitz] toute la petite piece'. See p. 205.
   Cf. E.L. to L.K., 13 Feb. 1771: 'il fait toujours presque le tour des loges ... Il parla beaucoup aux femmes' (SOALpZ, LRRA P. 16/22).
   On behaviour at the opera, admittedly with reference to Italy, see Rosselli, *Opera Industry*, pp. 9–11.

[64] See pp. 231–6.

[65] E.g. J. to L., 16 Feb. 1775 (Arneth, *MTuJ* II, p. 56); K-M VII, pp. 60, 156 and VIII, pp. 11, 100–1.

[66] One of J.'s very few references is in his letter to L. of 22 Dec. 1774 (Arneth, *MTuJ* II, p. 52). Also J. to L., 16 Mar. 1772, not in Arneth (HHSA FA Sbde 7). Ligne, *Mémoires*, vol. I, p. 241; K. F. Linger (ed.), *Denkwürdigkeiten aus dem Leben des k.k. Hofrathes H. G. von Bretschneider* (Vienna, 1892), p. 289; *Musikalische Korrespondenz* I (1790), 27–9; J. Pezzl, *Charakteristik Josephs II.* (Vienna, 1790), p. 325. I derive the two last references from the discussion by O. Biba, 'Kaiser Joseph II. und die Musik' in *ÖZKJ*, pp. 260–5.

[67] Scholes, *Eighteenth-Century Musical Tour*, vol. II, p. 88.

[68] See above, p. 198. J. to M.T., 31 Jan. 1767 (Arneth, *MTuJ* I, p. 214). A painting in the Kunsthistorisches Museum, Vienna, shows J. with his sisters at the harpsichord (see Plate 13). The Museum contains one of his pianos. Evidence is given in *ÖZKJ*, p. 658, that J. played the organ too.

[69] See, as well as the article in the *Musikalische Korrespondenz* (1790) cited in n. 66: Reichardt's autobiography in *Allgemeine musikalische Zeitung*, XV (1813), cols. 667–8; Dittersdorf, *Lebensbeschreibung*, pp. 210–11, 214–15; H. C. Robbins Landon, *Haydn at Esterháza, 1766–1790* (London, 1978), pp. 412–13, 413n.

and respected, Gassmann.[70] So he was capable of independent judgement in
musical matters. His taste, however, as one might expect, had been formed by
hearing and playing works of composers older than himself, like Monn
(1717–50), Gassmann (1729–74) and Sonnleithner (1734–86). From the
last-named he commissioned no fewer than thirty-six string quartets. He was
known to be especially fond of fugues, and in general to prefer the contra-
puntal music of the late Baroque or Rococo to the classical style associated
with Haydn and Mozart.[71] During the 1780s his predilections became
immensely significant in musical history. It is clear that they were founded on
his regular playing of a limited repertoire for recreation.

As for the visual arts, he at first showed not the slightest liking for them. But
Rome awakened some architectural appreciation, and by the end of the
co-regency, to the satisfaction of persons as various as Pietro Verri and
Wraxall,[72] he was helping to bring together the Habsburg collections of
paintings into a new gallery in the Belvedere palace, and trying to buy
canvases for it at bargain prices.[73] It was open to the public, at that time a
remarkable innovation.[74] The scheme owed much to Kaunitz's enthusiasm,
and no doubt the chancellor educated the emperor in this field as in others. All
concerned seem to have been impressed by the didactic as much as by the
aesthetic value of an art-collection.[75]

Guibert declared that Joseph never read a book, and Ligne that he read only
state papers. These statements cannot be literally true, and Guibert's was a
particularly hard saying, since his own essay on tactics was almost the only
work that we know Joseph claimed to have studied after the end of his formal
education.[76] He once borrowed a volume of the physiocratic periodical,
Nouvelles Ephémérides, from Karl Zinzendorf, and gave every appearance of
having read it when he returned it. His mother remarked in 1772 that at one
time he had loathed reading books, 'but he now sees the utility and necessity

[70] Letters of Leopold Mozart to L. Hagenauer, 30 Jan., 30 July, 14, 21 and 24 Sep. 1768 (W. A. Bauer and O. E. Deutsch, *Mozart. Briefe und Aufzeichnungen. Gesamtausgabe* (7 vols., Kassel, 1962–75), vol. I, pp. 257–8, 169–73, 278, 280–4). Dittersdorf, *Lebensbeschreibung*, pp. 190–1.
[71] The evidence is collected in Biba, *ÖZKJ*, pp. 261–4. The research of W. Kirkendale, *Fuge und Fugato in der Kammermusik des Rokoko und der Klassik* (Tutzing, 1966), has uncovered much new information about J.'s musical connexions – for this period see esp. pp. 60, 64–6, 80–1 (especially the diagram on p. 81 showing how J. fitted into the school of composer-teachers deriving from Fux), 87–90.
[72] See p. 259. P. to A. Verri, 17 Mar. 1779 (Giulini and Seregni, *Carteggio di P. e di A. Verri*, vol. X, p. 223). Wraxall, *Memoirs*, vol. II, pp. 435–6.
[73] Arneth, 'Maria Theresia und der Hofrat von Greiner', *Sitzungsberichte KAW* (1859), Heft III, 374–5.
[74] F. Klauner, *Picture Gallery of the Art History Museum, Vienna* (London, 1970), pp. 11–12; R. Neck, 'Das Sammelwesen' in *MTIZ*, p. 270.
[75] A Novotny, *Staatskanzler Kaunitz als geistige Persönlichkeit* (Vienna, 1947), pp. 133–5; Wraxall, *Memoirs*, vol. II, p. 436; G. Heinz, 'Die figürlichen Künste zur Zeit Josephs II.' in *ÖZKJ*, pp. 182–3.
[76] Guibert, *Journal*, vol. II, pp. 247, 255; Ligne, *Mémoires*, vol. I, p. 241.

of it'.[77] Readings took place at meetings of his favoured coteries, with his approval; he read to countess Windischgrätz during her last illness; his knowledge of Voltaire's writings passed muster with Frederick the Great; and when planning his visit to France, he remarked that he had no enthusiasm to meet *savants* whose works he could read.[78] In a letter of 1781 to the elector of Trier, written while he was on manoeuvres, he flaunted the names of three ecclesiastical controversialists, Febronius, the Jansenist Quesnel and the Jesuit Busenbaum, but claimed to have at hand only Frederick the Great's instruction to his generals and the *Rêveries* of the marshal de Saxe. Countess Kaunitz talked of his following the theories of Helvetius and Holbach. But his broad acquaintance with literature on many subjects must have owed much to conversation. As he said, it was quicker to extract the essence of others' learning in discussion than to do the reading himself.[79]

His principal and most characteristic recreation was to participate, almost every evening, in the talk of a coterie. Here, as Guibert acknowledged, he had no model among monarchs: Frederick would have been the last person to pass his evenings in a group mainly composed of women. The nature of Joseph's relations with these coteries must be considered as part of the broader topic of his friendships, especially with the other sex. More can be said about this matter than historians have realised: princess Liechtenstein's letters have been little used, and Arneth suppressed most of the passages in the emperor's which concerned his relations with women.[80]

PERSONAL RELATIONSHIPS, ESPECIALLY WITH WOMEN

The ever-critical Guibert declared Joseph equally incapable of friendship and of love. Among male acquaintances, however, 'he has two chamberlains for whom he appears to have a liking as he took them on his travels, M. De Siskowitz and M. de Nostitz, the latter a lieutenant-general. Both are mediocrities, and furthermore are in his confidence only to a limited extent.'[81] Leopold, still more captious, gave a much longer list of his brother's intimates in 1778:

[77] HHSA TZ, 12 and 15 Dec. 1775. M.T. to Ferd, 28 Oct. (1772) (Arneth, *MTKuF* I, pp. 163–4).

[78] J. to the *Dames*, 27 Aug. 1773 (SOALpZ, LRRA P. 16/22 and 23, copies); L.K. to E.L., 1 Nov. 1774 (*ibid.*, P. 16/23); Wraxall, *Memoirs*, vol. II, p. 421; Frederick to Voltaire, 18 Aug. 1770 (*VC* LXXVI, pp. 112–13); p. 369 below.

[79] Mohnike, *Zeitschrift für die Historische Theologie* (1834), p. 282; Wolf, *Fürstin Eleonore Liechtenstein*, p. 165. See p. 154.

[80] Guibert's remark: *Journal*, vol. II, p. 255. By far the best information on J. and the coteries is in Wolf, *Fürstin Eleonore Liechtenstein*, but I cite the original correspondence of the sisters because Wolf was sparing with dates and actual quotations. Bernard, *EEQ* (1976), seems to me to have garbled the story.

[81] Guibert, *Journal*, vol. II, p. 251.

Marshal Lacy has the greatest influence on him, although [the emperor] fears rather than likes him; generals Pellegrini, D'Alton, Fabris, Barco, Kinsky; count Hatzfeld; Hauer, Türckheim and other such people from the *Hofkriegsrat*; count Cobenzl from the *Banco*; but especially, baser men, the surgeon Brambilla, the servant Mayer who attends him [and] is all-powerful, a thoroughly bad fellow, pander, rogue and altogether wicked, his secretaries Vetter and Knecht, the valet Strack; prince Charles Liechtenstein and the master of the horse, Dietrichstein, to whom he's always writing and whom, although he doesn't esteem him, he uses as a trumpet, writing to him those fine statements and principles that he wants spread abroad to win popularity and to put what has been done in a suitable light.

This passage is remarkable not only for its venom but also for lumping together generals, ministers, a prince and menials. No doubt this seemed natural enough to a monarch. Even countess Kaunitz, in her appraisal of Joseph, had slipped easily from discussing his humble to his aristocratic servants.[82] But clearly the emperor was not so democratic in outlook that he treated his valet and prince Liechtenstein in exactly the same way.

Every ruler is blamed for paying excessive attention to those who as servants have ready access to him. One of the emperor's quirks certainly gave them a special opportunity: he generally ate a 'solitary' dinner, during which he used to talk to the waiter.[83] But although almost no hard evidence exists to prove or disprove Leopold's claims, a snatch of Joseph's badinage with the violinist Kreibich, recorded by Dittersdorf, gives some help. The emperor had been learning to sing, with the appropriate by-play, a comic song he had heard in a suburban theatre.

'Well, what do you think of it?' he once asked Kreibich. 'Do I sing the aria as the clown does?' 'Oh, oh, oh!' replied Kreibich, with his usual happy inspiration, 'upon my soul Your Majesty is the clown to the life!' The emperor cried with laughter. 'My dear Kreibich', he said at last, 'you really are the rudest of men! Do you call me a clown in front of my musicians?' 'Eh, eh, eh!' replied Kreibich, 'I didn't mean that. I blurted it out without thinking. I must beg your pardon.' 'Oh!' answered the emperor, 'you're forgiven already. You know very well that there are some people one cannot take amiss.' 'You mean idiots?' 'You've got it', replied the emperor. 'Meanwhile, you've fully revenged yourself on me for having often called you a buffoon. But ... the difference is that I was a clown only so long as I was singing, while you'll remain a buffoon now and for ever, *per omnia saecula saeculorum!*'[84]

This exchange well illustrates Joseph's jocose familiarity with his servants and his fondness for insensitive mockery; but it does not suggest that he much respected Kreibich's opinion. Probably the same was true of his relations with most of his servants.

[82] Wandruszka, *L. II.*, vol. I, p. 345. See p. 310 above.
[83] Wraxall, *Memoirs*, vol. II, pp. 432–3.
[84] Dittersdorf, *Lebensbeschreibung*, pp. 214–15. I have been helped by the translation of A. D. Coleridge in *The Autobiography of Karl von Dittersdorf* (London, 1896), p. 255, but I have attempted a different method of doing justice to the pun on the name Kasperl, having

On the other hand, everyone agreed that his chief secretary held an influential position. When Röder, appointed in 1765, died in 1772,[85] great interest was taken in Joseph's choice of a successor. He provisionally selected captain Weber, who had been working at the Austrian legation in Berlin. Joseph called him

a discreet and almost too misanthropic man, living alone, who after thirty years' service has asked for neither title nor pension. We shall see how efficient he is; his character, so far as I know it, would suit me well. [He's] a bachelor and from Freiburg, aged forty-eight.

Khevenhüller recorded that 'from [the emperor's] description he must be an eccentric rather than a *philosophe*, which the world thinks him'. Maria Theresa felt greater anxiety:

he's a Catholic but doesn't let it show, as he never goes to Church or to the sacrament [and accepts] no moral code – an elderly misanthrope . . . He reads only English books and Machiavelli. These are the clutches into which my son has fallen. He's another recommendation of Nostitz's. He lives on eight kreutzers a day and wears the same suit for years on end. That greatly recommends him. Imagine what harm such a man can do.

After a few months' experience of him, Joseph passed on to Leopold some of the secretary's *rêveries*, remarking that he was 'not a genius, but even less of a bigot'.[86]

The emperor presumably paid even more attention to the military men of whom he saw so much. Among them, apart from Lacy, it was Nostitz who was often singled out as a close friend of Joseph's and a bad influence on him. They sometimes dined together on their own, and Nostitz went on several journeys with the emperor.[87] If prince Charles Liechtenstein had resigned from the army in 1771, Joseph intended to appoint Nostitz to succeed him. One of the causes of the rupture between Lacy and the emperor in 1773 was thought to be the attitude of Nostitz.[88] Later, their friendship seems to have cooled.[89] But

concluded that 'Jack-pudding' was no longer current English. Given this conversation, it is interesting that J. considered his predecessors' practice of amusing themselves with fools both sad and childish (HHSA TZ, 30 Apr. 1772).

[85] On Röder see below, p. 328.

[86] J. to L., 9 July 1772 (Arneth, *MTuJ* I, p. 373); K-M VII, p. 137 (2 Aug. 1772) and also p. 424; M.T. to Herzelles, 31 July 1772 (Kervyn de Lettenhove, *MARB in-8o* (1868), 34). L.K. thought him an *esprit fort*: to E.L., 13 July 1772 (SOALpZ, LRRA P. 16/23).
J. to L., 20 Dec. 1772, not in Arneth, *MTuJ* (HHSA FA Sbde 7).

[87] See pp. 206, 247 above. In *PC* XXIX, p. 26n, there is a report from Vienna of 5 Aug. 1769 that Nostitz has superseded Dietrichstein in J.'s favour.
HHSA TZ, 18 Oct. 1770. Nostitz accompanied J. on most of his journeys until he found the hardships of Croatia too much for him (K-M VIII, p. 87). Cf. J. to L., 29 Oct. 1776 (Arneth, *MTuJ* II, p. 122).

[88] M.T. to Lacy (late Dec. 1770) and Lacy to M.T., 5 Jan. 1771 (HHSA NL, Karton 2). See p. 223.

[89] Wraxall, *Memoirs*, vol. II, p. 448.

unfortunately only one uninformative private letter to him from Joseph appears to have survived,[90] and it is impossible to discover much about their relationship.

Several other soldiers, not all of them mentioned by Leopold, had particular importance for Joseph. He certainly admired D'Alton for his work in Bohemia in the early seventies.[91] During the years of war before the first partition of Poland, the emperor took special trouble to humour general Poniatowski, brother of king Stanislaus Augustus, and promoted him in 1771; but Joseph's motives seem to have been political rather than personal.[92] The gauche and poorly connected Laudon, rival of Lacy, was treated by the emperor with notable respect, but hardly as a friend.[93] Ligne saw much of Joseph both in social and in military activities; and if the prince was sometimes too frivolous for his master's taste, the two men evidently enjoyed each other's company.[94] But Lacy's influence was almost always paramount.

A special role, however, was reserved for count Dietrichstein. As master of the horse and a prominent courtier, he was more visible than Nostitz, and sometimes acted as the emperor's emissary. He was believed to stand up to Joseph and say what he thought. Since he was a Freemason, he must have been more liberal than Maria Theresa liked.[95] Joseph mocked him, of course, and was not always satisfied with him.[96] But he retained his office until after Joseph's death, and their relationship remained friendly. If Leopold was right that the emperor wrote numerous letters to Dietrichstein, they seem to have been lost.

Joseph was close to two ambassadors, Renier, the future doge, Venetian envoy to Vienna in the late sixties,[97] and Rohan, the future cardinal, representative of France in the early seventies. By virtue of their office, these men ranked with royalty and moved in the highest society. Maria Theresa found Rohan's association with her son particularly distressing, since she believed the ambassador to be a disgrace to his cloth. He loved making just the kind of *bons mots* that Joseph relished and she abominated. In the end Rohan misbehaved so blatantly that he was recalled.[98]

---

[90] ÖNB Handschriften Autografen 436/11.   [91] See pp. 354–5.

[92] M.T. to Lacy, 31 Dec. 1770 (HHSA NL, Karton 2), says the whole promotion was distorted for love of Poniatowski, but E.L. to L.K., 7 Aug. 1771, says J. doesn't like him (SOALpZ, LRRA P. 16/22). It must be to the general and not to the king that M.T. referred in writing to Herzelles on 16 Dec. 1771 (Kervyn de Lettenhove, *MARB in-8o* (1868), 31).

[93] See pp. 407, 415, 425 below.   [94] I can only refer to Ligne's *Mémoires* and *Fragments, passim*.

[95] See p. 390. Wurzbach III, pp. 202–3. 'Tableau Caracteristique des Personnages qui composent la Cour et le Ministere de Vienne' (ÖNB Cod. Ser. n. 3230), a MS of 1781 clearly the work of someone very well informed.

[96] J. to L., 4 June 1769 (Arneth, *MTuJ* I, p. 287); E.L. to L.K., 13 Dec. 1771 (SOALpZ, LRRA P. 16/22).

[97] T. M. Marcellino, *Una forte personalità nel patriziato veneziano del Settecento: Paolo Renier* (Trieste, 1959), pp. 33–4.

[98] Many references to Rohan's misdeeds in Arneth & Geffroy I and II. On J. and Rohan, *ibid.* II, pp. 62–3. E.L. says J. behaved to Rohan like a *jolie femme coquette* (to L.K., 10 May 1772:

Among the most intimate and long-standing male acquaintances of the emperor's were count Philipp Cobenzl and count Franz Rosenberg. But their role – and Lacy's – cannot be properly understood without bringing into the picture Joseph's relationships with women. His first marriage, despite his wife's coolness, seems to have given him both intellectual and sexual satisfaction. After her death he was only with the greatest difficulty persuaded to marry again, and in his first period of widowhood his approaches to women – at least to women of title – seem to have been limited to the briefest flirtations.[99] During his disastrous second marriage, he begged his mother for permission to take part informally in the quasi-intellectual discussion-groups or coteries fashionable with some of his more enlightened noble subjects. In the context it is plain that he sought female as much as male society. Maria Theresa's response is unknown, but at about this time she was asking for lists of ladies suitable as company for her son.[100] Clearly his sister Josepha, until she died in 1767, and then the marquise d'Herzelles, his daughter's governess from 1767 to 1770, partly supplied this need – but only partly.[101] Princess Liechtenstein, though she often met him at countess Paar's, was sure in the spring of 1768 that he had formed no attachment. At Laxenburg in the summer of that year, she reported,

the emperor seems like a savage, a man who has never seen another human being. He's in an unimaginably bad temper. You don't know what to do or where to go. You're always wondering. You get caught on the stairs, in the corridor, you don't know whether to advance or retreat. My God, what ... price ... the life of the Court ...?[102]

Three weeks later Joseph wrote to Leopold that he was now 'given over to the pleasure, which I think unparalleled, of living quietly for myself'. After dinner

I generally go for a short ride on horseback or by carriage ... on my own with Dietrichstein or a chamberlain ... Otherwise, I am almost always discreet. Love doesn't divert me; I never feel it ... I'm a perfect bachelor, unwilling to tangle with anyone though ready to take what advantage I can from chance meetings.[103]

He remarked soon afterwards, in the letter about his passion for the wellbeing of the Monarchy which was quoted at the beginning of this book: 'Fortunately I have no wife or other attachment of any kind, and so I am free of care and

---

SOALpZ, LRRA P. 16/23). See also M.T. to Herzelles, 31 Aug. 1772 (Kervyn de Lettenhove, *MARB in-8o* (1868), 35–6).

[99] See pp. 85–6.

[100] See pp. 154–5 above. M.T.'s *apostille* on a letter of Silva-Tarouca's dated '1766': Karajan, *Feierliche Sitzungsberichte KAW* (1859), 68.

[101] See pp. 156, 201–3.

[102] E.L. to L.K., 14 June 1768 (SOALpZ, LRRA P. 16/21). See also the letter of the previous day.

[103] J. to L., 6 July 1768 (Arneth, *MTuJ* I, p. 223) with a passage restored (from HHSA FA Sbde 7) which Arneth omitted without any indication.

worry.'[104] He was obviously obsessed with the question at this time. In his very next letter, only three days later, he took it up again:

I talk to women so little that the other day our august mother, at a circle . . ., separated me from the foreign ministers, with whom I ordinarily make conversation, and condemned me to talk only to the ladies the whole time she remained. I did my best, I don't know how successfully: I'm inclined to think that to be scarce is a merit with women. [I found] I had the ability to make them laugh, which in my opinion is the true road to their hearts.

Then he went on to describe his 'system':

Like Epicurus's, [it] has never been able to give a high value, nor therefore wholehearted love, to these enchantresses. The laziness that I confess to has made me estimate everything at its true worth, and so women have naturally failed to impress me. The same [laziness] has made me invariably prefer ease and rapidity in my conquests to more glorious undertakings. So you can guess into what class I've descended, where, since my mind and heart are not involved, reason and honour have rescued and preserved me all the more easily.[105]

Philipp Cobenzl supplied the best account of an aristocratic coterie in these years, and the best evidence of Joseph's early involvement. Cobenzl, born in the same year as the emperor, was the nephew of the minister in Belgium and began his official career there. He moved to Vienna in 1767.

The most intimate of my friendships was with count Windischgrätz . . . He was the same age as I, married to a charming wife, who was an intimate friend of another most pleasant woman, . . . married to count Leopold Pálffy, whose aunt, countess Losy, though a very old lady, was very agreeable and had a charming character and was equally tied to the Windischgrätzes. So we formed a society of five persons, three women and two men, who used to see each other almost every day. We regularly spent the evening at the house of one or other of these ladies . . . We used to take tea, we chatted, and one of us read from an interesting work of some sort. These ladies had enquiring minds and were eager to be instructed; among other things they wanted to know something of physics, which led me to give them a regular course in the subject through one whole winter. To amuse them with a variety of experiments, I had had a pneumatic pump, an electric machine and some other instruments constructed.

The group kept together not only in town during the winter but also in the country during the summer and at Laxenburg.

For two years we five constituted the society, but in the third year a sixth person came to join us, honouring us often with his presence. It was the emperor Joseph who, when he wanted, put everyone at their ease without fuss and had the ability to be one of the most agreeable men in Society.

---

[104] J. to L., 25 July 1768 (Arneth, *MTuJ* I, p. 225).
[105] J. to L., 28 July 1768 (Arneth, *MTuJ* I, p. 228 – the last part restored from HHSA FA Sbde 7).

According to Cobenzl, the coterie met regularly for ten years until countess Windischgrätz died in 1777.[106] If so, it started in 1767 and Joseph joined it in 1769. But it seems more likely that his adhesion followed the death of his daughter and the departure of Herzelles from Vienna early in 1770. This was the time when his mother said he began to shun her Court.

By Viennese standards this was a coterie of political and religious radicals. Cobenzl tells us he had at one time lost his faith, which was restored only by reading Pope's *Essay on Man*.[107] Count Windischgrätz was notoriously advanced in his political and philosophical views, as later appeared in his little-publicised writings.[108] Perhaps even these unimpeachably aristocratic circles qualified for the empress's condemnation of those who led her son into bad ways. On the other hand, when countess Windischgrätz died, Maria Theresa wrote of her as having provided Joseph with 'a secure and tranquil society'.[109] It seems to have been accepted that their relationship was purely platonic. Joseph called her a 'woman of rare merit when you get to know her, and in whom I can truly say I have never seen a prejudice. She listens to reason, seeks it and bows to it. There are not very many like that among this sex of so-called charmers.' She and the emperor parted sorrowfully for the last time when she was dying and he was setting out on his journey to France.[110]

Cobenzl's description of this coterie must have exaggerated the rigidity and selectness of its membership. Wraxall mentioned as another regular participant countess Windischgrätz's sister, countess Esterházy, married to the heir of Haydn's grand patron, prince Nicholas Esterházy.[111] Even if the small group met as frequently as Cobenzl said, its members must also have been present at wider gatherings. Presumably the coterie as a whole was welcome at Esterházy houses, where Joseph was often seen.[112] In February 1772 he wrote: 'I'm beginning to become a libertine, paying evening visits to princess Esterházy and Mme Tarouca. Thus, step by step, I shall try to procure for myself a little society.' A month later matters had already progressed further:

I divide my evenings equally between three or four coteries, ... that is, either at princess Esterházy's, madame Tarouca's, madame Rosa Harrach's or princess Kinsky's. In the first and third there is a large gathering, in the other two a restricted group, as for example yesterday at princess Kinsky's we were the husband and wife, Madame de Kaunitz, princess Charles Liechtenstein, princess Clary, prince Kaunitz,

---

[106] Arneth, *AÖG* (1886), 101–4 (Cobenzl's memoirs). This evidence is so clear and authoritative that I think Wraxall's assertion (*Memoirs*, vol. II, p. 419) that the liaison began during the lifetime of the empress Josepha must be considered doubtful.
[107] Arneth, *AÖG* (1886), 92.   [108] Wurzbach LVII, pp. 60–3.
[109] M.T. to Maria Beatrix, 7 Apr. 1777 (Arneth, *MTKuF* III, p. 272).
[110] Wraxall, *Memoirs*, vol. II, pp. 419–20. J. to L., 16 Feb. 1775 (Arneth, *MTuJ* II, p. 55). Arneth, *AÖG* (1886), 122–3.
[111] Wraxall, *Memoirs*, vol. II, p. 419.   [112] E.g. HHSA TZ, 25 Nov. 1773, 9 Dec. 1775.

Rosenberg, Braganza and I. We conversed for more than two hours, which is entertaining and innocent.[113]

This is the first clear reference to Joseph's association with a group closely resembling the most famous and enduring of these coteries, that of 'the princesses' or 'the *Dames*', often held at princess Kinsky's. In July, Maria Theresa told Herzelles: 'This emperor, so hostile to women, cannot nowadays be without them until midnight or even later, on the promenades, in gardens except the one where I live, at the theatre, in their houses.'[114] Such was the alarming form taken by Joseph's social rebellion against his mother.

She went on: 'He thinks himself above everyone and [that] he uses them simply for his amusement. That's what he says. I hope he keeps to it.' In fact, Joseph's enthusiastic entry into female society coincided with the most intense affair of his life, with Eleonore Liechtenstein.

As we have seen, they had known each other well for several years. She was four years younger than he, and had married Charles a year after he had married Isabella. Eleonore had admired Joseph's appearance at his coronation as king of the Romans, but otherwise nearly all her comments about him had been critical. Even before his disastrous second marriage she had pitied anyone who became his wife. She had dreaded his approaches at Laxenburg in 1768, and refused to accept the panegyric of her sister, countess Kaunitz, on his behaviour at Naples in 1769. But after his daughter's death in January 1770, Eleonore had written: 'The emperor's grief is extreme. It is frightful that every person who would naturally engage his feelings should be snatched away from him, and since he has none too many, it's to be feared that, through inability to give them rein, he may entirely lose the habit.' When her sister repeated her eulogy of him, she replied: 'You have proved many points. I hope that you will never be disillusioned over others.'[115]

At the Austrian Court Eleonore was regarded both as a beauty and as a woman of exceptional education and intelligence. Her marriage was successful, but her husband did not share her intellectual interests. In the sixties she had been attracted by the attentions of general O'Donnell, prince Charles had become unreasonably jealous, and – in the manner of the countess in Mozart's *Marriage of Figaro* – she had felt desolate and had tried to keep out of O'Donnell's way.[116] In 1769 and 1770 Charles Greville, son of the earl of

---

[113] J. to L., 24 Feb. and 26 Mar. 1772 (Arneth, *MTuJ* I, pp. 365–6). A letter of 16 Mar. (not in Arneth; HHSA FA Sbde 7) records an intermediate stage. The duke of Braganza, a Portuguese princeling in exile, figured prominently in accounts of Viennese society at this period.

[114] This and the next quotation from M.T. to Herzelles, 2 July 1772 (Kervyn de Lettenhove, *MARB in-8o* (1868), 33).

[115] See above, pp. 115, 310, 322. E.L. to L.K., 29 Nov. 1764 (SOALpZ, LRRA P. 16/18); 21 Jan. and Mar. 1770 (*ibid.*, P. 16/22).

[116] This affair keeps on reappearing in the correspondence of E.L. and L.K. during the sixties.

Warwick and nephew of Sir William Hamilton, British envoy in Naples, spent many months in Vienna during his grand tour. She liked him very much, and was greatly displeased when after his departure she received no letter from him for several weeks. Greville wrote of her:

tho' as like Mad. Kaunitz as possible, [she] is very handsome; she is to the full as devout & strict as her sister, & if anyone was to be in love with her the flame would never be extinguished by her favors, and indeed her character is so well established that tho' the town is as greedy after scandal as any in the world, it never even shewed its shadow on the Princess, and the young men, &c., pay no kind of attention to her, none having esprit to court her acquaintance for her conversation. I, however, am an exception, & find her conversation very agreeable.[117]

She was a striking example of what seem to us the contradictions of the Catholic Enlightenment. If she complained of some of the many sermons she heard, others comforted and delighted her. Yet she thought everything Voltaire wrote interesting, and revelled in authors as diverse as Fontenelle, Montesquieu, Buffon, Richardson and Haller.[118]

A new phase in her relations with the emperor began after 'the fatal promotion of New Year's Day' 1771. Prince Charles Liechtenstein had been offered a military appointment in Hungary while generals Poniatowski and Pellegrini were promoted over his head. He threatened to leave the service, but Joseph offered embarrassed objections and the empress refused to accept his resignation. The princess reported developments in letters to her sister.

Could my husband have expected such an affront? What malevolence, what perfidy, what grounds for discouragement about the future! . . . Don't, I beg you, . . . defend the emperor's good faith. I've always understood him, I wasn't mistaken for a moment. Everyone knows how it came about. It's all a trick, which he's enjoyed devising, to set the entire army aflame. He has no idea of honesty and honour.

But a few days later, Joseph made a point of talking to her at a Court ball.

Imagine it, we didn't stop for two whole hours. It made the greatest possible sensation. For my part, I was as much at ease as if I'd been talking to you, and I perhaps told him some things he'd never heard . . . We parted about midnight. The small number of people still at the ball were much intrigued about what we could have been saying to each other, since the conversation never flagged.

The emperor advised the prince to swallow his pride on this occasion. Eleonore said the sacrifice would cost her husband more than the sacrifice he might one day have to make of his life. She now believed that the fault lay not

[117] E.L. to L.K., esp. 9 Dec. 1770, 30 Jan. 1771 (SOALpZ, LRRA P. 16/22). Greville to Hamilton, 9 Oct. 1769; A. Morrison (ed.), *The Hamilton and Nelson Papers*, vol. 1 (London, 1893), p. 13.
[118] Several letters from E.L. to L.K. about *Clarissa* in Sep. 1762 (SOALpZ, LRRA P. 16/18); in Mar., Apr. and Dec. 1767 on good and bad sermons, in July 1768 on Fontenelle, in Jan. 1769 on Montesquieu (*ibid.*, P. 16/21); on Buffon, 22 July 1771 (*ibid.*, P. 16/22); 6 Sep. 1773 on Voltaire, 23 Oct. on Haller (*ibid.*, P. 16/23).

with Joseph alone but arose out of the squabbling between him and his mother. The prince agreed to remain in the army and go to Hungary, while his wife stayed on in Vienna.[119]

Joseph now appeared once or twice a week at countess Paar's, sometimes staying until 11.30. During cards at Court, since the princess and the emperor both refused to play, they talked much to each other.

The faults I find in him would be high qualities in many other people. He has too much intelligence and too much command over himself, with corresponding loss of feeling ... I sometimes tell him truths that frighten me when I come out with them. But he takes such things marvellously. He seems extremely fond of natural conversation. On his side he supplies all imaginable charm, especially with women, although without any hint of flirtation. But the results don't match what he's said – why [otherwise] do our provinces languish without the slightest relief?

On successive days at the end of March, she passed on to her sister the news first of O'Donnell's death, then of countess Paar's. She grieved for the former, to her husband's chagrin; but the relationship had come to an end long ago. The countess, on the other hand, had remained important to her, not least in providing her with both a base for her coterie and a box at the theatre. But she soon found substitute accommodation, and from time to time reported meeting the emperor there or at Schönbrunn or the Belvedere palace. They still discussed her husband's promotion. She could even feel pity for Joseph, 'so overwhelmed with complaints and lamentations'. He managed to recover the prince's goodwill on a hunting expedition in December. But Eleonore felt no confidence about the future. 'There is a poison infecting everything [the emperor] says. He always seizes the most favourable moments, when it will make the greatest impression, to injure those for whom he professes friendship.' However, in February 1772 he awarded prince Charles the Golden Fleece vacated by his uncle, prince Josef Wenzel.[120]

For the first four months of 1772 both sisters found themselves in Vienna, and so no letters between them survive. By the time the correspondence was resumed in May, they were speaking of their coterie as the *Dames* and expecting Joseph to join it regularly. Eleonore was always running into him. He kept on pressing her to go on a trip to Dornbach, Lacy's estate, to see a striking view. He 'is always as strange as you saw him here. There is an eternal contradiction in his ideas, and therefore in his actions. He sends nearly every day to know whether princess Kinsky is at home.' Eleonore wishes he were 'as

[119] This paragraph is based on E.L.'s letters of 6 and 11 Jan. 1771 (*ibid.*, P. 16/22), with confirmation from K-M VII, pp. 55–6 and HHSA NL, Karton 2 (letters of late Dec. 1770 and early Jan. 1771). Falke, *Geschichte des fürstlichen Hauses Liechtenstein*, vol. III, pp. 255–7, attributes prince Charles's misfortune to M.T.'s displeasure – maybe with an element of truth. See J. to L., 10 Jan. 1771 (Arneth, *MTuJ* I, pp. 322–3).

[120] For these two paragraphs, letters of E.L. to L.K., esp. 13 Feb., 3, 27, 28 and 29 Mar., 26 Aug., 1 Oct., 13 Dec. 1771 (SOALpZ, LRRA P. 16/22). K-M VII, p. 115.

he was two years ago'; she is desperate to get out of Vienna to escape his attentions. Her husband is growing suspicious about Joseph's letters to her. On 11 July matters came to a first climax, at Dornbach:

He continues always on the same footing with me, but there are ups and downs. Sometimes [he's] sharp and petulant, sometimes cold and rational. Yesterday he said to me (he had a brief opportunity to speak to me alone when we were walking) that he looked upon me as his wife, that he had that kind of feeling for me. 'One is not loving towards one's wife', he said, 'but I am interested in everything that concerns you. I feel confident in fact that you belong to me.'

The princess replied that she was flattered, but could not follow his 'metaphysics of emotions' and was very far from belonging to him in any sense. 'He is very pleasant in society, that is certain, but it's very difficult to deal with him; he changes his nature according to what has recently impressed him.' The curious story of Röder, his secretary, who had just died, had figured largely in their talk. Joseph had always cherished him as a bachelor who had never had any dealings with the other sex. The emperor considered himself betrayed when the poor man, on the point of death, made an honest woman of his long-standing mistress.[121]

Eleonore now fled to Pressburg to be with her husband. There she was cheered to find that he too was embroiled in a love-affair, with the archduchess Marie Christine. Joseph, rebuffed by Eleonore, told his brother:

Vienna is deserted, everyone has gone into the country. For myself, I'm rapidly losing ground as a lover and becoming a recluse again. My God! the company of women is ultimately unbearable to a rational man, and ... the remarks of the grandest and wittiest often turn my stomach.[122]

Two weeks later, the princess returned to Vienna and joined the other *Dames* that night at princess Francis Liechtenstein's. The next day the coterie made an excursion to Dornbach accompanied not only by Joseph but by Maria Theresa herself. Describing it to her sister, Eleonore left us a rare document, the record of a lovers' tiff between herself and the emperor. He first tried to make excuses for not having come to princess Francis's the previous evening.

I assured him that there was no point, that his conduct was absolutely inexplicable. Nothing was more natural, after one of the members of a society had been away, than that the others should meet to see her. To act otherwise was to appear unfriendly to the [returning] member and absurd to the others. He assured me that for him it was a matter of state; that the empress had teased him cruelly during my absence, that she had given him news of me so pointedly, that she passed on to him every word I said, that on the very day of my arrival she had said to him, 'She will come and bring me a

[121] Letters of E.L., 6, 19, 22 and 31 May, 24 June, 5 and 11 July 1772 (SOALpZ, LRRA P. 16/23). See Plates 17a and 17b.
[122] E.L. to L.K., 15 and [?]24 July 1772 (*ibid.*). J. to L., 13 July 1772 (Arneth, *MTuJ* I, p. 374).

letter, but I shall be discreet, I won't delay it.' So he had wanted to have the pleasure of telling her he hadn't seen me.

Eleonore retorted that Joseph put a bad construction on everything,

that his scruples were as tiresome as they could be, that he was affecting to despise me in order to avoid being suspected of singling me out ... Although I sought no distinction from him, his contempt offended me ... It didn't become him to be ashamed of me in order to maintain his ridiculous systems ... I put at least as high a value on my friendship as on what he could offer me ... I shall certainly not let myself be fooled.

She had first suspected his feelings for her when he began to show such anxiety to send her into exile. She would be glad to go only if it assisted her husband's career. She begged to be left quietly in Vienna.

He made some kind of reply ... I took him back with princess Kinsky, with whom he gets on best. In the midst of all that, he said some very nice things to me and assured me that my return gave him great pleasure. It has to be admitted that he's an oddity. I've never seen anything like him.[123]

The next crisis followed a note she received from Joseph asking whether prince Charles might like to become commanding officer in Belgium, a position she had once mentioned as suitable for him. She wrote to her sister:

What a passion for sending us away! ... This unhappy message makes me weep ... I'm sad, annoyed, perturbed, and I swear I don't know why. But there is really no way of living with that man. Imagine, my intimate friend deciding overnight, with despotic power, to transport me where he pleases ... He's a walking paradox.

She allowed herself a few days to cool down and to receive a letter of advice from her sister. Countess Kaunitz reckoned that this latest move of Joseph's was designed to extract from Eleonore the avowal of love that she had hitherto held back. He was displaying 'this desire to persecute ... the people he loves best, this passion for vexing himself and vexing everyone who has the good or bad fortune to please him'. When Eleonore told the emperor what she thought of his conduct, he was momentarily reduced to silence. From what he later said she imagined all sorts of possible motives behind his action: did Maria Theresa, for example, want prince Charles removed from the vicinity of Marie Christine? Anyway, Joseph now produced a new suggestion, that Liechtenstein might like to succeed the military governor of Vienna, marshal Neipperg, who was eighty-eight. Maria Theresa seized on this proposal, saying 'it was necessary to keep this little woman here for the general good and especially for the sake of peace'. By the end of August the matter was settled,

[123] E.L. to L.K., 29 July 1772 (SOALpZ, LRRA P. 16/23).

though it had to be kept secret, since Neipperg, though so old, was as yet showing no signs of ill health, and already had a deputy.[124]

Joseph now induced his mother to agree to a change of the usual arrangements for a Laxenburg visit so that he could have his entire coterie of ladies there with him. But Eleonore refused point blank to join the party, and left Vienna. She would not allow him to write her anything that could not be shown to her husband. The emperor informed Leopold in November: 'the adventures I recounted to you are now over. The illustrious princess has been away for three months and I haven't the slightest news of her, just as she knows nothing of me.'[125]

Joseph had evidently hoped to persuade Eleonore to be his mistress. It was his 'one moment of madness, . . . cancelled immediately', his only departure from his 'system'. She in her turn, with all her criticism of him, was obviously attracted by his vivacity, flattered by his interest and sympathetic towards his difficulties. 'He's a strange being', she wrote, 'but I often feel sorry for him. Circumstances make us what we are.' But her feelings for her husband, her fidelity to her marriage vows, and her awareness of Joseph's peculiarities kept her from succumbing to his admitted charm. Her sister believed that if Eleonore had surrendered, he would have come to hate her as the woman who had 'seduced him from his duty'.[126]

Their relationship never again reached such a dangerous level of intensity. But it remained uniquely close. As soon as she returned to Vienna, he resumed regular visits to her coterie. The correspondence between the sisters was now more sporadic, since Leopoldine, to Joseph's annoyance, moved back to Vienna with her husband, for whom a comfortable post had been found as director of the royal buildings.[127] But the emperor's frame of mind is laid bare in the letters he wrote to Lacy and to the *Dames* during his immense journey to Transylvania and Galicia in the spring and summer of 1773.

The five 'princesses' of the coterie, as now established, were the wives of princes Clary, Kinsky, Francis and Charles Liechtenstein and of count Ernest Kaunitz. Joseph had fallen into the habit of calling them 'the fourteen' or, more comprehensibly, 'the amiable plural'. He sometimes corresponded direct with their 'secretary', generally Eleonore, who for this purpose, evi-

[124] E.L. to L.K., 11, 17 and 24 Aug.; L.K. to E.L., 14 Aug. (*ibid.*). M.T. to Lacy, 29 Aug. (HHSA NL, Karton 2); K-M VII, p. 164 and VIII, p. 25.

[125] E.L. to L.K., 31 Aug. 1772 (SOALpZ, LRRA P. 16/23); K-M VII, pp. 142–3; M.T. to Herzelles, 31 Aug. and 27 Sep. 1772 (Kervyn de Lettenhove, *MARB in-8o* (1868), 35–8); J. to L., 17 Nov. (Arneth, *MTuJ* I, pp. 386–7).

[126] J. to L., 16 Feb. 1774 (Arneth, *MTuJ* II, p. 56); E.L. to L.K., 17 Aug. and L.K. to E.L., 13 July 1772 (SOALpZ, LRRA P. 16/23).

[127] L.K. to E.L., 29 Oct. 1772 (*ibid.*); J. to L., 17 Nov. 1772 (Arneth, *MTuJ* I, p. 387).
Whenever I write of 'Leopoldine', I shall be referring to countess Kaunitz, although that was also princess Francis's Christian name.

dently with reference to the case of Röder, pretended to be male.[128] Other messages from the emperor came through Lacy, now clearly a full member of the coterie. From Temesvar in May Joseph wrote to the marshal:

I miss you very much ... Please give my compliments to the fourteen princesses and tell them ... that the Israelites in the desert didn't pine for the fleshpots of Egypt more than I [long], in these regions, for their precious and pleasant company. At about nine o'clock I'm always seized by a periodic ill humour, which I try to dispel by writing up my diary or sprawling on my mattress, though we don't lack for amusements – at Herad the theatre, *Bastien et Bastienne*, at Temesvar *Eugénie* – but I didn't go to either.

He sent them presents of lace. Sometimes he said he had no time to write and make them laugh. But from Salz Regen in June he painted a word-picture of their dresses as he imagined them on a recent excursion to Dornbach; and he asked Lacy to make a 'little clandestine salutation' to Eleonore.[129] In a letter to be passed on to her, he wished an angel could lift her by her *chignon* – as Habakkuk was supposed to have been carried by his hair to Daniel – and bring her to him, needlework and all, so that they could talk together. He had heard a local general being told by his wife how emaciated he looked after a journey and that he must take care of himself and not get constipated. This is the kind of thing, Joseph tells Eleonore, he needs a woman to say to him.[130]

In July a little dispute blew up about a ballet which the princesses had much appreciated. Writing to Lacy, Joseph scoffed at the admiration of women for cavaliers and heroes. They do not 'value those whose heroism is confined to conquering themselves and mastering their own feelings and passions. These are the true [heroes]. But since they need neither armour, lances nor pistols, only reason and calculation', women are not dazzled by them. For Joseph, however, his own conviction of his rectitude is enough to satisfy him. If women disapprove of him, so much the worse for them. Very soon, though, he was thanking 'the secretary whom I love as much as I esteem' for the minutes of 'the society [that] constitutes the sweetness of my life'. Her handwriting resembles that of ordinary women as little as does 'her manner of thinking and acting'.[131]

His frustration and unhappiness could hardly be more obvious. Intellectually, he accepted Eleonore's rejection of him. For others he paraded the misogynist notions he had already developed to conceal the wounds left by his bereavements. But his love for her and his yearning for female companionship leap from the page.

---

[128] See, in general, the collection of letters from J. to the *Dames* in SOALpZ, LRRA P. 16/22-3 (copies), and J.'s letters to Lacy of 1773 (HHSA FA Sbde 72).

[129] J. to Lacy, 12 May, 12 and 19 June, 9 July 1773 (HHSA FA Sbde 72).

[130] J. to Eleonore, from Transylvania, 1773 (undated) in SOALpZ, LRRA P. 16/22-3 (copies). I am most grateful to Frau I. Hassler for making sense of the remarks of the general's wife.

[131] J. to Lacy, 9 July (HHSA FA Sbde 72); J. to Eleonore, 16 July 1773 (SOALpZ, LRRA P. 16/22-3, copies).

Back in Vienna, Joseph announced, in her words, that he wanted 'willy-nilly to belong to our society'. It usually met in one or other of the ladies' Viennese palaces, all of which stood within a few hundred yards of the Hofburg. He did not wholly abandon other social gatherings, but he now joined the princesses' on three or four evenings each week. He still came when Eleonore was away, but he complained of her absences and sometimes pursued her into the country. He confessed to her sister that he would dearly like to be sure that Eleonore was smitten with him, though 'he well knew that he was made neither to give nor to receive love, and that it was no longer his intention'. Leopoldine extolled the advantages of mere friendship, and that was where the matter rested.[132] He told Leopold in 1775: 'I have no desire to have an affair. Nor do I want to try and make new acquaintances.' He even felt less keen to travel.[133] In 1777 – ironically, just before the War of the Bavarian Succession – he paid Eleonore the greatest compliment of which he was capable, when he confessed to doubts about his military calling:

One spends one's whole life being disappointed – all those manoeuvres and perhaps never a war. While you're gadding about and missing the pleasures of life, you would never become a great general, and you're risking the weakening of a friendship that makes for your happiness.[134]

In his strange way, Joseph wanted to settle down.

Apart from the ladies, Joseph and Lacy, the coterie regularly included one other member, count Franz Rosenberg. 'A skilled courtier' of long experience, he had accompanied Leopold to Tuscany to act as his chief minister and guide under Maria Theresa's orders. In 1771 he returned to Vienna, but he was later employed to look after both Ferdinand and Max Franz during their travels. He succeeded Khevenhüller as great chamberlain in 1777. Philipp Cobenzl, who regarded him as an enemy, called him 'intelligent, well-informed, amiable in society, not lacking in ability, ... but much given to pleasures' and lazy. His essential qualification for membership of the coterie was that he was a bachelor. We are told that the ladies' husbands were strictly excluded; and the experiment of admitting the French ambassador, Breteuil, at his own request, was soon abandoned in the face of the emperor's displeasure. Even when limited in this way, the group cannot have been completely harmonious. Joseph put up with Leopoldine only for her sister's sake, and Eleonore must have remained cool towards Lacy.[135]

132 E.L. to L.K., 16 Oct. 1773; L.K. to E.L., 8 Oct. 1773, 26 Oct. 1774 (*ibid.*, P. 16/23). J. to L., 6 Oct. 1774 (Arneth, *MTuJ* II, p. 39); Wraxall, *Memoirs*, vol. II, p. 426; Wolf, *Fürstin Eleonore Liechtenstein*, pp. 114–15.
133 J. to L., 16 Feb. 1775 (Arneth, *MTuJ* II, p. 56). See p. 229.
134 E.L. to L.K., 13 Sept. 1777 (SOALpZ, LRRA, P. 16/24).
135 On Rosenberg Arneth, *AÖG* (1886), 121; Wurzbach XXVII, pp. 14–17; Wandruszka, *L. II.*, vol. I, pp. 171–82, 249–60. Wraxall, *Memoirs*, vol. II, p. 427; E.L. to L.K., 15 July 1775 (SOALpZ, LRRA P. 16/23). See above, p. 184.

Just as the emperor's chief male friends, apart from Cobenzl, were all several years older than he, so were the princesses, except for Eleonore and Leopoldine.[136] Like the coterie round countess Windischgrätz, the *Dames* were closely interrelated. Not only were Eleonore and Leopoldine sisters, but so were princesses Clary and Kinsky, who were their cousins; and princess Francis was sister-in-law of Eleonore and Leopoldine. Joseph made a point of the fact that all save princess Francis came from Swabia.[137] They were distinctly more conservative than Cobenzl's associates.

What they talked about is rarely documented. A theological discussion is once mentioned, but unfortunately without details. Joseph certainly regaled them with endless accounts of his travels.[138] The most interesting question is how far matters of state were permitted topics. We know that at least one such issue gave trouble. In July 1775 Eleonore, who was eight months pregnant, described to her sister a conversation with Joseph about the problems of Bohemia. At this stage he was maintaining both that they were being greatly exaggerated, and that something drastic needed to be done about them.

He jumped from one contradiction and one paradox to another. He was absolutely determined to persuade me, to make me acknowledge he was right. He was shouting at me, badgering me, preventing me thinking and therefore speaking. I was wild with annoyance and impatience. I couldn't breathe, I was dying of the heat.

The emperor told Leopold:

as I take the line that we must hold firm, and as I stand out against intrigue, I am pitilessly torn apart, and by the people I am most friendly with. I know it, but I don't take it seriously, and I behave normally both as regards business and in society, as if it didn't matter.

Leopold urged his brother to abandon the coterie, no doubt imagining that this was what Joseph wanted him to say. But the emperor replied that the distraction of female company in the evenings was essential to his peace of mind.[139] It is inconceivable that private meetings taking place four times a week between the co-regent and head of the army, his principal lieutenant, the wife of the head of the artillery (prince Kinsky), the wife of the military commander of Vienna, and the daughter-in-law and *confidante* of the

---

[136] Rosenberg b. 1723, Lacy 1725, Dietrichstein and Nostitz 1728, Cobenzl 1741. The princesses: Clary 1728, Kinsky 1729, Francis Liechtenstein 1733, Leopoldine 1741, Eleonore 1745.

[137] L.K. to E.L., 26 July 1777 (SOALpZ, LRRA P. 16/24); Wolf, *Fürstin Eleonore Liechtenstein*, pp. 111–12. Eleonore and Leopoldine were born princesses of Öttingen-Spielberg; princesses Clary and Kinsky were born princesses of Hohenzollern-Hechingen.

[138] E.L. to L.K., 30 Oct. 1774 (SOALpZ, LRRA P. 16/23); L.K. to E.L., 21 Aug. 1777 (*ibid.*, P. 16/24).

[139] E.L. to L.K., June/July 1775 (*ibid.*, P. 16/23). J. to L., 20 July (Arneth, *MTuJ* II, p. 71 – but 'd'intrigue' is a mistake for 'à l'intrigue'); L. to J., 30 July, and J. to L., 11 Aug., not in Arneth, *MTuJ* (HHSA FA Sbde 7).

Staatskanzler should have excluded all discussion of public questions. They must have made Lacy's task more difficult, especially while he was president of the *Hofkriegsrat*. In fact they must have provided one of the arenas in which, no doubt in veiled forms, disputes between empress, emperor, marshal and chancellor could be staged and reconciled. The history of Joseph's relations with the princesses gives the lie to his constant assertions, accepted by some historians, that private considerations never affected his public actions. He showed himself ready to play fast and loose with army promotions to please or annoy Eleonore; at her request, he procured the Golden Fleece for Ernest Kaunitz. On occasions, he sent her copies of official documents.[140] No wonder she and her sister were so impressed by his inconsistency.

Nothing irritated the Monarchy's grandees more than his attitude to the theatre. In 1775 prince Charles and others organised performances of operas and French dramas such as Joseph would not subsidise. The emperor refused to attend, though the princesses were sure he was dying to do so. 'It is difficult', wrote Eleonore, 'to live with a man who has no other principle than that of thinking and acting in a manner diametrically opposed to ours.' 'He likes monopoly in everything.'[141]

She and her sister had better opportunities of getting to know Joseph than anyone else, except perhaps his mother. They saw him when charming, considerate, entertaining and in love. They saw him biting his nails with impatience and grinding his teeth in frustration. During the period of the row with Lacy he was almost in tears, 'terribly miserable and despairing'. They felt the force of his spite. They naturally dreaded and resented his use of his power in petty ways.[142] But the two qualities that most impressed them were, first, his oddity, and secondly, his inconsistency. 'He has such peculiar ideas', said Leopoldine, 'which arise so entirely unexpectedly, that it's impossible to be prepared for them.' His letters, even without the signature and preamble, could have been written by no one else.

He's an astonishing mixture. He changes colour and form, and always in a way you wouldn't expect. The upshot of all his schemes is always different from what would naturally come out of them. With him, two and two don't make four, but four-and-a-half or three-and-three-quarters. Speaking geometrically, one must suppose that there are some fundamental defects which throw out all the calculations.

He would pass at once from a despondent account of his unimaginably difficult position to cheerfulness and laughter.[143] Sometimes they concluded

---

[140] E.L. to L.K., 17 June 1772 (SOALpZ, LRRA P. 16/23); L.K. to E.L., 16 Oct. 1777 (*ibid.*, P. 16/24). Cf. Mitrofanov I, p. 103.
[141] E.L. to L.K., 25 and 27 Oct. 1775 (SOALpZ, LRRA P. 16/23).
[142] E.g. L.K. to E.L., 8 and 27 Oct. 1773 (*ibid.*), and 13 July 1776; E.L. to L.K., 9 Oct. 1777 (*ibid.*, P. 16/24).
[143] L.K. to E.L., 20 Aug. and 8 Oct. 1772, 27 Oct. and 3 Nov. 1773 (*ibid.*, P. 16/23).

that there was more good than bad in his composition. Quite often Eleonore felt sorry for him, but she could never forget his faults:

This poor prince, at bottom he is worthy of compassion. He has a character, a way of thinking, even a type of intelligence which have no parallel. He will never be happy. I think he aims at the good, he takes more trouble than many others to find it, it is pointed out to him, and he's never yet done it.[144]

His eccentric vivacity always called forth highly coloured character-sketches. In talking of his inconsistency the princesses were thinking mainly of his extreme moodiness. Leopoldine compared him to the weather: if it happened to be raining, you had to put your coat on; if it was fine, you were lucky.[145] But they felt entitled also, and with some justification, to draw inferences from his private conduct about his likely public behaviour. He was 'fertile in plans and slow, or more accurately uncertain, in their execution'. As she read Haller's portrait of an enlightened ruler in *Usong*, Eleonore surmised that the author hoped Joseph would emulate the hero – but, she said, the princesses know better.[146]

Joseph's relations with the great ladies of this as of other coteries were evidently platonic. But he made no secret of his sexual frustration. 'Systematic in all things', he told Ligne 'that he used to go to a prostitute before going to the house of a society woman whom he might hope to seduce, so as not to be tempted to take advantage.'[147] He said something to a French envoy which has led some historians to the improbable conclusion that he spent half-an-hour daily with his gardener's daughter throughout his widowed life. Leopold, on the other hand, claimed that Joseph had low-class women procured for him.[148] What the emperor himself told his brother in 1775 – scrupulously omitted by Arneth – ought to be taken into account:

I'm a little uncertain of myself in relation to prostitutes, of whom there are a great many, and shoddy merchandise. So I go to bed peacefully, happy to lie on my own mattress where at least, without the slightest inconvenience and without disturbing my peace, I am my own master, stretching myself and rolling about as I please.

This was how Joseph defended his visits to his coteries:

What is to be done? Either you remain on your own, or you go slumming, or you put up with the company . . . that the locality supplies. You would take the first option. If, like you, I had a wife and children, perhaps I would choose it [too]. But to spend the evening alone with a *valet de chambre* after working the whole day, that's a life I couldn't bear in the long run without falling into despair. As for the second possibility,

---

[144] E.L. to L.K., June/July 1775 (*ibid.*).   [145] L.K. to E.L., 2 Aug. 1777 (*ibid.*, P. 16/24).
[146] E.L. to L.K., 9 Sep. 1772 and 23 Oct. 1773 (*ibid.*, P. 16/23).
[147] Ligne, *Fragments*, vol. I, p. 184.
[148] Mitrofanov I, p. 101, citing Durand, apparently from a despatch of Nov. 1771. Dr H. M. Scott kindly helped me over this dating. See Padover, *Revolutionary Emperor*, p. 61, and above, p. 197.

namely, to go out looking for women, I've tried it, there are so many physical drawbacks, it's brutalising and leaves such a great void, that there's no other option [open] but the third one, that is, to take what advantage one can, make light of the rest, and try to spend the evening distracted from business.[149]

Despite his animus against the aristocracy as a body, every single one of his close associates belonged to the higher nobility, and most of them were princes of the Empire, their wives or children. More surprising still, all of them, except Nostitz, were his mother's favourites as well as his. Dietrichstein had been appointed master of the horse while Francis Stephen was alive; Rosenberg and Lacy, like the marquise d'Herzelles, had been Maria Theresa's *protégés* and put loyalty to her before devotion to Joseph. Cobenzl's uncle had been given the best job in the Monarchy, that of minister in Belgium. Countess Windischgrätz was both great-niece and step-daughter of marshal Batthyány, Joseph's *Ajo*. Eleonore's elderly relative, countess Paar, had been mistress of the robes not only to Maria Theresa but to her mother; prince Charles's uncle, prince Josef Wenzel, was revered by the empress as a great general and the reformer of the Monarchy's artillery; and it is clear that Maria Theresa was prepared to foster the relationship between her son and Eleonore, for fear of something worse. Moreover, Dietrichstein was the favourite nephew of Khevenhüller, and Rosenberg the close friend of the hated Starhemberg. Leopold's connexions, too, were important in Joseph's circle: Rosenberg had been minister in Tuscany, and Leopold in his bachelor days had had a liaison with the future countess Windischgrätz.[150] Joseph always extolled the merits of coteries by comparison with larger gatherings and still more with the Court, whose 'present composition', as he sweetly informed his mother, 'is such that it would be useless to look for any satisfaction there, and where instead of pleasure one might well encounter only inconveniences'.[151] But his escape from formality, from his mother and from his spinster sisters led only to his meeting, day after day, without ceremony and in other palaces, some of her principal courtiers and sympathisers.

Guibert's assertion that Joseph could feel neither friendship nor love will

---

[149] J. to L., 16 Feb. (portion garbled by Arneth) and 11 Aug. (not in Arneth, *MTuJ*) 1775 (HHSA FA Sbde 7). This correspondence contains a number of mysterious references by J. to sexual scandal, some of them actually ciphered, none printed by Arneth (see 24 Feb., 16 Mar., 20 Apr., 2 July 1772). In an unpublished part of the letter in Arneth, *MTuJ* II, p. 5 (evidently of Apr. 1773), J. asks L., if J. dies first, to go on paying 500 fl. to a woman involved in sexual scandal; but other letters including L.'s of 12 Apr. 1773, apparently identifying her as 'Mme Braun', suggest that J. was not the man in the case. I have not deciphered the coded passages.

[150] Apart from entries in Wurzbach, there is material on Dietrichstein in K-M VI, pp. 2–3; on countess Paar in K-M VII, p. 68; on prince Josef Wenzel in K-M VII, pp. 52, 115 and in Falke, *Geschichte des fürstlichen Hauses Liechtenstein*, vol. III, pp. 163–228; on Rosenberg in Wandruszka, *L. II.*, vol. I, esp. pp. 173–5; and on L. and countess Windischgrätz, *ibid.*, esp. pp. 77–9.

[151] J. to M.T., 22 July 1775 (Arneth, *MTuJ* II, p. 74).

not stand scrutiny. It is true that he imposed his friendship on others, and gave them a rough ride. But what is remarkable, despite his variability of mood, is the constancy of his relationships. On Joseph's side his confidence, once given, seems unshakeable. When he died, his best male friends were still Lacy, Dietrichstein, Rosenberg and Cobenzl; he had visited the princesses regularly until illness prevented him; and he never wavered in his affection for Eleonore.

CHAPTER 11

Bohemia: travel and reform, 1769–1777

JOSEPH DRIVES THE PLOUGH, 1769

Joseph never attracted better publicity than during the year 1769, when his glamorous visits to Italy and to Frederick the Great were complemented by the most celebrated of all his actions and gestures: on his way to see Frederick, between Brünn and Olmütz in Moravia, he took the plough of a peasant, Andreas Trnka, and drove it himself. We may doubt that he was conscious of 'the Indo-Germanic origins of the symbolism'; but he certainly wished to publicise his interest in agriculture and his sympathy with the tillers of the soil at a time when the government was enquiring into relations between lords and serfs in Bohemia and Moravia.[1] The scene became the subject of several published prints. Within a year the plough was being preserved as a relic. By the time count Karl von Zinzendorf passed that way in September 1773 he could see

a tasteless and graceless monument that prince Joseph Wenzel [Liechtenstein] erected in memory of the day, 19 August 1769, when His Maj. the Emperor Joseph II himself pushed the plough for a whole furrow of the field that extends as far as the village of Slawikowitz, situated in a hollow on the left of the main road. The monument is an immense pedestal of marble with bas-relief representing the event and three inscriptions in Czech, German and Latin. The peasants(?) of Slawikowitz had put up a little stone that is still there, with an inscription in bad German.[2]

Joseph was already staking his claim to be 'the people's emperor'.[3]

[1] See H. Rokyta, *Die böhmischen Länder* (Salzburg, 1970), pp. 166, 230, 280. The quotation (p. 166) refers to a repeat performance in 1779 at Reichenberg in Bohemia.
  For lord–serf relations, see below, pp. 347–8.
[2] HHSA TZ, 17 Sep. 1773. The monument he ascribes simply to prince Liechtenstein had some kind of blessing from the Estates of Moravia. Cf. Falke, *Geschichte des fürstlichen Hauses Liechtenstein*, vol. III, p. 225, and Plate 14b.
  The documents in G. Franz (ed.), *Quellen zur Geschichte des deutschen Bauernstandes in der Neuzeit* (Munich, 1963), pp. 258–9 show that M.T. wished to erect a monument. According to M. Zemek, 'Joseph II. und Slavikovice' in *ÖZKJ*, p. 291, this was never built. See *ÖZKJ*, pp. 352–4.
[3] See K. Vocelka, 'Das Nachleben Josephs II. im Zeitalter des Liberalismus' in *ÖZKJ*, pp. 293–8.

THE BOHEMIAN FAMINE AND THE JOURNEY OF 1771

By comparison with 1769, 1770 was for Joseph a year of repose. He made an extended tour of Hungary, during which he enquired, among other things, into the progress of urbarial reform; but his influence in Hungarian affairs was virtually confined to military matters.[4] As we have seen, he met Frederick the Great for the second time.[5] But it was only with his Bohemian journey of October–November 1771 that he was again able to use travel to divert the domestic policies of the Monarchy into new channels.

A description was given earlier of his mounting exasperation, bordering on hysteria, at the condition of affairs late in 1770 and during 1771.[6] Many elements went to make up what he saw as the Monarchy's great crisis, and contributed to his own excitement. The introduction of conscription and the strengthening of the cordon were constant preoccupations during this period. In foreign policy he was combating what he believed to be the ruinous schemes of Kaunitz for an attack on Russia, and he was personally responsible for promoting and executing the alternative plan of a large-scale military demonstration in Hungary early in 1771. In April of that year he secured for himself a dominant role in managing the *Staatsrat*, which kept him hard at work throughout the summer. The dispute over administrative reform in Lombardy became violent in August. But what troubled him above all was the situation in Bohemia.

Bohemia (for this as for most purposes to be understood as including Moravia and the tiny portion of Silesia remaining under Austrian rule) constituted the larger part of the central core of the Monarchy. Its population of about four million amounted to about a quarter of the total. More important, it paid fully 40 per cent of the *contributio*. It also suffered most from the wars of the period. The War of the Austrian Succession, the Seven Years War and the War of the Bavarian Succession all included invasions of Bohemia. Because of its exposed position facing Prussia, substantial numbers of troops had to be maintained there in peacetime. Hence the prosperity of Bohemia mattered more to the Monarchy than that of any other region.[7]

Both in 1770 and in 1771 harvests failed over much of Europe. Especially in central areas of the continent, these years saw a grave subsistence crisis, perhaps the worst of the whole eighteenth century, and Bohemia was affected as severely as anywhere. Famine there threatened to cripple the state's capacity to defend itself, because in the first place the tax-yield would fall, and

---

[4] Valuable, unpublished *Relation* in HHSA FA Hofreisen 2, fasz. 3. Nothing appears to have been written about this journey. Cf. pp. 283–4 above.

[5] See pp. 284–5 above.   [6] See pp. 207–9.

[7] On Bohemia in general, R. J. Kerner, *Bohemia in the Eighteenth Century* (New York, 1932); K. Bosl (ed.), *Handbuch der Geschichte der böhmischen Länder*, vol. II (Stuttgart, 1974), esp. pp. 415–97: 'Das Zeitalter des Zentralismus', by G. Hanke.

secondly some or all of the troops stationed in the province would have to be withdrawn, leaving the Monarchy at the mercy of Frederick. So Joseph's desperation can be understood.[8]

He was disturbed by what he learned of the situation as he travelled to and from his meeting with Frederick in the late summer of 1770. It was during this journey that the Bohemian government banned the export of grain. Maria Theresa soon extended the prohibition to the whole Monarchy, while encouraging the import of cereals from other countries and removing restrictions on the internal grain trade. Joseph had pressed for these measures; he now worked to prevent his mother making exceptions to them in favour of friendly foreign princes.[9] At the end of January 1771 he told Leopold:

It was only yesterday that we received the report we have been demanding from Bohemia for so long, since the month of September, on the subject of the grain shortage. It is so badly done that one can deduce nothing from it, except an almost general dearth and no measures to deal with it, the tyranny of the lords and no control.

A special commission was established in Vienna to examine the problem.

At the end of February Joseph reported:

In Bohemia the need has now become so urgent that H.M. has had to send there a certain Kressel as commissar. I've been writing and talking about it continuously for nearly six months. No one has been willing to believe it or to act vigorously. We now see the results. *O patientia*, how many times a day I have to invoke you![10]

Kressel found an acute shortage of grain, compounded by high prices, inept government intervention, profiteering, hoarding, unemployment especially among Bohemia's sizeable industrial work-force, and an overriding shortage of money. The poor, he concluded, simply did not earn enough to be in a position to buy food even if it was available. This was largely because so much of their time was spent in carrying out compulsory services without payment on their lords' estates (or *Robot*).[11]

Further measures were tried: a new approach to price-fixing; the provision of seed-corn and potatoes; relaxation of the central government's tax-

---

[8] It might be thought that an army that lived off the land, like Frederick's, would have avoided invading a famine-stricken province. But J. clearly took seriously the risk of its doing so: see below, p. 342.

[9] On the famine and the visit of 1771, generally: Arneth, *GMT* x, pp. 41–59; E. Weinzierl-Fischer, 'Die Bekämpfung der Hungersnot in Böhmen, 1770–1772', *MÖSA*, VII (1954), 478–514; F. Blaich, 'Die wirtschaftspolitische Tätigkeit der Kommission zur Bekämpfung der Hungersnot in Böhmen und Mähren (1771–1772)', *VSWG*, LVI (1969), 299–331; Schünemann, *MÖIG* (1933), 39–43.

On the food shortage and the journey of 1770, a few lines in Radics, *Oesterreichisch-Ungarische Revue* (1890), 5–7; Weinzierl-Fischer, *MÖSA* (1954), 479–80.

[10] J. to L., 24 Jan. and 21 Feb. 1771 (Arneth, *MTuJ* I, pp. 329, 332–3).

[11] Weinzierl-Fischer, *MÖSA* (1954), 486–90; Blaich, *VSWG* (1969), 306–17.

This famine evidently fitted into the pattern brilliantly described by A. Sen, *Poverty and Famines* (Oxford, 1982): food shortage was by no means the whole story.

demands; and grants of money to pay for roadworks.[12] But on 30 May the emperor informed Leopold:

I have a great deal of business, associated with a mortal grief, arising from the news we've just received from Prague, where famine has appeared . . . It was only at the last minute that we heard that they have nothing left and the *Gubernium* [provincial government] is making no arrangements. It is only the military that has revealed it, and I wanted to set out at once, but HM, which has caused me great sorrow, didn't desire it, without giving me any convincing reasons, and I'm left to guess at them. You can imagine that I have a pretty good idea, and they are neither flattering nor loving. But, however mortifying the vexation of seeing myself prevented from making myself known and taking action at the most crucial moment, I have to swallow it, and to set it among the class of a hundred thousand annoyances to which I am condemned by a quite special twist of Fate. Adieu. Pity me, dear brother, for few things in the world have given me such distress.[13]

The army and its supplies were brought into play, and the position improved for a short time.[14]

At this point Maria Theresa finally removed from office count Rudolf Chotek, the dying head of the Austro-Bohemian Chancellery in Vienna, and count Kollowrat, the octogenarian chief of the *Gubernium* in Prague. The mere fact that she had allowed them to remain for so long goes far to support Joseph's strictures on the civilian administration. Hatzfeld, retaining his other posts, took on Chotek's as well.[15]

As the summer wore on, the situation in Bohemia worsened, and the prospects for the next harvest were alarmingly poor. Reports reached Vienna of ever higher grain prices, of smuggling, of epidemics, of peasants eating grass and roots and rotten meat, of starvation and death in the countryside as well as in Prague. Yet, according to Joseph writing on 25 September, 'despite all my protests, nothing is being done to help Bohemia'. 'These officials here don't know anything; our departments are not equipped, and even the provincial governments don't tell one anything unless one goes and asks from door to door.' Maria Theresa had at last agreed to let him travel to Bohemia, but was still delaying his departure.[16] It was not until 29 September that he asked Hatzfeld for information to assist him during his tour: the names of the administrative districts and their chiefs; figures of the annual tax-revenue

[12] Weinzierl-Fischer, *MÖSA*, (1954), 490–4; Blaich, *VSWG* (1969), 317–29.
[13] J. to L., 30 May 1771 (HHSA FA Sbde 7, not printed by Arneth, but partly paraphrased in Fejtö, *J. II*, p. 132).
[14] Weinzierl-Fischer, *MÖSA* (1954), 494–6.
[15] Arneth, *GMT* x, pp. 42–3, 757; Walter, *VKNGÖ*, xxxii, p. 437. Wright, *Serf, Seigneur and Sovereign*, p. 45, is wrong in ascribing these changes to the period of J.'s journey.
[16] Weinzierl-Fischer, *MÖSA* (1954), 497–9; J. to L., 25 Sep. 1771 (Arneth, *MTuJ* I, p. 344, but omitting from the original the phrase about delaying his departure). J. to L., 23 Sep., reports that M.T. has permitted the journey (HHSA FA Sbde 7, not printed in Arneth).

from Bohemia and Moravia; population returns; and details of all recent directives.[17] Two days later he left Vienna.

He devised a questionnaire under fifteen headings to be completed by the district chiefs. From their replies, from his own observations and enquiries, and from petitions presented to him, he compiled the first part of his *Relation* in Prague at the end of October. He had found frightful conditions: general shortage of food; widespread disease; steeply rising death-rates; profiteering and oppression on the part of the lords.[18] He told his mother: 'The king of Prussia with 20,000 men can conquer [Bohemia and Moravia] without a battle, and our whole army, since provisions are lacking and impossible to procure, will have to fall back on the Danube.'[19] Joseph's remedies for the immediate problem of the famine amounted to the wider and more vigorous implementation of policies already agreed. His reports from Bohemia led to grain being released from the Vienna magazine. On his return it was decided to try to obtain a whole year's supply of corn for Bohemia by purchase in Hungary; a special commission with this object was set up under count Festetics; and by the middle of 1772 it had collected over 500,000 *Metzen* to supply civilian needs at a cost of over 1,000,000 florins. More money was made available for public works, and further tax-remissions were agreed. On 14 May 1772 the emperor ordered 100,000 florins to be paid out of his own resources for the relief of Bohemia and Moravia.[20] He was still lamenting the lack of urgency displayed by the government. To Leopold he wrote:

It is only with the deepest grief in my soul that I remain an impotent spectator, and an innocent accomplice in the eyes of the world, of such a [calamity?], which will be the shame of my life and of which your dear children will feel the effects.[21]

To the *Staatsrat* he complained of 'the so-called *Schlendrian* . . . in which great goodwill is shown; much paperwork is prepared, considered and argued over; but fundamentally nothing of importance is decided or completed'.[22]

The famine checked the development of the Bohemian economy for some years, and between 1770 and 1773 the region's population fell by perhaps 600,000. But the situation was already improving before a good harvest ended the emergency in the autumn of 1772.[23] Despite his own dissatisfaction with

---

17 Weinzierl-Fischer, *MÖSA* (1954), 499n.
18 Weinzierl-Fischer, *MÖSA* (1954), 500–4; Arneth, *GMT* x, pp. 47–9.
19 J. to M.T., 17 Oct. 1771 (Arneth, *MTuJ* I, p. 346).
20 Weinzierl-Fischer, *MÖSA* (1954), 504–12; Arneth, *GMT* x, pp. 49–50.
21 J. to L., 11 May 1772 (not printed in Arneth, garbled in Fejtö, *J. II*, pp. 134–5), HHSA FA Sbde 7.
22 Weinzierl-Fischer, *MÖSA* (1954), 511n; Schünemann, *MÖIG* (1933), 41. This comes from J.'s declaration to the *Staatsrat* of 13 June 1772, in which he proposed the appointment of a dictator (see above, p. 215).
23 Bosl, *Handbuch der böhmischen Geschichte*, vol. II, p. 478. Cf. Weinzierl-Fischer, *MÖSA* (1954), 504n. J. himself did not consider the emergency at an end in Nov. 1772 (J. to L., 2 Nov. 1772, Arneth, *MTuJ* I, p. 385).

the results he achieved, it cannot be doubted that Joseph's frantic activity had reduced the scale of the disaster, and that his journey, when finally permitted, had given him information and opportunities that enhanced his influence in the matter.[24] We have seen that his efforts and achievement were generally applauded; an observer who often criticised him, Karl von Zinzendorf, wrote in his diary on 17 November 1771: 'His Maj. the Emperor got back ... after midday. He is the first sovereign to do his job properly.'[25]

JOSEPH'S PROPOSALS FOR REFORM IN BOHEMIA

Joseph's attempts to mitigate the famine commanded widespread sympathy. It was a different story with the proposals he made in his Bohemian *Relation* for drastic reform of the church, central and local administration and many other aspects of society and government in the Monarchy as a whole. I have already dealt with the impact of his demands for change at the centre: one of their effects had been the replacement of Hatzfeld by Blümegen as Austro-Bohemian Chancellor in December 1771. I shall discuss ecclesiastical questions later.[26] Here I shall consider only local administration and problems peculiar to Bohemia.

He had told his mother that the Monarchy's system of government must be constructed afresh, from below – from the provinces upwards rather than, as hitherto, from the centre downwards. But that certainly did not imply he approved of the existing local administration. Quite the contrary.

No one is adequately informed about the facts. The official knows [our system] and [that he] is not required to understand the serfs and their true circumstances as well as [he understands] the landlord. The district chief [*Kreishauptmann*] can get away without properly overseeing his district. The provincial governments know nothing but what the district chief writes, who, as previously stated, cannot really know anything of the region.[27]

The administration is unnecessarily complex and burdensome:

In each and every *Land* there is the political establishment, the military command, the spiritual lords, the *Banco* administration, the judicial system, and the usually still separate and independent commerce departments. All of them operate on their own account, and generally against each other, with individual and one-sided aims. Each

---

For an interesting contemporary account of the famine and J.'s role see Pelzel, *Kurzgefasste Geschichte der Böhmen*, pp. 621–3.

[24] Both Arneth (*GMT* x, p. 46) and Weinzierl-Fischer (*MÖSA* (1954), 514) give J. and his journey much credit for the measures taken against the famine. Blaich (*VSWG* (1969), 330 and n.) mentions the journey twice, each time with a different and an incorrect dating, and allows it no importance whatsoever. This is another example of the unwisdom of concentrating on bureaucratic documents to the exclusion of the writings of monarchs.

[25] HHSA TZ, 17 Nov. 1771. Cf. K-M VII, p. 104 (18 Nov. 1771). See pp. 212, 215 above.

[26] See pp. 452–4.

[27] K-M VII, p. 375 (the Bohemian *Relation*).

thinks it has achieved a great deal if it gets the better of another, and takes credit for doing so with its superiors in Vienna, who also carry on business in the same way. Who suffers? The subject and YM.[28]

A new system must be created, with these aims:

that, first, the peasant, citizen and landlord, and above all YM's *contributio*, should be sustained;

secondly, the military should be maintained in genuinely good order and discipline, in a way which is least harmful to the peasant and cheapest for YM;

thirdly and last, that the rest of YM's revenues, which are assigned to cover the [interest on the] state debts and other necessities, should be managed as securely as possible and in the way most convenient to the *Land*.

The old provinces, Bohemia, Moravia and Silesia, ought, he maintained, to be united into one major administrative region; but at a lower level the existing districts are often too large. The local administration must be better unified: commercial, banking and political matters must all be concentrated in the hands of the district chiefs.

However, Joseph at once goes on to suggest complicating the machinery again, and in an alarming fashion:

I divide the military into two parts, namely: [first,] discipline, order, turnout, duties and training, which ... should remain in the hands of its regular general and staff officers. [Secondly,] I would entrust provisioning and clothing and keeping of conscription records in each and every district to an ... officer who would be called the Canton Director ... He would have to correspond and send reports directly to the lieutenant-generals or generals (of which I would place four in Bohemia and two in Moravia) ... His functions would extend, on civil questions, to everything that affects the wellbeing of the subject ... as a conscripted man, so that he would consider and settle with the district official all the more serious punishments affecting individuals ...; likewise he would be directed to receive all subjects' complaints in these matters and put them before the district chief. If he could get no remedy there, then he could pass on such complaints ... to the lieutenant-generals ... The lieutenant-general, if he also could not settle the matter, would send it to the general commanding. Thus a kind of control would be introduced in relation to the numerous petitions of subjects.[29]

This proposal would not only have complicated the local administration. It would also have accorded the military an immensely important role in matters hitherto and normally reserved for the civil power. According to Joseph, this would be wonderfully beneficial:

What endless advantages might not accrue from the intimate co-operation of all these parts [of the administration] that I charge with the maintenance of the whole army in all provinces, if they would really work together! How much might not the province do to make things easier by provisioning, equipping and quartering the soldier, without anyone being worse off – indeed perhaps people would be better off! How well might

[28] For this and the next quotation, K-M VII, p. 377.   [29] K-M VII, pp. 378–9.

not the old and deserving be looked after, when through co-operation of the civil and the military powers little jobs could be found for them instead of their being lackeys! How much might not revenues be increased if every soldier and officer in the province ..., jointly with the bank officials, and under his superiors' orders, occupied himself with this task!

If the Canton Director supplied the troops in his district entirely from local sources, everyone would profit, and transport costs would be reduced. The soldiers could be used to the general advantage in work such as road-construction. If house-owners were well paid to billet and quarter troops, lords would surely give up their old and empty castles for barracks, and surplus monastic buildings would be made available for the same purpose and as homes for soldiers' children, places of education and hospitals.[30]

In the twentieth century this dream is hard to take seriously or treat sympathetically. It was certainly not fully shared by the *Staatsrat* and the other committees which had to consider Joseph's Bohemian *Relation* and irritated him so much by their delays in coming to any decisions about it. But an attempt ought to be made to account for its plausibility to the emperor and, in a less heady form, to Lacy and others.

Maria Theresa and Haugwitz, needing more money for defence, had set about increasing the tax-yield from the provinces. They worked to enhance the influence of the central government there, to weaken the provincial Estates and the lords represented in them, and to strengthen the local bureaucratic structure, making the *Gubernia* and the district chiefs of each province both more powerful and more dependent on Vienna. But in fact the old aristocratic Establishment retained substantial influence in the new administration, and the central government's control, though greater than before, remained limited, especially where the interests of the lords were directly involved. In Bohemia counts Chotek and Kollowrat merited criticism not only because they were old and feeble but also because they displayed too much sympathy with the nobles and the Estates.

If the civil bureaucracy set up to combat provincial and aristocratic pretensions could not be relied on, perhaps the army could. In Prussia the canton system gave the military a role similar to that envisaged by the emperor, though one less hostile to the aristocracy.[31] According to Joseph, it was only the army that had given proper warning of the Bohemian famine. Without the army the disaster could certainly not have been contained. Soldiers were already under orders to carry out civilian tasks like census-taking and creating a sanitary cordon. The discipline of the military might be proof against the influence of the lords. To Joseph the army was evidently, as

---

[30] K-M VII, p. 392.
[31] See O. Büsch, *Militärsystem und Sozialleben im alten Preussen, 1713–1807* (Berlin, 1962), e.g. pp. 25–6.

well as the best embodiment of the power and will of the Monarchy, the promoter of equality of opportunity and, 'so to speak, the advocate of the subjects'.[32] Given the social structure and the limitations of the civil service, this view had some force. In an impressively detailed report of July 1771 on the progress of the conscription in Bohemia, Lacy noted that in the Königgrätz *Kreis*, on the Prussian border, one hundred citizens of the Monarchy emigrated to Prussia for every ten that immigrated; this, he claimed, was

> because the peasants, when they turn up for their *Robot*, are subjected by the estate officials sometimes to blows and generally to rough words. A remarkable proof that it is not military service, which has existed in Prussian districts for a long time, but rather time-honoured oppression that makes the subject leave his fatherland.[33]

THE QUESTION OF SERFDOM IN BOHEMIA, TO 1777

This question of the relations between lords and peasants in Bohemia was to be the main domestic concern of the Vienna government for much of the seventies. Joseph's part in the making of policy on the issue was significant but puzzling. He usually adopted his customary radical standpoint, but in the final stages he took the side of caution and compromise, opposing his mother who was advocating fundamental changes. The standard works on the subject[34] misrepresent the position of both rulers, largely because Arneth suppressed many of the letters that Joseph wrote on the question.

Bohemian serfdom is an intractable topic, partly because of the great variations in customs and traditions between different regions of the province. One can start from the fact that virtually all the land was owned by the lords, lay and ecclesiastical, generally in large estates. Lords let out much of it to peasants, but without according them security of tenure. In fact most tenants can be classed as serfs, forbidden to move or to marry without the consent of their lord, and bound to do service (or *Robot*) for him on his land. The

---

[32] K-M VII, pp. 386, 393, *passim*. Cf. Arneth, *GMT* X, p. 51. On the canton system as actually introduced, Duffy, *Army of M.T.*, pp. 52–4.

[33] J. Kalousek (ed.), *Archiv český*, XXIX ([Prague,] 1913), p. 510.

[34] K. Grünberg, *Die Bauernbefreiung und die Auflösung des gutsherrlich-bäuerlichen Verhältnisses in Böhmen, Mähren und Schlesien* (2 vols., Leipzig, 1893–4) is the principal authority (vol. II of this work consists largely of documents). Wright, *Serf, Seigneur and Sovereign*, is the best in English (but see n. 45 below). See also Arneth, *GMT* IX, ch. 12; Kerner, *Bohemia in the Eighteenth Century*, esp. pp. 22–40; Macartney, *Habsburg Empire*, pp. 61–75; A. Klima, 'Probleme der Leibeigenschaft in Böhmen', *VSWG*, LXII (1975), 214–28.

I find the line of argument of A. Špiesz in 'Die Entwicklung der Agrarverhältnisse in Mittelund Osteuropa in der Neuzeit und das Problem der Existenz der Gutsherrschaft auf unserem Gebiete', *Historický Časopis*, XV (1967), 558 (German summary), very difficult to accept. Contrary to his view, production for export evidently occurred in some parts of Bohemia.

In using the terms 'peasant' and 'serf' and 'services' and *Robot*, I am not committing myself to particular definitions. For the purposes of this book it does not seem necessary to go into detail and controversy about the exact nature and extent of servitude, or the variety of 'peasant' obligations.

demands of the lords on the peasants had been increasing for centuries, partly because of the profits that could be obtained from the sale of grain, partly because the easiest way for the lords to meet the rising tax-demands of the government was to make greater use of the free labour at their disposal. Although the peasants were supposed to be protected by the law from unreasonable exactions, it was almost impossible for them to obtain redress, since the lords possessed judicial powers over their serfs. It seems that the attempt by Charles VI to establish norms in his *Urbarium* of 1738 had only strengthened the hands of the landowners.

Maria Theresa's remodelling of the *contributio* in some ways increased the difficulties. Many peasants held land designated as 'rustical', which the lord did not exploit directly. They could make some profit for themselves from working their holdings. But they owed taxes as well as service to the lord, and it was they who paid the *contributio* in respect of this class of land. Other peasants held, on very restrictive terms, land that formed part of the lord's demesne, designated 'dominical' land, from which he took the profits and on which he paid the *contributio*. From a fiscal point of view, therefore, it was desirable to free 'rustical' peasants so far as possible from the lord's oppression so that they might prosper and be able to pay the state their share of the *contributio*; but it was less obviously in the state's interest to protect the 'dominical' serf, especially if the landowners needed to grind him down – as they said they did – in order to be able to pay their portion. However, if the peasant was to be conscripted into the army, he must be tolerably healthy to be of any use. More broadly, the emperor and empress and their more advanced advisers condemned, on grounds of humanity and natural justice, 'the tyranny of the lords'.[35] Maria Theresa approved in 1769 this instruction to the Austro-Bohemian Chancellery:

Whenever there is a question of defining the obligations of the peasants to their landlords, the Chancellery must take as its guiding principle that the first consideration must be to sustain the peasantry, as the most numerous class of subjects and the foundation and greatest strength of the state. They must be maintained in such a condition that they can feed themselves and their families and afford the general taxes in peace and wartime. Hence it follows automatically that neither an *Urbarium* nor an agreement, and still less a custom, however old, can stand which is irreconcilable with the aforementioned maintenance of the subject.[36]

In the previous year a number of memoranda had reached the government in Vienna, describing scandalous cases of oppression on Bohemian estates. Faced with these reports, Maria Theresa had ordered enquiries to be instituted on the six estates alleged to be the worst. Despite the lack of

[35] Grünberg, *Bauernbefreiung*, vol. I, pp. 192–4, 203. He calls Blanc's programme 'naturrecht-liche, sozialpolitische-revolutionäre'. J. to L., 24 Jan. 1771 (Arneth, *MTuJ* I, p. 329).
[36] Hock, *Staatsrath*, pp. 68–9.

sympathy for the peasants shown by the Austro-Bohemian Chancellery and its head, count Chotek, intolerable conditions were found on at least one estate, that of prince Mansfeld at Dobrzicz. Unlawful and unreasonable amounts of labour-service were being exacted; peasants were being compelled to buy the lord's produce at outrageously high prices; anyone who complained was likely to be flogged or beaten up by the lord's agents; the prince barred access to the woods in mid-winter, in order to try to force the serfs to withdraw their statements of grievances. In this one flagrant case the empress succeeded in punishing the landlord, though over the opposition of Chotek. Prince Mansfeld was fined, and deprived of his rights over this part of his estate for some years.[37]

Maria Theresa, encouraged by Joseph, tried to extend the scope of her enquiries, but was frustrated at every level. She also legislated in 1770 to eradicate certain obvious abuses: forced child labour; compelling peasants to sell their produce to the lord below the market price and to buy the lord's dear; making them buy fixed amounts of the beer and wine produced on their lord's estate; and requiring gifts in return for permissions to travel and marry. But it is clear that these measures were widely ignored.[38]

In the early part of 1771 another anonymous memorandum was submitted to Joseph. This document so impressed him that he put to the Chancellery and the *Hofkammer* fundamental questions arising out of it, including these: would the complete abolition of serfdom be useful to the state or otherwise? Should labour services be replaced by payments in money or kind? If services were abolished, should the demesnes be sold off to individual peasants? Would it be beneficial if those who paid the *contributio* paid part of it directly to the army's local units?[39] Joseph's interest in the subject was intensified by the reports he received about the famine in Bohemia through the *Hofkriegsrat* and from Kressel. They told him that the selfish activities of the lords were largely responsible for the famine. Landowners were sending grain abroad or to other parts of the Monarchy where prices were high and purchasers could be found, rather than feeding their own starving peasants. Lords had been buying their serfs' corn at absurdly low prices, hoarding it and then selling it off at a huge profit. Further, they were continuing to use up grain in the brewing of the beer that they forced the peasants to buy, even at a time when bread was unobtainable.[40]

In June 1771 Maria Theresa decided to establish a commission to devise a new *Urbarium* for Bohemia. Its instructions were dated 6 October, just after

[37] Grünberg, *Bauernbefreiung*, vol. I, pp. 191–200; vol. II, pp. 155–66, 172–85. Arneth, *GMT* IX, pp. 342–4.

[38] Arneth, *GMT* IX, p. 345; G. Otruba, *Die Wirtschaftspolitik Maria Theresias* (Vienna, 1963), p. 108; Grünberg, *Bauernbefreiung*, vol. I, pp. 199–200; Hock, *Staatsrath*, p. 69.

[39] Arneth, *GMT* IX, pp. 345–7.

[40] Weinzierl-Fischer, *MÖSA* (1954), 485–90; Blaich, *VSWG* (1969), 306–17.

Joseph had left for the province. He had no doubt influenced them, but he disagreed with them. He reckoned that the business would be best done separately in each locality on the basis of local practices and conditions, and so without long delays that would encourage intrigue and arouse speculation.[41] But while he was in Bohemia, he came across hundreds of instances of oppression. He considered that the underlings employed by the lords to manage their estates were the worst of all the officials he encountered – true 'despots'.[42] On his way back he passed through the contrasting scene of Upper Austria:

The land is beautiful and well cultivated, and the corn stands very well and the fields [are] very well prepared ... The reason for this is the private property that the peasant in Upper Austria has, and the fact that he is not hindered in his operations by forced labour and owes only [taxes] to his lord.[43]

His position already appears somewhat inconsistent. On the one hand, he thinks the absence of labour services, and the concession of property rights to the peasant, beneficial. On the other hand, he recommends speedy action on no fundamental principle, varying from district to district. But his sympathy with the oppressed is unmistakable.

As he had predicted, the commission argued for three years without coming to an agreed conclusion. Opinion among reformers differed as widely as possible, while the Estates produced proposals involving virtually no change. Meanwhile, Maria Theresa rewarded the landowners who made agreements with their own serfs – just one in Bohemia proper, just one in Moravia, and that was all.[44]

In February 1774 it was thought urgent to come to some decision willy-nilly. Maria Theresa, virtually alone, now wanted the complete abolition of serfdom, 'the only thing that keeps me at the helm of the state'. She asked Joseph for a written opinion. He started from the point that the revenue and therefore the strength of the Monarchy depended on the result. There were diametrically opposed views: one party maintained that, if the peasants' obligations to the lords were not reduced, Bohemia would be ruined and her tax-payments would dwindle; the other declared that without the forced labour of the serfs the lords would be unable to pay their share to the government. The emperor denied, with characteristic false modesty, that he possessed sufficient knowledge to decide between these views. But of one thing he felt sure. Conditions varied so much in Bohemia that to make general

---

[41] This must be the meaning of his remark in K-M VII, p. 390, and I suppose he is also referring to the serfdom problem in J. to L., 25 Sep. 1771 (Arneth, *MTuJ* I, p. 344), denouncing the establishment of a *concertation*. A meeting of the *Staatsrat* on the subject with departmental heads took place on 30 Sep. 1771 (Grünberg, *Bauernbefreiung*, vol. II, p. 202). For the original decision, *ibid.*, vol. I, p. 203.

[42] K-M VII, pp. 377–8.   [43] Arneth, *GMT* X, p. 50.

[44] Arneth, *GMT* IX, pp. 349–50.

arrangements would be an 'absurdity'. He finally recommended that a special *Urbarium* should be negotiated for each estate by the lord and his peasants during the next six months. If they failed to meet the deadline, then the bureaucracy should intervene. He resisted the attempts of his mother and Hatzfeld to supplement this provision with any direction from the government about these 'free' negotiations. In April 1774 a patent on the lines of Joseph's memorandum was published. It was accompanied, however, by an instruction to the officials about the principles they were to adopt in drawing up *Urbaria* after the six-month period of grace. In this document it was laid down that no peasant should be required to give more service to his lord than previously; and the labour force was divided into several categories, to each of which maximum obligations were assigned.[45]

Not surprisingly, the progress of the voluntary agreements was slow. In June it was made quite clear that they would be accepted as valid even if they contravened the principles of the additional instruction, which was itself amended.[46] It became ever more apparent to the Bohemian peasants that, contrary to what they rightly believed about the wishes of both Maria Theresa and Joseph, the landlords had won the day.

Early in 1775 a large-scale peasant rebellion broke out in Bohemia: labour was refused, mansions were pillaged, and Protestantism emerged into the daylight. This was Maria Theresa's anguished reaction, in a letter to her ambassador in Paris, Mercy – one of her great *cris de coeur*:

I have sacrificed thirty-five years to the public, I am so borne down, so troubled, that I do more harm than good. The recent revolt in Bohemia, which is suppressed but very far from being extinguished, is one of the events that hasten my decisions, not through fear – this is a feeling I do not know – but because I cannot put things right and I do great harm by my [continued] presence. The emperor, who is too concerned with popularity, has said too much, without making formal promises to these people on the numerous journeys he undertakes, both about freedom of religion and their freedom vis-à-vis the lords; on top of that [have come] the conscription arrangements, during which the officers have talked and promised too much and excited the people. All this has caused confusion in all our German provinces since 1770, of which this is the upshot, which was predicted then and since . . .

You will blame me for not imposing order. On that point much could be said. My age, my illness, my prostration after my adorable husband's death made me entirely passive for two years. After that, having lost almost all my confidential ministers and friends, I have not been able to supply the necessary counterweight . . . The love, the

---

[45] Arneth, *GMT* IX, pp. 349, 352–7. Grünberg, *Bauernbefreiung*, vol. I, pp. 212–13. Hock, *Staatsrath*, p. 74.

Wright's account in *Serf, Seigneur and Sovereign*, p. 48, ignores J.'s successful opposition to allowing the 'instruction' to govern the agreements made during the six-month period of grace.

Macartney, *M.T. and the House of Austria*, p. 121, says 'the name *urbarium* was confined to cases where a land survey was carried through'. J. and M.T. accepted no such restriction.

[46] Arneth, *GMT* IX, p. 357. Hock, *Staatsrath*, p. 74.

weakness of a mother and an old woman have crowned it all. The state has suffered only too much, and I ought not to leave things like this any longer.

If he is in sole charge, then he will see all the difficulties and will not be able to hide behind me. He has too much intelligence, and his judgement is not yet so weakened, that he will not in the end recognise the truth. His heart is not entirely spoiled, though on this last point it is time there was an improvement.

You will at once burn this letter.[47]

This maudlin document shows how well she understood her son's relationship with herself. But it is utterly unreasonable in its condemnation of his activities on his travels. When she wrote it, he was in Croatia. Her outburst reveals only too clearly why she had tried to prevent him going on his life-saving journey to Bohemia in 1771, and why she disliked all his visits to her provinces. Despite her own proposal to abolish serfdom, she still criticises him bitterly for his advocacy of peasant freedom.

Well before he arrived back, his mother had accepted the anxious advice of Mercy and others, and decided 'to surrender herself humbly to Providence', that is, not to abdicate.[48] This was Joseph's account of the situation on his return:

The urbarial arrangements are swimming as always in uncertainty, to the great disadvantage of the subjects and the lords; and the little outbreaks still to be seen here and there are only the natural results of the government's indecision. For five years it has been deluding the subject with the prospect of alleviations without ever letting him experience them, and has been threatening the lord with reductions without daring to make him suffer them. Impatience gets the better of some, intrigue [is the resource of] others. The former agitate, the latter obstruct, and that is how things are tossed about. The empress gets confused, people grumble in really quite unseemly language. As soon as something is decided and even published, it is rescinded or changed.

Three weeks later he claimed that Maria Theresa had 'made the effort more than ten times to order that matters must be settled; it's never lasted longer than the time it takes to write out or print the orders and patents'. 'A little philosophy' alone sustains him and prevents his going mad. The issue will never be resolved unless an individual is sent to Bohemia with plenary powers.[49] But Joseph was now advocating that a new *Urbarium* should be promulgated, incorporating a standardised reduction in the *Robot*, a proposal associated with a radical official called Blanc. The emperor represented this as a step leading inevitably towards total abolition of forced labour in the long run. He maintained that under such an *Urbarium* the landlords would not only be receiving higher money payments than previously, but would also be able to sell more estate wine and beer to the enriched peasants. So eventually all

[47] Arneth & Geffroy II, pp. 329–30 (4 May 1775).
[48] Mercy to M.T., 18 May; M.T. to Mercy, 2 June; cf. M.T. to M.A., 2 June, 1775 (Arneth & Geffroy II, pp. 337–41).
[49] J. to L., 20 July and 9 Aug. 1775 (Arneth, *MTuJ* II, pp. 71, 81–2).

parties would come to desire the general substitution of rents for services. But 'I consider it impossible to abolish by an act of power the *Robot* which [forms] an essential element in our constitution'.[50]

This scheme was opposed root and branch by Kaunitz, on the ground that rebellion should not be seen to prosper. But Kressel, who had been sent off to Bohemia again, strongly urged that a new patent be issued, and so did the head of the Bohemian *Gubernium*. Gebler advised that 'experience had shown middle ways to be the worst policy'. In essentials the emperor won this engagement. The new *Urbarium* was dated 13 August 1775, and was ceremonially proclaimed throughout the province by two military commissioners, generals Wallis and D'Alton. It occupied eighty pages – according to Joseph, it was bound to 'have less effect than expected, because it has been jumbled up in an incredible and almost unintelligible manner'. It divided all peasants into eleven classes, prescribing distinct obligations for each. But none were to be worse off than before, and their precise duties and rights were to be published and upheld. Although the lords made sure that the *Urbarium* was implemented unevenly and with difficulty, and although it gave rise to many problems, on balance it brought substantial relief to the serfs of Bohemia. To give one example, at Hradec in the south of the province, before the patent a total of 347 days *Robot* was exacted per hectare; after 1775, only 144 days.[51]

The publication of this enormous and highly significant piece of legislation did not terminate the business. Maria Theresa decided to set an example to the landlords by an experiment on two estates formerly belonging to the Jesuits, now hers to dispose of. Working through an official called Raab, she had the demesne land sold off to the tenants. She later extended the scheme, known as 'the Raab system', to other royal properties.[52] So far as the *Urbarium* itself was concerned, its introduction seemed to bring hardship to some landlords. A proposal was discussed to raise a loan in Belgium to assist the province and particularly these landlords. It was during the endless debates on this and related issues, though not purely because of disagreement over Bohemia, that confrontations occurred first between Joseph and Maria Theresa, and later between Joseph and Kaunitz.[53]

The season of bad weather and Christian hope, with the imperial family marooned in the Hofburg, often brought out the worst in the two rulers. At

[50] Arneth, *GMT* IX, pp. 366–7. Hock, *Staatsrath*, p. 77 (6 Aug. 1771). On Blanc, K. Grünberg, 'Franz Anton von Blanc, ein Sozialpolitiker der theresianisch-josefinischen Zeit', *Schmollers Jahrbuch*, XXXV (1911), 1155–1238.
[51] Arneth, *GMT* IX, pp. 367–8; Hock, *Staatsrath*, pp. 76–8; J. to L., 6 Oct. 1775 (Arneth, *MTuJ* II, p. 87); Grünberg, *Bauernbefreiung*, vol. I, pp. 222–36; vol. II, pp. 257–70; Wright, *Serf, Seigneur and Sovereign*, pp. 50–2; Klima, *VSWG* (1975), 225–7.
[52] This experiment is the main subject of Wright, *Serf, Seigneur and Sovereign*.
[53] It is Arneth who associates these disputes with Bohemia: *GMT* IX, pp. 368–75. (See *ibid.*, pp. 597–8 for reports from the Venetian Ambassador on conditions in Bohemia after the issue of the patent.)

the end of 1775, the empress allowed herself the following drastic criticism of the emperor's principles:

The three most important are free exercise of religion, which no Catholic prince may permit without [incurring] grave responsibility; the annihilation of the existing nobility, under the specious pretext of preserving the majority, of which I accept neither the necessity nor still less the advantage; the so often repeated freedom in all things, which makes me more apprehensive than optimistic. I am too old ever to come round to such principles. Indeed I hope and pray to God that my successor himself will never put them into effect. Neither he nor still less his successors would be the happier for it.

Since it was the empress, not Joseph, who advocated immediate abolition of serfdom, her point about the nobility is hard to understand; but exactly what he had said to provoke her seems to be undiscoverable.

On Christmas Eve the emperor replied. He saw, he said, that all the advice he gave, which was inspired simply by what he conceived to be his duty to God, his country and his sovereign, aroused in her 'an absolutely invincible mistrust'. He has nothing to reproach himself about. It is simply his fate, to which he submits. But, since she finds his principles so utterly false, of what use is he to her? What good can he do? His activity must be positively harmful to her and to the state. It follows that he must be released from the co-regency. 'Then you will not hear a word from me, everything will run better and more smoothly, and I shall live more contentedly, more peacefully and perhaps more usefully than at present.' But he cannot change his principles.

His mother answered: 'There is a great misfortune in our relations; with the best intentions we do not understand each other.' She is thoroughly unhappy,

for I can never accept too lax principles in matters of religion and morals. You make only too apparent your antipathy to all old customs and to all the clergy, your too free principles in matters of morality and behaviour. I have every reason to feel alarmed at your precarious situation, and I tremble for the future.

But 'this night and these days are too glorious to be occupied with a decision such as you require of me; I shall give it to you in the New Year'.[54]

She consulted Lacy and Kaunitz, while Joseph returned to the charge both on Christmas Day and Boxing Day. On Lacy's advice she pointed out to the emperor that a public rupture between them would damage both of them and the state, and urged that she deserved to be able to count on his advice. The marshal further advised that if this step did not succeed, the empress should simply 'let the correspondence drop, and leave the rest to time'. This is what seems to have happened.[55]

Six weeks later, Joseph gave himself the satisfaction of writing Leopold a

[54] Arneth, *MTuJ* II, pp. 94–102 and 102n.   [55] Arneth, *GMT* IX, pp. 374, 542–3, 637–8.

letter containing one of his more desperate condemnations of his mother's rule:

Although the empress had told me that a courier was shortly to leave for Rome, calling on you *en route*, the time appears not yet to have arrived. I think that they wish to inform you of the present state of foreign and internal affairs, but that they can't manage to do it. For business as HM glimpses it, namely desultorily and superficially, in bits and pieces, looks well enough; but if it's brought together into one picture, I reckon that the best pen is hard put to it to dress it up in such a way as to hide the pitiable condition – of uncertainty and irresolution combined with timidity, weakness and pusillanimity – in which the Monarchy, with all its resources and means, languishes and sinks towards its doom. I see this prospect, not without the most cruel pain. I will say more: I see how to remedy it. At the same time I have no hope left that steps will be taken to save us. There is still time in my opinion, but soon there won't be. I've already worn out my lungs, and my pens have dirtied mounds of paper, but it's absolutely useless. There must be eyes and ears to read and hear me, and these must be directed by the will to know the truth and the capacity and will to pursue it once it has been demonstrated. If there are moments when one believes one has laid a good stone which will improve the building, and written resolutions confirm the fact – a few days later, everything is put in doubt or changed, and in the end all that happens is that trifles are discussed, committees are held eternally, thought is given to the tools and the accessories, personalities are most carefully considered, and not the policies of which they should be only the instruments. This is more or less the picture. I don't know how much they'll tell you; but, if I had to do it, as I went through all the headings, I should prove to you the truth of all that I describe here.[56]

In March 1776 it was Kaunitz's turn to stage a protest. He resigned, ostensibly because of a row with the emperor over current projects for establishing trading companies in the Netherlands and at Trieste, with particular reference to the manner in which Leopold was to be informed and involved. But the chancellor had suffered a series of contradictions and defeats from Joseph on Bohemian questions as well. 'Imagine HM's anxiety', the emperor wrote to his brother. 'She excused [Kaunitz's] action yet again. But it is said that he is most upset.' The dispute was patched up, with some concession to the chancellor.[57]

News of further discontent in Bohemia, associated with increasing emigration from the province, led to discussion of yet another revision of the *Urbarium*. Early in 1777, Kaunitz advised the recall of Wallis and D'Alton, the two military commissioners who had been enforcing it on the spot, and proposed that a confirmation of the patent of 1775 should be accompanied by stronger encouragement to the nobles to adopt the Raab system on their estates.[58] The empress was still hoping for a fundamental reform. She told Ferdinand at the end of January 1777:

---

[56] J. to L., 8 Feb. 1776 (HHSA FA Sbde 7), not in Arneth.
[57] Arneth, *GMT* IX, pp. 375, 469–75; J. to L., 29 Mar. 1776 (Arneth, *MTuJ* II, p. 108).
[58] Arneth, *GMT* IX, pp. 376–80 (31 Jan. 1777).

I believe that if the emperor – I will not say would support me – would merely remain neutral, I should succeed in abolishing serfdom and *Robot*. Then all would be well. But unfortunately the lords, seeing that I'm not taken in by them, have ranged themselves on the emperor's side, and the spirit of contradiction that reigns here makes my task very hard.

A fortnight later she returned to the same subject:

Bohemian affairs trouble me greatly, the more so as the emperor and I cannot agree on the means to be adopted. The oppression of these poor people and the tyranny [of the lords] are well known and acknowledged. It's only a question of laying down suitable principles. I had reached the point of success, when suddenly the lords, who by the way are all the ministers, contrived to weaken the emperor's resolution, and so in a moment the work of two years has been nullified.[59]

What happened in the end was that the 1775 patent was merely reaffirmed, Wallis and D'Alton kept their posts, but Blanc, who had been advocating further reform with special vigour, was demoted to a post in his Swabian homeland.[60]

This was how Joseph explained himself to Leopold, in letters written over the same period as his mother's to Ferdinand, and not published by Arneth. On 16 January 1777 he described Maria Theresa as more troubled than he had ever seen her before. She thinks everyone is against her. She reproaches him continually for opposing her. It is painful to go and talk to her.

Her party consists of only three or four councillors, and all the ministers and reasonable men are against the general revolution that she wants to effect ... Committees are continually being held, to try to devise something that can be proposed to her, but her ideas are so strong, so ruinous, that it isn't possible to find anything to put to her that comes anywhere near them ...

Briefly, the empress would like to overturn the whole *Urbarium*, published a year ago with all possible solemnity. She would like to abolish serfdom; arbitrarily regulate contracts and the level of the rents that the peasants who have leased lands have paid to their lord for centuries; change the entire rural economy of the propertied; finally give relief to the subject in respect of all his dues and obligations without paying the slightest regard to the lord, and so put [the lord] in the position of losing at least half the revenue he enjoys, thus lowering all land-values and making as many bankrupts as there are lords who have debts or liabilities, who are numerous. You will not regret being at Florence. I should like to be in the Antipodes.

On 6 February he reported that his mother wanted 'the impossible'. She 'won't readily accept the simple, the natural, what in the end good sense and

---

[59] M.T. to Ferd., 30 Jan. and 13 Feb. 1777 (Arneth, *MTKuF* II, pp. 66, 69).

These letters are wrongly ascribed to 1775 by Otruba, *Die Wirtschaftspolitik M.T.s*, p. 109, and Tapié, *Rise and Fall of the Habsburg Monarchy*, p. 211. They are correctly dated in Fejtö, *J. II*, pp. 140–1, but the texts given are corrupt. E.g. when she writes of abolishing '*die Leibeigenschaft* et les corvées', Fejtö prints 'le servage et la misère'.

[60] Arneth, *GMT* IX, pp. 380–2; Arneth, *MTKuF* II, pp. 69–70 (M.T. to Ferd., 13 Feb. 1777).

the wisdom of experience both dictate, but racks her brains to discover what is perfect'. A week later:

I have the most cruel debates to sustain, and I swear that never in my life so far have I seen anything like it, for she is at one and the same time in a state of anger and incredible indecision. Councillor Blanc had been good enough to tell several lies about me, and among other things he went to tell prince Kaunitz, to win him over, that I didn't mean a word of what I wrote, and that I only did it to test the officials and the ministers. This was too strong; and, having let the cat out of the bag, HM had to send him away, with his salary, which he will go and devour at Freiburg. Everyone agrees with me. It is only HM and some underlings who think differently ... I suffer martyrdom, and the best I can hope for is to avoid similar scenes every time I visit her.[61]

Eugen Guglia, the best of Maria Theresa's modern biographers, knowing of the letters she sent to Ferdinand but not of those between Joseph and Leopold, wrote:

It must be left to the future biographer of Joseph to clarify his position in these matters. We can only suppose that people frightened him with the prospect that imperial authority would be shaken by a further concession to the refractory peasants.[62]

This is a challenge to which it is still impossible, with the material available, to give an entirely satisfactory response. The emperor certainly displayed in the course of this story the inconsistency of which his mother and the princesses regularly complained.[63] For example, in 1771 and 1774 he described general regulation of the *Robot* as impossible and absurd, but in 1775 declared it essential. He seems to have refused to entertain a scheme to help straitened landowners in 1775–6, but appeared to sympathise with them in 1777. Taking his career as a whole, it is hard to reconcile his attitudes over Bohemian serfdom between 1771 and 1777 with his views and actions in other cases and at other times. In the *Rêveries* he had recommended a secret policy of humbling and impoverishing the nobility. He often spoke with approval of peasant freedom and proprietorship, and had worked to promote them in the Banat.[64] In 1781, almost as soon as his mother was dead, he abolished most of the restrictions on the individual liberty of the serfs. He later tried to commute labour services into cash payments and to remove the tax-privileges of the Hungarian nobility.[65] More generally still, he was always denouncing compromise and demanding that radical reforms be put through at a stroke – yet in the affairs of Bohemia he avowedly sought to find a middle way, and cast doubt on the government's power and right to abolish serfdom and *Robot*.

[61] J. to L., 16 Jan., 6 Feb. and 13 Feb. 1777 (HHSA FA Sbde 7, not in Arneth). Substantial portions of the first of these letters are printed in Fejtö, *J. II*, pp. 139–40.
[62] E. Guglia, *Maria Theresia* (2 vols., Munich, 1917), vol. II, p. 355.
[63] See pp. 201, 226, 333–5.   [64] See pp. 98, 101, 249, 349.
[65] Macartney, *Habsburg and Hohenzollern Dynasties*, pp. 175–9; *Habsburg Empire*, pp. 127–30.

In this matter, however, Maria Theresa prided herself on her own inconsistency: the great revolt of 1775, she told Kaunitz, 'entirely alters the position of affairs and also the measures to be taken'.[66] Such calamities as the famine and the revolt certainly justified changes of tactics if not of principle, and Joseph would have deserved to be called intransigent if he had never modified his own attitude. But he remained consistent to this degree: that he always treated the questions of reducing or abolishing the *Robot* and other aspects of serfdom in a wider context. He believed in the necessity to maintain a larger and therefore more costly army than Maria Theresa or Kaunitz desired, and he viewed the peasant problem in its fiscal relations. When Maria Theresa urged the abolition of serfdom and the *Robot*, she does not seem to have explained how levels of taxation would be maintained under the new dispensation. This, for Joseph, was the crucial difficulty – not fear of further insubordination.[67]

Her insinuation that Joseph was influenced by his private friendships with ministers and landlords and their relatives is partly justified, but the position was much less straightforward than she implied. His great dispute with Eleonore occurred in 1775, when he was standing firm, as he put it, in support of the new patent; and there is no sign that he then let himself be deflected. The views of the princesses were far from merely reactionary. They can be found in their letters to each other casting doubts on Joseph's faith in the potato, but also arguing for lower taxation as the best way to reduce burdens on the peasants, and favouring the Raab system.[68] We do not know the details of whatever influence was brought to bear on the emperor early in 1777. But it looks as though we are here observing an effect of the *modus vivendi* established between him and his mother in 1773–4.[69] She had been released from some of her routine duties, thought she had little time left on earth, and was therefore tempted to make large proposals that others would have to implement. Joseph, as the workhorse of the *Staatsrat*, was playing exactly the role she claimed she wished him to play, that of a prudent chief minister in touch with the bureaucracy.

She unquestionably showed herself the more humane and the more revolutionary of the two in her attitude towards Bohemian serfdom after about 1775 – though not, as we shall see, in her approach to Bohemian Protestant-

---

[66] Arneth, *GMT* IX, p. 593.

[67] In his *Gutachten* on *Robotangelegenheiten* of 18 Jan. 1777 (HHSA FA Sbde 5) J. did stress the risk to *Ruhe* and *Ordnung*, but he made in this and other papers many other points. Cf. Fejtö, *J. II*, pp. 141–6. Wangermann's cautious moderation in *NCMH*, vol. VIII, pp. 282–3, contrasts with his tendentious standpoint in 'Matte Morgenröte' in *MTIZ*, pp. 67–71, where he identifies (1) what M.T. was proposing in 1777 with what J. enacted in the 1780s and (2) the criticisms made by J. of M.T.'s scheme with those made by aristocrats of J.'s edicts of the 1780s.

[68] See above, p. 333; L.K. to E.L., 12 Mar. 1771 and E.L. to L.K., 21 Dec. (SOALpZ, LRRA P. 16/22); and L.K. to E.L., 6 Aug. 1772 (*ibid.*, P. 16/23).

[69] See pp. 228–9.

ism.[70] One can only admire the vigour and independence of mind displayed by the harassed, ailing widow. But all contemporaries agreed that she found it terribly hard to take decisions and that her will now lacked its old firmness.[71] Joseph had worked to strengthen it in the case of the great patent of 1775. Two years later he was surely right when, for once adopting her normal position and the standpoint of all his critics then and since, he argued that the radical changes she was advocating simply could not be carried through and that, if the attempt was made, it would inevitably bring chaos and impoverishment to Bohemia and the whole Monarchy. His view receives support in the writings of two of his most brilliant and, in utterly different ways, radical contemporaries: both Frederick the Great and Rousseau considered serfdom detestable, but neither could conceive of its being abolished at a stroke.[72]

---

[70] See pp. 466–73.   [71] See pp. 193, 490 above.

[72] Frederick in 'Essai sur les formes de gouvernement' [1777] in Preuss, *Oeuvres de Frédéric*, vol. IX, pp. 205–6; Rousseau in *Considérations sur le gouvernement de Pologne* [1771] in C. E. Vaughan, *The Political Writings of Jean Jacques Rousseau* (2 vols., Cambridge, 1915), vol. II, pp. 497–9.

CHAPTER 12

Further travels: eastern provinces and France 1773–1777

TRANSYLVANIA AND GALICIA, 1773

In 1773 the business of partitioning Poland detained Joseph in Vienna, but in the following year he resumed his programme of travel with one of his longest journeys, lasting from early May to late September 1773. After paying his third visit to the Banat, he went on to see for the first time Transylvania and Galicia.

Maria Theresa was still placing obstacles in the way of his travel plans. At the beginning of 1773 he was making arrangements for a journey to the newly annexed province of Galicia, but the empress vetoed it as too dangerous. She was only with difficulty persuaded to let him go to Transylvania.[1] As he travelled, however, he continued to prepare for a visit to Galicia. Then on 12 June he wrote from the remote Transylvanian townlet of Kézdivásárhely to tell his mother how enthusiastic he was to go on to the new province, 'purely and simply for the good of the service'.[2] By the same post he cruelly urged Kaunitz to back his request. The chancellor must have known that Joseph would take the opportunity of such a visit to condemn the existing administration of the province by the *Staatskanzlei*. But he could hardly incur the emperor's wrath by obstructing the journey. Maria Theresa returned one of her most heartfelt replies to her son:

My peace of mind, my good humour haven't lasted long ... I can't view as you do this terrible journey or any of those you undertake at such cost in fatigue, wasting your best days, and stealing and embittering the few moments that remain to me. Help me rather to put in better order the provinces that you have [already] visited and that we're [already] dealing with. If these are solidly [established], Transylvania and Poland will follow. But, if we organise the latter, we shall not achieve the great object as with the others. Forgive me; it is my duty to tell you the truth. It isn't possible for you, despite

---

[1] M.T. to Lacy, 23 Apr. 1773 (Arneth, *GMT* IX, p. 624); M.T. to Ferd., 26 Apr. 1773 (Arneth, *MTKuF* II, p. 199): M.T. to J., 20 June 1773 (Arneth, *MTuJ* II, p. 10); Glassl, *Einrichtungswerk*, p. 69.

[2] J. to M.T., 12 June 1773 (Arneth *MTKuF* II, p. 8).

your ability and application, on these journeys of two or three months, to see everything and draw the [appropriate] conclusions . . .

You always rely on my affection, which is always on your side against my better judgement. Since I couldn't come to a decision contrary to my conviction, I consulted Kaunitz. This is his note. As a result of it, I've sent off all the letters.

She and Kaunitz clearly feared that, if she had forbidden him to go, Joseph would have disobeyed her.[3]

The emperor spent altogether nearly two months in Transylvania. Now the north-western part of Romania, it had by the 1770s been under effective Habsburg rule for about eighty years. But it had scarcely more in common with the main provinces of the Monarchy than Galicia had. Many aspects of Transylvania's old constitution remained in force. Three nations made up its 'Estates': the nobles of the Hungarian counties in the west; the 'Szekler' in the east, also for practical purposes Hungarian; and the 'Saxons', descendants of German settlers. However, the largest ethnic group, with half the total population of nearly 1½ million, were the Vlachs or Wallachians or Romanians, who had no status and were mostly unfree and poor. The strictly Catholic dynasty had to recognise no fewer than four religions in Transylvania: Roman Catholicism, including the Uniates who used the Greek rite but had been reconciled to Rome; Lutheranism; Calvinism; and, incredibly, Unitarianism. But the single largest body of adherents belonged to the Greek Orthodox Church, which was not recognised. The Saxons were virtually all Lutherans, and vice versa. The Orthodox Church was just as closely identified with the Romanians. Under Maria Theresa, Protestants discovered in other parts of the Monarchy were still usually 'exiled' to Transylvania.

Though nominally part of Hungary, it was separately governed. In the early sixties a serious attempt began to impose on the province institutional arrangements closer to those in the rest of the Monarchy: a regular military frontier zone was established, and attempts were made to impose heavier taxation while reducing the obligations of the peasants to their lords. These efforts led to fitful rebellion and continuous disputes. The Estates were not summoned after 1762. Matters were complicated by running battles within the administration: the military commander fought the civil governor; those on the spot denounced the Vienna *Hofkanzlei*; almost everyone intrigued and informed against Maria Theresa's favourite official of Transylvanian origin, baron Samuel von Brukenthal, a Lutheran 'Saxon', educated at German universities, detested by the Roman Catholic bishop, the generals, the Hungarians and the civil governors alike. In the early seventies Brukenthal was the effective head of the province's administration in Vienna, but from time to time he was sent to his homeland to impart energy to the local

---

[3] The quotation: M.T. to J., 20 June 1773 (Arneth, *MTuJ* II, pp. 9–10). M.T. to Ferd., 24 June 1773 (Arneth, *MTKuF* II, p. 213); Glassl, *Einrichtungswerk*, p. 69.

bureaucracy. The empress once remarked of the Transylvanian nations: 'to get the better of them, one would have to be a despot, and instead of the sceptre employ the knout to coerce them ... but I certainly can't change in that way'.[4]

Joseph prepared himself for his journey by reading memoranda specially composed by all the contending parties. He took his usual small suite, headed this time by generals Nostitz, Pellegrini and Siskowics.[5] He wrote some unusually vivid letters describing his activities to Lacy and the princesses in Vienna. From Clausenburg:

My occupations don't in reality resemble those of Hercules, neither in crushing monsters nor in spinning for Omphale. I go about, I learn, I see, I inform myself and I make notes. That's more like being a student than a conqueror. That may perhaps be of use now, but will certainly be of use in the future – or perhaps not, that depends on the decrees of providence – and I shall never regret the hardships or the years of my prime spent in instructing myself and accumulating useful information, even for so uncertain a future, or missing what the world calls pleasures.[6]

From Hermannstadt, a town he thought pathetically mean for a capital:

I've been here for five days, dictating and writing the entire day, or else borne down with audiences. I am like a prisoner of state, shut up in my hotel, unable to escape for an instant ... My house is continuously besieged by Wallachians and peasants giving in memorials, of which, taking only the political, I've already collected more than 7000.

From Kőrösmező, as he was about to pass into Galicia: 'You give me notice [to expect] many memorials in Galicia. Would you believe that I've already got up to 15,000?'[7]

An eye-witness described his receiving petitions as he travelled about:

All along the road petitioners of every age and sex, and of all the nations of Transylvania, knelt holding up their petitions. In front of each one the emperor stopped and told him to rise: '*Steht auf!*' to the Saxon, and '*Scula, scula*' to the Wallach. With his own hands he received each person's petition and questioned him briefly about its contents. Then, after a moment's reflection, he would say: '*Ich werde untersuchen*' [I will look into this] to the Saxon, or '*Voi cauta*' to the Wallach. With that, he placed the petitions in a sack tied to the inside of the carriage door and drove on.[8]

4 On eighteenth-century Transylvania in general and under M.T.: in English Prodan, *Supplex Libellus Valachorum*; K. Hitchins, *The Rumanian National Movement in Transylvania, 1780–1849* (Cambridge, Mass., 1969); in German Arneth, *GMT* x, ch. 5; Göllner, *Die siebenbürgische Militärgrenze*; Schuller, *Brukenthal*; K. Müller, *Siebenbürgische Wirtschaftspolitik unter M.T.* (Munich, 1961); E. Buchinger, *Die 'Landler' in Siebenbürgen* (Munich, 1980).
      Quotation from M.T. to Lacy, 18 Dec. 1769 (Arneth, *GMT* x, p. 771).
5 On the Transylvanian part of the journey, chiefly Arneth, *GMT* x, pp. 151–4; Schuller, *Brukenthal*, vol. 1, pp. 281–317; HHSA FA Hofreisen 5.
6 J. to Lacy, 26 June 1773 (Arneth, *GMT* x, p. 773).
7 J. to Lacy, 2 July and 16 July 1773 (HHSA FA Sbde 72).
8 Hitchins, *Rumanian National Movement*, p. 35, quoting the autobiography of M.C. von Heidendorf, from *Archiv des Vereines für siebenbürgische Landeskunde* (1881), 450. I have not seen the MS or the original article.

Joseph himself wrote home that he often had to talk Latin, as well as some Romanian.[9]

He had sent all officials a questionnaire with twenty-five headings. On the basis of the answers, of his discussion with the chief councillors, of the petitions and of his own observations he wrote an eighty-page *Relation* for his mother and the principal ministers in Vienna. 'On my honour', he wrote, 'I have had no preconceptions, only seen, heard and collected; and what I've presented are important conclusions arising.'[10] As usual, he found much to criticise; but he allowed himself to give more praise to individuals than generally. The land, he said, had great potentialities that were not being exploited. Although some of the reforms had been

in a certain fashion completed, still not one has been properly carried through, because a welter of contradictory views, intrigues, personal disagreements and religious differences have got in the way ... I must observe that the best intentions often go wrong; and the absence of local knowledge makes such a difference in provincial affairs that it is often impossible in practice to implement the best, most far-reaching and from a distance apparently most suitable plans, and that the total ignorance of all Your Majesty's advisers and experts in the central departments, the Transylvanian *Hofkanzlei* partially excepted, is a real difficulty, impediment and drawback for the service.[11]

Ethnic and religious divisions had greatly impressed him. Whereas his mother's policy, supported by most of her advisers, still envisaged spreading civilisation in Transylvania through the advance of Catholicism, Joseph recommended limiting the special favour shown to Catholics and urged measures to improve the education and standing of the Orthodox clergy and laity. The Hungarian nobility he found fanatical in their constitutionalism. The Saxons had learned that 'brains, zeal, understanding, sense and ideas pave the way to high office'. Both Hungarians and Saxons, he thought, oppressed the Wallachians. 'One's heart bleeds to hear for oneself and to observe the unfairness – indeed the impossibility of getting justice done to some poor men.' The government's aim ought to be to accord equal rights before the law and equal opportunities to all faithful subjects of whatever race or religion. All should see themselves as Transylvanians rather than Hungarians, Szekler, Saxons or Vlachs.[12]

Joseph's final proposals embodied two alternative schemes. The first and more radical was that the part of Transylvania not under military rule should be joined with the similar portion of the Banat and some Hungarian counties to form a new unit, loosely dependent on Hungary; and the separate

---

[9] J. to Lacy, for the circle of ladies, n.d. (SOALpZ, LRRA P. 16/22–3 (copies)).
[10] Hock, *Staatsrath*, p. 28.
[11] Schuller, *Brukenthal*, vol. I, p. 308. The comments J. made on individuals are reproduced in K-M VII, pp. 447–51.
[12] Schuller, *Brukenthal*, vol. I, pp. 307–17 (quotations from p. 309); Arneth, *GMT* x, pp. 152–4 (quotation from p. 153).

Transylvanian *Hofkanzlei* should be abolished. The second scheme amounted merely to more efficient and single-minded administration on the lines already established. It was naturally the second, milder alternative that Maria Theresa adopted, placing Brukenthal in charge of the provincial administration in July 1774.[13]

Galicia, where Joseph spent six weeks, posed different problems. Until the previous year it had formed part of Poland. It therefore contained a large number of Roman Catholic nobles, mostly impoverished, who had been exempt from taxation and whose position was entrenched under the old constitution by their control of the Diet. The province had well over two million inhabitants, of whom the majority were Uniate Ruthenes, though the governing class was Roman Catholic and Polish. The condition of the serfs was considered even worse than in the other eastern provinces of the Monarchy. To the 'horror and disgust' of Maria Theresa, Galicia's population included over 200,000 Jews, who dominated what there was of commerce and urban life. Joseph's reaction was that he now understood why he bore the title 'King of Jerusalem'.[14] When he arrived in Galicia at the end of July 1773, its precise frontiers had still to be settled, and the administration under Kaunitz's overall control had been established only temporarily, with count Pergen as the governor.[15]

Joseph used his journey, as we have seen, to impose on his mother and on Kaunitz the policy of extending the frontiers of the annexed province, particularly towards the river Sbrutz. He also prepared the way for the annexation of the Bukovina at the end of the Russo-Turkish War, rejecting the alternative of purchasing Little Wallachia.[16] And he wrested the government of the province from Kaunitz's hands.

It is this last achievement and its implications that mainly concern us here. Maria Theresa and the chancellor were inclined to treat Galicia gently, respecting some at least of its old institutions and attitudes. The empress wrote to Kaunitz:

I entirely agree. Pergen is to be told to proceed very slowly in all matters, especially so far as concerns the clergy. Over such a stupid, servile people they possess great power. We therefore ought to try to deal tactfully with them, to win them over rather than to impose things on them by force, until we're in a position to set up something solid.[17]

---

[13] Arneth, *GMT* x, pp. 153–5; Schuller, *Brukenthal*, vol. I, pp. 308, 312–32. See n. 28 below.
[14] For J.'s joke, W. Häusler, *Das galizische Judentum in der Habsburgermonarchie* (Vienna, 1979), p. 18.
    For M.T.'s horror, her letter to Ferd., 26 Aug. 1773 (Arneth, *MTKuF* II, p. 226).
[15] For Galicia in general Arneth, *GMT* x, ch. 3; Glassl, *Einrichtungswerk*; Macartney, *Habsburg Empire*, pp. 46–7 and ch. I generally. For J.'s journey, Rumpel, 'Reisen Kaiser J. II. nach Galizien'; Polek, *Jahrbuch des Bukowiner Landesmuseums* (1895), 25–140.
[16] See above, pp. 300–2.   [17] No date given. Arneth, *GMT* x, p. 86.

Kaunitz even proposed treating Galicia like Belgium, where an almost medieval constitutionalism still flourished and Haugwitz's reforms had never been introduced.[18] Joseph had succeeded in stiffening Pergen's instructions, and the governor made a point of asking the emperor numerous questions about how best to carry out his task.[19] But this was not enough for Joseph. Although he sometimes treated Galicia as an acquisition that might be bartered against some more desirable piece of territory, he fully intended that it should be seriously reformed.[20] Despite the fact that the claims on which the Monarchy's annexation was based derived entirely from Maria Theresa's Hungarian Crown, he was equally determined not to allow the province to become part of Hungary, which would have preserved the nobles' tax-exemptions.[21] He aimed to remodel it drastically, to make it 'a companion German hereditary province'.[22] He wished to eradicate Polish dress and customs, and to make Latin (rather than Polish or German) the language of affairs.[23]

His journey was even more uncomfortable than usual. So that he could write, a servant had constantly to flick away the flies. A flea got into his dumpling. He had to ride long distances into the mountains because there were no roads there at all.[24] What he saw and heard did not cause him to change his fundamental position that Galicia must become, administratively, part of the central bloc of the Monarchy. Petitioners gave him plenty of ammunition with which to assail the work of Pergen. But Joseph's attitudes were not unaffected by his visit. He became much more concerned with the welfare of the province itself, as opposed to its exploitation for the advantage of the whole Monarchy; and he took up a scheme he had previously opposed, for creating local Estates on the model of one of the central provinces, in order to give the nobility some feeling of participation in the new regime.[25]

His *Relation* embodied a denunciation of Pergen as lazy and incompetent. All he had contrived to do in a year, said Joseph, was to set up a new court of justice. When he received decrees from Vienna, far from acting on them, he kept them secret even from the subordinate officials.[26] The emperor submerged the poor man under no fewer than 154 'questions', some in several

---

[18] Kaunitz to Pergen, 5 Dec. 1772 (Glassl, *Einrichtungswerk*, p. 37). See pp. 484–5.

[19] Arneth, *GMT* x, pp. 78–81.

[20] Arneth, *GMT* x, pp. 88–9. Glassl repeatedly points out that J. did show himself ready to barter Galicia for other acquisitions (e.g. *Einrichtungswerk*, p. 10); but from what Arneth reports, and from Rumpel, 'Reisen Kaiser J. II. nach Galizien', it is clear that this readiness in no way implied laxity in reform. Cf. the case of Belgium in the 1780s, or the Breisgau.

[21] Arneth, *GMT* x, pp. 95–7. Cf. Glassl, *Einrichtungswerk*, pp. 44–6, 80–1.

[22] Glassl, *Einrichtungswerk*, p. 74.

[23] Glassl, *Einrichtungswerk*, e.g. pp. 100, 107, 236–43.

[24] J. to his circle of ladies, 16 July and 10 Aug. 1773 (SOALpZ, LRRA P. 16/22–3 (copies)).

[25] See esp. Rumpel, 'Reisen Kaiser J. II. nach Galizien', pp. 24, 48.

[26] Glassl, *Einrichtungswerk*, pp. 70–3.

parts and requiring vast researches to answer. The military administration received a further forty-eight.[27]

At the beginning of 1774 Kaunitz surrendered the direction of Galician affairs; Pergen was replaced as governor; and a separate department was established in Vienna to deal with the province.[28] Joseph's *Relation* and his questionnaire ensured that fundamental reform was planned and initiated, to assimilate Galicia to the pattern of Austria and Bohemia. But he was given no special status in the government of the province; and as in Transylvania and the Banat, personal and administrative rivalries delayed the process of reform, rendered difficult enough in any case by problems of distance, information and comprehension. One governor was said to have spent more time on disputes with officials in Vienna than on implementing orders. After only two years it was found desirable, with strong support from Joseph, to absorb the Galician department into the Austro-Bohemian Chancellery. Anyway, the local nobles and clergy proved unco-operative; there were 154 questions for a mere handful of bureaucrats to answer; and the major schemes never received the sanction of Maria Theresa.

By the time the emperor paid another visit to the province in 1780, on his way to Russia, very little seemed to him to have been achieved, except an elaborate edict on the position of the Jews. He exaggerated, of course. For example, a few monasteries had been suppressed. There remained under consideration an *Urbarium*; the project to set up Estates; proposals to redraw the diocesan boundaries and dissolve more monasteries; a new tax-system; a new district organisation; and an educational programme.[29] Joseph made a variety of further proposals, but he expressed a surprising measure of confidence in the new governor, count Brigido, the fourth man to hold the post since the annexation, and strongly backed the local administration against the bureaucracy in Vienna. He wanted Slovak speakers as officials in Galicia. 'For God's sake', he urged her, 'don't send any more Germans here.' He recommended employing more Galician nobles in the departments of justice, while strongly criticising the great lords who owned land in the province but resided elsewhere. He begged her to settle once and for all the question whether Galicia should be united to Hungary, 'an idea . . . so absurd, . . . so impracticable, even harmful'. But these views made no headway so long as Maria Theresa lived. Indeed, when Joseph passed through Galicia again on his way back to Vienna, he claimed that the situation had gone from bad to

---

[27] *Ibid.*, p. 70; Arneth, *GMT* x, pp. 89–92; Rumpel, 'Reisen Kaiser J. II. nach Galizien', p. 46.

[28] See Arneth, *GMT* VIII, pp. 413–23. Some unpublished letters of J. to L. in HHSA FA Sbde 7 (1 Dec. 1773, 27 May 1774) make it clear that J. was less than entirely satisfied with the change of administration in Galicia (and Transylvania).

[29] This account of the aftermath of J.'s 1773 visit to Galicia is based on Arneth, *GMT* x, pp. 92–9, Rumpel 'Reisen Kaiser J. II. nach Galizien', and Glassl, *Einrichtungswerk, passim*. See also Schünemann, *MÖIG* (1933), 45.

worse. Nothing had been done to meet the universal and justified clamour against the administration of the salt tax. And

in just over two months ... I think six or seven new [officials] have arrived, all originating from Bohemia and Austria. I testified to you that they were too numerous, and useless, and this is what happens. If we go on like this, the result will always be that these gentlemen, in order to do nothing, or worse than nothing, while making it appear that they are doing something, will cream the revenues of the Estates.[30]

CROATIA AND THE LITTORAL, 1775

In 1775 Joseph travelled to the only part of the Monarchy, except for Belgium, that he had not yet seen: Croatia and the Littoral, territories now within Yugoslavia. He went first to Croatia, a province associated with Hungary that had been ruled by the Habsburgs since the sixteenth century. Much of it was organised as a military frontier. Then he inspected the Littoral, including the short stretches of coastline that gave the main lands of the Monarchy their only direct access to the sea.[31] Before returning to Vienna, the emperor spent a few days in Venice with his three brothers, taking the opportunity to smooth relations with the Republic.[32]

On this journey Joseph was chiefly concerned with trade and ports. He criticised the lengthy delays and inconveniences that traders were forced to suffer, even in healthy periods, at the plague-cordon. He wanted its strictness much relaxed. He had for a long time been at odds with the *Kommerzienrat*, the department in charge of Austrian and Bohemian commerce,[33] which also administered the Littoral. The emperor, as in the case of the *Banco* and the Banat, objected to an economic department exercising political power over a province. He further considered it absurd that an agency entrusted with furthering the interests of Austria and Bohemia should control Fiume, Hungary's natural port. It will be remembered that Hungary was separated from the German lands by a customs barrier, and treated as their economic rival. In his *Relation* he recommended the abolition of the *Kommerzienrat*'s rule in the Littoral, and the absorption of the department within the Austro-Bohemian Chancellery. He proposed dividing the coastal strip into three parts, Trieste becoming Austrian, Fiume Croatian and therefore associated with Hungary, and the remainder attached to the military frontier. After some argument these recommendations were implemented in 1776.

---

[30] J. to M.T., 19 May and 6 August 1780 (Arneth, *MTuJ* III, pp. 242–4, 300–1); *Relation* in HHSA FA Hofreisen 11; Rumpel, 'Reisen Kaiser J. II. nach Galizien', ch. 6.

[31] On Croatia, W. Kessler, *Politik, Kultur und Gesellschaft in Kroatien und Slawonien in der ersten Hälfte des 19. Jhdts* (Munich, 1981); G. E. Rothenberg, *The Military Border in Croatia, 1740–1881* (Chicago, 1966). *Relation* in HHSA FA Hofreisen 9, printed in K-M VIII, pp. 258–66.

[32] See pp. 303–4 and 304n above.   [33] See pp. 93, 239–40.

Joseph was not deterred by the fact that they involved taking Fiume out of the Holy Roman Empire. He had no hesitation in putting the interests of the Monarchy as he saw them before his duties as 'perpetual enlarger of the *Reich*'. Karl Zinzendorf, whose job disappeared in the reorganisation, was soon compensated with the governorship of Trieste.[34]

FRANCE, 1777

After a year without long journeys, Joseph spent four months of 1777 on another great excursion, to France. He left Vienna on 1 April, passed through southern Germany and northern France, and reached Paris on the 18th. He stayed there or at Versailles for the next six weeks, then toured the French provinces, and returned through Switzerland. This visit to the dominant country and the leading city of the Enlightenment naturally attracted more publicity than any of his other journeys, and has aroused special interest among historians.[35]

In both directions he took the opportunity *en route* to inspect territories belonging to the Monarchy, and it is convenient to deal briefly with this aspect of his journey before considering the much more notable tour of France. These possessions included the westernmost parts of the old core of Habsburg lands, namely the Tyrol and Vorarlberg, most of which still remain part of the Austrian republic, together with scattered enclaves now German or Swiss (see Maps 1 and 2). Joseph spent little time in the Tyrol, which he had already visited in his youth. In any case his mother treated it, like Belgium and Hungary, as a province where, out of respect for its ancient and intractable constitution, the more drastic administrative reforms like conscription could not be introduced.[36] But he examined and reported with his usual vigour on Vorarlberg and the detached territories, known collectively as *Vorderösterreich* or the *Vorlande* – even though he considered them a liability rather than an asset:

---

[34] The only modern published discussion of this journey known to me is in Schünemann, *MÖIG* (1933), 53–5. See also Arneth, *GMT* IX, pp. 464–8 and X, pp. 129–30; K-M VIII, pp. 123–6. There is much relevant material in HHSA TZ.

[35] The main published source for the visit is Arneth & Geffroy III, pp. 47–87. See also comte de Pimodan, *Le Comte F.C. de Mercy-Argenteau* (Paris, 1911), ch. 9; Arneth, *MTuJ* II, pp. 130–49. The chief published account is H. Wagner, 'Die Reise Josephs II. nach Frankreich 1777 und die Reformen in Österreich' in *Österreich und Europa. Festgabe für Hugo Hantsch* (Graz, 1965), pp. 221–46.

[36] A few pages in Arneth, *GMT* X, ch. 1 on the Tyrol, esp. pp. 22–4, 31–5. J. in his talk with Tron in Venice in 1769 explained that the Tyrol, like Hungary, was separated from the rest of the Monarchy by a customs barrier because it did not help the sovereign, i.e. pay its full share of taxes (ASV, Corti Senato I (Secreta) Fᵃ 335).

According to *ÖZKJ*, p. 458, he ordered repairs to the road leading from Innsbruck to the Brenner pass.

F. Reitböck, 'Die kulturellen und sozialen Reformen unter der Regierung der Kaiserin

When one looks carefully at this province, it becomes obvious that there is very little advantage to be derived from it. But so long as there is any, prudence seems to demand that we get as much as possible, while at the same time making the people as happy as possible. Now with the present system we fail in both aims. An expensive, over-staffed and ill-manned administration wastes revenue and causes discontent.

Twenty councillors who, with their subordinates, cost 140,000 florins in a province that yields in total only 300,000 florins, since each of them has to find something to do, examine [issues], invent [problems], ask questions, write [reports] and exasperate everyone ... The University [of Freiburg] is in more or less the same state: with twenty-four professors, of whom some have seven or eight students at their lectures, others more, it clearly isn't worth what it costs and isn't in a position ever to attract more students.

Joseph recommended reducing the size of the civil service drastically, and uniting the university with that of Innsbruck. Attempts should also be made, he said, by promoting frontier adjustments and establishing historic claims, to gain territory that would expand the Monarchy's central bloc. But the lands that were irredeemably detached should be exchanged – though only if a very good bargain could be struck.[37]

The emperor's plan to visit France went back at least to 1770, when his youngest sister Marie Antoinette married the dauphin, the grandson and heir of Louis XV.[38] But the journey was not seriously mooted until the autumn of 1773, when Joseph embarked on an elaborate correspondence with count Mercy, the Austrian ambassador in Paris, about routes, timing, accommodation and other arrangements. Maria Theresa was not at first supposed to know anything about it, and evidently remained in the dark for some weeks, because she secretly warned Mercy to expect an approach from the emperor more than a month after it had taken place. The ambassador informed her that

all the motives stated by HM rest on considerations of propriety and utility: to see Mme the Dauphine; to make the personal acquaintance of the king; to appraise the situation of this Court now and for the future; to observe everything interesting that a great monarchy can show in the way of resources, administration, agriculture, finance, commerce, police, marine and military.

Joseph insisted as usual on preserving the strictest incognito. It was essential, he said, that he should be able to see sights and institutions without giving prior warning, 'in their natural state'. He would attend only a restricted

Maria Theresia in Tirol', University of Innsbruck PhD, 1943, gives many examples of attempts at religious reform.
[37] J. to M.T., 24 July 1777 (Arneth, *MTuJ* II, pp. 153–6). See also the previous letter of 20 July, esp. p. 151. Arneth, *GMT* x, pp. 36–40. See E. Gothein, *Der Breisgau unter Maria Theresia und Joseph II.* (Heidelberg, 1907), esp. pp. 24–5, for the importance of the visit. Cf. p. 392.
On the whole district, some excellent chapters in Metz, *Vorderösterreich*. For this part of his journey see Plates 15b and 16a.
[38] On the diplomacy behind the marriage and the event itself, see Arneth, *GMT* VII, ch. 13.

selection of operas and plays. His attitude to meeting celebrities is especially interesting:

He has no expectation of getting to know Parisian ladies and gentlemen during the few days he'll be there, and so has no desire to be admitted to social gatherings ... All the same, he doesn't decline to see particularly interesting and lively persons whom he may encounter on his way or by chance; but if it didn't seem too barbarous, he wouldn't be especially curious to meet the recognised *savants* personally, since they always seem to him more worth reading than seeing, when one cannot keep up their acquaintance.

He had told Mercy that he was open to suggestions, and in fact accepted several modifications proposed by the ambassador, even including some mitigation of his incognito.[39]

Maria Theresa confided to Mercy her very grave doubts about the journey:

[It] greatly displeases me, except on account of my daughter, and I do not anticipate any advantage from it. His dislike will only grow stronger when he sees the frivolity, absurdity and intrigues of this nation. The suite will be composed of general Nostitz and Joseph Colloredo, ... both of them sworn enemies of the French, and Cobenzl ... There is even an idea of returning through Switzerland to see Voltaire, Tissot, Haller and all those extremists ... All this distresses me.

Mercy tried to comfort her on the last point:

As for the plan to go and see Voltaire, Tissot and Haller, I think it will collapse of its own accord; first because it will take HM too much out of his way, secondly because there will be arguments to put against Voltaire that will remove the desire to get to know him. Tissot is a doctor, Haller a poet, neither of them so remarkably famous as to deserve the emperor's attention. Further, I shall have a sample to show HM here, which will enable him to judge the worth of these modern *savants* and *philosophes* who, in their private lives, their works and their detestable principles, give examples fit only to overturn society and provoke trouble and disorder.[40]

Over the next three years, until the very eve of his departure, Joseph blew hot and cold about the journey, postponing it repeatedly, sometimes when his mother asked him to, sometimes for plausible political reasons, at other times apparently from mere caprice or a desire to tease and cajole her and his sister with mystery and uncertainty.[41] One justification for delay was that in 1774

---

[39] Letters from J. to Mercy, 30 Sept., 6 Nov., 'Dec.' and from Mercy to J., 17 Oct. 1773 (Arneth & Flammermont II, pp. 421–34). M.T. to Mercy, 6 Nov. and Mercy to M.T., 18 Dec. 1773 (Arneth and Geffroy II, pp. 62–3, 84–5). Cf. M.T. to Lacy, 18 Dec. 1773, warning him also of the journey, in strict secrecy (HHSA NL, Karton 4).
  J. to Mercy, 30 Nov. 1776 (Arneth & Flammermont II, p. 478), uses the phrase 'dans leur état naturel'.
[40] M.T. to Mercy, 3 Jan. 1774; Mercy to M.T., 19 Jan. (Arneth & Geffroy II, pp. 89, 101–2). Cf. M.T. to Mercy, 3 Feb. (*ibid.*, pp. 105–6).
[41] M.T. to Mercy, 2 letters of 5 Apr. 1774, 31 Oct. 1776 (Arneth & Geffroy II, pp. 124–6, 509) and Mercy to M.T., two letters of 24 Jan. 1777 (*ibid.*, III, pp. 10–12); J. to Marie Antoinette, July 1775 (Arneth, *MAJL*, p. 1); M.T. to Maria Beatrix, 10 Mar., 17 Mar., 24 Mar. 1777 (Arneth, *MTKuF* III, pp. 269–70). See p. 229.

Louis XV died, the dauphin succeeded as Louis XVI, and Marie Antoinette became queen of France. The plan to visit France came to the fore again late in 1776, when the emperor offered Maria Theresa an embarrassingly wordy, immature and self-conscious justification for it:

Two very different objects will be the object of all my enquiries, namely the Court and the country. As for the former, it must be of great interest to a contemporary, to a man in my situation, to get to know personally the king and the principal officials, to see for himself how this machine works, how it is organised, what gets it moving, and what one can hope or might have to fear from it. This monarchy will always, from its fortunate situation, have such a direct influence on the whole of Europe, and especially on us, that to observe its strengths and weaknesses is most important, especially when one is of age, already trained in public affairs, and accustomed to using one's eyes to see and one's mind to observe. The country, and inspection of it, are the only means of getting to know the true strengths of the state, and correcting the illusion that the capital might give, and of finding out what could still be done there...

Of course it would give him pleasure to see and advise his sister.

I shall try, in general, to play the role there ... of a thoughtful and even a rather reticent man, to say as little as is necessary but to listen a great deal, to be very polite, and to appear to be there with no other idea than that of seeing my sister and satisfying my curiosity about the interesting things to be found there. For it will not be supposed, I trust, that I'm undertaking this journey at my age to educate myself or to acquire airs and graces, still less that I cherish and am flattered by the idea of triumphing in that country. I believe that in the eyes of sensible men a very natural, very simple style of conduct, founded on my system of the most perfect incognito, cannot possibly injure the reputation that, perhaps quite gratuitously, I have already acquired in the world...

On political matters I shall enter into conversation as little as possible; and when occasion arises, I know YM's system well enough, and I remember too well the clear and repeated instructions of prince Kaunitz to the ministers, to have any difficulty in replying laconically on appropriate lines. All the same I've read them once more in the last few days, and I'll go on doing so.

Finally, as usual, he submits himself to his mother's orders.[42]

This strange document reads like a point-by-point rebuttal of the criticisms levelled by Maria Theresa at his travel plans in her private and confidential letters to Lacy and Mercy – except that Joseph says nothing about calling on Voltaire.[43] It is not necessary to presume that he had seen the letters, since she made no secret of her attitude. But it remains remarkable that he should still have felt the need, even at the age of thirty-five, having been emperor for eleven years, to write to her so defensively and submissively. She had not

---

[42] J. to M.T., 24 Nov. 1776 (Arneth, *MTuJ* II, pp. 124–6). In HHSA FA Hofreisen 9 this document, docketed 'Projet und Relation von der Reise S.M. des Kayser nach Paris', is described ([?] by J.) as a 'Note'.
The repetitions of 'object' and 'observe' are in the French.

[43] See M.T. to Lacy, [?] 4 Apr. 1774, quoted above, p. 253. M.T. to Mercy, 3 Jan. 1774, quoted above, p. 369.

attempted to forbid the journey, although she kept hoping it would be abandoned.[44] She no longer expected to control all his actions, but he clearly did not consider himself a free agent.

In a letter to Leopold, Joseph said that he had deliberately chosen two unimpressive companions, Joseph Colloredo and Philipp Cobenzl, so that it should not look as though he aimed at any particular success in France.[45] In sending his detailed instructions to Mercy, the emperor stressed that his sole objects in visiting France were to see the queen and to gain knowledge and understanding of the country 'in its present state of splendour'. Most of the directions he gave were familiar: he wanted no demonstrations, no receptions, no speeches of welcome; he would neither accept nor tender invitations; his carriage was to be plain; his accommodation must be simple; he wished 'to be unnoticed in the crowd' at Court ceremonies; he would call on individuals and see sights as a private person. He specially asked the ambassador to have some clothes – *habits bourgeois* – made for him 'in the most modest, the simplest and the most natural style possible'.[46]

However, Joseph obviously saw the journey as politically significant; and so, apprehensively, did Maria Theresa, Kaunitz and Mercy. The empress had often expressed anxiety about her son's attitude to the French alliance. She congratulated herself that at the time of the visit he seemed better disposed on this point than usual.[47] The chancellor coached Joseph in diplomatic behaviour and supplied him with an elaborate memorandum of advice and instruction. It included a full justification of the alliance, and discussion of the major issues of foreign policy. The question of the Bavarian succession was becoming urgent, and Kaunitz positively encouraged the emperor to bring up the subject, so that France might have the opportunity to declare herself sympathetic to Austrian claims, or at least to reveal her policy in the matter.[48] Mercy felt sure that Joseph's visit would have an important effect, but he could not determine whether for good or evil. The emperor would undoubtedly make an impression by his personal qualities. But he might become disillusioned with France as an ally when he observed the faults of the nation and the government at close quarters. He might also take the queen to task too severely.[49]

The behaviour of Marie Antoinette was causing deep concern in Vienna. Like her sisters, the queen of Naples and the duchess of Parma, she incurred her mother's displeasure by her wayward conduct, and especially by her

[44] E.g. M.T. to Maria Beatrix, 17 Mar. 1777 (Arneth, *MTKuF* III, p. 269).
[45] J. to L., 5 Dec. 1776 (Arneth, *MTuJ* II, pp. 126–7). He also summoned count Belgiojoso to come from Brussels to attend him in Paris.
[46] Copies in HHSA FA Hofreisen 9 and ÖNB MSS ser. n. 1710.
[47] M.T. to Mercy, 30 Nov. 1776 and 4 Mar. 1777 (Arneth & Geffroy II, p. 532; III, p. 28).
[48] Published by Beer, *AÖG* (1872), 74-98, Bavarian point on pp. 94–5. The coaching described in K. to Mercy, 1 Jan. 1777 (Arneth & Flammermont II, pp. 482–3).
[49] E.g. Mercy to M.T., 19 Jan. 1774, 18 Oct. 1776 (Arneth & Geffroy II, pp. 100–1, 503–4).

interference in politics. Maria Theresa always advised her married daughters to leave the business of government to their husbands, but it is hardly surprising that her example proved more influential than her precepts. In any case there was an inconsistency in her attitude, because in all these instances the matches had been made partly on political grounds, and the wives had been intended and instructed to behave in the way most likely to promote Austrian interests. This was especially true of Marie Antoinette's marriage, the pet project of the French minister, Choiseul, a strong proponent of the Austro-French alliance. Her presence at Versailles was designed as a guarantee and reinforcement of the connexion.[50] It was a dangerous game to play. The poor princess arrived in her adopted country at the age of fourteen, charming and beautiful, but educated in little but the French language, to find the Court hostile and her husband stolid, unprepossessing and sexually retarded. Within a year Choiseul had been dismissed, and his policy seemed out of favour. Marie Antoinette liked admiration, jewellery, opera and theatre, travel, gambling and late nights. Louis rose early and was chiefly interested in eating, hunting and manual work. As queen her opportunities for extravagance and indiscretion grew, while the king was kept busy with affairs of state. She spent too little time with him, became involved in scandals, and joined in the successful intrigue against the Enlightened minister, Turgot, who lost office in 1776. On all these points the empress wrote strong reproofs to her daughter.[51] Joseph joined in the condemnation when Marie Antoinette refered to the king as 'the poor man' in a letter to count Rosenberg.[52] Vienna believed that the queen could best serve the Monarchy by establishing herself as a dutiful, respectable and fertile wife, thus commending the alliance by mute example. Having stored up credit in this way, she might safely intervene directly in politics for the benefit of the Monarchy, but only on the rarest occasions.[53]

Maria Theresa took a special interest in her daughter's sexual development, and particularly in the marital relations between king and queen.[54] If the empress had not shown this concern, it seems doubtful whether anyone at all would have tried to help Marie Antoinette in these matters. Here again the

---

[50] Arneth, *GMT* VII, ch. 13.

[51] Nearly all of these are printed in Arneth & Geffroy, but a particularly strong one about the Rosenberg letter was published only recently: it is dated 30 July 1775 and appears in Christoph, *MTuMA*, pp. 160–3. See Introduction, p. 10 and n. 21.

[52] J.'s first draft, which was held to be too strong, is in Christoph, *MTuMA*, pp. 157–60; the version that was sent is in Arneth, *MAJL*, pp. 1–4.

[53] See Arneth, *GMT* VII, ch. 13 and X, pp. 235–59, and of course Arneth & Geffroy and Arneth & Flammermont, *passim*. J. in his *Réflexions* for M.A. (Arneth, *MAJL*, p. 8) said she should *never* openly intervene.

[54] Stefan Zweig in *Marie Antoinette* (Paris, 1932) brought the matter into prominence, though some references were allowed into Arneth & Geffroy's edition of the queen's and Mercy's letters. See, more recently, Christoph, *MTuMA*; V. Cronin, *Louis and Antoinette* (London, 1974), pp. 119, 157–60, 406–11.

sympathy of a mother was intensified by the anxiety of the ruler. It was imperative, if the influence of the queen was to be maintained and the alliance strengthened, that she should bear Louis a son. But their attempts at sexual intercourse were few and unsuccessful. Marie Antoinette faithfully reported to her mother the beginning and recurrence of her periods. In 1773 she jubilantly announced the consummation of the marriage. But no pregnancy ensued, and it became clear that she had been mistaken.[55] The problem was gleefully discussed by ambassadors and political observers throughout Europe.[56] Doctors thought the fault lay with the king, and during 1775 suggested that he had a physical impediment that could be removed by a minor operation.[57] The evidence is not quite conclusive, but it is very unlikely that he ever underwent the surgery.[58] Either way, by the time Joseph reached France, consummation had still not taken place. Maria Theresa hoped against hope that her son's advice would put matters right.[59]

For Joseph's biographer his French journey is interesting on three main counts: first for its effects and political significance, if any; secondly for its impact on the emperor; and thirdly for its influence on his reputation. We have copious sources to work from. As well as writing lively letters to his brother, he prepared a journal running to more than 600 sides;[60] Mercy composed long reports; and France was full of writers who recorded their impressions for the public, correspondents or posterity.

Marie Antoinette had told Mercy that, while she acknowledged her formidable mother's right to criticise her conduct, she was on easy terms with her brother and felt entitled to answer him back.[61] In the event they got on remarkably well together. Joseph much admired not only her beauty and vivacity but also her intelligence and even, in some respects, her judgement. He sensitively informed the princesses in Vienna that he could imagine himself marrying Marie Antoinette if she had not been his sister. He condemned aspects of her behaviour and urged her, both in conversation and in lengthy written *Reflections*, to devote more time and effort to relations with

---

[55] M.A. to M.T., 17 July 1773 (Christoph, *MTuMA*, p. 100). See Christoph's introduction, pp. 12–13.

[56] See Aranda's letter printed in Padover, *Louis XVI*, p. 97n. Cf. HHSA TZ, 22 June 1771, describing a conversation at Laxenburg involving J. and Salm.

[57] M.T. to Mercy, 31 Aug. 1775 (Arneth & Geffroy II, p. 373). M.A. to M.T., 15 Sep. 1775 (Christoph, *MTuMA*, p. 165 and n.).

[58] M.A. mentioned inconclusive discussions about it in letters to M.T. on 15 Dec. 1775 and 14 Jan. 1776. On 10 Apr. 1776 M.A. says she still thinks it unnecessary (Christoph, *MTuMA*, pp. 172, 176 and 180). This disposes of Zinzendorf's diary entry of 8 Mar. 1776 (HHSA TZ): 'L'Imp^ce a dit a Me de C. que l'opération sur le vit du roi de France s'est fuite heureusement, ce n'est que l'équivalent d'une petite saignée.' See n. 66 below.

[59] M.T. to M.A., 2 Jan 1777 (Christoph, *MTuMA*, p. 205); M.T. to Mercy, 11 Apr. 1777 (Arneth & Geffroy III, p. 40).

[60] The journal is in HHSA FA Hofreisen 9.

[61] Mercy to M.T., 16 Jan. 1773 (Arneth & Geffroy I, p. 404). Cf. Mercy's journal of the visit (*ibid.*, III, p. 82).

the king, to abandon gambling and other imprudences, and to occupy herself with 'reading and rational company'. Otherwise – and here the emperor underlined his prophetic words – '*the revolution will be cruel*'. But he was tactful enough, and she reasonable enough, to avoid a major disagreement. She was desolated when he left. However, he was not hopeful for the future: 'the vortex of dissipation around her prevents her from seeing and thinking about anything but going from one pleasure to another ... How can I be expected to counter it on my own?'[62]

With Louis the emperor displayed such patience, charm and goodwill that he broke through the king's reticence. They had intimate political and personal discussions in which Louis proved unexpectedly articulate, intelligent and well informed. Joseph wrote to Leopold:

This man is rather weak but not imbecile. He has ideas and judgement, but there is something apathetic about both his body and mind. He can talk reasonably, but he has no taste for instruction and no curiosity. In a word, the *fiat lux* has not come upon him, the matter is still unformed.[63]

Joseph's advice to the king to travel round France had little or no impact.[64]

The emperor scored a triumph over the sexual problem. On walks and in talks Louis gave Joseph 'the most circumstantial details of his physical condition' and asked advice. The emperor went on, in the letter just quoted, to tell the whole story – in a manner too robust for publication until the 1950s:

Imagine! In his marriage bed – this is the secret – he has strong, perfectly satisfactory erections. He introduces the member, stays there for perhaps two minutes without moving, withdraws without ever discharging but still erect, and bids good night. It's incredible, because in addition he sometimes has night-time emissions, but in his bed, never when on the job, and he's happy, saying simply that he only does it out of duty and gets no pleasure from it. Ah! if I could have been present once, I should have arranged it properly. He needs to be whipped, to make him discharge in a passion, like donkeys. Further, my sister is pretty placid, and they're two incompetents together.[65]

---

[62] The *Réflexions* in Arneth, *MAJL*, pp. 4–18, quotations from p. 14. Comments on M.A. in J. to L., 11 May and 9 June 1777 (Arneth, *MTuJ* II, pp. 134, 138–9). Mercy's journal frequently refers to discussions between J. and M.A. and the need to soften J.'s approach, but the letters written after the emperor's departure are clear evidence of the good relations between brother and sister (Arneth & Geffroy III, pp. 47–93). Most striking, J.'s avowal to the princesses, 8 June 1777 (SOALpZ, LRRA P. 16/22–3 (copies)).

[63] J. to L., 9 June 1777 (Arneth, *MTuJ* II, p. 139). Mercy's journal (Arneth & Geffroy III, pp. 73–4, 80).

[64] J. L. H. Campan, *Memoirs of Marie Antoinette* (London, 1903), p. 98. Unreliable though these memoirs are, this passage seems first-hand and is supported by other evidence, e.g. Arneth & Geffroy III, p. 79.
　Louis XVI in fact made only one journey before the Revolution beyond the royal palaces, to Cherbourg in 1786.

[65] This portion of the letter was published by Fejtö (*J. II*, p. 167). (See the next note.) Mercy's journal (Arneth & Geffroy III, p. 80).

Joseph gave the necessary advice, which a few months later yielded the desired result. Both the king and the queen wrote to thank him for it.[66] A daughter was born in the following year, sons in 1781 and 1785. It graphically illustrates the loneliness of kingship that only the visit of a brother-monarch could enable Louis and his wife to discuss their sexual difficulties frankly and discover how to resolve them. Joseph's experience and family connexion gave him the advantage over the royal doctors. His own personal relationships, notoriously, were often unsatisfactory. But few friends or marriage counsellors have a greater achievement than this to their credit.

Kaunitz wrote his instructions for Joseph at the end of 1776, expecting that the emperor would soon leave for Paris and would be able on arrival to broach the Bavarian succession question with France for the first time. With the postponement of the journey, the chancellor decided that immediate consultation was necessary, and so entrusted it to Mercy. Kaunitz supplied a reasonably full account of the Monarchy's claims, and asked France to approve negotiations about them between Austria and the elector Palatine, the

---

[66] This was Joseph's claim (J. to L., 4 Oct. 1777, HHSA FA Sbde, 7, not printed in Arneth, quoted by Fejtö, *J. II*, p. 168): '[Louis] a enfin reussi a la grande oeuvre et la Reine peut devenir grosse ils me l'onts ecrits tous deux et me fonts des remerciments l'atribuant a mes conseils il est vrai que j'ai traite cette matiere a fond, dans mes conversations avec lui et que j'ai parfaitement reconnu que paresse mal adreisse et apathie etoit les seuls empechemens qui s'y oposoient.'

Cronin, *Louis and Antoinette*, pp. 158–9, 406–11, discusses the whole affair at some length. He concludes (1) that neither an operation nor J.'s advice was needed; (2) that an operation was never performed, and there is no evidence that it was; and therefore (3) that J.'s account was an invention to entertain his brother and glorify himself. If (3) were true, it would be of great significance to a biographer of J., because it would eliminate an instance of J.'s succeeding notably in a personal relationship and – far more important – would cast doubt on the reliability of the entire correspondence between J. and L. So the matter ought to be considered further.

Cronin makes several manifest errors:

(i)   He evidently does not know Christoph's collection, and denies the existence of any letter of thanks from Louis. But a letter of thanks from Louis is printed by Christoph, *MTuMA*, p. 234n, dated 21 Nov. 1777. In fact it had already been published – more fully – in Pimodan, *Mercy-Argenteau*, p. 171n, where it is dated, surely correctly, 21 Dec. 1777. See Arneth, *MAJL*, p. 2on for earlier publications. So, to justify J.'s letter of 4 Oct., there must have been a previous letter of thanks from Louis. We know there was an earlier letter from Louis at approximately the right moment, but not its content (see Arneth & Flammermont II, p. 507).

(ii)   He says that Marie Antoinette's letter of thanks ought to survive, because all her letters to J. do. But it is clear that Arneth (see *MAJL*, p. x) is right that many are lost. However, M.T. mentions a letter from M.A. to J. of just the right date in just the right context (Arneth & Geffroy, III, p. 117).

(iii)   He questions whether J. ever discussed the matter deeply with Louis, but Mercy's diary is conclusive that he did.

(iv)   He says that both J. advised Louis to have an operation, and that he didn't so advise him. On this point the wording of the letter of 4 Oct. 1777, quoted at the beginning of this note, strongly suggests that J. considered an operation unncessary. I don't think there is any evidence he advised one. I think Cronin is right that none took place. (See p. 373, no. 58 above.)

All these misstatements are on p. 408 of *Louis & Antoinette*. What Cronin has to say about the precepts of 'medical science' on p. 159 does not convince.

I am grateful for help from Professor R. A. McCance and Mr C. Parish on this question.

generally accepted heir to Bavaria. Vergennes, the French foreign minister, though he did not propose to breach the alliance with Austria, was both anxious to avoid assisting her in any war and hostile to her aggrandisement, especially in the *Reich*. Even the bait of compensation for France, perhaps in the Netherlands, did not much tempt him. He thought it better that Vienna should keep Belgium and so remain bound to France for its defence. He announced that he would answer Austria when his ambassador, Breteuil, returned to Vienna from leave in France. Breteuil reached Vienna only after Joseph had departed for Paris. So the emperor was left virtually without a role in foreign policy during his visit to France. He and Louis discussed international questions, but in general terms, and the king followed Vergennes's line. On 18 May, while Joseph was in Paris, the royal council decided to give an ostensible blessing to the negotiations between the Monarchy and the Palatinate, but to obstruct Austria's plans secretly. The emperor's diplomacy had not deflected the course of French foreign policy. It made little difference that personal relations between the rulers of the two states had improved. Equally, it was not the visit, as the British envoy asserted, that persuaded Louis and Vergennes that the emperor represented a danger to France.[67] Maria Theresa, however, was encouraged for the future by signs that Joseph had been impressed by the strength of France and had seen the injustice of some of his previous prejudices against the country and the alliance.[68]

It is of special interest to know how Joseph reacted to the people he met and the sights he saw in the country of the *philosophes* and of the future Revolution. He was certainly as active as possible in visiting the monuments and public works of France, and in enquiring into its government and administration. Long lists were compiled for him of eminent persons he might encounter, chiefly in Paris. They included great nobles, officials and ambassadors, writers like Buffon, D'Alembert, Diderot and Rousseau, architects like Soufflot, painters like Greuze, sculptors like Houdon, and others in special categories like Franklin and the fallen minister Turgot. A list of those he actually saw runs to about 600 names, some of them additional, like Necker and the future minister, Loménie de Brienne, archbishop of Toulouse. He travelled to the far west and south of France, keeping mainly to the coast and some of the principal rivers, taking in Rouen, Le Havre, Brest, Nantes, Tours, Bordeaux, Bayonne, an excursion into Spain, Toulouse, Toulon, Marseilles and Lyons. Documentation had been supplied to him beforehand about the state of the

---

[67] Tratchevsky, *RH* (1880), 272–3; Fagniez, *RH* (1922), esp. 4–22; P. Oursel, *La Diplomatie de la France sous Louis XVI* (Paris, 1921), ch. 1; fullest and most important, A. Unzer, *Der Friede von Teschen* (Kiel, 1903), esp. pp. 13–34. Most recent, O. T. Murphy, *Charles Gravier, Comte de Vergennes* (Albany, 1982), pp. 292–5. Keith to Stormont, 'separate and most secret', 4 Dec. 1779 (PRO SP 80/221).
[68] M.T. to M.A., 29 June 1777; M.T. to Mercy, 29 August 1777 (Arneth & Geffroy III, pp. 87, 109).

marine, certain recent ordinances, the trade of Lyons and so forth. But he collected and commissioned far more during the course of the visit: lists of notable churches, works of art, *hôtels*; programmes of plays and operas; maps and plans of towns and ports; memoranda about canals, factories and ships; and a particularly full selection of material about Turgot's reforming schemes.[69]

All this activity was scrupulously recorded by himself and Mercy – or at least nearly all of it: there is a suspicion that some visits to individuals might have been left out to avoid displeasing his mother.[70] But unfortunately, though characteristically, Joseph made few comments in the course of his *Relation*. He seems, too, to have kept his word and curbed his tongue in public.[71] However, it is possible to piece together a selection of his reactions from his *Relation*, his letters to Leopold, and the reports of Mercy and others.

He was able to observe the Court and the government closely. He naturally scoffed at the etiquette of Versailles, more forthrightly than the king and queen liked.[72] His remarks about the government were penetrating, and revealing of his own attitudes:

An aristocratic despotism reigns [at Versailles]; that seems paradoxical, but it's true all the same. Everyone is absolute in his own department, but continually afraid – not of being controlled by the sovereign, but replaced ... The king is absolute master only in order to pass from one slavery to another. He can change ministers, but unless he has transcendent genius, he can never take charge of the conduct of affairs ...

The government, consisting of an octogenarian minister, carries on after a fashion. No true system, no courage, no spirit of firmness.[73]

Some of the people he met he found both interesting and agreeable. He made a special effort to talk to Turgot; he sent a letter to Marie Antoinette recommending Brienne to the king as a minister;[74] and he was so impressed

---

69   Nearly all the material for this paragraph is in HHSA FA Hofreisen 10, but there is a little in 9. See also his letters to L. (Arneth, *MTuJ* II, pp. 138–40, 142–6).

70   Wagner, 'Reise', p. 240, suggests that a visit to Rousseau, said to have occurred on 25 May, was suppressed for this reason. A. D. Hytier, in her useful 'Joseph II, la Cour de Vienne et les philosophes', *SVEC*, CVI (1973), 225–51, implies on p. 245 that the Rousseau interview never took place. I doubt whether a visit to Rousseau would particularly have shocked M.T.; and his name was on the list of people whom J. thought of seeing (which Hytier has not used). See n. 69 above and p. 378, n. 77. I have not found all the letters J. claims to have written from France to the princesses. But no evidence has come to light from any of those closely involved (J., Rousseau, Mercy, Grimm) that supports the case for the meeting. Professor R. A. Leigh has very kindly informed me that his conclusion also is that it never took place.

71   E.g. Mme du Deffand to Horace Walpole, 1 June 1777 (Mrs Paget Toynbee (ed.), *Lettres de la marquise du Deffand à Horace Walpole*, vol. III (London, 1912), pp. 340–1).

72   Campan, *Memoirs of M.A.*, p. 98.

73   J. to L., 11 May and 9 June 1777 (Arneth, *MTuJ* II, pp. 133, 139).

74   J. to L., 29 Apr. 1777 (Arneth, *MTuJ* II, p. 131); Wagner, 'Reise', pp. 224–5; Mercy to M.T., 15 July 1777 (Arneth & Geffroy III, p. 95).

by Necker that he thought of inviting him to come to Vienna as an adviser.[75] He expressed admiration of Madame du Deffand, Horace Walpole's correspondent and a noted hostess.[76] At a special meeting of the Académie Française he went out of his way to be civil to D'Alembert about his protector, the king of Prussia, but needled the officials by asking why Diderot and Raynal were not members. He seemed bored during some of the addresses on this occasion. 'In general', wrote an observer, 'it appears that what we call *belles lettres*, which have much more to do with knowledge of words than of things, are in his eyes of no great value.'[77] Madame du Deffand put it rather differently: 'The intellectuals must be very surprised by the slight interest he shows in them.' 'As he has singled no one out, those who have pretensions are beginning to become faint in his praise.' Her description of her first meeting with him explains a great deal. The only topic he could find to discuss was her tatting. That evening he and the historian Gibbon were in the same room for several hours, but seem not to have talked. Joseph wrote to Leopold that, since it was impossible to get to know men in six weeks, he was concentrating on seeing objects.[78]

In Paris certain establishments especially interested him. He much admired Mansart's great dome of the Invalides and the institution it crowned. He told Louis it was the finest edifice in his capital, and criticised the etiquette that had prevented the king from ever visiting it.[79] Despite the risk of infection Joseph went to the Hôtel Dieu, the vast hospital in the heart of the city. But here 'he was not gratified by the prevailing lack of cleanliness, by the number of beds in one room and the number of patients packed into one bed'. On the other hand, he found the surgery school and the veterinary school instructive.[80] He paid particular attention to the school for the deaf and dumb run by the abbé de l'Épée. While he enjoyed some electrical experiments by Ledru, he found a demonstration by Lavoisier at the Académie des Sciences 'meaningless'. He considered the professors of theology at the Sorbonne had too much freedom in their choice of textbooks, and criticised the administration of the royal

[75] J. to Mercy, 12 June 1781 (Arneth & Flammermont I, p. 43). Admittedly, J. had been impressed by Necker's recently published *Compte rendu*, but his personal knowledge derived from the visit of 1777. He was writing from Ostend, just before proceeding to Paris for the second of his French visits. See his very warm letter about Necker to Mercy of 4 Mar. 1780 (Arneth & Geffroy III, p. 405n).
[76] Mme du Deffand to Horace Walpole, 8 June 1777 (Toynbee, *Lettres*, vol. III, p. 342).
[77] There are several accounts. The classic is M. Tourneux (ed.), *Correspondance littéraire, philosophique et critique par Grimm, Diderot, Raynal, Meister, etc.* (16 vols., 1877–82), vol. XI, pp. 473–4. Hytier, *SVEC* (1973), 235, casts doubt on this story, but does not cite the *Correspondance littéraire*, which seems to me a plausible source for it.
[78] Mme du Deffand to Horace Walpole, 11 and 18 May 1777 (Toynbee, *Lettres*, vol. III, pp. 332–5); J. to L., 9 June 1777 (Arneth, *MTuJ* II, p. 138).
[79] Campan, *Memoirs of M.A.*, p. 98; Tourneux, *Correspondance littéraire*, vol. XI, p. 475.
[80] HHSA Frankreich Varia 38 (1776–9), f. 21 of Barré's journal of J.'s visit. Wagner, 'Reise', pp. 232, 235–6.

archives.[81] All in all, he thought the buildings of Paris remarkably elegant and luxurious, but disappointing in terms of their utility.[82]

Outside Paris he was impressed by many of the ports he saw, notably Toulon, but 'I don't know what it is, I feel no confidence in the French navy'. He was struck by the fertility of the Loire valley and of Languedoc, the opulence of Bordeaux, the poverty of the Landes, the engineering of the Canal du Midi and the 'curious' ruins of Nîmes.[83]

Some historians have detected in his visit to France the origins of many of his attitudes and projects. It has been claimed, to take a few examples, that Turgot inspired much of his social and economic policy;[84] that Brienne's plans to dissolve some French monasteries influenced the legislation of Joseph's sole reign; that the Allgemeine Krankenhaus, the huge hospital built in Vienna in the 1780s, was modelled on the Hôtel Dieu; and that the Vienna school for the deaf and dumb was based on the Paris example.[85]

The truth is more complicated. The clearest case of imitation among these instances is the deaf and dumb school he established in Austria in 1779 under a director trained in Paris. But even here it was Joseph's earlier interest that led him to visit l'Épée's school, and it owed its fame to the emperor's patronage rather than vice versa.[86] As we have seen, he strongly criticised the Hôtel Dieu. Further, he must have become aware that its future was being strenuously debated and that a large body of experts and officials were convinced it must either be removed, divided or rebuilt. In fact Mercy maintained that Joseph's strictures stirred Louis into taking action about it. The emperor clearly ignored the argument that the sheer size of the hospital contributed to the high death-rate among the patients. There is no need to bring the Hôtel Dieu or its critics into any explanation of the plan of the Allgemeine Krankenhaus.[87] As for Brienne's ideas on monasteries, there is no proof that he discussed them with the emperor, and on the contrary an overwhelming mass of evidence that Joseph had been thinking of similar projects for more than ten years before they met.[88]

[81] Wagner, 'Reise', pp. 231, 235–8; Arneth & Geffroy III, p. 63.

[82] *Ibid.*, III, pp. 76–7. Cf. J. to L., 11 May 1777 (Arneth, *MTuJ* II, p. 132).

[83] J. to L., 9 June, 3 July 1777 (Arneth, *MTuJ* II, pp. 139–40, 142–5); Wagner, 'Reise', p. 228.

[84] See Gershoy, *From Despotism to Revolution*, p. 101 for one of the stronger claims. See references in n. 91 below, esp. Van Houtte's book.

[85] Claims put together by Wagner, 'Reise', pp. 226, 231–2 and n. 79, p. 244.

[86] See Mercy's journal (Arneth & Geffroy III, p. 63). A similar case is the veterinary school. J. also sent a surgeon to be trained in Paris at the surgery school (Wagner, 'Reise', pp. 235–6).

[87] Mercy to J., 12 Sep. 1777 (Arneth & Flammermont II, p. 509). See P. P. Bernard, 'The limits of absolutism: Joseph II and the Allgemeines Krankenhaus', *Eighteenth-Century Studies*, IX (1975–6), esp. 208–15; L. S. Greenbaum, 'Scientists and politicians: hospital reform in Paris on the eve of the French Revolution', in *The Consortium on Revolutionary Europe, 1750–1850: Proceedings, 1973*, ed. C. C. Sturgill (Gainesville, Florida, 1975), pp. 168–91. I am most grateful to Professor Bernard for sending me a copy of his article.

[88] Wagner, 'Reise', p. 226. See ch. 14 below.

Turgot's influence presents the most difficult problem of those mentioned. Joseph's interest in his work certainly antedated the visit,[89] though some contemporaries supposed that the emperor's attentions to him sprang from Leopold's adoption of his proposals in Tuscany.[90] Specifically, Joseph's tax measures, his policy of internal free trade in corn and his reform of the gilds bear signs of Turgot's influence. But in each case many other pressures contributed, and the emperor had been advocating such measures long before he visited France or Turgot recommended them to Louis XVI.[91]

Joseph was aware of the works of many *philosophes*, and himself something of a physiocrat, before he went to Paris; he was a *Gallomane* neither before nor afterwards. What he gained from his journey was much information, most of which could easily be accommodated within his existing framework of thought; greater awareness of what could be achieved in certain specialised fields; considerable knowledge of the royal family and of ministers, rather less of other prominent persons; and a generally more favourable view of the country and its people. His attitudes were modified in detail and subtly, not fundamentally and in general.

Joseph's visit was unquestionably a personal success. Mercy's report to the empress, written during the provincial tour, cannot be challenged:

Although impressions are seldom really constant in this fickle nation, I see that those which have been formed about HM the emperor have an unusual solidity ...; all Paris is still talking of this monarch with the same enthusiasm and affection ... The public continues to be preoccupied with the details of the emperor's journey; people amuse themselves by composing a thousand anecdotes that I don't believe are genuine, but are all to HM's credit.

His simplicity, affability, composure, energy, knowledge and quickness impressed nearly everyone who observed him, whether the sophisticated Madame du Deffand, the cloth manufacturers of Carcassonne,[92] or the audiences who cheered appropriate verses in the opera *Castor and Pollux* and in Voltaire's play, *Oedipe*:

> Ce Roi plus grand que la fortune
> Dédaignoit COMME vous une pompe importune.[93]

[89] In HHSA FA Hofreisen 10, Konv. 3, a copy of Turgot's letter of 1774 to Louis XVI, on the conditions necessary to the minister's success, is to be found among the papers prepared for J. before he reached France.

[90] E.g. Mme du Deffand to Horace Walpole, 18 May 1777 (Toynbee, *Lettres*, vol. III, p. 335).

[91] For discussion of these points: Mitrofanov I, pp. 424–5; R. Rozdolski, *Die grosse Steuer- und Agrarreform Josefs II.* (Warsaw, 1961), pp. 14ff., 17 n. 25, 91; Schünemann, *MÖIG* (1933), esp. 46–7; H. van Houtte, *Histoire économique de la Belgique à la fin de l'Ancien Régime* (Ghent, 1920), esp. pp. 86–91.

[92] Mercy to M.T., 15 July 1777 (Arneth & Geffroy III, p. 95); Mme du Deffand to Horace Walpole, 1 June 1777 (Toynbee, *Lettres*, vol. III, pp. 340–1); P. Masson, *Histoire du commerce français dans le Levant au XVIIIe siècle* (Paris, 1911), p. 393.

[93] These ovations were widely reported, e.g. [A.J.L. du Coudray,] *Anecdotes intéressantes et historiques de l'illustre Voyageur, pendant son séjour à Paris* (2nd edn, Paris, 1777), pp. 19, 32–3.

As Mercy said, several collections of anecdotes about the visit were published, which stressed Joseph's informality and his *bourgeois* behaviour; his love of talking to people who did not recognise him and seeing their astonishment when they found out who he was; his benevolence, enlightenment and intelligence – with suitable references to 'the modern Titus', Marcus Aurelius, Trajan, Haroun-al-Raschid and Peter the Great.[94]

The enthusiasm no doubt reflected public dissatisfaction with Louis XVI, who never appeared informally or travelled in his provinces, and, if he had, would have looked bored and uttered scarcely a word. Louis seems to have felt no resentment at Joseph's triumph, but other princes did. The chief criticisms of his behaviour come from correspondents of the jealous king of Sweden, Gustavus III. The countess de la Marck told him that Joseph 'kept repeating commonplaces which he uttered with an emphasis that made one die of laughing'. Louis's brother and heir presumptive, the count of Provence, competed with the emperor's provincial tour by making a simultaneous journey to the south coast. The countess scoffed at that as well: the pomp and ceremony led to 'frightful expense, the devastation of the posts and the provinces' and the count becoming 'as fat as a barrel'. He of course wrote venomously of Joseph to Gustavus III:

The emperor is very winning, fond of making protestations and vows of friendship; but, when closely examined, his protestations and his frank manner conceal the desire to do what is called pumping and to hide his own opinions; but he is inept, because with a little flattery, which he laps up, one can easily read him instead of being read oneself. He then becomes excessively indiscreet. His knowledge is very superficial.[95]

Joseph himself justified some of these criticisms when he wrote from France the letter to Leopold, already quoted, in which he admitted to being 'a charlatan of reason and modesty'.

This is what has aroused the enthusiasm, which is really embarrassing ... I've even tried hiding away ... Everywhere I've talked with the most educated persons for long hours, but only with three or four in each place. I've got them talking, I've entered into their way of thinking, I've pleased them. They've spread the tale. Everyone would

[94] E.g., as well as the brochure just cited in n. 93, Duval-Pyrau, *Journal et anecdotes intéressantes du voyage de Monsieur le Comte de Falckenstein* (Paris, 1777); M. Mayer, *Monsieur le Comte de Falckenstein, ou Voyages de l'Empereur Joseph II, en Italie, en Boheme et en France* (Leipzig, 1777) (translated into German, Leipzig, 1778); M***, *Voyage en France de Monsieur le Comte de Falckenstein* (2 vols., London, 1778). There are also German works, naturally more inclined to dilate on the German part of the tour: *Anthologische Beschreibung der Reise des Herrn Grafen von Falkenstein nach Frankreich* (Schwabach, n.d.); *Briefe an meinen Freund zu D....r über die Reise des Grafen von Falkenstein nach Frankreich* (Ulm, 1777); *Joseph der Zweyte auf seiner Reise nach Paris* (Naumburg, 1777).
[95] Countess de la Marck to Gustavus III, 7 Aug. 1777; count of Provence to same, 5 Oct. 1778, quoted in Arneth & Geffroy III, pp. 91n, 57n. The full letter from the count of Provence is in Geffroy, *Gustave III*, vol. II, pp. 385–91.

have liked to hear me talking, and since they couldn't, I've been treated without justification as an oracle, because rarity is a very precious thing.[96]

After leaving France, Joseph spent a short time in Switzerland, visiting Protestant as well as Catholic cantons. He was struck by 'the beauty and curiosity of its terrain and by the peculiar outlook of its inhabitants, who are unlike any other nation'. Experience of Switzerland no doubt intensified his hatred of religious intolerance, about which he was writing passionate letters to his mother during the last stages of his journey.[97] But he thought that all the cantons' governments made 'their subjects put up with a miserable life, always on the admirable pretext of making them happy, and protecting and defending them'. The aristocratic regimes seemed to him worse than the 'purely democratic'. He met Tissot, with whom he was disappointed, and Haller, with whom he was 'very satisfied. He has a very lively and well-stocked mind. He was the creator of the University of Göttingen.'[98] We know what Haller thought of him too. The old man, who was very ill, had dreaded the visit. If he had cherished illusions about Joseph's attitudes when he wrote *Usong*, he now feared his desire for aggrandisement and regretted his lack of *philosophie*. But the emperor made himself personally very agreeable, did not subject Haller to the expected barrage of questions, and showed sound understanding and clear ideas, 'perhaps also consciousness of his greatness, and no liking for contradiction'.[99] Within a few months Haller was dead, and Joseph had his library purchased by the government for the University of Pavia and the Brera at Milan.[100]

But he did not call on Voltaire. It had been publicly stated that he would; Frederick had told Voltaire that 'the light of reason' would guide the emperor to him; and Joseph's route passed by the turning to the great man's house. In the emperor's words, 'the self-styled *philosophe* . . . had donned a new wig, had arranged a little dinner-party, and had caused all his peasants to perch in the trees in order to give an ovation'. But the imperial carriage drove straight on.[101]

[96] J. to L., 10 July (Arneth, *MTuJ* II, pp. 148–9). See p. 312.

[97] J. to L., 30 July 1777 (Arneth, *MTuJ* II, p. 159). For the dispute about toleration see pp. 465–73.

[98] J. to the princesses, 16–17 July (SOALpZ, LRRA P. 16/22–3 (copies)).

[99] For Haller's views, H. Fischer (ed.), *Briefwechsel zwischen Albrecht von Haller und Eberhard Friedrich von Gemmingen*, Bibliothek des litterarischen Vereins in Stuttgart CCXIX (Tübingen, 1899), esp. 112, 116–18, 123, 126; L. Hirzel (ed.), *Albrecht von Hallers Gedichte* (Frauenfeld, 1882), pp. CDXCVIII–D; E. Hintzsche (ed.), *Albrecht von Hallers Briefe an Auguste Tissot, 1754–1777* (Stuttgart, 1977), p. 467.

[100] *Biographie universelle ancienne et moderne* (45 vols., 2nd edn, Paris, 1843–[65]), vol. XVIII, p. 370; P. Vaccari, *Storia dell' Università di Pavia* (2nd edn, Pavia, 1957), p. 165; Arneth, *GMT* X, p. 193.

[101] E.g. Du Coudray, *Anecdotes*, p. 162; Frederick to Voltaire, 1 June 1777 (*VC* XCVI, p. 193); J. to the princesses, 16–17 July 1777 (SOALpZ, LRRA P. 16/22–3 (copies)). Cf. Bonnet to Haller, 16 July 1777 (*VC* XCVII, p. 20).

If the meeting had taken place, it would have assumed immense significance. Though Voltaire had been patronised for decades by Frederick II and Catherine II, he was still denied the public recognition in France that was to be finally accorded him in the following year; and Maria Theresa, of course, considered him beyond the pale. He had had hopes of Joseph since at least 1769, when Grimm had assured him, on the basis of Frederick's impressions, that the emperor was 'one of us'.[102] Voltaire had taken an interest in publishing the letter to Papini.[103] He had also gone to special trouble to obtain a copy of *Le Monarque accompli*, a work by Lanjuinais, a Protestant former monk established in Switzerland, which attributed to Joseph the widest possible range of enlightened attitudes. However, its tedious three volumes contain virtually no specific evidence about the emperor's opinions or deeds and consist merely of indiscriminate eulogy. It was the portrait of an ideal ruler rather than of Joseph, and referred to the politics of France, not the Monarchy. Voltaire endorsed it 'roast monarch'.[104] Still, the book's existence testifies to the expectations nourished about Joseph by enlightened circles; and Grimm's *Correspondance littéraire* asserted that his visit to France was inspired by *philosophie*.[105]

Frederick was one of those who ascribed Joseph's failure to call on Voltaire to the veto of Maria Theresa. Mercy had claimed that he would be able to dissuade the emperor from paying the dreaded visit.[106] But the empress, relieved and thankful, gave Mercy a different account of her son's motives:

It isn't out of regard for me that the emperor decided not to see Voltaire. He said to me himself that he'd been annoyed by the arrangements Voltaire had made to receive him, going so far as to send two men to meet him. Voltaire wrote a letter to general Colloredo expressing his regret that he had been cheated of the honour of receiving the emperor in his house by the false move of these two men, in which he affected to have had no part.[107]

Joseph gave the same explanation to the princesses, adding the implausible gloss that he took the road that passed Ferney only because he was on the way to see 'Versoix, this new town that the French are building'.[108]

---

[102] Voltaire to D'Alembert, 28 Oct. 1769 (*VC* LXXIII, p. 142). See also the letter to Frederick on 30 Oct. (*ibid.*, p. 145). On Voltaire's earlier relations with the Court of Vienna, including some surprising attempts to flatter Francis and M.T., see J. Schmidt, 'Voltaire und Maria Theresia', *MVGSW* XI (1931), esp. 95–8.

[103] Voltaire to Hennin, 24 Feb. 1770 (*VC* LXXIV, p. 126). See p. 258 above.

[104] Mme de Vismes to Voltaire, 24 June 1776 (*VC* XCIV, pp. 165 and 166n). Lanjuinais, *Le Monarque accompli*. See my article, 'Christians and "philosophes"', in Beales and Best, *History, Society and the Churches*, pp. 186–7. Cf. Hytier, *SVEC* (1973), 230.

[105] Tourneux, *Correspondance littéraire*, vol. XI, p. 468.

[106] Frederick to Voltaire, 13 Aug. 1777 (*VC* XCVII, p. 49). See p. 369.

[107] M.T. to Mercy, 29 Aug. 1777 (Arneth & Geffroy III, pp. 109–10). There is support for this account in *VC* XCVII, pp. 23, 25–7, 31, 38, 54–5.

[108] J. to the princesses, 16–17 July 1777 (SOALpZ, LRRA P. 16/22–3 (copies)). In fact, Versoix was an uncompleted project which had been fostered by both Choiseul and Voltaire. See T. Besterman, *Voltaire* (London, 1969), pp. 465–6, 497–8, 587–8.

This kind of incident occurred several times during his travels. He and Frederick had failed to meet in 1766 through a similar misunderstanding. Earlier in the French journey, Choiseul had expected the emperor at his country 'cottage', but Joseph had turned in his tracks a few miles short of it, apparently because a visit had been solicited. In this instance his mother had regretted the snub to the promoter of the Austro-French alliance.[109] One must suppose that the explanation Joseph gave her about Voltaire was true – or at least an aspect of the truth. During his travels he absolutely insisted on his incognito and independence.

Furthermore, this was not the first time, and would not be the last, when he dissociated himself from the great *philosophe*. For example, during his Italian tour

the talk over dinner turned to the works of Voltaire, and one after the other each of those present was moved to condemn the impious sentiments of the author and, while criticising them, revealed that he had read them. The emperor remained silent throughout, then, seeming to awake from a deep reverie, he intervened, speaking in a serious tone: 'Tell me, are these works printed, and are there people in Tuscany who read them?' At this remark, or tacit reproof, delivered with a mixture of gravity and charm, everyone was struck dumb.[110]

If Joseph adopted some of the same causes as Voltaire, like inoculation and religious toleration, he never sympathised with the *philosophes*' rejection of traditional philosophy and Catholic theology. We have seen that he doubted the value of short interviews with authors whose works he knew; and he was evidently happier meeting scientists than literary men. Kaunitz applauded his conduct, saying that Joseph

would have found it unseemly to go and see on his travels a man whom he could not tolerate in his states; moreover ... the emperor is too wise to want to engage in a battle of wits with the head of a sect so destructive to society and to all good government.[111]

Leopoldine, reporting this, was sceptical. She thought that if Joseph had paid the visit, he would have been excused, even praised. He himself did not say that he had never intended to call on Voltaire, merely that he declined to reveal his intentions in advance. The importunity of the *philosophe*'s servants enabled the emperor to reject one aspect of his image, that of enlightened ruler, in favour of another aspect, that of the incognito traveller. It is impossible to be sure that he always meant to pass Voltaire by.

'So much the worse for the emperor', said Frederick when he heard what

[109] See above, p. 280; Arneth & Geffroy III, pp. 91 and n., 98–9; L.K. to E.L., 2 Aug. 1777, explicitly comparing J.'s treatment of Choiseul and Voltaire (SOALpZ, LRRA P. 16/23).

[110] HHSA FA Hofreisen 1, report of 3 May 1769. I could not find Voltaire on the lists of persons to be visited in HHSA FA Hofreisen 9 and 10, though Haller is there.

[111] See my article in Beales and Best, *History, Society and the Churches*, esp. pp. 185–9; above, p. 369; and L.K. to E.L., 30 July 1777 (SOALpZ, LRRA P. 16/23), used also in the next paragraph.

had happened.[112] But the affront to *philosophisme* rankled.[113] Goethe condemned it in his autobiography:

That Joseph II had kept away from [Voltaire] did not at all redound to the honour of this prince, for it would have done no harm to him and his undertakings if, with such a fine brain and such noble views, he had been somewhat more intellectual, and shown greater respect for the mind.[114]

Enlightened persons were equally disappointed by the most famous remark he made during this journey. The revolt of the American colonists against British rule was attracting widespread support in France. When forced to pronounce on the subject, the emperor declared: 'My trade is to be a royalist.'[115] His progressiveness manifestly had its limitations.

---

[112] Frederick to Voltaire, 13 Aug. 1777 (*VC* XCVII, p. 49).
[113] See the anonymous *Epitre à Sa Majesté Impériale L'Empereur Joseph II* (Paris, 1777), where J. is asked whether he does not fear retribution from soldiers as well as writers. Other evidence in Hytier, *SVEC* (1973), 247–8.
[114] *Goethes Werke*, vol. IX, p. 486.
[115] Quoted, e.g. in Tourneux, *Correspondance littéraire*, vol. XI, p. 471.

CHAPTER 13

Foreign policy during the co-regency:
II. War and diplomacy, 1776–1780

Foreign affairs dominated the last years of the co-regency. First came the question of the Bavarian succession, involving war between Prussia and the Monarchy in 1778–9. Then Maria Theresa procured the election of her youngest son, Max Franz, as coadjutor and therefore successor to the elector-archbishop of Cologne; while negotiations began for a Russian alliance. In international politics these developments set the scene for Joseph's sole reign. As emperor and commander-in-chief as well as co-regent, Joseph was at the centre of the Bavarian affair; as emperor he was necessarily concerned with the Cologne election; and it was his journey to St Petersburg in 1780 that broke the ice with Catherine II.

BAVARIA[1]

On 30 December 1777 Max Joseph, elector of Bavaria, died, the last of his line. The succession question, long debated at leisure, now had to be speedily resolved. The position was so excessively vexed and complicated that it is supposed to have been the subject of 288 published treatises.[2] The development of the crisis was also complex, but it falls naturally into four phases: first, the background, and the initial reactions to Max Joseph's death; secondly, the period of negotiation and preparation for war from late January to July 1778; thirdly, the war with Prussia and the concurrent diplomacy, down to November 1778; and finally the last stages of the war and the conclusion of the peace of Teschen in May 1779. For a biographer, the war constitutes the chief

---

[1] On the Bavarian question in general: in English, Temperley, *Frederic and Joseph*; in German, Arneth, *GMT* x, chs. 9–17; A. Beer 'Zur Geschichte des bayerischen Erbfolgekrieges', *HZ*, xxxv (1876), 88–152; Reimann, *Neuere Geschichte*, vol. II, pp. 3–265, 685–98; Aretin, *Reich*, esp. vol. I, pp. 110–30; Unzer, *Friede von Teschen*; Guglia, *M.T.*, vol. II, pp. 311–27; M. Spindler (ed.), *Handbuch der bayerischen Geschichte*, vol. II (Munich, 1969), pp. 1043–5; E. F. S. Hanfstaengl, *Amerika und Europa von Marlborough bis Mirabeau* (Munich, 1930).

  Bernard, *J. II and Bavaria* draws on original material but is not always reliable. See nn. 8, 9, 17, 40, 68, 73, 123 and 129 below. I am deeply indebted to Dr H. M. Scott for most careful, thoughtful and constructive comments on this chapter.

[2] Temperley, *Frederic and Joseph*, p. 73.

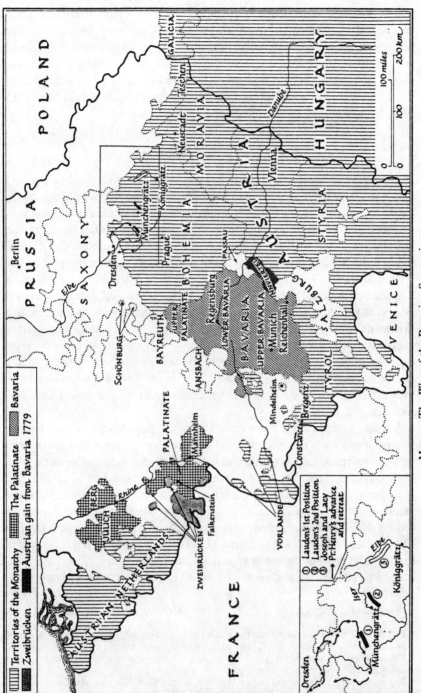

Map 4. The War of the Bavarian Succession.

test of Joseph's generalship, and the whole crisis is important for having occasioned the bitterest, the most prolonged and the best-documented wrangle of the entire co-regency. The literature in English is unsatisfactory; and, as usual, historians have commonly attributed the Monarchy's forward policies to Joseph's influence alone.[3] It is necessary, if his role is to be properly described and evaluated, to consider the matter in some detail. Map 4 and Figure 1 will help to clarify the complex issues involved.

The question, to January 1778

It was generally agreed, and many treaties had confirmed, that the heir to at least a major portion of Max Joseph's inheritance was the head of his family, his distant relative, Karl Theodor, already elector Palatine. But all manner of doubts could be raised about his rights to substantial parts of it, since the lands had been acquired at different times under many and various titles. To take some of the odder but clearer and more relevant cases, Max Joseph had held certain areas in Germany (like the duchy of Mindelheim) as fiefs of the kingdom of Bohemia, that is, from Maria Theresa herself; while conversely, others, mostly located within the borders of Bohemia, counted as 'allodials' (freeholds) that could be inherited by females. When Joseph ordered an enquiry into the question in 1772, his officials divided the Bavarian lands and dignities into six classes. When Keith, the British envoy in Vienna, tried to explain the matter to his government in 1776, he found it necessary to use twelve.[4] By 1778, as we shall see, yet further refinements would have been required.

A major complication arose from the constitution of the *Reich*. Units of government within the Holy Roman Empire were technically neither sovereign nor independent, but ranked as fiefs held by vassals from the emperor. In his *Wahlkapitulation*, like his predecessors, Joseph promised to submit cases of disputed succession to the opinion of the imperial diet. Some authorities maintained that, pending a settlement, he had the right or even the duty to occupy the lands concerned. Another difficulty was presented by Karl Theodor's own lack of a direct heir. His successor for most purposes was his nephew, the duke of the small principality of Zweibrücken. The duke would have to be considered and consulted in any negotiations about Max Joseph's inheritance.

Vienna was necessarily a party to the dispute. Joseph in his capacity as

---

[3] Temperley, *Frederic and Joseph*, though an admirable and invaluable book, makes little attempt to distinguish the roles of J., K. and M.T., scarcely uses Arneth, *MTuJ*, and treats the Monarchy's policy virtually as Joseph's (e.g. pp. 73–4, 207–9). For a recent example, McKay and Scott, *Rise of the Great Powers*, pp. 229–31.

[4] The 1772 report is summarised in Arneth, *GMT* x, pp. 286–8; Keith's is dated 22 Dec. 1776, separate and confidential, by Hanoverian courier (PRO SP 80/218).

emperor had a unique if ill-defined status in the matter. Maria Theresa had rights and pretensions of her own as queen of Bohemia, archduchess of Austria and so forth. In 1765 Joseph had acquired personal claims to some allodials by his marriage to a Bavarian princess. But of course, like all Powers of any size, the Monarchy wished above all to exploit any pretensions it could muster, in such a way as to enhance its strength, wealth, population and international standing. As Bavaria's neighbour it was in a peculiarly strong position to do so.

At the end of 1764, in connexion with Joseph's second marriage, an important discussion of the question took place in Vienna. Since we know that he compelled his mother to make the choice for him between the Bavarian and Saxon matches,[5] it is absolutely clear that he then had no regard for the political advantages that might accrue from his marrying Josepha. After the decision had been taken, Kaunitz wrote a memorandum on the issue. He had obviously used some of the same arguments to influence Maria Theresa's choice of bride for her son, and the question had been discussed in other contexts on several previous occasions, but he writes as though he is only now bringing the matter before her in all its ramifications. The time has come, he says, to face the issue, or other Powers will act first to Austria's disadvantage. The initial task is to establish what claims Maria Theresa might have to the succession. Kaunitz proposes employing a young and well-disposed historian called Schrötter to study them. The business must be kept profoundly secret, and no Protestant on the Aulic Council must hear of it. Joseph's marriage will give the Monarchy additional standing in the case. The chancellor then reveals his hand:

9.   I for my part believe that, if we behave judiciously and the event sooner or later occurs, a significant accession of land and population can hardly fail to come, if not to ourselves, then to our posterity, since [it is] perfectly clear in advance that a part of the allodials belongs by right to the heirs of Her Highness the bride; that the claim of the Palatinate line to the whole of the Bavarian succession, except the Upper Palatinate, can be disputed; and that there are yet more factors which could be exploited to help carry through an *arrondissement*. For, even if the duchy of Upper and Lower Bavaria fell without challenge to the line mentioned, [the Monarchy] would recover, as well as a portion of the allodials, all the Bohemian fiefs; and the disposal of the new[ly acquired] imperial fiefs devolves on the emperor's majesty and the Empire. All these points, taken together, could help to procure the acquisition of the whole strip of Bavaria along the river Inn to the Tyrolese frontier, which Austria has already held in the past.
10.   Certainly the most striking and most desirable outcome, if it were feasible, would be the union with Austria of the entire complex of Bavarian lands. Such a result can only seem a chimera at the moment. But there is no harm in contemplating it. And, although the idea could never be translated into fact without some compensation for the Palatinate and other Courts, we have either in the Austrian *Vorlande* or, if need be,

in the Netherlands, possessions that could be surrendered in order to balance everything up satisfactorily and so bring the priceless benefit of the *arrondissement*.

Kaunitz admits that his ideas are still crude. But they are not new; he has seen in his grandfather's papers references to 'the Bavarian *arrondissement*'. There would be difficulties of course. It would certainly be necessary to placate the Palatinate, France, the maritime Powers and the Empire; and it would be essential 'to keep the king of Prussia out of the game'.[6]

So Kaunitz had already, fourteen years before the crisis occurred, contemplated almost every possibility that was to be considered in the event. Even during the reign of Francis, the chancellor had shown himself sensitive to the status of the emperor in the business. His attitude to the Monarchy's claims emerges quite plainly: they are to be pressed not so much for themselves as in order to secure what is advantageous in terms of *Realpolitik*. Maria Theresa does not appear to have been horrified by his approach. She approved the employment and payment of the well-disposed historian. The *Staatsrat* discussed the question, presumably under the rubric that encouraged it to look into possible territorial claims.[7] At this stage, when Kaunitz was bringing these far-reaching ideas before the empress, Joseph played no discernible part at all – except to marry Josepha, under protest.

Joseph included a question about Bavaria in the questionnaire he sent to Kaunitz and the chief imperial officials at the end of 1766. But he scarcely mentioned the succession issue, and nor did the answers.[8] His first notable intervention in the affair occurred six years later. In the summer of 1772 his crony, count Dietrichstein, paid a mysterious visit to Frederick the Great. They discussed a wide range of issues including the Bavarian succession. The king surmised, surely correctly, that Dietrichstein's journey had been undertaken on behalf of Joseph.[9] Soon Frederick raised the Bavarian question with the Monarchy's official envoy in Prussia. Kaunitz delayed answering, and meanwhile the emperor instructed the imperial officials to report on it. They concluded that, once the Bavarian line failed, the whole of upper and lower Bavaria, as an imperial fief, would be at the disposal of the *Reich*. They

[6] The memo., presumably of Dec. 1764, is printed in K-M VI, pp. 342–4. See on its significance and on the background to it: Reimann, *Neuere Geschichte*, vol. II, pp. 3–5; Arneth, *GMT* X, pp. 281–4; Hanfstaengl, *Amerika und Europa*, esp. pp. 34–50. It is interesting that Frederick the Great attributes the scheme to Francis (Preuss, *Oeuvres de Frédéric*, vol. VI, p. 137).

[7] K-M VI, pp. 348–9. See above, p. 92.

[8] See pp. 120–3 above. Bernard, *J. II and Bavaria*, p. 11, completely misunderstands his source, Beer's article (*HZ* (1876), 89–90), in attributing to J. in his *Deliberanda* the view that 'Bavaria was a necessity for the Empire [*sic*] and that it should be acquired as soon as possible'. Colloredo and K. do mention in their answers the Bavarian allodials, but no more.

[9] See above, p. 294 and n. 76. Aretin (*Reich*, vol. I, p. 113), in ascribing Dietrichstein's journey to K.'s initiative, relies on G. B. Volz, 'Friedrich der Grosse und der bayrische Erbfolgekrieg', *FBPG*, XLIV (1932), 266–7. This useful article consists of little more than a summary of the relevant remarks in Frederick's *PC*, but in this case Volz summarises inadequately. Bernard, *J. II and Bavaria*, makes the same mistake.

advised that, immediately on the death of the elector, Joseph as emperor should occupy the fief, pending consultation with the diet. At least for the time being and perhaps permanently, the revenue would go to the emperor. Kaunitz's tame historian agreed. The chancellor himself was uneasy about the occupation, and doubted the long-term advantage to the Monarchy of an increase in the revenue and therefore in the independence of the emperor. But he acquiesced. All the necessary orders were prepared, ready for instant use when the moment came. Frederick was told, in reply to his enquiry, that a distinction had to be made between the claims of the Monarchy to certain small territories, and the rights of the emperor and the Empire over disputed fiefs.[10] Frederick had evidently wondered whether he might come to an understanding with Vienna over the Bavarian succession, and the Dietrichstein mission suggests that Joseph had had the same idea. But Kaunitz, in this case as in almost every other, wished to 'keep the king of Prussia out of the game'.

Prussia was not the only apprehensive Power. Max Joseph of Bavaria himself was always making agreements with Karl Theodor to secure him the succession. Saxony too was concerned, especially about the allodials, claimed by the dowager electress, the elder sister of Josepha. France, like most German states, feared any further Habsburg aggrandisement, especially in the *Reich*.[11]

There was one ruler, however, to whom Prussian schemes came to seem a greater threat than Austrian, namely Karl Theodor.[12] It was suspected that he was preoccupied with securing lavish provision for his bastard children. But he also had his own grand design to use his inheritance in order to establish a powerful state on the Rhine. He believed with reason that Frederick was interested in depriving him of two areas he had recently inherited that were essential to this plan, the duchies of Jülich and Berg. Moreover, to carry out his project, Karl Theodor hoped eventually to exchange Bavaria for Belgium. So at the end of 1776 he approached Vienna. He wanted an agreement under which his inheritance would be secured against Prussia and Saxony, in return for some compensation to the Monarchy, but as a preliminary to the Belgian

---

[10] Arneth, *GMT* x, pp. 286–93. Arneth gives a misleading impression by describing J.'s and his officials' enquiry of Dec. 1772 before he recounts Frederick's approach of Sep. 1772. Aretin, *Reich*, vol. I, pp. 113–14, explains K.'s attitude – and slightly more fully in his article, 'Kurfürst Karl Theodor und das bayerische Tauschprojekt', *ZBL*, xxv (1962), 747–8.

[11] The main sources for French attitudes are: Oursel, *La Diplomatie de la France*; Tratchevsky, *RH* (1880), esp. 272–5; Fagniez, *RH* (1922); Unzer, *Friede von Teschen*, ch. 1; Murphy, *Vergennes*, ch. 23.

[12] See Aretin, *ZBL* (1962), pp. 745–59; A. Unzer, 'Die Entstehung der pfälzisch-österreichischen Convention vom 3 Jan. 1778', *MÖIG*, xv (1894), 68–113; Arneth, *GMT* x, pp. 293–303; Beer, *HZ* (1876), 95–102. K.'s memo of late 1776 (Beer, *AÖG* (1872), 87–90) urges that the Habsburg claims be advanced in preference to the imperial.

PC xl, pp. 22–3, lends support to the fears of Karl Theodor about Jülich and Berg.

exchange. Maria Theresa and Joseph both agreed that this proposition should be explored, and negotiations proceeded throughout 1777.

By this decision Joseph showed himself ready to abandon the assertion of his rights as emperor – to the relief of Kaunitz and his mother. The triumph of the chancellor's policies owed much to the work of his tame historian, who discovered documentation of 1426 in which much of lower Bavaria was assigned by the emperor Sigismund to duke Albert V of Austria. This gave the Habsburgs a hitherto unsuspected claim to a substantial portion of the inheritance. Kaunitz was untroubled by the fact that the grant had been forgotten or repudiated within a few years. In his negotiations with Karl Theodor he based the Monarchy's pretensions on this discovery.[13]

Joseph worked for the acquisition of territories which would round off the Monarchy rather than fragment it further. He insisted also on making a good bargain. While he was visiting the Swabian lands of the Habsburgs on his way back from France in July 1777, he wrote to his mother:

All [these lands] are detached parts of the Monarchy, which it would be very advantageous to exchange for a larger *arrondissement*; the Vorarlberg, that is Bregenz and Constance, will never fall into this category and ought always to remain incorporated in the Monarchy. But one could not give up these lands [just] for the portion of Bavaria up to the Inn. The whole of upper and lower Bavaria as far as the Lech, and [also] the upper Palatinate would be necessary. Otherwise it would be a bad bargain.[14]

On Christmas Day he was consulting Lacy about a map of possible acquisitions sent by Kaunitz, and objecting to those which were detached from the Monarchy's central bloc.[15]

The treaty with the Palatinate was almost, but not quite, concluded when Max Joseph died on 30 December 1777. On New Year's Day, the occasion of the formal celebration that Joseph so hated, he wrote to Kaunitz:

I have just received the news that the elector of Bavaria has played on us the trick of dying, and that [our envoy] has not made use of the secret instructions given him some years ago. This is my first idea: since we've agreed on the principal point, namely that we should mutually recognise the rights we believe we have, and since it is [now] only a question of their greater or lesser extent; as there is no time to discuss the matter, we should take possession of lower Bavaria, as you marked it on the map, and promise to discuss in a friendly manner the extent of our frontiers. I've advised HM to say nothing about it in order to get through the reception and the [festivities of the] day. Consider all that is to be done, my dear prince, and tomorrow about midday I shall come and talk with you. Adieu.[16]

---

[13] The documents, for what it is worth, appear to have been genuine. See J. Kallbrunner, 'Zur Vorgeschichte des bayerischen Erbfolgekrieges', *MÖIG Ergänzungsband* XI (1929), 421–31.

[14] J. to M.T., 24 July 1777 (Arneth, *MTuJ* II, p. 156).

[15] J. to Lacy, 25 Dec. 1777 (HHSA FA Sbde 72). Cf. two letters of J. to K. (docketed 27 and 30 Dec.) in HHSA SKV 124.

[16] J. to K., 1 Jan. 1778 (Arneth, *GMT* X, pp. 303–4, 796). J. wrote to L. that day, listing the tiresome duties it imposed on him (HHFA SA Sbde 7, not in Arneth).

So Joseph wanted to use force at once, but in furtherance of the policy marked out by Kaunitz, not to establish imperial claims.

At the New Year's Day reception a famous scene occurred. The emperor was called out of the room, returned and whispered to his mother. 'She instantly let fall the cards, and rising up with evident marks of emotion, quitted the apartment.'[17] This was later explained as her reaction to the news of the elector's death. In fact she went out to discuss Joseph's plans to invade Bavaria immediately. She refused to sanction them.[18]

A few days later, the convention between the Monarchy and the Palatinate was signed. Austria was given most of lower Bavaria, subject to further archival research on precise boundaries. She also received the detached duchy of Mindelheim – so Joseph's comments on Kaunitz's map had not carried the day. Both sides agreed to further discussion about possible exchanges.[19] Maria Theresa congratulated Kaunitz as 'the greatest statesman in Europe',[20] and Joseph sent in his troops. He declared that this was the opportunity of a century. At the end of January he was still cock-a-hoop:

Our Bavarian affairs have up to now turned out in the best possible way. The elector has been dead a month and we've signed and ratified a convention, we're in possession of the whole district with the fiefs that lapse to us, and no one up to the present has said a word. Our decrees are published, the oath of fidelity has been sworn and everything is quiet. It remains to be seen how we shall act and what exchanges we shall make in the future for the benefit of both parties.[21]

Joseph and Kaunitz believed that the international situation favoured the success of their coup. England would disapprove, but was fully occupied with the war in America. France was about to join in on the side of the colonists, but in any case ought, as the Monarchy's ally, to be sympathetic: Vienna actually expected Paris to give military aid if Prussia attacked. Russia, though she had made peace with Turkey in 1774, was still embroiled over the Crimea. Within Germany it was thought that an arrangement could be made with Saxony, Austria's long-standing friend; the duke of Zweibrücken had given Karl Theodor *carte blanche* in negotiations with the Monarchy; and it was doubted whether Frederick, at his advanced age, would risk war.[22]

As with the partition of Poland, the policy pursued had been Kaunitz's, not Joseph's. The chancellor had doubted the justice, the advantage to the Monarchy and the chances of success of Joseph's plan to press his rights as

[17] Wraxall, *Memoirs*, vol. I, pp. 308–9. The accounts of Bernard, *J. II and Bavaria*, p. 38 and n., and Padover, *Revolutionary Emperor*, p. 96, are confused.
[18] M.T. to J., 2 Jan. 1778 (Arneth, *MTuJ* II, pp. 170–2).
[19] Unzer, *MÖIG* (1894), 98–9; Aretin, *ZBL* (1962), 756–7.
[20] M.T. to K., 16 Jan. 1778 (Arneth, *GMT* x, pp. 317, 798).
[21] J. to Mercy, 5 and 31 Jan. 1778 (Arneth & Flammermont II, pp. 518, 521). Aretin, *ZBL* (1962), 758, seems wrong to say that 6 Jan. was the occupation date. His source says 16 Jan.
[22] See the works listed in nn. 1 and 11 above, and Madariaga, *Catherine the Great*, pp. 378–81.

emperor.[23] When Karl Theodor offered him the opportunity, Kaunitz had wrested the matter out of the imperial sphere and resumed control of it as the Monarchy's foreign minister. Maria Theresa and France both encouraged him, because his way seemed more likely to be the way of peace.[24] No doubt Kaunitz was always conscious of pressure from Joseph to secure as good results from negotiation as could be expected from imperial intervention. It is true that Vienna used the threat of occupation in the emperor's name in order to dragoon Karl Theodor into giving a hasty signature to the convention. But Joseph was prevented from sending in his troops until the convention had been ratified. Admittedly, he then let the soldiers occupy rather more territory than the Monarchy had so far been assigned.[25] Otherwise, all that was done in 1777 and the early weeks of 1778 followed from Kaunitz's proposals of 1764.

The Monarchy was now irretrievably committed to the annexation of lower Bavaria under the terms of the convention with Karl Theodor. In retrospect, the line of policy that led to this commitment seems at best of doubtful wisdom, at worst a crass mistake. In detail, the researchers found the archives unfavourable to many of Vienna's claims.[26] More generally, no other Power proved ready to accept the convention; Austria was compelled to fight for her gains; and eventually she had to surrender almost everything. The historian finds himself wondering whether it might not have been wiser after all to have implemented Joseph's instructions of 1772. The emperor could then have stood forth as the guardian of the imperial constitution. If by any chance he could have retained the revenues of much of Bavaria for the Empire, its whole history would have been changed. But Joseph cannot be imagined as wanting to benefit the *Reich* rather than the Monarchy. It is difficult to gainsay the warnings given him by Pergen and Kaunitz in 1767, that the imperial dignity could bring advantage to the Monarchy only if it was not used aggressively.[27] Occupation on behalf of the emperor would surely have been challenged as strongly as annexation by the Monarchy, and Maria Theresa would scarcely have permitted her armies to be fully engaged in an imperial cause. A more hopeful alternative course of action to that actually pursued would have been a deal with Prussia, such as seemed possible in 1772. But the empress and the chancellor would never have acquiesced in that policy.[28]

[23] See n. 10 above.
[24] Arneth, *GMT* x, esp. p. 302; Fagniez, *RH* (1922), 22–5; Unzer, *Friede von Teschen*, pp. 32–3; cf. K. to Mercy, 19 Feb. 1778, reporting a row with Breteuil in which it was common ground that France had encouraged Austria to negotiate with the Palatinate rather than seize Bavaria by force (Arneth & Flammermont II, pp. 524–5).
[25] Aretin, *ZBL* (1962), 752, 756, 758; J. to L., 15 Jan. 1778 (Arneth, *MTuJ* II, p. 176).
[26] Aretin, *ZBL* (1962), 774.
[27] See above, pp. 121–3.
[28] For the whole paragraph cf. Aretin, *Reich*, vol. I, pp. 113–15; Unzer, *Friede von Teschen*, esp. p. 26. Frederick said afterwards that Austria should have squared either France or Prussia (Preuss, *Oeuvres de Frédéric*, vol. VI, p. 177).

Frederick's views, as expressed in his political testament of 1752,[29] tend in certain respects to vindicate the line followed by Joseph and Kaunitz. He wrote of the likelihood that the Bavarian line would fail, and saw that the resulting union of the lands of the Palatinate and Bavaria would set up a dangerous Catholic rival to the Habsburgs within the Empire. In discussing Prussia's own dynastic claims, he urged his heirs to press only those that would lead to an *arrondissement*. With reference to the acquisition of Mecklenburg, he advised immediate occupation if the succession question there came to a head, 'because the right of possession gives a great advantage in the Holy Roman Empire, and one can argue one's case comfortably when one is quietly extracting revenue from one's acquisition'. As Maria Theresa was always complaining, Joseph and Kaunitz were only acting in the Prussian manner.[30]

In the testament Frederick made no mention of any claims of his to any part of Bavaria or the Palatinate, not even to Jülich and Berg. But he laid great stress on his right of succession to the principalities of Ansbach and Bayreuth. These lands, located between Bavaria and Prussia, would in his eyes constitute an *arrondissement*. By the 1770s the extinction of their ruling dynasty seemed imminent, and Frederick often linked this question to that of the Bavarian succession. If he was to allow the Monarchy to make any gain from the failure of the Bavarian line, he wanted assurances that his right to Ansbach and Bayreuth would be recognised.[31] Kaunitz's refusal, in the early weeks after he had obtained the convention with Karl Theodor, to make the slightest acknowledgement of Prussia's interest in these duchies showed how gravely he had overestimated the strength of the Monarchy's position. It was quite unreasonable to expect other Powers to acquiesce in a scheme of aggrandisement, based on novel and improbable historical claims, that had been negotiated only with Karl Theodor, whose projects were as fantastic as his credit was low. Kaunitz had again become the dupe of his own elaborate and over-refined diplomatic combinations.

The approach to war, January–July 1778

No sooner had Joseph written his jubilant letter than his and Kaunitz's illusions began to crumble. Frederick's attitude was decisive, and his remarks and actions were various and devious enough to justify most Austrian

---

[29] For this and the following paragraph, Bosbach, *Les 'Rêveries Politiques'*, pp. 137–8.
[30] E.g. M.T. to J., 2 Jan. 1778 (Arneth, *MTuJ* II, pp. 171–2).
[31] E.g. Arneth, *GMT* X, pp. 291–2; Volz, *FBPG* (1932), 266–7. Conversely, if Austria gained nothing, Frederick still hoped to secure the succession to Ansbach and Bayreuth (*ibid.*, p. 292).

It seems to me that Temperley (*Frederic and Joseph*, esp. pp. 109–10 and 182–3), in neglecting Frederick's early desire to link Ansbach-Bayreuth with Bavaria, is too critical of J.'s and K.'s attempts to connect them during most of 1778.

strictures on the 'monster'.[32] His agents first induced the duke of Zwei-brücken to withdraw his consent to the plans of Karl Theodor. Most of the princes of the *Reich*, already alarmed by the activity of the emperor, worked to prevent Austrian aggrandisement. Saxony, in the last war Vienna's friend, had recently been offended when her claims to the county of Schönburg had been brushed aside by the Monarchy's troops, acting to maintain the rights of Maria Theresa as queen of Bohemia. The elector finally allied with Prussia. Opposition appeared within Bavaria itself. If George III as king of England seemed unconcerned, as elector of Hanover he supported Frederick. Keith was instructed not to discuss the affairs of Hanover; but as Maria Theresa told him, 'there can be no Doubt of the Sovereign of both Countries knowing what passes in each of them'. Catherine II, born and brought up a German princess, wished to secure for Russia a recognised position in the Empire, and so showed sympathy with the princes. Despite the pleadings of Marie Antoinette, France publicly dissociated herself from Austria's actions, declined to acknowledge any obligation to defend the newly annexed lands of the Monarchy, and declared herself strictly neutral.[33]

Just as it was clear to Joseph and Kaunitz that Bavaria was the only land in which they could hope to compensate the Monarchy for the loss of Silesia, so it was plain to Frederick that a large Austrian aggrandisement in Bavaria would threaten the position he had won for Prussia in the *Reich*. On these arguments, war between the Monarchy and Prussia over the annexation of lower Bavaria seems inevitable, especially since Frederick had been deliberately 'kept out of the game'. War preparations began in earnest in February, and in April both king and emperor took command of their troops. But Frederick hesitated, or appeared to do so. Although war was widely expected from the start, negotiations of great variety and complexity were always in train and occasionally gave hope of a peaceful settlement.[34]

One part of this diplomatic activity concerned possible exchanges of territory between the Monarchy and Karl Theodor.[35] For a time it was

[32] A frequent usage of M.T.'s. See e.g. M.T. to J., 20 Apr. and 21 June 1778 (Arneth, *MTuJ* II, pp. 211, 300).

[33] For this paragraph see the works listed in nn. 1, 11 and 22 above; and Volz, *FBPG* (1932). On Saxony, in addition to Arneth, *GMT* x, pp. 274–9, 357–62, E. Reimann, 'Friedrich August III. und Karl Theodor', *Neues Archiv für Sächsische Geschichte und Alterthumskunde*, IV (1883), 317–19, 338–9 (making telling points against Arneth's attitude and methods). On Hanover see Keith's despatches to Suffolk of 15 Feb. ('most secret and confidential', composed over four days, 15–18 Feb.), 4 and 24 June, 18 July 1778 (PRO SP 80/270). The same duality of policy is observable as is shown to exist at a later date in T. C. W. Blanning, '"That horrid electorate" or "Ma patrie germanique"? George III, Hanover, and the *Fürstenbund* of 1785', *HJ* XX (1977), 311–44.

[34] See above, nn. 1 and 11 for principal references. I have used HHSA SKV 125–6, much of which was printed or summarised by Arneth, but which contains some important documents he did not cite (cf. Aretin, *ZBL* (1962), 759n). SKV files have been renumbered since Aretin used them.

[35] See Aretin, *ZBL* (1962), 756–72.

believed in Vienna and Munich that such an agreement might be carried into effect without involving other Powers. The attitude of the principals in Vienna is of special interest, because the issue came to the fore again, though of course in rather different circumstances, in 1784–5. A wide range of proposals was discussed, from minor frontier adjustments to schemes involving the whole of the Austrian Netherlands or even Galicia. Maria Theresa was always opposed to the exchange of Belgium, which she considered a loyal and profitable possession, worth more even than Silesia. She preferred the Belgians as subjects to Bavarian 'rustics'.[36] More surprisingly, Kaunitz had concluded by 1776 that the Netherlands were too valuable to be bartered even against the whole of Bavaria. In retrospect, the 'benefit of the *arrondissement*' seems, as he had described it in 1764, 'priceless', especially by comparison with retaining detached provinces that could not be adequately defended against France or other Powers. But the chancellor seems to have been quite serious in arguing that any exchange agreed must leave the Monarchy with no less revenue than it had possessed beforehand. Since enquiries showed that Bavaria yielded annually one or two million florins less than the Netherlands, he was never prepared to contemplate the straight exchange, the only arrangement that really interested Karl Theodor.[37] Joseph too was influenced by these arguments and usually took the same line. But there was a moment when he wrote to Leopold for his opinion on the straight exchange, adding that the shortfall in revenue could be made up by loans. Leopold disagreed,[38] and anyway the issue soon became academic as other Powers complicated the exchange negotiations by advancing their own claims to 'compensation' for Austrian aggrandisement.

Negotiations with Frederick involved not only regular diplomatic channels but also intermediaries of uncertain standing, including prince Henry, the king's brother, who wished to avoid war. If Joseph and Kaunitz had been less confident of their rights and chances at the start, they might well have obtained terms better than the peace of Teschen ultimately gave them. But the concessions they made came slowly, and in obvious response to their weakening international position. Though they eventually offered to abandon some of their gains in Bavaria and to recognise Frederick's claims on Ansbach and Bayreuth as a prelude to mutually satisfactory exchanges, by then he was in such a strong position that he declined to bargain, preferring to maintain

---

[36] E.g. M.T. to J., 29 Apr., 19 June, 21 June, 26 June 1778 (Arneth, *MTuJ* II, pp. 228, 296–7, 302, 305). Cf. pp. 485–7 below.

[37] See K.'s memo. of late 1776 in Beer, *AÖG* (1872), 89; Arneth, *GMT* x, pp. 346–8; Aretin, *ZBL* (1962), 759–61. A proposal of 28 May, echoing one of 17 Mar., came near a straight exchange, but added refinements like the cession of either Ansbach or Bayreuth to Austria (*ibid.*, pp. 767 and n., 770).

[38] J. to L., 12 Mar. 1778 (misdated by Arneth in *MTuJ* II, p. 184, to 27 Mar.) and L. to J., 24 Mar. (see Arneth, *GMT* x, pp. 344, 800). This letter of L.'s is one of the very few which Arneth later acknowledges, having not printed it in *MTuJ*.

his stand as defender of the liberties of the *Reich* against a 'despotic' emperor.[39]

The making of Austria's policy during these months, down to the middle of July, though it was punctuated by the customary storms between mother, son and minister, reveals the relationship of Maria Theresa and Joseph at its happiest. For a time she appeared to share the optimism of the emperor and the chancellor that they would get away with the seizure of lower Bavaria. But when war began to seem near, on 14 March, she dictated a heartfelt disavowal of the whole affair, which she read to both men. 'It is a question', she said, 'of nothing less than the ruin of our dynasty and Monarchy, and even of a total revolution in Europe.' Frederick's army has thirty or forty thousand more men than hers. To confront him, huge parts of the Monarchy will have to be denuded of troops and left open to attack: Galicia, Hungary, the Netherlands, Italy, the newly occupied parts of Bavaria themselves. There is no hope of any real gain. Even if the Austrians win battles, that will only lead to a more general war and to final defeat.

I should be unworthy of the name of sovereign and mother if I didn't take measures appropriate to the circumstances . . . I will gladly commit myself to anything, even if it tarnishes my reputation. People can accuse me of senility, weakness, pusillanimity. Nothing will stop me rescuing Europe from this dangerous situation.

Joseph and Kaunitz persuaded her that she was exaggerating. She contented herself with adding a final flourish which she did not communicate to them:

If war breaks out, place no more reliance on me. I shall withdraw to the Tyrol, to finish my days there in the deepest retirement, where my only occupation will be to lament the unfortunate fate of my House and my peoples, and to try to end my unhappy days in a Christian manner.[40]

Having been overborne this time, she could assert in July that from the beginning of the crisis she had not 'meddled in any political, financial or other arrangements, knowing very well that in the end people [would] want to indulge in recriminations about them'.[41] She spoke of leaving a negotiation entirely to Kaunitz, and wrote to Joseph at the front: 'My dear son, don't be afraid that I'll interfere in your military or political operations. You know that

[39] Arneth, *GMT* x, pp. 363–437; Reimann, *Neuere Geschichte*, pp. 83–109; Aretin, *Reich*, vol. I, pp. 115–17; Volz, *FBPG* (1932), 285–300; *PC* XL–XLI, *passim*.

[40] M.T. to J., 14 Mar. 1778 (Arneth, *MTuJ* II, pp. 186–91). I do not know where Bernard (*J. II and Bavaria*, pp. 79–80) gets the idea that K. modified this document significantly in draft. Karajan, *Feierliche Sitzungsberichte KAW* (1865), 21, mentions only one trivial emendation in K.'s hand.

[41] This note (of [?]9 July) quoted by Arneth (*GMT* x, p. 808) says she has ceased to participate since 3 Feb., as does a letter to Ferd. (also 9 July, Arneth, *MTKuF* II, p. 129). War preparations began on 3 Feb. But cf. M.T. to Mercy, 31 Jan. 1778 (Arneth & Geffroy III, p. 161), suggesting earlier abstention.

I've handed them over to you completely, and that all I'm concerned about is that I should be kept informed.'[42]

Her proclaimed abdication of responsibility was most nearly realised in military affairs. She did complain of what she saw as too ruthless requisitioning policies. She had to tell Joseph that Belgium could not raise the loan he asked for – at which he spoke bitingly of the province's 'perfect neutrality'. But she accepted or gave the orders necessary for mobilisation of troops, animals and supplies, as he requested. She claimed, and he seems not to have disputed, that she did all she could on this score.[43]

In foreign policy-making the position was less clear. The general line pursued followed from the stand taken in December and January by Kaunitz and Joseph. But she wrote letter after letter to the emperor expressing her anxieties, giving her opinions on new propositions, and urging him to work for peace. When he appeared sympathetic, she offered him 'full powers to make peace on the battlefield, without laying down any condition to you so long as peace is made'. But in other contexts she continued to exert influence in detail as well as in general. She argued with Kaunitz too, but showed him at least as much confidence as she extended to her son. Needless to say, emperor and chancellor had many differences of opinion on specific questions. Once Joseph was in Bohemia, negotiations with Prussia were channelled through him, and he sometimes amended, delayed or even rejected Kaunitz's proposals. But the chancellor, the man in Vienna, with the sympathy of the empress and the resources of the office behind him, remained the guiding spirit until the last weeks of peace.[44]

When Joseph acted on his own initiative, it was treated as a nine days' wonder. He carried with him to the army in April a letter ready to send to Frederick, which had been long debated and frequently rewritten in Vienna, but was to be passed off as his own work. He modified it slightly before sending it, in ways which Kaunitz later criticised. As soon as the king received it, he sat down and replied in his own hand, without the benefit of advice. He accused Joseph of behaving despotically as emperor in claiming the right to dispose of all imperial fiefs as he chose. Joseph answered immediately, also without consultation, emphasising that he had acted throughout not as emperor, but in his capacities as elector of Bohemia and archduke of Austria, on the basis of a treaty made freely with Karl Theodor. He vigorously rebutted the imputation of despotism, a 'word . . . I abhor at least as much as you'.[45] He

[42] M.T. to J., 29 May and 8 June 1778 (Arneth, *MTuJ* II, pp. 262, 276).

[43] M.T. to J., 22 Apr., 10, 15 and 22 May; J. to M.T., 27 Apr. (*ibid.*, pp. 218–19, 226, 246, 250, 255).

[44] The quotation from M.T. to J., 8 June 1778 (*ibid.*, p. 277). In general, *ibid.*, pp. 186–320 *passim*; HHSA SKV 125–6; Arneth, *GMT* X, chs. 11–12; Beer, *HZ* (1876), 137–42.

[45] Correspondence between J. and Frederick in *PC* XL, pp. 392–4, 394–6, 407–10, 419–20; Arneth, *GMT* X, pp. 389–94, 397–9, 805; HHSA SKV 126 (with some early drafts in 125). K.'s criticism of J.'s modifications is in HHSA SKV 126 (15 Apr. 1778).

then wrote to his mother asking her indulgence for having replied to Frederick without her authority. Maria Theresa, after reading the king's letter, at which she was indignant and scornful, turned to her son's with

admiration, and you carry your delicacy too far when you insist on apologising for it. You know, and I repeat it again, that you rightly possess my entire confidence ... You could not have given your pupil a lesson in politics with greater gentleness and dignity, nor expressed your feelings about this despot with more banter and irony. . .

When the king responded more reasonably, she took up his classical allusions and talked of Lucullus having taught a lesson to Mithridates. 'I love my Cato, my Christian philosopher. Your letter is to be published ... Kaunitz is thrilled with it.' She wrote of Joseph's next salvo: 'Your letter is another unique piece ... You can imagine what my heart feels, you being my son – and what a son, a phoenix!'[46] On the chancellor's advice, however, Joseph then broke off the correspondence.[47] It is obvious that Kaunitz feared and disliked any step being taken in foreign policy without his cognisance.

A changing pattern of influence is revealed in this letter of 22 May from mother to son:

I haven't seen Kaunitz since the third of May; I sent for Binder, who seemed to me very cagey and embarrassed. I gave him some notes to discuss with Kaunitz and to indicate that I should like to speak to him, or that he should draft yet another reasoned memorandum for my guidance and yours – although you don't need it, and everything you compose is beautifully clear and vigorous ... I had all this passed to Kaunitz by Binder the day before yesterday, but after two whole days not a sign of life. I can't, as you do, go round to him to do the job [myself], and I confess I wouldn't have your patience, nor enough talent to draft and dictate things as you do.

When the chancellor's memorandum arrived, she called it 'faultless'. But she told Joseph that one of Kaunitz's despatches was confused.[48]

In fact the chancellor made a poor showing during these months. His paperwork took far too long, and he grumbled when he was given a deadline.[49] Yet he found time at the height of the crisis to ask Maria Theresa to sanction experiments with a new method of keeping stables dry, a product of 'my imagination [which is] very fertile in the arts in general and in that of architecture in particular'.[50] Emotion seems for once to have clouded his judgement. When the French ambassador told him that no help would come

---

[46] J. to M.T., 16 Apr. 1778; M.T. to J., two letters of 18 Apr., two of 20 Apr., 21 Apr., 24 Apr. (Arneth, *MTuJ* II, pp. 200–4, 211, 213–14, 221). These letters of J. to Frederick must be distinguished from the false letter quoted in Padover, *Revolutionary Emperor*, p. 102 and Crankshaw, *Maria Theresa*, p. 314. See pp. 19–20 above.

[47] Arneth, *GMT*, x, p. 402.

[48] M.T. to J., 22 and 31 May 1778 (Arneth, *MTuJ* II, pp. 256, 264); Arneth, *GMT* x, pp. 414–22.

[49] E.g. M.T. to J., 22 May, just quoted; K. to M.T., 25 Apr. and K. to J., 25 Apr. (both in HHSA SKV 126); M.T. to Mercy, 31 July 1778 (Arneth & Geffroy III, p. 232).

[50] K. to M.T., 5 June 1778 (HHSA SKV 126).

from Paris, he threw a tantrum and talked of the end of the alliance.[51] He loved denouncing Frederick's ignorance, bad faith, poor logic and 'utter foolishness', and appeared blind to his astuteness.[52] As each of Kaunitz's calculations proved false, he embraced new error. One Prussian emissary after another strengthened his conviction that the king would never fight.[53] The chancellor devised a succession of elaborate partition plans, maintaining that 'it is only by this door that we can hope ultimately to escape from the labyrinth [created by] the injustice and folly of the King of Prussia'.[54] Kaunitz's position was certainly 'a singular one, [demanding] consummate address, in order, while he preserves the affection of the mother, not to irritate, or alienate the son'.[55] But it was not until May that he began to acknowledge the full seriousness of the situation and adopt a more realistic line.[56]

Away from Vienna, Joseph became increasingly reluctant to accept any of Kaunitz's advice unamended; and when the chancellor tried to lower Austria's demands in May and June, the emperor talked of timorousness and broke off correspondence.[57] Until the last days of June Joseph kept on asserting that, so long as the Monarchy stood firm, Frederick would recede.[58] As usual, he hoped – indeed had expected – to gain territory by warlike demonstrations rather than by war.[59] He had moments of doubt and anxiety. His time was fully occupied with military preparations before as well as after he left Vienna for the army, and he once confessed to Leopold:

I almost succumb under the weight of administration that is now falling on me. I recognise the gravity of a false step, and I can assure you that my brain seethes the whole day with business and the orders to be given, while my thoughts in bed on the consequences and the next moves don't help me to sleep well.

At times the state of the army alarmed him. But in general he appeared confident, expecting peace but rejecting terms that seemed shameful, and

---

[51] K. to Mercy, 19 Feb. 1778 (Arneth & Flammermont II, pp. 523–6).

On 15–18 Feb. Keith reported to Suffolk (PRO SP 80/270, one vast despatch, 'most secret and confidential', not numbered) what appeared like an approach from K. to England, at least designed to keep her from joining Prussia, and threatening closer alliance with France if she did. The usually elusive and secretive chancellor gave Keith four interviews in four days. This demonstration was no doubt directed against both France and Hanover. See n. 33 above.

[52] E.g. K.'s note of 19 Apr. 1778 (HHSA SKV 126). Frederick shrewdly wrote to J. of K.'s *humeur* (*PC* XL, p. 396).

[53] Arneth, *GMT* X, pp. 379–80, 804–5.   [54] Note of 19 Apr. 1778 (HHSA SKV 126).

[55] Wraxall, *Memoirs*, vol. I, pp. 352–3.

[56] Arneth, *GMT* X, pp. 403–5, 806: a letter of K.'s to J. of 2 May, suggesting a new approach to Prussia, which J. declined to make.

On K. in general during this crisis, see the trenchant remarks of Crankshaw (*Maria Theresa*, pp. 315, 318).

[57] M.T. to Mercy, 31 July 1778 (Arneth & Geffroy III, p. 230) says J. had broken off correspondence for six weeks. But he wrote in a most flattering manner to K. on 24 June (Arneth, *GMT* X, pp. 433–4, 808). See *ibid.*, pp. 472–6.

[58] E.g. J. to M.T., 28 June 1778 (Arneth, *MTuJ* II, p. 307).

[59] J. to L., 5 Jan. 1778 (*ibid.*, p. 174).

declaring himself ready, if necessary, for war.[60] During June Maria Theresa gave him his head.

A new tone now pervades the correspondence between mother and son. She frequently preaches at him to change his approach, to sacrifice his own feelings and reputation in the interests of his peoples, to prefer a moderate peace to a victorious war, to imagine himself in the place of those with whom he is negotiating, to give up *Habsucht* (greed). Occasionally he replies with some of his customary sharpness. But her manner is uncharacteristically admiring, flattering and encouraging, while his is unusually warm, confiding and reasonable. He solicits her aid, she apologises for her 'Jeremiads'.[61] They may differ violently over policy, but they collaborate like true joint rulers. The change is evident in some of the letters already quoted. Here are some more instances. This is Joseph writing when Frederick has answered his second letter more mildly and there seems hope of a settlement:

It will be a good thing to begin negotiating. Either we'll make peace and there'll be no war at all, or we'll [start the war] later, and we shall be infinitely better off so far as both our arrangements and the army are concerned ... But I beg YM not to pass on this glimmer of hope to anyone.[62]

He asked her to tell everyone she expected war, as the best hope of bringing Frederick to terms. This gave her no difficulty, she replied, as she was quite convinced war would come. They comforted each other with accounts of patriotic manifestations in various parts of the Monarchy.

In the Vorlande and Vorarlberg [she wrote], where recruits could never be got, everyone is rushing to fight for the emperor. It's affecting, and a grace from God, and a tangible reward for the efforts [you've made] and the popularity you have everywhere you've been.[63]

He remembers her birthday, and pleases her by taking part in the celebrations of the feast of St John Nepomuk in Prague. She is alarmed for his safety, which she thinks threatened not only by disease but also by fantastic machinations attributed to the 'monster'. Above all, he must look after himself:

Nothing has sustained me in all my cruel misfortunes and losses but you. When I see you and hear you and [when I remember] that what I'm suffering is for you, this is the only reward I want for all I've undertaken, from your birth onwards, and I spare no effort now ... All the rest is nothing in comparison with you.

[60] J. to L., 12 Mar. 1778 (*ibid.*, pp. 185–6). See n. 38 above. Similar remarks in J. to L., 26 Mar. 1778 (HHSA FA Sbde 7, not printed by Arneth). Cf. on the state of the army J. to M.T., 18 Apr. 1778 (Arneth, *MTuJ* II, pp. 204–5). In his letters in June there is a good deal about shameful peace, e.g. J. to M.T., 18 June 1778 (*ibid.*, pp. 295–6).

[61] The *Habsucht* remark is in M.T. to J., 31 May 1778 (*ibid.*, p. 265). She speaks of 'my Jeremiads' on 10 June (*ibid.*, p. 282). For the rest of this paragraph, which is based on the letters between M.T. and J. printed by Arneth, I shall give references only to actual quotations.

[62] J. to M.T., 19 Apr. 1778 (*ibid.*, p. 208).   [63] M.T. to J., 8 May 1778 (*ibid.*, pp. 243–4).

She tells him she has tried to emulate his promptness in sending off orders, even though she disagrees with them. She even brought herself to this admission:

The Monarchy, my dear son, has fallen terribly under petticoat government. It needs all your support and energy, and for that we must have peace. You cannot be in two places at once, and I must tell you that you won't be effectively backed here in the event of war.[64]

So, during this phase, although the empress continued to utter dire warnings, she gave Joseph her help and confidence in his capacity as commander-in-chief. In foreign policy too she acquiesced in the line established in January; and when Kaunitz began to waver from it during the last weeks of peace, she followed her son's advice rather than her chancellor's. The emperor's clearest personal contribution in this phase was to prevent by his obstinacy a shift of approach in May and June. Kaunitz ascribed the rejection of his advice and Joseph's new coolness towards him to the machinations of Lacy. The marshal obviously had every opportunity to influence the emperor. As for the empress, she told Lacy in April to write regularly to her through 'our common friend, princess Francis'; 'that will cause less curiosity'. She would write back in the same way. They should both use low-grade paper to make the deception more plausible.[65] It may well be that she was relying on Lacy's advice when she endorsed Joseph's policy.

The emperor's calculations, however, proved as false as the chancellor's. Neither of them appreciated how widespread and violent an opposition their scheme would evoke. They did not realise how disturbed other Powers and German opinion had been by the Austrian policy of aggrandisement seen in the annexation of Galicia and Bukovina and in the assertion of imperial and Habsburg claims within the *Reich*. It was natural that most policy-makers in Vienna should think themselves entitled to seize the opportunity of the Bavarian crisis to pay back Frederick for the rape of Silesia. Though he now had a good case in law and morality, it was not so good as Maria Theresa's case against him in 1740. But as she saw, Silesia was unique, and no other such enterprise would be allowed to succeed. She also pointed out that Frederick and his party understood public relations better than Kaunitz and Joseph did.[66] Prussia easily won the war of opinion. The Monarchy could still be plausibly represented as Goliath, with Prussia as David.[67]

---

64 M.T. to J., 4 July 1778 (*ibid.*, p. 315); 22 May (pp. 257–8).
65 M.T. to Lacy, 18 Apr. 1778 (HHSA NL, Karton 2). So far as I know, these letters do not survive. But (presumably different) letters from Lacy to princess Francis are often summarised and quoted by E.L. in her letters to L.K. from July to October 1778. For K.'s resentment, see L.K.'s replies (SOALpZ, LRRA P. 17/24).
66 M.T. to J., 2 Jan. 1778 (Arneth, *MTuJ* II, pp. 171–2); M.T. to Mercy, 31 July 1778 (Arneth & Geffroy III, p. 231). Cf. Preuss, *Oeuvres de Frédéric*, vol. VI, p. 178.
67 In general on reactions of other Powers, Reimann, *Neuere Geschichte*, vol. II, pp. 13–15; Fagniez, *RH* (1922), 5–8; Unzer, *Friede von Teschen*, chs. 2 and 4. On German opinion Wangermann, *WBGN* (1982), 65–7. The comparison with David and Goliath is to be found,

The war and the concurrent negotiations, July–November 1778[68]

After declaring war, Frederick invaded Bohemia on 5 July. In total, the Monarchy now had about 250,000 men under arms. Of these over 160,000 were awaiting a Prussian attack in Bohemia. Vienna had decided that Austrian strategy must be purely defensive. Any kind of pre-emptive strike had been ruled out on political grounds: the Monarchy could not afford to alienate international opinion further by another act of aggression. On military grounds, given Prussia's supposed numerical superiority on this front, it was thought safest to dig in on the best possible defensive positions and abandon any ideas of counter-attack. This plan of course corresponded with Joseph's and Lacy's predilections, and it was Lacy who was responsible for the disposition of the Austrian forces. On the eve of war they were divided into two: the larger part to the east, facing Frederick and the Silesian frontier, was to be commanded by Joseph and Lacy; on the west marshal Laudon's wing would guard the approaches from Saxony. Two days after war broke out, Laudon suddenly proposed that the two armies be reunited so that they could make an unexpected assault on the invading Prussians. Not surprisingly, this idea was rejected as too risky by Joseph and Lacy.[69]

When Maria Theresa received the news of the invasion, she wrote to her son applauding his arrangements and offering words of encouragement. Here was the opportunity for which he had been longing and preparing ever since he had been placed at the head of the army. But at this critical moment, while his mother, despite her deep anxieties, abandoned talk of abdication and behaved like a sovereign, Joseph came near to panic.

Desperate circumstances [he told her on 7 July] demand desperate remedies. In this present ruinous and extremely dangerous war, the survival of the Monarchy now hangs on a few unlucky minutes. The enemy with whom we have to deal is substantially stronger than we, and notoriously ready to [use] every means, moreover [is] a great soldier. We are effectively without allies, so the Monarchy has to find its resources within itself and rely on them alone. It would be inexcusable to lose a moment ...

for example, in Clausewitz (C. von Clausewitz, *On War*, ed. M. Howard and P. Paret (Princeton, 1976), p. 583n).

[68] On the war Temperley, *Frederic and Joseph*, ch. 5, is valuable, together with Arneth, *GMT* x, esp. ch. 14; O. Criste, *Kriege unter Kaiser Josef II.* (Vienna, 1904), pp. 47–134; J. Nosinich and L. Wiener, *Kaiser Josef II. als Staatsmann und Feldherr* (Vienna, 1885), ch. 4; Kotasek, *Lacy*, pp. 151–67. On the negotiations, Arneth, *GMT* x, chs. 13 and 15; Unzer, *Friede von Teschen*, chs. 2 and 5; Aretin, *ZBL* (1962), 772–6; documents in HHSA SKV 126–7. Arneth, *MTuJ* II–III is full of material for this phase. Bernard, *J. II and Bavaria*, ch. 7, completely misrepresents the campaign on the ground, reversing the roles of prince Henry and king Frederick and mixing up Bohemia and Moravia.

[69] On this idea of Laudon's, Nosinich and Wiener, *Kaiser J. II.*, pp. 147–8; Criste, *Kriege*, pp. 82–3; Temperley, *Frederic and Joseph*, pp. 123–5. This incident is discussed quite differently by Criste and by Nosinich and Wiener: Criste aligns J. with Lacy against Laudon, Nosinich and Wiener picture J. backing Laudon. Since neither book gives adequate references, it is hard to decide between them. Criste's is the later and the more convincing.

There must be 40,000 recruited immediately, without regard to the usual exemptions. Taxes and loans must be raised to new levels. 'All citizens from the throne down to the lowest peasant ... must contribute according to their abilities to maintain the whole.' Hungary and Transylvania cannot be excepted. Allies must be sought, or else mercenaries will have to be hired. Joseph asks his mother to summon all her ministers, explain to them the state of affairs, and urge all provinces and 'every well-disposed patriot' to maximum effort. 'As a true patriot' himself he feels bound to put the truth of the situation before her. 'I shall gladly contribute everything I have and possess, including the utmost powers of my mind and body.'[70]

It took two to three days for letters from Joseph at the front to reach Maria Theresa. As soon as she received this wild appeal, she wrote frantically to Kaunitz:

It's what I've always foreseen, but I expected it after a lost battle, which is inevitable ... Without a shot fired we're told that already all is lost, and recruits and volunteers must save the Monarchy after 170,000 men, trained and tormented, are in confusion and panic. Goodbye, Monarchy, I don't see how to save it. I await you and your advice what I ought to reply tomorrow evening, since I'm at my wits' end.[71]

She answered Joseph on the 11th. She reminded him that she had always feared and predicted this outcome but, urging him to recall the feats of the Monarchy's great captains in the past, stressed that one battle would not be decisive. She pointed out the difficulties some of his requests posed, while undertaking to meet as many of them as possible. She went on: 'I feel rejuvenated, I shall leave no stone unturned, the sword will not be enough now.' If he possibly can, he should make peace. 'It's a matter of extricating ourselves, of saving Joseph.' Above all else, he must preserve himself.[72]

As yet, she kept back news of the boldest step she had taken. She had written a second note to Kaunitz:

I'm firmly resolved to attempt the impossible, to avert the outbreak even now. Without delay, you will seriously consider how the war could at once, without further loss of time, come to an end, and you will put before me the ways and means.

Advised by Kaunitz, she wanted to make Frederick what would look like a personal proposal, through an emissary, baron Thugut. The chancellor failed to produce the document fast enough, or in a simple enough style, to please her. But on 13 July Thugut duly left Vienna in great secrecy, disguised as a Russian diplomat, carrying a peace plan which lowered Austrian claims on Bavaria and acknowledged Prussia's right to Ansbach and Bayreuth. It was

---

[70] M.T. to J., 7 July 1778; J. to M.T., same day (Arneth, *MTuJ* II, pp. 323–6 and 325–7n).
[71] HHSA SKV 126 ([?]10 July 1778). The version in Arneth, *GMT* x, p. 694, shamelessly omits 'tourmentés' and 'et tremerola' – presumably as too discreditable to the Austrian army. Yet the full text had been printed by Karajan, *Feierliche Sitzungsberichte KAW* (1865), 44.
[72] Arneth, *MTuJ* II, pp. 331–2.

accompanied by a covering letter, genuinely composed by Maria Theresa, in which she spoke of her maternal anxiety for Joseph – and also for Max Franz and Albert, both serving with the army – and told Frederick she was writing without the emperor's knowledge.[73]

Meanwhile, Joseph's letters grew more alarmist still. On the 9th he had not been able to sleep: 'When I shut my eyes, what terrible thoughts come into my mind about our situation and our future actions!' Two days later: 'If some way could be found of restoring peace on moderately fair terms, it would be a great benefit, but I don't see how it's to be done.' On the 12th:

It is certain that war is a horrible thing. The evils that it leads to are frightful, and . . . it is much worse than I had visualised. If there was a way of shortening it or inducing France and Russia to mediate a reasonable arrangement, that would be the best. I certainly don't say this as a coward, but as a man and a citizen, for its frightful to see what people have suffered in eight days and what they will suffer in future.

This very minute the officer of the guard comes to bring me your precious letter [of the 11th]. If I wanted to reply to it, I could not. I can only assure you that it has brought tears to my eyes, and that my admiration for its sublime manner of thinking equals my gratitude. How happy I am to have such a mother and such a sovereign, and I should have much to blame myself for if this precious blood that you have poured into my veins should ever be false to itself. No, dear mother. You can rest assured that I shall redouble my efforts, to serve you . . . as you deserve . . . I see again the great, the incomparable Maria Theresa. She will discover and employ the necessary means to sustain her armies, her states and her reputation.[74]

This is the moment of closest accord between mother and son: Joseph has apparently come round to Maria Theresa's view of the situation; she seems to be ready to second all his endeavours; and their mutual love finds full expression.

Three days later he received her letter of the 13th, which informed him of Thugut's mission. In it she remarked that she would have sent off Thugut more calmly if by then she had had Joseph's letter of the 11th, sighing for peace. But in any case she intends to take the whole blame on herself. Joseph reacted hysterically:

---

[73] M.T. to K., 11 July 1778 (Arneth, *GMT* x, p. 809). Much material in HHSA SKV 126. Arneth, *ibid.*, ch. 13 is devoted to Thugut's mission. See for this and later negotiations A. Beer, 'Die Sendung Thugut's in das preussische Hauptquartier und der Friede von Teschen', *HZ*, XXXVIII (1877), 403–76 – but Arneth, *GMT* x, pp. 817–19, corrects it on several points. *PC* XLI, p. 265.

  The exact role of K. is difficult to evaluate. He suggested the sending of Thugut; M.T. gave into him over the form of the instructions. In her letter to Mercy of 31 July (Arneth & Geffroy III, p. 230) she says: 'Je n'ai pas fait ce pas de ma tête seule; Kaunitz l'a proposé pour me consoler.' But it seems probable that she took the original decision and galvanised K. thereafter. Bernard, *J. II and Bavaria*, pp. 112–13 seems to misunderstand Guglia, *M.T.*, vol. II, p. 316. See Arneth, *GMT* x, pp. 449–52, 809; Aretin, *ZBL* (1962), 775.

[74] J. to M.T., 9, 11 and 12 July 1778 (Arneth, *MTuJ* II, pp. 330, 333–5).

The king of Prussia is certain . . . to make ridiculous and unacceptable propositions [in return]. We are telling him that all the forces of the Monarchy are nothing and that, when he wants something, we're obliged to consent . . . I declare I find the action as injurious as possible . . . This step moreover proves that YM is entirely displeased with my efforts, that she disapproves and condemns them. What course remains to me but to abandon everything and to get away, I don't know where, to Italy, without passing through Vienna, [but] keeping up appearances and giving the action a semblance of plausibility?

He devoutly hopes the king will refuse the terms. Otherwise, 'with the honour of the Monarchy, your reputation and mine compromised by this move, if I want to rescue both, I'm unhappily compelled to make a public demonstration of the difference in our opinions and to publicise YM's personal weakness, in order to preserve the stability of the state'.[75]

Frederick welcomed the empress's approach, and undertook not to put her family at risk while negotiations continued. But, stiffened by his ministers, he soon made awkward counter-proposals.[76] Joseph's attitude fluctuated wildly. On the same day as he had threatened to escape to Italy, he wrote a second time to his mother submitting to her authority. Presumably it was between these two letters that he corresponded with Laudon: Joseph told him of the peace move, expressed his indignation and spoke of leaving for Florence; Laudon replied urging him to 'show a truly great soul', to stay at his post and, if peace was made, to resume his work of improving the army so that one day war could be waged against Prussia with hope of success.[77]

The emperor did not abandon the army, but he continued to rant against the negotiations. He said they made his position with the army intolerable. One day he claimed they would make a lasting settlement impossible; another day they would allow Frederick to retreat in good order. He declined to give any opinion on detailed peace propositions. He refused to receive Thugut. He repeatedly asked for more troops: 'If YM prefers energy and vigour to discouragement and humiliation, means will be found to defend ourselves, even perhaps advantageously.' But he warned her that it might soon be necessary to retreat behind Prague, and to leave Bohemia to the mercy of Prussian troops for the winter. Maria Theresa could not resist pointing out that she had never had so many troops in any of her previous wars as Joseph now commanded. 'That', she wrote bitterly to Mercy, 'restores the credit of prince Charles [of Lorraine] and [marshal] Daun, who were called unadven-

---

[75] M.T. to J., 13 July 1778; J. to M.T., 15 July 1778 (Arneth, *MTuJ* II, pp. 336–8, 341–2).

[76] Frederick to M.T., 17, 25 and 28 July 1778 (*PC* XLI, pp. 265–6, 288, 296–8). Aretin, *ZBL* (1962), 774–5.

[77] J. to M.T., 15 July 1778 (Arneth, *MTuJ* II, p. 343); letters between Laudon and J. in Arneth, *GMT* X, pp. 458–60.

turous; at least they held things together.' She intensified her efforts for peace.[78]

Her task was further complicated by the emperor's breach with Kaunitz. On one occasion the chancellor composed necessary documents in German, so that in Maria Theresa's French translation they would sound like her own work and not his. On another, he begged her not to send one of his reports on to Joseph.[79]

At the beginning of August she tried to enlist her son's support in advance for a revised approach to Frederick. She would now demand only the strip of Bavaria between the Austrian frontier and the river Inn – or an even smaller portion – in return for her recognition of Prussia's claim to Ansbach and Bayreuth. She made a point of marking the map herself, so that Kaunitz should not be held responsible. Her own preference, she told Joseph, would be to surrender the whole of Bavaria on condition that Frederick gave up Ansbach and Bayreuth; but she felt sure the king would not accept that.[80]

The emperor began his reply by refusing to take the slightest part in the negotiation, 'the consequences of which have always seemed to me, and always will seem to me, dishonourable, harmful and shameful . . . I would . . . say nothing else if my respectful affection did not drag an opinion from me.' She must make up her own mind for peace or war; it is entirely her decision. He 'will subscribe to it, having no right for the present' to challenge it. But

if there's already a desire to take this step, [then] the only course that seems to me acceptable is still to give everything back to the elector of Bavaria and let the king of Prussia have nothing, assuming that . . . with the enemy in Bohemia, we can contemplate doing anything but fight each other – and let the *Reichstag* settle the matter in the cases of Saxony and the other claimants.[81]

So, while emphatically declining to advise his mother, he advised her all the same. What is more, he supported her own preferred position.

Maria Theresa gave the marked maps to Thugut nonetheless, but Frederick rejected both her proposals of territorial adjustment. It thus appeared that she and Kaunitz had been wrong to blame the emperor for the failure of earlier negotiations. They had now themselves failed in a line of policy deliberately initiated without Joseph's knowledge and pursued against his advice. The plan of mutual renunciation, preferred by both ruler and co-regent, was finally

---

[78] The quotations come from J. to M.T., 26 July 1778 (Arneth, *MTuJ* II, p. 372) and M.T. to Mercy, 31 July 1778 (Arneth & Geffroy III, p. 231). Other points from *MTuJ* II, letters of July and *MTuJ* III, letters of Aug.

[79] Arneth, *GMT* X, pp. 470–4.

[80] M.T. to J., 2 Aug. 1778 (Arneth, *MTuJ* III, pp. 2–6). Cf. her appeal of 31 July 1778 (*ibid.*, II pp. 380–4). In a note of 3 Aug. (HHSA SKV 127) she explained to K. that she had deliberately refrained from showing him her most recent letters in order to be able to say that he had not been informed of them, and especially of the line she had drawn on the map.

[81] J. to M.T., 4 Aug. 1778 (Arneth, *MTuJ* III, pp. 12–14).

put to the king, but he rejected that too. He told his brother: 'Now we shall have to beat the Austrian buggers, to bring them to a more reasonable frame of mind.'[82]

At this stage, in August, the war was going badly for the Monarchy. Prince Henry, commanding the Prussian troops on the western sector of the front, had broken through into Bohemia and was pressing Laudon's army hard. If the latter's positions became indefensible, as seemed likely, they would have to be abandoned. The other Austrian army, under Joseph and Lacy, would then also have to retreat to avoid being cut off. Hence Prague and the whole of Bohemia would be at Frederick's mercy. Until early September this nightmare seemed always on the point of realisation.

So Joseph was under immense strain in his military capacity, over and above the stress of the peace negotiations. He described his day to Leopold:

War is a horrible thing – the ravaging of fields and villages, the lamentations of the poor peasants, in short the ruin of so many innocent people, the ferment one is caught up in day and night. For my life goes like this: I have to be up and about before dawn, because this is the critical moment. At this time of year you have to be on horseback at three in the morning; then comes the heat of the day; and with the cool of the evening you have to be in bed, before eight o'clock. During the hours when I'm in bed, people come and wake me two or three times with messages. Sometimes I have to write something. You can imagine how easy it is to get to sleep again. Only exhaustion makes it possible. The importance of everything, however small, because it may turn out to be of the greatest consequence, the resulting anxiety to know whether one's judgement has been right – this makes it a dog's life. But you gradually get used to it.[83]

He depended heavily on Lacy, and often told him so. 'The nearer we approach to the rise of the curtain, the more I need the advice of a mind and spirit like yours, and the indulgence of your friendship for my inexperience.' 'I count for nothing without you, and the sure confidence that your opinions give me are [*sic*] my guides in this difficult career.' But Joseph was nonetheless the effective and a most active commander-in-chief – according to the princesses, too active, at least in small matters.[84] He did not again lose his nerve.

His letters to his mother give a striking if egocentric picture of the vicissitudes and crises of the campaign. On 2 August he repeated his earlier warnings of retreat, but said he had resolved not to evacuate Bohemia without first fighting a battle. The very next day, Laudon had already withdrawn so far that Joseph's position was threatened. On the 5th he despatched reinforcements, to encourage Laudon to make a stand. But on the 10th the marshal sent from Münchengrätz to say he could hold the line no longer and doubted the

---

[82] *PC* XLI, pp. 316, 331–42, 363–2 – the quotation from Frederick to prince Henry, 11 Aug. 1778 (p. 349); Arneth, *GMT* X, pp. 478–96; Aretin, *ZBL* (1962), 774–5.

[83] J. to L., 18 July 1778 (Arneth, *MTuJ* II, pp. 351–2).

[84] Arneth, *GMT* X, pp. 812, 816 (J. to Lacy, 27 June and 2 Nov. 1778). E.L. to L.K., 13 Oct. and L.K. to E.L. 18 Oct. 1778 (SOALpZ, LRRA P. 17/24).

wisdom of risking a battle; he favoured retreat. Enclosing this letter to his mother Joseph wrote: 'the only thing to be done is to go at once to Laudon myself, with a single carriage, to get some idea of the state of affairs, because it's of the utmost importance that we should not leave our position except in the last extremity'. He found Laudon 'very disturbed and irresolute', and out of touch with his generals. On the 14th:

I must speak clearly: marshal Laudon lost his head – quite comprehensively – when prince Henry advanced . . . He fled – you can call it that – without firing a shot, without having seen the enemy, as far as here [Münchengrätz]. In so doing he abandoned the Elbe, allowed the enemy to debouch from the mountains without the least resistance . . . he has not been able to withdraw all his artillery, and he was on the point of leaving here if I hadn't been on the spot; the tents had already been taken down. I can't describe to YM my condition, my anguish, the pressure on me, and the violent situation I find myself in. A hundred projects, all of them disputed, and continual vacillation. He's in despair over what he's done . . . he wishes he were dead, but the evil is past remedy, and as soon as the line is breached, if peace doesn't come beforehand – and, if peace is going to be made, the sooner the better – we shall be behind the Elbe and the king will have the whole land to himself.

Encouraged by the emperor, Laudon held his ground, but for the next few weeks Joseph regularly reported that there seemed little hope of preventing an advance by prince Henry, which would lead to retreat by both wings of the Austrian army.[85]

In these circumstances Maria Theresa naturally persisted in attempts at negotiation. At the end of August she sent count Rosenberg to Joseph, bearing proposals from Kaunitz about various ways and means of obtaining peace by concessions, partition schemes, appeal to the *Reichstag*, mediation and so forth. She had told Marie Antoinette:

There was a bit of ill feeling between us over the negotiation, but I hope that that will soon change, and I intend sending Rosenberg to the emperor . . . This dispute was aggravating my worries, and I look forward to its early end, and I believe that we're in agreement on the essential point. It was only about methods that we were taking different views.[86]

The empress must have been underplaying the disagreement with Joseph for French consumption, but at bottom she was right, as the story of Rosenberg's mission shows. He reached the emperor's camp on 28 August. His arrival was perfectly timed. While they were talking, a message came from Laudon that, subject to confirmation of news about Prussian movements, his retreat was inevitable. The emperor was therefore compelled to set in train arrangements to withdraw his own army. He had no more time for detailed discussions and

[85] Arneth, *MTuJ* III, pp. 7–8, 10–11, 15–16, 37–8, 37–9n, 44, 48–9, 55, 58, 70, 73–4 etc. Cf. Criste, *Kriege*, pp. 100–1.
[86] M.T. to M.A., 23 Aug. 1778 (Arneth & Geffroy III, p. 246).

did not read Kaunitz's memoranda. Under the strongest pressure from Lacy as well as from Rosenberg, Joseph gave his mother *carte blanche* to make a speedy peace by a renewed approach to the king of Prussia. Rosenberg at once left the frenzied camp and returned post-haste to Vienna with the emperor's letter:

There are only two courses to choose from, either to make peace as soon as possible at any price – and for that every day is precious – or wage all-out war ... Mediation, neutrality, all that is very fine and large; [but] immediate remedies are necessary. Give the king of Prussia what he asks for, and bring hostilities to an end, everything is then settled. Otherwise abandon hope of expelling him from Bohemia and Prague this winter...[87]

Communication delays between the front and Vienna mattered greatly at this stage. Having received this letter of Joseph's, Maria Theresa was ready not only to abandon any claims on Bavaria but also to let Frederick assert his rights over Ansbach and Bayreuth without further question. She had a letter to the king drafted, which embodied this proposition. But Kaunitz declined to approve such an abject surrender, insisting that the scheme must first be submitted to the emperor. More encouraging reports now began to come from Joseph. He wrote on the 29th: 'Marshal Laudon sent me three letters today; the first said he was staying put, the second that he was leaving, and the third that he was staying put again, so I shan't be moving either.' On the 30th he was calculating that, if only he could maintain his position for six more days, Frederick himself would have to retreat. The weather was atrocious; snow fell on 1 September. The Prussians were suffering from illness, desertions and shortage of supplies. The emperor's hopes mounted. So, when Maria Theresa's new proposal reached him on 5 September, he rejected it. She wrote:

I cannot blame you for returning my letter, although I should have liked it sent on to its destination. But you think as a *statesman*, I as mother and woman ... but I must, all the same, point out exactly when this letter was written. Rosenberg and your letter of the 28th told us you were retreating, and Bohemia was lost for the whole winter ... Things have changed...

No doubt she had also been influenced by the first reports from Joseph that Max Franz was ill.[88]

This incident led to reconciliation between Joseph and Kaunitz. The

---

[87] J. to M.T., 28 Aug. 1778 (Arneth, *MTuJ* III, pp. 73–4); Rosenberg to M.T., same day (*ibid.*, p. 74n); Arneth & Geffroy III, p. 248n. It appears that J. at first wrote an unequivocal *carte blanche* and then tore it up. However, the letter of 28 Aug. is clear enough, and was relied on in Vienna (HHSA SKV 127, K.'s *Vortrag* of 2 Sep. 1778). Arneth, *GMT* X, pp. 515–19, is valuable but lacks the evidence of Arneth & Geffroy, and seems to underrate the success of Rosenberg's mission.

[88] Arneth, *GMT* X, pp. 519–22, 814. J. to M.T., 29, 30, 31 Aug. and 5 Sep. 1778 (Arneth, *MTuJ* III, pp. 76–7, 80, 92). M.T. to J., 2 and 7 Sep. (*ibid.*, pp. 82, 95). Drafts of her letter to Frederick in HHSA SKV 127. Frederick to prince Henry, 4 Sep. 1778 (*PC* XLI, p. 415).

emperor wrote to the chancellor on 7 September that he had always found it hard to believe that recent peace plans emanated from 'your office, where I have so often, with so much pleasure, and from teaching both clear and sound, imbibed principles and fashioned my proposals'. Kaunitz replied circumspectly and reprovingly. He had given advice only when asked for it; he did not claim for himself infallibility, but rectitude; he was glad that Joseph adhered to the position that, if all Bavaria was to be surrendered, it must be in return for Frederick's renunciation of his claims to Ansbach and Bayreuth.

But I cannot conceal from you that it would have been much more agreeable to me to know [your views] than to have to guess them, and that it seems to me that for the advantage of your service it would be desirable that in the future you should think it proper not to expose me again to the risk of having to guess.[89]

In the middle of September both Prussian armies retreated. Bohemia was saved. Joseph justly ascribed the credit for this achievement, in private and in public, to Lacy's choice of positions that Frederick and his brother could not breach.[90] This was not the end of the campaign, but it was the turning-point. In the later stages the emperor was left at the front, to his great alarm, without the support of Lacy's presence, but no disaster occurred. Having failed to pursue the Prussians very vigorously, and then established his army in its winter quarters, Joseph arrived back in Vienna, surprising his mother in church, on 22 November.[91]

Disputes about peace-plans had continued during these months despite the restoration of more normal relations between emperor, empress and chancellor. Joseph would neither take any personal part in the negotiations nor publicly approve them. His general line in October was to oppose Kaunitz's elaborate schemes for drumming up support in Poland or the *Reich*, and anything involving the delays of an international congress; to scoff at any idea of relying on French sympathy or assistance; and to reject the notion that Russia would intervene on the side of her ally, Prussia. However, he admitted that, if she did, the situation would be grave indeed.

At the end of October it looked as though the dreaded moment had come. After Austria had requested Catherine's mediation but before the letter had reached its distant destination, the Russian ambassador in Vienna delivered to Kaunitz a strong criticism of the Monarchy's policy. It was learned that Russian troops were being sent to the aid of Prussia. In this emergency the

[89] Arneth, *GMT* x, pp. 522–6, 814–15. The actual letters between J. and K. are in HHSA FA Sbde 70 (J. to K., 7 Sep. 1778) and HHSA SKV 127 (K. to J., 11 Sep.).

[90] Criste, *Kriege*, pp. 106–10; Arneth, *GMT* x, pp. 526–31. J. to M.T., 19 Sep. 1778 (Arneth, *MTuJ* III, p. 122). L.K. to E.L. 26 Sep. 1778 (SOALpZ, LRRA P. 17/24).

[91] J. to M.T., 30 Oct. 1778 (Arneth, *MTuJ* III, p. 169). M.T. to Maria Beatrix, 22 Nov. (Arneth, *MTKuF* III, p. 334). Cf. J. to Lacy, 26 Oct., 4 and 19 Nov. (Arneth, *GMT* x, pp. 815–16, 818). For the question whether J. was to blame for the failure to pursue the Prussians, see below pp. 415–17.

empress asked Joseph to come to Vienna for consultation. He refused, unless explicitly ordered to do so, saying that his presence with the army was indispensable. But he did state his grudging readiness to subscribe to his mother's decisions.[92]

Early in November, under this pressure, he discussed affairs in a new tone of sweet reasonableness. On the 2nd he actually begged his mother to settle the question of peace before he returned to the capital; he acknowledged that he was 'perhaps idiosyncratic', and that 'circumstances and personalities' made 'very vigorous policies' 'inopportune'. He showed his usual inconsistency, it is true. On the 6th he addressed a lucid and considered statement to Kaunitz embodying more positive views: he returned to his doubts about Russian intervention and expressed fears about too rapid pacification; the military situation, he said, rather favoured the Monarchy; abject surrender was out of the question; he raised again the possibility of exchanging all Bavaria for the whole of the Austrian Netherlands, whatever their relative revenues. When Lacy, who had been pleading ill-health to excuse himself from another campaign, consented to serve again, the emperor gave way to warlike fervour: 'I shall try to obtain proper advantage from it, especially with the Russians ... With you and an army I'm afraid of nothing. We shall just have to go and beat one [country] after the other.' But on the 16th he laid bare in a remarkable letter to his mother a different range of thoughts and feelings:

It seems to me essential that we make an immediate reply to Russia and either accept mediation; or first state how far we'll go, in the manner of an ultimatum; or remit the whole question to negotiations at the *Reichstag* and to its decisions; and that, when we give up Bavaria, the mediators should bring about a suspension of hostilities, or even a peace between the king of Prussia and ourselves ... If a peace like that must now be made, the sooner the better ... All this amounts to unhappy expedients. Undoubtedly the quickest and most satisfactory course would be to say: 'I'm in possession of Bavaria by right of cession. If it is taken from me, I'll defend myself.'

... I speak against myself ... but as I see things there is nothing else for it [but peace]. I think I'm all the more obliged to say so because, considered quite impartially, this war is directed against me personally rather than against the Monarchy. I've so often sacrificed myself to its wellbeing that I don't even consult my own feelings about the great effect it will have on my reputation, with results that will rebound on me alone.

As the empress told Kaunitz, 'the emperor's letter gives us freedom to proceed ... I was most touched by his conclusion'. In her resolution she omitted

---

[92] For this and the previous paragraph, J. to M.T., 18, 23, 30 Oct. and 1 Nov. 1778 (Arneth, *MTuJ* III, pp. 153–4, 160–1, 170–1, 174–5); M.T. to J. and K. to J., 29 Oct. 1778 (*ibid.*, pp. 167–8; Arneth, *GMT* x, pp. 543–57); J. to Lacy, 1 Nov. 1778 (*ibid.*, p. 817).

On Russia's attitude, Unzer, *Friede von Teschen*, chs. 5 and 6. Aretin, *Reich*, vol. I, pp. 119–26, lays great stress on K.'s attempts to involve the Empire in mediation, but they came to nothing, and J. and M.T. had little time for them. See n. 130 below.

quoting from this handsome recantation: 'although it will stay among the documents, the emperor never wants it to be cited'.[93]

Even with Joseph so co-operative, Maria Theresa could not get matters arranged before he returned to Vienna. She described the situation to Mercy:

> I sympathise with all the pain that the emperor and prince Kaunitz feel at appearing to be the authors of a peace which can scarcely be very honourable. But since I acknowledge its indispensable necessity, my love for my House and the Monarchy as well as for humanity makes me shoulder the whole blame ... I don't recognise [Kaunitz] in this business. He's concerned with protecting his reputation, and apparently inspired by Binder's pipedreams. He too easily persuades himself that he'll be able to find some way out as events develop, which makes him spin out decisions.

Only after Joseph's return did the chancellor produce a draft with 'a rapidity very different from his customary pace'. The empress wanted speedy acceptance of mediation and a declaration of readiness to abandon Bavaria, in hopes of avoiding any long drawn-out negotiations and especially the calling of a congress. Kaunitz and Joseph, on the other hand, still hoped to salvage something to the advantage of Austria from the peacemaking process. Eventually, on 25 November, the response to Russia was despatched, at the same time as a reply to the other Power willing to mediate, France. In these documents mediation was welcomed and a congress deprecated, but it was left unstated what terms the Monarchy was prepared to accept.[94] Even so, with Russia poised to impose a settlement, an early peace was now probable.

Plans were being made in case another campaign proved necessary, and they were largely carried through in order to buttress Austria's negotiating position.[95] It was expected that nearly 400,000 troops would be fielded in 1779, an unparalleled achievement requiring enormous expenditure of money and effort.[96] But as it turned out, the campaign of 1778 constituted the only significant fighting of the war.

It had been a curious affair. Wraxall gathered views about it while visiting both Saxony and Austria during this winter. 'No campaign in the course of the present century', he wrote, 'has more disappointed expectation, produced fewer events, or been attended with so inconsiderable an effusion of blood.'[97] On the Prussian side the troops were said to have been occupied digging up potatoes; on the Austrian side, picking plums.[98] A war without battles

[93] J. to M.T., 2 and 16 Nov. 1778 (Arneth, *MTuJ* III, pp. 178, 193–4); J. to K., 6 Nov. (*ibid.*, pp. 184–9n); J. to Lacy, 8 and 10 Nov. (Arneth, *GMT* x, pp. 821–2); Beer, *HZ* (1877), 457–8.

[94] M.T. to Mercy, 25 Nov. 1778 (Arneth & Geffroy III, pp. 268–9); Arneth, *GMT* x, pp. 572–81; Unzer, *Friede von Teschen*, esp. pp. 248–57. On France's attitude, Murphy, *Vergennes*, ch. 24.

[95] These preparations were a matter for much discussion in the correspondence betwen M.T. and J. in September, October and November. K. wrote long memoranda on the question on 7 Sep. and 2 Oct. (HHSA SKV 127), summarised in Arneth, *GMT* x, pp. 524–5, 539–40.

[96] See Criste, *Kriege*, pp. 116–18; Nosinich and Wiener, *Kaiser J. II.*, pp. 217–21.

[97] Wraxall, *Memoirs*, vol. II, p. 164.   [98] W. von Janko, *Laudon's Leben* (Vienna, 1869), p. 375.

corresponded to the ideal of some contemporary military theorists, and it aroused interest again in 1915 as an anticipation of trench warfare. But it has usually been treated as the *reductio ad absurdum* of eighteenth-century warfare.[99] Frederick and Henry were much criticised by their subordinates, and Joseph and Lacy by theirs, for failing to provoke a decisive action.[100]

In detail, Wraxall quoted comments heard in Vienna that the Austrian campaign had been so inglorious that defeat would have been preferable; that the Prussians had been allowed to plunder Bohemia, and then to retreat, with impunity; that Laudon would have fallen on prince Henry's retreating army if Joseph had not driven over and prevented him; that 'the Emperor breathes war, but knows not how to conduct it, though for our misfortune, he aspires to superintend all the operations in person'. Prince Albert blamed Joseph for having acted before the war as though his army could stand up to the Prussians, and then claiming it was inadequate and needed massive reinforcements.[101]

Of course an outright Austrian victory would have been more glorious than the shadow-boxing of 1778. But the Monarchy's armies had seldom managed to defeat Frederick's, and the spectacle of the king and his brother retreating from Bohemia, however skilfully, made a considerable impression in other countries.[102] The Prussians, after all, were thought to have possessed numerical superiority at this stage. For the campaign of 1779 it would be the other way round, unless Russia intervened in strength. The Monarchy's bargaining position had been improved by these months of inconclusive manoeuvring.

Laudon, alone among Austrian generals, had a reputation for successful aggression. Kaunitz admired him, and believed he was treated unfairly by Joseph and Lacy. But Laudon did not perform well in this campaign. Attractive though his idea of a surprise offensive in the first days of the war may sound, it was clearly very risky, especially since entirely unprepared. Despite the claims of his partisans, his conduct during the rest of the campaign belies the view that with adequate support he could have won dazzling victories. He evidently disgraced himself in late July and August when he allowed prince Henry to break through and threaten his well-chosen position. At this moment, by forbidding withdrawal, Joseph saved his marshal's reputation and career as well as the campaign. Later, the emperor unsuccessfully urged him to pursue the retreating Prussians; but when he

---

[99] The marshal de Saxe was one theorist who reckoned avoidance of battles the mark of good generalship (see Clausewitz, *On War*, p. 670, essay by B. Brodie). Temperley, *Frederic and Joseph*, pp. 119, 150 and n., 242–4. McKay and Scott, *Rise of the Great Powers*, p. 231.

[100] E.g. Wraxall, *Memoirs*, vol. II, pp. 164–6.

[101] *Ibid.*, vol. II, pp. 217–21. Albert's memoirs quoted by Arneth, *GMT* x, p. 808. These points are all echoed in the correspondence between E.L. and L.K. (SOALpZ, LRRA P. 17/24).

[102] E.g. M.A. to M.T., 17 Oct. 1778 (Arneth & Geffroy III, pp. 257–8); Unzer, *Friede von Teschen*, pp. 122, 243–4; Temperley, *Frederic and Joseph*, pp. 140–3. Cf. Criste, *Kriege*, pp. 133–4 and 134n.

drove over, found Laudon incapable of initiative, prostrated with diarrhoea.[103]

There was certainly a contrast between Joseph's firmness during the negotiations of May and June, and his near-panic at the outbreak of war. But he had never claimed the army to be sure of success; rather, he hoped and believed that war would be avoided, while maintaining that Prussia's terms were simply too humiliating to be accepted even if rejection meant war. Maria Theresa blamed prince Albert himself, Laudon, Lacy and Hadik – not Joseph – for having exaggerated the preparedness of the army, 'playing courtiers'. Experience had made her deeply pessimistic about her soldiers. She wrote to her son before the war:

Here is Lacy worn out. Laudon will hardly last, and the fat Hadik is perhaps an even greater liability . . . It is for this reason that we've lost all our battles and that the fruits even of the victories have eluded us. Our troops, when well led, have always done their duty.[104]

This defeatism was hardly calculated to encourage confident leadership in Joseph.

He sometimes complained that it was her orders that tied him down to defence, and there were occasions when he deplored the caution of his generals, even Lacy.[105] But there is no evidence that he himself had the capacity for aggressive generalship, and his whole bent was towards Lacy's defensive approach. His initial panic must be held against him – though even the great Frederick had lost his nerve at Mollwitz in 1741. Once the emperor had passed that moment, it is agreed that he showed personal courage, steadfastness and immense energy. He also won admiration by sharing the hardships of his troops.[106] With Lacy and Laudon both elderly and prone to illness, Joseph's normal reluctance to delegate was intensified and justified. There was some ground not only for his mother's concern at his overtaxing himself, but also for her alarm 'that your presence seems to be required everywhere to put matters right'.[107]

People thought Joseph drove his subordinates too hard, and feared that his inexperience and temperament would lead to rash initiatives. But in fact his moderation in military questions was striking. He continually deferred to Lacy. He refrained – perhaps on Lacy's advice – from publicly condemning

103 Cf. Janko, *Laudon's Leben*, esp. pp. 385–6; Temperley, *Frederic and Joseph*, pp. 146, 247; J. to M.T., 14 and 24 Sep. 1778 (Arneth, *MTuJ* III, pp. 110, 126). See below, p. 419n. The role of Laudon, and K.'s exaggerated opinion of him, are constant themes of the correspondence between E.L. and L.K. during the war (SOALpZ, LRRA P. 17/24).
104 For J.'s position before the war, his letters of April to June in Arneth, *MTuJ* II. M.T. to J., 20 June 1778 (*ibid.*, p. 298). M.T. to Mercy, 31 July 1778 (Arneth & Geffroy III, p. 231).
105 J. to M.T., 29 July and 16 August 1778 (Arneth, *MTuJ* II, pp. 376–7; III, p. 54); J. to Lacy, 19 Nov. (Arneth, *GMT* x, p. 818); E.L. to L.K., 19 Sep. 1778 (SOALpZ, LRRA P. 17/24).
106 Temperley, *Frederic and Joseph*, pp. 146–7; Wraxall, *Memoirs*, vol. II, pp. 22, 462–4.
107 M.T. to J., esp. 8 Aug. and 10 Oct. 1778 (Arneth, *MTuJ* III, pp. 23, 146–7).

Laudon's errors, which the empress would have treated more severely, in order not 'to destroy the marshal's credit, which I want to preserve to him for some great occasion, when he may become very necessary'. This magnanimity should be remembered in Joseph's favour when Laudon's capture of Belgrade in 1789 is applauded. And at the end of the campaign, when he was pressing for an attack on some positions newly seized by the Prussians, he bowed to the advice of subordinates whom he thought too timid, because 'with people so obstinate how could the simplest thing be carried through?'[108] He showed no genius, but some judgement.

His difficulties were compounded by the incompatibility between the three roles he was required to play, those of commander-in-chief, emperor and co-regent. The role of emperor proved almost pure embarrassment. It was easy for Frederick to exploit the ambiguities in Joseph's position, laying emphasis on his supposed claim to occupy and dispose of lapsed imperial fiefs. That Joseph was acting as commander-in-chief and co-regent of one of the parties in a German civil war obviously compromised his imperial position. It was a further complication for him that he would have to subscribe as emperor to the ultimate settlement. In this dispute the advantages to the Habsburgs of possessing the imperial crown were far outweighed by the disadvantages.[109]

As usual, the greatest problems arose with the role of co-regent. In recent years Joseph had been permitted to run some, and influence many, aspects of the Monarchy's affairs, especially its foreign policy. Until war broke out, Maria Theresa had allowed him and Kaunitz to promote their Bavarian scheme with much protest but little interference. On 11 July she reasserted her latent absolute power. She deliberately took her decision to seek peace without consulting Joseph, and at first without even telling him. The manner of her approach to Frederick – parading her maternal anxieties – whether instinctive or calculated, was bound to seem particularly dishonourable to Joseph. She was in effect asking for special treatment for him on the battlefield. She also told Lacy that 'the most important consideration for the Monarchy [and] for me is the security of the emperor's person'. As Joseph said, his health as son and heir was being valued above his honour as soldier and ruler.[110] She was humiliating him at a time when he needed maximum prestige as commander-in-chief. If she proposed ever to take such a line, she should never have groomed him for the leadership of the army in the field, or made him co-regent. He expressed his anguish to Leopold: 'To be duped for

[108] J. to M.T., 14 Aug. 1778; M.T. to J., 16 Aug. (Arneth, *MTuJ* III, pp. 49, 51–2); J. to Lacy, 19 Nov. (Arneth, *GMT* x, p. 818). See the correspondence of E.L. and L.K., esp. E.L.'s letters of 22 and 26 Sep. and 13 Oct. 1778 (SOALpZ, LRRA P. 17/24). J. is shown with his principal generals in Plate 16b.
[109] See esp. Aretin, *Reich*, vol. I, p. 123.
[110] M.T. to Lacy, n.d. [1778] (HHSA NL, Karton 2); J. to M.T., 16 Aug. 1778 (Arneth, *MTuJ* III, p. 54).

sixteen years is intolerable, and it's high time I ceased to be so and that I performed this service to the state, of sparing it the embarrassment of two wills.' The episode destroyed his confidence that he could ultimately rely on his mother's word.[111] His bitterness is understandable, even if her actions are deemed right.

On the other hand, Joseph had given her justification for embarking on peace negotiations by his alarmist letters of the early days of the war. Moreover, after the initial approach to Frederick through Thugut, a kind of dialogue took place between mother and son, however grudging on his side. At this time the process of decision-making in the Monarchy certainly reached a low point in terms of goodwill and fair dealing. It is hard to know whether to castigate or to ridicule the conduct of 'the three sovereigns', as the French ambassador called them:[112] Kaunitz's pretence that he was taking no initiatives in offering advice, his unwillingness to let the emperor see his memoranda, his sulks, *amour-propre* and delays, his over-elaborate scheming; Maria Theresa's translating the chancellor's German into French, marking lines on maps, writing to Lacy through an intermediary on low-quality paper, concealing Joseph's and Kaunitz's letters from each other, exploiting her motherhood; the emperor's hysteria, his refusal for several weeks to communicate with the chancellor, and his attempts to avoid responsibility for the peace he could not help advising. He wrote frequent indiscreet letters to Eleonore about the military position and his feelings of desperation; princess Francis heard regularly from Lacy, whose 'discontent . . . resembles despair'; countess Kaunitz saw the chancellor 'overwhelmed', 'depressed', 'pained' and 'indignant', especially with Joseph and Lacy; and she and her sister knew Maria Theresa to be 'capable of anything, at once violent and timorous'. They thought the Monarchy 'within an ace of destruction'.[113] But somehow a line of policy was adopted which owed something to all three principals; and though arrived at in this preposterous fashion, it proved reasonably successful. Maria Theresa's original approach to Frederick began the process of restoring the Monarchy's international position. The offer to abandon the whole of Bavaria if Prussia would withdraw her claims to Ansbach and Bayreuth carried it further. As soon as the details of the negotiation were known, the Monarchy's standing in the Empire and with other Powers dramatically improved. The king's refusal to surrender his claims branded him as rapacious while Austria now appeared disinterested.[114] Vienna's acceptance of mediation not only removed the immediate threat of armed

---

[111] J. to L., 8 Aug. 1778 (Arneth, *MTuJ* III, p. 29); J. to K., 30 Mar. 1780 (HHSA FA Sbde 70).

[112] Unzer, *Friede von Teschen*, p. 250.

[113] Neither J.'s letters to Eleonore nor Lacy's to princess Francis seem to survive, but they are often quoted and summarised in E.L.'s letters to L.K. The main quotations come from E.L. to L.K., 21 July, and L.K. to E.L., 18 Oct. 1778 (SOALpZ, LRRA P 17/24).

[114] *Ibid.*, pp. 111–13, but cf. 241. Aretin, *ZBL* (1962), 775.

intervention by Russia, but also strengthened the Monarchy's negotiating position.

As between the members of the triumvirate, Maria Theresa was primarily responsible for this shift of policy. The chancellor proved fertile in expedients but, as the empress complained, did not pursue a consistent and straight-forward line. Joseph gave him the credit for the proposal that placed Frederick in the wrong,[115] but it was in fact the emperor who insisted on adhering to this stance. He also supported his mother in rejecting some of Kaunitz's elaborate and time-wasting combinations involving the *Reich*, Poland and territorial exchanges. If there must be peace, he often said, let it come as quickly as possible. On the other side, he backed Kaunitz when Maria Theresa proposed surrendering the whole of Bavaria unconditionally, a defeatist step that would have left the Monarchy utterly humiliated. As she acknowledged, he was thinking as a statesman while she was inclined to ignore ordinary criteria of foreign policy.[116] So, despite his violent objections to the negotiations, his contribution to the peace offensive was neither negligible nor unconstructive.

No war has more fully borne out Clausewitz's dictum: 'Policy will permeate all military operations, and, in so far as their violent nature will admit, it will have a continuous influence on them.' But despite occasional statements from both sides that the peace negotiations inhibited military action, it seems that the main features of the campaign were unaffected by them. The Austrians' defensive posture owed more to Joseph's and Lacy's principles and to their consciousness of numerical inferiority. Frederick and Henry both tried hard to break through, and gave up because of military, not political calcula-tions.[117] But Austrian morale cannot have been strengthened by the know-ledge that Maria Theresa despaired of victory, and Frederick must have been heartened by the divisions in his enemy's camp.

The peace of Teschen

From the acceptance of mediation in late November 1778 it took almost six months of tortuous negotiation to achieve a settlement. A formal congress had to be held, which assembled on 10 March at Teschen. An armistice took effect at the same time. The peace was finally concluded on 13 May.[118]

Austria's attitude was that she would surrender nearly all the territory she

---

[115] J. to K., 5 Oct. 1778 (Arneth, *MTuJ* III, pp. 141–2nn).

[116] M.T. to J., 7 Sep. 1778 (*ibid.*, p. 95).

[117] Clausewitz, *On War*, p. 87. These conclusions appear generally justified by the correspon-dence in Arneth, *MTuJ* and *PC*. Cf. Temperley, *Frederic and Joseph*, ch. 5. Nosinich and Wiener, *Kaiser J. II.*, pp. 178–9, 198, accept J.'s claims that the peace negotiations prevented pursuit of the Prussians. But the claims seem spurious at least in Laudon's case (see above, pp. 415–16); and Criste, *Kriege*, writes of J.'s hot pursuit of Frederick (p. 110).

[118] For the peace in general, in English Temperley, *Frederic and Joseph*, ch. 7; Unzer, *Friede von Teschen*, chs. 6 and 7; Arneth, *GMT* x, ch. 16; Fagniez, *RH* (1922), 177–205.

had seized in Bavaria, would permit Prussia in due course to incorporate Ansbach and Bayreuth, and would yield rights over Bohemian fiefs and other minor points, provided that she was allowed to annex a small but significant portion of Bavaria, preferably the strip of land east of the Inn from the Danube to the Tyrol. Some such package was acceptable in principle to Prussia and the mediating Powers. But the negotiation was spun out on these and a variety of other questions: the status of the treaty of 3 January 1778; the claims of Saxony to Max Joseph's allodials in Bavaria and Bohemia; compensation to Saxony for the cost and devastation of war; compensation for the duke of Zweibrücken, and his role in the treaty-making; the rights of Karl Theodor in Jülich and Berg; and Prussia's demand to be named a guarantor of the settlement.

In this phase the Viennese triumvirate behaved according to the traditionally accepted pattern. Maria Theresa was overwhelmingly concerned with securing peace, and speedily; she was ready to make almost any concession. Joseph wished to yield as little as possible, and insisted not only on hard bargaining but also on sabre-rattling. Kaunitz picked a course between them.

The emperor's main contributions to the process were these. Militarily, he kept the threat of a renewal of the war alive by pressing forward his preparations for another campaign. In mid-January Austrian troops attacked the town of Habelschwert in the county of Glatz and took some Prussian prisoners, including a general. After some Prussian retaliation, on 28 February Neustadt in Silesia was set on fire by the Austrians. This was the result of a plan devised by Joseph without telling his mother – though of course she got to hear of it. 'Never', wrote the British envoy in Vienna, 'did there exist so strange a Mixture of Warfare and Negotiation.'[119]

On the diplomatic front, the emperor had insisted, 'by way of bargaining', that a larger slice of territory should be asked for than was likely to be conceded. He even required Kaunitz to demand some land west of the Inn, but Maria Theresa outflanked him by informing the French ambassador, who was acting as one of the two mediators, that she disapproved.[120] Later, she was ready to accept Prussia as a guarantor of the settlement; Joseph thought it an issue worth renewing the war over; while Kaunitz, by sending copies of both rulers' correspondence to the Austrian representative at Teschen, count Philipp Cobenzl, gave him the hint that he might yield the point. But on this occasion the emperor's calculation was vindicated: Frederick gave way.[121] Joseph's behaviour convinced the king that there was a real prospect of the

119 Nosinich and Wiener, *Kaiser J. II.*, pp. 210–17; Criste, *Kriege*, pp. 121–6; Arneth, *GMT* x, pp. 602–4, 608–9, 823; Keith to Suffolk, 3 Mar. 1779, cypher (PRO SP 80/221), quoted in Temperley, *Frederic and Joseph*, p. 202.
120 Arneth, *GMT* x, pp. 585–90, 820.
121 *Ibid.*, pp. 613–14, 624–30, 823–6; J. to M.T., 11 Apr. 1779 (Arneth, *MTuJ* III, pp. 206–7) (see date correction in Arneth, *GMT* x, p. 826); HHSA SKV 128.

negotiations breaking down, and clearly procured somewhat better terms for the Monarchy than Maria Theresa and Kaunitz would have obtained on their own.[122]

In the final treaties Vienna surrendered to Karl Theodor almost the whole of Bavaria including the duchy of Mindelheim and Bohemia's rights over Bavarian fiefs. Saxony was declared heir to Max Joseph's allodials, but was to give them up to Karl Theodor in return for six million florins. Bohemia's claims in Schönburg passed to Saxony. Karl Theodor's right to Jülich and Berg was affirmed, as was the right of the duke of Zweibrücken to succeed to the whole inheritance. Prussia was acknowledged heir to Ansbach and Bayreuth. The Monarchy retained a strip of formerly Bavarian land east of the Inn, christened the Innviertel by Joseph himself. France and Russia became guarantors of the settlement. Joseph had formally to accept it both as emperor and in his capacities as co-regent and heir to Maria Theresa.[123]

Although the principal objection to Austria's annexations had been that they flouted the laws of the Empire, the peace of Teschen was nonetheless imposed on the *Reich* from outside. Far the most important result of the settlement was that Russia acquired a legal standing in the affairs of the Empire. This of course had the effect of making her alliance still more valuable, and her enmity still more alarming, to a German Power.[124]

Both Prussia and Austria could claim to have gained and appear to have lost. Frederick considered the succession to Ansbach and Bayreuth of high importance. He had maintained the cause of his ally, Saxony. According to his own estimate, he had upheld the liberties of the Empire against a despotic emperor. From Joseph's standpoint, Frederick was 'an anti-Caesar protected by Russia'.[125]

The Monarchy had escaped a number of humiliations: outright condemnation of the treaty of 3 January 1778; a Prussian guarantee of the settlement; and any cession to Zweibrücken. The duke had actually asked for the county of Falkenstein – in Maria Theresa's words, 'very disagreeable to take away the only thing which is the emperor's own'.[126] But Austria had spent over 100,000,000 florins and in the process returned its finances to a condition of

---

[122] Arneth, *GMT* x, pp. 587–8; 601–2, 616–17; cf. *PC* XLII.

[123] The treaties are conveniently reproduced in C. Parry (ed.), *The Consolidated Treaty Series*, vol. XLVII (New York, 1969), pp. 153–99. The terms are often misstated, even e.g. by Temperley, *Frederic and Joseph*, pp. 203–4 and Bernard, *J. II and Bavaria*, p. 131. On J.'s christening of the Innviertel, Arneth, *GMT* x, p. 640.

[124] On the effects of the peace see esp. Aretin, *Reich*, vol. I, pp. 126–30; Madariaga, *Catherine the Great*, p. 381.

[125] Preuss, *Oeuvres de Frédéric*, vol. VI, p. 179; Frederick to prince Henry, 11 Feb. and 4 Mar. 1779 (*PC* XLII, pp. 331, 420). Aretin, *Reich*, vol. I, pp. 19–20, 128. The remark attributed to J. comes from prince Charles of Hesse to Görtz, 30 Jan. 1779 (*PC* XLII, p. 321), and Frederick kept on repeating it; I have not found it in J.'s letters.

[126] M.T. to K., [?]22 Mar. 1779 (Arneth, *GMT* x, p. 619).

severe embarrassment. The gain of the Innviertel appeared a pitifully small return for so huge an expenditure.[127]

Kaunitz's original plan of 1764 had envisaged the annexation of the whole area east of the Inn between the Danube and the Tyrol, and Joseph was still hoping for as much early in 1779.[128] But in the event less than half of that was obtained, an area of about 1000 square miles with a population of 120,000 yielding a revenue of about half a million florins a year. Foreign territory still cut it off from the Tyrol, and it did not include the coveted salt-mines of Reichenhall.[129] However, it unquestionably constituted an *arrondissement*, and it was the only piece of land within the *Reich* that the Monarchy gained during the reigns of Maria Theresa and Joseph II. Kaunitz had argued in September 1778 that the war should be brought to an end because, unlike the Seven Years War which had been fought to recover Silesia, it had no major objective in view.[130] But whereas the Seven Years War had left the Monarchy's frontiers unaltered, the War of the Bavarian Succession at least procured the Innviertel.

The province was absorbed into upper Austria, and Joseph duly visited it in the autumn of 1779. He naturally found its frontiers unsatisfactory, and put in hand negotiations to readjust them with the ecclesiastical rulers of Salzburg and Passau. He also gave various orders intended to improve the economy and communications of the district. As he told his mother: 'When one considers what might perhaps have come to pass, it is a petty thing, but in itself this morsel is satisfactory and very convenient for upper Austria.'[131]

'The three sovereigns'

The quarrels between 'the three sovereigns' had reached a new level of intransigence and bitterness during this crisis. They deserve further attention here, since they greatly affected Joseph's standing both at home and abroad.

[127] On finance Arneth, *GMT* x, pp. 650–1; many memos in HHSA SKV 128–9; J. to M.T., 24 May 1779 (Arneth, *MTuJ* III, pp. 211–15); tables in HHSA NL, Karton 10.

[128] Arneth, *GMT* x, pp. 584–5, 589–90, 820, citing material of late Dec. 1778. The hopes were not dashed until Jan.

[129] Both Bernard, *J. II and Bavaria*, p. 131 and McKay and Scott, *Rise of the Great Powers*, p. 231 wrongly state that the Innviertel linked up the Tyrol with the rest of the Monarchy. On the salt-mines, Arneth, *GMT* x, pp. 569, 585. On the population, which J. himself underrated at 80,000, see G. Heilingsetzer, 'Oberösterreich zur Zeit Kaiser, Js. II.', *ÖZKJ*, p. 133.

[130] 'Opinion du Pce de Kaunitz-Rietberg sur l'état des circonstances militaires et politiques', 7 Sep. 1778 (HHSA SKV 127). This is one of several pieces of K.'s, written between Sep. and Nov. 1778, on the situation and esp. on the prospects of another campaign. It is printed in Aretin, *Reich.*, vol. II, pp. 1–2. Its content gives no clue that it is leading up to a proposal for *Reich* mediation, and I cannot help thinking that *ibid.*, vol I, pp. 119–26, exaggerates this aspect of K.'s scheming. The 'Opinion' itself reads to me like an attempt of K. to construct an argument agreeable to M.T. – and perhaps even to persuade himself of the failure of his policy over Bavaria. See n. 92 above.

[131] Arneth, *GMT* x, pp. 640–2, 660–3; Arneth, *MTuJ* III, pp. 228–34. The *Relation* of J.'s journey, including its Bohemian portion, was reprinted in facsimile in *Innviertel 1779*:

Matters had been made worse by the deeper involvement in these disputes of other members of the royal family. Marie Christine, the empress's favourite daughter, had always exerted influence behind the scenes; but more than one witness observed that she played an especially active part in the Bavarian affair. Her husband, the Saxon prince Albert, went off to his command in the war as a faithful servant of the Monarchy. But Marie Christine sympathised with him in the conflict of loyalties he felt in fighting against his native state. According to Leopold,

The public, which doesn't want peace, says that it is she who has obliged the empress to prohibit her generals from invading Saxony, to surrender Bavaria, and to make peace on any conditions, even shameful ones, so that Saxony, where she keeps all her capital, should suffer no damage ... and in order to get her husband back home quickly.

Naturally, she and the emperor had come to dislike each other.[132]

Leopold himself was enlisted as a pawn in the Court game. As early as February 1778 Joseph had suggested that he might need his brother in Vienna 'to back me up and obtain for me the means to enable the army to do a good job'.[133] Leopold was cannily reluctant, but held himself in readiness to come if Maria Theresa wished it. The emperor kept on urging his mother to give the word, but she suspected that Leopold was 'an intimate friend and partisan of the emperor's, and ... had sold out to him completely for the sake of [his] own future interests'.[134] She finally summoned him only during the crisis of late August. He set out at once and was in Vienna, or at the front with Joseph, from 6 September 1778 till 8 March 1779. His position was difficult indeed. The emperor expected from him total support in tough measures both against Prussia and to strengthen the army. Leopold privately disapproved of the whole enterprise and detested Joseph. After some weeks Maria Theresa tried to induce Leopold to prepare a scheme for the financial salvation of the Monarchy. This he was too prudent to undertake, but she had him initiated into the work of most of the departments, she showed him secret papers and asked his advice. It is clear that he did not get to know everything,[135] but what he learned confirmed not only his prejudice against Joseph and his dislike of

Reisejournal Kaiser Joseph II. Generalstabsbericht Oberst v. Seeger (Schärding, 1979). Though Seeger, the frontier expert (see above, p. 283), was on hand, it is interesting that J. seemed to think his presence of little value (J. to M.T., 3 Nov. 1779: Arneth, *MTuJ* III, pp. 232–3). See Plate 24.

132 The source for much of this and the next paragraph is L. II's memos reprinted or summarised in Wandruszka, *L. II.*, vol. I, pp. 324–67. On M.C. *ibid.*, pp. 347, 350–2, quotation from p. 352; Wraxall, *Memoirs*, vol. II, pp. 239, 345–7; Wolf, *Marie Christine*, vol. I, pp. 149–62; many letters in SOALpZ, LRRA P. 17/24, esp. L.K. to E.L., 29 Sep. 1778, reporting that M.C. is supposed to have suggested giving up three Bohemian *Kreise* for the sake of peace.

133 J. to L., 26 Feb. 1778 (Arneth, *MTuJ* II, p. 182).

134 Wandruszka, *L. II.*, vol. I, p. 340 (L.'s own words). J. frequently suggests that L. be summoned in his letters to M.T. in the spring and summer of 1778 (Arneth, *MTuJ* II).

135 Aretin, *Reich*, vol. I, p. 119n, gives one example.

the war but also his convictions that his mother had crippling faults as a ruler and that her system was beyond reform. By the time Joseph returned to the capital, he had developed a sense of resentment that Leopold had not backed him wholeheartedly. The emperor is said to have greeted him with the words, 'Now I'm here, my brother can go, since he only came to take my place.'[136] It was partly to avoid public scandal that Leopold stayed on until March. The experience of this visit, though it weakened them, did not destroy Joseph's feelings for his brother. But it intensified Leopold's secret bitterness towards the emperor – especially since Maria Theresa revealed to the younger brother Joseph's plan to reunite Tuscany with the Monarchy.[137] These family differences, though not known to the world in detail, were widely suspected, and strengthened foreign Courts' belief in the uncertain direction of Vienna's policy.[138]

It had long been public knowledge that Joseph and his mother were at loggerheads. But during this crisis their disagreements were for the first time officially acknowledged, and actually exploited as a weapon of policy. As we have seen,[139] when the empress reasserted her authority in July and approached Frederick without consulting her son, she made a virtue of their disputes, thus both humiliating Joseph and giving a hostage to the enemies of the Monarchy. The emperor felt that his honour and his role as commander-in-chief required him to avoid any public association with Maria Theresa's peace negotiations. She continued to play the maternal card emphasising that this policy was her own and that she would take all the blame for it. Although, in private, mother and son found it possible to discuss the question to some constructive effect, in the eyes of the world and of other Powers the rift between them seemed unbridgeable. Frederick claimed to doubt in July and August 1778 whether Joseph would accept peace even if Prussia came to terms with Maria Theresa.[140] The emperor himself recognised at one point that the war was directed against him personally rather than against the Monarchy.[141] Frederick was unquestionably influenced during the negotiations of early 1779 by the belief that Joseph was determined to renew the war and was sabotaging the peace.[142] For this reason the co-regent was made to subscribe separately to the ultimate settlement. It was thus partly through Maria Theresa's tactics that Joseph was branded after the War of the Bavarian Succession as even more of an expansionist and warmonger than before. For

[136] HHSA TZ, 28 Aug. 1779, quoted in Wandruszka, *L. II.*, vol. I, p. 330.
[137] See esp. Wandruszka, *L. II.*, vol. I, pp. 331, 364. J.'s letter to L. of 1 Oct. 1780 (Plate 22b) illustrates this coolness.
[138] Cf. Preuss, *Oeuvres de Frédéric*, vol. VI, p. 153; Keith to Suffolk, 16 Dec. 1778, cypher (PRO SP 80/270).
[139] See above, pp. 405–6.
[140] See Frederick to Finckenstein and Hertzberg, 28 July 1778, and Thugut's report on his negotiation with Frederick (*PC* XLI, pp. 295, 335).
[141] J. to M.T., 16 Nov. 1778 (Arneth, *MTuJ* III, p. 194).   [142] See above, pp. 420–1.

the French ambassador this picture was heightened by the evidently false modesty with which the emperor received congratulations on his conduct of the campaign of 1778.[143] Few realised how important Kaunitz's role had been in the negotiations with Karl Theodor, and no one knew quite how anxious for peace Joseph had shown himself in his private correspondence. Everyone was asking Frederick's question: 'What effect will this war have on the future? Will the emperor become more circumspect because of it?'[144]

Joseph's ostensible attitude earned him internal criticism too. The most telling rebuke came from marshal Laudon:

The spectacle of a dispute between mother and son is a lamentable occurrence from every point of view; and the world is happily not so corrupt that it will not side with the mother in such a case, even when the son is right. This dispute will make all the deeper impression on the generous-hearted peoples of Austria, the more they feel contented under the truly patriarchal [sic] rule of the empress, the more they respect the best mother of the nation. This heartfelt love has worked wonders at dangerous crises, indeed has saved the state. Your Majesty, chosen by Providence to inherit not only the Austrian Monarchy but also this attachment of its subjects, will certainly not renounce the latter part of the inheritance, which alone can give full value to the former, or seek to find a substitute for it in some districts of Bavaria. So wise a monarch, who by his actions has attracted the world's admiration and aroused the liveliest expectations in the peoples of Austria, cannot possibly set before them the example of a son living in dispute with his revered mother and then expect them to fulfil the filial duties which he himself neglects.[145]

It says much for the marshal's candour that he was ready to write this letter, and much for Joseph's tolerance that he did not take offence. But the criticism was unanswerable.

Mother and son patched up their relationship. She told him that peace had been made possible by 'his wise and prudent conduct of the last campaign'.[146] She even wrote to prince Ferdinand of Brunswick, for Prussian consumption:

My son is not to be blamed for having found it hard to give up the war. I must say that, seeing the troops and their good spirit, there was enough to stir not [only] a young prince seeking glory, but my old heart was stirred, and I'm the more pleased with this dear son that he has sacrificed himself for me and doesn't show the least resentment or regret.[147]

Kaunitz too had to be mollified. On the conclusion of peace she thanked him effusively:

---

143 Breteuil to Vergennes, 26 May 1779 in M. de Flassan, *Histoire générale et raisonnée de la diplomatie française, ou de la politique de la France*, vol. VII (Paris, 1811), pp. 261–2.

144 Preuss, *Oeuvres de Frédéric*, vol. VI, p. 179.

145 Janko, *Laudon's Leben*, p. 397 (not there dated, but evidently written late in 1778).

146 M.T. to J., 13 Feb. 1779 (Arneth, *MTuJ* III, p. 195; dated in Arneth, *GMT* X, p. 822).

147 M.T. to prince Ferdinand of Brunswick, nephew of Frederick, 3 July 1779 (Arneth, *MTKuF*, IV, p. 541).

Although this is not the most glorious of your achievements, it is certainly the most laborious and the most useful for the Monarchy and for me that you have ever [carried through], among so many that I owe to your penetration and devotion; and they have ensured my gratitude and friendship to you so long as I live.[148]

In view of the way Joseph had treated him, and of what Maria Theresa had said about him behind his back, it is scarcely surprising that the chancellor wanted even more acknowledgement than this. He took the opportunity of the ratification to ask again to be allowed to retire, 'having regard to his age and infirmities'. She would not hear of it. Kaunitz then offered as an alternative the appointment of a vice-chancellor to assist him, asking for count Philipp Cobenzl.[149] This request testifies to the undiminished political artistry of the old statesman in his sixty-eighth year. Cobenzl was a favourite of Joseph's, his assistant in the reform of the tariff and his companion on the journey to Paris. He had entered diplomacy by the farcical accident that his cousin of the same name, Ludwig, had been crippled with gout when he was due to leave for the congress of Teschen as Austrian plenipotentiary. Philipp had asked:

Couldn't I go instead? I've never worked in diplomacy, but I've worked in other affairs ... I can use my cousin's servants, his furniture and his carriages, it's not even necessary to send an announcement. Cobenzl has been announced, and a Cobenzl will go.[150]

He had given satisfaction to all three 'sovereigns' in Vienna. Joseph in particular had written fulsomely to congratulate him, describing him as one of his 'tools' whom he had been 'keeping in reserve'.[151] By securing Cobenzl as assistant, Kaunitz at one stroke relieved himself of work, nullified a possible supplanter, and strengthened his hand with the emperor. The way was incidentally prepared for the promotion of the younger Zinzendorf, Cobenzl's rival as an economic expert and a *protégé* of the chancellor's.[152] Joseph regretted losing him on the financial side, but the empress was determined to retain Kaunitz. The emperor brought himself to write to the chancellor in these unctuous terms:

The few words you spoke to HM alarmed and touched me; and she has deserved them for some time. My only impulse was to seize you and to hold on to your coat-tail. You yourself know too well what sort of a man can manage millions to suppose that, when we are lucky enough to have you, we can [bear to] lose you. Your proposal about Cobenzl seems to me to raise no difficulty, and I cannot understand why HM did not accept it. You can rely on my desire to show you at every opportunity my esteem, my gratitude and my friendship.[153]

---

[148] M.T. to K., 6 May 1779 (Arneth, *MTuJ* III, pp. 215–16nn).
[149] For this episode see Arneth, *GMT* x, pp. 643–6, 827; J. to L., 24 May 1779 (Arneth, *MTuJ* III, pp. 215–16); Arneth, *AÖG* (1886), 125–31 (Cobenzl's memoirs).
[150] Arneth, *AÖG* (1886), 126 (Cobenzl's memoirs).   [151] *Ibid.*, p. 127.
[152] *Ibid.*, pp. 113, 130–1.
[153] J. to K., 15 May 1779 (HHSA FA Sbde 70; misdated 1 May by Arneth, *GMT* x, p. 827).

Kaunitz insisted that a notice be published explaining the change and heavily underlining the confidence reposed by both emperor and empress in his conduct of affairs. Rule by triumvirate was more securely established than ever.

THE ESTABLISHMENT OF MAX FRANZ IN COLOGNE, 1779–80

If it was unclear who had won the War of the Bavarian Succession and who had gained most from the peace of Teschen, there was no doubt at all that in the next eighteen months the international position of the Monarchy markedly improved, while Frederick's worsened. Vienna's first diplomatic coup during this period was the election of Max Franz as coadjutor in Cologne and Münster.

In the ecclesiastical principalities of the *Reich* each successive ruler had to be genuinely elected by the cathedral or monastic chapter; and it was possible during the lifetime of a ruler to elect a coadjutor, who then automatically succeeded.[154] Neither the pope nor any one monarch could control the choice. Since all these states had some significance in the balance of power and their rulers received substantial revenues, the composition of the chapters and the election of bishops, abbots and coadjutors ranked as important questions in international diplomacy. Not only German states but other Powers, especially France, Britain and Holland, took an active interest. After the expenditure of large sums of money to sweeten the chapter concerned, the man selected was most often a member of some lesser German princely or noble house who appeared both reasonably independent to the chapter and an acceptable compromise candidate to the Powers most affected. But in the distant day when Habsburgs had produced a surplus of male heirs, younger archdukes had often been provided with one or more prince-bishoprics to govern, thus at the same time increasing the dynasty's influence and reducing Vienna's financial liabilities. From the second half of the sixteenth until the early eighteenth century it was the Bavarian ruling house that succeeded most frequently in placing one or more of its numerous princelings in some of these prestigious and lucrative employments. In 1761, however, the last of these died, Clemens August, archbishop-elector of Cologne, bishop of Münster, Paderborn, Hildesheim, Regensburg and Osnabrück, provost of Berchtesgaden and grand master of the Teutonic Order. As yet Maria Theresa's available son, Max Franz, was too young to be a serious candidate for a bishopric, and anyway she and Joseph refused to consider such a career for

---

154 The great authority on these matters is H. E. Feine, *Die Besetzung der Reichsbistümer vom Westfälischen Friede bis zur Säkularisation, 1648–1803*, Kirchenrechtliche Abhandlungen, 97 and 98 (Stuttgart, 1921), though he is not much concerned with the international aspect of the elections. See also Aretin, *Reich*, vol. I, esp. pp. 34–51, 'Die Kirche im Reich'. See Blanning, *Reform and Revolution in Mainz*, esp. pp. 65–6.

him. 'If after full trial he wants to be a monk, he would not be prevented, but not elector or bishop.'[155] She gave some assistance instead to a campaign to procure as many ecclesiastical principalities as possible for Clemens Wenzeslaus of Saxony, younger brother of prince Albert. In this fantastic merry-go-round he failed to win election at Mainz, Cologne, Liège, Paderborn, Hildesheim and Passau, but achieved success at Freising and Regensburg in 1763, and Trier and Augsburg in 1768. However, the pope had been legislating against vast accumulations of dioceses, and Clemens Wenzeslaus was allowed to keep only Trier and Augsburg.[156]

These elections concerned both the emperor and the ruler of the Monarchy, but in rather different ways. The emperor had once possessed power to influence the choices, including the right to exclude a particular candidate. But now his accepted role, as in so many fields, was that of constitutional monarch, to hold the ring and ensure that the election was legally conducted.[157] Joseph made a point of refusing to interfere, at least publicly, declaring that the chapter ought to be allowed to choose freely. This pious standpoint had at least three advantages: it was cheap, it called into question the influence exercised by other rulers, and it did not prevent him expressing his preferences discreetly. In 1770 he tried to stop the election of the successful candidate at Speyer; in 1772 he secured Salzburg for Hieronymus, son of the imperial vice-chancellor Colloredo.[158] Maria Theresa held more traditional views about patronage and about the Monarchy's interest in securing the election of sympathetic candidates to strengthen its international position. She was prepared to spend money in important cases. It seems, though, that her main considerations were dynastic. She supported Clemens Wenzeslaus as a close relative, belonging to a house that had recently turned Catholic and had staunchly assisted her against Prussia.[159]

Her attitude was clearly displayed at the election in 1775 of a coadjutor to the abbess of Essen. The empress had at least two special grounds of interest: first, her sister-in-law had been the coadjutor, but had never become abbess

155 M.T. on a report of K.'s, 6 Jan. 1770, quoted in Arneth, *GMT* x, p. 695.
156 On this campaign see Raab, *Clemens Wenzeslaus*, vol. I; F. Schröder, 'Wie wurde Clemens Wenzeslaus Kurfürst von Trier?', *Historisches Jahrbuch*, xxx (1909), 24–42, 274–86. He also became coadjutor to the prince-provost of Ellwangen in 1770, receiving the support of Vienna.
157 Feine, *Besetzung der Reichsbistümer*, ch. 4.
158 *Ibid.*, pp. 133, 138–9; E. Guglia, 'Zur Geschichte der Bischofswahlen in den deutschen Reichsstiften unter Joseph II.', *MÖIG* xxxiv (1913), 296–314, dealing only with the 1780s. Schröder, *Historisches Jahrbuch* (1909) 274–7, brings out the differences between M.T. and J. over the Trier election. Raab, *Clemens Wenzeslaus*, vol. I, pp. 272–6, 306, 318 etc. has interesting examples of Viennese 'interference', mostly by M.T. On Speyer and Salzburg, K-M vii, pp. 18, 118–21, 237–41, 416–21. E. Glas, 'Studien über den Einfluss Joseph II. auf die deutschen Bischofswahlen', University of Vienna PhD, 1949, is of limited use.
159 Raab, *Clemens Wenzeslaus*, vol. I, esp. pp. 187, 247–8, 250, 354. Cf. Lippert, *M.T. und Maria Antonia von Sachsen*, *passim*.

because the incumbent had outlived her; secondly, Maria Theresa felt an obligation to provide a respectable position for Kunigunde of Saxony, the princess whom Joseph might have married instead of the disastrous Josepha. After much diplomacy, the empress agreed to pay the expenses of the election, so long as the emperor did not get to hear of it, 'since he criticises her excessive liberality at every opportunity'. At a cost of 80,000 florins Kunigunde was elected, and duly succeeded as abbess in 1776.[160]

All these elections necessarily involved a great many parties, and the case of Cologne in 1779–80 well illustrates the point. The origins of the project to elect Max Franz were multifarious. For some years the elector of Cologne's minister, baron Belderbusch, had been indicating to Vienna that he would like to secure as coadjutor a Habsburg prince, and claiming that he could achieve this result. These hints were received with suspicion, and Maria Theresa continued to assert that she would never permit one of her children to become a prince-bishop so long as she lived.[161] She destined Max Franz for the governorship of Hungary and a military career, in which she assured him that the combination of his birth with education and determination would guarantee him success comparable with prince Eugene's. The fact that she obtained for him in 1769 the coadjutorship to her brother-in-law as grand master of the Teutonic Order, though it committed him to bachelorhood, did not imply that he would follow an ecclesiastical career.[162] But during the campaign of 1778 he was taken ill, and for about a year suffered badly from some disease of the knees which was treated by countless operations and left him manifestly unfit to be a soldier. Although it was an obvious course in these circumstances to turn him into a priest and find him a prince-bishopric, Maria Theresa and he still resisted this solution. Then in August 1779 she was goaded into action by a letter from Leopold asking whether one of his many sons might be provided with an ecclesiastical principality. She pointed out that they were far too young, and set about working vigorously for the election of Max Franz in Cologne.[163] It is not clear whether she was influenced beforehand, or merely assisted afterwards, by the increasing attention

[160] F. Schröder, 'Eine kanonische Wahl im Zeitalter des Josephinismus', *Historisches Jahrbuch*, XXVII (1906), 551–60, 729–38. See above, pp. 84–6.
[161] Arneth, *GMT* x, p. 696; M. Braubach, *Max Franz* (2nd edn, Vienna, 1961), pp. 53–5; W. Baum, 'Die Wahl des Erzherzogs Maximilian Franz zum Koadjutor des Kurstiftes Köln und des Fürstbistums Münster (1979/80)', *MIÖG*, LXXXI (1973), 139–40.
[162] See her immense instructions for Max (April 1774) in Arneth, *MTKuF* II, esp. pp. 320–1, 324.
[163] Arneth, *GMT* x, pp. 696–9; Braubach, *Max Franz*, pp. 54–6; Baum, *MIÖG* (1973), 141. In letters to Mercy of 1 Nov. 1779 and 31 Jan. 1780 (Arneth & Geffroy III, pp. 364–6, 395) M.T. puts a somewhat different complexion on the affair, talking of pressure from the electors of Cologne and Mainz, and describing Max's own repugnance as the only objection from a Viennese standpoint. This sounds like special pleading designed to placate France.

Kaunitz and other officials were giving to the possibilities of strengthening Austria's position in the *Reich*.[164]

When consulted, the chancellor pronounced in favour of the scheme on many grounds. Assuming, he said, that Münster could as usual be held jointly with Cologne, the resulting benefits to the Monarchy would be immense: greater influence in the Empire and in imperial elections, the establishment of a bridgehead confronting Prussia in north Germany, a reduction in Vienna's expenditure on the imperial family, and an increase in Austria's attraction as an ally either to France or Britain.[165] Joseph concurred, though doubting that the plan would succeed; Max Franz was prevailed upon to take the necessary minor orders; secrecy was maintained for long enough to outmanoeuvre Frederick the Great; and the pope was persuaded to give his blessing. Max Franz was eventually elected coadjutor to both sees in August 1780, at a cost to the Monarchy of over a million florins.[166] Although he did not succeed to the bishoprics until 1784, the election was recognised as a boost to Austria's international standing. It was noted as far away in Constantinople that Prussia had suffered a reverse.[167] Frederick talked impotently of 'a Court whose sole aim is to incorporate one German province after another', 'this new despotism', and ascribed to Joseph both a desire to provoke war and limitless ambitions in the ecclesiastical states of the Empire.[168]

In fact, however, the emperor never spoke of the plan as his own, he confined himself to giving good if pessimistic advice about the details, and he was travelling in the Innviertel and in Russia during critical stages of the negotiations. He told his mother he had not mentioned it to Catherine because it was 'such a petty thing'. Not only the resources – what Joseph called 'the cost of buying the Holy Spirit' – but also the drive came from Maria Theresa.[169] The contrast with the War of the Bavarian Succession is striking. That dangerous and expensive project, to which her son was so deeply committed, achieved only a dubious gain, while this smooth, peaceful and

---

164 This is the particular emphasis of Aretin, *Reich*, vol. I, pp. 128–31.

165 His *Vortrag* of 26 Nov. 1779 is printed in Aretin, *Reich*, vol. II, pp. 24–8. See also K.'s retrospective justification of 1787 for J. in Maass, *Josephinismus*, vol. II, pp. 512–14 and Baum, *MIÖG* (1973), 146–7.

166 Arneth, *GMT* X, pp. 669–712; Braubach, *Max Franz*, pp. 56–64; Aretin, *Reich*, vol. I, pp. 132–6; Baum, *MIÖG* (1973), 144.

167 Ranke, *Die deutschen Mächte*, vol. I, p. 95.

168 Frederick to Finckenstein, 30 May, and to Goertz, 5 Aug. 1780 (*PC* XLIV, pp. 278–9, 398, and *passim*). The threat of war was taken seriously, as is shown by Elliot to Harris, 24 July 1780 (*A Series of Letters of ... Malmesbury, his Family and Friends*, ed. [3rd] earl of Malmesbury, vol. I ([London,] 1870), p. 469).

   Both M.T. and J. showed themselves sensitive to these charges: M.T. to Ferd., 17 Oct. 1780 (Arneth, *MTKuF* II, pp. 300–1); J. to L. Cobenzl. 25 Oct. 1780 (Beer & Fiedler, *JuLC* I, p. 71).

169 See Arneth, *MTuJ* III, esp. pp. 222, 245, 250–1, 263 – both quotations from p. 263 (J. to M.T., 28 June 1780); Arneth, *GMT* X, pp. 699 (M.T. has spoken to J. early in Nov. 1779, as soon as he has returned), 706 (she must go ahead without consulting J. in Russia).

comparatively cheap operation resulted in an undoubted triumph. Nothing could underline more strongly the wisdom of the advice that Joseph continually received about the affairs of the Empire: that cautious, constitutional methods could achieve much, while the ruthless assertion of rights by threats and force would inevitably provoke determined opposition. But the emperor simply did not think in this way. He was less interested in securing prince-bishoprics for his relatives and supporters than in assisting the often-canvassed plans to secularise these anomalous relics of the past.[170] Furthermore, the primitive, dynastic aim that had brought the Monarchy an advantage in terms of *Realpolitik* through the Cologne election was itself alien to Joseph's thinking. He did not want younger sons provided with their own states; he wanted the unitary Monarchy expanded. All the same, outsiders saw the emperor as the prime mover over Cologne, as over Bavaria. In the case of the war, although Maria Theresa's tactics had helped to create an exaggerated impression of Joseph's ambitions, the picture that the world received of his attitude was not fundamentally unjust. In the case of Cologne his mother made all the running, but he nonetheless took the blame.

JOSEPH'S VISIT TO RUSSIA, 1780

While Maria Theresa was procuring this benefit to her family and the state, Joseph was pursuing an initiative of a different kind which, according to his lights, was far better calculated to enhance the position of the Monarchy. On 1 February 1780, having obtained half-hearted sanction from his mother but without telling Kaunitz, the emperor called privately and unattended on the Russian ambassador to Vienna to suggest a meeting with Catherine II. She was known to be planning a journey through her western territories; Joseph was intending to tour Galicia; he could easily arrange to meet her at her convenience. Catherine replied favourably and speedily – but by way of Kaunitz, which involved the emperor in some unconvincing explanations: during his rare conversations with the chancellor, he said, although he had meant to mention the proposal, it had slipped his mind.[171] He declared to the ambassador that his objects in making the journey were purely private, to get to know the famous empress whom he so much admired and to see the country for which she had done so much. But he told Lacy that Frederick

---

170 See M.T. to Ferd., 17 Oct. 1780 (Arneth, *MTKuF* II, p. 301). A project for secularisation of ecclesiastical states was discussed and rejected by K. in correspondence with J. in Dec. 1779 (HHSA SKV 130).

171 On the proposal for the journey, Arneth, *GMT* X, pp. 668–71, 830–1; M.T. to Mercy, 3 Mar. 1780 (Arneth & Geffroy III, pp. 404–5); M.T. to Ferd., 17 Mar. 1780 (Arneth, *MTKuF* II, p. 258), explicitly saying Vienna had arranged it. Ranke, *Die deutschen Mächte*, vol. I, pp. 130–1, made a mistake in ascribing the initiative to K.

would choke with rage, and speculated whether Catherine expected from him 'diplomacy, partition, war or gallantry'.[172] Manifestly Joseph hoped that Russia's alliance with Prussia, though recently renewed, could be superseded by a Russo-Austrian alliance. He had always shown greater enthusiasm for a Russian connexion than Kaunitz, and had long shared with Lacy dreams of aggrandisement in the Balkans at the expense of Turkey. In 1768–72 he had done his best to frustrate Kaunitz's anti-Russian policy, and would have preferred to partition the Ottoman Empire instead of Poland. During the War of the Bavarian Succession he had seen the threat of Russian intervention force the Monarchy to accept mediation and an unsatisfactory peace. Catherine II was now recognised as a guarantor of the constitution of the *Reich*. Allied with her, Frederick the Great could lord it over Germany. By contrast, if the Monarchy could win Russia's friendship, Joseph could hope to revive his schemes for expansion or *arrondissement* in Germany with a real prospect of success. Experience during the war had rekindled his interest in the possibility of overthrowing Kaunitz's whole system, which tied Austria to alliance with a perfidious France.[173]

It is never easy to uncover the origins and motives of Joseph's actions. Though the meeting with Catherine was certainly in a sense his own work, the moment was favourable both in Russia and Vienna. Having secured a position for herself in the *Reich*, she was turning her attention again to her southern borders. In 1779 her second grandson was born and was christened Constantine in the midst of a flurry of propaganda about reviving a Greek empire. A faction at the Court of St Petersburg, headed by prince Potemkin, was working for a change of alliances against the minister associated with the existing system, count Panin. Frederick imprudently made it clear that he valued Russia's alliance only against the Monarchy and would not support the dismemberment of Turkey. No wonder Catherine 'reddened with joy' when she received Joseph's proposal.[174]

---

[172] Arneth, *GMT* x, pp. 668–9, 830–1 (J. to Lacy, 29 Feb. 1780); J. to L. Cobenzl, 13 Apr. 1780 (Beer & Fiedler, *JuLC* I, p. 4).

[173] On J.'s general attitudes in foreign policy see above, pp. 273–7.
    It would be to anticipate later discussion to expatiate on J.'s developing views. His extremely important letter to L. Cobenzl of 12 Nov. 1783 (Beer & Fiedler, *JuLC*, I, pp. 434–6) criticises the French alliance while trying to win Catherine for a Bavarian exchange. But while I think J. always entertained the possibility of a change of system, I doubt whether he ever firmly decided for it. For earlier references see J. to Lacy, 8 Apr. 1778 (HHSA FA Sbde 72); Arneth, *GMT* x, pp. 664–7; M.T. to Mercy, 3 Mar. 1780 (Arneth & Geffroy III, p. 405); J. to K., 19 Jan. 1781 and K. to J., 20 Jan. (Beer, *JLuK*, pp. 31–4). In connexion with the Russian visit he gave many assurances to France, as emerges from Arneth & Geffroy III, and Arneth & Flammermont II. But Frederick seems to have believed he was working hand in glove with England (*PC* XLIV, e.g. p. 136).
    The most perceptive discussions of J.'s policy remain those of Beer (e.g. in the introduction to *JLuK*) and Ranke in *Die deutschen Mächte*.

[174] On Russia: Madariaga, *Catherine the Great*, pp. 383–4, and 'The secret Austro-Russian treaty of 1781', *SR*, XXXVIII (1959–60), pp. 114–16; E. Hösch, 'Das sogenannte "griechische

In Vienna policy-makers could not escape the dilemma that had vexed them ever since the weakness of the Turks had become apparent at the beginning of the century. As a neighbour the weak Ottoman Empire seemed preferable to powerful Russia. The Austrians were doubtful of the value of acquisitions in the Balkans. Yet, if Turkey was in any case doomed, then their best policy must be to partition it in association with Russia.[175] Maria Theresa strongly opposed any attempt by Austria to weaken the Turks, and regarded Catherine II with 'aversion and horror'.[176] But Kaunitz could not rule out the possibility of a deal with Russia. In the survey of policy which he wrote for Joseph at the end of 1776 he discussed the question whether it would be to the advantage of the Monarchy that Russia's aim should be achieved and the Ottoman Empire destroyed.

It is certain [he declared] that the Turkish empire is rapidly approaching its ruin, that with our co-operation this could hardly fail to be the result, that we should obtain as our share vast conquests such as Turkish Dalmatia and Croatia, Bosnia, Serbia, Wallachia, Moldavia and even some further Turkish provinces adjoining our frontiers, and we could rid ourselves permanently of a traditional enemy.

But the chancellor still doubted the wisdom of taking steps to bring about this consummation. It would substitute a dangerous for an almost harmless neighbour; the process would offer wonderful opportunities for Prussian aggrandisement in Poland; and France would be alienated from Austria. Kaunitz recommended that an alliance with Russia should be considered only if it was directed against Prussia rather than Turkey. But he reckoned that Russia would be in no state to embark on another war for at least twenty years.[177]

Within a few months, however, in the spring of 1777, another Russo-Turkish war seemed imminent, and Lacy was instructed to comment on the military outlook. He saw little difficulty, if Russia and Austria fought together, in driving the Turks out of Europe in one campaign; he favoured claiming as the Monarchy's share of the spoils Wallachia, part of Bulgaria and the whole of Serbia, Bosnia and Greece. Even more far-reaching schemes were put forward by Ludwig Cobenzl, who in 1779 was appointed Austrian ambassador to St Petersburg. Although he considered that, other things being equal, Vienna should strive to maintain the Ottoman Empire intact, he

Projekt" Katharinas II.', *Jahrbücher für Geschichte Osteuropas*, neue Folge, XII (1964), esp. 183–90; D. L. Ransel, *The Politics of Catherinian Russia* (New Haven and London, 1975), pp. 252–3; D. M. Griffiths, 'The rise and fall of the northern system', *CSS* IV (1970), 547–69.

    On Prussia: W. Stribrny, *Die Russlandpolitik Friedrichs des Grossen* (Wurzburg, 1966) and his edition of an extremely interesting document: J. E. Graf von Goertz, *Mémoire sur la Russie* (1786; Wiesbaden, 1969).

[175] Roider, *Austria's Eastern Question*, passim; A. Beer, *Die orientalische Politik Oesterreichs seit 1774* (Prague, 1883), esp. pp. 30–45. I am grateful to Professor Sir Harry Hinsley for impressing on me the importance to Austria of keeping Russia at a distance.

[176] See her letter to Mercy of 3 Mar. 1780 cited in n. 173 above.

[177] Beer, *AÖG* (1872), 82–5; Dyck, *Canadian Slavonic Papers* (1980), 451–69.

calculated that the international situation would make this position untenable. He therefore discussed two possibilities: in the first case, if the Turks were expelled only from Europe, Austria might expect to annex parts of Wallachia, Bulgaria and Rumelia, and the whole of Bosnia, Serbia, Albania, Greece and the Morea; in the second case, if the Turks were removed from Asia as well, though Prussia would have to be compensated, Vienna might hope to control the mouth of the Danube and to secure access to it through the Bosphorus. He thought the second outcome would be the more satisfactory to the Monarchy. From these memoranda it can be clearly seen that Joseph was not alone in working for a Russian alliance, or uniquely rapacious in his schemes of Balkan aggrandisement.[178]

Kaunitz, though, remained cautious. Commenting on Lacy's remarks, he urged that decisions should be deferred until the attitudes of other Powers were known. In a secret supplement to the instructions for Vienna's ambassadors to St Petersburg, first used in 1777 and renewed in 1779, he argued that Russia was the natural ally of Austria and that her association with Prussia could and should be weakened; but he stressed the primacy for the Monarchy of the Prussian problem, and offered no very warm encouragement to Catherine's plans in the Balkans. Certainly, if she intended to destroy the Ottoman Empire, then the Monarchy would have to oppose her, unless a prior understanding had been reached between the two Powers. But Kaunitz feared that the fall of the Turkish state might bring down the Monarchy too. It is significant that he saw no need to modify this document after the war over Bavaria.[179]

Whether the chancellor genuinely welcomed Joseph's journey or not, he had to approve it and make use of it once it had been arranged. He supplied the usual lengthy notes to guide the emperor's conduct, on the lines of his previous memoranda. Joseph artfully asked his advice whether while in Russia he should try to confine himself to non-political conversation, or at least wait until Catherine initiated political discussions. A letter was sent after him to Lemberg in Galicia telling him that he must of course ensure that political questions were ventilated. But Joseph as well as Kaunitz realised that the position was very delicate. Panin was still Catherine's minister, Prussia still her ally. She might well pass on anything the emperor said straight to Frederick, who would make use of it in France and elsewhere. The game could easily be lost by indiscretion. Joseph wrote that his first aim must be to mitigate Catherine's prejudices by rebutting the calumnies Frederick circu-

---

[178] Beer, *Die orientalische Politik*, pp. 36–42. Beer is responsible for the plausible attribution of this memorandum to L. Cobenzl, but does not offer a specific date for its composition. Lacy's is dated 2 May 1777.

[179] Beer, *Die orientalische Politik*, pp. 36–9, 42–3. The supplement to the instructions is printed in E. Winter, 'Grundlinien der österreichischen Russlandpolitik am Ende des 18. Jahrhunderts', *Zeitschrift für Slawistik*, IV (1959), 94–110.

lated about him and the Monarchy. For the moment, the most that could be hoped for from the meeting would be the establishment of good personal relations between the two rulers. Only slowly could this lead to a better understanding between the two states.[180]

As always, Joseph insisted on travelling as count Falkenstein, at high speed, without ceremony and with a very small suite, in this case just six carriages. He was happy to 'be mixed up among the gentlemen of the [Russian] Court'. He wanted no presents; the only jewels that would please him would be the Silesian towns of Schweidnitz, Glatz, Neisse and Kosel.[181] He had prepared himself perhaps more carefully than ever, reading up on Russia, trying to procure adequate maps, making endless calculations about times and distances.[182] He left Vienna on 26 April, spent nearly three weeks reporting on Galicia and then proceeded to Mohilev, where he was to meet Catherine. Arriving there on 2 June, he found it 'a dirty town, built of wood, with streets full of mud'. On 4 June he witnessed 'in plain clothes' the empress's ceremonial entry, and then sat next to her at a dinner for fifty. He was much in her company in Mohilev and on the road until 15 June, when he left her to continue her progress while he went to visit Moscow. 'It is much larger than anything I've seen. Paris, Rome, Naples in no way approach its size.' True, most of the houses are mean, but beautiful palaces exist among them, and the streets are fine. The company, especially female, is excellent. The orphanage and the military hospital surpass those of Vienna. Then at Catherine's request he changed his plans and travelled on to St Petersburg, where he met her again and made the acquaintance of her Prussophile son and heir, Paul, and his wife. He stayed in and around the capital from 28 June to 18 July. On the way back he again spent some days in Galicia, but humoured his mother by missing out a planned detour to the Bukovina. He reached Vienna on 20 August, having covered about 3000 miles.[183]

His incognito had deprived him of few attentions. He was given official lodgings at Mohilev – necessarily, because the whole town had been requisitioned for Catherine's visit. She brought with her 'her entire theatre and musicians' to amuse and impress him. In St Petersburg he stayed with his ambassador, looking out from the embassy windows on to the sails passing along the Neva. He toured the royal palaces and laid foundation-stones; gala

---

[180] HHSA SKV 131; Beer, *Die orientalische Politik*, p. 45; Arneth, *GMT* x, pp. 647–82, 832; Beer & Fiedler, *JuLC* I, p. ix. Ranke, *Die deutschen Mächte*, attributes a K. memorandum to J. (vol. I, p. 137), as Beer & Fiedler point out (vol. I, p. ix, no. 3), but his summary of K.'s advice is excellent (pp. 133–7).

[181] J. to K., 1 Mar. 1780 (Beer, *JLuK*, pp. 3–5); J. to L. Cobenzl, 13 Apr. 1780 (Beer & Fiedler, *JuLC* I, pp. 1–5).

[182] HHSA FA Hofreisen 11 contains lists of academicians, many route calculations, accounts of Russia etc.

[183] Journal in HHSA FA Hofreisen 11; letters of J. to M.T. (Arneth, *MTuJ* III, pp. 246–301). On the visits to Galicia see pp. 365–6 above.

succeeded fête; he and Catherine sampled each other's church services, not very reverently. He had many discussions with Potemkin and even talked to Panin.[184] We have few eye-witness accounts, but it is clear that the visit was a public as well as a private triumph for both rulers.

When Joseph used the ordinary post in Russia, he had to assume that his letters would be read by Catherine, and therefore the flattering remarks he put into them about her and her country have to be heavily discounted.[185] He had few opportunities to write home by a safe courier, and then he naturally concentrated on describing his meetings with the tsarina. For this journey we lack the usual chatty letters written to Lacy for consumption by the circle of ladies. His diary is characteristically matter-of-fact.[186] His comments on Mohilev and Moscow, just quoted, constitute a high proportion of his surviving uninhibited remarks about what he saw in Russia, though we know that after he returned to Vienna he told Maria Theresa something of the country's peculiar cuisine: 'jams are made for almost every dish'. She reported, however, that 'at the moment nothing is good except what is at Moscow or Petersburg'.[187] Joseph was clearly determined to admire the country and its ruler. On this evidence, he was more impressed by backward Russia than by France, the leader of European civilisation.

He made every effort to be agreeable, and with Catherine spared no flattery. She too was in a mood to be impressed, and found him excellent, talkative, amusing company, far preferable to the king of Sweden. She thought him superior now to Frederick the Great, whom she regarded as doddering. The emperor, she wrote to Grimm, has 'the most solid, the most profound, the best-informed mind I know: by heaven, anyone who is going to steal a march on him will have to get up very early in the morning'. He supplied her with material about the Monarchy's *Normalschulen*, which she decided she wanted to imitate in Russia.[188]

During his frequent and lengthy talks with Catherine he set out to justify Austrian policy and condemn Prussian. He explained away Vienna's anti-Russian stance in the last Turkish war. She in return justified her opposition to Austria at her accession, and made it plain that she would not openly break with Frederick. The first tentative, half-frivolous exchange about possible mutual aggrandisement set the tone for subsequent discussions:

[184] These points have been collected from J.'s letters to M.T. in Arneth, *MTuJ* III; from Beer & Fiedler, *JuLC* I, Catherine's letters in *SIRIO* IX and XXIII (ed. J. Groot); M.T. to Ferdinand, 27 Apr. 1780 in Arneth, *MTKuF* II, p. 266.
[185] Arneth, *MTuJ* III, p. 265n. The post was under Panin's direct control (Ransel, *Politics of Catherinian Russia*, p. 254).
[186] Journal in HHSA FA Hofreisen 11. There are letters to Lacy, of no great interest, from Smolensk and Riga only (HHSA FA Sbde 72).
[187] M.T. to Ferd., 21 and 30 Aug. 1780 (Arneth, *MTKuF* II, pp. 290, 293).
[188] Catherine II to grand duke Paul and his wife, letters of 24 May to 7 June 1780 (Russian calendar) in *SIRIO* IX, pp. 52–62. I am indebted to my wife for translating Russian passages. Catherine to Grimm, 25 and 27 May, 25 July 1780 in *SIRIO* XXIII (ed. Groot), pp. 180–3.

She tempted me [with the question] whether Italy and especially the papal state wouldn't suit me as the patrimony of the emperor of the Romans ... At first I replied jokingly, but then seriously I just said that the *status quo* in Italy was something that interested so many Powers so intensely that I wouldn't be able to validate rights even if they stemmed from Augustus, but that her Rome, that is Constantinople, was much easier for her to conquer. She apologised for this question and appeared embarrassed to have asked it, and assured me that she wanted only peace, and had no idea of this conquest.[189]

She kept on reverting to Joseph's opportunities 'to immortalise himself' in Italy, and it became obvious that she was full of her project to establish a 'Greek empire' for Constantine on the ruins of the Ottoman state.[190] However, nothing concrete was put forward in the course of these conversations. The most specific proposal discussed was mooted during talks between Potemkin and Cobenzl: a mutual guarantee of each other's possessions, suggested originally by Kaunitz. Catherine asked whether that extended to future conquests, and Potemkin indicated that any Austrian gains outside Germany and Poland could be included. But nothing had been formulated, let alone agreed, by the time Joseph left Russia. He and Kaunitz deliberately checked the pace of the negotiations, believing that time was needed for reflection and decision in both countries.[191]

Sir James Harris, the British ambassador to St Petersburg, did all he could to assist Joseph's cause, in the hope that an Austro-Russian alliance would lead to an Anglo-Austrian alliance. He was able to report to his government: 'Count Falkenstein ... has for ever given a severe stroke to the King of Prussia's influence, so deep a one that I almost doubt its recovery.' Although Frederick sent his nephew to Russia immediately after Joseph's visit, the damage had been done; and the emperor's friend, the prince de Ligne, was much better received than the Prussian when both paid court to Catherine later in the year.[192] Kaunitz recognised the emperor's success and induced Maria Theresa to send a letter of thanks to the tsarina.[193] Joseph's long-term expectations of alliance were treated sceptically by his mother in her more confidential letters, but she acknowledged that 'he has had the good fortune to

---

189 J. to M.T., 8 June 1780 (Arneth, *MTuJ* III, p. 252).
190 J. to M.T., 4 and 18 July 1780 (*ibid.*, pp. 269, 285). See Hösch, *Jahrbücher für Geschichte Osteuropas* (1964).
191 J. to M.T., 4 and 12 July 1780 (Arneth, *MTuJ* III, pp. 270–1, 278–9). For the whole negotiation see also Beer & Fiedler, *JuLC* I; Arneth, *GMT* X, pp. 683–9; Ranke, *Die deutschen Mächte*, vol. I, pp. 138–41; Beer, *Die orientalische Politik*, pp. 45–7.
192 Harris to Stormont, 14/25 July and 15/26 Sep. 1780 in earl of Malmesbury, *Diaries and Correspondence of James Harris, First Earl of Malmesbury* (4 vols., London, 1844), vol. I, pp. 324, 332. Cf. Catherine to Grimm, 7 Sep. 1780 (*SIRIO* XXIII (ed. Groot), p. 192).
193 K. to L. Cobenzl, 22 Aug. 1780, and M.T. to Catherine II, 21 Aug. (Beer & Fiedler, *JuLC* I, pp. 45–6; II, p. 413).

remove the false prejudices against us, which were very strong'.[194] The achievement was all the more valuable in that neither France nor Prussia grasped what had happened. Both Powers underrated the impact Joseph had made on Catherine, and she on him, and failed to appreciate that she was working determinedly to change her system of alliances.[195]

On this, the most adventurous of his journeys, Joseph had registered the most striking success of all his travels. Within a year an Austro-Russian alliance had been negotiated. Ultimately it was to prove a dangerous achievement, and Catherine benefited from it more than Joseph did. But in 1780 he was not duped. He was well aware of the tsarina's ambition and arrogance, and knew exactly what he was doing when he flattered her preposterously.[196] He was even inclined to indulge her when she went so far as to ask for the Order of the Golden Fleece. Yet the statutes of the Order restricted it to males; Maria Theresa herself did not hold it; and the request was blocked. But Joseph always set less store by these baubles than anyone else.[197] At the time of his visit the Monarchy desperately needed to loosen the close ties between Russia and Prussia. It was feared in St Petersburg that Joseph was duping Catherine, not the other way round.[198] She, on the other hand, badly wanted Austrian support in her efforts to impose a new foreign policy. But Joseph could easily have wasted his opportunity. Instead, as the Prussian ambassador said, he displayed immense skill as diplomat and intriguer.[199]

As against Kaunitz, the emperor had shown that he could sometimes take a personal initiative and carry it through triumphantly. As against Maria Theresa, the visit established Joseph as the director of a vital aspect of the Monarchy's policy. She remarked, half-admiringly, half-cynically: 'He has seen things quite differently from the way we have seen them for twenty or thirty years.'[200] This was the first stage of Joseph's diplomatic revolution.

---

[194] M.T. to K., 16 Aug. 1780 (Arneth, *GMT* x, p. 833); to Ferd., 21 Aug. (Arneth, *MTKuF* II, p. 290); to Mercy and M.A., 31 Aug. (Arneth & Geffroy III, pp. 462–3).

[195] Tratchevsky, *RH* (1880), 280; *PC* XLIV, *passim*; Madariaga, *SR* (1959–60), esp. 114, 139.

[196] J. to M.T., 18 July 1780 (Arneth, *MTuJ* III, p. 286); J. to L., 3 Jan. 1781 (Arneth, *JuL* I, p. 2).

[197] J. to M.T., 12 July 1780 (Arneth, *MTuJ* III, pp. 279–80); L. Cobenzl to J., 22 July and 2 Aug., J.'s reply of 21 Aug. (Beer & Fiedler, *JuLC* I, pp. 32, 40, 45).

[198] Ranke, *Die deutschen Mächte*, vol. I, pp. 137–8; Hösch, *Jahrbücher für Geschichte Osteuropas* (1964), 189–90; Griffiths, *CSS* (1970), 559.

[199] Goertz, *Mémoire* (1786), pp. 26–9. In J. to Catherine, 13 Nov. 1780 (Arneth, *JuK*, pp. 16–17), he played on her desire to emancipate herself from her ministers.

[200] M.T. to Ferd., 21 Aug. 1780 (Arneth, *MTKuF* II, p. 290).

CHAPTER 14

Joseph and Josephism under Maria Theresa

THE HISTORIOGRAPHICAL PROBLEM

Of the three classic 'enlightened despots', Frederick and Catherine are universally styled 'the Great'. A few writers tried to attach the same epithet to Joseph,[1] but it did not stick. On the other hand, no movement or tendency has been named after Frederick or Catherine, whereas 'Josephism' has become a firmly established concept of historiography.

The origins of the term seen never to have been studied in detail,[2] and in any case would interest us mainly as an element in the mythology that grew up around the emperor after his death. But it is clear that, when invented, the word referred to developments in the relations between church and state thought to be directly associated with Joseph and his rule. Modern historians give the term a much broader significance. In the Introduction to this book Josephism was defined as

a movement for a change ... affecting many aspects of [the life of the Monarchy], but especially associated with claims made and measures taken by the state to control and reform the Roman Catholic Church within its borders, involving not only obviously ecclesiastical matters like the exclusion of papal bulls, the dissolution of monasteries and the introduction of religious toleration but also wider issues such as the reform of education in all its aspects, the liberalisation of censorship and the reorganisation of poor relief.

This definition would probably command the acceptance of many, though not of all, students in the field – but only if it was applied to a period beginning about 1750, before Joseph could exercise any personal influence, and continuing well into the nineteenth century, long after his death. Three distinguished works that still dominate the field, all entitled *Der Josephinismus* and

---

[1] This question will be discussed in the second volume of this study.
[2] E. Kovács in her article 'Giuseppinismo' in *Dizionario degli Istituti di Perfezione*, ed. Pelliccia and Rocca, vol. IV, cols. 1357–67, speaks confidently of the origins of the term. But her source seems to be R. Bauer, 'Remarques sur l'histoire "du" ou "des" Joséphismes', in *Utopie et Institutions au XVIIIe siècle*, ed. P. Francastel (Paris, 1963), pp. 107–12, which makes no pretence of covering the question in depth.

all published during or soon after the Second World War,[3] agree in extending the chronological range of their treatment far beyond the emperor's years of power.

They agree on little else, and at least one of them would reject my proposed definition. For Fritz Valjavec, Josephism embraced the whole story of Enlightenment in the Monarchy during the late eighteenth and early nineteenth centuries, and was not bound up with governmental activity or with church–state relations. This usage has not been generally accepted. Of course the Enlightenment is relevant to the matters traditionally discussed under the heading of Josephism; but it is unhelpful to equate two terms which, though related, are clearly distinguishable and which it is convenient to distinguish.[4] Eduard Winter shifted the concept's meaning more plausibly, to 'reform Catholicism in the Monarchy from 1740 to 1848'. This description overlaps to a much greater extent with the original meaning, and with my definition, but still tends to underplay the role of the state and that of the emperor himself.[5] The most central of the three treatments came from Ferdinand Maass who, in editing five volumes of relevant official documents, defined Josephism as *Staatskirchentum*, 'state domination of the church' or 'Caesaropapism', during the period 1750–1855. Maass insisted that the concept of Josephism would lose its identity if it was dissociated from government action.[6] But this did not lead him on to accept the natural corollary that the views and work of Joseph himself were of special importance in its development. On the contrary, Maass minimised the emperor's role in new ways. Apart from extending the history of Josephism into periods when the emperor was too young to exert influence, or dead, he allowed him very little importance during the admittedly seminal years of his co-regency. In Maass's first volume, which goes down to 1769, he quoted Joseph only once, and then from a false letter.[7] Thereafter the emperor was kept off stage until toleration became an issue in the later seventies. Further, Maass stressed the significance both of Maria Theresa's reforming intentions as expressed in her political testament and of the ecclesiastical plans and legislation affecting Lombardy in the 1760s, which he saw as anticipating most if not all that was applied during the next two decades to the rest of the Monarchy. These initiatives he attributed chiefly to Kaunitz, assisted by other officials, and in virtually no point to the emperor. 'If Kaunitz was the father of Josephism,'

---

[3] The first edition of Winter's *Josefinismus* appeared in 1943; that of Valjavec's *Josephinismus* in 1944; and the first volume of Maass's *Josephinismus* in 1951.
[4] See Bauer, *Critique* (1958), 630–2, 633n.
[5] Winter's position is both confusing and demonstrably wrong. Sometimes he emphasises the supposed economic basis of Bohemian Josephism. At other times he will give weight to J. himself, though in the 1780s rather than earlier, both in the book and in his pamphlet, 'Josef II.', *Der Bindenschild*, III (1946). But he places great stress on the now exploded view that Martini was J.'s tutor. (See *Josefinismus*, pp. 38, 100–14.)
[6] Maass, *Josephinismus*, vol. I, pp. xviii–xx.   [7] *Ibid.*, vol. I, p. 97n. See below, pp. 460–1.

he asserted, 'Maria Theresa was the mother.'[8] That, deliberately, left Joseph nowhere.

More recent writing has illuminated other aspects of the subject, such as the influence of 'Jansenism' in Austria and the reform of the censorship, the liturgy and theological education.[9] But no historian has studied the emperor's own aims and work in the light of this new research. It is the obvious duty of a biographer to do this, and to consider whether Joseph himself deserves to be treated after all as a serious contributor to the movement that bears his name.

MARIA THERESA'S REIGN BEFORE 1765

Much must be conceded to the army of historians who have given weight to other influences. It is certainly true, first, that the regime of Charles VI, under which a peculiarly superstitious, bigoted and restrictive Catholicism was inextricably bound up with secular affairs and enthusiastically supported by the state, had been considerably modified before Joseph had any part in decision-making. The most striking step by far was the destruction of the Jesuits' virtual monopoly of censorship and university education in 1759.[10] Until then the Society had enjoyed the special favour of the Monarchy's rulers for over a century. Every royal confessor was a Jesuit. So were all professors of philosophy and theology. The Society educated nearly all the clergy and controlled the censorship of nearly all books. It also ran most secondary schools. Jesuits were associated with maintaining the trappings of baroque piety and the theological attitudes that justified it. In the universities they alone taught philosophy and theology, and their power enabled them to prevent the study there of rival schools of thought, even including the traditions of the great Benedictine, Augustinian and Dominican Orders.

Small groups of both laymen and clergy, some influenced by Jansenism or by Muratori, had been campaigning against the Jesuits' teaching and the monopoly that sustained it. The Society was especially criticised for favouring a moral system, 'probabilism', that was said to blur the just distinctions between right and wrong. There was obvious reason why not only the great monastic Orders but also the bishops and the secular clergy should be jealous

8 As well as in *ibid.* (esp. vol. I), Maass stresses the importance of the Lombard legislation in *MÖSA* (1948), 289–444. The quotation is from the article, p. 297n.

9 Hersche, *Spätjansenismus*; Klingenstein, *Staatsverwaltung und kirchliche Autorität*; E. Kovács, *Ultramontanismus und Staatskirchentum im theresianisch-josephinischen Staat* (Vienna, 1975) and her article in *MÖSA* (1979), 109–42 on ceremonial.

10 For this and the next paragraph see particularly the books cited in the previous note, which all contain full bibliographies, and Winter, *Josefinismus*, esp. pp. 37–45. Prof. Klingenstein has written a useful article, supplementing her book, on 'Van Swieten und die Zensur' in *Gerard van Swieten und seine Zeit*, ed. E. Lesky & A. Wandruszka (Vienna, 1973), pp. 93–106. In English, on the importance and role of the Jesuits generally, Chadwick, *Popes and Revolution*, ch. 5; and for the Monarchy, Evans, *Making of the Habsburg Monarchy*, passim.

of the Jesuits' power. Van Swieten, working under the empress's patronage from within the university and the censorship commission, had already achieved some victories against them, like the licence to circulate *De l'esprit des lois*. When Migazzi became archbishop of Vienna in 1757, he joined Van Swieten in urging Maria Theresa to go further. She was induced to act in 1759, when she removed some Jesuits from their Chairs and from their places on the censorship commission, and replaced them with non-Jesuits. This measure clearly marked a major shift of policy.

Apart from the assault on the Jesuits, however, no radical ecclesiastical changes were actually carried out by Maria Theresa before the sixties – unless the reduction in the number of feast-days, agreed with the papacy, is counted as radical. But she had certainly envisaged in her political testament, written in the early fifties, 'a great reform' of the monasteries to be effected 'in good time and after due consideration', in order to take away their surplus wealth. Further, with reference to Hungary, she had looked forward to improving spiritual provision, with the aid of both clergy and laymen. She made approaches to the pope in the late fifties for assistance in some such project, associated with heavier taxation of the clergy by the state. These plans have been held to foreshadow the whole programme of Josephism.[11]

I believe that too much has been made of the undoubtedly remarkable passages in her testament. They certainly show hostility to the monasteries and their wealth. But her words do not explicitly prescribe unilateral action on the part of the state without the agreement of the papacy, or even the actual suppression of monasteries; and the mention of enlisting the help of laymen, which has been used to argue that she was already prepared to usurp the role of the clergy in all church reform, as the principles of Josephism would require, is quite plainly restricted to Hungary and to the making of better provision there for education and hospitals. For Maria Theresa, Hungary was a special case because, despite all her own and her predecessors' efforts, it remained half Protestant. Moreover, the statements were secret and private, as were the negotiations that have been connected with them; and nothing was achieved. By contrast, she was making a more public fuss in 1758 in order to secure from the new pope, Clement XIII, recognition of the title 'Apostolic' which she claimed as queen of Hungary. This she considered important to her prestige now that the king of Portugal, by becoming 'Most

---

[11] See for this and the next paragraph pp. 53–4 above and the literature cited on p. 53, n. 142. For some strident statements asserting the all-embracing significance of M.T.'s remarks see Wangermann, *Austrian Achievement*, pp. 74–5, 78–9; Maass, *Josephinismus*, vol. I, pp. 5–10. Maass quotes the passage on Hungary in full (p. 6), but by p. 9 is talking as though it applied to Austria. J. A. von Helfert, *Die Gründung der österreichischen Volksschule durch Maria Theresia* (2 vols., styled vols. I and III, Prague, 1860), vol. I, p. 222 stresses the importance of the reduction of feast-days.

Faithful', had joined the 'Most Christian' king of France and the 'Catholic' king of Spain.[12]

Changes in her attitude were encouraged by events abroad. At the same time as the Jesuit monopolies were being attacked in the Monarchy, an international crusade against the Society was getting under way. Secular rulers advanced many standard charges against them: they owed obedience to a foreign sovereign, the pope, rather than to their own prince; some of their teachers not only taught probabilism, but advocated assassination in certain cases, and Jesuits were supposed to have plotted to kill the king of Portugal; their royal confessors abused the secret of the confessional in the interests of the Society and the papacy; they were rich, and had become so by sharp practice or worse. In 1759 Portugal expelled them and confiscated their property. Five years later, after a tremendous battle publicised all over Europe, the Society was suppressed in France. The pope was being urged by many Catholic rulers to dissolve it completely.[13]

A wider assault now began on the position of the church, and especially of the papacy. In 1763 there appeared over the pseudonym 'Febronius' a work entitled *The State of the Church*, which argued that individual bishops ought to possess the powers at present exercised by the pope, and that secular rulers had not only the right, but the duty, to promote church reform. The author was soon discovered to be Nikolaus von Hontheim, suffragan bishop of Trier in the *Reich*. His views attracted much interest, especially in Germany.[14] In one state after another during the sixties, legislation was enacted, often without papal sanction, to prevent the church from receiving further donations of land, to take back some of what had already been given, to tax the clergy more heavily, to abolish their legal privileges, to end or restrict the right of criminals to sanctuary in religious institutions, to abolish monastic and episcopal prisons, to limit the number of monks, to refuse entry to papal bulls, to put ecclesiastical appointments in the hands of the secular ruler, to curb the Inquisition and so forth. By comparison with any period since the Reformation, the pace of ecclesiastical change was hectic.[15]

The Monarchy at first lagged behind other Catholic states. Before 1765 the main development was the further weakening of the Jesuits' position. In 1760 Joseph's bride, Isabella, set the precedent of appointing a non-Jesuit confessor. He was soon employed in the same capacity for other members of the

12 Arneth, *GMT* IX, pp. 8–10. Dr P. G. M. Dickson reminds me that M.T. did tax the clergy more heavily than other Catholic rulers did.

13 Chadwick, *Popes and Revolution*, pp. 346–59; Pastor, *History of the Popes*, vol. XXXVI, pp. 294–504; D. V. Kley, *The Jansenists and the Expulsion of the Jesuits from France, 1757–1765* (London, 1975).

14 Chadwick, *Popes and Revolution*, pp. 408–11; Pastor, *History of the Popes*, vol. XXXVI, pp. 247–75; Winter, *Josefinismus*, pp. 41–2, 93–7.

15 Chadwick, *Popes and Revolution*, esp. pp. 47–59, 227–9, 239–49, 332. For Italy, Venturi, *Settecento riformatore*, esp. vol. II.

royal family.[16] Jesuits played a much smaller part in Leopold's education than in Joseph's.[17] In 1764 the last Jesuit left the censorship commission.[18] Influential lay intellectuals like Van Swieten and Sonnenfels, together with a few advanced clergymen, argued for further liberalisation of censorship and education. But Migazzi, once the power of the pope and the independence of the church had been challenged, moved on to the defensive, even taking up the cause of the Jesuits. Maria Theresa, subjected to these contradictory pressures, pursued an uncertain and vacillating policy. For example, the censorship commission induced her to permit the circulation of Febronius's book in 1764, but Migazzi had the decision reversed – though not for long. In 1764 also, Maria Theresa showed pleasure when Adam Kollár put forward on her behalf extensive claims to rights over the church in Hungary; but the reaction of the Hungarian Diet forced her publicly to dissociate herself from them.[19]

More generally, the foundation of the *Staatsrat* and 'the entry of Kaunitz into domestic politics' might have been expected to lead to movement, especially since the essential problem facing Maria Theresa and her ministers was bankruptcy, and the church was an obvious source of additional revenue. It is true that the empress made new approaches to the pope about clerical taxation, which were again rebuffed. In 1762 she asked the Austro-Bohemian Chancellery to look into ways of reducing the number of monks – but with no result. Kaunitz, who had previously shown little interest in church questions and had supported the policy of trying to secure the co-operation of the papacy, was beginning to advocate unilateral action in emulation of the reform programmes of other states. But the *Staatsrat* was not asked to consider broad ecclesiastical issues until after Joseph became co-regent.[20]

It was only in Lombardy that a more decided line was pursued. No doubt the main reason was that the province was ruled from Vienna almost despotically by Kaunitz. But he could rely on the support of the sophisticated and progressive resident minister, Firmian, and some of the local officials; and most other Italian governments were introducing anti-papal and anti-clerical legislation. In 1762 Kaunitz and Firmian corresponded about enacting a prohibition, on the Spanish model, of all papal pronouncements unless they had been approved by the ruler. Relations with Rome steadily worsened. By

[16] Hersche, *Spätjansenismus*, p. 139.
[17] Wandruszka, *L. II.*, vol. I; pp. 40–52. On Leopold's sympathetic attitude to the Jesuits, though, see *ibid.*, vol. I, pp. 236–7.
[18] Klingenstein, *Staatsverwaltung und kirchliche Autorität*, p. 188.
[19] Arneth, *GMT* VII, pp. 114–22 and IX, pp. 148–50; Maass, *Josephinismus*, vol. I, pp. 40–6. More generally, see the works cited in n. 9 above.
[20] This interesting point, made by Hock, *Staatsrath*, p. 48, seems fully borne out by the small number and limited range of the ecclesiastical questions listed at the end of K-M VI as appearing on the agenda of the *Staatsrat* before 1766. On the question of clerical taxation and monastic numbers see Maass, *Frühjosephinismus*, p. 76 and ch. 5.

the end of 1764 the chancellor was talking wildly of the 'despotism' that the papacy was seeking to establish, which he said would deny the lay sovereign any rights in ecclesiastical matters. Firmian went to Innsbruck for Leopold's wedding, and Kaunitz discussed with him at length there, and afterwards in Vienna, new arrangements for the government of Lombardy, with special reference to church questions. On 30 November 1765 a *Giunta Economale* was set up in Milan, charged with considering every matter in this field that was not deemed purely spiritual. The new body, chiefly composed of laymen, would supersede the bishops and the ancient local Senate in advising the empress. Thus far had Kaunitz travelled, and induced Maria Theresa to accompany him, by the end of 1765.[21]

THE EARLY YEARS OF JOSEPH'S CO-REGENCY, 1765–70

There appears to be no surviving direct evidence of Joseph's views on ecclesiastical questions before he became emperor, except that we know he hated over-elaborate ceremonial and lengthy worship. He says nothing about the church either in his first memorandum of 1761 or in the *Rêveries* of 1763. But as soon as his father died, he burst on to the scene with his reform of Court etiquette and ceremonial, and his memorandum of 1765 on the state of the Monarchy. The former involved the drastic reduction of the number of solemn public appearances by the Court at religious services. Khevenhüller, we have seen, thought his mother 'inclined' in the same direction. But this radical measure, followed by other piecemeal modifications of particular ceremonies, was plainly a personal initiative of Joseph's, and went much further than the empress would have contemplated. She later complained of 'the drawbacks that always follow abolishing formalities at a great Court. I see the results only too well here. Everything falls into inanition, and no one is satisfied.'[22] As a recent historian has written,

If one surveys the change in the ceremonial observance of public worship in the period from 1765–6 to 1780–1, one sees the almost total destruction of *Pietas Austriaca*, of Habsburg piety, as it had developed since the beginning of the seventeenth century, carried out by Joseph himself ... It illustrated the operation of Josephist principles before they were enacted into law, and foreshadowed liturgical decrees like the 'Josephist Prayer Book' of 1783.[23]

This fundamental reform of 1765, ignored by Maass, owed nothing, so far as we know, to Kaunitz, and little to Maria Theresa.

In his memorandum of 1765 Joseph touched on several pertinent issues: the

---

[21] Maass, *MÖSA* (1948) and *Josephinismus*, vol. I, esp. chs. 4 and 6 and the related documents. Venturi, *Settecento riformatore*, vol. II, pp. 86–8.
[22] M.T. to Mercy, 1 Jan. 1780 (Arneth & Geffroy III, p. 384).
[23] E. Kovács, *MÖSA* (1979), 133.

oppressiveness of the censorship system; the disadvantages of religious intolerance; the weaknesses of education in the Monarchy; and the excessive size, number and wealth of monasteries, many of which he considered useless. It is instructive to see how Kaunitz, in the comments requested from him by Maria Theresa, dealt with these questions. He virtually ignored censorship and toleration. In his lengthy discussion of education, though he spent much time on how to secure from it practical benefits to the various classes of society, he gave an important place to religious and moral instruction. He drily suggested that cardinal Migazzi might usefully employ his 'apostolic zeal' in preparing suitable textbooks in these fields for lower schools. But the most remarkable section of his comments, involving an unexpected conflict of view with Joseph, relates to the monasteries. The emperor had proposed a commission of enquiry into all houses, followed, where appropriate, by their reform and the reallocation of their surplus resources. 'Whatever the pope and all the monks in the universe might say', he would raise the age at which binding vows could be taken to twenty-five. The chancellor first casts doubt on the assumption that monks and nuns are too numerous. He claims that in the German hereditary lands, according to the census, the total is only 23,000. Of course, if the state were being refounded, celibacy would be restricted. But, far from the monasteries removing from useful lay employment numerous able citizens, there is a shortage of jobs, and in any case most monks are virtually unemployable. Hence the convents are performing a service to society by maintaining them.

If monks live at public expense, they also render services, and that is so true that, unless it was decided to reduce the obligation to attend worship, it would scarcely be possible to do without their help or ministry. It is true that there could be fewer monks if there were more secular priests. But it is not less true that the cost of priests is much higher than that of monks, for it is clear that three monks can live in a community on what it would be necessary to pay one priest living on his own...

Even the replacement of the services provided by a mere one-tenth of mendicant houses would be financially prohibitive. Certainly, monks 'spread and favour the spirit of bigotry'. However, the remedy for this fault is not suppression of monasteries but the introduction of a 'reasonable catechism' that the monks are obliged to preach, thus gradually purifying popular education. As for the age of profession, while Kaunitz thinks it is within the competence of the lay ruler to fix it, he doubts the justice of undermining in this way individual rights, 'for at the end of the day [monks] are citizens like the bourgeois and the gentleman, they ought like them to enjoy the protection of the state, and in this state they pay as much for the privilege as any other class of citizens'. Perhaps a compromise measure could be adopted which would cause the establishment of each monastery to fall to the level originally intended.

These arguments are characteristically clinical, and it is no surprise to find Kaunitz already stating the position he later forced upon the empress, that the secular ruler could properly raise the age of monastic profession without the concurrence of the pope: 'If the sovereign has the power to forbid subjects to alienate and even enjoy their property until they have attained the age of majority, why should he not equally be able to forbid them to alienate their persons?'[24] But his hesitation to advise the use of this power, and his assessment of the utility of monks and their houses, are astonishing in view of his later actions. Indeed, these attitudes seem unlikely to have corresponded to his true opinion even in 1766. Zinzendorf had recorded five years earlier that Kaunitz 'said a great deal against monasteries . . . that he always felt pity when he saw young people there with nothing to do, isolating themselves from society'.[25] However, perhaps on the orders of Maria Theresa, Kaunitz had now committed himself to this eccentric defence of the existing monastic system. Here is a case where, as even Maass admits,[26] it was the chancellor who was slow in coming round to Joseph's opinion, not vice versa. The policy towards the monasteries proposed by the emperor in his memorandum was much more explicitly radical than what his mother had suggested in her political testament; Kaunitz argued against it; and yet it was the policy soon to be enacted, partly under Maria Theresa and partly in the 1780s.

After Joseph became co-regent, Lombardy remained for some years a centre of ecclesiastical reform. In 1767 Kaunitz induced the empress to remove powers of censorship from the clergy there, and to appoint a commission overwhelmingly composed of laymen to undertake the task. The pope called this 'an entirely new system', unparalleled in any Catholic state. In the same year the government declared that no new ecclesiastical foundations could be made, and no property given to existing institutions, without its permission. Secret new instructions were sent to the *Giunta Economale* in June 1768, in which it was proclaimed that the lay power had the right to act in all matters affecting the church except dogma, biblical interpretation, worship, the sacraments and internal discipline – and even in these areas the clergy were not conceded complete independence, since society as a whole was interested in the issues involved. Early in 1769 the first steps were taken towards dissolving a small number of monasteries supposed to be useless, corrupt and superfluous. By now, to Kaunitz's great satisfaction, his edicts were being

---

[24] See above, pp. 167–8 for J.'s memorandum. K.'s reply is printed in Beer, *AÖG* (1872), the relevant passages on pp. 102–9. Dr P. G. M. Dickson tells me that K.'s figure of 23,000 'religious' was really the total for all clergy.
[25] HHSA TZ, 4 May 1761.   [26] Maass, *MÖSA* (1948), 301.

imitated by other Powers. He declared complacently that he had done more in Milan in the last three years than had been achieved by his predecessors in the last three hundred.[27]

As we have seen, there is no reason to think that the emperor had much part in these reforms, though he applauded them in general. But in the late sixties the *Staatsrat* began to discuss proposals for church reform in the Monarchy as a whole, and Joseph was necessarily involved in these debates though, as always, we are ignorant of his detailed role. In the 'General picture' he told Leopold of the pope's intransigence over

the establishment of the *Erbschafts-Steuer* [death duties] for priests, over the transfer we had proposed of all feast-days falling on weekdays to Sundays, over the distribution of the revenues of the salt-fund in Bohemia, over the affairs of the censorship and the Theology Chairs in our universities, even over marriage dispensations.

Although Vienna, says Joseph, has hitherto shown patience, it is apparent that the best method of dealing with the pope would be to ask for his consent to changes while telling him that, if he did not give it, they would be made all the same, for the good of the state. In writing like this, the emperor was adopting a position not yet formally sanctioned, and never wholeheartedly accepted, by Maria Theresa.[28]

In 1768, however, she duly announced that she would henceforth tax the clergy, in Hungary as well as in other lands, on her sole authority. The chancellor was meanwhile devoting immense effort to trying to establish a theoretical basis for the assertion of lay power over almost every aspect of church affairs. He drew on the legislation of other states, on legal authorities and even on the *Encyclopédie*. He actually wrote a pamphlet for publication entitled *On the Sovereign Power of Roman Catholic Princes in relation to Religion and the Clergy*, which took the line of the secret instructions to the *Giunta Economale*. With his habitual modesty, he claimed to have solved a problem men had puzzled over unavailingly for more than a millennium. In 1768 also, an official called Heinke was instructed to prepare a document on the principles of a new system of church–state relations for 'all the German hereditary lands including Hungary'. His conclusions, which closely resembled Kaunitz's, received a guarded approval from Maria Theresa in the next year; and in 1770 he became the effective director of a new government

[27] Maass, *Josephinismus*, vol. I, chs. 7–9 and related documents, which can be supplemented from his article in *MÖSA* (1948). Venturi, *Settecento riformatore*, vol. II, pp. 88–94. A. Ellemunter, *Antonio Eugenio Visconti und die Anfänge des Josephinismus* (Graz, 1963) gives further information and explains the policy of Rome.

[28] HHSA TG, ff. 190–1. Pastor describes J.'s attitude in this memorandum (the ecclesiastical portions of which were quoted by Arneth in *GMT* IX, pp. 27–8, 550–1) as 'completely Febronian' (*History of the Popes*, vol. XXXIX, p. 429); but that seems to me unhelpful, since J. never, so far as I know, sympathised with the rights of bishops against the pope unless to promote the power of the ruler.

agency, the *Consessus in publicis-ecclesiasticis*, which settled down to devising detailed proposals for church reform.[29]

Among the factors which strengthened the empress's willingness to act against the church, especially in the late sixties, was her indignation at the attitude of pope Clement XIII, who was trying to reassert the position of Rome after the complaisant reign of Benedict XIV. Clement not only refused to help her over clerical taxation, but he appointed Lombard bishops without consulting her. He complained to her about the treatment of his representative at the election of Joseph as king of the Romans, comparing her unfavourably with her predecessors. She was furious; it had been nothing to do with her; she declined to receive the pope's letter. The crowning instance of what she saw as his presumption was his revival of the old papalist pretensions against her relative, the duke of Parma, in 1768.[30] Other Catholic Powers, of course, were pressing her to take much stronger action, and she wished to please them because they were allies and because they supplied husbands for her daughters. Even Leopold of Tuscany was by 1769 engaging in reform more advanced than Vienna's, and recommending it to his mother.[31]

The mere fact that Joseph had become co-regent, given the views he expressed in his memorandum of 1765, decidedly altered the balance of forces around her. His role in the *Staatsrat* has already been mentioned. The extent of his activity elsewhere can only be surmised from certain instances that happen to have been recorded. One concerns a notable event of 1767, the appointment of the provost of the convent of St Dorothea in Vienna, Ignaz Müller, as confessor extraordinary to Maria Theresa. Until then, her confessor since childhood had been a Jesuit, Father Kampmiller. At the height of her dangerous illness in 1767, Müller was called in and

although she still always confessed to Father Kampmiller ... she did nothing in any other matter of significance without consulting the ... Provost, and made a habit of holding secret heart-to-heart talks with him on the 18th of every month, her day of retreat.[32]

Müller was a notorious enemy of the Jesuits and friend to church reform, and as confessor he made it easy for Maria Theresa to approve Josephist

---

[29] As well as Maass, *Josephinismus*, vol. I and *MÖSA* (1948), *Josephinismus*, vol. III now comes into play, esp. pp. 1–29, 139–215 on the preparatory work of Heinke. Hock, *Staatsrath*, pp. 48–53; Arneth, *GMT* IX, pp. 45–7, 57. Wangermann, *Austrian Achievement*, p. 81, has the chronology wrong.

[30] Arneth, *GMT* IX, pp. 11–26. Cf. Maass, *Josephinismus*, esp. vol. I, pp. 81–6 and vol. II, pp. 28–31, and the relevant documents. See p. 256 above.

[31] Wandruszka, *L. II.*, vol. I, pp. 229–35; cf. Arneth, *GMT* IX, p. 54, and Diaz, *Studi settecenteschi* (1981), 20–4.

[32] K-M VIII, pp. 181–2 (31 Aug. 1773). Hersche, *Spätjansenismus*, pp. 128, 135, 138, rather exaggerates in talking of Kampmiller's complete supersession, for surely K-M is to be believed.

measures.[33] Why the appointment was made is something of a mystery. Kampmiller was getting old and blind. But the historian of Austrian Jansenism has discovered that, according to one plausible contemporary authority, Kampmiller lost favour because he had revealed to the Jesuit General in Rome information about the expulsion of the Society from Spain which Maria Theresa had confided to him under the seal of the confessional. It has not been noticed that another credible source, the British ambassador in Vienna, reported that Joseph himself had effected the change of confessor.[34] The emperor certainly had the opportunity, since he was continuously with his mother during her illness. If he did help to bring about the appointment of Müller, he made thereby an important contribution to the progress of Josephism.

He can be seen in the background of reform again in the next year. Paolo Frisi, one of the most important figures of the Milanese Enlightenment, was then visiting Vienna, where he wrote an essay at Kaunitz's suggestion on the temporal power of princes and the spiritual authority of the church. In the dedicatory preface Frisi tells of having discussed the question with the emperor. A few months later when Clement XIII died in 1769, Joseph interviewed Migazzi about the coming conclave, and made a point of needling the cardinal by saying it did not matter who became the next pope, since Maria Theresa could tax and regulate the clergy whether or not Rome agreed.[35]

THE REFORMS OF THE SEVENTIES

During the last decade of Maria Theresa's reign, despite her hesitations, an impressive range of ecclesiastical reforms was enacted, either for the whole Monarchy or for the great majority of provinces. Many dealt either with restricting the flow of money and property to the church and tapping its wealth to the advantage of the state, or with asserting the authority of the secular power over and against the clergy. Under the first heading the main change was the renewed prohibition in 1771 of further gifts of land to the church, unless permitted by the government. In the second category the chief measures abolished monastic and episcopal prisons (1771) and limited the right of criminals to asylum on church property (1775). Other provisions more directly concerned spiritual matters. The age of monastic profession was raised to twenty-five in 1771. The number of public holidays on church

---

[33] On Müller S. F. Wintermayr, 'Die Aufhebung des Chorherrenstiftes St. Dorothea in Wien', *MVGSW*, XVII (1938), 52–87; Hersche, *Spätjansenismus*, esp. pp. 125–34; Ellemunter, *Visconti*, showing Müller in a somewhat different light. See also Kovács, *Ultramontanismus*, esp. pp. 81–6, and pp. 462–3 below.

[34] Hersche, *Spätjansenismus*, p. 138; Stormont to Conway, 18 July 1767, cypher (PRO SP 80/204).

[35] F. Venturi (ed.), *Illuministi italiani*, vol. III (Milan, 1958), p. 322n; Venturi, *Settecento riformatore*, vol. II, pp. 90–1; Wolfsgruber, *Migazzi*, p. 227.

festivals was again reduced, as was the extent of jollification permitted on those that remained and on Sundays (1772). Pilgrimages were curbed (1772). The education of clergy in the universities was remodelled to ensure that the government's claims and attitudes were supported by the teachers of theology, canon law and church history, and by the set textbooks; and all those training for the priesthood were required to spend some time receiving instruction in the universities. Church reformers much disliked the proliferation of religious organisations for laymen which were not integrated with the parish system, such as 'brotherhoods', numbering 668 in Lower Austria alone, and the 'Third Orders' associated with certain Orders of monks and friars. Legislation was brought in to prevent any new brotherhoods being founded (1771) and to cause the Third Orders to wither away (1776). The government set about reforming all levels of education with varying degrees of thoroughness. In her final years Maria Theresa allowed a barely perceptible extension of *de facto* religious toleration. The clergy were forbidden to criticise these measures (1776).[36] Meanwhile, the pope contributed to the march of reform by suppressing the Society of Jesus in 1773.

In most of these changes Kaunitz and his *protégés*, especially Heinke, were prime movers. Their efforts can easily be studied in their voluminous state papers, many of which Maass has published. Most of the documentation spawned by the *Staatsrat* has been lost, but we know that its role was vital, though it was sometimes deeply divided.[37] As always, Joseph's activity is hard to trace. But the part he is known to have played in one case, of 1770, strongly suggests that his influence was crucial in the whole process.

The measure concerned was one of those advocated by the emperor in his memorandum of 1765, and at that time contested by Kaunitz: the raising of the age of monastic profession. But the current form of the proposal, emanating from Heinke's commission, specified twenty-two as the minimum age, not twenty-five as Joseph had wanted. After prolonged dispute, the majority of the *Staatsrat* agreed with the recommendation and further advised that the empress could act on it without consulting the pope. The chancellor then decided to try for the higher age. He now accepted that the number of monks must be drastically reduced. As soon as Joseph returned from his journey to Hungary, Kaunitz wrote to him:

My most humble ... *Vota* concern such important matters that they seem to me especially worthy of your Imperial Majesty's gracious and most particular attention

---

[36] A most useful guide to almost all these measures is Heinke's own immense memorandum of 1787 on his work in the ecclesiastical department: Maass, *Josephinismus*, vol. III, pp. 343–402. On the important changes in university clerical education see esp. Kovács, *Ultramontanismus*, chs. 3.2, 4 and 5. F. Hartl, 'Pax et securitas', *Jahrbuch des Vereines für Geschichte der Stadt Wien*, XXXII (1977), 42–62, stresses the limitations of the legislation on asylum. It is puzzling that the renewal of frequently reiterated legislation on mortmain should appear so significant.
[37] See Hock, *Staatsrath*, pp. 48–68.

and, if they should please Your Imperial Majesty, also of your most gracious strongest support. For, since they differ greatly from the common view, they will doubtless meet much opposition; and, if the cause is not to be lost once and for all, everything may depend on [your support], so that by taking the first step in such important and difficult matters a solid foundation may be laid to the great building which I believe I am right in thinking it is Your Majesty's gracious intention gradually to erect.

Kaunitz urged on Joseph the utmost secrecy about this approach. Between them, they carried the day on the essential issue. At a later stage, however, a protest from the pope on the subject so affected Maria Theresa that she drastically corrected Kaunitz's draft reply, thereby conceding some of Rome's arguments. The chancellor threw a tantrum, turning the matter into a question of her confidence in his whole policy and in his efficient performance of his duties. Joseph was on hand to lend him aid. The empress apologised, and accepted Kaunitz's draft.[38] Here is absolutely clear proof of the secret collaboration of emperor and chancellor in church matters, of the importance to Kaunitz of Joseph's support, and of the minister's deliberate adoption of a proposal he had resisted when it had been made earlier by the emperor, a change of view justified by the assertion that he was concerned to further Joseph's long-term plans.

It was during 1771, when many of the church reforms were being discussed, that Joseph came nearest to running the *Staatsrat* himself.[39] In the absence of other records, the best evidence available for his attitudes on religious questions at this time comes from a section of the Bohemian *Relation* he wrote at the end of the year.[40] Here he emphasises above all the need to improve education, and especially the training of the clergy.

He has found 'true Christian and moral virtues' woefully lacking among the subjects of the empress. The common people are grossly ignorant, and even the better-off are kept by overworked, selfish and stupid clergy in a deplorable state of superstitious piety. For example, they join brotherhoods and pay for numerous Masses to be said after their death. They are taught to ascribe to the saints emotions like spite, jealousy and vengefulness, and so are frightened into paying money for their salvation 'instead of [feeling] the childlike respect, love and obedience which are all that, in my opinion, God asks of us'. Among particular enormities Joseph mentions a crucifix hung with tobacco-pipes and resting on nude figures; and the widely displayed coat-of-arms of the dean of

[38] The letter from K. to J., 4 July 1770 in Maass, *Josephinismus*, vol. II, p. 139. See also in this vol. ch. I and pp. 144–59; F. Maass, 'Die Stellungnahme des Fürsten Kaunitz zur staatlichen Festsetzung der Altersgrenze für die Ablegung der Ordensgelübde in Österreich im Jahre 1770/71', *MÖIG*, LVIII (1950), 656–67; Arneth, *GMT* IX, pp. 70–8; Hock, *Staatsrath*, pp. 53–5.
[39] See above, pp. 207–8.
[40] Printed in K-M VII, the relevant passages on pp. 381–5. Schüller, 'J. II.', uses (e.g. pp. 62–3) another memo. of J.'s in the same spirit, which I could not find, dating from 1770 and referring to Austria.

Vysehrad, which depicts St Peter publicly whipping a duke of Bohemia for having seized something belonging to the Chapter. No doubt, he says, this will continue until reparation is made.

Sermons, he goes on, are full of adventure stories and fairy-tales.

They would do much better if they confined themselves to the great Commandments, Love God and Thy Neighbour, for this alone is the true way to promote effective Christianity and to cultivate honourable citizens, faithful subjects and worthy servants of God and the state.

In this manner stupidity, idleness and disloyalty could be eradicated among the upper as well as the lower classes. The clergy come of peasant stock and are compelled to live like peasants, because they are underpaid. Their parishes are huge. The seminary in Prague, though good, is far too small to train all priests. The dioceses of Prague and Olmütz are much too large, and anyway the bishops have a bad reputation. Two more bishoprics are needed in Bohemia, and another two in Moravia.

A completely new system is required.

What good are the random proposals of our wretched *Religions-Commission* for improving the clergy? What difference will one feast-day more or less make? or a few nuns? The essential is this, that personal conduct and attitude must be changed. Unless the clergy can regulate themselves and be regulated, nothing can be done. Unless they are relieved of worldly anxieties and freed from all considerations of self-interest, educated better and put in a better position to lead a better life and fulfil their duties more adequately, there can be no assurance that the service of God, of their fellow-men and of the state will ever be properly undertaken, and God's perfect handiwork will be continually misapplied and brought into disrepute by the most absurd and disgraceful practices, a source of derision to our enemies and of scandal to all thinking and rational men – from which irreligion and unbelief easily arise.

As often, in his passion Joseph's grammar gets completely out of hand, and the section ends with a verbless sentence incoherently denouncing the extortionate vagabondage of the mendicant Orders.

In order to deal with the problem of the clergy's degradation, what is necessary is 'the amalgamation of all ecclesiastical revenues and foundations' under one administration that can distribute them according to need. According to Joseph, the church in these provinces is very wealthy, owning at least a seventh of the lands, and in particular, the provision for private Masses runs to 8,000,000 florins in Moravia alone.

What a rich fund from which to abolish mendicant monks, to establish and order a proper hierarchy, to foster religion worthy of our most perfect Creator and Saviour! There would be resources available for the most useful foundations, the increase of parishes and schoolmasters, the support of seminaries and houses for retired clergy, finally for foundling hospitals, orphanages, workhouses, houses of correction, spinning-houses and prisons – yes, and hospitals – in which the young would be trained

Joseph and Josephism under Maria Theresa

as true Catholic members of the state, those who had been abandoned would receive life, the idle would be put away, criminals punished and reformed, and finally the worn-out and aged cared for.

All this would come much closer to God's plan than the existing monasteries, convents, bishops and parish priests.

Everyone is a servant of God like us – but also of the state. If we are to fulfil our obligations, it is our duty – and for this purpose we need neither Rome nor bishops – to create in each province better distribution and order. This has nothing to do with dogma, rites or morals.

He ends this section by describing how people are dying in Prague without the ministrations of any of the numerous clergy there.

This harangue is typical of the emperor in its breathlessness, its radicalism, its censoriousness and its impatience. But it stands out among his writings in its religiosity. Though he never forgets to mention duty to the state as well as duties to God, the church and one's neighbour, and though he stresses that lay rulers are not only entitled but bound to reform the church, he talks ardently of increasing the numbers, improving the quality and enhancing the effectiveness of the secular clergy. He accepts that they will continue to dominate education. Further, he attaches immense value to the fulfilment of the central priestly functions. His hopes of reformation are evangelical, almost apocalyptic. After reading this document, it is impossible to doubt the genuineness of his religious fervour – which he clearly conceives to be a true Catholic's.

So far as his governmental activity in the seventies is concerned, we must then suppose – and other evidence bears out this view[41] – that he became impatient over some of the minutiae of church reform. As in all other spheres, he claimed that only petty changes were being attempted when what was required was something approaching a revolution. In this area he was frustrated by the lengthy negotiations with Rome and the opposition of Migazzi as well as by the laboriousness of the Viennese bureaucracy. But he will surely have supported restrictions on 'the masquerades called brotherhoods', the Third Order and pilgrimages, the remodelling of clerical education, and every aspect of the assertion of lay sovereignty over the church and against the pope. A particular suggestion he made, for the creation of new bishoprics in Bohemia and Moravia, was taken up by his mother with the pope, and after long negotiations one new diocese, of Brünn, was set up in 1777.[42] His ideas about clerical education resemble those that Kaunitz was to

---

[41] E.g. a report from Visconti quoted in Ellemunter, *Visconti*, p. 84 (28 Aug. 1772).
[42] K-M VII, p. 383; Arneth, *GMT* IX, pp. 123–4 and X, p. 62. J. to L., 10 Dec. 1772 (HHSA FA Sbde 7), rude remark on brotherhoods omitted by Arneth, *MTuJ* I, pp. 388–90.

put forward when the Jesuits were suppressed, as they obviously foreshadow the establishment of the general seminaries during the eighties.[43]

On three particular, interrelated topics it is possible to illustrate Joseph's influence more specifically: education, the Jesuits and toleration.

EDUCATION

Joseph had fulminated about the existing system in his memorandum of 1765, criticising especially the universities, the religious bias of schools and the lack of worthwhile education for women. Kaunitz had accepted the need for reform, but of a rather less radical character than Joseph had proposed. In the Bohemian *Relation* the emperor emphasised clerical education as the key to all reform in the field. But he added some remarks on the content of the basic education that the clergy gave to pupils in ordinary schools.

Education in YM's lands, despite all the effort and expense that YM has devoted to it, has still not attained the point at which it would be really useful to the state. This is partly because public education and all lower schools, entirely in the hands of the clergy, still follow the time-consuming old method of instructing children for nine or ten years in the comparatively useless Latin language, without teaching them to think properly or to read and write correctly in their mother-tongue. The higher schools are certainly staffed with professors who are the best in our states, but these men do not compare with those of other countries either in industry or ability.

He disclaims the knowledge to pursue the question in detail; and anyway he says it has recently been thoroughly ventilated. But the root of the problem in his opinion lies not in the schools themselves but in the low value placed by society and the court on educational attainment. So long as posts in the public service are awarded on the basis of family connections, social accomplishments and wealth, parents and children will see no advantage in good education; and the state will continue to be served by incompetent and lazy officials. If civil servants were recruited on the basis of ability, then the whole system would be transformed.[44] This argument, of course, recalls the *Rêveries* as well as the memorandum of 1765.[45]

These remarks relate to a long and bitter dispute in the administration over educational reform, which was at its height in 1771. We have seen that Maria Theresa had made a beginning with modernising the universities. So far as the higher schools were concerned, her main contribution had been to found in 1746 the *Theresianum*, a large school for nobles run by Jesuits in the old Favorita palace.[46] She had also, on Kaunitz's recommendation, established in

---

[43] See Kovács, *Ultramontanismus*, p. 50 for emphasis on K.'s role, but without reference to the Bohemian *Relation*.

[44] K-M VII, pp. 385–8.   [45] See above, pp. 99–100, 167–8.

[46] E. Schlöss, *Das Theresianum*, Forschungen und Beiträge zur Wiener Stadtgeschichte, vol. V (Vienna, 1979), p. 18.

1754 an Oriental Academy intended to train future diplomats.[47] The government showed concern about secondary education generally, and about schools for the mass of the people; but little could be done unless the state could lay its hands on large quantities of money. The issue began to be more seriously discussed in 1769, when count Leopold Firmian, the prince-bishop of Passau, who in his spiritual capacity was responsible for large areas of Austria, appealed to Maria Theresa to take action to improve the dismally low standards of popular education. He himself in his own territory was doing what he could, in particular by introducing a new and more comprehensible catechism.[48] At an early stage, in 1770, the empress made the famous declaration that education was *ein Politicum*, a matter for the lay ruler.[49] As usual, it was proposed in Vienna that a special commission should be set up to deal with the matter. But the mere process of establishing this body proved remarkably vexed and lengthy.

Count Pergen, as part of his duties in the *Staatskanzlei*, had in 1769 been put in charge of the affairs of the Oriental Academy. This intervention was considered necessary because Father Frantz, Joseph's old Jesuit tutor, the head of the Academy, had mismanaged its affairs and run it into debt. Another Jesuit was appointed to succeed him, but Pergen was instructed to supervise the institution. It was not long before he became an active proponent of change first in the Academy, and then in all the schools of the Monarchy. In August 1770 he submitted a powerful paper outlining a scheme of radical educational reform, especially at the higher levels. His main concern was that pupils should be taught what would be useful to them and to the state, and to have it taught in German. But he had concluded that nothing could be achieved so long as regular clergy had any part at all in the process of education. Only secular clergy and laymen, he proposed, should be allowed to teach. He also recommended bringing in experts from Germany, including Protestants, to advise and assist. Since he had produced this document, which had been widely approved, it was agreed that he should be nominated chairman of the new education commission.[50]

However, he made a condition. He would only accept the post if his recommendation that all regular clergy should be excluded from teaching was carried into effect. Virtually no one supported him in his demand. The

---

[47] Roider, *Austria's Eastern Question*, p. 10.
[48] Hock, *Staatsrath*, p. 62; Wodka, *Kirche in Österreich*, p. 297. This point is not mentioned in the valuable account by Arneth, *GMT* IX, chs. 8–9. On education in the Austrian lands in general, I have found the following useful, as well as Helfert, *Volksschule*: G. Strakosch-Grassmann, *Geschichte des österreichischen Unterrichtswesens* (Vienna, 1905).
[49] Osterloh, *Sonnenfels*, pp. 70–1. Cf. Helfert, *Volksschule*, vol. I, pp. 117–18, and Wodka, *Kirche in Österreich*, p. 297, pointing out the restricted context and limited meaning of this assertion.
[50] For this and the next paragraph: Arneth, *GMT* IX, pp. 227–35; Hock, *Staatsrath*, pp. 63–4; Helfert, *Volksschule*, vol. I, esp. pp. 208–13, 249, 619–28.

proposal seemed, and seems, scarcely practicable. Especially at secondary level, the Jesuits supplied not only the mass of teachers but many of the best. Their competitors included rival Orders like the Piarists. The cost of replacing all these regulars would have been prohibitive, even if adequate substitutes could have been found for them. Joseph as well as Kaunitz pronounced against him.

The emperor gave his opinion also on another controversial aspect of Pergen's scheme, the suggestion that foreign professors should be enlisted. Joseph wrote on 15 July 1772:

Count Pergen's plan, though I have never read it, by common consent contained much good. But as for using learned foreign advisers, this seems to me a very useful proposal, but very inopportune. We must first of all try to ensure that every subject learns the three Rs. For that purpose all scholars are useless. [First, we need] schools and the dissemination of the Sagan teaching method, together with funds to pay able teachers, ... the assertion of control over clerical education to make it essentially consistent with the best interests of society as a whole; after this, the improvement of all grammar teaching and the elimination of unnecessary subtleties in Latin; next, scholarships for exceptionally gifted subjects of any class, who would receive the means to devote themselves fully to study of the branches of knowledge most illuminating to them, according to their varying talents; then, orphanages, foundations, colleges, academies, from which useless studies would similarly be excluded and where only promising students would be kept on, it being understood that they will not be supporting themselves but will be maintained out of public funds or by foundations.

Thereafter, when it comes to finding them jobs, there should be no class distinctions made within the civil service – at least not as between nobles and others. Only seniority should be given precedence. Not until all this has been achieved – if then – should foreign scholars be imported. 'We can or ought to know our provinces, our constitutions, our weaknesses, our resources, better than any foreign scholar, however intelligent.' The money and time spent on such a man would only delay the advance of national education.[51]

Joseph's reference to 'the Sagan teaching method' is important and interesting. It was at Sagan in Prussian Silesia that Ignaz Felbiger was provost of the Augustinian college of canons. He and his house had become famous for a new teaching method and a new catechism for primary schools, and the Vienna government had already asked his advice about educational reform. When the suppression of the Jesuits made major change inescapable, Felbiger was 'borrowed' from Frederick the Great and put in charge of the establishment of the new primary-school system.[52] It is highly significant that in 1771 the emperor gave priority to reform at this level and applauded the Sagan

[51] J.'s views in Arneth, *GMT* IX, pp. 235–7.
[52] On Felbiger and his method, Arneth, *GMT* IX, ch. 9; U. Krömer, *Johann Ignaz v. Felbiger. Leben und Werk* (Freiburg im Breisgau, 1966).

method, while rejecting the help of less orthodox *savants* who were more interested in secondary and higher education.

At first sight, it seems perverse of Joseph to refuse the aid of foreign scholars. He had often spoken of the superiority of German universities and their professors to those of the Monarchy, and he had held up Protestant universities as models.[53] More generally, it is odd that he should have put forward such radical views about opening careers in the government service to talent and encouraging individual students of special merit to study what suited them best, and yet shown himself so obscurantist about international contacts. No doubt he was influenced in taking this stand by tactical considerations: the debate about inviting outsiders was delaying other decisions; Maria Theresa certainly dreaded the advent of Protestant *Aufklärer*. This memorandum was written at the high point of his exasperation with his mother's ways, when he was sending his most despairing letters to Leopold and had just gone so far as to propose to her the nomination of a dictator. In that context his slighting references to Pergen – surely Joseph must, or should, have read the scheme – suggest that he considered it and its author presumptuous. If anyone was to be allowed to lay down the principles of educational reform for the Monarchy, and preside over their implementation, it must be the emperor himself. But his wish to give priority to primary education was and is intelligible; he wanted better Catholic teaching, not Protestant; and he cannot have relished the notions of academic freedom that emerged during the discussions about employing foreign scholars.[54]

Maria Theresa thankfully welcomed her son's statement, and the voluminous documentation on this issue was, by her order, filed. Pergen had by now been assigned to other duties; but she established a commission, under the chairmanship of baron Kressel, unassisted by any north German scholars.[55] Within little more than a year after the emperor's note, the suppression of the Jesuits made more effective action immediately necessary and possible.

The suppression left education within the Monarchy in disarray. Jesuit schools as such ceased to exist; and it was questionable how far, if the pope was obeyed, ex-Jesuits could go on teaching. On the other hand, the government gained by the suppression control of all the Society's property including its

---

[53] See above pp. 382, 455.   [54] See above pp. 215–16 and Helfert, *Volksschule*, vol. I, p. 632.
[55] Arneth, *GMT* IX, p. 237; Hock, *Staatsrath*, p. 54. I cannot pretend that I fully grasp the process of creation of the *Studienhofkommission*. Clearly, neither did Arneth nor Hock. It appears to have been nominated in 1771, with Pergen as its head, and its chairman changed in 1772. But in 1773 it seems identical with the commission that dealt with the Jesuits and their lands.

What Arneth says about the summoning of F. J. Riedel from Erfurt to assist in the educational reform, M.T.'s change of heart about it, his journey to Vienna and his finally 'achieving his aim' is also puzzling. Wurzbach XXVI, pp. 87–8, and Nicolai to Gebler, 10 Mar. 1773 (Werner, *Aus dem Josephinischen Wien*, p. 41) show that he was fobbed off with an assignment to which he was quite unsuited, editing the work of Winckelmann on Greek antiquities.

schools. Some of the resulting revenue was appropriated to filling the gaps left by the Jesuits or to remodelling the educational system. Many schemes of reform were submitted, most of them far too ambitious. But at the end of 1774 the first general school ordinance for the central lands of the Monarchy was enacted. Under it, primary schools of a new type were to be established as quickly as possible in each town and village to teach the three Rs in German – or, in Slav lands, in German and the local vernacular. In each county or circle one higher school was to be set up. Normal schools were to be founded for the training of the teachers. Felbiger was put in charge of the whole operation, despite objections from the pundits of the commission just created. With the aid of private donations and enforced grants of money, land and buildings, and using former Jesuit houses and schools, ex-Jesuit teachers and some of the Society's revenues, considerable success was achieved even before Maria Theresa died. By then, 500 new schools had been started in the Austrian and Bohemian lands, a much larger number of existing schools had converted to the new methods, and in some areas school attendance had risen dramatically.[56] This development, however, seems to have been achieved only at the cost of secondary education. Many former Jesuit *Gymnasien* survived, often now run by Piarists; and despite proposals to the contrary, they remained grammar-schools much as before. But the numbers attending them were already falling, and continued to do so, especially as most of their pupils now had to pay fees.[57] Somewhat similar reforms followed in other provinces of the Monarchy.[58]

Throughout Maria Theresa's reign, and especially after 1765, the government had been steadily increasing its claims to control education, previously almost entirely a matter for the church and private individuals. The suppression of the Jesuits, carried through in the end on papal instructions, enormously strengthened the state's role in this field. The subsequent reforms, which in essentials remained operative for nearly a century, were as important in the Monarchy's history as anything done under the empress and her son. For example, they established the principle of compelling children to go to school, though only for short periods of the year. They enhanced the opportunities for girls to receive education. And they typified in many ways the Josephist spirit. The more secularist, or lay, proposals for change had been

[56] See references in n. 52 above. H. Pirchegger (ed.), *Geschichte und Kulturleben Deutschösterreichs von 1526 bis 1792* (Vienna, 1931), p. 345; Strakosch-Grassmann, *Geschichte des österreichischen Unterrichtswesens*, esp. pp. 126–32; Helfert, *Volksschule*, vol. I, pp. 582–5; Bosl, *Handbuch der böhmischen Geschichte*, vol. II, pp. 394–5; A. Weiss, *Geschichte der Theresianischen Schulreform in Böhmen*, vol. I (Vienna, 1906), esp. p. 29. I hope my reading of the available statistics is correct.
[57] Strakosch-Grassmann, *Geschichte des österreichischen Unterrichtswesens*, esp. pp. 106–18.
[58] E.g. for Hungary see D. Kosáry, 'Die ungarische Unterrichtsreform von 1777' in *Ungarn und Österreich unter Maria Theresia und Joseph II.*, ed. A. M. Drabek, R. G. Plaschka and A. Wandruszka (Vienna, 1982), pp. 91–100.

rejected, partly on grounds of practicality. The clergy, though subordinated to the state, still played by far the largest part in education. Indeed, it was one of the principles on which the government most strongly insisted that the clergy, however reluctantly, must qualify as teachers and must themselves give the religious education required in the schools. Of course the nature of this teaching was strictly prescribed. But in consequence, not only were ex-Jesuits, Piarists and other regular clergy allowed to go on teaching, ostensibly until such time as suitable secular clergy and laymen could be trained to replace them; but also most ordinary priests were fully integrated into the system as the official teachers of religion in schools. Church and state were inextricably bound together in education. In Joseph's sole reign it was thought necessary – though it proved impracticable – to lay down that the village schoolmaster should not double as church organist. No doubt it would be impossible to determine which suffered more by this evidently common arrangement, the teaching in the schools or the music in the churches.[59]

Joseph cannot be found taking a continuous interest in the detail of the school reforms of the seventies; and he acted to prevent Felbiger's authority and system being extended to include special schools for soldiers and their children.[60] On the other hand, he had warmly and repeatedly advocated the extension of basic primary education in the vernacular; he had recommended the Sagan method; he gave these measures priority over secondary education; he supported the use of clergy as teachers, under state direction, and opposed the more radical plans of the education commission; as we shall see, he strongly urged the appropriation of the Jesuits' surplus revenues for educational reform; and he was to continue the development of the system on much the same basis after 1780. On this issue mother and son seem to have reached a consensus. His approval of her policy is shown by the fact that he organised annual balls to raise money for the education fund.[61]

JOSEPH AND THE JESUITS

In one of the best-known of the false Constantinople letters, Joseph was made to write to Choiseul, the French chief minister, in January 1770:

If I were regent, you might boast of my support. With respect to the Jesuits, and your plan for their suppression, you have my perfect approbation...
I know these people as well as any man; I know all the plans they have executed; their

59 The point about the organist is on p. 131 of Strakosch-Grassmann, *Geschichte des österreichischen Unterrichtswesens*; pp. 127–9 for the compulsion on clergy to teach in schools.
60 Arneth, *GMT* IX, pp. 257–60. See Arneth, *Sitzungsberichte KAW* (1859), 356–64, for the affair of the military schools and for at least one other example of J. taking an interest in educational detail at the end of the co-regency.
61 On the 1780s, in addition to works already cited, E. Wangermann, *Aufklärung und staatsbürgerliche Erziehung* (Vienna, 1978), esp. ch. 3. Helfert, *Volksschule*, vol. I, pp. 164–5, 395.

endeavours to spread darkness over the earth, and to govern and confuse Europe from Cape Finisterre to the North Sea . . .

In this and in another often-quoted but spurious letter to count Aranda, the Spanish minister, dated 1773, he rehearses some of the historical indictment commonly put forward against the Jesuits. Even scholars of the calibre of Pastor and Maass have accepted the first of these diatribes as genuine, and have therefore supported the widespread view that Joseph was violently hostile to the Society.[62]

A few contemporary suggestions can be found that he was less sympathetic to it than his mother was.[63] As we have seen, he may have encouraged her to abandon her Jesuit confessor in favour of Provost Müller. He joked about the Jesuits' confessional method.[64] He criticised their behaviour in Prague.[65] But the evidence of his respect for them is much more striking. He was content with the education he had received at their hands. When Lacy wrote to him in 1769 about the possible appropriation of Jesuit property for military purposes, it was in terms implying that the idea would be new to the emperor.[66] A report from his confessor in March 1769 declared that he was indifferent to the suppression.[67] During his Italian journey of the same year he supported his mother's policy of neutrality publicly and privately. But his words led count Papini to think him an ardent defender of the Society.[68] The Jesuit Father Höller remained his confessor until he died in 1770.[69] Joseph surprised Catherine II by the warmth of his praise for the Society in 1780.[70] If he criticised the Jesuits of Prague, he did not suggest that they behaved worse than other monks. It is true that he sometimes fiercely denounced all regulars, as when he called them, in a passage discreetly and without indication omitted in Arneth's edition, 'by their nature the scourge of all Catholic provinces, and the most implacable leeches of the poor labourer and artisan'.[71] But his general attitude, as illustrated in his legislation of the eighties, was that, while

---

[62] Beales, *HJ* (1975), 477; *The Pamphleteer*, XI (1822), 83–5 (contains *Letters of Joseph II* (London, 1821–2)). Pastor, *History of the Popes*, vol. XXXVIII, p. 257 and n; Maass, *Josephinismus*, vol. I, p. 97n.

[63] E.g. Stormont to Conway, 18 July 1767, cypher (PRO SP 80/204), which also supplies the evidence for the next sentence.

[64] M.T. to marquise d'Herzelles, 2 Apr. 1771 (Kervyn de Lettenhove, *MARB in-8o* (1868), 28).

[65] K-M VII, pp. 382, 385.   [66] See above, pp. 256–7.

[67] Pastor, *History of the Popes*, vol. XXXVIII, p. 257n.

[68] See above, p. 258.

[69] M.T. to marquise d'Herzelles, 1 Mar. 1771 (Kervyn de Lettenhove, *MARB in-8o* (1868), 23). This is less striking if it is true, as M.T. says, that J. had not made a general confession for six years before 1771. See above, p. 205.
   Hersche, *Spätjansenismus*, p. 135, erroneously says J. dismissed Höller. See K-M VII, p. 54.

[70] Catherine II to grand-duke Paul and his wife, 30 May 1780 (*SIRIO* IX, p. 57). I owe my wife thanks for translating the passage for me.

[71] See the Bohemian *Relation* (K-M VII, pp. 382–5); J. to L. 6 Oct. 1774 (HHSA FA Sbde 7 – these words are part of a portion omitted after 'faudrait' in line 3 of Arneth, *MTuJ* II, p. 39).

purely contemplative and especially mendicant Orders were useless and pernicious, teaching Orders, at least in the short run, were to be cherished.[72]

The threat to the existence of the Jesuits came from outside the Monarchy. Perhaps if Maria Theresa had actively fought for them instead of declaring her neutrality, she could have preserved them, at least in her own lands.[73] But her system of alliances, together with pressure from some of her advisers and her own misgivings about the Society, prevented her abandoning her passive stance.[74] There is no substantial evidence that Joseph tried to influence her in either direction. It must be concluded that he was relatively sympathetic to the Society, less so perhaps than Maria Theresa, but more so than almost any other Catholic ruler or minister of the time. In certain respects he was actually more sympathetic to them than his mother was. She was hostile to them on religious and theological grounds in a way that he was not. Her growing Jansenist tendencies, fostered by her confessor Müller, went with the increased religiosity of her widowhood. She sometimes asserted, outrageously, that her son was anti-religious. But the main difference between them in this field was that he accorded to religion and the church a much more circumscribed role than she did. He maintained that the pope should not interfere in the ecclesiastical reforms of the Monarchy's rulers. He allowed the clergy scarcely any standing in political matters. Maria Theresa on the other hand, seems to have listened not only to Müller's views on reform but also to his denunciations of the partition of Poland and the War of the Bavarian Succession. As countess Kaunitz said, there would have been a furious outcry if a Jesuit confessor had presumed to give such advice when the hegemony of the Monarchy in Germany was at stake.[75]

Joseph may well have been genuinely neutral about the suppression of the Society; but once news reached Vienna that it was imminent, and a draft of the papal bull ordaining it came to hand, in the spring of 1773, he urged immediate action to prepare for this momentous change. Under the terms of the draft, when the Society had been dissolved its property was to be administered by the bishops. This the emperor strongly rebutted. In general, he argued, it was the state that should take charge of the property. In the particular case of the Monarchy, so much of which belonged to dioceses whose bishops were based outside it, to give them control would be to deny the state property to which it was manifestly entitled. Many people believed that the Jesuits would try to transfer their wealth to friendly countries before the bull

---

[72] E.g. E. Bradler-Rottmann, *Die Reformen Kaiser Josephs II*. (Göppingen, 1973), pp. 153–4.

[73] As is claimed by Maass, *Josephinismus*, vol. II, pp. 29–31. But his judgement about the fate of the Jesuits is not very persuasive, since he is totally unable to see why they were so much disliked and to enter into the mind of Clement XIV.

[74] See Arneth, *GMT* IX, esp. ch. 4.

[75] See Hersche, *Spätjansenismus, passim*; pp. 204–5 above; and L.K. to E.L., 19 Sep. 1778 (SOALpZ, LRRA P. 17/24). Winter, *Josefinismus*, p. 101, represents J. as strongly anti-Jesuit on the erroneous basis that Martini was J.'s tutor.

took effect. Joseph therefore pressed for publication of its provisions in advance, and for measures to forestall export of the Society's funds.

The bull explicitly dissolved the Society and deprived it of its corporate property. But the pope used vague language about what individual Jesuits might do in future. The emperor wrote that the most notable aspects of education, namely religion and the humanities, had hitherto been almost entirely entrusted to Jesuits. In the short term it would be quite impossible to replace them by equally able men either from other Orders or from the secular clergy. It was surely not only 'desirable, but necessary for the good of religion and the state', that the better ex-Jesuits should be allowed to go on teaching, especially in the higher schools. As for the property of the Society, the pope wanted it applied to religious purposes only. In Vienna it was accepted that the ex-Jesuits themselves must be the first charge on it. Joseph urged that the surplus after that should be used for education. He asked for a commission to be established to consider all these points.[76]

Kaunitz agreed with the emperor; Maria Theresa established the commission under Kressel, with Müller and Martini as members; and Joseph went off to Transylvania and Galicia in May believing that the policy he had put forward would be carried into effect.[77] Certainly the empress insisted that the pope gave to herself rather than to the bishops control of the property and persons of the Jesuits.[78] But during the summer the emperor began to complain of delays and indecision, and especially that so many of the ministers had been allowed to leave the capital for long periods. Maria Theresa blamed Joseph's absence as well, and used it as an excuse for delay. When he returned at the end of September, he claimed that nothing had been done about his recommendations.[79] However, in the end the Society was suppressed, its property was seized by the state, the disappointingly small surplus revenue was applied to educational purposes, and many ex-Jesuits were employed – all roughly in the way the emperor had wanted. Because of the delay in publishing the final version of the bull, cardinal Migazzi, acting on an earlier draft, tried to take over the Viennese lands and buildings of the Society himself. But this was prevented. The archbishop was more successful in his efforts to secure that ex-Jesuits might continue to teach in schools and universities, and act as parish priests wherever they were needed. Maria Theresa on the whole supported him, though she said 'no one insisted so strongly as I did ... that all professorships of theology should immediately be taken away from them'. But instead of acting on her own authority, she asked the pope for permission to use them as teachers and parish priests, and was

[76] This memo. of J.'s is printed in K-M VII, pp. 453–6 (3 Apr. 1773).
[77] J. to L., 22 Apr. and 23 Sep. 1773 (Arneth, *MTuJ* II, pp. 6, 17–18).
[78] Arneth, *GMT* IX, pp. 93–7.
[79] J. to L., 23 Sep. 1773 (Arneth, *MTuJ* IX p. 17); M.T. to Neny, Sep. 1773 (Arneth, *GMT*, IX, p. 568); Arneth, *GMT* IX, pp. 98–9.

told she could do as she thought fit. Kaunitz and Kressel's commission opposed this approach, but Joseph, so far as we know, did not.[80]

The lands and property of the Jesuits were exploited in a variety of ways. Those estates that the empress kept under her control became centres for the Raab experiment.[81] Buildings not needed for education were adapted to many new functions: for example, the Society's chief house in Vienna became, as Lacy had envisaged, the seat of the war department.[82] Maria Theresa, to Joseph's annoyance, made huge loans to great lords from the Jesuit fund – with the result that sometimes there was no ready money with which to pay the pensions of the former members of the Society.[83] But in principle the revenue was preserved for this and for educational purposes. The manner of the dissolution served in many respects as a model for the later suppressions of Joseph's reign.

Two detailed implications of the measure testify to the intellectual standing of the Society and help to explain the emperor's hesitant attitude to the problem. First, many of the Jesuits' books were given to university libraries. It was in this way that the University of Vienna first acquired copies of some of the greatest products of the culture and Enlightenment of the seventeenth and eighteenth centuries, such as works by Newton, Boyle, Voltaire, Winckel-mann and Samuel Johnson. Secondly, the government had been discussing for some years the formation of a learned academy in Vienna, to rival institutions like those of Berlin and St Petersburg. The proposal was sometimes considered in relation to the idea of establishing a German national theatre and in connexion with plans for educational reform. Finance was perhaps the chief difficulty, but there were others. The new body would have had to include foreign *savants*, but it obviously had to rely mainly on subjects of Maria Theresa. When in 1775 the empress saw the proposed list of local members, she wrote: 'I could not possibly decide to start an academy with three ex-Jesuits and a worthy professor of chemistry. We would be the laughing-stock of the world.' Joseph presumably agreed, since that was the end of the matter.[84]

---

80 Wolfsgruber, *Migazzi*, pp. 168–81; Arneth, *GMT* IX, pp. 106–9, 114–23.
81 Wright, *Serf, Seigneur and Sovereign*, pp. 54, 59, 63. See above, p. 352.
  See also H. Kröll, 'Beiträge zur Geschichte der Aufhebung der Gesellschaft Jesu in Wien und Niederösterreich', University of Vienna PhD, 1965, and H. Haberzettl, *Die Stellung der Exjesuiten in Politik und Kulturleben Österreichs zu Ende des 18. Jahrhunderts* (Vienna, 1973).
82 There are several letters on this in HHSA NL, Karton 2. On disposal of the buildings and many other matters there is much useful information in Kröll, 'Beiträge zur Geschichte der Aufhebung der Gesellschaft Jesu'.
83 Holzknecht, *Reformideen Kaiser Josephs II.*, p. 86 and n.; K-M VIII, p. 118 (28 Nov. 1775).
84 Kröll, 'Beiträge zur Geschichte der Aufhebung der Gesellschaft Jesu', pp. 116–201; Arneth, *GMT* IX, pp. 263–7. In correspondence between J. and L. of Dec. 1773 and Jan. 1774, not published by Arneth, it emerges that J. probably and L. certainly doubted the wisdom of founding an academy. They also speak of the *Monita Secreta*, the famous forgery of 1614 directed against the Jesuits, as a document new to them (HHSA FA Sbde 7).

TOLERATION

Whereas the question of the Jesuits, which was so emotionally charged for many of his contemporaries, did not particularly excite Joseph, the issue of religious toleration stirred him deeply. In the memorandum of 1765 he had declared that the state had no business to try to convert heretics: it needed subjects, and the best possible servants; their religious beliefs were irrelevant. He reiterated these points from time to time as occasion offered, for example in his reports from the Banat and Transylvania. But his views made little impression[85] until the question became burning and immediate in 1777.

Even those historians who maintain that Maria Theresa's reforming intentions in ecclesiastical matters embraced virtually everything done by the Monarchy's government down to 1790 cannot find a shred of evidence for her envisaging the measures of toleration for Protestants and Jews that were enacted during the 1780s.[86] The empress was prepared to treat Protestant envoys and visitors civilly. Protestant worship had to be permitted, even in Vienna, in the embassies of Protestant Powers. She especially liked to give employment to heretics who converted to Roman Catholicism, like Haugwitz, Gebler, and the two Zinzendorfs, nephews of the famous evangelist.[87] She made presents of money to Protestants who submitted to Rome.[88] She had to accept that treaties and constitutions required her to accord a degree of toleration in Hungary, and more in Transylvania. There were other special cases like the duchy of Teschen. One of her most trusted servants was Brukenthal, a Lutheran employed in the affairs of Transylvania.[89] But she took a strict Counter-Reformation view of the ideal relationship between religious and secular obedience, namely that they should be one, and was convinced of her duty to promote it. About nothing was she more consistent than her determination to make her states, if possible, more solidly Catholic. In her mind, this was a principal object of her church reforms. She harried the remaining Protestants in the Austrian mountains. Except where she was required to by sworn agreement, she refused before 1778 to allow any public Protestant worship. She had recalcitrant heretics transported from the central

---

[85] E.g. deportations to Transylvania continued, or actually intensified, while J. was there in 1773 (Buchinger, *Die 'Landler' in Siebenbürgen*, p. 394).

[86] Wangermann comes nearest to claiming this, by depreciating the edict of 1781 (*Austrian Achievement*, pp. 96–7) and denying that it was 'ideologically motivated', while taking M.T.'s 'toleration policy' (!) too seriously (in his chapter 'Matte Morgenröte' in *MTIZ*, pp. 67–71). See below, pp. 472–3 for remarks on Maass's standpoint. Cf. the comments of O'Brien, *TAPS* (1969), 5.

[87] There is much evidence about Protestant worship in Vienna in HHSA TZ, 1761–4, where also M.T.'s management of the Zinzendorfs can be followed.

[88] Wagner in Winters and Held, *Intellectual and Social Developments*, p. 18.

[89] On Teschen, see W. R. Ward, 'Aufklärung und religiöser Aufbruch im europäischen Protestantismus des 18. Jahrhunderts', *ÖGL*, xxviii (1984), 6–8. On Hungary Marczali, *Hungary in the Eighteenth Century*, ch. 4. Schuller, *Brukenthal, passim*.

Catholic lands to Transylvania, for example a batch of nearly 200 in 1773.[90] She would not allow her censors to admit Protestant books, except in special cases and under the most restrictive conditions.[91] She was violently anti-Semitic, describing Jews as 'a public plague' and declaring in 1777 that she would allow none to settle in Vienna without her written permission.[92] In one important respect she pursued a more single-mindedly Catholic policy even than her predecessors. The upshot of the Diplomatic Revolution was that the Monarchy became part of an international Catholic bloc. After 1749 she made alliances with Russia and then with Turkey, but not with Protestant states.[93]

Of the central Catholic lands of the Monarchy, Bohemia and Moravia, particularly the latter, still contained significant numbers of Protestants, despite the repression of the previous two centuries. A remarkable 'revival' had occurred there in the 1720s, largely independent of any organised church, and notable for open-air services and itinerant preachers.[94] Some Protestants had declared themselves during the revolt of 1775, but were soon restored to passive obedience. Two years later, Catholic missionaries, acting very like *agents provocateurs*, 'discovered' more than 10,000 avowed Protestants in a remote area of Moravia. To announce oneself a Protestant, and to indulge in public Protestant worship, were serious criminal offences. When the news of this discovery reached Vienna in May 1777, the empress was appalled.[95]

Her instincts would have led her to act with vigour, using a combination of force and persuasion. But several factors inhibited her. Joseph was in France, and would not return for some months. She knew very well how strongly he felt about religious toleration, and also that the increased boldness of the Moravian Protestants owed something to his known sympathy. In recent years she had been persuaded by her more progressive advisers, working through the *Staatsrat*, to turn a blind eye at least to the mere existence of Protestants and to their worshipping privately in their homes as they wished. Forced conversion, she was taught, brought no merit to the converted, no credit to the

---

90 Benna, *Festschrift F. Loidl*, pp. 207–9; Buchinger, *Die 'Landler' in Siebenbürgen*, esp. pp. 319–36; Schünemann, *Österreichs Bevölkerungspolitik*, esp. pp. 95–106.

91 Klingenstein, *Staatsverwaltung und kirchliche Autorität*, esp. p. 202; Kovács, *Ultramontanismus*, pp. 116–19.

92 Macartney, *Habsburg and Hohenzollern Dynasties*, p. 148.

93 R. A. Kann, 'Ideengeschichtliche Bezugspunkte der Aussenpolitik Maria Theresias und ihrer Söhne (1740–1792)' in R. G. Plaschka, G. Klingenstein and others (ed.), *Österreich im Europa der Aufklärung: Kontinuität und Zäsur in Europa zur Zeit Maria Theresias und Josephs II.* (2 vols., Vienna, 1985), vol. I, pp. 557–66, stresses the Catholic alignment of M.T.'s foreign policy, but does not even mention the Turkish alliance.

94 See Ward, *ÖGL* (1984), 9.

95 The rest of this section is largely based on Arneth, *GMT* x, pp. 60–75 and Maass, *Josephinismus*, vol. II, pp. 46–61, 217–25, 240–53, together with the letters of M.T. and J. in Arneth, *MTuJ* II, pp. 140–2, 146–7, 150–2, 157–65. See also O'Brien, *TAPS* (1969), 20–2; Winter, *Josefinismus*, pp. 162–72.

I give specific references only to quotations, to other sources and on points of difficulty.

church, and no advantage to the state.[96] The emigration of many thousands of Protestants following the Salzburg persecution of the 1730s had made a deep impression in the Habsburg lands, as Joseph's education showed.[97] The outcome was seen as objectionable not only on grounds of humanity and justice, but also because it damaged the state's economy. Further, the newly discovered Moravian Protestants lived in a district near the Prussian border, and doubtless admired Frederick the Great. Nobody in Vienna wished Prussia to benefit from this affair, either in reputation or population.

Maria Theresa consulted Kaunitz, who supplied his usual logical statement of principle. He argued against any kind of compulsion, and blamed the emergence of the Protestants on the inadequacies of the local clergy. The empress therefore precipitated the creation of the bishopric of Brünn, recommended by Joseph six years earlier,[98] and announced the building of forty new churches. She also sent two officials to the area to find out what was going on, armed with books of religious instruction. For obdurate heretics, however, she spoke of exile to Transylvania.

Joseph received news of these measures from his mother while he was travelling in western France. He wrote from Rochefort on 19 June:

You know my views on this subject. I shall never change them. I'm delighted that Kressel has been sent there, despite the odd satellites and the extracts from Bossuet and Muratori that go with him. He couldn't do anything less sensible than what the instruction of the [Austro-Bohemian] Chancellery contains, which comes to no decision on any point ... and never begins to attack the evil at its root. For politically, differences of religion within a state are an evil only in so far as there is fanaticism, disunion and party spirit. This vanishes automatically when all sectaries are treated with perfect impartiality, and He who directs all hearts is left to do the rest.[99]

The emperor's remarks point to one of the difficulties. The affair was a matter for the Austro-Bohemian Chancellery, and so Kaunitz had no administrative standing in it.

Joseph followed up this letter with another fuller and much more radical statement of his position:

The open declarations of irreligion in Moravia only strengthen me in my principles: freedom of belief, and there will then be but one religion, that which guides all inhabitants without distinction for the good of the state ... Half-measures don't square with my principles. There must either be complete freedom of worship, or you must expatriate everyone who doesn't believe as you do ... So that their souls may not be damned after their death, is one to expel, and lose all benefit from, excellent cultivators and good subjects while they're alive? By what authority? Can one go so far as to dispense Divine mercy, to try to save people despite themselves, to control their consciences? Temporal administrators! So long as the state is served, the laws of Nature and society observed, your Supreme Being in no way dishonoured but

[96] Hock, *Staatsrath*, pp. 57–9. [97] See above, p. 61 and Ward, *ÖGL* (1984), 10–12.
[98] See above, p. 453. [99] J. to M.T., 19 July 1777 (Arneth, *MTuJ* II, pp. 140–1).

respected and adored, what ground have you for interference? The Holy Spirit must enlighten hearts, your laws will only delay His work.[100]

The empress now consulted Migazzi[101] and despatched an equally impassioned answer:

I have to say, to my great grief, that there is now nothing in your approach to religion remaining to be corrupted if you persist in approving this general toleration that you tell me is one of your principles from which you will never deviate. I hope you will, and I shall continue to pray, and to have others more worthy than myself pray, that God will preserve you from this evil, which would be the greatest that the Monarchy has ever suffered. While you are thinking about keeping and even attracting cultivators, you will be ruining your state, you will be the cause of so many souls being lost. What is the point of your possessing the true religion if you value and love it so little that you consider it unimportant to maintain it and strengthen it? I do not notice such indifference among all Protestants . . .

She claimed that he would see for himself in Switzerland that toleration did not generate cultivators. 'There is no less flourishing or more backward country than these provinces. What is needful is the true faith, immutable principles.'[102]

She returned to the charge in another letter. Without a dominant religion, she says the state will find itself unable to control its subjects except through the inhumanity of the gallows and the wheel.

By dint of seeing and hearing, combining together the spirit of contradiction and that of invention, you are damning yourself, and taking the whole Monarchy with you at the same time, [ruining] all the great efforts of your ancestors who have passed these provinces down to us with great difficulty and improved them by introducing our holy religion – not, like our adversaries, by cruelty and force, but by effort, trouble and expense. Certainly no spirit of persecution; but still more, no indifference or systematic toleration: this is the policy I intend to follow so long as I live.

She fervently hopes her son will do the same,

and abandon false reasoning and evil books, such as those written by men to show off their wit at the expense of everything that is most holy and deserving of respect, who aim to introduce an imaginary freedom which can never exist and which issues in licence and total confusion.[103]

This exchange reads like a direct confrontation between the radical French Enlightenment and the high Counter-Reformation. But his mother's expostulations led Joseph to retreat from the apparent implications of his more

---

[100] J. to M.T., undated, 'June 1777' (Arneth, *MTuJ* II, pp. 141–2).
[101] As O'Brien, *TAPS* (1969), 20n, brings out.
[102] M.T. to J., 5 July 1777 (Arneth, *MTuJ* II, pp. 146–7).
[103] M.T. to J., undated, 'July 1777' (Arneth, *MTuJ* I, pp. 157–8). It seems to me from J.'s letter, next quoted, that he must have been replying to this letter of M.T.'s, although it is placed later than J.'s in Arneth's edition.

extreme statements. He could only suppose, he said, when he first read her reply, that in his original letter he had written something he hadn't intended. He claims that the problem arises from her misunderstanding of the word 'toleration'.

God preserve me from thinking that it is a matter of indifference whether subjects become Protestants or remain Catholics, still less whether they believe or at least follow the religion derived from their fathers. I would give all I possess if all the Protestants of your states could become Catholics!

For me toleration means only that in purely temporal matters, I would, without taking account of religion, employ and allow to own lands, enter trades and become citizens those who are competent and who would bring advantage and industry to the [Monarchy]. Those who unhappily have false beliefs are much less close to conversion if they stay in their own countries than if they move to one where they are exposed to the impressive truths of Catholic religion, just as the undisturbed practice of their cult at once makes them better subjects and discourages them from irreligion, which is so much more dangerous a temptation for our Catholics than the exercise of their [religions].

The fact that Protestant states remain intolerant arises from the relative inferiority of their statesmen and from the conservatism of republics as compared with monarchies. Joseph does not think his policy will result in anyone becoming a Lutheran or Calvinist, and there will be fewer blasphemers in all denominations. He does not believe God will blame him for pursuing it.[104]

Meanwhile, the situation in Moravia worsened, Kressel and his satellites reported that the Protestants were defiant; their numbers were increasing; they were obstructing access to Catholic churches; they were holding huge prayer-meetings in the open air. She now sent a special commission headed by Blümegen, the Austro-Bohemian Chancellor, himself, still with orders to do everything possible by reform and persuasion. But after he announced at the end of August that more drastic measures were inescapable, the empress authorised them on 12 September. The military was to be used to disperse unlawful gatherings and to restore Catholic worship. Obdurate heretics were to be forced to enlist or be sent to Transylvania, and their children were to be kept back so that they could be instructed in the true faith.

Joseph, who had stayed in Vienna for only a few weeks after returning from France, was now attending manoeuvres in Moravia itself. He wrote to his mother denouncing the new orders, which he ascribed, transparently, to foolish ministers.

Can anything be imagined more absurd than the content of these orders? How can one convert people by forcing them to become soldiers, sending them to the mines or to public works? That didn't happen even in the times of persecution when Lutheranism

---

[104] J. to M.T., from Freiburg, 20 July 1777 (Arneth, *MTuJ* II, pp. 151–2). See previous note.

began. I could not say enough about the significance of such a step. I find myself obliged to declare in the most positive terms, and I shall prove it, that whoever has dreamed up and devised this rescript is the most unworthy of your servants, and therefore a man beneath contempt, because it is as stupid as it is ill-conceived. I beg YM at any rate to consult other persons ... I must at the same time urge you, very humbly, that if such things must be done during my co-regency, you will permit me to take the course I have desired for so long, and separate myself from all affairs of state, to let the universe know that I have no standing and weight in them. My conscience, my duty, and what I owe to my reputation, require it.[105]

She of course rejected this suggestion, stating that the orders in question had been approved by the whole Bohemian government and by the *Staatsrat*. He must recognise that a ruler has to enforce the existing laws or enact something better, and must follow the opinions of others rather than his own. His reply professed respect and submission. But he declared her policy to be '*unjust, impious, harmful, impossible, ridiculous*'. It brought home to him the misery of his position as co-regent. To surrender it is 'the only one of his wishes ... that his philosophy, his reasoning have never come near to obtaining'. Otherwise he will find himself sitting in the *Staatsrat* watching the bad effects of this decision, either continually objecting to the policy or 'silently swallowing in long draughts a slow poison which will eat me away'. He can be of no further use as co-regent since they disagree so violently. Freed from it, he would please her much better:

I've always been able to carry out the job of a good son without having to work at it. It comes naturally. The position of co-regent, to be tolerable, needs only to become imaginary. After twelve years of study I haven't yet attained proficiency, and never shall, except by the method that I'm sure you'll permit me to adopt, and thus my withdrawal will be the beginning of my happiness.

The empress sadly responded: 'it is cruel that we should love each other and mutually torment each other without doing any good'.[106]

The saga continued. The Moravian Protestants, knowing Joseph's opinions, and taking advantage of his accessibility to all subjects, sent a representative to him with a petition asking him to intercede with Maria Theresa on behalf of their religious freedom. The empress put the representative in prison. But she also consulted Kaunitz again. He now argued that the lay ruler had no business to interfere in matters of conscience. Forcible conversion was quite contrary to the teachings of the New Testament. Though it was quite legitimate in theory for the prince to exile heretics, in practice to send them out of the state was to lose valuable hands, and to re-settle many thousands internally was not feasible. So the Protestants would have to be left

---

[105] J. to M.T., from Turas, 23 Sep. 1777 (Arneth, *MTuJ* II, pp. 160–1).

[106] M.T.'s letter, 25 Sep. 1777 (Arneth, *MTuJ* II, p. 162); J.'s reply, 26 Sep. (*ibid.*, pp. 163–4); M.T.'s weary answer, undated, '27 Sep.' (*ibid.*, p. 165). The words underlined by J. in his letter were reduced by Arneth to 'injuste et nuisible'. Original in HHSA FA Sbde 4.

in peace, provided that they did not make disturbances or try to worship publicly. It must be hoped that the influence of their Catholic fellow-citizens, strengthened by the reform of the church, would ultimately reclaim them for the true faith. This influence should be allowed to operate compulsorily only on the children of heretics under the age of eighteen, who would be required to attend Catholic instruction classes.[107] Although the officials of the Austro-Bohemian Chancellery opposed this very limited form of toleration, on 14 November 1777 Maria Theresa embodied it in secret instructions to the Moravian government.

For over two years, peace reigned. During 1778, however, Joseph enhanced his public reputation for tolerance by securing permission for Protestants to build their own church in the free port of Trieste.[108] Early in 1780 some of the Moravians again declared themselves Protestants, and asked for the right to worship publicly. The Chancellery officials recommended strong measures. Kaunitz, as before, argued for mildness. But this time he proposed that a formal patent be issued, of which he supplied a draft, acknowledging the existence of these heretics, permitting them to worship undisturbed in their houses, but removing hope of further concessions. This document Joseph excoriated on 14 February in his usual style. It was 'harmful or at least useless'. He proposed the recall of all the commissions and officials previously involved, the replacement of all existing clergy, and

that in future not the least difference should be made between wholly Catholic villages and those infected with Protestant error, or enquiry made whether and how many people go to Mass, whether or not they send their children to church, Christian teaching and school, whether they sing at home, pray or don't pray, whether they go to Hungary or Teschen or not.[109]

The empress resorted to Kaunitz again, who now proposed adding to his draft an explicit permission to the Protestants to take Easter Communion in Teschen and Hungary. Joseph agreed, on three conditions: first, that the patent in its new form should be issued unamended; secondly, that whatever happened, and whoever objected, the government would adhere strictly to the patent in this form; and thirdly, that it should be published in every province. After six days wrestling with her conscience and consulting Migazzi, the empress told Kaunitz that she had insuperable doubts about the permission to worship in Teschen and Hungary, and about generalising the patent. Kaunitz replied:

Just as it could not but be agreeable to me to see the emperor finally accede to the opinion of all those of the recognised councillors of Your Majesty who were for the publication of the patent that I had proposed ... because YM had indicated to me that

---

[107] K.'s memo. of 13 Oct. 1777 in Beer, *AÖG* (1872), pp. 158–62.
[108] O'Brien, *TAPS* (1969), 19–20.
[109] J.'s memo., 14 Feb. 1780 (Maass, *Josephinismus*, vol. II, p. 248).

she very much desired me to do so, so I could not but be naturally very pained, and most astonished at the same time, that YM should have abandoned the idea at the very moment when all opinions were united on this matter, on account of scruples which are devoid of all foundation ... It is totally impossible for her not to grant [the patent] in the present state of things relative to the Moravian sectaries, as it will be elsewhere, when sooner or later the same state of affairs comes into being.

The chancellor kept on urging her to follow the proposals in Joseph's note of 14 February. But the most she would do was tell the local officials in an instruction of 8 March not to make any enquiries into the private behaviour of the Protestants, even including their visits to Hungary or Teschen.[110]

On 13 May 1780 the last scene of this tragicomedy began. Four thousand of the Moravian Protestants met in the open, loyally celebrated the empress's birthday and then held a service. The few available troops attempted, but failed, to arrest the preacher. Joseph was far away in Russia. Some days after the assembly had dispersed, on orders from Vienna the preacher and the ringleaders of the demonstration were arrested and deported to Hungary. But their hardship was mitigated by a personal gift of a hundred gulden for each family from Maria Theresa herself.[111]

Maass's position on this issue is especially awkward. He has at last to allow Joseph a large role in his account and to admit that the toleration patent of 1781 sprang from the emperor's initiative. But in so far as change occurred in this field during the co-regency, he attributes it to Kaunitz's 'prudent circumspection' rather than to the 'stormy vehemence' of Joseph. Further, he says, 'the discussion shows that the toleration of the modern state ultimately followed from the premisses of the chancellor's system of thought'.[112]

What seems to me to emerge from the story is rather this: that only the emperor's known views and 'stormy vehemence' caused Maria Theresa to consult Kaunitz and so limit the influence of the Austro-Bohemian officials; that the chancellor at first made more modest proposals than the emperor hoped for, and achieved some success; that he eventually took over Joseph's scheme of 14 February 1780, but failed to carry it with the empress, even though he sent her one of his sternest rebukes; and that he had by no means reached the point of advocating the full-blown 'toleration of the modern state'. In this area Maria Theresa was reactionary, though willing to listen to arguments in favour of mild measures, and capable of humanitarian gestures. Kaunitz was prepared to advocate a very limited toleration, no doubt trying to find a course of action acceptable to both rulers. Joseph made the running. It is true that the emperor too fell short of proposing or accepting the 'toleration of the modern state', however radical some of his propositions sounded. He

---

[110] K. to M.T., 28 Feb. 1780 (Maass, *Josephinismus*, vol. II, p. 252). It is curious that Maass does not mention this resolution of the dispute by M.T. (Arneth, *GMT* x, p. 74).

[111] Arneth, *GMT*, x, pp. 74–5.   [112] Maass, *Josephinismus*, vol. II, pp. 46, 57.

intended that Catholicism should remain the established religion of the Monarchy. He spoke of Protestants as 'irreligious'.[113] He did not think the state could be indifferent to avowed atheism or even, as he showed in 1783, deism. But the scope of his toleration was far wider than anything contemplated under his mother's rule.[114]

As for his toleration of Jews, that has no prehistory during the co-regency at all.

CONCLUSIONS

Most recent historians concur that Josephism owed little to Joseph. They can hardly deny him substantial responsibility for the measures of his sole reign. But they stress, first, that what was enacted under Maria Theresa was of major importance in itself; secondly, that she and her ministers laid down the principles, and in some cases made administrative preparations, for the reforms of the eighties; and thirdly, that the main forces behind these developments were Kaunitz, the reforming inclinations of the empress, other officials, and wider social tendencies.

Certainly, a strong movement for church reform extended far beyond the Court circles and government departments of Vienna. As well as the direct influence of other Catholic rulers, Maria Theresa and her advisers felt the force of a massive shift of opinion throughout Catholic Europe. It is doubtful how far it touched the peasantry and the urban poor, who seem often to have been ready to defend traditional religious practice.[115] But baroque piety was evidently becoming widely unacceptable among the educated. The *élan* that had covered the Monarchy with baroque and then rococo churches spent itself during the empress's reign. The first two major neo-classical schemes of church architecture to be erected in the Habsburg lands were carried out during the co-regency. It is impossible to associate buildings in this style with the myths, fantasies, miracles and ecstasies of baroque piety. Sometimes, indeed, neo-classicism is identified with the bourgeoisie and the Revolution. It is all the more striking that both schemes were built by French architects for ecclesiastical patrons who were hostile to most aspects of Maria Theresa's reform programme: for Migazzi, the grotesque but revolutionary cathedral at Vác, his second see; and a completely reconstructed monastery for Gerbert, the ultramontane abbot of St Blasien, with the church modelled on the

---

[113] See p. 467 above.   [114] O'Brien, *TAPS* (1969), 26–9.
[115] On popular piety in the Monarchy see, e.g. A. Sikora, *Der Kampf um die Passionsspiele in Tirol im 18. Jahrhundert* (Vienna, 1907); more generally, Chadwick, *Popes and Revolution*, esp. ch. 1; T. C. W. Blanning, *The French Revolution in Germany* (Oxford, 1983), esp. ch. 6. J. McManners, *Death and the Enlightenment* (Oxford, 1981) offers a brilliant account of changes in religious attitudes in France, which has much wider implications.

Pantheon.[116] It is indicative of an intellectual transformation that, without much pressure from above, the execution of convicted witches ceased in Moravia in 1740, and even in Hungary in the 1760s.[117] Muratori and Febronius, and their many sympathisers, agreed that some Counter-Reformation doctrines and practices were excrescences, that monks and nuns were too numerous, that Catholics ought to make more use of the Bible and the vernacular, and that Protestants should be accorded a measure of toleration. Like the Jesuits, the mendicant Orders were now generally denounced.[118] One of Maria Theresa's favourite officials, Greiner, assured her that no scholar any longer accepted the dogma of the pope's personal infallibility and that no rational man doubted the lay ruler's right to jurisdiction over the clergy in all secular matters.[119]

Within the Vienna administration, Kaunitz could draw on much support among the empress's officials. Those placed in charge of censorship, church reform and education were generally, like Van Swieten, Sonnenfels, Heinke, Kressel, Martini and Greiner, decided progressives, although they disagreed over methods and details. Brukenthal and Karl Zinzendorf, who were given responsibility respectively for the affairs of Transylvania and Trieste, held similar views. More important still were certain members of the *Staatsrat*. That body usually came down on the side of reform and subordination of the church, for toleration of Protestants and for liberalisation of the censorship system. Perhaps the most notable advocate of these measures was Tobias Gebler, who joined the *Staatsrat* in 1765. He was a convert from Protestantism, had been educated in Germany and, as we have seen, was a regular correspondent of the great publicist of the north German Protestant Enlightenment, Friedrich Nicolai. Migazzi, on the other hand, had no supporters on the *Staatsrat*, at any rate after 1770.[120]

That Maria Theresa had reforming inclinations is well attested; and her appointment of all these advanced officials constitutes further evidence of the fact, together with the views expressed in her political testaments and the approval she gave to Kaunitz's and Heinke's general propositions about the relations between church and state. However, I have already suggested that the words of her testaments have been invested with a broader significance

---

[116] Vác is extraordinarily little known. I happen to have had the chance to visit it, through attending a conference at Mátrafüred, for which I owe thanks to the Hungarian Institute of Historical Sciences and to Dr K. Benda in particular. Cf. Wolfsgruber, *Migazzi*, pp. 63–4. For St Blasien see W. Braunfels, *Monasteries of Western Europe* (London, 1972), esp. pp. 219–20. See Plates 19a and 19b.

[117] Evans, *Making of the Habsburg Monarchy*, pp. 404–5.

[118] Chadwick, *Popes and Revolution*, esp. pp. 27–30, 75–8, and chs. 3 and 6.

[119] Arneth, *Sitzungsberichte KAW* (1859), 350.

[120] Hock, *Staatsrath*, pp. 48–68; Werner, *Aus dem Josephinischem Wien, passim*; P. P. Bernard, 'The philosophe as public servant: Tobias Philip Gebler', *EEQ*, VII (1973), 41–51. I am grateful to Prof. Bernard for sending me a copy of this article.

than the context justifies. It seems to me that much the same *caveat* applies to her progressive appointments and her acceptance of radical statements of principle. Despite them, she almost always made difficulties about particular proposals, she usually tried to secure the concurrence of the pope before coming to a final decision, and she often listened to the advice of opponents of reform, especially Migazzi. Her reforming instincts were counteracted by her piety, which became obsessive after her husband's death. She seems to have become in her heart more and more conservative as she grew older, and she allowed this change to make some impact on her measures and appointments: for example, the censorship commission became less liberal after the death of Van Swieten in 1772.[121] But we here come up against a peculiar characteristic of her rule. To make or accept a secret, wide-ranging statement of principle was one thing; to enact specific legislation quite another. She would employ her more progressive officials on special commissions, which would naturally put forward radical recommendations; she would acknowledge their labours in flattering terms; she sustained them against their enemies;[122] and yet she would allow their schemes to be modified, delayed or frustrated with the help of her more traditionalist advisers. In the end she was quite often induced to approve measures she had resisted and continued to dislike, but the sum total of her legislation came nowhere near to fulfilling either the recommendations of her commissions or the implications of the generalisations she had herself uttered or endorsed. I wonder, with Maass, whether she grasped the significance of the grand principles of Kaunitz and Heinke to which she assented.[123] I further wonder whether, when she herself made an apparently sweeping generalisation, she really meant it. In her own way she was as prone to exaggerated language as her son. At one time or another, she announced that her sole or prime purpose as ruler was to secure the welfare of the army, to educate or establish her children, to promote the spiritual wellbeing of her provinces, to improve the peasant's lot, or to work for Joseph's ultimate benefit.[124] What was uppermost in her mind at a particular moment she would describe as her only care. Her unarticulated instincts about priorities between policies were shrewd enough, but she was barely capable of sustained and orderly exposition. She seems to have used general statements, as others use expletives, to reinforce her reactions to immediate concerns, rather than with the serious intention of laying down principles.

One would naturally say that the role of Kaunitz in the early history of Josephism could hardly be overestimated, if Maass had not in fact contrived to

---

121 Klingenstein, *Staatsverwaltung und kirchliche Autorität*, p. 202. Cf. pp. 444, 452, 468.
122 Van Swieten: Arneth, *GMT* IX, pp. 167–8. Heinke: Maass, *Josephinismus*, vol. III, pp. 29–30. Greiner: Arneth, *Sitzungsberichte KAW* (1859), 328–31.
123 Cf. Maass's remarks in *Josephinismus*, vol. I, pp. 91–3, vol. II, pp. 60–1, and vol. III, pp. 40–1 and 41n.
124 See above, pp. 52n, 67, 140, 185, 349, 402, 468.

exaggerate it. The Lombard measures were as much his personal achievement as any such programme can be. The same can be said of the theoretical statement of 1768. He invented the *Staatsrat* and had a great deal to do with appointments to it. He had a hand in the promotions of almost all the chief radicals in the administration. His hold over Maria Theresa was unique. No one else could have persuaded both *Staatsrat* and empress to raise the age of profession unilaterally to twenty-five. He usually favoured more radical measures than were actually enacted, but without his crafty handling of the empress church reform would have proceeded far more slowly.

To write like this, though, is to assume that Kaunitz and Maria Theresa could operate without reference to Joseph. This is palpably absurd. However much the co-regent could be constrained in that capacity, he was the emperor in unchallenged possession and the unquestioned heir to the Monarchy. The empress almost venerated the chancellor, but in the last resort he was more expendable than Joseph. We have found her expressing her relief that her son had come round to approval of Kaunitz between 1763 and 1765, then urging the chancellor to pay court to Joseph rather than to herself, and more than once proposing Starhemberg as an alternative chief minister when she or her son became especially exasperated with Kaunitz.[125] If we ask why Joseph, having wished in 1763 to wrest the Italian department from the chancellor's control, spoke of his work with approval two years later, a likely answer would be: because Kaunitz's approach to church reform, as shown in Lombardy, pleased the emperor. If we ask how the chancellor followed Maria Theresa's instruction to pay court to Joseph, part of a likely answer would be: through his ecclesiastical policies, and in particular by adopting Joseph's proposal for raising the age of profession. If we ask why the emperor always shrank from displacing Kaunitz when Starhemberg was offered as the successor, an aspect of a likely answer would be: because Starhemberg was a conservative in religious matters. When the *Staatsrat* debated such questions with Starhemberg as a member, between 1767 and 1770, he appears to have taken the most reactionary line. An account of one division of opinion survives. Migazzi had complained of Sonnenfels's teaching in the University of Vienna on several counts, for example that he criticised existing laws of the Monarchy on torture and the death penalty, and that he identified a state's population with its wealth and argued on that basis against the celibacy of the clergy. The cardinal wanted him censured, and ordered not to attack the present constitution of church and state. Starhemberg agreed. But Kaunitz, Blümegen and the emperor successfully defended Sonnenfels.[126] Starhemberg's departure for

---

[125] See above, pp. 140, 144–7, 222.
[126] Hock, *Staatsrath*, pp. 61–2. Cf. Wandruszka, *L. II.*, vol. I, p. 337. Arneth's suggestions about the reasons for J.'s hostility to Starhemberg (*GMT* x, pp. 213–14) are unconvincing.

the Netherlands was immediately followed by the main burst of church reform in Maria Theresa's reign.

Within the broad European movement of Catholic reform, there were numerous shades and variations of opinion, many of them represented in the Monarchy. Some of its promoters, like Kaunitz, Sonnenfels and Gebler, appear to have cared little about doctrinal detail, and to have incorporated much of the teaching of the *philosophes* into their attitudes. But a closer look even at these three radicals, associated together in the work of reform, reveals striking differences between them. For example, Sonnenfels and Gebler belonged to a Masonic lodge. Kaunitz would have nothing to do with such nonsense.[127] At the other end of the spectrum, Migazzi counted as a reformer in so far as he wished to make the works of Muratori more widely known, worked against the hegemony of the Jesuits, discouraged certain aspects of traditional piety, and was concerned to improve pastoral care and religious education. The followers of Febronius stressed the authority of individual bishops. Those influenced by Jansenism promoted a strict moralism, more austere but more intense religious observance, and a theology that emphasised grace rather than works. If the force of European opinion made it necessary for the rulers of the Monarchy to embark on some programme of church reform, they were clearly in a position, by their appointments and in their legislation, to impart to the movement in their dominions a particular character. In the period of the co-regency this character was largely the product of a compromise between the views of Maria Theresa, Kaunitz – and Joseph.

Maybe the empress, if unconstrained by the combination of Joseph and Kaunitz, could have kept the whole process of reform in check. Opposition to it came not only from vested interests and the superstitious poor. An intellectual reaction was already evident, among the early leaders of which was the rebuilder of St Blasien, who in 1769 published a book against Febronius and who extracted from the empress a concession about the age of profession in his monastery.[128] Some ex-Jesuits, like the Belgian Feller, campaigned remorselessly against the new tendencies.[129] It was possible therefore for a ruler to find support in turning against reform. In 1771 the young duke of Parma, choking on the education he had received from Condillac and other radical *philosophes*, suddenly tired of goading the pope, seized the opportunity

---

[127] Bodi, *Tauwetter in Wien*, esp. pp. 77–8; Werner, *Aus dem Josephinischen Wien*, esp. p. 125; H. Wagner, 'Die Lombardei und das Freimaurer Patent Josephs II.', *MÖSA*, XXXI (1978), 143.

[128] Winter, *Josefinismus*, p. 97. Gerbert, however, was a liturgical reformer.
See also Maass, *Josephinismus*, vol. III, pp. 27–8; Hock, *Staatsrath*, p. 55. E. Kovács, *Der Pabst in Teutschland* (Munich, 1983), esp. chs. 2 and 3, has good material on the Ultramontanes.

[129] On Feller, L. Delplace, *Joseph II et la Révolution brabançonne* (Bruges, 1891); M. le Maire, 'Un publiciste au XVIIIe siècle: Francois-Xavier de Feller', unpublished memoir, 1951 (Bibliothèque nationale, Brussels).

of popular agitation to dismiss his Enlightened minister and settled down to a regime of bigotry and devotions.[130] In the Monarchy, Migazzi, Khevenhüller, Starhemberg and perhaps Blümegen would have made a nucleus for a reactionary party, and it seems conceivable that the empress contemplated going over to them.

What ultimately blocked this option was the co-regent. So long as he remained a firm supporter of reform and, however reluctantly, preferred Kaunitz to Starhemberg, reaction was not feasible. Maria Theresa's main policies were inextricably bound up with each other, and tied to this constellation of personalities. Preserving the Bourbon alliance went with keeping Kaunitz in power, with neutrality on the Jesuit question and with church reform – all of which policies taken together kept Joseph not entirely dissatisfied. This nexus, and the emperor's initiatives on Court religion, the age of profession, toleration and the suppression of the Jesuits, made his role in Josephism decisive. If Maria Theresa is to be acknowledged as its mother and Kaunitz as its father, then she hardly knew what she was doing when she conceived it, she often tried to put it away, and without Joseph the marriage might well have foundered and the child would certainly never have reached maturity.

We must ask, finally, how far the measures of the co-regency anticipated those of the sole reign. This question of course cannot be completely answered here, but some points should be made now. First, although Kaunitz's and Heinke's statements of principle offered enormous powers to the state in church questions, they did not spell out what should be done with them. It does not seem reasonable to stress the significance of the secretly agreed principle rather than its public and effective implementation. During the co-regency, nothing at all was done about tolerating the Jews, very little about tolerating Protestants; no monasteries were dissolved outside Lombardy and Galicia, except the Jesuit houses suppressed by the authority of the pope; the diocesan map was barely touched; and 5000 books were prohibited.[131] Travellers continued to be shocked by the confiscation of their libraries at the frontier, at the lack of education among the nobility of both sexes, at the prevailing superstition. Wraxall wrote at the end of the seventies: 'Natural philosophy has scarcely made greater progress in Vienna, than sound reason and real religion.' He estimated that 3000 persons were engaged in seeking the philosopher's stone.[132] Nicolai later went to hear the professors who had been appointed to teach the reformed course for clergy at the University of Vienna, and thought their bigotry and obscurantism scarcely distinguishable from that of Jesuits.[133] If Protestant testimony seems too biased, Leopold criticised in 1778 the limited progress made, for example in educational reform, and

130 Venturi, *Settecento riformatore*, vol. II, pp. 234–5.   131 Bodi, *Tauwetter in Wien*, p. 51.
132 Wraxall, *Memoirs*, vol. II, pp. 246–7, 249, 257–8, 278–89.
133 Nicolai, *Beschreibung*, vol. IV, pp. 738–44, cited in Kovács, *Ultramontanismus*, pp. 38–9.

castigated Maria Theresa's excessive piety and readiness to listen to Migazzi and his allies.[134] When Heinke surveyed in 1787 the work carried out by his department since 1765, he listed the legislation under eighty-one headings. Of these, fifty-four mentioned only measures passed after 1780; fifteen referred only to measures enacted under Maria Theresa; and twelve included items from both periods.[135] In other words, both the scope and the momentum of reform increased enormously after 1780.

The co-regency was a period of contradictions. Some arose from the operation of rival pressures. There were times when Migazzi had the upper hand with the empress. He was able, until the end of her reign, to make life very difficult for radical professors who purveyed heterodox views and used forbidden books.[136] On the other hand, the society around Kaunitz, as depicted in Zinzendorf's diary, appears almost wholly emancipated in discussing the latest works of the French Enlightenment. The co-regent himself could be inconsistent or weak. In 1767, as we have seen, he agreed to go back on a reform made in 1754, and to permit trumpets and drums to be used in specially festive church services.[137] But some apparent contradictions have a more fundamental explanation. For Maass and many other scholars, Josephism was simply anti-Catholic, because it denied the infallibility of the pope and asserted the right of the secular power to reform the church, because it played with fire in using the works of the *philosophes* in a religious context – and because its *Staatskirchentum* seemed to anticipate totalitarianism.[138] But these criticisms are unhistorical. This was a period before Roman Catholicism confined itself within the doctrines and attitudes of ultramontanism and the First Vatican Council.[139] In Kaunitz's salon Zinzendorf, at the same time as discussing Voltaire, received guidance on conversion to Rome.[140] Joseph attracted notice both for his public displays of respect to religious processions and for his knowledge of the writings of *philosophes*. Many people, including the emperor, saw no inconsistency in this. Though Maass was right to stress that the work of the state is essential to the concept of Josephism, he was wrong to deny that many of the state's aims in this field, and many of Joseph's own, breathed the spirit of Reform Catholicism and Catholic Enlightenment.[141]

---

[134] See Wandruszka, *L. II.*, vol. I, pp. 336–7; also his article, 'Österreich am Ende der Regierungszeit Maria Theresias', *Anzeiger ÖAW*, CXI (1974), 54–7.

[135] Calculated from Maass, *Josephinismus*, vol. III, pp. 343–402.

[136] See the account of Stöger's legal battle in Kovács, *Ultramontanismus*, ch. 5, Seibt's in Winter, *Josefinismus*, pp. 79–84, and Eybel's in Wolfsgruber, *Migazzi*, p. 384.

[137] Wolfsgruber, *Migazzi*, p. 463.

[138] This view is propounded with uncompromising obtuseness by H. Rieser, *Der Geist des Josephinismus und sein Fortleben. Der Kampf der Kirche um ihre Freiheit* (Vienna, 1963).

[139] See P. Hersche, 'Neuere Literatur zur katholischen Aufklärung in Österreich', *Internationale kirchliche Zeitschrift*, LXII (1972), 115–28.

[140] HHSA TZ, 27 Feb. 1764.

[141] See the articles by Blanning and Wangermann in Porter and Teich (ed.), *The Enlightenment in National Context*; and my article in Beales and Best, *History, Society and the Churches*.

Conclusion

THE LAST YEAR OF MARIA THERESA'S LIFE

On 15 September 1779 Joseph wrote from Bohemia a letter beginning:

> Dearest mother,
> I have received the gracious letter that she has had the goodness to write to me. I am delighted that her fall on the staircase has had no serious effect, and I venture to beg her to get into the habit of looking more at the ground. I have often noticed that YM comes downstairs without looking down, and feels for the first step with her foot, which is very dangerous.

He then dealt with a variety of matters, complaining about most of them. For example, the *Staatskanzlei*'s latest note always mixes up the Danube and the Inn. This and other failings make him wonder why the salaries of ministers are continually raised. 'Three-quarters of the salaries ... is money down the drain.'[1]

The empress 'shared her anxieties' with Kaunitz:

> I return to you the memorandum, with the emperor's reply for you alone, and your new note. You will tell me what decision I should record.
> I was expecting some loving concern about my fall. Instead I am preached at, and that's all. The content of this cruel letter does me more injury than my fall. I tell that only to my friend, and you will return this letter to me this evening.

Kaunitz answered, lamenting Joseph's

> cast of mind, as false as it is unjust, which comes through at every point. A mother, and what a mother! brothers, servants of all kinds – everyone is treated in the same way. One day he will get his deserts, which means he will have no friends, and for servants only base men and knaves. What a prospect![2]

In no previous dispute, to our knowledge, did Maria Theresa and her chancellor express to each other such bitter criticism of Joseph.

She soon recovered from the fall and seemed well enough for most of the

[1] J. to M.T., 15 Sep. 1779 (Arneth, *MTuJ* III, pp. 217–19).
[2] Karajan, *Feierliche Sitzungsberichte KAW* (1865), 38–9 (letters of 18 Sep. 1779).

year 1780. Her son caused her much vexation, but also paid her some compliments. He told her in July how thankful he was that their relations were not like those between Catherine II and the grand duke Paul. In September she lunched with him at his new house in the Augarten.[3] But over the same period he was expostulating to Leopold about new enormities at Court. Cardinal Herzan, the Monarchy's ambassador to the papacy, had spent the last year in Vienna.

He has received everything he asked for, down to the Grand Cross of St Stephen. It was impossible to avoid conferring it on him, but at least I had the good sense to send it to him and not to put it round his neck myself. He's a first-class rogue and cheat ... but he's the admiration and darling of the empress, of Marianne, of Marie [Christine]...

The emperor was disturbed by the prospect of a change of papal nuncio. 'There's a secretary called Egisti at the nunciature here. Through the intermediary of a woman, this man lets me know the intrigues that the nuncio, Migazzi, Herzan and the famous prelates of every kind get up to.' If a new nuncio was appointed, Joseph wanted Leopold to help in attaching Egisti to his household, because 'in this world it is difficult to find not only honest servants but also skilful rascals'.[4]

During the second half of November Maria Theresa became seriously ill. She developed a frightful cough, she often had to gasp for breath, she felt so hot that all the windows had to be wide open, she could not bear to sleep lying down. She and her doctor were soon convinced she was dying. But Joseph at first refused to accept what they said, and delayed summoning relatives and making arrangements for the last sacraments. On the 26th, however, she insisted on receiving communion in public, Leopold was informed of her condition, and the emperor began to spend the night in the room next to hers. She continued to put her affairs in order, write letters and sign papers; but her nights were terrible, and Joseph hardly slept. In the small hours of the 28th, in the company of Joseph and Max Franz, Albert and Marie Christine, Marianne and Elizabeth, she received extreme unction, and after the ceremony spoke to them all for twenty minutes, thanking them for their love and commending them to God and to the emperor. When Joseph tried to respond, he was overcome by tears and could only kiss her hand. Albert said he had never seen a man so moved as the emperor was at that moment. During that day she

[3] J. to M.T., 4 July 1780 (Arneth, *MTuJ* III, p. 271); K-M VIII, p. 194.
[4] J. to L., 31 Aug. and 14 Sep. 1780 (HHSA FA Sbde 7, the first not printed by Arneth and the second only partly). These letters destroy the view, strongly held by Eduard Winter, that Herzan and J. were close associates: see his 'Kaiser Josef II. und der Kardinalprotektor der deutschen Reichskirche, F. Herzan Reichsgraf von Harras' in *Prager Festgabe für Theodor Mayer*, ed. R. Schreiber (Salzburg, 1953), pp. 148–55, and his *Josefinismus*, pp. 105–6. Hersche (*Spätjansenismus*, p. 340) appears to accept this picture. S. Brunner, *Die theologische Dienerschaft am Hofe Joseph II* (Vienna, 1868), pp. 85–6 and 86n, reveals that Egisti betrayed his master, but only to K.; and although Brunner makes a lot of the letter of 31 Aug. (pp. 53–4), he does not know the full text.

talked much to her son, who told Kaunitz that 'her courage, resignation, steadfastness and patience' were 'astonishing'. The chancellor's notorious fear of illness and death was held to justify his absenting himself on this occasion. She survived the night, urging Joseph to snatch some sleep by allowing Max Franz to watch with her instead. The next morning she called for breakfast, which she took with her children. Throughout the day she again talked to the emperor for long spells. 'No doubt she was already losing her memory, and she spoke to him, contrary to her usual practice, in French.' He 'exhorted her several times like the most zealous of priests; he carried out all temporal and spiritual duties in such a perfect manner as to be a model to all sons'. At about nine in the evening, she got up suddenly, collapsed and had to be lifted on to her chaise-longue. Joseph said to her: 'Your Majesty is uncomfortable.' 'Yes', she replied, 'but in a good enough position for dying.' A few minutes later, in the presence of Joseph, Max Franz and Albert, her life came to an end.[5]

BALANCE-SHEET OF THE CO-REGENCY

As the previous nine chapters have made plain, there is no simple formula that can accurately describe the balance of power and influence between Joseph and his mother during the co-regency. He could do almost nothing in the affairs of the Monarchy without at least her formal ratification. She, by contrast, could always legally act without consulting him, and not infrequently did so. Even where she had explicitly surrendered control to him, as with the army and the theatre, she still interfered continually to delay, obstruct and modify his plans.[6] Yet he managed to exert a measure of influence in virtually every sphere. At each juncture and in each type of business the pattern was different. Many factors contributed to the variation: for example, the principals' age and state of health; the intensity of their interest; the standing of the ministers chiefly concerned, and especially whether Kaunitz was involved; which province or provinces were affected; the opportunities for other members of the royal family to make their views felt; and the changes in the administrative role of the co-regent effected in 1771 and 1773-4.[7] One of the most significant elements was Joseph's travels. When he was visiting a province and just after he had done so, he could usually make a special impact on its affairs, as with the Banat in and after 1768, Italy in 1769-71, Bohemia from 1771 onwards, Galicia in 1773-4, and the southern provinces in 1775-6. But the price of his journeys was that he was sometimes

---

[5] See contemporary accounts by archduchess Marianne (Arneth & Geffroy III, pp. 492-5) and princess Francis Liechtenstein (Wolf, *M.C.*, vol. II, pp. 221-7); quotations from Albert's memoirs in Arneth, *GMT* x, ch. 20 and pp. 837-8; J.'s letters to L. in *MTuJ* III; and letters in Beer, *JLuK*, esp. J. to K., 28 Nov. 1780 (p. 20). See Plate 23.

[6] On the co-regency, p. 135; on the army, pp. 184-7, 223-4, 226-7; on the theatre, pp. 230-6.

[7] See pp. 207-8, 228-9 for the administrative changes.

away from Vienna at crucial stages in the progress of other business, such as the suppression of the Jesuits in 1773 or Moravian toleration in 1777 and 1780.[8] Whereas in domestic matters, however impatient Joseph himself became, issues could generally be mulled over for many years and the *Staatsrat* and other bodies were endlessly consulted, in foreign affairs decisions often had to be taken rapidly and the circle of policy-makers was for most purposes confined to the empress, the chancellor and the co-regent. Here the fact that Joseph was emperor, and his position as head of the army, ensured him an important role. If he ranked as the weakest member of this triumvirate, his views always made some impression. But in July 1778 Maria Theresa reasserted her full sovereignty when she made peace overtures to Prussia without her son's agreement. In this field his travels were unimportant until the journey to Russia in 1780.[9]

This book has concentrated on the areas in which he possessed significant influence. Something must be said here about those in which he was denied it. It is possible to give some remarkable instances: by the end of 1775, for example, he had not been told what salaries and emoluments were received by the principal officials; and his mother always guarded jealously the fund from which she could distribute pensions and other largesse to faithful servants.[10] Easily the most important exclusions were geographical. Certain types of action taken by the central government applied to all or virtually all provinces alike, with no or minor variations. Ecclesiastical legislation fell into this category, even though it was enacted for different provinces at different dates and in distinct decrees. In so far as Joseph made an impact in this field, it was felt throughout the Monarchy.[11] Some types of enactment, on the other hand, were necessarily localised, like *Urbaria*, which were irrelevant to Belgium and Italy and varied in date and content for other provinces. The emperor accepted this practice; indeed, he thought that too little attention was paid to the diversity of conditions even within provinces.[12] But many other reforms that, at least in Joseph's opinion, could have been extended to the whole Monarchy were restricted to its central core; and even there the Tyrol was handled with kid gloves. As we have seen, such restrictions applied to the new customs system, the abolition of torture and the introduction of cantons and conscription.[13] The co-regent's desire to treat the Monarchy as one homogeneous state was continually frustrated. In fact the success he had in promoting changes in the central provinces must actually have increased the divergence between that bloc and the other lands.

In Italy the absolutist system inherited from Spanish rule, the absence of an

[8] See chs. 8, 11, 12 and pp. 463, 467–71.   [9] On foreign policy, chs. 9 and 13.
[10] K-M VIII, p. 118. Wagner in Winters and Held, *Intellectual and Social Developments*, pp. 5–29. See pp. 218, 223 above.
[11] See ch. 14.   [12] See pp. 349–50.   [13] See pp. 240, 236n, 227.

effective royal viceroy before 1771, and support from enlightened local officials made it possible for Kaunitz to carry through a programme of reforms on lines which Joseph in the main approved but which he succeeded, after visiting the province, in modifying.[14] Hungary and Belgium, however, respectively the largest and the richest of the Monarchy's territories, escaped not only Haugwitz's reforms but also many of the empress's later initiatives; and as a corollary, her son was allowed little say in their administration.

Their constitutions were totally different from those of the other provinces of the Monarchy. In some fields, instead of giving orders to them, the ruler had to make requests.[15] In the case of Hungary, Maria Theresa, desperate for support, had accepted the old constitution at her accession, with additions that strengthened the diet and the nobles. She later tried to secure their co-operation in reform, especially at the diet of 1764; but it ended in recrimination. Thereafter she made what changes she could effect by royal order alone, which included ecclesiastical measures and an *Urbarium*. As we have seen, she had Hungarian affairs discussed by the *Staatsrat* but avoided making the fact known. She and her advisers were most reluctant to risk another diet. She put the best face she could on the failure of her plans, telling Max Franz in 1776: 'Anything can be done with this nation if it is treated well and shown affection ... You will see this and be astonished at the advantages I have obtained and still obtain from it.' Her viceroy, prince Albert, and his wife, Marie Christine, helped to persuade her that the position was satisfactory. Joseph often travelled through Hungary, but he never included in his reports the radical proposals he made for other provinces; he confined himself to the areas in which the government was accustomed to take action.[16] However, during the Bavarian War he demanded that Hungary play its part in saving the Monarchy, that the old citizen-army, the 'Insurrection', should be called out. His mother replied: 'The Insurrection cannot operate outside the country.' He then asked for more Hungarian regiments to be raised. She explained the difficulties that would have to be overcome:

the lords don't have the right to enlist people as in other lands; everything has to go through the counties and the magistrates. I wouldn't advise any lord to try it; a riot would break out first; and we have no military men we can put in charge ... Where power and right are both lacking, it is necessary to [make] friendly approaches, not criticisms.

[14] See pp. 263–71.
[15] Cf. K. Schünemann's remarks on Hungary in *Jahrbuch des Wiener Ungarischen Historischen Instituts* (1931), pp. 196–7.
[16] See pp. 283–4, 339. M.T. to Max Franz, 18 Apr. 1776 (Arneth, *GMT* VII, p. 574). On Albert and M.C., see *ibid.*, X, ch. 4 and Wolf, *M.C.*, vol. I, ch. 2.

She contemplated summoning a diet, but was thankful when the idea could be dropped. So she assumed, or pretended, that Joseph was ignorant about Hungarian affairs.[17]

The Austrian Netherlands consisted of ten provinces, nearly all of them with basically medieval constitutions and powerful Estates. By far the most important were Flanders, which the government had found particularly co-operative, and Brabant, which boasted an especially recalcitrant constitution, the *Joyeuse Entrée*, dating from the fourteenth century and last revised in the sixteenth. They cost little to run and defend, since their continued possession by the Monarchy was acknowledged to depend on the maintenance of the French alliance; and they were supposed to produce a surplus on which Vienna could draw for general purposes. The province's chief banker, the widow Nettine, supplied the government with substantial loans. Almost from the beginning of Maria Theresa's reign the viceroy had been prince Charles of Lorraine, Francis Stephen's brother, who maintained an extravagant Court in Brussels and did not expect to be ordered about by Vienna.[18] He much resented those aspects of Joseph's and Lacy's army reforms that threatened the independence of provincial commanders-in-chief like himself. Military matters alone gave the emperor standing to interfere in Belgium, but of course he despised almost everything his uncle stood for. Maria Theresa considered her brother-in-law a great general, but Joseph told her he had 'lost seven battles'. General d'Ayasasa, one of the beneficiaries of the notorious promotion of 1771, reporting to the war department in Vienna, probably in that year, produced an annihilating critique worthy of the emperor himself, which went far beyond his departmental brief. The prince displayed 'excessive generosity', had arrogated to himself 'limitless authority', showed 'extreme indifference' to business and exhibited 'ill temper' about the recent military reforms, most of which he ignored; in this insubordination he was abetted by the minister, Starhemberg, who was 'infatuated with his pride'; the widow Nettine had been making outrageous profits from army contracts; everything was corrupt and slack. The viceroy complained to Maria Theresa, and

---

[17] J. to M.T., 7 July 1778, attached German note, and 19 July; M.T. to J., 11 and 24 July 1778 (Arneth, *MTuJ* II, pp. 326n, 332, 356, 361–2). Cf. Arneth, *GMT* x, p. 514.

[18] See H. Pirenne, *Histoire de Belgique*, vol. v (Brussels, 1920), book III, chs. 2 and 3; Davis, *J. II.: An Imperial Reformer*, chs. 1 and 2; J. Schouteden-Wery, *Charles de Lorraine et son Temps (1712–1780)* (Brussels, 1943); C. Bronne, *Financiers et comédiens au XVIIIe siècle: Madame de Nettine* (Brussels, 1969), esp. ch. 4; H. Benedikt, *Als Belgien österreichisch war* (Vienna, 1965), pp. 100–14, 151–4.

Dr P. G. M. Dickson argues that the Belgian surplus revenue, when it existed, was usually more than matched by payments from Vienna to service Belgian loans. But M.T. and J. certainly regarded Belgium as a kind of gold-mine, and the government's fund called *Gastos Segretos* had the special advantage of being secret. On 3 June 1780 M.T. wrote to Starhemberg that, since she could not herself afford to pay for the election of Max Franz at Cologne, she would do so out of the surplus produced by Belgium (HHSA Rep. DD, Abt. A, Depechen, 1779–81).

Starhemberg twice asked to resign. The empress retained them both in their posts, but required her brother-in-law to report, 'as matters arose', to the war department.[19] In aspects of Belgian affairs that could not be reckoned military, Joseph can have had little influence, since they were in Kaunitz's hands and did not even come before the *Staatsrat*.[20] And the emperor did not visit the province during his mother's lifetime.

In 1777, however, she consulted him about an issue involving prince Charles which has a wide interest. The viceroy and his courtiers had been openly frequenting the meetings of Masonic lodges. This enormity was brought to Maria Theresa's notice, and Kaunitz recommended her to prohibit such activities, as no doubt she was herself inclined to do. But her son took a different view:

I have the honour to tell her that whatever methods are employed to prevent and harass such clubs tend only to make them more attractive and, since their innocence is recognised by all sensible persons in society, to bring ridicule on governments and on those who, by forbidding things that they believe to be bad simply because they don't know anything about them, endow them with a measure of importance. I therefore very humbly suggest that no action should be taken . . . But if she thinks it appropriate, the leaders of Brussels society could be gently informed that we should prefer them not to amuse themselves so publicly with Freemasonry, but that they should conceal it better, so that the affair won't cause so much talk.

This was what was done.[21] It is remarkable to find the emperor adopting a more liberal line than Kaunitz on such an issue, and interesting that he did not seize this opportunity to be spiteful towards prince Charles.

The viceroy died in July 1780. He left his estate in disorder, and Joseph took the matter into his hands, refusing to carry out some of the provisions of his uncle's will.[22] He tried also at this favourable moment to assert himself in Belgian affairs, but the succession to prince Charles had been promised long ago, with Joseph's agreement, to Albert and Marie Christine, and Maria Theresa declined to alter the conditions of the appointment. In telling her son so, she justified the mildness of her whole policy towards the Netherlands:

In the essentials of the constitution and form of government of this province, I do not believe that anything needs changing. It is the only happy province, and it has provided us with so many resources. You know how these peoples value their ancient, even

19 This dispute is treated from M.T.'s standpoint in Arneth, *GMT* x, pp. 214–16, 785–6; and see J. to M.T., 23 July 1780 (Arneth, *MTuJ* III, p. 289). D'Ayasasa's report is in HHSA NL, Karton 1, dated 1778 by an archivist; there is a bulky file in Karton 8; see also M.T. to Lacy, 6 June 1772 and undated (no. 107), Karton 2.
20 See above, pp. 92, 228.
21 Arneth, *GMT* x, pp. 230–1, 790. But J.'s letter is discussed and even printed in vol. IX, pp. 398–9, 603, with reference to Bohemia! It is dated 21 Feb. 1777 (HHSA FA Sbde 4). Cf. P. Duchaine, *La Franc-Maçonnerie belge au XVIIIe siècle* (Brussels, 1911), esp. ch. 3, from which it appears that M.T. later worked to suppress the Belgian lodges.
22 J. to L., 31 Aug. and 2 Nov. 1780 (HHSA FA Sbde 7, not printed by Arneth) and 14 Sep. 1780 (Arneth, *MTuJ* III, pp. 310–11); J. to M.T., 6 Aug. and 13 Oct. 1780 (*ibid.*, pp. 299, 315–16).

absurd, prejudices. If they are obedient and loyal and contribute more than our impoverished and discontented German lands, what more can one ask of them? A governor will have to have full authority in view of the remoteness and separation of this province, and with such powerful neighbours. It's already been too much eroded; only a shadow of the past remains ... The results have proved that this branch has been successfully managed, to mutual satisfaction.

Even in these last months of her life, she was still capable of categorically rejecting Joseph's proposals. In this letter she was aligning herself with Leopold, who was now studying with admiration the constitutions of the Netherlands and Hungary, as part of his preparation for giving a constitution to Tuscany.[23] She seems here almost to recant the principles of her own early reformism and her political testaments, which she now saw resurgent in an alarming guise in the plans of the emperor.

This dispute over the affairs of Belgium and Hungary between the empress and Leopold on one side, and Joseph on the other, introduces one of the main themes of the second volume of this biography.

With the exclusion of these provinces from Joseph's purview as co-regent went his mother's refusal to entertain his schemes for centralising and making homogeneous the government of the entire Monarchy. She also drew the line, as we have seen, at many of his other demands, such as for religious toleration, censorship relaxation and the wholesale dissolution of monasteries. All these matters he took in hand immediately on his accession in 1780; but unlike his plans for Belgium and Hungary, his main proposals for reform in the central provinces had already been discussed in detail by the two rulers with their ministers, as had her own radical scheme for the abolition of serfdom, which the emperor in turn had obstructed.[24]

In other areas, however, admittedly after much argument, he had contributed as co-regent to notable changes: in fiscal, military and ecclesiastical questions, and in the administration of the central lands. He had also founded a national theatre.[25] In foreign policy he had helped to secure the annexation of Galicia, which was to remain part of the Monarchy until 1918; been instrumental in that of the Bukovina, which proved equally enduring and was thought to have had especially happy results; and played an important role in that of the Innviertel, which is still Austrian today. He had set in train negotiations for an alliance with Russia.[26] Despite his repeated claims that his position as co-regent was intolerable and that the denial of fundamental

[23] See above, p. 424. M.T. to J., 22 July 1780 (Arneth, *MTKuF* I, p. 3). Cf. M.T. to Mercy, 3 Nov. 1780 (Arneth & Geffroy III, p. 485). Wandruszka, *L. II.*, vol. I, p. 373–4.
[24] See above, chs. 6, 7, 11 and 14.   [25] See pp. 232–5.
[26] See chs. 9 and 13. On the Bukovina see the articles of Kaindl and Polek in *Jahrbuch des Bukowiner Landesmuseums*, I and II (1895–6) and Macartney, *Habsburg Empire*, pp. 650–1 for a favourable view of the effects of annexation. On the other side the introduction to the anonymous collection *Rapt de la Bukovine d'après des documents authentiques*.

reform was ruining the state as well as his reputation, he evidently regarded the period as one of some positive achievement – at least from the standpoint of 1787. In that year he asked all departments to submit to him a statement of what they had accomplished since 1765, thus recognising a measure of continuity between the co-regency and his sole reign.[27]

Among Maria Theresa's motives in naming him co-regent had been the desire to curb and tame him.[28] His work in this capacity had certainly strengthened his ingrained preference for the affairs of the Monarchy, where the sovereign possessed real power, over those of the Empire, where he was virtually impotent. This had resolved one possible difficulty foreseen in 1765, though by 1780 the empress and Kaunitz thought Joseph was going too far in treating the business of the *Reich* as contemptible.[29] The co-regency, and his work on the *Staatsrat* and as head of the army, had accustomed him to collaborating with his mother's ministers, inured him to her policies and trained him in the methods of the existing administration, thus instilling into him traditional habits of mind dating back to the reforms of 1749 and beyond. He had not wholly 'abandoned' his *Rêveries* of 1763 or the still revolutionary aims expressed in the memorandum of 1765 and the Bohemian *Relation* of 1771; but the responsible approach he had adopted in the 'General picture' of 1768 had become second nature to him, as exemplified in his administrative activity after the crisis of 1773–4.[30] In addition, he had formed a circle of friendships within a group approved by his mother.[31] Since the other side of the coin is so much more conspicuous, it is important to stress these points. The co-regency was for Joseph a period of apprenticeship and political education, and of useful work in the cause of reform.

These elements, however, were overshadowed by the furious rows he had with his mother, with Kaunitz and with other ministers. Joseph felt desperately frustrated by the terms of the co-regency, and often asked to give it up. At other times he put forward proposals which would have meant his usurping the controlling power in the government. The emperor and empress took apparently irreconcilable positions on the unification of the Monarchy's administration, on the balance between civil and military, on territorial aggrandisement, on the place of Catholicism in the state, and on the role of the monarch. She found his attitudes both subversive and wounding, and often talked of abdication.[32]

Each accused the other of inconsistency and vacillation. Each claimed to be

[27] The request about Lombardy and Belgium is in HHSA SKV 143 (J. to K., 11 Apr. 1787). See p. 479 above for the report on ecclesiastical changes. For the Hungarian response see MOL, Kabinettsarchiv, Ungarische Einrichtungen, Konvolut F.

[28] See above, pp. 136–7.   [29] See ch. 5 and pp. 410–13, 419, 428–31.

[30] For these documents see pp. 98–106, 164–91, 209–12, 343–6, 452–5.

[31] See pp. 322–37 above.

[32] The main disputes are dealt with in chs. 6, 7, 11 and 14 for internal affairs and in chs. 9 and 13 for foreign.

prevented by the other's opposition from achieving anything worthwhile. Each asserted that the welfare of the Monarchy was being seriously damaged by their disputes. Their embarrassed courtiers agreed. Eleonore Liechtenstein said in 1772 that opportunities were aways being missed because mother and son were at odds: 'When, like us, one knows what's going on, it's astonishing that the Monarchy still exists.' Khevenhüller wrote in the same year of 'the present intrigues and confusions', adding that 'there seems unhappily to be daily less hope' that 'things will be better clarified and attain some consistency'. Leopold noted after his experience of Vienna in 1778–9:

The contrast of attitudes between her and the emperor in nearly all matters is common knowledge, since both of them talk about it openly; and that has the effect that, among the officials and in all classes of persons, there are people who say that they belong either to the emperor's or empress's party and that this is how to get on and be promoted. This makes a very bad impression [internally] and also among the foreign ambassadors, and is very injurious in affairs of state, and demoralises everybody.[33]

Yet Stormont likened these confrontations to lovers' quarrels, and with much justification. After Joseph had survived a dangerous riding accident in 1772, Maria Theresa confessed: 'I adore him, despite the fact that he torments me.' According to Rosenberg, she loved him more than all her other children put together. If his protestations of affection often ring hollow, his behaviour towards her during her grave illnesses bears them out.[34] Both the emperor and his mother used exaggerated language in dramatising their differences. He often put to her, as his first choice, a revolutionary proposal that he must have realised she would never entertain, and advanced a more moderate proposition as second best which she could accept as a basis for discussion.[35] Their positions were commonly closer together than appeared, and the compromises they ultimately made were generally reasonable. There is a case that their pursuit of conflicting policies during the War of the Bavarian Succession helped rather than hindered the achievement of a settlement favourable to the Monarchy.[36] It must not be forgotten that the dynasty acquired many times more territory under the co-regency than during the sole reign of Joseph II. In the sardonic words of Frederick the Great, Maria Theresa 'would be in tears, but she would take'. Like the backbiting between British generals and politicians during the Second World War, the disputes of emperor and empress seemed to overshadow, but did not nullify, their common purpose.

All the same, both the abdication of the empress and the resignation of the co-regent appeared on several occasions to be real possibilities. They patched

[33] E.L. to L.K., 22 May 1772 (SOALpZ, LRRA P. 16/23); K-M VII, p. 152 (5 Dec. 1772); Wandruszka, *L. II.*, vol. I, pp. 363–4.
[34] Stormont to Suffolk, 19 Oct. 1771, particular (PRO SP 80/209); M.T. to Lacy, [18 Aug. 1772,] quoted in Arneth, *GMT* IX, p. 621 (dated from K-M VII, p. 138); L.K. to E.L., 31 Oct. 1778 (SOALpZ, LRRA P. 17/24).
[35] E.g. pp. 218, 249, 362–3.   [36] See above, pp. 418–19.

things up in the end, but only at the cost of changes in the personnel and organisation of the government. So Joseph contributed, by joining in these rows, to perpetuate into the seventies the uncertainty and instability he deplored in the previous decades.[37] But it took two to make these quarrels. Comparison between the behaviour of Maria Theresa and that of Mr Gladstone suggests that repeated offers to abdicate by a revered elder statesman whom many consider indispensable are calculated to engender a peculiar degree of bitterness and perplexity. Leopold, despite his violent hostility to his brother's policies, accepted his criticisms of their mother's conduct during her last years. He thought her now unfit to govern, and wished she had laid down her burden and withdrawn completely and finally to the Tyrol. If she had, he said,

she would have brought peace to her conscience; and while she would have left the emperor on his own – since he's certainly the heir, knows the provinces and is experienced in affairs – she would have made it necessary and possible for him to work and make every effort to restore to order the disorganised affairs of the Monarchy, which will deteriorate with every year, [a task] for which energy, courage and youth are needed; and the emperor will age, his zeal will be blunted, his temper will get worse and worse, and he'll lose his inclination to work.

The empress reminded Leopold of men who are always talking of suicide but never carry out their threat. But so long as her offers to abdicate were half-hearted, the arguments against Joseph's accepting them remained over-whelming.[38]

So the co-regency endured until her death. Contemporaries puzzled over the question what difference Joseph's accession would make to the policy of the Monarchy. Outside the circle of courtiers and ambassadors, very little authentic information was available about his attitudes. Of the first-hand accounts used in this book, hardly any were published before 1780. An assiduous reader of pamphlets and the Press would have seen his letter to Papini, something on his attempts at imperial reform, some account of his travels, and a good deal on his role in the Bavarian affair. Such a reader might still credit *Le Monarque accompli*, which depicted Joseph as a *philosophe* and the ally of Protestants. Others nourished implausible hopes of him as a promoter of German culture.[39]

Among the better informed, French and Prussian statesmen expected the emperor to embark on a grand scheme of territorial expansion; but they were over-influenced by his fondness for military life and anxiety to increase the size

---

[37] See above, pp. 210–15. [38] Wandruszka, *L. II.*, vol. 1, pp. 363–4. Cf. p. 225.

[39] See above, pp. 132, 234, 383. Those who happened to have access to the anonymous *Portrait de Joseph II attribué à un Ambassadeur à la Cour de Vienne, et tracé en 1773* (Vienna, 1773) would have learned some correct information about J. Moore's *View of Society* was published in 1779. For other hopes [J.K.] Riesbeck, *Travels through Germany*, trans. Maty (3 vols., London, 1787), vol. 1, pp. 255–6.

of his army, and by Maria Theresa's presentation of herself as curbing his ambitions.[40] Leopold and many established officials of the Monarchy had good reason to fear that the new regime would be despotic and militaristic at home.[41] The prince de Ligne's apparently flippant prognosis to the British envoy in Russia was especially shrewd: 'As a man he has the greatest merit and talent; as a prince he will have continual erections and never be satisfied. His reign will be a continual Priapism. Or, if you prefer, it will be an erysipelas, like that of the body to which he is subject.'[42] Keith was more canny: 'I cannot help thinking that the Emperor will one Day shine forth as a Sort of Comet – & (Lord knows) I am not Astronomer enough to trace out His Orbit.' With all their knowledge of Joseph, these observers could not make accurate and specific predictions. As Wraxall wrote, 'In order to know him completely, it is requisite that he should survive Maria Theresa. Then, and not till then, we shall be able to appreciate in their utmost extent, the virtues, and the defects of Joseph the Second.'[43]

Even with all the information that has been set out in this volume, it would have been impossible to feel sure which aspects of his character and attitudes would dominate the policies of his sole reign. The contradictions in his personality and in his views seemed so extraordinary; and the new context would be so different. Up to now it had been a question of Joseph against his mother. In future he would stand against the world.

---

[40] See above, pp. 302–5, 424–5, 431.
[41] On the fears of L. and Zinzendorf, Wandruszka, *L. II.*, vol. I, pp. 346–7, 365. See above, pp. 103, 183–90, 302–3, 342–6.
[42] Ligne, *Fragments*, vol. I, p. 183. According to a version quoted in F. Bluche, *Le Despotisme éclairé* (Paris, 1968), Ligne's prediction was that J. would always be sneezing.
[43] Keith to Suffolk, 8 June 1774, private and confidential (PRO SP 80/215); Wraxall, *Memoirs*, vol. II, p. 468.

Bibliography

The Introduction to this book includes a general bibliographical essay, and the footnotes provide full references to the secondary literature. Here I shall list manuscript sources and, under the heading 'Printed sources', only eighteenth-century publications, published collections of documents and other works that contain significant amounts of original material in quotation. I shall confine myself to material that I have found useful and that relates to the period covered by this volume.

The short titles of other works cited more than once in the footnotes are listed in the bibliographical index.

MANUSCRIPT SOURCES

Asterisked sources were consulted on microfilm or Xerox, now either in the Seeley Historical Library, Cambridge, or in my possession.

BUDAPEST

Magyar Országos Levéltár (Hungarian National Archives: MOL)
'Memoires de ma Vie' by Prince Albert of Saxe-Teschen*
Kabinettsarchiv – Ungarische Einrichtungen 1765–1788 – I (Signatur: I–50)

LONDON

British Library (BL)
Hardwicke MSS: Add. MSS 35547–35556 are Sir Robert Murray Keith's diplomatic letter-books for this period, duplicating his despatches in the Public Record Office. There is important material in his private correspondence (Add. MSS 35503–35546), of which I have used for this volume 35508, 35514, 35516–35517.

Public Record Office, Chancery Lane (PRO)
Official Correspondence: Germany/Empire, 1763–80: SP 80/199–223
France, 1777: SP 78/302
Naples, 1769: SP 93/24
Venice, 1769, 1774: SP 99/73–74, 77

PARIS

Archives des Affaires Etrangères (AAE)
Correspondance Politique (CP): Autriche, volumes 293–317
Mémoires et Documents: Autriche, volumes 1, 38–9

SAN MARINO, CALIFORNIA

Huntington Library
Correspondence of Sir Robert Murray Keith with his sisters*

VENICE

Archivio di Stato (ASV)
Corti, Senato I (Secreta) Fᵃ 335: Tron's report on Joseph's visit of 1769* and related
material.

Biblioteca Nazionale Marciana
MSS. cl. VII. Ital. 1881, 1883; 1911, 1987*

VIENNA

Haus-, Hof- und Staatsarchiv (HHSA)
[Belgium:] Rep. DD, Abt. A. Depechen, 1779–81
Familien-Archiv (FA), Sammelbände 4, 5, 7, 10, 26, 55, 68, 70, 72, 87, 88; Hofreisen
    1, 2, 9, 10, 11
Frankreich, Varia (1776–9)
Handbilletenprotokolle (HBP), vol. IV, 1780
Kaiser Franz Akten 212
Nachlass Lacy (NL), Kartone 1–10
Staatskanzlei, Vorträge (SKV), 124–32 (1777–80)
Tagebuch Zinzendorf (TZ), 1761–76

Nationalbibliothek (ÖNB), Handschriftensammlung
Autographen 4/57, 6–13 (juvenilia), 21 (letter to M.T.); 436/11 (to Nostitz)
Ser.n. 1611, 1612, 1617, 1621, 1622, 1710, 1796, 3230, 3419, 12039, 12061, 12176,
    12181

YALE

Beinecke Library
MSS of N. W. Wraxall, *Memoirs of the Courts of Berlin, Dresden, Warsaw, and Vienna,
in the Years 1777, 1778, and 1789*

ŽITENICE (CZECHOSLOVAKIA)

Státní oblastní archiv v Litoměřicích, pobočka Žitenice
(State archives of Litoměřice, Žitenice branch: SOALpZ)
Fürstliches Liechtensteinisches Archiv. Letters of Princess Eleonore Liechtenstein
and Countess Leopoldine Kaunitz, 1762–80: LRRA, P. 16/18–23; P. 17/24–6
[these are available in the original, but also in fair copies made in the 1860s for the
years from 1767 onwards; among the copies are copies of J.'s letters to the *Dames*,
the originals of which are stated to be in the collection of Countess Szecsenyi-
Wurmbrand]
Letters of Prince Charles Liechtenstein to his wife, 1761–80: LRRA, P. 16/12–13
[The catalogue lists letters of M.T. and J. to Princess Eleonore as LRRA, P. 16/1 and
3, but they appear to be missing.]

PRINTED SOURCES

Acton, H. *The Bourbons of Naples, 1734–1825*, London, 1956.
Antespurg, J. B. von. *Das Josephinische Erzherzogliche A.B.C. oder Namenbüchlein*
(1741), ed. G. Mraz, Dortmund, 1980.
Aretin, K. O. Freiherr von. *Heiliges Römisches Reich, 1776–1806*, 2 vols., Wiesbaden,
1967.
Arneth, A. Ritter von (ed.). *Briefe der Kaiserin Maria Theresia an Ihre Kinder und
Freunde*, 4 vols., Vienna, 1881.
Arneth, A. Ritter von. *Geschichte Maria Theresias*, 10 vols., Vienna, 1863–79.
Arneth, A. Ritter von. 'Graf Philipp Cobenzl und seine Memoiren', *AÖG*, LXVII
(1886), 1–177.
Arneth, A. Ritter von (ed.). *Joseph II. und Katharina von Russland: Ihr Briefwechsel*,
Vienna, 1869.
Arneth, A. Ritter von (ed.). *Maria Theresia und Joseph II.: Ihre Correspondenz sammt
Briefen Joseph's an seinen Bruder Leopold*, 3 vols., Vienna, 1867–8.
Arneth, A. Ritter von. 'Maria Theresia und der Hofrat von Greiner', *Sitzungsberichte
KAW* (1859), Heft III, 307–78.
Arneth, A. Ritter von (ed.). *Marie Antoinette, Joseph II. und Leopold II.: Ihr
Briefwechsel*, Vienna, 1866.
Arneth, A. Ritter von (ed.). *Die Relationen der Botschafter Venedigs über Österreich im
achtzehnten Jahrhundert*, Vienna, 1863.
Arneth, A. Ritter von and Flammermont, J. (eds.). *Correspondance secrète du Comte de
Mercy-Argenteau avec l'Empereur Joseph II et le Prince de Kaunitz*, 2 vols., Paris,
1889, 1891.
Arneth, A. Ritter von and Geffroy, M. A. (eds.). *Marie-Antoinette. Correspondance
secrète entre Marie-Thérèse et le Cte de Mercy-Argenteau, avec les lettres de Marie-
Thérèse et de Marie-Antoinette*, 3 vols., 2nd edn, Paris, 1874–5.
Bauer, W. A. and Deutsch, O. E. *Mozart. Briefe und Aufzeichnungen. Gesamtausgabe*,
7 vols., Kassel, 1962–75.
Beales, D. 'Joseph II's "Rêveries"', *MÖSA*, XXXIII (1980), 142–60.
Beer, A. 'Denkschriften des Fürsten Wenzel Kaunitz-Rittberg', *AÖG*, XLVIII (1872),
1–162.
Beer, A. *Die erste Theilung Polens*, 3 vols., Vienna, 1873.

Beer, A. 'Die Staatsschulden und die Ordnung des Staatshaushaltes unter Maria Theresia', *AÖG*, LXXXII (1895), 1–135.

Beer, A. (ed.). *Joseph II., Leopold II. und Kaunitz: Ihr Briefwechsel*, Vienna, 1873.

Beer, A. 'Die Zusammenkünfte Josefs II. und Friedrichs II. zu Neisse und Neustadt', *AÖG*, XLVII (1871), 383–527.

Beer, A. and Fiedler, J. von (eds.). *Joseph II. und Graf Ludwig Cobenzl: Ihr Briefwechsel*, 2 vols., Vienna, 1901.

Benedikt, E. *Kaiser Joseph II., 1741–1790*, Vienna, 1936.

Besterman, T. (ed.). *Voltaire's Correspondence*, 107 vols., Geneva, 1953–65.

Beyträge zur Schilderung Wiens, Vienna, 1781.

Bicchieri, E. 'Lettere famigliari dell' Imperator Giuseppe II a Don Filippo e Don Ferdinando Duchi di Parma (1760–1767) con note e documenti', *AMMP*, IV (1868), 105–24.

Blanning, T. C. W. *Joseph II and Enlightened Despotism*, London, 1970.

Bosbach, E. *Die 'Rêveries Politiques' in Friedrichs des Grossen Politischem Testament von 1752*, Kölner historische Abhandlungen 3, Cologne, 1960.

Breunlich-Pawlik, M. and Wagner, H. (eds.). See Khevenhüller-Metsch and Schlitter.

Brissot, J.-P. *Mémoires (1754–1793)*, ed. C. Perroud, 2 vols., Paris, [1911].

Campan, J. L. H. *Memoirs of Marie Antoinette*, London, 1903.

Catherine II. ['Correspondence with grand-duke Paul and his wife',] *SIRIO*, IX, 1–194.

Christoph, P. [D. Pollack] (ed.). *Maria Theresia und Maria Antoinette: Ihr geheimer Briefwechsel*, Vienna, 1952.

['Cogniazzo'.] *Freymüthiger Beytrag zur Geschichte des österreichischen Militairdienstes*, Frankfurt, 1780.

Conrad, H. *Recht und Verfassung des Reiches in der Zeit Maria Theresias. Die Vorträge zum Unterricht des Erzherzogs Joseph im Natur- und Völkerrecht sowie im Deutschen Staats- und Lehnrecht*, Cologne, 1964.

Conrad, H. 'Verfassung und politische Lage des Reiches in einer Denkschrift Josephs II. von 1767/68' in *Festschrift Nikolaus Grass*, ed. L. Carlen and F. Steinegger, 2 vols., Innsbruck, 1974, vol. I, pp. 161–85.

Coxe, W. *History of the House of Austria, from the Foundation of the Monarchy by Rhodolph of Hapsburgh, to the Death of Leopold the Second: 1218 to 1792*, 2 vols. in 3, London, 1807.

Dittersdorf, K. D. von. *Lebensbeschreibung*, ed. E. Schmitz, Regensburg, 1940.

[Du Coudray, A. J. L.] *Anecdotes intéressantes et historiques de l'illustre Voyageur, pendant son séjour à Paris*, 2nd edn, Paris, 1777.

Ellemunter, A. *Antonio Eugenio Visconti und die Anfänge des Josephinismus*, Graz, 1963.

Ember, G. 'Der österreichische Staatsrat und die ungarische Verfassung, 1761–1768', *Acta historica*, VI (1959), 105–53, 331–71 and VII (1960), 149–82.

Epitre à Sa Majesté Impériale L'Empereur Joseph II, Paris, 1777.

Fechner, J. U. (ed.). *Erfahrene und erfundene Landschaft: Aurelio de' Giorgi Bertolàs Deutschlandbild und die Begründung der Rheinromantik*, Opladen, 1974.

Fejtö, F. *Un Habsbourg révolutionnaire, Joseph II. Portrait d'un despote éclairé*, Paris, 1953.

Fischer, H. (ed.). *Briefwechsel zwischen Albrecht von Haller und Eberhard Friedrich von Gemmingen*, Bibliothek des litterarischen Vereins in Stuttgart CCXIX, Tübingen, 1899.

Flassan, M. de. *Histoire générale et raisonnée de la diplomatie française, ou de la politique de la France*, vol. VII, Paris, 1811.

'Flexier de Réval' [F.-X. Feller]. *Catéchisme philosophique, ou recueil d'observations propres à défendre la religion chrétienne contre ses ennemis*, 2nd edn, Paris, 1777.

Franz, G. (ed.). *Quellen zur Geschichte des deutschen Bauernstandes in der Neuzeit*, Munich, 1963.

Friedel, J. *Briefe aus Wien verschiedenen Inhalts an einen Freund in Berlin*, 3rd edn, Leipzig, 1784.

Geffroy, A. (ed.). *Gustave III et la cour de France*, 2 vols., Paris, 1867.

Geisler, A. F. *Skizen aus dem Karakter und Handlungen Josephs des Zweiten . . .*, Erste Sammlung, Halle, 1783.

Goethe, J. W. von. *Dichtung und Wahrheit (Goethes Werke*, vols. IX–X, Hamburg, 1960–1).

Giulini, A. and Seregni, G. See Greppi and Giulini.

Gottschall, K. (ed.). *Dokumente zum Wandel im religiösen Leben Wiens während des Josephinismus*, Veröffentlichungen des Instituts für Volkskunde der Universität Wien 7, Vienna, 1979.

Greppi, E. and Giulini, A. (eds.). *Carteggio di Pietro e di Alessandro Verri*, vols. I–X (vols. VIII–X ed. Giulini and G. Seregni), Milan, 1910–39.

Groot, J. (ed.). *SIRIO*, vol. XXIII: *Correspondance de Catherine II avec Grimm* (1878).

Groot, J. (ed.). *SIRIO*, vol. XLIV: *Correspondance de Grimm avec Catherine II* (1881).

Gross-Hoffinger, A. J. (ed.), *Archiv der Urkunden und Beweisstücke zur Geschichte Kaiser Josephs des Zweiten*, Stuttgart, 1837.

Grünberg, K. *Die Bauernbefreiung und die Auflösung des gutsherrlich-bäuerlichen Verhältnisses in Böhmen, Mähren und Schlesien*, 2 vols., Leipzig, 1893–4.

Guibert, G. A. H. *Journal d'un voyage en Allemagne, fait en 1773 . . .*, 2 vols., Paris, 1803.

Hadamowsky, F. *Die Josefinische Theaterreform und das Spieljahr 1776/77 des Burgtheaters. Eine Dokumentation*, Quellen zur Theatergeschichte 2, Vienna, 1978.

Haller, A. von. *Usong. Eine morgenländische Geschichte*, Berne, 1771 (anon.); improved edn with new preface and name of author, Berne, 1778; English edn, with name of author, London, 1773.

Handelmann, H. 'Vom Wiener Hofe aus der Zeit der Kaiserin Maria Theresia und Kaiser Joseph's II., aus ungedruckten Depeschen des Grafen Johann Friedrich Bachoff von Echt, königlich dänischen Gesandten (von 1751 bis 1781)', *AÖG*, XXXVIII (1867), 457–67.

Helfert, J. A. Freiherr von. *Die Gründung der österreichischen Volksschule durch Maria Theresia*, 2 vols. numbered I and III, Prague, 1860.

Herbert, Lord (ed.). *Henry, Elizabeth and George*, London, 1939.

Hesse, Charles, prince de. *Mémoires de mon temps*, Copenhagen, 1861.

Hintzsche, E. (ed.). *Albrecht von Hallers Briefe an Auguste Tissot, 1754–1777*, Stuttgart, 1977.

Hock, C. Freiherr von. *Der österreichische Staatsrath*, Vienna, 1879.

Hrazky, J. 'Die Persönlichkeit der Infantin Isabella von Parma', *MÖSA*, XII (1959), 174–239.

Innviertel 1779. Reisejournal Kaiser Joseph II. Generalstabsbericht Oberst v. Seeger, Schärding, 1979.

Kallbrunner, J. (ed.), *Kaiserin Maria Theresias politisches Testament*, Vienna, 1952.

Kallbrunner, J. and Winkler, M. (eds.). *VKNGÖ*, vol. XVIII: *Die Zeit des Directorium in Publicis et Cameralibus. Aktenstücke*, Vienna, 1925.

Kalousek, J. (ed.). *Archiv český*, vols. XXIV (1910), 209–564; XXIX (1913), 459–553.

Karajan, T. G. von. 'Maria Theresia und Graf Sylva-Tarouca', *Feierliche Sitzungsberichte KAW*, 1859.

Karajan, T. G. von, 'Maria Theresia und Joseph II. während der Mitregentschaft', *Feierliche Sitzungsberichte KAW*, 1865.

Kervyn de Lettenhove, baron. 'Lettres inédites de Marie-Thérèse et de Joseph II', *MARB in-8o*, XX (1868), 3–60.

Keysler, J. G. *Travels through Germany, Bohemia, Hungary, Switzerland, Italy and Lorrain*, 4 vols., 2nd edn, London, 1756–7.

Khevenhüller-Metsch, Graf R. and Schlitter, H. (eds.). *Aus der Zeit Maria Theresias. Tagebuch des Fürsten Johann Josef Khevenhüller-Metsch, kaiserlichen Obersthofmeisters, 1742–1776*, 8 vols., Vienna, 1907–72 (vol. VIII ed. M. Breunlich-Pawlik, and H. Wagner, *VKNGÖ*, vol. LVI).

Labande, J. H. (ed.). *Un Diplomate français à la cour de Catharine II, 1775–1780. Journal intime du chevalier de Corberon*, 2 vols., Paris, 1901.

Lamberg, Count M. *Mémorial d'un mondain*, 2 vols., 2nd edn, London, 1776.

Landon, H. C. Robbins. *Haydn. Chronicle and Works*. Vol. I: *Haydn, The Early Years, 1732–1765*, London, 1980. Vol. II: *Haydn at Eszterháza, 1766–1790*, London, 1978.

Lanjuinais, J. *Le Monarque accompli, ou prodiges de bonté, de savoir, et de sagesse qui font l'éloge de . . . Joseph II*, 3 vols., Lausanne, 1774.

Leigh, R. A. (ed.). *Correspondance complète de Jean-Jacques Rousseau*, 43 vols., Geneva and Oxford, 1965–84.

Lettres de Pascal Paoli, publiées par M. le docteur Perelli, 3e série, Bastia, 1890; 5e série, Bastia, 1899 (all in *BSSHNC*).

Leuridant, F. (ed.). *Annales Prince de Ligne*, Brussels, 1920–32.

Lewis, W. S., Smith, W. H. and Lam, G. L. *Horace Walpole's Correspondence with Sir Horace Mann*, vol. VII, London, 1967.

Ligne, Charles Joseph, prince de. *Fragments de l'histoire de ma vie*, ed. F. Leuridant, 2 vols., Paris, 1927–8.

Ligne, Charles Joseph, prince de. *Mémoires et mélanges historiques et littéraires*, 5 vols., Paris, 1827–8.

Linger, K. F. (ed.). *Denkwürdigkeiten aus dem Leben des k.k. Hofrathes H.G. von Bretschneider, 1739 bis 1810*, Vienna, 1892.

Linzbauer, F.-X. *Codex sanitario-medicinalis*, 3 vols., Budapest, 1852–61.

Lippert, W. (ed.). *Kaiserin Maria Theresia und Kurfürstin Maria Antonia von Sachsen. Briefwechsel 1747–1772*, Leipzig, 1908.

Maass, F. (ed.). *Der Josephinismus. Quellen zu seiner Geschichte in Österreich, 1760–1850*, FRA, 5 vols., Vienna, 1951–61.

Maass, F. 'Vorbereitung und Anfänge des Josefinismus im amtlichen Schriftwechsel des Staatskanzlers . . . mit . . . Firmian, 1763 bis 1770', *MÖSA*, I (1948), 289–444.

Macartney, C. A. (ed.). *The Habsburg and Hohenzollern Dynasties in the Seventeenth and Eighteenth Centuries*, London, 1970.

Malmesbury, 3rd earl of (ed.). *Diaries and Correspondence of James Harris, First Earl of Malmesbury*, 4 vols., London, 1844.

Malmesbury, 3rd earl of (ed.). *A Series of Letters of the First Earl of Malmesbury, his Family and Friends from 1745 to 1820*, vol. I, [London,] 1870.

Marczali, H. *Magyarország története II. József korában*, 3 vols., Budapest, 1881–8.

Maria Theresia und ihre Zeit, catalogue of the exhibition held at Schönbrunn, 1980.

Mariani, C. *Il viaggio di Giuseppe II a Roma e Napoli nel 1769*, Lanciano, 1907.

[Maria Anna, archduchess.] *Schau- und Denkmünzen Maria Theresias* (1782), ed. G. Probszt-Ohstorff, Graz, 1970.

Maroger, D. (ed.), *The Memoirs of Catherine the Great*, trans. M. Budberg, London, 1955.

Marshall, J. *Travels through Holland, Flanders, Germany . . . in the Years 1768, 1769, and 1770*, 3 vols., London, 1772.

Mayer, M. *Monsieur le Comte de Falckenstein, ou Voyages de l'Empereur Joseph II, en Italie, en Boheme et en France*, Leipzig, 1777.

The Memoirs of Charles-Lewis, Baron de Pollnitz, 2 vols., London, 1737.

Mikoletzky, H. L. 'Kaiser Franz I. Stephan in Briefen (an seine Mitarbeiter)' in *Etudes européennes: Mélanges offerts à Victor Tapié*, Paris, 1973, pp. 270–9.

Mitrofanov, P. von. *Josef II. Seine politische und kulturelle Tätigkeit*, trans. from the Russian 1907 edn by V. von Demelic, 2 vols., Vienna, 1910.

[Moore, J.] *A View of Society and Manners in France, Switzerland, and Germany*, 2 vols., London, 1779.

Morrison, A. (ed.). *The Hamilton and Nelson Papers*, vol. I, London, 1893.

Moser, C. F. von. *Was ist: gut Kayserlich, und: nicht gut Kayserlich?*, 2nd edn, 'Gedruckt im Vaterland', 1766.

Nicolai, F. *Beschreibung einer Reise durch Deutschland und die Schweiz, im Jahre 1781*, 8 vols., Berlin, 1783–7.

Nosinich, J. and Wiener, L. *Kaiser Josef II. als Staatsmann und Feldherr*, Vienna, 1885.

Novotny, A. *Staatskanzler Kaunitz als geistige Persönlichkeit*, Vienna, 1947.

Österreich zur Zeit Kaiser Josephs II., catalogue of the exhibition held at Melk, 1980.

Otruba, G. *Die Wirtschaftspolitik Maria Theresias*, Vienna, 1963.

Padover, S. K. 'Prince Kaunitz' résumé of his eastern policy, 1763–71', *JMH*, v (1933), 352–65.

'Pansmouser, G.' [J. Lind]. *Le Partage de la Pologne, en sept dialogues en forme de drame*, London, [1774].

Parry, C. (ed.). *The Consolidated Treaty Series*, vol. 47, New York, 1969.

Pastor, L. von. *History of the Popes*, 40 vols., London, 1938–53.

Patriotisches Archiv für Deutschland, vols. VIII (1788) and X (1789).

Payer von Thurn, R. *Joseph II. als Theaterdirektor*, Vienna, 1920.

Pelzel, F. M. *Kurzgefasste Geschichte der Böhmen*, Prague, 1774.

Pettenegg, E. G. Graf von. *Ludwig und Karl, Grafen und Herren von Zinzendorf, Ihre Selbstbiographien*, Vienna, 1879.

Pichler, C. *Denkwürdigkeiten aus meinem Leben*, ed. E. K. Blümml, 2 vols., Munich, 1914.

Pilati, C. A. *Voyages en differens pays de l'Europe en 1774, 1775 et 1776*, 2 vols., The Hague, 1777.

Polek, J. 'Joseph's II. Reisen nach Galizien und der Bukowina und ihre Bedeutung für letztere Provinz', *Jahrbuch des Bukowiner Landesmuseums*, I (1895), 25–140.

Portrait de Joseph II attribué à un Ambassadeur à la Cour de Vienne, et tracé en 1773, Vienna, 1773.

Preuss, J. D. E. (ed.). *Oeuvres de Frédéric le Grand*, 31 vols., Berlin, 1846–57.

Prokeš, J. 'Instruka vydaná r. 1762 pro českou a rakouskou dvorní kancelára, *Věstník královské české společnosti nauk – třída ilosoficko-historicko jazykozpytná* (1926), no. 4.

Ranke, L. von. 'Maria Theresia, ihr Staat und ihr Hof im Jahre 1755. Aus den Papieren des Grosskanzlers Fürst' in *Sämmtliche Werke*, vol. XXX, Leipzig, 1875, ch. 1 (originally in *Historisch-politische Zeitschrift*, II, 4 (1836)).

Rapt de la Bukovine d'après des documents authentiques, Paris, 1875.

Raumer, F. von. *Beiträge zur neueren Geschichte aus dem britischen und französischen Reichsarchive*, 5 vols., Leipzig, 1836–9.

Riesbeck, [J.K.]. *Travels through Germany*, trans. Maty, 3 vols., London, 1787.

Romanin, S. *Storia documentata della Repubblica di Venezia*, 10 vols., Venice, 1853–61.

Sammlung aller k.k. Verordnungen und Gesetze vom Jahre 1740, bis 1780 ..., 9 vols., Vienna, 1787.

Schlitter, H. (ed.). *Correspondance secrète entre le Comte W.A. Kaunitz-Rietberg et le Baron Ignaz de Koch, 1750–1752*, Vienna, 1899.

Scholes, P. A. (ed.). *An Eighteenth-Century Musical Tour in Central Europe and the Netherlands*, vol. II, London, 1959.

Schöne, A. *Briefwechsel zwischen Lessing und seiner Frau*, Leipzig, 1885.

Schuller, G. A. *Samuel von Brukenthal*, 2 vols., Munich, 1967.

Schüller, S. 'Kaiser Joseph II. Beiträge zur Charakteristik seiner politischen Ideen.' PhD thesis, University of Vienna, 1931.

Schünemann, K. 'Die Wirtschaftspolitik Josephs II. in der Zeit seiner Mitregentschaft', *MÖIG*, XLVII (1933), 13–56.

Seregni, G. See Greppi and Giulini.

Smyth, Mrs G. (ed.). *Memoirs and Correspondence (Official and Familiar) of Sir Robert Murray Keith, K.B.*, 2 vols., London, 1849.

Tommaseo, N. 'Lettere inedite di Pasquale de' Paoli', *ASI*, 5th series, VI (1890), 266–306.

Tourneux, M. (ed.). *Correspondance littéraire, philosophique et critique par Grimm, Diderot, Raynal, Meister, etc.*, 16 vols., Paris, 1877–82, vol. XI (1879).

Toynbee, Mrs Paget (ed.). *Lettres de la marquise du Deffand à Horace Walpole*, vol. III, London, 1912.

Tratchevsky, A. 'La France et l'Allemagne sous Louis XVI', *RH*, XIV (1880), 241–85.

Valsecchi, F. *L'assolutismo illuminato in Austria e in Lombardia*, 2 vols., Bologna, 1931, 1934.

Venturi, F. (ed.). *Illuministi italiani*, vol. III: *Riformatori lombardi, piemontesi e toscani*, Milan, 1958.

Voltelini, H. 'Eine Denkschrift des Grafen Johann Anton Pergen über die Bedeutung der römischen Kaiserkrone für das Haus Österreich' in *GV*, pp. 152–68.

Volz, G. B. and others (eds.). *Politische Correspondenz Friedrichs des Grossen*, 46 vols., Berlin, 1879–1939.

Volz, G. B. (ed.). *Die politischen Testamente Friedrich's des Grossen*, Berlin, 1920.

Wagner, H. (ed.). *Wien von Maria Theresia bis zur Franzosenzeit: Aus den Tagebüchern des Grafen Karl von Zinzendorf*, Vienna, 1972.

Walter, F. *VKNGÖ*, vol. XXXII: *Die Geschichte der österreichischen Zentralverwaltung in der Zeit Maria Theresias (1740–1780)*, Vienna, 1938.

Walter, F. 'Kaunitz' Eintritt in die innere Politik', *MÖIG*, XLVI (1932), 37–79.

Walter, F. 'Der letzte grosse Versuch einer Verwaltungsreform unter Maria Theresia (1764/65)', *MÖIG*, XLVII (1933), 427–69.

Walter, F. (ed.). *VKNGÖ*, vol. XXIX: *Vom Sturz des Directorium in Publicis et Cameralibus (1760/61) bis zum Ausgang der Regierung Maria Theresias. Aktenstücke*, Vienna, 1934.

Wandruszka, A. *Leopold II.*, 2 vols., Vienna, 1963, 1965.

Wehofer, T. M. (ed.). 'Das Lehrbuch der Metaphysik für Kaiser Josef II., verfasst von P. Josef Frantz', *Jahrbuch für Philosophie und spekulative Theologie*, Ergänzungsheft II, Paderborn, 1895.

Werner, R. M. (ed.). *Aus dem Josephinischen Wien*, Berlin, 1888.

Wiener Zeitung (Wienerisches Diarium).

Wiennerische Beleuchtungen oder Beschreibung Aller deren Triumph- und Ehren-Gerüsten, Sinn-Bildern und anderen sowohl herzlich- als kostbar und annoch nie so prächtig geschenen Auszierungen welche bey denen zu Ihren der Höchst-gewünschten Geburt Des Durchleutigsten Ertz-Hertzogs zu Oesterreich ec. JOSEPHI Den 13. Martii das erstemal und sodann Bey Allerhöchst Ihro Majestät der Königin von Hungarn ... MARIAE THERESIAE ... Beseegneten Hervorgang ..., Vienna, 1741.

Winter, E. 'Grundlinien der österreichischen Russlandpolitik am Ende des 18. Jahrhunderts', *Zeitschrift für Slawistik*, IV (1959), 94–110.

Witte, baron J. de (ed.). *Journal de l'abbé de Véri*, 2 vols., Paris, n.d.

Wolf, A. *Aus dem Hofleben Maria Theresia's*, 2nd edn, Vienna, 1859.

Wolf, A. *Marie Christine, Erzherzogin von Oesterreich*, 2 vols., Vienna, 1863.

Wolf, A. 'Relationen des Grafen von Podewils, Gesandten K. Friedrich's II. von Preussen, über den Wiener Hof in den Jahren 1746, 1747, 1748', *Sitzungsberichte KAW*, V (1850), 466–543.

Wolfsgruber, C. *Christoph Anton Kardinal Migazzi, Fürsterzbischof von Wien*, Saulgau, 1890.

Wraxall, Sir N. W. *Historical Memoirs of My Own Time*, ed. R. Askham, London, 1904.

Wraxall, N. W. *Memoirs of the Courts of Berlin, Dresden, Warsaw, and Vienna, in the Years 1777, 1778, and 1779*, 2 vols., 3rd edn, London, 1806.

Wurzbach, C. von. *Biographisches Lexikon des Kaiserthums Oesterreich, 1750–1850*, 60 vols., Vienna, 1856–91.

Zweybrück, F., 'Briefe der Kaiserin Maria Theresia und Joseph II. und Berichte des Obersthofmeisters Grafen Anton Salm, 17 März 1760 bis 16 Jänner 1765', *AÖG*, LXXVI (1890), 111–25.

Bibliographical index

This index gives the location of the full footnote reference for every work not listed in the bibliography and cited more than once.

General index